THIRD EDITION

PRISON AND JAIL

PRACTICE AND THEORY

ADMINISTRATION

EDITED BY

PETER M. CARLSON, DPA

Professor, Department of Government
Christopher Newport University
Newport News, Virginia

JONES & BARTLETT
LEARNING

World Headquarters
Jones & Bartlett Learning
5 Wall Street
Burlington, MA 01803
978-443-5000
info@jblearning.com
www.jblearning.com

Jones & Bartlett Learning books and products are available through most bookstores and online booksellers. To contact Jones & Bartlett Learning directly, call 800-832-0034, fax 978-443-8000, or visit our website, www.jblearning.com.

Substantial discounts on bulk quantities of Jones & Bartlett Learning publications are available to corporations, professional associations, and other qualified organizations. For details and specific discount information, contact the special sales department at Jones & Bartlett Learning via the above contact information or send an email to specialsales@jblearning.com.

Production Credits
Executive Publisher: William Brottmiller
Publisher: Cathy L. Esperti
Senior Acquisitions Editor: Erin O'Connor
Editorial Assistant: Audrey Schwinn
Production Manager: Tracey McCrea
Marketing Manager: Lindsay White
Manufacturing and Inventory Control Supervisor: Amy Bacus
Composition: diacriTech
Cover Design: Kristin E. Parker
Associate Permissions and Photo Researcher: Ashley Dos Santos
Cover and Title Page Images: From top and to the right: © Peter Kunasz/Shutterstock, Inc.; © Fer Gregory/Shutterstock, Inc.; © Corbis/age fotostock; © Alexander Chaikin/Shutterstock, Inc.; © maxriesgo/Shutterstock, Inc.; © luxorphoto/Shutterstock, Inc.; © Constock/Thinkstock; © Thinkstock/age fotostock
Printing and Binding: Edwards Brothers Malloy
Cover Printing: Edwards Brothers Malloy

Library of Congress Cataloging-in-Publication Data
Prison and jail administration : practice and theory / [edited by] Peter M. Carlson.
    pages cm
Revised edition of: Prison and jail administration : practice and theory / edited by Peter M. Carlson, Judith Simon Garrett. 2nd ed.
Includes bibliographical references and index.
ISBN 978-1-4496-5305-7 (pbk.)
1. Prisons–United States–History. 2. Prison administration–United States–History. 3. Punishment–United States–History.
4. Prisoners–United States–Social conditions. 5. Correctional personnel–United States. I. Carlson, Peter M.
HV9304.P725 2014
365.068–dc23
                        2013022683
6048

Printed in the United States of America
17 16 15 14 13   10 9 8 7 6 5 4 3 2 1

Contents

Acknowledgments

I would like to express sincere appreciation for the exceptional contributions of those that have written for this text and shared their knowledge, expertise, and wise judgment with all who read it. These writers have been selected to contribute to this volume by virtue of being outstanding leaders and teachers in the correctional field.

This text is designed to help develop the knowledge base of present and future correctional administrators. The staff of America's prisons and jails are unsung heroes in many ways: they keep our communities safe, they assist as well as supervise as inmates go about their daily institutional routines, and serve as role models for the thousands of offenders inside the walls, fences, and wire of our correctional facilities. They are public servants doing a tough job around the clock; those that have careers inside deserve our appreciation and our respect.

I thank my mentors in corrections, my friends, and my family for their support throughout my career and life. I value each and every one of you.

Peter M. Carlson
Smithfield, Virginia

Contributors

Judy C. Anderson is Warden for the South Carolina Department of Corrections at the Camille Griffin Graham Correctional Institution. Previously, Ms. Anderson served as the Chief of Institutional Operations for the South Carolina Department of Juvenile Justice, where she was responsible for secure institutions, classification, and disciplinary procedures. Prior to that assignment, she served in many capacities for the South Carolina Department of Corrections, including as warden of two institutions, deputy regional director, and chair of state classification. Ms. Anderson received her Bachelor's degree from the University of Southern Mississippi and her Master's degree from the University of South Carolina.

Stephanie R. Appel began her career in 1995 in the Kentucky Finance and Administration Cabinet where she worked until coming to the Kentucky Department of Corrections, Division of Personnel in June 2000. Ms. Appel is currently the Human Resources Director for the Kentucky Justice and Public Safety Cabinet in which she oversees the management of over 8,000 employees. She attended Midway College and the University of Kentucky and holds a Bachelor's degree in business administration.

John J. Armstrong is retired from a 27-year career with the Connecticut Department of Correction where he began as a correctional officer and was ultimately appointed as the Commissioner of the agency, a position he held for eight years. He is currently a corrections consultant, has worked in Iraq, and continues to teach criminal justice at Naugatuck Valley Community College in Connecticut. Mr. Armstrong holds an MS degree from the University of New Haven.

Dyona Augustin, MS, is currently a doctoral candidate in clinical psychology at the Center for Psychological Studies at Nova Southeastern University (NSU). She received her Master's degree from NSU in 2012. Augustin has contributed to several works related to forensic psychology, including co-authoring a chapter in the book entitled, *Correctional Mental Health: From Theory to Best Practice*. In addition to working on numerous research projects within the field of forensic psychology, Ms. Augustin is also interested in multicultural psychology.

James Austin is President of the JFA Institute in Washington, DC. Before taking this position, he was co-director of the Institute on Crime, Justice and Corrections at the George Washington University in Washington, DC, served as executive vice president of the National Council on Crime and Delinquency, and was employed by the Illinois Department of Corrections. Mr. Austin has authored numerous publications, was honored with the American Correctional Association's Peter P. Lejins Research Award, and received the Western Society of Criminology Paul Tappin Award for outstanding contributions to the field of criminology.

Dr. Austin received his undergraduate and graduate degrees in sociology from Wheaton College, DePaul University in Chicago, and the University of California at Davis.

Lindsey Battles is an undergraduate student at Christopher Newport University in Newport News, Virginia. She is studying Political Science and is expected to graduate December 2013.

Rachel Bosley joined The Moss Group, Inc. as Associate, Research and Program Design in 2010. Her role focuses on technical assistance project management of the Prison Rape Elimination Act, as well as research analysis, PREA policy review, training and curriculum development, and editorial support.

Armand R. Burruel worked in the state of California civil service for 34 years, managing Corrections Human Resources and Labor Relations programs for over 24 years. During his last 10 years in state service, he was an Associate Warden at three different prisons and the central headquarters. His experience in Labor Relations began in 1978 as California implemented collective bargaining for state civil service employees. He participated and led many of the labor contract negotiations with the various labor unions representing state employees, including the Correctional Peace Officers Union. Upon his retirement, the California Assembly issued him a resolution recognizing his distinguished service and contributions.

Peter M. Carlson is a Professor in the Department of Government at Christopher Newport University, Newport News, Virginia. He has served as Chair of the University Faculty and as the President of the Faculty Senate. He is retired from a 30-year career with the U.S. Department of Justice, Federal Bureau of Prisons where he served as the Assistant Director of the agency, Regional Director of the Western Region, and Warden of three federal prisons. He received his BA degree from Willamette University in Salem, Oregon, an MS degree from Western Oregon University, and an MPA and doctoral degree in public administration from the University of Southern California. He is the author of numerous articles, reviews, and is the editor and chapter author of this text. He is a consultant to the federal court system on the death penalty and to state prison systems on correctional administration and inmate management issues.

William C. Collins began working with legal issues in corrections in the early 1970s, representing the Washington State Department of Corrections. Upon leaving government service, he spent over 25 years writing, training, and consulting with prisons and jails around the country on inmate rights issues. He was a frequent consultant for the National Institute of Corrections. Mr. Collins received both his Bachelor's and law degrees from the University of Washington.

Michael B. Cooksey is a Senior Advisor for Corrections for the International Criminal Investigative Training Assistance Program (ICITAP), and works primarily with their Iraq program. Prior to his current position with ICITAP, Mr. Cooksey served as assistant director for the Correctional Programs Division at the Federal Bureau of Prisons. He provided bureau-wide oversight for inmate programs, custody and security, community corrections, and private prisons. During his career, he served as warden at four federal prisons. Mr. Cooksey also has served on advisory committees at several colleges and received his BS in business and MA in psychology from Middle Tennessee State University.

Clair A. Cripe is the retired General Counsel for the Federal Bureau of Prisons. After legal work as a JAG officer in the U.S. Navy, he entered government service in Washington, DC, first as a trial attorney in the Food and Drug Administration, and then as a lawyer in the Federal Bureau of Prisons. He worked for 28 years in the

Prisons Bureau, the last 15 years as its General Counsel. He taught a course in Corrections Law for 15 years at the National Law Center at the George Washington University and criminal justice classes at several other schools. He holds degrees from Oberlin College and Harvard Law School.

Julius Debro is the Associate Dean of the Graduate School at the University of Washington. Dr. Debro began his career in probation with Alameda County in Oakland, California. After seven years, he joined the California Department of Corrections at San Quentin, California, as a counselor, then joined the U.S. Probation Department in San Francisco on a special research project. He has conducted extensive research in the areas of corrections, juvenile delinquency, and policing. Dr. Debro received his Bachelor's degree from the University of San Francisco, his Master's in sociology from San Jose State University, and his Doctorate in criminology from the University of California, Berkley.

John J. DiIulio, Jr., is the Frederic Fox Leadership Professor of Politics, Religion, and Urban Civil Society at the University of Pennsylvania. He is the author, coauthor, or editor of 12 books and has written op-eds for many major newspapers and popular magazines. Dr. DiIulio received his Bachelor's degree in political science and economics, a Master's degree in political science-public policy from the University of Pennsylvania, and a Doctorate from Harvard University.

Mara Dodson began working for The Moss Group, Inc. in 2008, initially working on the National Prison Rape Elimination Commission Report by conducting a national survey to identify current practice in agency responses to sexual abuse. She continues to provide project management and subject matter expertise for major Grants and agency-funded projects, focusing primarily in the areas of implementing the Prison Rape Elimination Act and female offenders in both adult and juvenile settings. In this capacity, through The Moss Group, Ms. Dodson manages facility sexual safety assessments to assist agencies in further enhancing PREA implementation by addressing PREA standards, culture and leadership to promote sexual safety.

Julie C. Eng is a national board-certified teacher and reading specialist who maintains a research interest in the field of social policy and criminal justice. She is an English teacher at Smithfield High School, Smithfield, Virginia. Ms. Eng has a Bachelor's degree in sociology from Emory University and an MA in education from the College of William and Mary.

Thomas J. Fagan, PhD, is currently a professor of psychology and the Director of the Division of Social and Behavioral Science at Nova Southeastern University in Ft. Lauderdale, Florida. For 23 years he was a psychology practitioner and administrator with the Federal Bureau of Prisons where he was an active participant in developing correctional mental health programs, creating mental health policies and procedures, and training professional, paraprofessional, and correctional staff. Dr. Fagan was also the Bureau's Chief hostage negotiator and coordinator of its crisis negotiation training program. Over the years, he has served as a consultant to numerous federal, state, and local law enforcement agencies in the areas of crisis negotiation, critical incident stress debriefing, and management of correctional mental health services and programs.

Dr. Fagan has published regularly in correctional and psychological journals, has authored several book chapters, and co-edited three books with Robert K. Ax, PhD—*Correctional Mental Health Handbook* (2003); *Corrections, Mental Health, and Social Policy: International Perspectives* (2007); and *Correctional Mental Health: From Theory to Best Practice* (2011). He also published a book on crisis negotiation in correctional settings - *Negotiating Correctional Incidents: A Practical Guide* (2003).

Since 1997, Dr. Fagan has served as the American Psychological Association (APA)'s representative on the Board of Directors of the National Commission on Correctional Health Care (NCCHC) – a national organization dedicated to insuring quality health and mental health care to incarcerated individuals. He served as NCCHC's Board Chair from 2002–2003. He is a Fellow in APA's Divisions 12 and 18. Division 18 recognized his work in correctional mental health with a special achievement award in 1993 and he received APA's Award for Distinguished Contributions to Practice in the Public Sector in 2006. He received his Bachelor's degree from Rutgers University and his Master's and Doctoral degrees from Virginia Tech.

Mark S. Fleisher, PhD, is a Research Professor at the Mandel School of Applied Social Sciences, Case Western Reserve University. He is the author of five books: *Warehousing Violence* (1989); *Beggars and Thieves* (1995); *Dead End Kids* (1998); *Crime and Employment: Issue in Crime Reduction for Corrections* (2004); and *The Myth of Prison Rape: Sexual Culture in American Prisons* (2009).

Jeffery W. Frazier has 23 years of experience in corrections, both at the state and local levels. He served in the U.S. Army and the Virginia Air National Guard and is a veteran of Desert Storm. Mr. Frazier received his bachelor's degree in business administration from Strayer College and was one of the first in the nation to receive a certification as a jail manager through the Jail Manager Certification Commission. He was also the recipient of the 1998 American Jail Association Correctional Administrator of the Year award and was certified as a Firearms Instructor through the Virginia Department of Criminal Justice Services.

Judith Simon Garrett is the Assistant Director in the Information, Policy, and Public Affairs Division of the Federal Bureau of Prisons. She oversees the offices of Legislative Affairs, Public Affairs, Research and Evaluation, and Policy and Information Management. She has a law degree from Washington University in St. Louis and a Bachelor's degree from the University of Wisconsin–Madison.

Robert S. George, **FAIA**, joined the Federal Bureau of Prisons as a staff architect and managed the design of several new correctional facilities in the concept of direct supervision. He moved to the Bureau's Western Regional Office in 1977 where he served as a staff architect and facilities administrator. In 1984, he returned to private architectural practice, and, in 1998, he was elevated to the College of Fellows of the American Institute of Architects. He continues to practice in the San Francisco area. Mr. George received his BA in architecture from the University of California, Berkeley.

Lior Gideon, PhD, is an Associate Professor at John Jay College of Criminal Justice in New York. He specializes in corrections-based program evaluation, and focuses his research on rehabilitation, reentry and reintegration issues and in particular by examining offenders' perceptions of their needs. His research interests also involve international and comparative corrections related public opinion surveys and their affect on policy. To that extent, Dr. Gideon published several manuscripts on these topics, including two previously published books on offenders needs in the reintegration process, titled: *Substance Abusing Inmates: Experiences of Recovering Drug Addicts on their way Back Home* (Springer), and *Rethinking Corrections: Rehabilitation, Reentry and Reintegration* (Sage) (with Hung-En Sung). His, other work was recently published in *The Prison Journal*, the *International Journal of Offender Therapy and Comparative Criminology*, and the *Asian Journal of Criminology*. Recently, Dr. Gideon was nominated as the Co-Chief Editor for a Springer journal titled: *Health & Justice*. Dr. Gideon earned his PhD from the Faculty of Law, Institute of Criminology at the Hebrew University in Jerusalem, and completed a post-doctoral fellowship at the University of Maryland's Bureau of Governmental Research.

Robert C. Grieser is the Chief of Strategic Business Development and Marketing for Federal Prison Industries, Inc. He began his career in corrections in 1976 with the Virginia Department of Corrections and served as Director of Operations for the Institute for Economic and Policy Studies, a nonprofit consulting firm. He has served on the National Correctional Industries Association (NCIA) Board of Directors since 1989, serving as NCIA President in 1998. Mr. Grieser earned an MSW degree from Virginia Commonwealth University.

Marie L. Griffin is an Associate Professor in the School of Criminology and Criminal Justice at Arizona State University. Her research interests include issues of organizational climate in the correctional setting; use of force in corrections; prison and jail misconduct; and gender and crime. She received her PhD in Justice Studies from Arizona State University.

Suzanne R. Hastings is currently the Warden of the Federal Correctional Institution in Jesup, Georgia which is her fifth assignment as Warden within the Federal Bureau of Prisons. She started her correctional career with the Kentucky Department of Corrections as Recreation Supervisor at Northpoint Training Center in Burgin, Kentucky before joining the Bureau of Prisons as a Recreation Specialist in 1988. Ms. Hastings is a 1983 Recreation & Park Administration graduate of Eastern Kentucky University and has been in the field of corrections for 28 years.

Samantha Hauptman is an Assistant Professor of Criminal Justice at the University of South Carolina Upstate. Before joining the faculty at USC Upstate, she worked at the USC Union campus for 2 years and was the Criminal Justice Academic Program Director and an Instructor at Piedmont Technical College for 6 years. Prior to her teaching career, Dr. Hauptman spent 6 years in administration at the South Carolina Department of Corrections. She received both her Master of Criminal Justice and PhD in Sociology (specializing in criminal and social deviance) at the University of South Carolina. Dr. Hauptman's research interests include criminology, criminal/social deviance, social control, and immigration.

John R. Hepburn is a Professor in the School of Criminology and Criminal Justice at Arizona State University. His research has focused on issues of correctional administration and control of inmates as well as successful offender reentry to the community.

Martin F. Horn is Distinguished Lecturer at John Jay College of Criminal Justice of the City University of New York and Executive Director of the New York State Sentencing Commission. For nearly seven years prior to joining the faculty in September 2009 he served simultaneously as Correction Commissioner and Probation Commissioner for the City of New York. He previously served as Secretary of Corrections for the Commonwealth of Pennsylvania and for many years was the Executive Director of New York State's paroling authority. Mr. Horn has over 40 years of experience working in corrections and community supervision. He has been a warden and has taught, written and spoken extensively about issues of prison and parole reform throughout his career.

Brandon Howard has been a Kentucky State Correctional Officer since 2004. He initially sought a career in corrections due to job security and later because it provided a dynamic and challenging work environment. He is a 2011 graduate of Morehead State University with a BA in Geography. His work related interests include security threat groups and promotion in administration.

Dominick P. Ignaffo, MPA, has over 30 years of CRJ experience with the Dutchess County Office of Probation and Community Corrections, as a Probation Officer, School Resource Officer, and a Unit Administrator. He is currently an Adjunct Professor at John Jay College of Criminal Justice.

James A. Inciardi is Director of the Center for Drug and Alcohol Studies and Professor of Sociology and Criminal Justice at the University of Delaware. He also holds positions as Adjunct Professor in the Department of Epidemiology and Public Health at the University of Miami School of Medicine and is a Distinguished Professor at the State University of Rio de Janeiro and guest professor in the Department of Psychiatry at the Federal University of Rio Grande do Sul in Porto Alegre, Brazil. Dr. Inciardi earned his PhD from New York University and has published numerous books, articles, and chapters in the areas of substance abuse, criminology, criminal justice, history, folklore, public policy, AIDS, medicine, and law.

Gilbert L. Ingram is a criminal justice consultant who retired after 35 years of service with the Federal Bureau of Prisons. His experience included serving as the warden of two federal prisons, director of two federal prison regions, and Assistant Director of Correctional Programs. He has also served as Adjunct Faculty Member at seven universities. Dr. Ingram received his PhD in psychology from the University of Maryland.

Michael H. Jaime has been retired from the California Department of Corrections since 2004. He served in many responsible positions including the role of Chief of Labor Relations. He also has finance and labor relations experience in three other state departments in California. Mr. Jaime received his Bachelor's degree in social work and Master's degree in public administration from California State University, Sacramento.

Sally C. Johnson, MD, Professor of Psychiatry at University of North Carolina in Chapel Hill NC specializes in Forensic Psychiatry. She divides her time among teaching at Duke, UNC, and University of Tennessee law schools, research on violence and aggression and mental health issues among Veterans, and conducting criminal and civil forensic evaluations. She has a special interest in correctional mental health and completed career military service as a United States Public Health Service physician with the U.S. Department of Justice, Federal Bureau of Prisons.

J. C. Keeney has retired from a 36-year career in corrections. He began his career as a recreation officer in 1960 and was promoted through the ranks to become the superintendent of the Oregon State Penitentiary. He also served in the Arizona Department of Corrections as the Assistant Director of Adult Institutions and has worked in private corrections as the Warden of Arizona State Prison (Phoenix West).

Harley G. Lappin was the seventh Director of the Federal Bureau of Prisons. He was responsible for the oversight and management of the BOP's 114 institutions and for the safety and security of the more than 198,000 inmates under the agency's jurisdiction. He received a BA in forensic studies from Indiana University in Bloomington, Indiana, and an MA in criminal justice and correctional administration from Kent State University in Kent, Ohio. He is currently employed by Corrections Corporation of America.

Stefan LoBuglio, Chief of the Pre-Release and Reentry Services Division for the Montgomery County (Maryland) Department of Correction and Rehabilitation, oversees community-based reentry programs that serve up to 200 local, state, and federal inmates. Prior to his appointment in January 2005, Mr. LoBuglio was Deputy Superintendent of Community Corrections for the Suffolk County Sheriff's Department in Boston, Massachusetts for 12 years and was involved in a number of reentry initiatives. Mr. LoBuglio has his Bachelor of Science in Mechanical Engineering from Duke University and a Doctorate from Harvard's Graduate School of Education where he focused his studies on the evaluation of correctional reentry programs. Over the past several years, he has co-authored a number of publications on reentry, and his most recent work is focused on developing appropriate and realistic measures of performance for these types of programs.

Paul McAlister is Treatment Director for Zumbro Valley Mental Health Center's Residential Treatment Program in Rochester, Minnesota. He has taught for 28 years at Crossroads College, Augsburg College, and 7 years at the Mayo Medical School in the areas of medical ethics, philosophy, and theology. He has spent many years working with Community Corrections boards and committees as well as the Community Relations Board at the Federal Medical Center, Rochester, Minnesota. He is currently providing member care and working in the area of child safety and protection for PBT, an international group working in translation and literacy with special focus on Papua New Guinea. His doctorate is in the areas of philosophy, ethics, and theology.

Duane C. McBride is Chair of the Behavioral Sciences Department and Director, Institute for Prevention of Addictions, Research Professor of Sociology at Andrews University in Michigan. His areas of expertise are criminology and drug abuse. His current research focuses on the areas of juvenile delinquency and AIDS infection of IV drug users. Dr. McBride currently teaches courses on Criminology, Introduction to Sociology, Drug Use in American Society, Theories of Addictive Behavior, and Juvenile Delinquency.

Douglas McDonald, PhD, is a principal associate at Abt Associates, an organization that conducts research and provides science-based assistance to governments around the world. McDonald's primary research interests include criminal justice institutions/policies/practices and substance abuse.

James A. Meko is retired from the Criminal Justice Program faculty at Gannon University in Erie, Pennsylvania. As a U.S. Army Captain in Viet Nam, he was awarded the Bronze Star in 1971. He served 25 years with the Federal Bureau of Prisons, worked in five facilities and retired in 1996. He was warden at both a federal jail and a medium security facility, Chief of Staff Training, Senior Deputy Assistant Director and Executive Assistant to the Director of the agency. He implemented the first international prisoner transfer programs for the United States, wrote papers on the utilization of correctional intelligence and received recognition from the U.S. Attorney General for efforts in resolving a staff hostage situation. A member of the U.S. Senior Executive Service, Mr. Meko received the Bureau of Prison's Meritorious Service Medal in 1996. He holds a Bachelor's degree from Gannon University and a Master's degree from the University of Notre Dame.

Kevin I. Minor is Professor of Justice Studies at Eastern Kentucky University, where he has worked since 1992. Prior to that, he taught at Missouri State University and worked in both adult and juvenile correctional facilities. Dr. Minor has authored or co-authored four books and over 50 journal articles and book chapters. He has also consulted extensively for national, state, and local level criminal justice organizations.

Joann B. Morton is Professor Emeritus of Criminal Justice at the University of South Carolina. Prior to joining the faculty at USC, she was Director of Special Projects at the South Carolina Department of Corrections and before coming to SCDC, she was Director of the Southeastern Correctional Management Training Program at the University of Georgia. She is co-founder of the Association on Programs for Female Offenders and is the author of 2 books and several articles on women offenders.

Anadora Moss is founder and President of The Moss Group, Inc., a Washington, DC-based criminal justice consulting firm established in 2002. Ms. Moss has an extensive history working on sensitive correctional management issues, particularly sexual abuse and sexual misconduct issues. In the Georgia Department of Corrections she provided oversight for reform in women's services. As an Assistant Deputy Commissioner in the Georgia Department of Corrections during the *Cason v. Seckinger* lawsuit in the early 1990s, and as a Program Manager with the National Institute of Corrections (NIC) from September 1995 to

February 2002, she was involved in the development of early strategies to address staff sexual misconduct in the field of corrections.

Phyllis J. Newton currently serves as the Director of the Office of Research and Evaluation at the U.S. Department of Justice's National Institute of Justice (NIJ). In this role, she directs internal and external research related to crime, violence, victimization, and justice systems, focusing principally at state and local level concerns. Prior to her tenure at NIJ, Ms. Newton served as Director of Communications and Special Assistant to the Assistant Director at the Federal Bureau of Prisons. For 7 years, Ms. Newton served as Staff Director of the U.S. Sentencing Commission. Her primary substantive focus areas include sentencing, corrections, violence against women, and human trafficking.

Stephen Parson is a senior associate with Commonwealth Research Consulting. He has over 25 years of experience in criminal justice, specializing in institutional corrections and evaluation research. Mr. Parson has consulted on a variety of correctional research, evaluation, and technical assistance projects for federal, state, and corporate clients. Recent projects include a training needs assessment and job task analysis for youth workers, the evaluation of various training delivery modalities, and the development and validation of an instrument for assessing safety in women's correctional facilities. Mr. Parson was previously a research associate in the Center for Criminal Justice Education and Research at Eastern Kentucky University. He holds a Bachelor's degree in sociology and political science, and a Master's degree in correctional and juvenile justice studies.

Beverly Pierce is retired from a 20-year career with the Federal Bureau of Prisons. She has served in many financial management positions and as the Associate Warden at the Federal Correctional Institution, Terminal Island, California.

Dan Phillips is an Associate Professor of Sociology and Criminal Justice and the Criminal Justice Program Coordinator at Lindsey Wilson College in Columbia, Kentucky. He has edited two books entitled *Mental Health Issues in the Criminal Justice System* and *Probation and Parole: Current Trends*. Dr. Phillips' past speaking engagements have focused on mental health and criminal justice topics as well. He has trained police officers on how to deal with citizens with mental illness. He is the former editor of the *International Journal of Sociological Research* and the *Kentucky Journal of Anthropology and Sociology*.

James E. Rivers is Deputy Director of the Comprehensive Drug Research Center at the University of Miami School of Medicine and is a Research Associate Professor in both the Department of Sociology and the Department of Epidemiology and Public Health. Dr. Rivers has research, teaching, and administrative/policy experience in a broad range of substance abuse areas and, in recent years, has been Director of the Metropolitan Dade Country Office of Substance Abuse Control and Loaned Executive to the Law Enforcement, Courts and Corrections Task Force of the Miami Coalition for a Safe and Drug Free Community. Dr. Rivers earned his PhD in sociology from the University of Kentucky.

Tom Roth is a Senior Consultant for MGT of America, Inc., a management research and consultant firm in Austin, Texas. He is retired from a 27-year career with the Illinois Department of Corrections where he served as Assistant Director of Administration and as Warden of four separate prisons. He was an auditor with the American Correctional Association for nine years and holds a Master's degree from Michigan State University.

Steve Schwalb is the Executive Director of Pioneer Human Services in Seattle, Washington, a correctional services industry. He started his lengthy correctional career in 1973 and has served as the Assistant Director of the Federal Bureau of Prisons and as the Chief Operating Officer of Federal Prison Industries, a government-owned corporation that employs thousands of federal inmates in manufacturing and service tasks. He has also served as the warden of a federal prison and as the Director of the King County Department of Adult Detention in Seattle. Mr. Schwalb received his Bachelor's degree in personnel management and labor relations from the University of Washington.

John R. Shaw is a corrections consultant specializing in ethical and legal issues. He has testified as an expert witness in many federal criminal matters. Mr. Shaw is retired from the Federal Bureau of Prisons where he served as Regional Counsel and Deputy Regional Director. He holds a BS from the University of Maryland and a JD from the University of South Carolina.

Sam S. Souryal is a Professor of Criminal Justice and Ethics in the College of Criminal Justice at Sam Houston State University in Texas. He is most interested in the areas of policing, corrections, and ethics. He has written several books on criminal justice administration and management, ethics and justice, as well as books on comparative cultures and religions.

Richard L. Stalder is the Secretary of the Louisiana Department of Public Safety and Corrections. He began his career with the department in 1971 as a correctional officer and has served as superintendent and warden of major juvenile and adult facilities among other management roles. In 2002, he received the American Correctional Association's E.R. Cass Correctional Achievement Award and the Association of State Correctional Administrators' Michael Francke Award. He possesses Bachelor's and Master's degrees from Louisiana State University.

E. A. Stepp has held correctional leadership positions for many years. He is retired from the Federal Bureau of Prisons where he served as the warden of the Federal Correctional Complex in Coleman, Florida, and at the United States Penitentiary, in Marion, Illinois. He has also held the position of Chief of Emergency Preparedness for the agency. He is currently employed by the GEO Group. Mr. Stepp received his Bachelor's degree in criminal justice from Indiana State University.

Steve Steurer is the Executive Director of the Correctional Education Association since 1986. He worked as the Coordinator of Academic Education for inmate education at the Maryland Department of Education for 30 years and continues to consult with government and nonprofit agencies.

Timothy Thielman is the Food Service Administrator for a 556 bed adult correctional facility in Saint Paul, Minnesota. He also oversees food service for two juvenile facilities, the inmate commissary, laundry, purchasing, and warehouse management for the adult correctional facility. Lt. Thielman is a Certified Correctional Food System Manager (CFSM) and has been working in institutional food service for 30 years and correctional food service for 20 years. He is the Past President of the Northern Lakes Chapter of the Association of Correctional Food Service Affiliates (ACFSA) and is currently the ACFSA Region Three Director and serves as the chair of the ACHSA Education Committee.

Robert R. Thompson is a graduate of Thomas Jefferson University Medical College and received his medical residency training at the Mayo Clinic. He is the author of 23 articles and a book dealing with a variety of medical and social issues. Prior to retirement, he worked as a physician at the Federal Medical Center in Rochester, Minnesota where he was medical director of the hospice program.

Sonya Thompson is the Senior Deputy Assistant Director for Information Resource Management (and Chief Information Officer) with the Federal Bureau of Prisons. She is responsible for overseeing the BOP's enterprise IT program, including systems development, network management, and IT security. She has a Bachelor of Science in Electrical Engineering and Juris Doctor from Washington University in St. Louis.

Tessa Unwin is the Public Affairs Liaison for the Ohio State Department of Rehabilitation and Correction. She has served in the public information department for many years. Previously, Ms. Unwin worked as a producer in public radio. Ms. Unwin received her Bachelor's degree in journalism from The Ohio State University.

Susan Van Baalen served as a correctional chaplain in state and federal prisons for twenty-eight years, and for fourteen years was the Chief Chaplain for the Federal Bureau of Prisons (BOP) in Washington, DC. After retirement from the BOP, Dr. Van Baalen was the Executive Director of Prison Outreach Ministry (POM) for five years. The Welcome Home Reentry Program, POM's major program component, provided mentoring support for more than 150 returning citizens annually. Dr. Van Baalen is currently an independent consultant and volunteer in a Florida State prison for female offenders. She has consulted both nationally and internationally on issues related to religious accommodation of non-Christian inmates and inmate adherents of emerging religious movements. Dr. Van Baalen completed her doctoral studies at Georgetown University, Washington, DC.

Arthur Wallenstein is the Director of Montgomery County Maryland Department of Corrections and Rehabilitation. He previously served as Director of King County Department of Adult Detention in Seattle and Director of Bucks County Pennsylvania Department of Corrections. He is a member of the National Institute of Corrections Advisory Board. He received his BS from Georgetown University and an MA from the University of Pennsylvania.

Reginald A. Wilkinson is the President and CEO of the Ohio College Access Network. Most recently, he was the Executive Director of the Ohio Business Alliance for Higher Education and the Economy. Dr. Wilkinson retired in April 2006 as the Director of the Ohio Department of Rehabilitation and Correction, a position he held since 1991. He is a member and former Chairperson of the National Institute of Corrections Advisory Board. He is a past president of the American Correctional Association, the Association of State Correctional Administrators, and the International Association of Reentry. Wilkinson's academic background includes BA and MA degrees from The Ohio State University. He was also awarded the Doctor of Education degree from the University of Cincinnati.

Robert L. Wright served 35 years in corrections. He held many progressively responsible positions with the Oregon Department of Corrections and served as the superintendent of the Eastern Oregon Correctional Institution. He also served as the superintendent of the Clallam Bay Corrections Center in Clallam Bay, Washington. He recently retired as the Executive Director of the Eastern Oregon Alcoholism Foundation. He received his Bachelor's and Master's degrees from Oregon State University. He has previously been the President of the West Central Wardens and Superintendents Association and has served as a reviewer for the Commission on Accreditation for U.S. and Canadian correctional facilities.

Reviewers

Reverend Professor Kimora
John Jay College of Criminal Justice

John F. Littlefield
University of Maryland—University College

William E. Kelly
Auburn University

Kevin Cashen
Tiffin University

Larry E. Spencer
Alabama State University

Mary Ellen Mastrorilli
Boston University Metropolitan College

Corrections Past and Present

YOU ARE THE ADMINISTRATOR

■ What Is Our Purpose in Corrections?

You are the assistant warden of the large state penitentiary located 8 miles from town. You are responsible for programs and inmate care at the 2,500-bed facility.

One Saturday night, you and your spouse are out for the evening with several neighbors. As you are enjoying dinner before heading to a local movie theater, one of the men in the group, an attorney, commented rather emotionally about a recent lawsuit filed in federal court about the conditions of confinement at the local county jail. Inmates have complained that there is a lack of education programs in the jail. Your neighbor, the attorney, clearly believes that inmates are treated too well and have expectations of resort-like conditions in the jail. He said the judge had contacted him to ask if he would consider representing the inmates on a pro bono (no fee) basis. He added that he did not understand why taxpayers should pay to educate convicted offenders.

Even though you do not work at this facility, your group all turns and looks to you for response to this critical correctional issue.

How should you respond to this in a semi-public setting? Recognizing that it is always easy to criticize prison or jail operations, do you have an obligation to explain the dilemma presented to public servants working in corrections by the American public—that is, what should corrections be focusing on, punishment or rehabilitation? Should you take a definite side? How can you explain the apparent lack of a consistent correctional philosophy that has been demonstrated in the history of corrections?

The Legacy of Punishment

Peter M. Carlson and Tom Roth

CHAPTER OBJECTIVES

- Understand the role religion has played in the development of punishment.
- Understand why the concept of punishment has become such a major force in the American administration of justice.
- Name several common forms of corporal punishment found in early American history.
- Understand how the concept of a "day fine" compares to other economic sanctions utilized by our court system.

How should we deal with those who violate our person, property, or liberty? Should we punish or help those who have harmed us in some way? Should we publicly humiliate them, banish them, hurt them, confine them, or try to reform them? We have responded to criminal behavior in all of these ways over time!

Although this discussion often lends itself to important theoretical debate, the history of our society is that we change our minds on a regular basis as to how we should treat scofflaws and crooks. Within our American heritage, we reserve the prerogative to shift our opinion over time.

Punishment for misbehavior and violations of the law, or for any perceived malfeasance on the part of others, is a social response that can be found throughout the history of our world and in all major civilizations.

The law is a social construct. Laws are established by every society, and violations of the law are defined by a government or by those in power. The definition of what is legal, or illegal, changes over time in all societies as our collective views and attitudes shift. For instance, in the United States, we outlawed the manufacture, transportation, and sale of alcohol during the era of prohibition . . . and subsequently legalized it again.

Our American society believes in punishment. The concept of "just desserts" has its roots in the early history of the original colonies and certainly before that in British jurisprudence. When an individual violates our person or property, or that of our loved ones, citizens of the United States believe that a penalty must be exacted for the abridgment of our rights. Retribution is important in our culture.

When people band together as friends, family, society, or as a nation, social rules are developed and applied to all members. This requires submission to the accepted mores and, in turn, demands a sanction if one does not comply with expectations. Nonobedience requires a price: punishment. Vengeance, both from the aspect of private retaliation and from public justice, is a key aspect of our human nature. When we are injured by another, figuratively or literally, our nature is such that we want and expect the offender to be dealt with in a just manner. The concept of *lex talionis*—an eye for an eye—has been well accepted in many cultures around the world.

Punishment is defined by Webster's dictionary as the infliction of a penalty; "retributive suffering, pain, or loss."[1] Punishment is truly a cultural process. In our social world, the idea of punishment has an ancient history.[2] Various types of physical and mental castigation date back to the primitive origins of mankind.

The evolution of punishment has intertwined with that of religion over the years. The power of the Roman Empire was extensive and predated Christ by 500 years. The Roman Emperor Justin organized Roman law through a written document known as the Justinian Code, and this had a lasting influence over the centuries as it was one of the first written codes. However, as the Roman Empire disintegrated, chaos ruled Europe and there was no central authority other than the Church. Church punishments were often bloody and violent.

The concept of free will has evolved from the religious belief that one must choose to believe in God and make the decision to follow the path of righteousness. The parallel thought is that one must choose to violate the law, and should therefore be held responsible for those actions.

This idea has formed the center focus of the American criminal justice system and is the logic behind the development of rehabilitative programs in the judicial system. Organized religion has affected corrections and the management of the American judicial system in many ways.

Prisons and jails play a big part in punishment today, and short of capital punishment, confinement is the most serious sanction utilized by American courts. Imprisonment as punishment is a concept that developed in the United States and has subsequently been adopted throughout the world. The rate of incarceration in America (492 per 100,000 population as of December 2011) is believed to be the highest in the world, if one can place credibility in the reported statistics from other countries. While the nation's federal and state prisoners have declined as of 2011, the number of confined offenders still totals over 1.5 million.[3]

Furthermore, criminal courts of the United States are heavy handed, and the prisoners serve longer sentences than in other countries. The stringent get-tough-on-crime policies enacted throughout the last 25 years continue to have a huge effect on the growth of the population of our nation's correctional facilities. Present-day sentencing options include mandatory sentencing requirements for many drug offenses, "truth-in sentencing" provisions that preclude release on parole, and "three-strikes-and-you're-out" laws for repeat offenders.

Yet jails and prisons were not always the linchpin of the administration of justice. Colonial America borrowed its judicial practices from English law. English houses of confinement, or gaols, were utilized for short-term detention of law violators awaiting trial. In the extraordinary history of punishment in early England, confinement as punishment would have been considered too easy on the offender; the Anglo-Saxon legacy was one of revenge. Felons were killed, tortured, banished, transported away from their homeland, and publicly humiliated. Corporal punishment was imposed with impunity, and the severity of the sanctions was extreme. Offenders were buried alive, beheaded, drowned, burned at the stake, boiled, stoned, and otherwise mutilated in every imaginable way. All punishment was public, and even minor sanctions such as placement in a pillory were conducted in front of amused crowds. These sanctions were greatly valued and have contributed to the seemingly bloodthirsty nature of revenge and retribution. Justice certainly has evolved from this patchwork of societal response to crime, but the American sense of justice is deeply steeped in the physical and aggressive punishments of early England.

Houses of detention were originally utilized to safely keep pretrial detainees. In the 16th century, the Church of England began to use the bishop's facility at St. Bridget's Well for confining and beating misdemeanants for crimes such as prostitution and begging. Such institutions became commonplace and were referred to as "bridewells."[4] As these facilities spread, they rapidly deteriorated and became known as "houses of darkness" because of the conditions of confinement. These British gaols were filthy, without natural light, and disease-ridden. The English prison reformer John Howard noted that more prisoners died of sickness and disease than were executed by the very common practice of hanging.[5] Men and women, juveniles and adults, and murderers and petty thieves were all confined together in these houses of pestilence.

British justice often utilized transportation from one's homeland as punishment. Hundreds of thousands of lawbreakers were shipped to the American colonies, and later to Australia, where they were forced into servitude for a number of years as part of their sanction. This generally involved taking the role of an indentured servant, rather than prisoner, and individuals served up to five years in this capacity. Once released, the former prisoners were often given land for a new start.

These practices were the cornerstone of justice administration in the American colonies. Criminal codes and sanctions were essentially the same as those the new American immigrants brought with them to the new world. Justice demanded harsh penalties, and an extraordinary number of offenders were subject to death, banishment, or various forms of corporal punishment. When jails were used for the detention of pretrial offenders, the conditions were often as bad as those in the English goals.

After the American Revolution, the new society began to turn away from many concepts and practices imported from England. Philosophies changed, and as new ideas emerged in the fledgling states, prison and jail reformers had a major influence on the nature of punishment. In Pennsylvania, the Quakers took up the mantle of correcting the negative and deleterious aspects of jail conditions. The earliest institutions designed for long-term confinement as punishment (except for the failed Simsbury Mine) evolved from the Walnut Street Jail in Philadelphia, Pennsylvania.

The Walnut Street Jail and the subsequent Eastern Penitentiary were the earliest penitentiaries in the United States. The Quaker reformers intended for this punishing confinement to instill penitence and repentance in the hearts of those sentenced to periods of incarceration. Prisoners were isolated in individual cells, and this forced solitude was designed to reform the evil nature of those who had violated the laws of society. Prayer and interpersonal reflection were believed to be the answer to criminal behavior. Prisoners did not see or speak to each other, reflecting the concern that they would contaminate each other; this was known as the "separate system."

This type of confinement was eventually challenged by another prison philosophy that became known as the Auburn model. This developed in the state of New York and involved a continuance of the silent system but added the idea of congregate work; permitting prisoners to work greatly cut down the cost of prison operation. Individual cells were much smaller than those in Philadelphia, and the Auburn prison became legend for its regime of harsh discipline. This prison design and operating philosophy became the standard for prisons built in the United States for years to come; several of those built prior to 1870 are still in operation today.

These principles of economical operation, restricted interaction between convicts, congregate work, extreme discipline, and tight control became enduring precepts of penal operation and punishment for years to come. Strict obedience to prison employees was enforced, and corporal punishment was used to enforce institutional regulations. Chains, beatings, solitary confinement, and limited food became instruments of punishment and control within the American prison environment.

The face of punishment today has evolved over the years from the tyranny of physical and mental abuse to much more civilized forms of sanctions. Public displays of offender humiliation are much less in evidence; the death penalty is not exercised nearly to the extent it was a century earlier; and the conditions of confinement are much improved over a decade earlier.

■ Today's Sanctions

Fines, probation, and incarceration are the basic punishments found in the current criminal justice system in America.

Fines are monetary sanctions imposed by the courts for offenses ranging from misdemeanor violations such as shoplifting up to and including felony offenses such as arson, murder, and rape. Fines may be the only sanction imposed by the court, or they can be combined with other alternatives such as probation, restitution, or confinement. The laws and guidelines that authorize the use of fines vary widely across criminal court jurisdictions and tend to be very inconsistently applied.

Research is not clear as to whether fines are an effective punishment in terms of having an effect on criminal behavior. Monetary loss may not be a significant issue to those well endowed with more than adequate resources and may absolutely crush an individual who is poor. Some jurisdictions have tried to compensate for this concern by utilizing fines that are based on the defendant's offense as well as his or her capacity to earn. This "day fine" is based on the individual's income and assets and is considered to be a much more equitable method of assessing monetary sanctions.

McDonald notes that some courts utilize a two-step process to establish the amount of the fine.[6] Step 1 is the quantification of the offense for the formula; the more serious offenses have increasing value. Step 2 establishes the worth of the convicted defendant based on his or her specific economic circumstances. Clearly, the shortfall to such a system lies in the problem of accurately determining the true assets of the offender.

Another monetary punishment that can be imposed on convicted persons is a requirement to make restitution to the victim or the community. Restitution is often required as a partial sanction and can be used as a condition of another punishment such as probation. This sanction involves paying a specified amount of money to the person damaged by a criminal act or repaying the local community by the performance of services.

Another economic punishment used by many judges is the imposition of a requirement for the offender to pay for court costs or to forfeit certain assets that he or she may have. The forfeiture of owned property is often tied to the personal property being connected in some manner to the crime. As an example, in federal courts, it is commonplace for an offender to forfeit an automobile or airplane if the vehicle is associated with the criminal activity.

Over 4.8 million adults were under state or federal community supervision in the United States as of 2011.[7] Probation supervision allows the offender to remain in the community with special conditions and accountability requirements. Probation is generally associated with incarceration in the sentencing process; if the individual does not meet all conditions of probation, he or she has probation revoked and the sentence is then served in prison or jail.

Intensive probation is another form of this community supervision sanction. It is occasionally utilized by the courts for those individuals who may be considered high risk. In general, intensive probation means the supervising probation officer has a smaller caseload and therefore is able to spend more time supervising and assisting the offender. This variation of probation also demands more intense reporting requirements and often has more structured accountability of the probationers' whereabouts and living and working conditions.

Incarceration, a criminal sanction that involves the sentencing of an offender to a term of confinement in a prison or jail, is utilized by the courts when the offense or the individual's personal characteristics are such that the judge believes that society must be protected from the possibility of further victimization by the criminal.

Today, confinement is the primary punishment of the American society. It is the nearly exclusive sanction to punish serious and repetitive offenders. The incarceration of a convicted individual, the taking of one's liberty, is what the public believes corrections is all about. The placement of a criminal behind bars is believed to have the most significant effect on crime and is the expected punishment within the realm of American jurisprudence.

The evolution of the prison and jail in the United States has followed the shifting social forces at work in the country. Those who have advocated reform of these institutions believe that an individual's social deviance is a problem that can be addressed and corrected. They have advocated that correctional institutions must provide a healthy environment and work toward the goal of reformed criminals.[8] See **Table 1-1**.

TABLE 1-1 Attitudes Toward Most Important Purpose in Sentencing Adults

	Discourage Others From Committing Crime	Separate Offenders From Society	Train, Educate, and Counsel Offenders	Give Offenders the Punishment They Deserve
National	12.4%	12.5%	19.9%	50.8%
Sex				
Male	13.3	11.0	20.5	51.2
Female	11.5	13.8	19.4	50.5
Race				
White	13.2	13.6	17.3	51.4
Black	7.5	6.6	29.2	52.8
Hispanic	9.6	9.6	28.8	47.9
Age				
18–29 years	10.9	8.6	27.1	48.4
30–39 years	13.6	11.8	17.9	55.2
40–59 years	13.6	16.8	17.7	47.8
60 years and older	9.2	12.1	18.4	52.9

(continues)

TABLE 1-1 Attitudes Toward Most Important Purpose in Sentencing Adults (cont.)

	Discourage Others From Committing Crime	Separate Offenders From Society	Train, Educate, and Counsel Offenders	Give Offenders the Punishment They Deserve
Education				
College graduate	12.5	20.0	21.8	42.5
Some college	17.2	11.6	19.3	48.1
High school graduate	10.2	9.5	19.1	56.6
Less than high school graduate	4.9	5.8	22.3	62.1
Income				
Over $60,000	12.8	16.6	25.7	42.8
Between $30,000 and $60,000	13.3	12.2	19.1	51.2
Between $15,000 and $29,000	10.9	14.2	15.5	57.3
Less than $15,000	11.9	6.8	25.4	50.8
Community				
Urban	9.7	18.1	14.8	49.7
Suburban	11.7	15.5	21.6	47.3
Small city	13.8	13.8	24.9	43.4
Rural/small town	12.6	8.1	18.6	58.0
Region				
Northeast	14.2	13.6	15.9	49.4
Midwest	8.5	11.0	26.7	48.7
South	11.7	10.9	16.6	57.6
West	15.8	15.4	21.2	44.4
Politics				
Republican	16.7	16.0	13.9	50.7
Democrat	8.9	10.7	23.8	53.7
Independent/other	11.7	12.2	22.6	47.3

Source: Data From Bureau of Justice Statistics, U.S. Department of Justice, *Sourcebook of Criminal Justice Statistics - 1996* Washington, D.C., U.S. Government Printing Office, 1997. 153.

The two opposing forces, one advocating punishment and the other advocating rehabilitation, have driven the many changes that have beset the operation of American penitentiaries. Yet the primary focus of confinement has remained a custodial function. Citizens of the United States have always viewed imprisonment as the punishment of choice.[9]

This text examines major aspects of jail and prison operations as the United States nears the turn of the 21st century. This punishment environment—the incarceration of those who violate the laws—is certainly worthy of our examination and study. The practice of punishment in America will surely continue to evolve.

Chapter Resources

DISCUSSION QUESTIONS

1. What sentencing factors have caused the United States to become the country with the highest incarceration rate in the world? What societal factors have led to these sentencing issues?
2. What are the three primary forms of judicial punishment in the United States today?
3. Do you believe "economic" sanctions are an effective form of punishment? What is the problem with this type of sentence?
4. Are "mandatory sentencing" and "three-strikes-and-you're-out" laws fair and just?
5. Do you support the idea of corporal punishment in lieu of confinement for some crimes?
6. Why does the American public not consider alternative forms of sanctions (sentencing options other than imprisonment) to be appropriately punishing?
7. Does a day fine serve to punish those offenses that are considered to be of a white-collar nature?
8. Although religion has had a huge effect on the American system of criminal justice, should religious programs be supported by the government and funded by the taxpayer for those who are confined?

ONLINE RESOURCES

- Crime and Punishment—The National Archives, http://learningcurve.pro.gov/uk/canedp/default.htm
- The Federal Bureau of Prisons, http://www.bop.gov
- Jeremy Bentham—The Rationale of Punishment, http://www.la.utexas.edu/labyrinth/rp/
- The World Corporal Punishment Research, http://www.corpun.com/

NOTES

1. *Merriam-Webster's collegiate dictionary*. (2003). Springfield, MA: Merriam-Webster Inc. Publishers.
2. Newman, G. (1985). *The punishment response*. Albany, NY: Harrow and Heston Publishers.
3. Carson, E., & Sabol, W., Bureau of Justice Statistics. (2012). *Prisoners in 2011*. Washington, DC: Government Printing Office, NCJ Publication 239808.
4. Allen, H., & Simonsen, C. (2000). *Corrections in America: An introduction* (9th ed.). New York, NY: Macmillan Publishing Company.
5. Howard, J. (1780). *The state of the prisons in England and Wales.* (p. 10). London, England: William Eyres.
6. McDonald, D. (1992). Introduction: The day fine as a means of expanding judges' sentencing options. In D. McDonald (Ed.), *Day fines in American courts: The Staten Island and Milwaukee experiments.* Washington, DC: U.S. Department of Justice, Office of Justice Programs.
7. Maruschak, L., & Parks, E., Bureau of Justice Statistics. (2011). *Probation and parole in the United States, 2011.* Washington, DC: U.S. Department of Justice, NCJ Publication 239686.
8. Johnson, A. (1987). *Hard times. Understanding and reforming the prison* (p. 19). Belmont, CA, Wadsworth Inc.
9. Sherman, M., & Hawkins, G. (1981). *Imprisonment in America* (p. 86). Chicago: The University of Chicago Press.

American Jails—Dramatic Changes in Public Policy

Arthur Wallenstein

CHAPTER 2

CHAPTER OBJECTIVES

- Recognize the enormous number of individuals who pass through the jail system in the United States every year.

- Identify changing, evolving, and overtly new elements in public policy that are highlighting and redefining the local jail as a driving element in the criminal justice system in the United States.

- Understand the importance of local jails as a filtering element that can successfully identify and engage several million individuals suffering from mental health difficulties, alcohol and substance abuse addiction, and a growing array of physical health problems that are nowhere better presented and are easily recognizable in jails throughout the United States.

■ Introduction

Corrections as an element of public policy and criminal justice operations has far too long focused almost exclusively on lengthy sentence prisons as the dominant element of the field of corrections. The public, virtually at the drop of a hat, assumes that the discussion is of prisons when sentencing and judicial outcomes are mentioned. Whether it is Internet discussion, global cable television, scores of talk shows, or personal memoirs of past experiences, it is logically assumed that prisons are the focus and drive the adult correctional system in the United States.

Virtually every character of note, policy in less than positive standing, or moment of high drama is considered to be a prison-based behavior. Historically, this trend developed with the literary and public policy debates in the 19th century between the Pennsylvania and New York models for prison architecture and degrees of prisoner isolation/separation in prison operations. This continues right through the recent past where films, literature, personal narratives, and documentary presentations focus on the prison or the "Big House" that so quickly comes to dominate our imagination and understanding of the corrections equation.

Nothing could be further from an accurate portrayal or presentation of correctional reality than the primacy of just prisons, especially when compared to a much larger local jail system, and then of course to the largest component engaging convicted offenders—probation and other forms of community corrections and community-based supervision. The jail is now understood as something infinitely more complex, challenging, and useful in understanding the larger criminal justice system in the United States. There are more than 3,320 local jails or regional justice systems in the United States, which push us and demand our attention on the local public policy process, right down to the town square in virtually every identified community in the United States.

Jails, crosscutting every jurisdiction in this country, are no longer mom-and-pop operations, regardless of their size, capacity, number of bookings/releases, degree of offender sophistication, and urban/rural/Indian geographic location. Common behaviors characterizing both pretrial and sentenced inmate behaviors, which are now increasingly understood through such measures as Level of Service Inventory–Revised™ (LSIR), create opportunities for real—not imagined—evidence-based practices that start to build a new and far more meaningful role for the local jail or county jail or jail setting in one of the unified state systems in this country.

The importance of local jails and the role of local corrections being developed as a function of the national jail system have redefined our understanding of the local lockup. It is now translated and understood to bring the world of criminal behavior, the characteristics of offenders, the combined pathologies that characterize criminal process, and the human and social services challenges that affect, in part, every single community in this country to the forefront. A jail offers an opportunity to dramatically confront criminal behavior from its inception at the adult level through new and evolving public policy priorities such as reentry and return to the community as opposed to some previously generated simplistic axiom known as release to the streets.

■ Jail Population

Nothing in this chapter presents hard data that jails are simply more important than prisons. This would offer as little useful guidance on this topic as past generations have developed in citing prisons as the prevailing critical element of practice. What is now a matter of essential understanding is that jail systems book and release some 15 times the number of individuals as are admitted and then released from prisons throughout the United States after the completion of sentence served. This is new ground, and although initially highlighted in work published by the American Correctional Association (ACA) in 1996, it has taken to early 2012 for the importance of bookings and releases to challenge average daily population (ADP) as the prevailing data element of analysis when discussing incarceration in one form or another.

On a typical given day at present, more than 2.3 million individuals can be found in an incarceration setting in this country. More than 1.6 million can be found in state or federal prisons, whereas approximately 735,000 can be found in county jails or local municipal jail settings. This would suggest that prisons are the dominant location and structure of incarceration, and such an inference would be totally wrong. Bookings and releases—the dominant data element in jail operations—number between 10 and 13 million bookings and are estimated to include more than 9 million individual persons. These numbers dwarf the number of prison admissions by some 10 to 15 times and demonstrate how the landscape of criminal justice–focused behavior could be dramatically affected if greater attention and focus were directed toward local jails in the United States.

Although the average length of stay in a jail is far less than in a state or federal prison, the dominant size and scope of admissions and releases back into local communities characterize both criminal justice outcomes and opportunities to truly affect public safety at the local level. Jails are not some minor afterthought to a media, entertainment, literary, and video focus on prisons, with their dramatic tales of social interaction and institutional violence and disturbances. It is time we started to focus on the potential to truly affect public safety outcomes at the point of reentry, and here local jails offer a unique set of opportunities given their proximity in terms of geography and social interaction to local communities throughout every county and municipal jurisdiction in the United States. See Table 2-1.

Studies of jail population levels and of total bookings and releases and the characteristics of those who enter jails improved dramatically during the first decade of the 21st century. Nowhere has more accurate and dynamic descriptive material been developed than through the U.S. Department of Justice—Bureau of Justice Statistics in an almost unending improvement and the expansion of quality studies and scope of data collection.[1] Some will find it important that jail populations were continuing to decline in some measure since the enormous growth of the previous 20 years. The significance of the tidal wave of individuals entering the system and returning to the community through jail systems remains dominant and, until recently, an almost undocumented and poorly utilized data element in the broader public safety equation. See Figure 2-1.

TABLE 2-1 Estimated Percentages of Local Jail Inmates, by Selected Characteristic and Ratio Estimates, 2011

Characteristic	Estimate	Standard Error
Sex		
Male	87.3%	0.12%
Female	12.7	0.12
Race/origin		
White[a]	44.8	0.43
Black/African American[a]	37.6	0.39
Hispanic/Latino	15.5	0.34
Other[a,b]	2.0	0.14
Two or more races[a]	0.2	0.02
Conviction status[c]		
Convicted	39.4	0.42
Unconvicted	60.6	0.42

Detail may not sum to 100% due to rounding.

[a]Excludes persons of Hispanic or Latino origin.

[b]Includes American Indians, Alaska Natives, Asians, Native Hawaiians, and other Pacific Islanders.

[c]Includes juveniles who were tried or awaiting trial as adults.

Source: Minton, T.D. (2012). *Jail Inmates at Midyear, 2011 - Statistical Tables.* (Washington, DC. Bureau of Justice Statistics, Table 12).

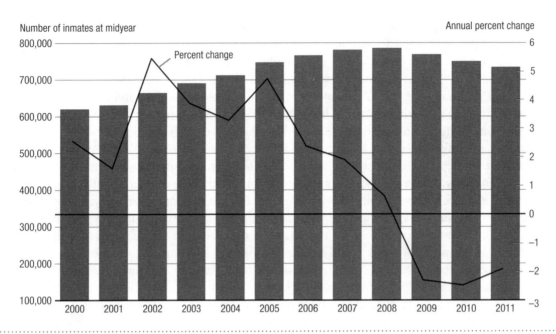

FIGURE 2-1 Inmates confined in local jails at midyear and change in the jail population, 2000–2011
Source: Bureau of Justice Statistics, Annual Survey of Jails and the 2005 Census of Jail Inmates.

Slightly more than 62% of the 10–13 million jail admissions are awaiting disposition of their cases, meaning they have a pretrial status. It then follows that approximately 38% of all those entering jails are serving sentences at the local level and are not being transferred to state prisons. Local jails conduct a heterogeneous slice of criminal justice practice in the United States, and the better we understand who is in jail and what are the driving components of their incarceration (both pretrial and convicted/sentenced), the greater will be our understanding of the enormous focus of opportunity that local jails provide to attack public safety challenges across the board in every jurisdiction in the United States.

Local jails hold less than 50% of the numbers held in state prisons on any given day, but in any given year local jails receive, work with, and release between 10 and 15 times the numbers of individuals engaged by the entire adult state prison system in the United States.

■ Pretrial Process

Because more than 60% of the 10–13 million bookings who enter county jails each year are in pretrial status, this might well be considered the single most important public policy and operational issue in the entire field of jails. It must be remembered and restated over and over again that the vast percentage of individuals who are booked into county jails or local jails or tribal jails or federal detention centers are awaiting some disposition of criminal justice matters and at this point are considered not guilty. It does not mean they have not committed the crime or behaviors that initiated their arrest. It does mean that under the due process guidelines of our criminal justice system, guilt has not been established and every effort must be taken to treat individuals as if this ultimate determination were still in doubt and required formal intervention and ultimate decision making through the pretrial justice system.

It is essential, as we study the jail system and engage in real issues, that pretrial process and pretrial decision making stand out as enormously important, crosscutting every single jail setting in the United States. As we will see, jail populations might not be significantly grounded on the level of crime but rather have a strong linkage to bail practices, standards of pretrial review in more than 3,000 jurisdictions, and local levels of commitment and support for advancing evidence-based practices regarding pretrial release. Incarceration in a jail is not given—nor is it understood to be required—but very often arrest is equated with incarceration in a local jail, and this myth needs to be exploded, for it does not conform to historic reality, due process pretrial practices, and a growing tension between bail as it exists in the 21st century and other options that are available in support of a least restrictive environment and good public policy decision making.

For the majority of this nation's history, bail (money, property, some combination of money and property, or other tangible financial instruments) has been the traditional means of securing release from a local jail facility after arrest. For several generations, neither was it generally challenged nor were alternatives easily available. At a 1964 conference on pretrial justice, then–Attorney General Robert Kennedy noted in a very direct manner: "What has been demonstrated here is that usually only one factor determines whether a defendant stays in jail before he comes to trial. That factor is not guilt or innocence. It is not the nature of the crime. It is not the character of the defendant. The factor is, simply, money." The words of the attorney general came at a time when traditional bail and the bondsman organizations began to be considered as a methodology and practice that could be changed and should be changed or altered with other options. Personal wealth and/or resources could never, in our constitutional democracy, be considered valid criteria for a determination of guilt or innocence in any criminal matter.

Jails cannot possibly be understood as an element of the correctional system unless bail, pretrial release criteria, application of data-driven practices, and alternative strategies are deeply considered and understood. Wealthy individuals should have no greater or lesser opportunity for release from pretrial detention based on factors of personal wealth. Ensuring presence in court is the goal of the pretrial system, and although money bail may be a factor, developments for the past generation have demonstrated that evidence-based assessment and supervision programs provide a very useful and positive alternative to money and personal financial capacity.

In the early 1960s, a movement was initiated in New York City known as the Manhattan Bail Project. It was developed by the very respected and creative Vera Institute of Justice. The focus was conducting interviews of pretrial detainees after their arrest, not to determine any matters of guilt but to decide whether they were good risks to return for future court hearings and trial without the need for further pretrial detention. Anyone studying jails or hoping to understand jails and their role in the U.S. criminal justice system must accept and understand that pretrial release decision making can now, after some 50 years of practice, be conducted with significant reliance on ties to the community and past pretrial reporting and other community-based practices as a proper means of providing due process of law and moderating the size of traditional jail populations.

The majority of pretrial detainees can exist quite safely in the community prior to further hearings and the ultimate disposition of their cases. Trials are rare (less than 5% of all dispositions) in our criminal justice system. In most cases, pretrial release awaits either a plea agreement between prosecution and defense or a determination that no criminal act actually occurred. It is a cornerstone of American criminal justice practice that pretrial detention should not be based on personal wealth, and that means that every year improved interview templates and standards of pretrial release community linkage questions can be improved upon and can be found to support public safety and reduced jail population levels.

In many jurisdictions, jail release or the avoidance of jail (regardless of guilt or innocence on the underlying charges) could be accomplished without any bail at all. Release on personal recognizance flows from strong community ties, a history of employment, an existing family structure, no prior history of missing judicial hearings, and following pretrial supervision guidelines that simply did not exist in the past and are still in debate in many jurisdictions across the country. It is not surprising that from the windows of jail cells you can see flashing neon signs for bail in bail bond offices immediately across the street. Neon lights are a marketing tool.

In the same manner, bail bond agencies advertise in telephone books and use creative spelling to be first in the alphabetical listings. What started as the AAA Bond Agency may now extend to the AAAA Bond Agency or the AAAAA Bond Agency seeking to be listed first in local telephone directories, as inmates (newly arrested pretrial detainees) or family members consult the phone directory or web-based Internet listings to find an agency to support bail release for a friend, relative, or loved one. It is not uncommon for bail agencies in a given jurisdiction (supported by large insurance companies) to argue and compete bitterly for special access to recently arrested individuals at intake facilities, which has become an ongoing challenge for local jails across the nation.

Organizations such as the Pretrial Justice Institute (PJI) have established focused advocacy programs to limit the use of money bail because it speaks to the effect of poverty to many and their continued presence in jail, as they await disposition of their cases. PJI has recognized that evidence-based practice developed through years of linking community stability indicators with returning to court can diminish the reliance on money. In 2011, national attention returned to the groundbreaking efforts of former Attorney General Robert Kennedy in seeking to stimulate a renewed national commitment to diminish personal wealth and money as the primary means of deciding who should remain in jail pending final judicial action. Attorney General Eric Holder strongly reiterated the admonition of Robert Kennedy in reminding the nation that jails should not simply be a reservoir for poor people whose financial status might continue to drive decisions regarding pretrial detention.[2]

The American jail system needs to generate constant and compelling attention to no-money bail options that now exist in an increasing number of jurisdictions to give credence to the goal of removing the jail as a monument to poverty, as opposed to a potentially valuable public safety institution where decisions are made based on data-driven principles and not pure dollar considerations. Guilt or innocence has never been found, ultimately, to be based on wealth in any specific case, but jail population growth over the past 50 years certainly has been fueled in part by reluctance to test the full extent of pretrial interview and data collection methodologies that have fostered and will continue to foster moderation, objectivity, and a nonmonetary focus on jail populations.

■ Health Care as a Core Element of American Jail Operations

It is hard to imagine a healthcare system admitting 10–13 million potential patients in the course of a single year. Yet that is precisely what happens in the jail portion of the adult correctional system in this country. The system is staggering in size and scope because health care has, since the mid-1970s, been a mandatory area of correctional practice with full constitutional supports. In 1976, the U.S. Supreme Court made quality healthcare delivery crystal clear—without debate or exception in a landmark case from a prison system, but with 100% applicability to every jail in the United States.[3]

Justice Thurgood Marshall, writing in the early days of major judicial intervention in correctional operations, noted that there was no alternative in providing quality health care. Any "deliberate indifference" on the part of correctional administrators to legitimate healthcare needs and the practice of health care would then and for the future be a valid subject of federal litigation. As late as 2011, judicial intervention in correctional health care found face in the state of California when the entire healthcare system for the second largest correctional agency in the country was placed under a receiver given the absence to meet constitutional standards. Justice Marshall told us 40 years earlier that there was no alternative to proper care because prisoners, detainees, inmates, offenders, and any other people incarcerated against their will had to rely on government for their physical safety, the safety of their physical environment, and their physical, medical, and mental health needs.

With more than 3,300 jails operating in the United States and between 10 and 13 million individuals seeking some form of required care, the cost of and attention to healthcare delivery is a mandatory element of any discussion of American jails. Every incoming jail prisoner or detainee receives some form of medical intervention—initial intake interview, initial medical screening, evaluation, treatment, or community-based referral upon release. These millions of individuals even with a generally youthful median age bring enormous healthcare needs into the jail with them. Many have never had routine and regular healthcare screening and review. For some, mandatory jail-provided healthcare services will be their first introduction to a community standard of care. Healthcare issues including HIV/AIDS,[4] hepatitis, sexually transmitted diseases (STDs), tuberculosis, physical problems relating to alcohol and substance abuse, heart disease, specialized women's issues, and an evolving practice covering disorders of the aging.

For many inmates, dental care has never existed as an area of proactive treatment. Women often arrive with very little knowledge about family planning and pregnancy issues. Many have been sexually abused and bring with them both the physical and emotional issues of trauma that accompany such predatory behaviors that they were subjected to for extended periods of time.

Because being in jail does not diminish governmental responsibility for healthcare delivery, decisions cannot be made as matters of choice given public disdain or negative feelings regarding the offender behavior or the alleged detainee behavior that brought them into the criminal justice system. Granted, cosmetic or voluntary procedures such as plastic surgery for visual improvement, complicated dental surgery or tooth replacement, or a wide range of other non-mandatory interventions are not required, but other costs are likely the highest and largest non-staff-related budget items in every jail system in the United States. Inmates arrive in conditions that appear almost theatrical or contrived from a film situation.

Jail healthcare staff often is shocked at how individuals can survive after living on the streets, self-medicating with wide ranges of illicit chemical/prescription combinations or the complex rigor of years of alcoholism. Jails cannot look the other way—cannot blame extensive healthcare deficiencies on the absence of a proper healthcare delivery system—they must confront every legitimate healthcare concern that comes through the doors of the jail booking and reception unit regardless of costs and the origin of the malady, disease, or healthcare deficiency.

The Bureau of Justice Statistics has periodically issued special reports on the medical problems of jail inmates.[5] Prison inmates have often received quality care in local jails prior to conviction and sentencing. Police officers arrive at the jail transporting individuals that have been arrested directly from the streets or from a local police station and often deliver inmates with injuries from the arrest situation. This creates a legal problem, and legislation in most states requires that police receive a medical clearance from a local hospital prior to taking the prisoner to jail for initial intake, booking, and processing. Public comment may strongly suggest that the problem rests with the prisoner, and although that may sound thoughtful as a point of discussion, the mandatory legal requirements demand that the governmental unit provide full care. Disagreements can occur between police officers bringing a prisoner to jail and jail healthcare staff if injuries exist and require community review. This speaks to the complexity of mandatory jail healthcare intervention and, frankly, is not open to debate or discussion. No jail-based booking unit correctional officer or police officer may contradict core constitutional practice concerning the level of health care to be provided to every inmate in every jail setting in the United States.

Major maladies reported upon jail admission have included arthritis, asthma, cancer, diabetes, heart disease and related problems, hypertension, kidney problems, liver issues, paralysis, stroke, hepatitis, HIV/AIDS, STD, tuberculosis, and an expanding list as greater medical diagnoses continue to develop. It might appear that jail inmates are all products of a geriatric setting or were arrested in a senior citizens' residence, but that is far from the truth. The United States has great divisions regarding quality and accessibility of health care based on wealth, employment, military service, education, and other factors relating to access. Jail inmates may not be equally as ill as state prisoners, but they bring every known medical condition into the jail with them, and healthcare delivery requires professional intervention at every level of practice.

■ Behavioral Health/Mental Illness and Substance Abuse Driving Jail Operations

It is striking that if not for issues of serious mental illness and substance abuse, the jails of this country would likely hold less than 50% of their current adult daily population (ADP) of approximately 750,000 and yearly intake numbers of between 10 and 13 million. In no way is it suggested that criminal behavior is dependent on mental illness or alcoholism and substance abuse as a primary driver of activity. Data-driven research would never support such a macro assertion. What is clear is that the jails of the United States are populated with a significant majority of individuals who present records of serious mental illness and extended histories of alcoholism and/or substance abuse. This cannot be minimized; it is very likely, along with poverty, the single most compelling characteristic base of the jail population in the United States.

Going back to the early 1960s, it was always hoped that community treatment efforts would replace the large public mental health facilities that dominated the behavioral health landscape in this country for generations. The development of new medications, community-based treatment modalities, and the introduction of procedural due process requirements dramatically diminished state hospital bed space and placed thousands of individuals on the streets without sufficient care. For numerous environmental reasons that have been well documented in the literature on public policy in this field, jail systems across the country were forced into the role of human service provider of last resort. Economic conditions throughout the United States beginning in the early years of this millennium diminished funding capacity for community-based treatment service. It is clear that the quest for community treatment systems so eagerly anticipated from the early 1960s never came online and forced more persons onto the streets and as a last resort into jails as even minor criminal behavior followed.

This movement to the streets and to jails has been with us for well over 35 years, but only now have improved research capabilities permitted more effective measures of the prevalence of these challenging issues among those in our local jail-based correctional systems. The earliest work conducted by able researchers in the 1980s and 1990s in the Cook County (Illinois) jail system documented severe mental disorders for 6.4% of male inmates and 12.2% of female inmates. Following studies documented a larger and growing number of mentally ill individuals in the jail system. A recent well-regarded study noted a prevalence of serious mental illness among male inmates of approximately 17.5% in two major target county systems. Prevalence among female inmates ranged much higher and was reported at over 30%. The final research outcome of this major study, with appropriate weightings, documented 14.5% for male inmates and 31% for female inmates crosscutting four major county correctional systems.[6]

The conclusions of the study were in some respects challenged, but what is clear is that the jails of this country, for many of the wrong reasons, have become the new mental health hospitals, completely contrary to all of the public policy actions that sought to remove the mentally ill from state hospitals beginning some 50 years ago. It is a challenge to human service methodology and humane public policy process in the United States to have relocated persons with serious mental illness from one negative environment to the criminal justice system and to county jails in particular.

Mental health services in local jails have dramatically improved as a result of mandatory federal constitutional standards concerning healthcare delivery. National standards of care have been voluntarily developed by the National Commission on Correctional Health Care and the ACA. Thirty-six states have standards that, to varying degrees, have further driven improvements in mental health care at the county jail level. Civil rights litigation filed against local jail systems after inmate suicides or documented histories of less than adequate care has pushed jail systems all across this country to improve their services covering the following:

- Intake questioning of detainees by correctional officers
- Intake review by professional healthcare staff members
- Crisis intervention interviews for detainees by licensed mental health professionals at point of jail intake

- Medical and mental health review through more detailed examinations after 14 days of incarceration
- Interface with community service providers as a function of a community standard of care forged between community and jail
- Forensic evaluations that also crosscut general mental health considerations and behaviors
- Individual and group therapy in selected jail environments
- Residential treatment options within specialized jail housing units from minimal treatment through full therapeutic communities
- Screening for community-based release with linkages actually developed and treatment providers identified—from jail to community
- A growing belief that within 10 years, either through court decision or evolving practice, a treatment plan for those with documented mental illness will be required upon leaving a local jail facility

Whether it is because of funding reductions in community-based programs, the closure of state hospitals as poor providers of optimal therapeutic intervention, improvement of crisis intervention teams in the community, or a homeless population with high levels of mental illness, the jail system in the United States is and will continue to be a mental health provider of first, middle, and last resort, however imperfect the venue might be for this critical intervention. It is a serious challenge for the entire jail system in the United States.

Substance abuse (drugs and alcohol) has historically been both a significant characteristic of persons in jail and a driver of jail populations. Drugs in most forms remain illegal, regardless of debate and discussion to the contrary. Methodologies of engagement, whether they be supply-side enforcement or treatment intervention and education to diminish use, still leave us with an enormous substance abuse population in local jails. New detainees often arrive under the influence, going through withdrawal, suffering serious crisis from drug and alcohol abuse, and presenting serious medical complications and a wide range of other problems. Many of these individuals have been self-medicating while living on the streets and often require immediate crisis intervention and lifesaving transport to medical facilities, given the most challenging of personal healthcare situations.

Drug courts are now in operation in more than 300 counties in the United States, seeking to offer a strict treatment regime as an alternative to serious jail and prison incarceration. Contrary to popular thought, many substance abusers have shown little interest in engaging in the rigor of the very invasive and challenging treatment program to avoid relatively short stays in jail. As sentencing options and lengths of time have expanded over the last decade, greater interest has been shown. Persons selected are not first-time users, but increasingly are veteran offenders who clearly might be on their way back to jail or prison for probation and parole violations, let alone new criminal offenses. Because jails are the primary custodial institution serving the courts, jail staff will become more involved in generating referrals for drug courts. Evidence-based practice documents that treatment does work for many individuals, and it is certainly an option starting at the jail level to the far-too-long-revolving door for alcohol and substance abusers who populate our jails.

■ Programs in Jails/The End of Dead Time/Opening a Positive Environment

The local jail traditionally has been seen as a location to provide security and ensure the presence of an individual in court. This is almost a one-dimensional construct with no implications for any detainee or prisoner self-growth and development. Our own data show that at present, 62% of all jail detainees are pretrial and have been convicted of no crime. A logical question is why it is even suggested that personal growth and development programs should be considered, let alone funded, by local government units. Any suggestion that pretrial prisoners have no personal growth and development needs is full of sound and fury and signifies nothing other than traditional jail reluctance to engage in meaningful programs that will require additional planning and work and coordination.

Of the 10–13 million individuals who pass through local jails in the course of a year, well over 50% leave on some form of pretrial release or bail or cases nol-prossed. That still leaves an enormous population for whom program opportunities should surely outweigh mindless hours of television and table games. There are core considerations that warrant our attention and are increasingly data driven to define their importance:

- Jail prisoners who are involved in some meaningful program will evidence a diminished capacity for violence, misbehavior, gang involvement, or any self-destructive behavior;
- Well-intentioned personal growth and development opportunities can affect behavior over short periods of time and can create a more positive personal climate and openness to challenge traditional offender behavioral outcomes.

Why waste time in jail when it can be used productively for both creating a safer correctional environment and improving skill areas in a nonthreatening manner for a majority of prisoners? Dead time demands our attention, for it contributes nothing to jail operations and often creates an environment more likely to generate violence, inappropriate behavior, and the potential for conflict.[7] Jails throughout the country are starting to engage well-tested program elements that improve the local environment. They offer the following growth options:

- Clearly contributing to the safety and security of the jail
- Reducing violence and associated costs of jail violence
- Providing rehabilitation and personal growth opportunities in a controlled setting
- In states with county jail "good time" legislation, reducing days in custody through meaningful prisoner program involvement
- Providing positive interactions in an environment not generally associated with personal growth and development
- Preparing inmates for community reentry

A county or local jail drawing on resources (paid and volunteer) in the surrounding community can find national support and program examples for any of the following program initiatives:

- Adult basic education
- GED—General educational development
- Special education (partnering with school districts for youthful offenders under age 21)
- ESOL—English instruction for people who do not speak English as their first language
- Faith community—Religious doctrine and fundamental religious books and documents
- Faith community—Religious services
- Faith community—Clinical pastoral counseling and mentoring
- Substance abuse treatment—Drug and alcohol education, recovery, and focus on reduced criminality
- Substance abuse treatment—Therapeutic communities—turning a cellblock or housing unit into a treatment modality
- Women's issues—A wide variety of issues tightly targeted to women are available through community colleges, community groups, and highly trained volunteers
- Cognitive behavioral programs—Several templates exist and correctional officers can be trained to work in a treatment modality in a typical jail housing unit
- One-stop job development awareness—Pre- and postrelease job search, interviewing, and resume writing built into IT-based learning—models readily available for use in jails

- Library and reading development—Jails are a perfect location for some form of library and for local literacy programs to conduct one-on-one reading efforts
- Inmate work programs—Institutional work assignments designed to promote positive work ethics and skills, which can be beneficial to inmates upon return to the community
- Health promotion—Public health providers will find an eager audience for a broad range of on-point health-related topics, including healthy sexual behavior practices, STDs, HIV/AIDS prevention, nutrition, aging, issues specific to women's health, smoking cessation, and new topics evolving over time
- Fatherhood and parenting programs—Helping incarcerated fathers develop and maintain healthy relationships with their children and partners to reduce recidivism and break cycles of violence and crime
- Digital skill development—This is the world at present with no other options available other than learning computer-based skills at all levels

The above are simply exemplars of program options that can be conducted in a single program room in the smallest of jails or in large program settings in much larger facilities. Dead time denotes the absence of management resolve to confront traditional practices solely focused on ancient definitions of safety and security. Programs create safer environments in the toughest and most demanding of jail settings. Programs also offer avenues for detainee and offender growth and development.

■ Life After Lockup—Jail Detainees and Prisoners Returning Home

For a period of some 30 years, criminal justice and public safety rhetoric was largely focused on enforcement, incarceration, longer sentences, and building and filling jails and prisons. That is not a political comment—it is data driven—for a generation has observed public policy moving toward tough responses to crime and a dramatic focus toward incarceration. Some will agree and some will not, but that is an introduction, not the real issue before us. What virtually everyone will accept is that the focus was on removing people from the streets for longer periods of incarceration, and very little focus, and very little creativity, was dispatched toward reentry and return to the community.

In the last decade, the phrase "offender reentry" reentered the correctional lexicon.[8] It was less a matter of political persuasion than the recognition that enormous numbers of prisoners were returning and would be returning to the community. Twenty-plus years of unabated jail construction, prison construction, and enhanced duration of sentencing penalties would begin to see offenders being released and returning to the community, regardless of whether they were prepared to assume roles in society with some diminished capacity to commit crime. A one-dimensional public polity focus can continue only so long. The focus of "get tough, longer sentences and more prisons" would in part run its course as costs became impossible to sustain in light of competing educational, military, healthcare, and child development priorities.

Led by Jeremy Travis, then of the Urban Institute, reentry as a public attention option received a superior dose of public policy attention. Travis would likely argue that many others were involved, but there is no question that his work on offender reentry at the state prison level pushed the conscience of a broad policy community that recognized that offenders were coming home.[9] Jeremy Travis set many thinking or at least realizing that a tidal wave of offenders was going to leave incarceration and go directly back to the communities from which they came. This was a significant challenge.

In 2002, one of those unique moments and gatherings took place in Branson, Missouri, that was to have significant implications for reentry considerations and future programming at the level of county jails and local jails. Called by the National Association of Counties—Justice and Public Safety Steering Committee, the issue of reentry at the jail level crystallized during a presentation by a scholar and public policy analyst who had worked with Travis on state prison reentry considerations. National AIDS Control Organisation elected officials from around the country realized that the jails in their jurisdictions were returning between 10 and 13 million individuals to local communities and that it was unconscionable that reentry would be excluded from local jail consideration simply because corrections had been so long defined in an almost purely prison context. At a quiet meeting in more rural Missouri, an idea was developed that jails counted and should be part of the reentry equation.

The Urban Institute, this time under the direction of Amy Solomon, accepted the challenge and developed a program in concert with the John Jay College of Criminal Justice, the Montgomery County (Maryland) Department of Correction and Rehabilitation, and the Bureau of Justice Assistance. By mid-2008, offender reentry and detainee reentry at the jail level were established as data-driven elements of serious public policy. National meetings were held, and descriptive analytical and training materials were developed to focus on reentry from jail to the community all across the United States.[10] Since 2007, the Bureau of Justice Statistics had meaningfully inferred and documented that well over 10 million individuals were leaving county jails and that their success would be flat, negative, and contrary to public safety priorities if they were simply walked to the jail door and released.

Work completed by the Urban Institute highlighted the size of the returning jail population and the enormous complexity of the characteristics and issues that challenged any hope of successful return. The jail portion of the corrections profession was urged to accept, consider, and develop strategies to confront the following barriers and challenges to return to the community:

- Employment and education
- Substance abuse
- Mental health
- Physical health
- Housing
- Chronic offenders
- Specialized issues affecting women upon their release

It may appear that these are the same issues challenging offenders leaving state prisons, but jails had never even been part of the equation. It was an issue essentially swept away or never given proper consideration until vast numbers leaving jails, and some good public policy discussion, forced the issue onto the mantle of public policy and public safety. Jails were not mom-and-pop institutions, but were a public safety core element that affected public safety in every single community in the United States.

Persons leaving local jails often could not cash a check with the funds they had brought with them at the time of arrest, for they had no identification that would be accepted in the community. Waves of departing jail detainees and offenders had lost mental health and physical health benefits as a function of jail placement (whether guilty or not guilty) and could find no apparent way to reassert their needs and receive help and medications that were provided appropriately while incarcerated, but were not available upon release.

Many leaving local jails had neither social security cards nor any frame of reference to past history that would facilitate workforce development and seeking a job upon release. Housing options were severely limited, as even the most minor of offenders coming out of local jails were denied access to Section 8 housing options as a result of their criminal behavior and jail incarceration. Hundreds of professions were closed to jail-based offenders because of strict though ancient prohibitions closing off work to many who would otherwise be employable. Thousands of individual barriers existed across all 50 states, limiting the capacity of individuals to gear-up their personal situations to have a great opportunity for postrelease success.

The Second Chance Act, formally passed in 2008 and signed into law by then-President George W. Bush, provided strong bully pulpit leadership to find means to assist those leaving jail and prison to overcome barriers that had been reinforced so firmly during a period of much tougher attitudes toward criminal justice and its outcomes. County and local jails were included in the language of the Second Chance Act rather than being left along the roadside as had happened so often in the past regarding the jail component of the criminal justice and public safety process. The exceptional work of the Urban Institute and the "Life After Lockup" project identified barriers, strategies, and best practices to engage the millions returning to the community from local jails.

Jails gained enormous traction with the formation of the Federal Interagency Reentry Council, established in January 2011 by Attorney General Eric Holder with driving encouragement by Assistant Attorney General Laurie Robinson, Office of Justice Programs, U.S. Department of Justice. This effort has brought more than 19 cabinet-level agencies and offices to directly confront and engage the following offender issues:

- To identify research and evidence-based practices, policies, and programs that advance the Reentry Council's mission related to prisoner reentry and community safety.
- To identify federal policy opportunities and barriers to improve outcomes for the reentry population.
- To promote federal statutory, policy, and practice changes that focus on reducing crime and improving the well-being of formerly incarcerated individuals, their families, and communities.
- To identify and support initiatives in the areas of education, employment, health, housing, faith, drug treatment, and family and community well-being that can contribute to successful outcomes for formerly incarcerated individuals.
- To leverage resources across agencies that support this population in becoming productive citizens and reducing recidivism and victimization.
- To coordinate messaging and communications about prisoner reentry and the administration's response to it.[11]

Each element was an effort to directly confront the rigor and complexity of providing those returning to the community with a best chance to be successful. The jail system was right in the middle of this new and evolving development. Local correctional systems based in jails could no longer just open the door and send detainees and offenders out to the street with nothing of substance to support their return home. Part of the total public safety equation included reentry planning and development of improved means to confront those issues that brought individuals into the criminal justice system. Jails have a unique role to play, for they exist amid local communities where millions of persons will be returned. Looking elsewhere or assuming that others will carry on the work is no longer acceptable. Jails have a solid reentry responsibility and a growing body of technical assistance and support to conduct that new mission.

■ Conclusion

Jails are now recognized as a changing and dynamic element of the corrections and criminal justice process. Jails house sentenced populations right in the middle of every jurisdiction in the United States. Pretrial jails populations drive national jail population levels and clearly improved process can dramatically alter years of traditional case disposition process. Bail as a matter of pretrial release is under serious review as data-driven and evidence-based practices of risk assessment offer improved decisions without the introduction of personal wealth. This is creating fascinating changes in the entire methodology of corrections at the local level and a maturity in policy and process development.[12]

Our society still has miles to travel to find a more appropriate mental health provider of last resort than local jails. Treatment can be so difficult to engage in the free community and so easily engaged in the criminal justice system. This aspect of jail operations and human service public policy considerations must change; treatment in jail should be a last resort, not a standard aspect of the treatment equation. Jails are located generally right in the midst of most political jurisdictions in this country, and they have the potential to seriously expand discussion of those issues that contribute to criminal behavior and the absence of positive outcomes given past practices that have not contributed to improved situations. Jails have become a key element in criminal justice systems in every community in the United States.

Chapter Resources

DISCUSSION QUESTIONS

1. Why have jails historically been accorded a minor role in discussions of corrections, and how is that changing?
2. Are jail population levels a function of static forces such as the rate and level of crime, or are there means to influence population levels as a matter of policy and criminal justice process?
3. How do the existence of personal growth and development programs influence the safety of staff and inmates in jails?
4. Why have jails seen a significant growth in the number of mentally ill detainees and offenders entering the criminal justice system?
5. Why does offender reentry make sense as a matter of public policy in jails throughout the nation?

ONLINE RESOURCES

- American Correctional Association, http://www.aca.org/
- American Jail Association, http://www.aja.org/
- Bureau of Justice Statistics (BJS)—U.S. Department of Justice, http://www.bjs.gov/
- Consensus Project (Mental Illness and Criminal Justice), http://www.consensusproject.org/
- Council of State Government Justice Center, http://www.justicecenter.csg/
- Montgomery County (MD) Department of Correction and Rehabilitation, http://www.montgomery countymd.gov/doctmpl.asp?url=/content/docr/index.asp
- National Institute of Corrections, http://www.nicic.gov/
- National Reentry Resource Center and Federal Interagency Reentry Council, http://www.nationalreentry resourcecenter.org/reentry-council
- Office of Justice Policy—U.S. Department of Justice, http://www.ojp.usdoj.gov/
- Pretrial Justice Institute (PJI), http://www.pretrial.org/

NOTES

1. Minton, T. (2012). *Jail inmates at midyear 2011—Statistical tables*. Washington, DC: Bureau of Justice Statistics.
2. Pretrial Justice Institute. (2009). *Pretrial justice in America: A survey of county pretrial release policies, practices and outcomes*. Washington, DC: Author.
3. Freudenberg, N. (2006). *Coming home from jail: A review of health and social problems facing US jail populations and of opportunities for reentry interventions*. Washington, DC: Urban Institute—Jail Re-entry Roundtable Initiative.
4. Maruschak, L. (2009). *HIV in prisons, 2007–2008*. Washington, DC: Bureau of Justice Statistics; Dwyer, M., & Fish, C. D., Gallucci, A., & Walker, S. (2011). HIV care in correctional settings. In *Guide for HIV/AIDS clinical care*. Washington, DC: Health Resources and Services Administration, U.S. Department of Health and Human Services.

5. Maruschak, L. (2006). *Medical problems of jail inmates.* Washington, DC: Bureau of Justice Statistics, Special Report; Noonan, M., & Carson, E. A. (2011). *Prison and jail deaths in custody 2000–2009—Statistical tables.* Washington, DC: Bureau of Justice Statistics.

6. Steadman, H., Osher, F., Robbins, P. C., Case, B., & Samuels, S. (2009). Prevalence of serious mental illness among jail inmates. *Journal of Psychiatric Services, 60,* 761–765; Justice Center—Council of State Governments. (2009). *Frequently asked questions about the new study of serious mental illness in jails.* New York, NY: Author.

7. French, S., & Gendreau, P. (2006). Reducing prison misconducts: What works. *Criminal Justice and Behavioral Health, 33,* 185–218.

8. Travis, J. (2000). *But they all come back: Rethinking prisoner reentry, sentencing and corrections—Issues for the 21st century.* Washington, DC: National Institute of Justice; Langan, P., & Levin, D. (2002). *Recidivism of prisoners released in 1994.* Washington, DC: Bureau of Justice Statistics, Special Report.

9. Travis, J. (March, 2009). *What works for successful prisoner reentry, testimony before the US house of representatives—Committee on appropriations.* Washington, DC: John Jay College.

10. Solomon, A., Osborne, J., Lobuglio, S., Mellow, J., & Mukamal, D. (2008). *Life after lockup: Improving reentry from jail to the community.* Washington, DC: Urban Institute—Justice Policy Center.

11. Federal Interagency Reentry Council. (2012). *Reducing barriers to successful reentry—Second chance and secure communities.* Washington, DC: Council of State Governments.

12. Mauer, M., & Epstein, K. (Eds.). (2012). *To build a better criminal justice system: 25 experts envision the next 25 years of reform.* Washington, DC: The Sentencing Project.

Prison Architecture
Robert S. George

CHAPTER OBJECTIVES

- Understand the limitations of building correctional facilities with specific materials.
- Distinguish different housing unit models on the basis of their architectural characteristics.
- Differentiate between security levels that are suitable for various housing units.

To design a prison or jail facility, architects must consider many factors, including:

- Characteristics and numbers of inmates
- Management and punishment philosophy
- Availability of funding
- Site and utility characteristics
- Staffing requirements
- Type of housing unit

Correctional institutions are communities unto themselves and require many different services, including:

- Food service
- Medical support
- Maintenance
- Work and industrial areas
- Education and recreation facilities
- Isolation cells for rule violators

A correctional institution needs at least one basic housing configuration to accommodate various correctional programs, however, institutions are often a collection of different types of housing units. The design of the elements that support the institution, collectively referred to as the institution's core by some systems, tends to evolve from the architectural design of the inmate housing unit or units.

Housing Configurations

The evolution of prison housing concepts corresponds closely to the development of correctional management practices over the centuries. Prison architecture is influenced significantly by the operating agencies' policies and management styles. Societal attitudes toward incarcerated people and emerging construction systems affect decisions about the architectural details of a housing unit as well.

There have been few changes in housing unit design over the centuries, but most have been dramatic departures from their predecessors. The changes have tended to follow the philosophy and attitudes of the citizens of the country and the wishes of the elected representatives who authorize the design and construction. Sometimes architectural design changes follow a swing toward more punitive attitudes. At other times, they respond to a belief that the behavior of sentenced criminals can be improved through their living environment, and these facilities are designed as places of rehabilitation.

The desire to separate criminals from society and punish them has been the most consistent influence on correctional architecture through the years. Architecture is a language of symbols. Some prison architecture conveys a message of decent, safe, and sanitary conditions, whereas some expresses extreme punishment. In recent years, correctional architecture has come to reflect classification systems that assess inmates' behavior and try to predict their needs while they are in custody.

Historical Models

The history of prison architecture progresses through a series of specific facilities and models.

The Bastille

This famous French fortress was built around 1370 as part of the fortifications for the wall around Paris. Its physical characteristics are linked clearly to the harsh approach to punishment practiced there. It was four floors high, with all levels contained in a continuous, stone masonry wall. Its massive form derived from eight cylindrical towers linked together with a series of straight wall sections. The walls had several windows on each level arranged directly over the ones beneath. Much like a medieval castle, it had two interior courtyards, and like many castles, it had a projected, crenellated parapet (a series of stone shields running along the top of the wall) to protect defenders stationed on the roof against arrows and other flying projectiles. Also like a castle, it was accessible only by a drawbridge. In all likelihood, it had limited means for personal hygiene, and its walls allowed the weather elements to enter and circulate cold air and airborne contaminants. The Bastille's architectural features symbolize its primary, and probably only, design goal of containing masses of people and resisting attackers bent on forcing the prisoners' release.

The Second Western Penitentiary of Pennsylvania, an example of Bastille-like design on the other side of the Atlantic, was built near Pittsburgh in the 1830s. Its architectural proportions with four levels high with thick walls and a crenellated parapet are different from its model in Paris, but its origins are undeniable. Secure, punitive, and gloomy, it operated throughout most of the 19th century to warehouse people in a hopeless, degenerative environment.

Convict Hulks

Numerous wooden ships docked in harbors, such as Portsmouth, were used widely in England in the last half of the 18th century to confine convicted persons. These crowded, dirty surplus boats served to separate England's convicted from society regardless of their crime. They were infested with rodents and insects, and their basic wood construction facilitated incubation, absorption, and spread of disease. These hulks were probably unsupervised, and their construction made them a perpetual fire hazard. The convict hulk has had a long-term influence on prison design over much of the globe. Eventually, after a few ghastly episodes stemming from the nature of the hulks' construction, prison reform advocates prevailed with a more humane design approach.

Panopticon

This housing unit concept was created by English philosopher and social reformer Jeremy Bentham around 1790. Despite Bentham's English origins, no facilities with this housing design were ever built in England.

The Panopticon unit consists of two-person cells arranged side-by-side in a circular plan that generates a building in the form of a drum. Because of its shape, it is also called a roundhouse. Four tiers high with a supervision pod in the center, it was intended to be an efficient means for housing a large number of people under constant supervision (see **Figure 3-1**).

The cells in the Panopticon face each other across a wide circular space and overlook an enclosed officer's observation station at the center. With the cells arranged along the thick masonry perimeter walls with narrow windows, if any, this configuration resembles the Pennsylvania model. Moving around on the ground level is simple and direct. On any of the upper tiers, however, officers must follow the curving balcony along the cell fronts for some distance to reach a stair. If officers in the observation station need move quickly from the station to a problem they have seen from within the station, they have a substantial distance to travel.

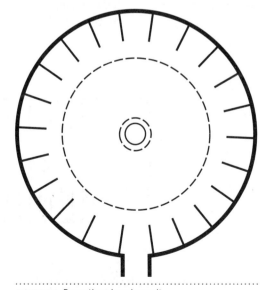

FIGURE 3-1 Panopticon housing unit

The Panopticon concept includes another unattractive feature that undermines its use. Built with concrete or masonry, furnished with steel bunks, and secured with steel cell fronts, the Panopticon has extremely high normal, or ambient, noise levels because of reverberation and echoes within its hard walls. The circular shape is a natural sound amplifier. Given the normal activity in a prison housing unit (e.g., talking, showering, closing doors, doing janitorial work), the ambient noise level in a Panopticon at midday, for example, is so reinforced by its shape that normal conversation reaches shouting levels. The deleterious effect of exposure to this acoustic on the occupants of this space—both staff and inmates—must be significant.

Pennsylvania and Auburn Models

The Pennsylvania system (see Chapter 1) focused on imprisonment with hard labor, so prison design emerged as an important issue. To replace the open bay or congregate style of housing dozens of people that had prevailed in previous centuries, the Walnut Street Jail was erected in 1790 with small cells to house individual prisoners. In 1829, the Eastern Penitentiary at Cherry Hill in Philadelphia, Pennsylvania, was developed based on cellular housing (see **Figure 3-2**).

At the opposite ends of the 18th century, cellular imprisonment had been used in the papal prison of St. Michael in Rome and at Ghent in Belgium. These European models featured cells arranged along the exterior walls of the building, an arrangement now known as an outside-cell plan. Eastern Penitentiary's design borrowed this concept and took it a step further by organizing the cell buildings in a spoke pattern (see Figure 3-3). In this plan, buildings enclosing a number of cells were arranged side by side in a linear pattern and in one or more levels radiating from a central hub space or rotunda. The application of this architectural configuration facilitated systematic identification and management of the institution's population in groups of predetermined size. This configuration has been used quite extensively in England, France, and other European countries.

Architecturally, the outside-cell configuration is based on flanking cells arranged in a linear plan and facing a common central corridor and another row of cells on the other side. Depending on the number of inmates and floor area constraints, cells are stacked in one or more tiers accessible by stairs at either end of the range.

Cell-front design can be open with bars and a barred door, or they can be solid with a panel door. Because each prisoner can touch an exterior building wall in this configuration, the construction details of the wall and any windows it may include become essential to the institution's perimeter security. With the development of modern plumbing systems, outside-cell configurations now include toilet, lavatory fixtures, and showers.

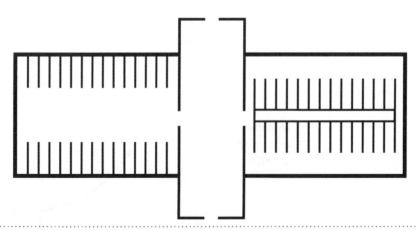

FIGURE 3-2 Pennsylvania housing unit with exterior cells (left) and Auburn housing unit with interior cells (right)

Typically, these fixtures are arranged along the fronts of the cells to permit a full view into the cell and to facilitate maintenance of the mechanical system from the walkway outside the cell.

The Pennsylvania concept led to the radiating wing organization for large housing units. In this organization, linear cellblocks are arranged like spokes in a wheel around a central hub.

The Auburn system used a slightly different model, featuring two back-to-back rows of multitiered cells arranged in a straight, linear plan. A typical cell of an individual prisoner could measure 3.5 by 7 by 7 feet. (By contrast, today's standards call for a room 7 or 8 feet wide, 10 feet long, and 8 feet high.) This housing concept dominated U.S. prison and jail design in the 19th and early 20th centuries. Like the Pennsylvania model, side-by-side cells extend far enough to accommodate the desired number of beds. The number of cells in a row can range from five or six to several dozen. Two of these blocks of cells can be joined at a central space that permits access to both.

Over the decades, electrical, plumbing, and ventilation systems were introduced into the housing unit design. These systems were usually accommodated in the architectural design by separating the back-to-back rows of cells a few feet to form a continuous space called a chase. The chase can be entered from either end of the cellblock for maintenance of the systems and acts as a spine to serve the toilet and light fixtures at the back of each cell. The piping system in the chase tends to limit the overall length of the cellblock because of the relationship between a pipe's diameter and the volume of water it can handle. Other than this, there are no architectural or construction constraints to the length of a cellblock.

This concept allows the rows of cells to be stacked in tiers accessible by stairs, and these tiers can range as high as six levels. Multitiered applications of rows of cells have become commonly known as cellblocks. In the Auburn model, or inside-cell plan configuration, cells are organized in the middle of the overall space with their fronts facing the building's exterior walls. Unlike in the Pennsylvania model, the cells and their occupants do not face each other. The distance between the cell front and the outside wall at the ground floor level usually equals or exceeds the depth of the cells to allow for a continuous balcony along the front of the cells on the levels above the ground floor. Because the occupants of the cells cannot reach the walls as long as the cell front is closed, the exterior walls can have windows for light and ventilation without compromising the building's security.

Auburn-style cellblocks were designed to provide a certain number of cells in one housing unit. However, in many of the larger institutions with long cellblocks, a crossover corridor has been incorporated at midpoint to allow movement to the cells on the other side of the unit without having to walk or run all the way to one end of the building. Group showers are often located in this same crossover corridor. The building is accessible from one end, where it joins a corridor that, in turn, leads to more cellblocks or other components of the institution. Somewhere close to the other end, the building may have another door to the outside to permit entrance into the building by staff in the event of a disturbance. Beginning in the late 1970s, modern fire and life safety concerns have influenced correctional architecture significantly, and these second doors are more common and are considered emergency exits to allow evacuation. Some old cellblocks have been divided with fire-rated cross walls and doors so that one end can act as an area of refuge for the other in an emergency.

Dozens of Auburn-style housing units have been built throughout the United States. This housing concept dominated much of prison and jail design in the 19th century. Its features have become so familiar that when most people think of correctional facilities, they think of the inside-cell architectural model. There are still several functioning examples of the Auburn housing unit, probably because overcrowded conditions keep the demand for housing so high that replacement is not economically feasible. But it is interesting to note that many of them have been substantially remodeled and internally subdivided to upgrade their life safety characteristics and convert them into more manageable modules.

When supervising in both the Auburn and Pennsylvania model housing units, officers patrol on the ground floor or the continuous balcony in front of the rows of cells. Officers need to look directly into each cell during their patrols. The application of gang-locking hardware systems in the early 20th century permitted officers to selectively open one or several doors in a range of cells at once to let certain inmates out for meals, work, or recreation. The linear housing unit configuration and the supervision practices it fostered has led in some instances to inadequate attention from staff and contributed to significant neglect and harsh treatment.

Later, institutions made up of combinations of the Pennsylvania and Auburn models arranged in a radial plan developed to take advantage of the merits of both (see **Figure 3-3**). Another site plan arrangement known as the telephone pole plan does much the same thing (see **Figure 3-4**) by attaching housing units of different configurations to opposite sides of a central corridor or spine.

Together, the Pennsylvania and Auburn configurations are now known as the linear indirect configuration because both of them feature long, narrow organization and can only be effectively supervised by walking back and forth along its length. This supervision style means that staff can temporarily lose awareness of some parts of the unit. This architectural style was used extensively in American prisons and jails over the 20th century. However, other housing styles emerged over the century, giving the institution a wider variety of housing conditions within the same security perimeter.

■ Direct Supervision

One of the most interesting developments in modern correctional facility design occurred when the Federal Bureau of Prisons (BOP) opened the federal correctional institutions at Pleasanton, California, and Miami, Florida. Prompted in part by the need to abate the conditions that contributed to a long and deadly disturbance that occurred in the New York State Prison at Attica in 1971, BOP initiated the design of a new style of housing unit that is nearly a square.

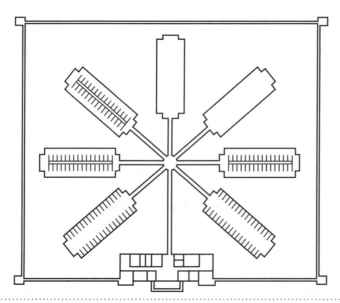

FIGURE 3-3 Radiating wing organization

This significant departure from the linear Auburn and Pennsylvania models features a large, open central indoor recreational or day room space (see **Figure 3-5**). Individual cells are organized around this square space. Showers and quiet recreation areas are interspersed among the cells. A correctional officer in this model can roam around the unit and see most of the interior space from just about any vantage point. The cells in the housing unit are stacked two high, one level above and below the common area. Because the officer on the common floor is within a half-flight of either level of rooms, response to any cell is quicker.

By design, the capacity of the unit was limited to 125 cells, an appropriate number for 1 or 2 officers to supervise. The unit, in turn, can be divided into halves or quarters by means of sliding doors or temporary partitions. Like its predecessor, the Pennsylvania model, the building envelope (i.e., the exterior walls and the roof) has been detailed to provide the building perimeter security. The secure envelope means that the interior partitions, doors, hardware, stairs, and other features could be built of lighter materials. This concept, which has become known as the direct supervision model (or new generation model), encourages a humane atmosphere by facilitating inmate-staff communication and security.

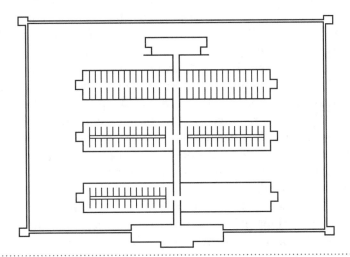

FIGURE 3-4 Telephone pole organization

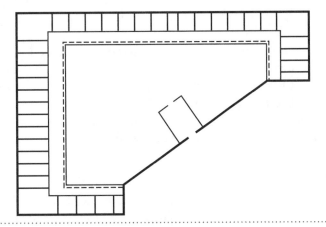

FIGURE 3-5 Direct supervision model

The exterior shape of this housing unit includes a sloping roof covered with conventional shingles so that persons can be seen on the roof. Inmate cell windows are quite large, and the walls are trimmed with large wood beams. Because more systems for commercial construction can be used in this concept, it is more economical to build.

■ Supermaximum Security

Prison systems have found it necessary to develop high-security institutions to handle groups of inmates who are especially violent.[1] BOP operated the U.S. Penitentiary (USP) on Alcatraz Island in the San Francisco Bay for 30 years for very dangerous inmates. Architecturally, Alcatraz was a combination of the Auburn system (with stacked inside cells) and the Pennsylvania system (with rows of cells that face each other across an open corridor or range) (see Figure 3-2). It had manually operated gang-locking doors and the central plumbing chase characteristic of the Auburn model. The buildings and support structures around the island were constructed of reinforced concrete. Its capacity ranged from 200 to 250 inmates, each in single cells. The rows of cells were stacked too high, and the main roof over the housing unit was high enough to permit skylights that were well out of the reach of inmates. It also featured a central dining room. Outdoor recreation took place on the south side of the island in a large, open yard enclosed by a tall, concrete wall. The institution included industries and some staff housing.

In 1963, USP Alcatraz was closed, and its super maximum security role in the federal prison system was transferred to the new USP Marion in southern Illinois. Marion was built with a control unit of 70 cells for inmates within the federal system with records of dangerous and aggressive behavior, long sentence duration, or other administrative conditions that required that they be housed under constant segregation conditions. The unit's design is based on inside cells with a dedicated shower at one end. This shower and a small recreation yard adjacent to the unit are available to only one inmate at a time. Meals are delivered on trays to each cell, and all movements within the unit are under multiple escorts.

High-security institutions were taken to a new level in California in the late 1980s and in Colorado in the 1990s. The California Department of Corrections' Pelican Bay Prison near the Oregon border includes two security housing units (SHUs) totaling 1,056 beds. The SHU is a new model of the administrative–maximum security facility to house management cases, habitual criminals, prison gang members, and the like. In these units, the inmate lives alone in a single cell. Each unit has its own grille-covered recreation yard. The inmate is permitted to use this yard for a short period each day. Doors to each cell are sliding, perforated steel plates with overhead and motor-operated sliding devices operated from a control center. With the exception of escorted, scheduled movements for recreation or other appointments, the inmate never leaves the cell.

The administrative–maximum security institution at the USP in Florence, Colorado, is the current federal edition of a supermaximum facility. As in Marion, the capacity of the Florence basic module is small to facilitate supervision. Each housing unit has 64 cells, each cell is accessible through its own sally port, and each cell includes its own shower as well as toilet and lavatory. Cells are arranged in the outside-cell configuration on two levels split at the unit entrance, but a wall down the middle of the unit screens the view of the cells across the corridor. Inmates can use a large outdoor recreation area between the units on established schedules.

■ Other Design Factors

The housing unit of a prison or jail is the most important element of correctional design. Depending on the capacity of the institution, the collection of housing units typically accounts for at least half of the land covered by a correctional facility. The architecture of the inmate housing area largely steers the design of the rest of the institution. The other elements consist of the spaces needed to support the housing units. These elements include space to prepare and serve food, run programs, provide medical services, hold visits, put out fires, ensure the institution's security, and provide for its administration, sanitation, and maintenance. In many modern institutions, large industrial buildings are included so inmates can manufacture goods or provide services for outside agencies. Some correctional systems provide housing for conjugal visits, too.

A correctional facility is a large, expensive, and complex place to build and to maintain. Prisons and jails are more costly to build than most other types of buildings. Construction and maintenance costs rise primarily in proportion to the level of security required by the institution's population. Other factors that influence construction and maintenance costs include proximity to an urban area, regional climate, and soil and land characteristics.

There are other significant operational costs that must be considered in the design of a prison or jail. Correctional facilities are always "open for business"; they are occupied every day and all day. This means that power and lighting, mechanical and plumbing, and security and communication systems are always running. They are in constant need of maintenance. Their various systems are used heavily, and they need to be repaired or replaced frequently. Prison and jail facilities are never truly complete because their changing populations and space needs demand expansion or alteration, which leads to ongoing renovation. And like all buildings, correctional facilities must face the unpredictable effects of wear and tear, earthquakes, hurricanes, floods, fire, and other natural disasters.

The prison design tends to react to new or changed conditions, operations, or programs. In the process, correctional design often employs technology originally devised for other building types. Rarely is a new technology invented for use in a correctional environment. Usually, a new technology is adapted slowly for prison use after first proving itself in some other arena. For example, most forms of the electronic life safety and surveillance and control systems now common in modern jails and prisons were common in schools, hospitals, dormitories, and the like well before they made their way into corrections.

Evolving technology presents significant benefits and challenges to population management, too. Digital technology gives today's prison and jail administrator tools that far surpass the hand-operated means of keeping track of inmate and staff records commonly used only a few decades ago. At the same time, digital technology presents serious concerns when it drifts into the hands of the inmate population. Architecturally, the modern institution needs to provide space dedicated to contain, protect, and upgrade equipment that supports and monitors both wired and wireless electronic signals.

A correctional institution of any size is a place for people to live and for others to work. Correctional architecture needs to contribute to a sense of safety and health in both of these groups as they go about their lives. Obviously, correctional institutions can be dangerous places, and they can readily become a setting for the worst in mass human behavior. Almost every day in a correctional institution, life is a repetition of the day before. On occasion, although, disturbances occur, exposing people—staff and inmates alike—to serious threats. Balancing the dichotomous nature of the culture it serves is a massive challenge in the process of designing a correctional facility.

Over the centuries, prison architecture has had the same central purpose—to separate convicted offenders from the rest of society—but different forces have influenced how correctional facilities are designed:

- Social reformers dismayed at conditions they found in the justice system of their particular day
- Correctional science and classification systems that identify and separate offender types
- Management sciences used to train staff and manage resources
- Technological advances in construction systems, detention hardware, and electronic surveillance and control systems

■ Conclusion

Prison and jail architectures are driven by societal attitudes and directly relate to the purpose for which the institution is designed. If the prevailing attitude is supportive of harsh punishment, institutions are designed and built to emphasize harsh control features. If citizens wish to emphasize rehabilitation, the design will reflect more normal-appearing, less-controlling architectural features. The history of prison design is a fascinating one, and it parallels changes in expectations and attitudes that have shifted in American society.

Chapter Resources

DISCUSSION QUESTIONS

1. What kind of correctional programs would work best in each of the architectural configurations described in this chapter?
2. What are some of the possible health, safety, and emotional effects that might accrue from long-term confinement to any of these housing configurations?
3. In comparing possible goals for a correctional institution, what factors would you consider as you establish security and program requirements to be included in the architectural design of the facility?
4. Which housing configurations lend themselves to good sanitation and maintenance?
5. Which housing configurations would be the most difficult to maintain and keep clean?

ADDITIONAL RESOURCES

American Correctional Association. (1983). *The American prison: From the beginning. A pictorial history.* College Park, MD: Author.

American Correctional Association. (1983). *Design guide for secure adult correctional facilities.* College Park, MD: Author.

Fairweather, L., & McConville, S. (2000). *Prison architecture policy, design and experience.* New York, NY: Architectural Press/Elsevier.

Fairweather, L., & McConville, S. (2012). *Prison architecture.* New York, NY: Routledge.

Jewkes, Y., & Johnston, H. (2007). "The evolution of prison architecture." *Handbook on Prisons*, 174.

Johnston, N. (2004). "The World's Most Influential Prison: Success or Failure?" *The Prison Journal, 84*(4), suppl, 20S–40S.

NOTE

1. Johnson, R. (2002). *Hard time: Understanding and reforming the prison.* Belmont, CA: Wadsworth/Thomas Learning.

YOU ARE THE ADMINISTRATOR

■ A Serious Assault

The warden and 15 staff members at Green Point State Prison were served on Monday. The lawsuit alleged serious negligence on the part of senior administrators as well as the correctional officers on duty. The inmate, James Day, had been violently assaulted 11 months ago, on the day of his arrival at this high-security state correctional institution.

It was inmate Day's first time in a higher security institution. The inmate was initially serving his 3-year sentence at a low-security facility, but the staff at the first institution observed very erratic behavior. Staff members quickly determined that there may have been some mental issues with this fellow; he occasionally talked to himself, spoke haughtily to staff and other inmates, and generally could not get along with others. It was believed that he should be placed in a major institution where mental health resources were available on staff. Green Point did have four psychologists employed. Even though Day would ordinarily not have been placed in a high-security facility, he was sent to Green Point for medical and psychiatric assessment.

On the day of his arrival at the Green Point State Prison, intake screening staff made the decision to place the transferred inmate in a detention cell away from the general population until a psychologist could assess his behavior. Unfortunately, the only administrative detention cell available was a two-person cell that was already occupied by another inmate. The officers on duty, thinking that this was an appropriate decision, placed him in the cell with the other inmate. They noted in the record that the other inmate had no history of violent behavior.

One hour later, officers heard screaming in the cell. When they looked in the cell's door window, they observed inmate Day lying on the floor with blood running out of a huge gash on his forehead. He was immediately removed from the cell and taken to the institution's hospital, where the medical decision was made to place him in the nearby town's medical center for emergency care. He was returned 3 hours later with a diagnosis of trauma to his neck, face, and forehead. He suffered a severe contusion to his throat and was unable to talk or use his vocal cords. Over the next 8 months, he did slowly regain full function of his voice, and his other injuries healed. One large scar remained on his forehead.

The inmate who assaulted Day claimed that Day insulted him when he arrived and continued to verbally berate him. He said his anger simply got the better of him, and when Day was on his knees looking out the food trap on the door, he kicked the back of his head, jamming his forehead, face, and throat into the door. He added that he did not know why the staff had put that "crazy ol' son of a bitch" in his cell, anyway!

- Did the Green Point staff handle this mental health case appropriately on his arrival?
- Would you offer any advice as to how inmate Day should have been treated differently?
- Did the detention officers deserve to be named in this lawsuit?
- Is it right that the warden, who did not ever know of this specific case, should be sued?
- Why is this an issue relating to inmate classification?

Custody and Security

Michael B. Cooksey

CHAPTER OBJECTIVES

- Discuss the role classification plays in maintaining an institution security.
- Describe why it is important to control clutter and excessive inmate personal property in correctional environments.
- Explain why accounting for staff in a correctional institution is important.
- Identify the best sources of intelligence regarding inmate activities.

Most inmates prefer a quiet, clean, and orderly prison where they can serve their time in a safe environment. A well-run institution has a certain feel about it: The quiet rumble of daily activities with no loud noises, clean and shining hallways, and lack of clutter in inmate cells signify that the staff is in charge and running the prison. Few inmates benefit from disrupting daily activities. Proper security can ensure inmate safety and provide staff with good working conditions.

■ Security Begins with Inmate Classification

It is difficult to begin a discussion on institution security without first discussing proper classification of facilities and inmates. Institutions must be designed to house a certain type of offender. Violent, aggressive, and escape-prone inmates require more physical security features and staff resources.

Classification can best be defined as the systematic grouping of inmates into categories based on shared characteristics and behavioral patterns. Using the inmate's history, staff can make fairly accurate predictions about the inmate's future behavior and adjustment to incarceration. Inmates with similar characteristics living together in an appropriately designed facility are much easier to manage. Likewise, a strong inmate among a weaker population can wreak havoc. Escapes, assaults, and drug dealing very seldom occur in areas where the inmates are deliberately stratified.

But inmates may find ways to manipulate the system so that they can be in areas of the institution where there is little staff supervision. On April 5, 2006, Richard McNair, a notorious inmate who was considered an extreme escape risk and who had a history of compromising staff, escaped from the U.S. Penitentiary in Pollock, Louisiana. He was able to avoid the higher degree of supervision normally afforded an inmate of his status. The inmate worked in Federal Prison Industries, where he secreted himself in a pallet of mailbags being shipped from the prison. Subsequent searches of the prison confirmed that the inmate had escaped. The escaped inmate was stopped by local police while he was running along railroad tracks near the prison, but he was able to convince the police that he was a jogger.[1]

■ Accountability Is Key

Knowing where inmates are at all times is a must in secure facilities. A system of callouts, passes, and controlled movement at prescribed times greatly assists staff with inmate accountability. Housing unit officers should know which inmates are in the unit and the destination of inmates leaving the housing unit. When inmates are given assignments outside the unit, such as work or educational programs, the work supervisor, education staff member, or some other staff person should be responsible for the inmate. A formal call-out system will greatly improve inmate accountability when an inmate is needed at a certain place for a short period of time for medical appointments, counseling sessions, and so on.

In addition to formal counts at prescribed times, random census counts should be taken. During such counts, all institutions' activitvties will stop and inmates are counted in place to quickly determine whether inmates are where they should be. If census counts are not practical, supervisory correctional staff can periodically check various work details, classrooms, or housing units to ensure that inmates are in their assigned areas.

Inmates should be informed of their responsibility to be in their authorized area. Disciplinary procedures should be established to deter inmates from being in unauthorized areas. Of equal if not greater importance are procedures that account for all staff and their approximate locations in the institution. Accounting for staff is difficult, as staff usually have more mobility than inmates within the institution. During emergencies, accounting for staff should be top priority. Determining whether the staff have been taken hostage has a tremendous effect on how the warden plans to resolve demonstrations, riots, or other emergencies.

■ Preparing for Crisis

Even in the best-run prison, emergencies occur. At the very least, plans for dealing with escapes, riots, work or food strikes, hostage situations, outside demonstrations, natural disasters, bomb threats, and evacuations are necessary to ensure that staff are properly prepared to deal with emergencies. Prison administrators should identify those areas that most concern them and prepare detailed plans to address these issues. If the prison is close to major roadways, shipping lanes, or railways, plans should be developed in case of toxic or chemical spills. In areas susceptible to natural disasters such as wildfires, hurricanes, or earthquakes, evacuation may be necessary to save lives (see **Box 4-1**).

Emergency plans should be informative and easy to read. Although brief, the plans should set out specific responsibilities. The plans should be updated periodically as situations change. Emergency plans are only as good as the preparation to implement them. All staff should be fully familiar with emergency plans. At least yearly, staff should read and be given an opportunity to discuss the plans with peers and supervisors. Periodic mock exercises improve staff knowledge and make them more comfortable with their roles in emergencies. Developing memoranda of understanding and involving sister agencies and law enforcement in mock exercises will not only improve the outside agencies' knowledge of the correctional facility but foster good relationships.

■ Unacceptable Inmate Possessions

Controlling contraband should be a top priority in all correctional institutions regardless of security level. Contraband is any item or article that an inmate is forbidden to possess. All correctional facilities provide inmates with medical care, room and board, clothing, and basic hygiene items. Most facilities allow inmates

BOX 4-1   SENTENCING LAWS CAUSE DISTURBANCES

A series of major and minor institution disturbances in federal prisons began on October 19, 1995, and continued through October 26. Fifteen separate incidents, ranging from full-scale riots to small episodes of inmates refusing to return to their cells, taxed the resources of the Federal Bureau of Prisons and, considered together, constituted the most serious nationwide period of disruption in the agency's history.

These disturbances were primarily related to inmates' extreme dissatisfaction with federal sentencing laws and specifically the disparity between penalties for crack cocaine and powder cocaine. This generalized perception of racial unfairness (crack violators were predominantly African American, and crack cocaine penalties were much higher than powder cocaine penalties) created major tension. In this environment, any significant event might galvanize inmates to action. Just such a spark occurred after Congress voted on October 19 not to reconcile the cocaine sentencing disparities. That evening, there was the initial major riot at the Federal Correctional Institution in Talladega, Alabama.

Inmate perceptions of unfairness in the federal criminal justice system—external to the federal prisons—were based on changes designed to toughen penalties against law violators. Lengthy mandatory minimum sentences, the crack cocaine sentencing disparity issue, and loss of federal funding for selected inmate programs created significant resentment in many federal prisons. External issues fueled the tension, and an external event—the congressional vote that was taken that day—ignited the response.

On top of these external issues, the media reporting of the first disturbance meant that prisoners in other federal institutions quickly learned of the event. There were reactions in 14 other federal facilities in the next week. The Federal Bureau of Prisons took the unprecedented step of imposing a nationwide precautionary lockdown of its 92 prisons and focused all tactical resources on the critical locations as events developed. The crisis management response to this event was exceptional and led to the resolution of all situations with no serious injuries to staff or inmates.

to purchase items in the commissary or receive items through other authorized channels. Anything else that the inmate possesses is contraband.

Weapons, escape materials, or excess property that add fuel during fires are all equally dangerous in the right circumstances. Most staff are acutely aware of the havoc that these items, as well as drugs and alcohol, can cause and the resultant danger for staff and inmates. Other items such as materials to make dummies, either homemade rope or buffer cords, maps, and unauthorized clothing pose a danger by facilitating inmate escapes. Gambling paraphernalia lead to inmate assaults to collect debts.

Institutions should have regulations that restrict the amount of personal property that an inmate may possess. Cluttered cells and excess personal property are excellent hiding places for more serious contraband. In addition, these areas are much more difficult to search, tying up valuable staff time. Excess property can fuel fires and pose health-related hazards as breeding grounds for bacteria. Institution regulations should specify the amount of newspapers, magazines, pants, shirts, and even underwear an inmate may possess. Medications should be tightly controlled. Legal property provides great hiding places for contraband, as staff are reluctant to properly search legal items. The amount of legal property that an inmate can possess should be specified and tightly controlled. It is important to properly document seizure, confiscation, and disposition of contraband in case of civil lawsuits.

Staff must know what items enter and exit the prison. Incoming boxes and packages should be X-rayed before entering the correctional institution and searched prior to being given to inmates. Visitors should pass through a metal detector. Because most serious contraband, such as drugs, is introduced by inmate visitors, visitors who behave suspiciously should be subject to a more thorough search prior to visiting. Thoroughly searching inmates following visits also will deter the introduction of contraband. All vehicles should be thoroughly checked, and trash receptacles should sit in the sally port through at least one count before being removed from the institution.

Random frequent searches of inmate living areas can greatly reduce contraband. Inmates who have a history of hiding unauthorized items on their person or in their living area should be identified and searched more frequently. Common areas in the housing unit should be searched daily in a systematic manner to ensure that all areas are covered. Likewise, inmate work areas should be searched daily not only to check for contraband but also to make sure all equipment and fixtures are complete with no missing parts. Bars, windows, frames, and doors should be checked frequently to detect cuts and determine whether the locking devices have been tampered with. It is imperative that staff account for all tools in the institution. Only authorized tools should be utilized by staff and inmates. Staff should never bring personal tools into the institution. Should a tool be lost, all activity in the area should cease until a thorough search is conducted and the tool found. Limiting access to computers will protect the sensitive information they contain; two inmates at a federal penitentiary were able to obtain architectural drawings on a computer and make good their escape through a utility tunnel.

Drugs and alcohol are highly disruptive to the daily activities in a prison. Regular urinalysis and breathalyzer tests of suspected users and random tests of the entire population will determine the scope of use and deter abuse. During the holidays, inmates are more lonely and susceptible to temptation, and accordingly, searches should be made even more frequently to control fruit, sugar, and other items that may lead to a disruption.

■ When Communication Fails

Occasionally, it may be necessary to use physical force to gain an inmate's compliance. Naturally, the preferred scenario is for the inmate to comply with a verbal command, but in emotional and tense situations, this does not always occur.

Having a written use of force policy greatly increases the probability of gaining the inmate's compliance without injury to staff or inmate. The policy should explicitly state when it is permissible to use physical force and describe (in detail) the responsibilities of staff, from supervisors to those actually restraining the inmate. It is always best to videotape the use of force to prevent abuse and protect staff in case of a civil lawsuit.

Immediate use of force occurs when an inmate acts out with little or no warning and staff are required to physically restrain the inmate. These are highly charged, emotional incidents for both staff and inmate. Proper training allows staff to gain control of the situation while controlling their own emotions and preventing inmate abuse. These incidents should be well documented (e.g., in witness statements) by those involved.

A calculated use of force occurs when inmates are confined in an area and do not present an immediate threat to themselves or others, yet are refusing to comply with staff orders. Staff should talk with these inmates to gain their voluntary compliance and allow time for staff to fully assess the situation. Staff should determine whether the inmate has weapons and whether it is necessary to use gas, other less than lethal munitions, or a well-trained extraction team to move the inmate to the desired location. If more than one inmate is involved, the use of disturbance control or other tactical teams may be required.

Proper use of force has a great influence on staff and inmate morale. A highly professional attitude concerning use of force by administrative and supervisory staff will be modeled by line staff, prevent inmate abuse, and enhance inmate compliance with rules and regulations. Unfortunately, the history of corrections is marred by instances of staff physically abusing inmates. In many of these incidents, higher echelon staff have projected a cavalier or macho image that was imitated by line staff.

■ Hands-On Management

Accurate and reliable information about staff, inmates, the political landscape, and the local community is essential to running a well-organized and secure prison. The administrator who sits in the office waiting for information to arrive through the hierarchical organizational structure is doomed to be woefully uninformed. Administrative staff should tour the prison often to assess firsthand the atmosphere of the institution. Some inmates are chronic complainers, but others go about their daily activities in an orderly fashion while being respectful to staff and other inmates. When this latter group of inmates is unhappy, administrators should take heed and address the problems. Staff at all levels need to talk and, more important, listen to inmates. If staff listen, inmates will tell them what is happening in the prison.

Staff who supervise inmate work details, teachers, counselors, and correctional officers working in the housing units are often trusted by the inmates and are excellent sources of intelligence. A mechanism that allows these staff to submit confidential reports of conversations and observations of inmates is critical to gathering accurate intelligence. Once collected, this information can be analyzed and evaluated by specially trained intelligence staff. These informed judgments allow administrators to manage institution security and forecast future security needs. Long-range strategic planning based on accurate information allows the proper allocation of security assets.

■ Scanning Outside the Prison

Prisons do not operate in a vacuum but are integral parts of communities and larger correctional systems. Reading daily newspapers and professional magazines and maintaining good relationships with elected officials will keep prison administrators abreast of public sentiment and possible changes directed by politicians. Not too long ago, prisons were forgotten places to the public and the political arena. Today, correctional institutions are major employers and are very visible to local communities.

Prison and jail walls and fences are permeable in the sense that the external world has a strong influence on these institutions. Televisions, radios, newspapers, telephone calls, visits, interaction with staff, and newly arriving inmates all carry information from the outside community into the correctional environment. It is critical that penal administrators stay tuned to events outside that may influence the attitudes and beliefs of those who are confined. Some issues move inside the facility rapidly, and others take longer to affect the population. Staff must constantly be alerted to the changes within and outside their institution.

■ Protecting Inmate Victims

Certain inmates present unique challenges to prison administrators. Running prisons would be easy if all inmates were similar, serving their time and leaving when they completed their sentences. Good classification can ensure that similar inmates are in the same prison, but changing situations in inmates' lives plus loopholes in the classification system can sometimes place inmates in the wrong prison. One category of inmate that has always caused problems can best be described as the "weaker" inmate. Weaker inmates typically have committed an especially heinous crime and have received a long sentence that requires them to serve their sentence in a higher security institution. Once in prison, they become prey for other inmates after the other inmates learn of their crime. Child sex offenders find it especially difficult to serve their sentence in the general population once other inmates learn of their offense. Weaker inmates usually spend great portions of their sentence in special housing units for protective custody. The weaker inmates are frequently transferred between prisons, as they are unable to cope in the general population. Weaker inmates may act out against staff, as they know that staff are prohibited from physically punishing them. In addition, weaker inmates are often very litigious, filing institutional appeals and court documents complaining about their conditions of confinement. Staff at all levels need to be properly trained in working with weaker inmates, as most cases of proven staff abuse occur in this area.

■ Dangerous Inmates—The Assaultive, the Manipulative, and the Eager to Leave

In many ways, the aggressive inmate is easier to manage than the weaker inmate. The highly assaultive, combative inmate lives best in a prison with other aggressive inmates. Aggressors seldom prey on aggressors. Many states and the federal system have developed supermaximum penitentiaries to house aggressive inmates. Because the criteria for transfer to "supermaxes" are usually behavior based, many staff and other inmates are the target of these inmates' aggressions before their placement in the supermax. In systems that operate without a supermaximum prison, aggressive inmates spend much of their sentences in special housing units. Policies and guidelines for handling aggressive inmates should be specific and followed by all staff. Ensuring staff safety is paramount when dealing with aggressive and combative inmates.

Sophisticated or manipulative inmates target staff, other inmates, and the political system to gain items or favors that are otherwise prohibited. They often have tremendous resources in the community, including finances and support groups. The media may follow up their incarceration and show continued interest in their plight. These inmates may be leaders or may quietly give advice and counsel to inmate leaders. They are experts at detecting and exploiting staff insecurities and procedural weaknesses.

There are also inmates whose every waking moment is filled with fantasies of escape. These inmates tend to be smarter and more adept at recognizing weaknesses in physical structures and procedures. These inmates may take months and even years to closely observe staff for any habits or consistent failures to follow policy that these inmates may exploit. Many successful escapes involve the inmate simply walking out the front or rear entrance to the institution following visiting times or at shift changes. One notorious prisoner who had a history of escape was able to obtain what appeared to be civilian clothing and was actually escorted out of a correctional institution by staff who assumed he was a parole examiner. Other stories entail the inmate working for months, hoarding escape paraphernalia to breach physical structures to make good an escape. Almost every investigative report following an attempted or successful escape reveals poor security procedures or staff's failure to follow proper procedures.

■ Security Threat Groups

Gang activity is increasing in major cities, rural communities, and prisons. Gangs are responsible for the majority of homicides and assaults in prison. Well-organized, highly structured prison gangs have been around for decades. These gangs have strong leaders and exert pressure on other inmates through violence or the threat of violence. They are interested only in providing illicit drugs, alcohol, and contraband to other prisoners, and prison programs mean little to them (see **Box 4-2**).

In recent years, more street gang members have been incarcerated. In addition, more inmates have sought membership in groups from a certain city or geographical area. These gangs are unpredictable, less structured, and, in many ways, more difficult to manage than the traditional prison gangs. Several state prison systems have developed strategies to deal with gangs. Some correctional systems just deny the existence of gangs. In still other systems, the problem is so complex that it defies solution. Controlling gangs and their disruptive activities will haunt many prison administrators until solutions are found.

■ Conclusion

An institution's security staff perform heroic and often dangerous duty, 24 hours a day, each and every day of the year. Maintaining control of a correctional environment is a daunting task, given the uncooperative nature of many of the inmates and the challenges they present to the staff. The key to a prison or jail security system's success is a well-trained staff who are held accountable for detail and required to be alert to the inmate population. Positive accountability of inmates and an appropriate sense of order and discipline are mandatory. A prison or jail must develop a culture that treats prisoners with respect, always reinforces positive communication between staff and inmates, and offers inmates a humane, safe, and sanitary institutional program. Good security is a product of good leadership and results from high-quality staff who believe their work makes a difference. And indeed it does. Those who work "inside" and contribute to the daily supervision of inmates are public servants in the finest sense of the term.

BOX 4-2   CALIFORNIA GANG AND RACE DIVISIONS CREATE CHAOS

Wasco State Prison

In September 2005, a series of gang-related disturbances swept through two California state prison facilities at Wasco State Prison in Bakersfield, California. Although authorities did not identify specific causes of the disturbances, new reports indicated that a prison spokesman said such riots are often caused by issues of respect.

The four large-scale disturbances in two co-joined institutions involved two separate inmate gangs, the Southern Hispanics and the Fresno Bulldogs. The prison public information officer stated that these two groups cannot be placed in the same high-security prison together or problems erupt. However, this series of incidents occurred in Wasco prison, a facility for lower-security-level offenders. One riot took place while inmates were in the recreation yard for exercise, and the other three smaller incidents occurred in dorm facilities.

San Quentin State Prison

The largest riot at the San Quentin State Prison in 23 years left 42 inmates injured on August 1, 2005. A fight broke out between white and Latino inmates in a medium-security dormitory-style housing unit that houses approximately 900 prisoners, according to the institution's public information officer. As many as 80 inmates were involved in several buildings.

It took about 50 correctional officers armed with batons and pepper spray to quell the disturbance. The incident lasted less than 10 minutes. Staff believed that the incident was kicked off when one member of a prison gang disrespected another group.

The north–south gang rivalry in California has been ongoing for nearly 40 years.

Chapter Resources

DISCUSSION QUESTIONS

1. Do you believe it is important for administrators to see for themselves what day-to-day activities are occurring in their prisons?
2. Should prisons operate in a vacuum outside public scrutiny?
3. Do you believe that gangs are easier to control in a correctional environment?
4. How do staff members contribute to an inmate's ability to escape?

ADDITIONAL RESOURCES

Bowker, L. (1980). *Prison victimization.* New York, NY: Elsevier.

Carlson, P. (2004). Something to lose: A balanced and reality-based rationale for institutional programming. In J. L. Krienert & M. S. Fleisher (Eds.), *Crime and employment. Critical issues in crime reduction for corrections.* Walnut Creek, CA: Altamira Press.

Fleisher, M. (1989). *Warehousing violence.* Newbury Park, CA: Sage Publications.

Fox, J. (1982). *Organizational and racial conflict in maximum security prisons.* Lexington, MA: Lexington Books.

Garland, D. (2001). *The culture of control.* Chicago, IL: University of Chicago Press.

Haas, K., & Alpert, G. (1995). *The dilemmas of corrections.* Prospect Heights, IL: Waveland Press, Inc.

Irwin, J. (2005). *The warehouse prison. Disposal of the new dangerous class.* Los Angeles, CA: Roxbury Publishing Company.

Jankowski, M. (1991). *Islands in the street: Gangs and American urban society.* Berkeley, CA: University of California Press.

NOTE

1. *America's Most Wanted.* Retrieved from http://www.amw.com/fugitives/case.cfm?id=38335

Inmate Classification

Peter M. Carlson

CHAPTER 5

CHAPTER OBJECTIVES

- Explain classification, its role in the penal system, and the benefits of an objective classification system.
- Outline the difference between case management and unit management.
- Define a reliable and valid classification system.

■ Classification

Most penal facilities offer social service staff to provide classification and program/work advisory services for their inmate populations. As one of the main responsibilities in a correctional facility, classification involves categorizing offenders by assessing an individual's social and criminal background and current programming needs and assigning him or her to an appropriately secure institution, housing area, work assignment, and program (see **Figure 5-1**). How classification is organized and conducted varies a great deal by jurisdiction, type of facility, and institutional staffing levels.

Previously, all decisions about an inmate's security and prison assignments for work and housing were generally made by a senior management official designated by the warden, often the deputy warden.[1] This individual controlled all aspects of life inside the institution and made unilateral decisions based strictly on his or her often limited knowledge of inmates, their deportment, and their attitudes. Although this was an effective method of establishing consistent governance in a punitive environment, little attention was directed to interaction with the prisoners, and virtually no emphasis was given to the goal of positively influencing an inmate's life.

As this process evolved, this responsibility shifted from the deputy warden to a classification committee. In most correctional facilities, classification committees are large groups of subject matter experts who gather regularly to evaluate new inmates or to reclassify inmates for custody, housing, work, and program assignments. The committee is often chaired by a senior management official such as an associate warden and comprises the heads of institution departments such as the captain of security, the chief of classification, the supervisor of education, and the inmate's case manager. Many case management committees require the attendance of the inmate being reviewed.

As a primary link of communication between inmates and staff, as well as an important connection to the individual's future life in the community, the case management team is responsible for a significant part of an institution's operation. The team may be a small department of overworked case workers or a large, organized network of social work and case management staff who consistently work with inmates, including unit managers, case managers (also known as case workers or social workers), counselors, education representatives, psychologists, and secretaries.[2] Responsibilities of the team include inmate classification, social service support, institution program planning, and release preparation. Most correctional professionals believe that these tasks are critical to today's prison and jail operations.

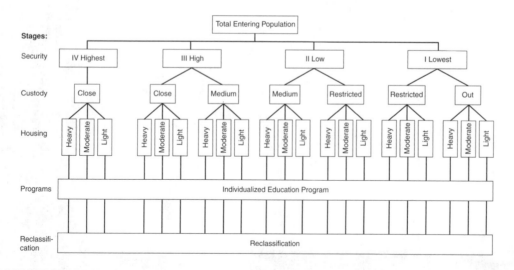

FIGURE 5-1 A classification system

The personnel who manage and work in prison and jail facilities recognize the need to separate the many different types of felons who are held in confinement facilities. Separating inmates (male from female, sick from healthy, youth from adult, and aggressive from passive) is a function that has important ramifications for all aspects of institution operations. Inmate classification is simply sorting inmates into appropriate categories. Once the correct category is determined, many other decisions can be made.

Accurate inmate classification is one of the primary factors that contribute to a safe and orderly penal environment. The classification of inmates is a process that ensures that a correctional system places inmates in an appropriate institution that can provide the necessary amount of security and supervision. All state prison systems, as well as the Federal Bureau of Prisons, utilize similar systems that separate inmates based on the level of security required to control and contain them. It would not be safe to place a hardened, violent offender in a correctional facility designed for minimum security individuals. Conversely, it would be a waste of taxpayer funds to confine a nonviolent offender in a maximum security institution.

Many state correctional agencies operate one or more central reception centers; all newly committed inmates are placed initially at one of these institutions, where they are reviewed and classified. Once the classification process has been completed, staff know what the inmate's security requirements are and what programs may be important during the offender's confinement. The reception center staff are then able to select an appropriate prison that will meet the inmate's security and program needs.

History of Classification

Early penal facilities housed violators in the same detention facilities without any consideration of their gender, age, health, criminal history, or current offense. Over time, correctional practitioners recognized the value of separating offenders. Early classification simply involved separating male and female offenders, juveniles and adults, and first-time or nonviolent offenders from more frequent or serious offenders.

Historically, institutional managers used their subjective judgment to assign inmates to various security levels. Staff members would simply consider the offender's age, prior record, current offense and sentence, and institutional adjustment. Simply stated, these decisions were made based on intuition and experience. However, decisions could be affected by unacceptable factors such as an inmate's race, gender, or poor social skills. Accordingly, discrimination could cloud each individual decision.

Early classification committees were made up of only senior staff members who did not know the individual inmate well. Eventually, team classification developed; case management and security staff who worked with the inmate on a regular basis were charged with making initial and ongoing decisions related to classification and daily operational inmate requests. This system continued to evolve and became the case management system.

■ Case Management

Case management focuses on the provision of social support programs to an inmate population, and case management staff maintain the official classification documents for each inmate. In many jurisdictions, these staff members are not only responsible for determining the prisoner's custody and security needs but are also charged with helping the inmates plan their institution-based work and program assignments, representing the inmate to the parole board, offering counseling services, providing connections to the community, and handling release planning. Case managers perform myriad tasks that pertain to inmates' daily lives and guide inmates' activities with the ultimate goal of helping them make successful transitions back to their home communities after release.

Case managers or counselors are responsible for inmates from the time they first arrive in a correctional setting. Initial screening of new arrivals is generally accomplished by social service staff members who ask new prisoners about their needs. Interviewers ask if the inmate feels he or she needs protection from other people he or she may have testified against and try to identify other potential enemies within the institution's general population. Screening questions also seek information about the offender's physical and mental health and other pressing management issues.

Case management staff gather background information about new inmates in pre- or postsentence reports (prepared for the sentencing courts by probation and parole officers) and seek other basic information about individuals. This attempt to gather information about the inmate is a direct result of a philosophical change in contemporary corrections. As prisons and jails began to do more than simply house offenders, most correctional agencies during the early 1960s began to implement rehabilitation programs; this was known as the medical model. Supporters of the medical model believed that criminality was an illness and that inmates could be cured of their social deviance by program involvement during confinement.[3] The resulting emphasis on treatment required staff to focus on the criminal rather than the crime.

Once the case manager gathers information about the individual's prior arrest record, adjustment to earlier periods of incarceration, and social data about family and friends, he or she prepares a classification study report (in most jurisdictions). This document identifies the prisoner, mentions social factors that may have led to his or her offenses, and recommends institutional programs that may help prepare the individual for release. Details about the inmate's program participation or lack of progress are added to the record throughout his or her confinement.

In many correctional systems, the initial assessment is completed at a reception and diagnostic center over a period of 4–8 weeks. In the jurisdictions that utilize these centers, the newly arrived prisoner is put through an extensive evaluation that often includes a complete personality assessment, intelligence and psychometric testing, review of past work habits and lifestyle, observation of how he or she interacts with staff and inmates, and identification of those factors that may have led the individual to crime. In other jurisdictions that do not have reception and diagnostic centers, inmates are committed directly to an institution and go through a similar classification process.

Once the background classification report is prepared, the inmate is then formally evaluated at a classification meeting. This meeting entails the development of an integrated work assignment, permanent housing, and educational, vocational, and social improvement programs for the offender.

Classification is the backbone of the security program of any prison or jail. It is imperative that staff know the background of each inmate and the threat each presents to the effective custodial management of the facility. Necessary basic information includes:

- Age
- Sex
- Social history
- Criminal sophistication
- History of violent or aggressive behavior
- Special needs (e.g., mental or medical issues)
- Potential challenges to security (e.g., escape history, gang membership)
- Special management factors (e.g., judicial recommendation, racial balance, program availability)
- Institutional capacity, availability, and security

If a realistic assessment is accomplished by case management staff, the inmate can be placed in housing with appropriate security and all other aspects of institution management will follow accordingly. It is important that inmates be placed in the least restrictive facility that is able to meet their security needs.

Once they classify and assign inmates, case managers track them throughout their confinement, offering assistance with the supervision of inmates, participating in discipline hearings, tracking progress, and continually assessing needs for program reassignment. Classification is not a one-time event but an ongoing procedure. The case manager serves as the offender's liaison to the classification committee for any changes in his or her program that are desired. Program modifications could include changes in work assignment, approvals for program participation, requests for transfer, consideration for custody reduction, or housing assignments. Case managers may also provide counseling support and approve and supervise outside visitors.

The final key component of case management staff is release planning, which actually begins at the time of initial classification. The appropriate goals of all institutional classification and programming should be to ensure the safety and security of all inmates and staff and prepare the offender for successful transition back to free society.[4] In all interactions with offenders, staff should encourage inmates to improve or increase their educational opportunities, job skills, self-sufficiency, and responsibility for their lives.

■ Unit Management

In recent decades, many correctional systems have adopted a unit management approach to classification. Unit management involves dividing a large prison or jail population into smaller groups, often separated by housing unit. This decentralized form of management delegates much more decision-making authority to the staff who know the offenders the best—those who supervise inmates in the housing units. Having staff offices in the unit also serves the important goals of augmenting the day-to-day supervision of inmates and makes staff more accessible to the inmate population.

Functional unit management is, simply put, the decentralization of case management services to a diverse, eclectic group of staff from different departments of the institution. The concept behind unit management is to subdivide the larger prison or jail into smaller groups of inmates, generally with their own housing unit, with staff offices within the unit. Similar to case management, inmate classification decisions are made by a unit management team. General policy establishes operational guidelines for these separate teams, and these staff members are empowered to make inmate classification, program, and housing decisions.

■ Comparison of Management Models

Unlike case management, the decentralized unit management model permits decisions about inmates to be made by the staff who know the inmates best. Clearly, when staff offices are next to inmate housing, staff can better supervise and get to know inmates. Positive, professional relationships are more likely to develop between inmates and staff. Daily interaction is helpful. Relationships among staff members are often greatly improved by unit management. Interdisciplinary staff of various departments who are assigned to a specific unit develop close working relationships that facilitate a productive working environment. In general, research has demonstrated that staff and inmate morale is improved with unit management. Inmates are much more pleased with responsive staff who know them, and staff are glad to have the authority to make program decisions.[5]

However, there are some negative aspects to the decentralization of prison management. It is much more difficult to maintain consistency in classification decision making when multiple teams are involved in inmate management determinations. It is critical that senior management establish overarching policy to guide the unit teams in their decision making. It is also important that penal institutions with unit management have open and effective lines of communication for staff and inmates. If unit staff are aware of inmate unrest or brewing tensions, they must share this knowledge with senior staff members.

There are three main functions of unit management: correction, care, and control.[6] *Correction* refers to the rehabilitative function of prisons and jails; *care* describes the assistance, resources, and support given to inmates; and *control* means the level of required custodial supervision. All of these functions are crucial to the administration of justice and successful prison or jail management. Unit management offers an efficient means of achieving these goals.

■ Objective Classification

A good, functional classification system should be easy to use and sensitive enough to reflect the need for change as an offender progresses through the service of his or her sentence. A typical inmate classification system is designed to consider the inmate's criminal and social history, the current crime, and the length of confinement and, over time, reflect how the offender responds to confinement. Classification is designed to predict an individual's risk for violence or escape and is based empirically on his or her past behavior. An individual's classification is made by reviewing that person's propensity for violent behavior.

Objective, fact-based classification facilitates agency-wide consistency that can be defended rationally and is perceived as equitable by all those involved in the process, including the inmates. Once the classification system has been validated, personal characteristics can be quantified, and each inmate can be scored accurately. Furthermore, the system can facilitate rescoring based on an offender's progress while incarcerated.

An objective prison classification system must be both reliable and valid. Reliability means that the classification instrument consistently does what it purports to do; in other words, no matter which staff member utilizes the classification instrument for a specific inmate, the same result will be reached. Validity refers to the fact that the classification instrument is accurate in assessing a prisoner's future behavior and propensity for violence.

Contemporary correctional classification is based on the philosophy that an inmate is to be classified at the least restrictive security and custody level that meets the individual's needs. Correctional administrators must also ensure that an individual's classification considers the all-important issue of public safety. Although practitioners do not want to overclassify an inmate, it is equally important not to underclassify the offender. Sometimes, this will mean that classification personnel will have to override the classification instrument. For example, a sex offender with a clean record throughout confinement may be eligible for consideration for a minimum security or trustee work assignment. But the nature of his or her offense may well preclude such consideration based on the potential serious threat to the community by the offender if he or she were to escape.

Research has demonstrated with significant validity and reliability that an individual's past behavior predicts future behavior.[7] Therefore, objective classification instruments should:

- Be validated on prison populations
- Utilize the same standards for all inmates
- Use a rational, uncomplicated process that is based on factors that are related directly to the classification decision
- Recommend classification decisions that are based on the offender's background
- Promote consistent decisions for similarly situated offenders
- Use a process that is understood easily by staff and inmates
- Allow staff to monitor the inmate's progress efficiently and effectively[8]

Once the individual's security needs have been determined, staff members may develop plans to designate an appropriate institution for long-term incarceration. Inmates are generally assigned to an institution that meets their security needs, is as close to their home community as possible, and offers the appropriate programs to address their specific program needs. Each state correctional system utilizes its own institutional classification system, and there is not necessarily consistency among states as to the name of each security level.

Although formal classification systems are based on firm data points, most systems also allow the final classification to be modified by the professional judgment of staff. It is important to allow staff judgment to enter the final decision and, if necessary, override the formula of the classification instrument.

■ External Versus Internal Classification Systems

External classification is a process that determines how much security a specific inmate requires to ensure his or her safety and the safety of others. This facilitates making a decision as to which level of security the inmate should be assigned. This classification decision is generally made at a central reception center that processes newly sentenced offenders into the correctional system.

An internal classification system is utilized to determine an inmate's housing, work, and program assignments. Many special programs such as drug abuse treatment or protective custody housing have specific criteria for inmate placement, and an internal classification system matches the right inmate population to the program resource.

■ Reclassification

Inmate classification and reclassification represent an outstanding means of keeping up to date with an inmate as he or she progresses. Recognizing that an inmate can and will change over time, for better or worse, staff must track these changes. If an offender's behavior deteriorates, staff should consider a transfer to a higher security institution. If an inmate exhibits good behavior and a positive attitude, staff may want to consider a transfer to a less secure facility at some point.

Initial classification should also be used to identify an inmate's program needs. Most prison facilities offer a large array of self-improvement programs that can have a positive effect on an inmate. Treatment programs include academic education, vocational education, mental health care, substance abuse programs, individual and group counseling, anger management, and many other opportunities. Many of these programs are not only effective in terms of changing behavior, but they also play an important part in keeping inmates productively and positively engaged. The outcomes of positive and effective institutional programs serve all parties well—staff, inmates, and the general public.

■ Gender Differences

Female offenders are often subject to a separate classification standard than are male inmates. Research and experience have established that men and women react differently in similar situations in a prison environment. In general, women are much less violent than men.[9] Although women are not often involved in large amounts of violent behavior in prison, they do act violently on occasion. This violence is predictable with a valid and reliable classification system. Research also concludes that female offenders should be classified using a separate classification system from males to ensure that gender-specific predictors are identified.[10]

■ Conclusion

Inmate classification, if appropriately accomplished, serves all aspects of institutional management. Inmates and staff are safer, institutional organization by security level is cost-effective, and program resources may be focused on the specific group of inmates who will most benefit from an activity. Classification of offenders will minimize the risk of escape and violence, provide a good rationale for the assignment of correctional staff, and provide the ability to minimize risk within the facility.

The ability to distinguish among groups of confined felons gives institutional personnel an outstanding tool in terms of staff safety and inmate accountability. Staff have an affirmative responsibility to operate correctional facilities in a safe manner and in such a way that protects the public's safety. Classification is at the center of these key obligations and provides staff members with the ability to execute their extremely important public service roles effectively.

Chapter Resources

DISCUSSION QUESTIONS

1. Why is a classification system important to inmate safety?
2. Do you believe that staff can combine effectively the roles of supervisor (and disciplinarian) with the supportive responsibility of being a counselor and support person?
3. What are the benefits of unit management?
4. Why is it important to have a case management team?
5. What are the goals of an effective classification system?

ADDITIONAL RESOURCES

Austin, J. (1998). *Objective jail classification systems: A guide for jail administrators.* Washington, DC: National Institute of Corrections. Retrieved from http://nicic.gov/Library/014373

Austin, J., Hardyman, P., & Brown, S. (2001). *Critical issues and development in prison classification.* Washington, DC: National Institute of Corrections.

Brennan, T., Alexander, J., & Wells, D. (2004). *Enhancing prison classification systems: The emerging role of management information systems.* Washington, DC: National Institute of Corrections.

Kane, T. (1986). The validity of prison classification: An introduction to practical considerations and research issues. *Crime and Delinquency, 32,* 367–390.

Levinson, R. (1998). *Unit management: The concept that changed corrections.* College Park, MD: American Correctional Association.

NOTES

1. Levinson, R. (1994). The development of classification and programming. In J. Roberts (Ed.), *Escaping prison myths: Selected topics in the history of federal corrections.* Lanham, MD: University Publishing Associates, Inc.
2. Keve, P. (1991). *Prisons and the American conscience: A history of US federal corrections* (p. 234). Carbondale, IL: Southern Illinois University Press.
3. Balch, R. (1975). The medical model of delinquency: Theoretical, practical, and ethical implications. *Crime and Delinquency, 21,* 116–129.
4. Glaser, D. (1964). *The effectiveness of a prison and parole system.* Indianapolis, IN: Dobbs-Merrill Company, Inc.
5. Toch, H. (1997). *Corrections: A humanistic approach* (pp. 30–34). Guilderland, NY: Harrow and Heston Publishers.
6. Levinson, R., & Gerard, R. (1973). Functional units: A different correctional approach. *Federal Probation, 37,* 15.

7. Buchanan, R., Whitlow, K. L., & Austin, J. (1986). National evaluation of objective prison classification systems: The current state of the art. *Crime and Delinquency*, *32*(3), 272–290.

8. Ibid.

9. Steffensmeier, D., & Allen, E. (1998). The nature of female offending: Patterns and explanations. In R. Zaplin (Ed.), *Female offenders: Critical perspectives and effective interventions* (pp. 5–29). Sudbury, MA: Jones and Bartlett Publishers.

10. Harer, M., & Langan, N. (2001). Gender differences in predictors of prison violence: Assessing the predictive validity of a risk classification system. *Crime and Delinquency*, *47*(4), 526.

Support Operations in Penal Facilities

PART III

YOU ARE THE ADMINISTRATOR

■ Food Problems at Jenkins Correctional Institution

Some say the incident at Jenkins Correctional Facility was long overdue. Officers and inmates alike confirm that the disturbance in the institutional dining room began yesterday at 11:45 A.M., when one inmate threw his food tray at a staff member and yelled "you can eat this shi* if you want, but I'm damn sick of it." Other inmates reacted to this aggressive behavior by throwing food, punches, and insults at various staff members who were supervising the area. The mini-riot lasted approximately 20 minutes and resulted in eight injuries to staff and convicts. Staff retreated from the dining room and locked the building, but the inmates continued to destroy furniture and equipment that is critical to the prison's operation. The riot was the second serious incident at the facility in as many years, and both involved food-related issues.

A prison spokesperson, Sandy Fellman, released a short statement saying that the incident was under investigation. The press release specified that "approximately 30–50 offenders created a disturbance in the institution food service area yesterday before noon. Security staff responded to the scene and secured the area within thirty minutes of the incident. Six staff members received minor bruises, and two inmates received minor lacerations from flying objects. Investigators are interviewing all inmates and personnel on the scene to determine the cause of the incident."

Inmate Da'Will Jackson said in a phone interview this morning that everyone was just fed up with the terrible food, the same meals over and over, poor quality food, and filthy conditions in the dining area. One correctional officer, unnamed because he spoke off the record, agreed that the food was an ongoing bone of contention at the prison and that staff members have been commenting on the rise in tension among the inmates.

- Why are support services such as food and mail so important in a correctional environment?
- How does tension build inside a prison or jail? If anger or resentment is noticed, what should a staff member do with this information?
- Is it possible to differentiate between normal institution grumbling and a serious problem with how inmates are treated?

Intake, Discharge, Mail, and Documentation

Jeffery W. Frazier

CHAPTER OBJECTIVES

- Explain the critical nature of receiving and discharging offenders from jail or prison.

- Identify some of the complexities associated with receiving and discharge operations at prisons and jails.

- Differentiate between various types of records maintained on arrestees and inmates.

The initial reception of prisoners into an institution, whether it is a jail or prison, is a critical process that individuals will remember throughout their confinement. The process begins as the citizen becomes a prisoner and is thrust into a new environment. Previous roles (e.g., father, wife, community leader) are all but eliminated. This identity change affects both the tangible and intangible. The citizen, now prisoner, is relieved of personal possessions as well as personal routines and activities. He or she is now told what to wear; when to get up in the morning; when to eat breakfast, lunch, and dinner; and when to use the telephone or watch television. Although some jails and prisons have policies that allow prisoners to keep their personal belongings, which may reduce the humiliation of incarceration somewhat, such policies will do little to ameliorate the substantial effect incarceration has on an individual's life.

■ Intake

Staff who work in intake and booking should be mature, well-trained personnel who are skilled in interpersonal communication. Furthermore, staff should be thoroughly familiar with the institution's policies and procedures, committal documents, confinement orders, and other such documents to ensure that there is a legal basis for confining the prisoner.

If not handled properly, the admission process can create undue humiliation and stress that can lead to disciplinary problems along with safety, security, legal, and health concerns. The basic intake process has several important goals:

- To prevent contraband from entering the institution
- To gather the necessary information about the offender
- To orient the offender to the policies and procedures of the institution
- To assess the offender's physical and mental health
- To perform an accurate inventory of the offender's personal property
- To promote personal cleanliness and minimize the risk of infestation or infection

Search

An initial search should be conducted immediately upon the arrival of a new prisoner, preferably in an area that prevents the introduction of contraband into the secure perimeter of the institution. Conducting a search requires tact and diplomacy on the part of the searcher. Furthermore, extreme caution should be exercised during any search due to the proximity of the prisoner to the searching officer. Upset, aggressive, or agitated prisoners should be given an ample "cooling down" period before a search is conducted, unless doing so would create a greater safety or security concern.

The complete search should be conducted in a private area. It should be performed by a member of the same sex as the person being searched. The officer conducting the search should explain to the prisoner, in a calm and respectful manner, the purpose of the search and the procedure that will be followed. The search should be conducted slowly and methodically, with instructions given to the prisoner throughout the process. If a strip search is required or allowed by policy or law (strip searches may not be conducted on individuals charged with certain crimes), the same procedures should be followed. However, touching the prisoner during a strip search is not necessary and should be avoided. Under no circumstances should a strip search be conducted by a member of the opposite sex. Body cavity searches, if and when necessary, should be conducted only by trained medical personnel in an area that affords privacy. Under no circumstances should a body cavity search be conducted in view of other inmates.

Gathering Information

It is critical to gather personal information about each inmate, but staff should be cautious not to ask questions related directly to inmates' criminal charges. All the data gathered will assist classification staff in determining at what custody level the prisoner should be held. Furthermore, the data will help in determining housing assignments. The National Institute of Corrections has made available a number of forms, free of charge, that can assist in the intake and receiving process.

Orientation

Upon intake, all prisoners should also be oriented to the basic rules and regulations of the institution. The arrestee should be given a copy of those rules, and staff should carefully go over the rules, answering all questions that the prisoner may have. It is important that intake and booking staff verify that the prisoner can read and comprehend the rules and regulations before proceeding.

Inventory

In a jail setting, intake and booking usually begin with a complete inventory of the prisoner's personal property. Each item should be carefully noted; the inventorying officer should not omit any items (e.g., nails, staples, washers, and gum wrappers) regardless of how trivial they may seem. All jewelry should be described by color, not type of precious metal or stone. Rings, necklaces, and bracelets should be described as gold or silver in color. A ring, for example, might be described as "one gold in color wedding band containing a single clear stone." All identifying inscriptions should also be recorded. All clothing should be described as thoroughly as possible, using sizes, brand names, and any other identifiable markings (e.g., stains, rips, tears). All money should be counted in the presence of the prisoner.

After the inventory, the prisoner should be required to sign a property/money slip indicating that he or she agrees with the inventory list. This slip should then be signed by the inventorying officer. A copy of this inventory list should be given to the inmate, a copy placed with the property, and a copy forwarded to the records department to be filed in the inmate's institutional file. A well-conducted inventory of all personal property will help to reduce or prevent false claims of damaged, lost, or destroyed property.

Health and Psychological Screening

All prisoners should be asked several basic questions about their current health condition, history, and medications. Such screening helps correctional and medical personnel address the individual's personal health needs and protects the health and well-being of others incarcerated in the jail. This screening should also include questions related to the individual's psychological health, including any history of suicide attempts. The importance of the health and psychological screening process cannot be overstated. The first 48 hours of a prisoner's initial incarceration are the most critical, because this is the period when most suicides occur.

Most health screening forms are divided into two categories: observations and questions. Observations are details that the officer may notice, such as obvious bleeding, open sores or lesions, vermin infestation, intoxication from alcohol or drug use, signs of drug or alcohol withdrawal, convulsions, or seizures. Personal observations can be as detailed as the agency policy dictates. Questions should be asked in an area that affords maximum privacy so that other prisoners do not overhear. Questions should be worded so that the prisoner may respond initially with a simple "yes" or "no" answer. All "yes" answers should be followed up with additional inquiries to determine the exact nature and extent of the problem. For example:

(Q) "Are you allergic to any medications?"

(A) "Yes."

(Q) "What medications are you allergic to?"

(A) "Penicillin."

Responses should be documented. All screening forms should give the intake and booking officer specific directions on what to do with critical "yes" or "no" observations and answers. If an officer notes that an individual is bleeding, for instance, he or she would immediately notify the appropriate medical and supervisory personnel. If the prisoner describes a history of or has positive test results for a highly infectious disease such as tuberculosis, the officer may be required to notify medical personnel immediately and medically isolate the individual from the rest of the population.

Once completed, the health screening report should be placed in the individual prisoner's file. A thoroughly completed health screening form is a valuable tool in preventing frivolous litigation, especially if an individual arrives with multiple superficial cuts and bruises and later claims that he or she was assaulted by jail staff. Furthermore, this report will help medical personnel during their initial evaluation of the prisoner.

Showering and Dress

Jails and prisons have different personal cleanliness standards and procedures. However, many jails and prisons require inmates to shower and change into jail or prison clothing. This reduces the likelihood of introducing body lice and other insects into the institution. The change from personal clothing to jail or prison clothing also reduces the possibility of theft, gambling, bartering, and the strong-arming of inmates. Furthermore, it reduces the problems that are associated with the laundering of personal clothing.

During the showering and exchange of clothing process, the intake and booking staff should search visually for rashes, cuts, abrasions, scars, tattoos, and so forth, all of which should be documented. At the conclusion of this process, inmates should be given clean linens, towels, and washcloths.

■ Release

The process of discharge from jail or prison is very similar to the intake and booking process. Discharge is a major responsibility—probably one of the most critical assignments that an officer can undertake. It is of the utmost importance that the releasing officer verify the identity and sentence of the subject being released. Failure to do so could result in the wrong inmate being released or an inmate being released before the complete sentence is satisfied. Furthermore, if a criminal background (i.e., wanted persons) check is not performed, a person who is wanted by a sister agency or state could be wrongfully released.

There are many reasons that an inmate may be released from custody. Special documentation and procedures apply to each case.

- *Personal recognizance.* Release on personal recognizance is granted by a judge or other judicial officer based on the promise that the subject will appear in court on the scheduled date. Many factors are considered prior to releasing someone on personal recognizance, such as the nature of the crime, the subject's criminal history, and the subject's standing in the community.
- *Bail.* Bail is a specified amount of money, usually established by the court or other judicial officer, that must be presented before the inmate can be released. The money is held by the court to ensure that the subject appears in court when scheduled.
- *Bond.* A bond is something that is posted by a licensed bonding company or bondsman in a state. The subject is released into the custody of the bondsman, who will ensure that the subject appears in court on the scheduled date. If the subject fails to appear, the bonding company will be required to pay the entire bond amount to the court. Most bondsmen charge at least a 10% fee of the original bond amount for incurring the risk that the subject might not appear in court.
- *Court order.* Inmates may be released by the court for reasons such as time served, sentence reduction, or dismissal of charges, or they may be granted a temporary release to attend the funeral of a loved one. The releasing officer should verify that a copy of such order has been obtained prior to release.
- *Time served.* The inmate has satisfied the conditions of his or her sentence and can be released.
- *Release to other law enforcement personnel.* In some cases, a subject is released into the custody of other law enforcement personnel who may have pending charges against the subject or to another agency

because the subject has already been tried and convicted of committing a crime and now must satisfy that sentence. When a prisoner is released to another agency, the transporting officer's identity should be verified and a receipt should be obtained indicating that the transporting officer has accepted custody of the prisoner.

- *Release documentation.* Regardless of the reason for release, the releasing officer should verify that the release documents are in order and properly signed. If the subject is being released because of time served, the computation of his or her sentence should be verified. A "wanted persons" check should be made through the agency's computer system that is tied into the National Criminal Information Center network. Finally, the subject's identity should be verified to prevent the wrongful release of an offender. Release documents should contain, at a minimum, date of release; time of release; reason for release; if released to another agency, the name of the agency and the person to whom the subject was released; the name of the officer who released the subject; and a description of all personal property that was released with the subject.

◼ Mail

The First Amendment to the U.S. Constitution gives inmates the right to send and receive mail. However, prisons and jails can place reasonable restrictions on these rights. The Supreme Court established that a restriction on inmate mail is acceptable "if [the restriction] furthers an important or substantial governmental interest; and if the incidental restriction on alleged First Amendment freedoms is no greater than is essential to the furtherance of that interest."[1]

Thus, local regulations must show that a regulation that authorizes mail censorship furthers an important or substantial governmental interest such as security, order, or rehabilitation. In order to establish appropriate institution rules that comply with federal law, it is very helpful to delineate two types of inmate mail: legal and social.

Legal Correspondence

Legal or official correspondence is an inmate's correspondence with police, probation and parole officers, judges and attorneys, and so forth. Official correspondence should be inspected in front of the inmate to ensure that contraband is not enclosed. But it must not be read—inmates have a right to confidentiality with their attorneys and other public officials. All official correspondence, both incoming and outgoing, should be documented in a logbook. For incoming mail, the name and address of the sender and the date received should be logged. There should also be a place for the inmate to sign that he or she received the official mail. For outgoing mail, the logbook should list the date mailed and the name of the addressee.

Social Correspondence

Social correspondence is the personal letters of a prisoner to and from family and friends. Personal correspondence can be inspected outside the presence of the inmate; however, as with official mail, it should not be read unless the legal tests of the previously cited Supreme Court decision can be met and staff follow the basic requirements outlined in that case. Many institutions open all personal correspondence, inspect for contraband, and remove money orders so that the inmate's personal account can be credited. The mail is then forwarded to the inmate.

◼ Documentation

It is important that each institution maintain accurate, up-to-date records on all inmates, from their reception into the institution until their departure or ultimate release. It is only through sound records management that a foundation can be created to protect the staff and agency from inmate litigation for alleged violations of constitutional rights.

Although in recent years the courts have been willing to entertain inmate complaints, they are not always willing to interfere with the operations of an institution unless there are clear constitutional violations, such as living conditions that are extremely barbaric and inhumane. There are a number of routine records that all institutions must maintain; others are determined by the institution's own needs or the statutory requirements of the locality and state.

Mandatory records are as follows:

- Admission and release records
- Medical records
- Disciplinary records
- Inmate grievance records
- Visitation records, both personal and professional
- Criminal justice system records (e.g., court orders and time computation records)
- Personal property records
- Inspection records that reflect the conditions of the institution, both from a security standpoint and from a life, health, and safety standpoint
- Logs that reflect all activities within the institution (e.g., meals served, recreation given, counts conducted, medication dispensed, mail delivered)

Documentation and records management provide administrators with data that can be used in making policy decisions, forecasting trends, performing staffing analyses, evaluating the climate of the institution, and projecting future budget needs. As the old saying goes, if it is not documented, it did not occur. Therefore, documentation is the first defense in preventing litigation. Once litigation has been filed, proper, complete, and up-to-date records will greatly improve an institution's chance of prevailing in the courts.

■ Conclusion

The reception and discharge of individuals is a critical process that requires the attention of responsible staff with excellent interpersonal communication skills and an eye for detail. It is the initial reception process that usually sets the tone of the prisoner's behavior during his or her stay at the institution and acts as the first physical barrier to contraband in the institution. The information-gathering phase of the receiving process provides the institution with a personal history of the offender, which will be ultimately used to assist the classification department. Finally, through the promotion of cleanliness, institutions can better identify infectious disease and reduce the infestation of body lice.

During the discharge of individuals from confinement, the releasing officer must be extremely cautious to prevent the unlawful or wrongful release of prisoners. All release documents must be examined for authenticity. The releasing officer must indicate the date and time of release, the reason for the release, and a description of all property released. If a prisoner is released to an individual from another agency, the officer must indicate the name of the agency and the individual. Wanted persons checks must be performed to verify that the individual being released is not wanted by another agency.

Inmates have the right to send and receive mail, but the institution can place reasonable restrictions on that right. Only official mail must be opened in front of the inmate. An institution can censor an inmate's mail if it can show that the censorship furthers an important or substantial government interest and meets certain established legal minimum standards.

Finally, it is through the maintenance of accurate records documenting all aspects of an inmate's stay that institutions are able to reduce the likelihood of litigation and increase their chance of prevailing in court if litigation is filed. Accurate records also provide managers with the necessary data to forecast trends, prepare budgets, and make policy decisions that affect an institution's entire operation.

Chapter Resources

DISCUSSION QUESTIONS

1. In what ways are the receiving and discharge operations at jails and prisons critical to the operation of those facilities?
2. What are some of the complexities associated with institutional operations as covered in this chapter?
3. What are the principles that underpin the policies and practices for processing mail for inmates?
4. What types of information about arrestees or prisoners are maintained by jails and prisons?
5. What roles do mail processing and documentation management play in the overall operation of a penal institution?

ADDITIONAL RESOURCES

American Correctional Association, http://www.aca.org

American Jail Association, http://www.aja.org

Cripe, C., Pearlman, M. G., & Kosiak, D. (1997). *Legal aspects of corrections management* (3rd ed.). Burlington, MA: Jones & Bartlett Learning.

Johnson, P. (1991). *Understanding prisons and jails: A corrections manual* (2nd ed.). Jackson, MS: Correctional Consultants, Inc.

National Institution of Corrections. (1989). *NIC jail resource manual* (4th ed.). Kents Hill, ME: Community Resource Services, Inc.

National Sheriffs' Association. (1980). *Jail officers' training manual.* Alexandria, VA: Author.

Palmer, J. (1996). *Constitutional rights of prisoners* (4th ed.). Cincinnati, OH: Anderson Publishing Company.

NOTE

1. *Procunier v. Martinez*, 416 U.S. 396, 94 S.Ct. 1800 (1974).

Food Service

Timothy Thielman

CHAPTER OBJECTIVES

- Outline the correctional food service requirements for adult and juvenile offenders.

- Explain the Religious Land Use and Institutionalized Persons Act (RLUIPA).

- Understand correctional food service's role in rehabilitation.

- Describe the budgetary challenges in correctional food service.

- Describe the importance of emergency preparedness in an institution as it relates to food service.

There are many approaches in a correctional setting that are used to manage offenders and keep them content. Food service can be one of the least thought about areas, yet is one of the most vital areas inside the walls of a correctional institution. As one could imagine, there is not too much to look forward to while doing time behind bars. Receiving mail, having a visit, and mealtimes are often the highlights of an offender's day regardless of whether he or she is in a small county jail in a remote area with six inmates or an institution such as San Quentin State Prison in California, which has an inmate population of more than 5,000.[1] Food service plays a vital role in keeping order behind the razor wire. Correctional food service touches every incarcerated person three times a day, and if the offenders are given subpar food, it can create a volatile situation that can leave staff and other offenders in harm's way.

Food service administrators (FSAs) face many challenges with tight budgets and ensuring compliance of all the local, state, and federal regulations pertaining not only to nutrition but also to health and safety standards. FSAs must know the requirements and ensure compliance with local regulations regarding things such as city codes for installing new equipment and construction projects, state and county health codes, state and federal regulations pertaining to jails and prisons, and U.S. Department of Agriculture requirements for juvenile offenders. Additionally, FSAs must also stay current with case law pertaining to correctional food service that stems from litigation over religious diets. Failure to do so could result in a costly lawsuit for that organization.

FSAs must also be able to react quickly in matters regarding a power outage or other utility failure and even a natural disaster. All the challenges in a food service operation have an effect on the budget as well as keeping a peaceful environment within the institution. Having an FSA who understands the job's demands and has the ability to keep the operation flowing smoothly and efficiently is essential to a successful operation.

■ Food Service Requirements for Adults

In 2011, there were just under 1.6 million people incarcerated in the United States.[2] Correctional food service operations across the country prepare millions of meals each day. Meals must be nutritionally balanced with adequate calories and must conform to strict guidelines that are set by state and federal regulations. The American Correctional Association (ACA) is an organization that has been in existence for more than 125 years and has played a vital role in setting standards for correctional institutions.[3] Menu cycles and caloric intake requirements vary from state to state; however, there are minimum guidelines for all institutions. From a food service manager's perspective, calories cost money, meaning that serving large portions of food to inmates does mean more calories for inmates; however, this also means higher food costs. Some larger facilities such as state or federal prisons have work crews that can work long, hard hours doing strenuous labor. These types of facilities may choose to serve higher calorie meals to keep the inmates content and nourish them for energy. On the other hand, a short-term facility such as a jail with a high turnover rate and inmates who are sedentary would be more apt to serve the minimum required calories. In addition to the activity level, caloric and nutritional values of meals and additional requirements will depend on the age and gender of the inmate. Menus do not necessarily need to be written by a registered dietician in every case, but the menus must be reviewed and approved by a registered dietician.

■ Food Service Requirements for Juveniles

There are also nutritional guidelines for juvenile offenders; however, the guidelines and requirements on meal service to juveniles and much more stringent, because institutions for juveniles receive monetary reimbursements from the government for the Department of Agriculture's Child Nutrition Program. Under this program, the organization will receive reimbursements and government commodities from the government if that facility has school-age children and a school within the facility. The reimbursements are given for breakfast, lunch and, if qualified, even snacks. Reimbursements are not automatically given to a facility with school-age children and a school. Government reimbursements require meticulous record keeping and regular audits to ensure compliance.[4]

There are two methods of serving juveniles. The first is the offer method, which is similar to a regular school, where the children come through the serving line, cafeteria style, to receive their food. The second method is the serve method; this is when the children are housed in a facility that serves the meals right in the living unit. For this method, the trays are premade and given to them without choices. In cafeteria-style serving, the juveniles may be able to pick and choose what they want; however, what they get on their trays will determine whether the meal meets the requirements to be reimbursable. For example, if the juvenile does not take at least three of the five food groups, the meal cannot be counted as reimbursable. In the serve method, if the juvenile were to eat only the dessert on the tray, that meal would not be reimbursable. It is important that whoever is monitoring the juveniles fully understands the requirements and that accurate meal counts are taken and reported.

Facilities that participate in the program are also eligible to receive commodities. Commodity entitlements are generally according to the previous year's average daily population (ADP). Commodities and monetary reimbursements are great ways for a food service manager to save money on the food budget but require a lot of paperwork and trained staff.

■ Therapeutic and Religious Diets

Some inmates require special diets because of a medical condition, allergies, or intolerance to certain foods. Others may need a special diet because of their religious beliefs. Some examples of common medical diets are renal diets, cardiac diets, and gluten-free diets. Examples of religious diets include Kosher, Halal, and some vegetarian diets. Inmates placed on a medical or therapeutic diet are usually done so by the medical staff. Religious diets are approved by the chaplain. Approval of a religious diet is based on the inmate's sincerely held religious beliefs. Because of the vagueness in what defines sincere belief, there is constant litigation across the nation from inmates who have been denied special diet requests. Both therapeutic and religious diets can be costly. Buying all gluten-free foods can become costly, especially if an institution has several inmates on a gluten-free diet for an extended period of time. Similarly, accommodating religious diets can take a chunk out of a budget. In 2008, those on religious diets within the Federal Bureau of Prisons (BOP) represented 3% of the inmate population. This may not seem like much, but it equates to 5,575 inmates out of a population of 188,000 and 9% of the total food budget with an estimated cost of $14.2 million.[5]

Certain diets such as Halal or Kosher require special preparations; food must be made in special kitchens with strict regulations and served from designated pans. This would be ideal if every institution had these accommodations; however, many organizations would not see this as making economic sense. Many institutions do not have the luxury of a separate kitchen for special diets or the means to prepare items in accordance with the laws of certain religions and must resort to purchasing fully cooked, prepackaged meals. These types of meals can become costly and will be discussed further, later in this chapter.

■ Religious Land Use and Institutionalized Persons Act (RLUIPA)

There have been a number of Supreme Court decisions that have influenced the way prison policies are written. The 1987 case of *Turner v. Safley* was one that has had an effect on inmates and their constitutional rights. In this case, two inmates in the Missouri Department of Corrections wanted to marry and communicate with each other from separate facilities. Their request was denied by prison officials because there were no compelling reasons why they should be allowed to do this.[6]

As a result of the *Turner v. Safley* case, a "balancing test" was established that would be used for future Supreme Court cases involving inmates and their constitutional rights. The "balancing test" involves four questions: Are inmates allowed other ways of exercising their right? How much will allowing the inmates to exercise this right affect others in the facility? Are there alternatives that accommodate both interests available? Is there a valid connection between the regulation and a legitimate correctional interest?

Some critics of the "balancing test" believed that it gave the government too much opportunity to restrict the free exercise of one's religion. As a result, the Religious Freedom Restoration Act (RFRA) was enacted by Congress and set forth two significant criteria: First, the restriction must show a "compelling government interest" to deny an inmate the right to exercise his or her religious beliefs. Second, the restriction must be the "least restrictive means of furthering that interest." In 1997, RFRA was struck down by the U.S. Supreme Court but still applied to the federal government by executive order. In 2000, Congress passed the RLUIPA to ensure that protections offered under RFRA would apply to the states. RLUIPA goes one step farther than RFRA by ensuring religious freedom protections for prisoners and others in our nation's institutions.[7]

Over the years, both RFRA and RLUIPA have been put to the test with litigation across the nation. One of the greatest challenges for prison officials has been interpreting what exactly a "sincerely held religious belief" is, because a sincere belief has little to do with how popular, organized, or old a religion may be. RLUIPA is intended to offer very wide protections.[7] Often an inmate will make requests for religious accommodations that are outside the normal practice of the religion he or she is claiming as a preference. Additionally, the protections under RLUIPA make allowances for those who may craft their own belief system, do not have a following, and may not even have a regular place to worship. In other words, the established rule of law regarding religious freedom illustrates that one's religious beliefs need not be conventional, logical, or even comprehensible to others. Prison authorities must do the best they can to interpret the law and watch how future rulings affect prison policy.

■ Cooking Methods

There are several cooking methods used for feeding inmates. Smaller facilities generally prepare meals on site, and the food is served immediately. Some larger operations may have a central kitchen or cook/chill facility where all the food is prepared and then shipped out to several facilities. The food shipped out could either be hot or cold—that is, the cold food was prepared days or even weeks earlier and was rapidly cooled in a special blast chiller. The food also could be sent hot or cold in bulk form or preplated.

Food that is sent out cold must be reheated to the proper temperature in a special rethermalization oven or microwave. This high-tech method of reheating food is also used by catering companies, schools, and airlines. The blast chiller cools food three times faster than a regular refrigerator or freezer. Rapid chilling is crucial and does not allow formation of large crystals of ice to form on the food. Most importantly, the quick chilling method gets the food out of the temperature danger zone where bacteria can grow.

There are many correctional food service units that operate central kitchens. The San Diego Sheriff's Department Food Services Division operates a 38,000-square-foot cook/chill production center that produces 41,000 meals per day that are shipped out to 12 facilities. The division also supports the search and rescue units for both planned and emergency services. In addition, the unit provides catering services for department functions and special events.[8]

■ Serving Methods

The way an institution serves meals will vary according to how an institution is designed and its policies. For example, inmates who are under 24-hour lockdown for disciplinary reasons will typically receive meals in their cells. The meal will usually come on an insulated tray or in disposable ware. There may also be institutions that serve the entire inmate population on insulated trays directly in their cells or living units.

Most commonly, inmates come through the serving line, cafeteria style. This method can be problematic, because there is interaction between the inmates who are serving and the inmates who come through the line. The dining room and serving line can be a volatile area because of the large number of inmates in a concentrated area versus the number of staff who are supervising them. Meal time in the cafeteria is an opportune time for inmates to pass contraband or create a disturbance that could put both staff and inmates at risk for becoming injured. Correctional staff must be on high alert and vigilant in the dining room. It is quite common for an institution to have strict rules in the dining room regarding inmate behavior. Some common rules are no talking, no passing food between tables, and no getting up once seated until instructed to get up. The inmates are typically taken to the dining room and released in an orderly fashion. Some institutions have walls that separate the servers from the patrons. With this method, the trays are portioned out and slid through an opening in the wall that is only large enough to slide the tray of food through.

■ Food Services Role in Rehabilitation

Many correctional food service operations are dependent on the use of inmate labor. Some institutions will pay inmates for working, whereas others do not. Inmates who are paid for working do not get paid much, and often a portion of the money earned is taken back to pay fines and restitution. For some inmates, it is the opportunity to get out of their cells or living units every day that makes kitchen duty appealing. Most inmates who are assigned to kitchen duty have never worked in the food service industry. Food service staff are tasked with teaching inmates many skills of the trade. These skills include but are not limited to large-quantity cooking and baking, butchering, storekeeping, and sanitation. Inmates who perform cooking and baking duties may be required to use basic mathematical skills to increase and reduce recipes according to the population of the institution.

The skills learned while on kitchen duty can be valuable for inmates who wish to pursue a career in the food service industry once released. Many institutions have formal training programs for inmates that integrate classroom learning with practical experience in food service. Some organizations may even offer sanitation certification courses that are recognized nationwide and are often required in order to work at some food establishments. On completion of these programs, the inmate is given a certificate or diploma. Once released, the inmate can use the certificate to show a potential employer that he or she has training and experience in food service.

The Virginia Department of Corrections (VADOC), for example, has 3,400 inmates across the state who work in food service. VADOC offers a number of valuable training opportunities for both male and female inmates. The Food Services Unit operates a re-entry program that equips offenders with knowledge, training, experience, and certifications to assist inmates with reintegration into society. The programs offered include computer training, culinary arts on-the-job training, and culinary arts correspondence courses.[9]

■ Self-Operated Versus Contract Management

A food service operation in a correctional institution will be either self-operated or contracted by a private food service company. One that is self-operated could be staffed with either civilian personnel or correctional staff. If civilian staff are used and inmates work in the

Courtesy of Tim Thielman.

Correctional Officer II / Cook, Gary Wiggins, prepares a meal at the Ramsey County Correctional Facility, a 556 bed Medium Security Correctional Facility in Saint Paul, Minnesota. Unlike contract management employees, correctional officer cooks are specially trained and perform duties as a correctional officer in addition to being a cook.

kitchen, there will typically be a uniformed staff member stationed in the kitchen for security. There are also correctional officers who are also cooks. These individuals are trained as cooks but also receive special training as correctional officers.

Using private food service companies has become popular nationwide in schools and prisons because it removes the financial burden of pensions and health insurance costs for the food service employees from the taxpayers. Private food companies can provide meal service with or without inmate labor; this is typically worked out during contract negotiations between the private company and the organization. If inmates are used for meal service, then there would also be a uniformed staff member stationed in the kitchen for security. No matter who does the food service in an institution, there are upsides and downsides to each option, and both are held to the same standards and regulations.

■ Adequately Trained Staff

There are many safety and security risks in a prison kitchen. Yeast, sugar, and pure extracts are kept under lock and key and are inventoried daily to prevent inmates from making homemade alcohol. Knives are tethered to a fixed object to prevent someone from sneaking them out of the kitchen and must be secured when not in use. Utensils and other small but potentially dangerous objects are regularly inventoried and kept in secure cabinets or on shadow boards. Delivery vehicles are searched, regular headcounts are conducted of all workers, and contents of trash carts are poked with iron rods before being pushed outside to ensure that there are no stowaways in the carts. Inmate workers are patted down or strip-searched when leaving the kitchen to ensure that no contraband is taken out. This is not like working for a school or restaurant. Being a food service worker in a correctional institution takes special training and careful attention to detail. Staff training in a jail, correctional facility, or prison is required for all food service employees regardless of whether the employee is a correctional officer or civilian. All employees have a minimum number of training hours that are required each year. Training for food service personnel will vary depending on whether they are correctional officers, detention deputies, or civilian workers. Commonly, food service workers receive food handler training and certification that must be renewed every few years. In addition to food safety training, correctional officers or detention deputies may be required to have training in control tactics, crisis intervention, or other specialized training that uniformed staff receive.

Food service managers must be highly trained and well versed in local, state, and federal regulations pertaining to food service. A food service manager must typically have a food manager license that is issued by the state and must be renewed every couple years by attending a refresher sanitation class. The person in charge of a prison kitchen operation is not only responsible for the safe handling and preparation of the food, but also for planning menus, managing several budgets, and having the ability to act quickly in emergency situations. Additionally, a food service manager must be able to effectively manage the staff and inmate food service personnel and ensure adherence to all applicable regulations.

■ Association of Correctional Food Service Affiliates

In 1969, an organization called the American Correctional Food Service Association (ACFSA) was formed and consisted of mostly retired military cooks, because in those days there was not much for contract management companies in the correctional setting and who better to run an institutional kitchen than someone who had just spent 20 years providing food service to thousands of troops. Today, the ACFSA is known as the Association of Correctional Food Service Affiliates and has members across the United States, Canada, and even as far away as Australia. The ranks of ACFSA consist of men and women working in correctional food service either as public employees or working for a contract management company. The mission of the ACFSA is to develop and promote educational programs and networking activities to improve professionalism and provide an opportunity for broadening knowledge.[10]

The ACFSA has two certification programs that are designed to increase the level of excellence and professional standards in the food service segment of corrections. These programs require continuing education to maintain certification and to promote education and training.

■ Hurricane Katrina

On August 28, 2005, the most destructive hurricane to ever strike the United States made landfall at 7:10 A.M. on the Gulf Coast in Southern Louisiana.[11] A little farther inland in New Orleans, Sheriff Marlin Gusman contacted food service manager Major Jim Beach and informed him that Hurricane Katrina was heading right toward New Orleans and that he and his employees should report to work to as an emergency precaution. This is not uncommon practice for hurricane season, and it typically turns out to be a two-day get-together at the jail in a picnic-type atmosphere. This time, it would not be the case. By Monday morning, there was 3 feet of water in the streets of New Orleans, and the jail kitchen staff were feverishly preparing 50,000 sandwiches. By 9:00 P.M., there was 4 feet of water in the streets, and the storm raged on. Around 2:00 A.M. Tuesday, Major Beach stepped off the last step from his office in the jail kitchen and was standing in about 12 inches of water. The kitchen at the jail was 4 feet off the ground. By sunrise, Major Beach and his staff were wading in waist-deep water in the kitchen trying to salvage any food that could be used to feed staff and inmates. Kitchen staff set up makeshift feeding stations while they continued to wade through water that was polluted with diesel fuel from generators and with raw sewage. As the water rose, 6,000 inmates were evacuated with boats to the only dry area around—a bridge that was high above the water. In the aftermath of the storm, more than 30,000 people took shelter in the Superdome. The Coast Guard rescued 42,000 people, 1,588 people died, and 4,000 men, women, and children were missing. Four million people lost their jobs, and there was an estimated $34.4 billion in damages.[12]

■ Disaster and Emergency Preparedness

As of 2013, Major Beach and his staff are still operating out of a temporary kitchen, and inmates are housed in temporary housing while the jail is being rebuilt. The new kitchen will be a $100 million cook/chill facility. Generators will no longer be on the ground level of the jail. This jail is being built and designed based on the lessons that were learned from Katrina. This is an extreme case of disaster and emergency preparedness, and no one could have ever been prepared for the destruction Katrina caused; however, emergency and disaster plans are crucial for every operation, and food service is a vital part of the plan.

In a correctional setting, the primary concern in any emergency or disaster is the safety and security of the staff and inmates. Having good policies and procedures in place is key to being able to react appropriately to every situation.[13] Some examples of emergencies could be a facility needing to quickly assemble work crews to fill sandbags to head off a spring flood, or a power outage or water shutoff inside the facility. Whatever the case may be, people need to eat, and a food service manager will need to think through many of these situations and have a plan together. If possible, it is good to have a joint plan with a nearby facility in case additional resources are needed.

■ Pandemic Flu

The pandemic flu of 1918 infected 500 million people around the world. In 2009, a new strain of flu was declared to be a global pandemic.[14] Jails and prisons around the country began contingency plans to battle against the H1N1 influenza virus. Food service managers and food companies worked together to develop procedures for meal service and pandemic menus should the epidemic hit. Even though the pandemic flu of 2009 came and went without major incident, it was a good drill in emergency preparedness, and many prisons and jails updated policies regarding mass illnesses.

Budget Planning and Challenges

Many government organizations operate on a 1- or 2-year budget cycle. Food service managers typically use a combination of meals served along with their purchasing and inventory data to come up with budgetary numbers.

Planning a budget for food service can be difficult, because there are many unknown factors when it comes to food costs. As mentioned earlier in this chapter, purchasing foods for special diets can be costly, and there is no way to predict how many and what types of special diets an institution will have in a year. It is a good idea to track that type of information yearly to determine an average cost. Some other unpredictable factors that influence the price of food are fuel surcharges and the climate from the previous year. In other words, a drought this year could affect food prices next year. For example, in 2012, much of the midsection of the United States was in a severe drought. The extreme dry temperatures caused low yields of corn. To look at the bigger picture and illustrate how the low corn yields affects the overall cost of everything, corn is used for food, not only for humans but also for animals, and is a staple food for feeding livestock. Corn is also used to produce ethanol fuel. Less corn means a higher demand for many reasons. Less ethanol produced means higher fuel consumption. These are just a few common things that can drive prices up and really affect a budget.[15]

Many food service operations rely on facility-grown produce from gardens and buying locally grown produce to help reduce food costs. Even in the northern states that have a considerably shorter growing season, institutions can save considerable amounts of money by growing gardens and purchasing locally grown fruits and vegetables. Flexibility of menu changes allows the opportunity for in season fruit and vegetable purchases and are cost-effective ways to help a budget.

Opportunity Buys

Opportunity buys on food are a good way to save some budget dollars. Most large food-manufacturing companies offer good deals on discontinued products, short-dated products, or items that were produced for a company and did not quite meet the specifications of their customer. For example, a manufacturer that produces chicken patties for a large restaurant chain makes a production error, and these patties are irregularly shaped, slightly lighter or darker than they wanted, or just under or over the desired weight. Instead of the chicken patties going to waste, they are sold at a discount price either directly to an institution or through a food distributor. Many larger organizations are unable to buy these types of products because they are limited by state or federal contracts or because they are unable to change menu items. A downside to opportunity buying is the short-term availability of a product. Nonetheless, if a facility has the ability to change menu items frequently, there can be some significant savings involved.

Conclusion

There are many facets involved in having a smooth-running food service operation in a jail or prison. Palatable food that is prepared in sanitary conditions is a key component to keeping order inside the confines of an institution. Food service managers are constantly looking for ways to reduce costs while still serving nutritious meals. Whether self-operated or under contract management, institutions are held to the same standard, and having highly trained competent staff is a must. Federal Court rulings regarding religious diets affect prison food service policies and can put additional strain on food budgets. The climate can also have an effect on a food budget in events such as a drought or other natural disaster.

Chapter Resources

DISCUSSION QUESTIONS

1. What are the differences between feeding juvenile and adult inmates?
2. How has the RLUIPA shaped the way special diets are handled?
3. What can affect a prison food budget?
4. What type of emergency situations must food service managers plan for?

ADDITIONAL RESOURCES

Government Finance Officer Association, http://gfoa.org/

United States Department of Justice, *Federal Bureau of Prisons food service manual*, http://www.bop.gov/policy/progstat/4700_006.pdf

NOTES

1. California Department of Corrections & Rehabilitation. (2010). *Prison facilities, California Department of Corrections: San Quentin State Prison*. Retrieved from http://www.cdcr.ca.gov/Facilities_Locator/SQ-Institution_Stats.html
2. Glaze, L., Parks, E., & United States Department of Justice. (2012). *Correctional populations in the United States, 2011*. Washington, DC: Government Printing Office. Retrieved from http://bjs.ojp.usdoj.gov/content/pub/pdf/cpus11.pdf
3. The American Correctional Association. (n.d.). *"Past, Present, and Future." An overview of the American Correctional Association*. Retrieved from http://aca.org/pastpresentfuture/history.asp
4. United States Department of Agriculture, Food and Nutrition Service. (2012). *About school meals*. Washington DC: Government Printing Office. Retrieved from http://www.fns.usda.gov/cnd/About/AboutCNP.htm
5. Issermoyer, T. (2008, August 27). *Federal Bureau of Prisons religious diet program*. Presentation prepared for the Association of Correctional Food Service Affiliates International Conference.
6. *Turner v. Safley*. (1987). 482 U.S. 78. Retrieved from http://caselaw.lp.findlaw.com/scripts/getcase.pl?navby=case&court=us&vol=482&invol=78
7. Issermoyer, T. (2008, August 27). *Federal Bureau of Prisons religious diet program*. Presentation prepared for the Association of Correctional Food Service Affiliates International Conference.
8. San Diego County Sheriff's Department. (2013). *San Diego County Sheriff's Department, Food Service and Commissary*. Retrieved from http://www.sdsheriff.net/jailinfo/food.html
9. Garris, K. (2011). *Food services unit*. Richmond, VA: Department of Corrections.

10. Association of Correctional Food Service Affiliates. (2013). Retrieved from http://www.acfsa.org

11. National Oceanic & Atmospheric Administration (NOOA). (n.d.). *Hurricane Katrina*. Retrieved from http://www.katrina.noaa.gov/

12. Beach, J. (2008, Fall). In the company of heros. *Insider*, pp. 18–21.

13. Schwartz, J., & Barry, C. (2009). *A guide to preparing for and responding to jail emergencies*. Washington, DC: National Institute of Corrections.

14. Centers for Disease Control and Prevention. (2013). *Pandemic flu*. Retrieved from http://www.cdc.gov/flu/pandemic-resources/

15. The Weather Channel. (2012). *2012 drought rivals dust bowl*. Retrieved from http://www.weather.com/news/drought-disaster-new-data-20120715

Financial Operations

Beverly Pierce

CHAPTER OBJECTIVES

- Describe key concepts related to the fiscal management of penal institutions.
- Name at least three approaches to prudence in the utilization of public funds.
- Explore the issues that can cause balanced budget failure.

Few correctional administrators have a professional background in the financial management of institutional operations. Traditionally, wardens and jail administrators have learned their craft through the apprenticeship system and have earned incremental promotions up the ranks of the institution. Upon reaching senior management, most individuals are fiscally unskilled and totally unprepared for the significant responsibility of jail or prison financial management.

The cost of running the country's prisons is a major issue in today's world of expanding institutional populations. As more and larger prisons and jails become necessary, these institutions garner more of the public and media attention. As budgets take up an increasing amount of legislators' discretionary allotments, the issue of confinement can and will become the center of attention for influential third parties.

Incarceration is expensive, and administrators are being tasked with developing initiatives that can significantly reduce expenditures beyond the institution budget. The inmate populations are soaring as well as the cost. It is time to seriously recommend creative alternatives to incarceration and revise sentencing guidelines that will cause a reduction in the prison population. The current financial trends are putting states in financial crises with deficits. They are bearing the largest costs for corrections, mostly incarceration, and receive diminishing returns on the dollar. Cost containment at the institution level is important, but it is not substantial enough for this economy. The kind of deep cuts necessary to affect costs translate to reducing the inmate population while maintaining public safety.

The United States incarcerates more people than any other nation. The incarceration rate has increased 350% since 1980. Sixty percent of the prison and jail population are nonviolent offenders. This should allow flexibility in achieving budget reductions by changing sentencing guidelines.

■ Understanding Financial Operations

The budget is best explained in three phases: budget development, budget execution, and budget oversight. Budget development is the beginning of the cycle—the formulation of a funding request. Budget execution is the administration of those funds through expenditures and distribution. Budget oversight is the implementation of systems and internal controls that ensure that funds are used in a manner consistent with budgetary goals while protecting the integrity of the disbursements.

The results of making uneducated financial decisions can challenge the best-intentioned administrator. Poorly thought-out decisions can lead to disastrous reactions from staff, inmates the governor's office, and the state legislature. In private corrections, the bottom line is critical to the senior administrator's survival.

The following problems can result from poorly made financial decisions:

- Allowing expenditures to be made that cannot sustain public scrutiny
- Failing to manage program funds within funds allocated
- Failing to understand the fundamentals of budgeting
- Establishing insufficient internal controls to prevent fraud, waste, and abuse
- Failing to provide adequate oversight for early detection of budgeting problems

Financial management of a multimillion-dollar institution budget requires specific knowledge and abilities such as understanding the concept of a budget, analyzing and comparing data, and differentiating between bona fide requirements and incidentals.

Mastering financial management means modifying many already-acquired management and administrative skills to apply to the financial arena, but nothing will serve the new administrator better than good old-fashioned common sense. Simply stated, do not spend more money than was allocated in the budget. Institutional managers must always consider the public perception of their financial decisions. A penal administrator should not spend money on programs that appear to provide inmates with a better quality of life than the general public enjoys. Public administrators must also be cautious not to spend money for buildings and landscaping that are so aesthetically pleasing that the correctional facility looks like a country club. Public stewardship also mandates that institution administrators only spend money on approved purchases, using the correctly appropriated funds. Every dollar spent should be able to sustain public scrutiny.

An administrator must have a planning staff. Staff should include both program and financial managers. These individuals are responsible for analyzing past expenditures and factoring in future budget requests to create a budget that will cover necessary operations and projects over the planning horizon (i.e., future fiscal years). Budget-tracking staff ensure that money is spent as planned and is appropriately conserved throughout the budget year. Anyone assigned budgeting or purchasing responsibilities should be required to participate in a financial training course. Program managers also need to understand and apply sound financial principles to maintain budget accountability on a project basis. Clearly defined budgeting expectations and spending parameters should be established and documented in the institution's policies and procedures. Finally, the chief executive officer of the facility must insist that common sense and good public stewardship are exercised by any staff member given signature authority to expend funds.

■ Political Influence

Correctional staff should never forget that typically, public funds are utilized to create, operate, and otherwise manage all correctional facilities. Even if an institution is built and/or managed by a private, for-profit correctional company, the revenue stream for the facility originates with public funding—taxes. Because the institution's financial support originates with local, state, or federal government, these entities also exercise control over institution budgets.

Correctional staff should also understand the power of publicly elected officials. City councils, state legislatures, and the U.S. Congress are composed of elected representatives of the people. In a democratic republic, the public elects representatives to make decisions on their behalf. The decisions of those representatives then affect the governance of all public institutions, including prison and jail facilities. These elected representatives are expected to make logical and informed decisions as to how public funds should be used. They are also charged with making and changing policies that specify how public money is to be spent. In summary, elected representatives have been given the power and authority to provide broad policy guidelines to the criminal justice system and to ensure that an institution's financial decisions reflect those policies.

Virtually every aspect of correctional management is subject to law, policy, guidelines, rules, or other controls that conform to the broad policy philosophy of the government representatives elected to serve the people. No correctional facility can create a budget in a vacuum, free from government influence or control. All must be aware that correctional leaders are controlled by politicians who manage the policy priorities and purse strings of government operations. To restate the obvious, all policy and funding decisions are political.

■ Budget Development

In government budget cycles, performing strategic planning and properly preparing budget justifications are vital functions of the senior institution executive. Many state budget cycles require multiple-year lead times for budget submission, so anticipating and planning for future requirements are critical. Per capita costs of inmate management (day-to-day costs associated with inmate housing, security, programs, and food and health expenses) must be factored into the daily cost projections along with adjustments for anticipated inflation. Capital outlay (equipment, furniture, and machinery) must be included, as well as capital improvement expenses (maintenance and new construction).

Poor planning inevitably leads to crisis management—a mode of operation that can quickly sabotage a balanced budget. All too often, a lack of planning translates into less value for the dollar. Urgent or emergency purchasing of goods and services sacrifices price savings for shorter delivery times. Because the financial resources for prison operations are precious, every effort must be made to allow the maximum time practical to find and negotiate the best values. Planning is critical in the budget development cycle and can make the difference between success and failure in maintaining a balanced budget.

Budgeting for Human Resources

The most important and expensive part of the institution budget is human resources—the institutional staff. Salaries make up the greatest percentage of institution costs, and agreeing on the number of staff members needed to efficiently, yet economically, operate each institutional department can be difficult. Line staff members and union officials always want to increase rosters. Senior administrators, constantly under pressure to reduce operating expenses, seek to do more with less. Roster management of operations in larger institution departments (such as the correctional security staff) can be a full-time job; supervisors must cover all posts while providing days off, sick leave, and training time, as well as loaning out staff for special projects.

Inevitably, managers must use overtime hours to cover all critical areas of the jail or prison with reasonable supervision. Obviously, paying for unplanned overtime can destroy a carefully balanced financial plan. Caution should be exercised when attempting to implement cost-containment measures by reducing the correctional security personnel. These efforts are often nothing more than smoke and mirrors. If staff rosters are reduced so drastically that overtime is the only alternative to handle special circumstances, no real dollars are saved. Overtime is a variable factor in budget planning and an expensive factor in budget administration.

In the event that major changes to the human resources budget are anticipated, such as a new plan to avoid the use of overtime in the new budget year, it is important to provide adequate planning and lead time for those who must implement that program change. An overtime policy change can cause large-scale ramifications to many personnel in the institutional setting. Morale can decrease if staff security is affected negatively. Ironically, morale can also take a negative turn if a decision is made to curtail the use of overtime, because some staff members depend on this additional income.

Although employee salaries constitute the largest portion of a budget, they do not have to be difficult to project, provided the staffing pattern remains consistent and there are no policy changes that significantly affect institutional operations. Usually, salary increases are negotiated, or at least predictable, prior to the budgeting cycle. Financial staff can provide reasonably accurate salary projections by taking the current work-year cost of each employee and adding a pay increase. A typical work-year for a full-time employee consists of 2,080 hours of paid employment—that is, 52 weeks times 40 hours per week. A specific amount of funding to support overtime, incentive awards, and premium pay should be included in the financial plan. Once staff have calculated salary projections, they have developed 60%–70% of a budget.

Budget and Planning Committees

The establishment of a budget and planning committee is a key step in building a solid financial plan for the institution. Such a committee would ideally consist of a financial manager, subject matter experts at the department head level, the warden, and administrators. The subject matter experts should provide the rationale behind the funding requirements needed to operate their departmental programs and properly justify any need for increased funding levels. Conversely, they should be able to explain the reason for requesting less funding. In a zealous attempt to employ cost-containment measures, staff may underestimate requirements, compromising the integrity of the entire institution's budget. Compensating for shortfalls in underfunded areas can hinder the institution's ability to meet budgetary goals.

The committee should serve in an advisory capacity to the chief executive officer and should meet periodically throughout the fiscal year. The committee should make recommendations to reallocate funds as needed to handle surpluses and deficits in different program areas.

Administrators must understand the political environment in which their agency operates, because changes in this environment may require the institution to ask for additional funding or alter the budget execution process. The budget should incorporate enough flexibility to allow staff to shift emphasis as missions change. Legislative changes in areas such as sentencing guidelines, environmental issues, accessibility for persons with disabilities, and life safety issues can influence funding requirements.

Often, financial managers must consider more unknowns when formulating the operations portion of the budget. Prior-year spending is the best starting point for developing the operations budget. Financial staff can provide an estimate of anticipated increases based on historical data and the consumer price index. After considering routine operations, staff must factor in any new requirements. A history of past obligations, anticipated new costs, and projections of a funding source for uncontrollable or unanticipated expenses (e.g., utility increases, institution emergencies, and catastrophic medical care events) should be well substantiated.

Multiyear formal contracting for purchasing goods and services can be a very useful budgeting instrument. Contracts ensure competitive pricing—the best value for the dollar—and can guarantee prices. Using contracts can increase the accuracy of the budgeting forecast, as it removes some of the guesswork. Warranties and maintenance agreements for equipment can also be a good budgeting tool. They have recognized costs and can reduce unanticipated expenditures.

One of the greatest threats to the integrity of a budget request is the organization's own financial philosophy. Too often, staff believe that if they do not use all approved funding in one budget cycle, it will not be appropriated in future budgets. This belief perpetuates wasteful spending and discourages cost-containment initiatives.

Finally, to make a successful budget request, one must present a clearly defined budgeting goal. Whether the goal is cost containment, enhancing programs, or renovation, staff need to know what they want to achieve with the funds requested. Only when staff have identified the budgeting objective do they have a solid foundation for the request.

■ Managing the Institutional Budget

Once a budget has been approved and funded, the institution is accountable for managing that budget. Laws, statutes, and administrative rules generally govern most institutional financial matters. It is therefore critical that the senior administrator knows the spending limits of the institution budget. These limits are documented in a legislature-approved budget that has been certified by the corrections department. The individual with signature authority to expend jail or prison financial resources must know the limits that apply to him or her along with the rules governing the transfer of discrete amounts of funds between fund categories (salaries, operations, capital outlay, and capital improvement) and ensure that all expenditures are reasonable and justified. **Table 8-1** shows the fiscal year 2001 budgets for adult facilities throughout the United States.

The management of planned expenditures is a dynamic process. The ebb and flow of jail and prison management requires some degree of flexibility in financial management; hence, it is critical that the senior administrator be prepared to shift funds between cost centers to the extent that the law or regulation will permit.

Additionally, senior administrators must ensure that there are internal controls that effectively prevent fraudulent or deficit spending. A checkpoint can be as simple as examining the percentage of the budget expended as a proportion of the full budget cycle. For example, if staff have used 70% of the yearly budget and are only halfway through the budget cycle, there should be a reasonable explanation. Sometimes, contract fees covering the entire budget cycle must be paid in advance, which can skew a given checkpoint. However, department heads should be aware of such situations and be able to explain any departure from what was planned.

Financial staff should be on the lookout for any invalid obligations, as they will distort the budget picture by overstating expenditures and underestimating available funds. Invalid obligations are funds that were

TABLE 8-1 **Adult Correctional Budgets, 2009–2010**

Average Daily Population 12/31/09			
	Prison/Residential	**Probation/Parole**	**Total**
Alabama	25,499	N/A	$466,200,000
Alaska	5,517	6,741	$261,160,400
Arizona	No response		
Arkansas	14,854	N/A	$289,941,901
California	No response		
Colorado	22,919	11,655	$759,875,487
Connecticut	18,077	2,706 (parole)	$666,854,033
Delaware	6,858	16,932	$260,100,200
Florida	101,437	155,837	$2,411,095,387
Georgia	52,473	5,277	$1,113,443,858
Hawaii	5,902	918	$193,825,319
Idaho	7,400	13,821	$165,622,405
Illinois	No response		
Indiana	26,356	10,527 (parole)	$609,000,000
Iowa	No response		
Kansas	8,622	6,000 (parole)	$278,875,041
Kentucky	21,651	39,364	$468,816,416
Louisiana	38,595	66,945	$663,681,680
Maine	2,268	7,360	$97,360,856
Maryland	20,579	N/A	$798,428,181
Massachusetts	11,239	N/A	$523,600,658
Michigan	45,530	79,093	$1,997,144,600
Minnesota	9,132	19,256	$454,310,763[1]
Mississippi	21,521	33,331	$337,698,500
Missouri	30,548	73,985	$685,459,127
Montana	1,623	8,674	$169,054,953
Nebraska	4,359	1,063	$173,269,390
Nevada	12,903	N/A	$268,015,746
New Hampshire	2,763	14,775	$106,711,100
New Jersey	23,981	N/A	$1,073,754,000
New Mexico	No response		
New York	59,328	N/A	$3,300,477,000
North Carolina	40,527	111,785	$1,400,990,511
North Dakota	1,205	4,822	$106,600,000
Ohio	50,889	33,209	$1,564,025,072
Oklahoma	25,479	29,272	$551,766,487
Oregon	13,786	31,649	$704,259,878[2]
Pennsylvania	51,487	N/A	$1,785,201,000[3]

Rhode Island	3,612	27,140	$195,999,266[4]
South Carolina	24,186	N/A	$316,684,632
South Dakota	3,438	2,821 (parole)	$66,449,246
Tennessee	19,670	61,140	$685,675,100
Texas	154,183	507,703	$3,113,507,578
Utah	6,571	15,421	$240,397,413
Vermont	2,220	9,692	$138,315,722
Virginia	31,220	60,773	$1,124,623,931
Washington	18,055	N/A	$899,407,953
West Virginia	5,062	2,393	$154,936,305
Wisconsin	23,184	68,208	$1,079,917,100
Wyoming	2,048	848	$140,346,669

Capital expenditures: Money spent on new construction, physical plant improvements, and equipment.

Operating expenditures: Money spent on routine expenses (e.g., staff, food, clothing, medical services, programs utilities, and maintenance).

1. MINNESOTA: The total budget includes adult and juvenile services and cannot be separated.

2. OREGON: The state operates on a two-year budget.

3. PENNSYLVANIA: The total figure represents $1,612,290,000 from the General Fund and $172,911,000 from American Recovery and Reinvestment Act (ARRA funds. Additionally, expenditures for custody/security staff, physical plant/maintenance, and community programs of internal services are included with institutional services.

4. RHODE ISLAND: The total noted was the actual enacted budget amount; however, the indicated allocation amounts are based on the spent totals equaling $185,003,800.

Source: Data from: *Corrections Compendium*, Volume 36, Issue 1. Spring 2011. pg. 17–29. ACA.

overestimated for the purchase of goods or services and then not deleted in the accounting system after payment. This situation occurs when cost estimates exceed actual expenses. Often, accounting staff do not know when an order is complete and fully invoiced. Unused funds associated with the order or contract remain encumbered. For example, this often occurs with medical expenses. Frequently, the treatment or procedure is different from what was expected or is even deemed unnecessary after the obligation has occurred. The opposite situation can arise when funds are encumbered for a procedure or service that was more expensive than originally planned; this can cause deficit spending or an overstated budget balance.

Reducing the chance of budget errors caused by invalid obligations requires the input of subject matter experts. The program manager must review the open obligation records in the accounting system to verify their accuracy. When searching for explanations for budget shortfalls or surpluses, invalid obligations are a good place to start.

Early detection of disparities in the budget is critical to an administrator's ability to take corrective action. Identifying potential surpluses in one area is equally important if staff need to compensate for budgeting shortfalls or unforeseen fund expenditures in other areas.

Although some correctional administrators may argue the point, most believe there are truly very few large-scale unforeseen expenses associated with prison and jail management. There are some obvious exceptions: natural disasters, inmate disturbances, and catastrophic medical care for inmates. Special contingency funding must always be set aside to prevent such events from breaking the bank and damaging an administrator's career.

Appropriate levels of reserve funding can be calculated by developing an equitable formula that sets aside a percentage of each discipline's budget for contingencies. This should be done at the beginning of the cycle. The reserves can be used to correct budget problems or be reappropriated to other projects. However, senior administrators must realize that using funds appropriated for inmate care for another purpose may draw criticism. For example, funding for medical care, food, and inmate comfort items should remain in the operations portion of the budget. The budget and planning committee should be able to identify personnel changes and salary variations in advance of a catastrophe.

Accountability in any financial process is important, but in the budgetary environment, it is mandatory. Although it is acceptable, and generally desirable, to decentralize cost center management control to the department head level within the institution, it is critical that the overall budget manager assign specific tracking responsibility along with the authority to spend. Individuals with signature authority to spend must be required to justify expenditures in writing, account for all fund outlays, and keep spending within preset limits.

Compliance monitoring or financial auditing is critical to the integrity of an agency's budgeting process. In many cases, the parent organization has an official financial auditing system in place. However, an in-house review should be conducted periodically using specific financial auditing guidelines that focus on vital functions and prevent fraud. The facility's financial management operation should be able to sustain an audit from a private accounting firm or government accounting agency. An acceptable internal auditing system should also be in place throughout the budgeting cycle.

Part of maintaining the integrity of a budget is being able to demonstrate the ability to protect and maximize the financial resources entrusted to staff stewardship. This will require internal controls to prevent waste, fraud, and abuse. Internal requirements might include:

- A system for accountability for purchasing and maintaining property and equipment with a high acquisition value
- Policies limiting or eliminating personal use of equipment
- A second level of procurement authority to ensure that contracts and small purchases are competitively priced and available to all eligible contractors and vendors
- Documentation to support the destruction or removal of property that is no longer useful or cannot be repaired

Jail or prison staff must be aware of special funds for which staff have stewardship responsibility. These funds may include inmate accounts, inmate wages, and canteen profit accounts designated by law or internal regulation for special institutional purposes. Inmates can be sensitive about these funds, and they have been the subject of inmate-originated lawsuits. Such accounts also receive, and deserve, close attention from outside auditors. It may be advisable to develop an inmate canteen committee that would allow inmates to have a voice in the use of canteen profits. At least a portion of these funds should be used to benefit the entire inmate population, for example, by purchasing recreation equipment or augmenting the children's area of the visiting room.

Senior institution staff must also pay particular attention to the expenditure of public money for employee travel and attendance at conferences or special training events. This type of activity can easily generate undesirable attention if such events are not reasonable and appropriate. Per diem expenses of on-duty staff who are working outside the institution offer great potential for abuse and subsequent negative publicity. Management should exercise care in the approval process for training locations; if a conference is in a resort area, it can draw criticism from the public.

Public scrutiny must be an important consideration in all aspects of institution spending. A correctional facility, whether government run or privately operated, is largely funded by the taxpayers. As shown in **Figure 8-1**, the cost of incarceration is rapidly increasing; therefore, management of institution resources must be logical, acceptable to the public conscience, and based on common sense. Institutional staff must develop a keen sensitivity to what people might consider inmate luxuries and avoid spending money on items that are not acceptable to the average citizen. In general, equipment and programs available to inmates should not be better than those available to the average free citizen.

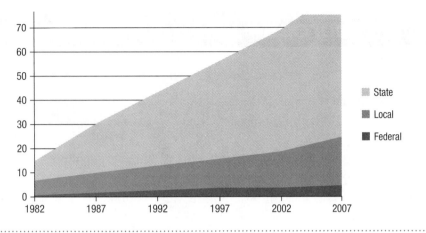

FIGURE 8-1 U.S. prison expenditures; chart represents billions of dollars

Source: Analysis of Bureau of Justice Statistics data by the authors of *The High Budgetary Cost of Incarceration*, John Schmitt, Kris Warner, and Sarika Gupta.

■ Conclusion

Basic training of senior correctional personnel in the use of financial reports and general budgeting principles and techniques helps ensure financial accountability in a prison or jail environment. Although most senior managers are not from a business or accounting background, there are many benefits in providing basic financial knowledge to correctional leaders. Most correctional budgets represent multimillion-dollar operations; hence, the return on basic financial training is significant.

The financial operation of a prison or jail is a critical management responsibility. Stewardship of the public's resources requires conservative decision making, a well-developed sense of integrity, and the ability to apply administrative accountability to the overall process. Effective and efficient operations and programs require fiscally responsible budget planning and execution.

Chapter Resources

DISCUSSION QUESTIONS

1. How do the staffing pattern and roster affect the institution budget?
2. As a senior administrator, what level of importance would you assign financial management in your institution and why?
3. How do you think public scrutiny and perception relate to institution expenditures?
4. What methods can be used to ensure fiscal accountability?
5. What challenges might a prison or jail administrator face with regard to financial operations?

ADDITIONAL RESOURCE

Phillips, R., & McConnell, C. (2005). *The effective corrections manager: Correctional supervision for the future*. Sudbury, MA: Jones & Bartlett Publishers.

Correctional Programs

IV

■ Is There Value in Institutional Programs for Inmates?

Many would argue that correctional programs are the "meat and potatoes" of the task assigned to public servants who work in prisons and jails in America. The concept of reforming criminals while they are confined dates back to the early leadership of the National Prison Association in the 1870s. We try to measure the success of the efforts to prevent offenders from committing future crimes once they have been released from confinement by tracking the released inmates' future arrest records. These recidivism statistics become important to legislative policy makers, practitioners, and the general public.

The Pew Center on the States completed the most recent comprehensive study of recidivism rates in 2011 and found that:

45.4 percent of inmates released from prison in 1999 and 43.3 percent of those sent home in 2004 were re-incarcerated within three years, either for committing a new offense or for violating conditions governing their release.

The Pew study further notes:

Recidivism rates between 1994 and 2007 have consistently remained around 40 percent…if more than four out of 10 adult American offenders still return to prison within three years of their release, the system designed to deter them from continued criminal behavior is falling short. That is an unhappy reality, not just for offenders, but for the safety of American communities.

Source: Pew Center on the States, *State of recidivism: The revolving door of America's prisons* (Washington, DC: The Pew Charitable Trusts, April 2011).

As you consider the value of correctional programs in prisons and jails, ponder these questions:

- If 40% of released inmates are returning to prison, 60% are successful (as defined by the 3-year window of the study). Is this success?
- In today's tight fiscal environment, should precious financial resources be expended on institutional programs? If so, what types of programs? If not, what programs would you not fund?
- How would you defend the fact that 40% of released inmates return to prison? Is this a statistic for which correctional authorities should bear responsibility?

Rehabilitation

James Austin

CHAPTER OBJECTIVES

- Identify the major factors that affect criminal behavior.
- Explain the role of correctional treatment programs in reducing crime.
- Describe common challenges faced by ex-offenders returning to the community.

There is much debate regarding the potential of correctional treatment interventions to reduce crime in general and among offenders who are under the control of the criminal justice system in particular. But correctional treatment interventions do not operate in a vacuum. Personal, social, and economic factors also affect criminal behavior. In addition, the political climate influences whether correctional administrators support rehabilitation and treatment programs, regardless of their efficacy. Given all these influencing factors, it is difficult to determine whether rehabilitation programs alone reduce crime.

■ Factors Relating to Criminal Careers

Criminologists have conducted considerable research that shows that criminal careers for both adults and juveniles do not follow predictable patterns. Many youths who are delinquent during their adolescent years cease their criminal activities by adulthood. Most adult offenders have not had juvenile crime careers (or at least not extensive ones) and are unlikely to continue their criminal behaviors indefinitely. Many factors other than treatment influence patterns of criminal behavior. The causal factors affecting criminal activity can be grouped into two categories:

1. Structural factors—demographic factors (such as gender and age) that are largely static and cannot be modified
2. Situational factors—societal influences (such as employment, marriage, and societal and economic considerations) that are more dynamic and flexible

Structural Factors

The vast majority of crimes are committed by young men between the ages of 15 and 24.[1] Thereafter, rate of offending declines dramatically, so that by age 30, many offenders have effectively "aged out" of crime and are no longer considered high risk. There are, of course, exceptions to this generalization, but these exceptions tend to be adults with extensive juvenile and adult criminal histories who are unable or unwilling to pursue a normative lifestyle.

The fact that most active criminals are young is especially relevant to the significant number of adult prisoners, probationers, and parolees. Many offenders who are under correctional supervision are well above their peak years of criminal behavior and can be expected to significantly reduce their recidivism rates due solely to maturation. With today's longer prison terms, increasing numbers of inmates will be less likely to recidivate due to their age. Several studies have shown that only a small proportion of the crimes committed each year can be attributed to released prisoners or parolees. These data underscore that correctional treatment and punishment initiatives will have minimal, if any, effect on crime rates.

Situational Factors

The ability of a former offender to maintain stable employment (coupled with the aging process) will significantly reduce that person's criminal tendencies. One important study in California found that providing even very modest economic assistance to released prisoners greatly reduced the rates of recidivism.[2]

Another major factor that reduces offenders' probability of continuing their criminal behavior is maintaining a stable and supportive marriage.[3] A stable marriage helps ex-offenders maintain jobs and places to live as well as reduce drug and alcohol abuse.[4]

Criminologists have also examined the societal and economic influences on crime rates. Some factors produce social stress that in turn affects crime rates. States with high rates of violent crimes, mental illness, and suicide tended to have high rates of the following social and economic factors:

• Business failures
• Unemployment claims

- Workers on strike
- Personal bankruptcies
- Mortgage foreclosures
- Divorces
- Abortions
- Illegitimate births
- Infant deaths
- Fetal deaths
- Disaster assistance
- State residency of less than 5 years
- New houses authorized
- New welfare cases
- High school dropouts

It is also noteworthy that studies did not find an association between incarceration rates and crime rates. In fact, there is a well-established negative correlation (i.e., states with high incarceration rates tend to have high crime rates). Some experts believe that high rates of incarceration may contribute to high levels of social stress and thus increase crime rates.

■ Role of Incarceration

Numerous studies have examined the relative effects of incarceration on crime rates in general and on individual offenders. In their pioneering study, Sampson and Laub followed 880 juveniles from adolescence through adulthood and found that neither the number of incarcerations nor the length of incarceration had a direct effect on a person's criminal career.[5] They went on to note that incarcerations actually have a deleterious effect on recidivism, as they severely disrupt efforts to maintain relationships with loved ones and secure stable employment.

A review of numerous studies of the many early release programs that are now operating throughout the country found that neither moderate increases nor moderate decreases (3–6 months) in prison terms have an effect on either crime rates in general or an individual offender's rate of reoffending. Again, age is a dominant factor; older inmates (age 35 and above) have by far the lowest rates of recidivism.

In addition, studies have shown little evidence that adjustments in the use of incarceration have an independent effect on crime rates. For example, states with the highest crime rates have the highest incarceration rates, and states with the lowest incarceration rates have the lowest crime rates. Historical fluctuations in crime rates and incarceration rates reveal no clear relationship between incarceration rates and crime rates. However, the tripling of not only the prison population but also the probation, jail, and parole populations over the past 15 years has had some effect on crime rates. At the same time, other developments such as an improving economy, reductions in unemployment and drug use, increases in deportation of illegal aliens, tighter gun control measures, and a growing number of prevention programs sponsored by private sector organizations have substantially reduced crime rates.

■ Role of Correctional Treatment

For years, criminologists have debated whether correctional treatment helps juvenile and adult offenders. The debate began with a 1974 publication by Robert Martinson that left the unfortunate impression that "nothing works."[6] Martinson's publication was based on a review of existing evaluations of prison treatment programs by himself and his colleagues—one of the first meta-analyses that attempted to summarize the findings of numerous experimental and quasi-experimental studies of rehabilitation programs. This pioneering work has been followed by several other major meta-analyses that reach a different conclusion that under certain conditions, some treatment interventions can have a significant effect on recidivism rates. In other words, many treatment programs fail, but a sizable number succeed.[7]

Many have disagreed with these later findings; they argue that the meta-analyses are suspect and overstate the merits of rehabilitation. In particular, the studies cited by these meta-analyses tend to have small sample sizes (less than 250 cases for experimental and control groups). Also, in many of the studies, the differences between the recidivism rates of control and experimental subjects were minimal (5%–10%). Furthermore, the recommended conditions necessary for treatment to succeed are difficult to define and replicate in other sites.

Well-designed and well-administered correctional treatment programs are the exception rather than the rule. Program integrity is often weak, which may explain the absence of strong treatment effects for many treatment programs. Correctional agencies are often ill-equipped to design and implement effective treatment programs. Most agencies do not themselves believe that effective treatment is possible or that it is part of their mission.[8] A survey showed that most prison wardens believe that only 25% of their inmates are amenable to treatment. The wardens also stated that involving inmates in rehabilitation programs was not a high priority for their organizations. However, they do view such programs as having an important place in a prison setting.[9]

The Federal Bureau of Prisons (BOP) has concluded, based on thorough research and analysis, that work experience and vocational training programs in federal correctional institutions have significant effects on an offender's ability to successfully reintegrate into the community following release from prison. Specifically, it found that prison programs can have a positive effect on postrelease employment and arrest in the short run, and on recommitment in the long run. The research was based on data from more than 7,000 offenders who had been released from prison for 8–12 years. Inmates who had worked in federal prison industries or participated in a vocational training program (the study group) were significantly more likely to be employed than inmates who had done neither (the comparison group). The study group inmates were also significantly less likely than the comparison group to recidivate. Inmates who worked in prison industries were 24% less likely to recidivate than comparable inmates who had not worked in industries, and inmates who participated in vocational training or apprenticeship training were 33% less likely to recidivate than inmates who had not.[10]

On the basis of another study that also employed a very rigorous methodology, the BOP has concluded that residential drug abuse treatment has a positive effect on inmates' propensity to recidivate. A 1998 study involving 1,800 offenders who had participated in intensive substance abuse therapy for either 9 or 12 months revealed that offenders who completed the program were 15% less likely than inmates who did not complete the program to be rearrested during the first 3 years after reentry into the community. Similarly, graduates of the program were less likely to use drugs following release. The large sample size (1,800 offenders), rigorous research design, and multisite sample make these findings particularly noteworthy.[11]

■ Conclusion

Among the various forms of rehabilitation programs, interventions (or treatment programs) that help equip an individual to secure meaningful employment in today's increasingly competitive economy will be the most successful. Programs that simply offer drug treatment or cognitive learning-based interventions that do not enhance the offenders' ability to perform basic tasks essential for any form of employment are unlikely to reduce recidivism. Furthermore, the private and public sector must recognize the need to provide employment opportunities for this segment of the population.

Based on research to date, the following conclusions can be made regarding the effect of treatment and punishment on crime rates and individual offenders:

- The vast majority of crimes are not committed by persons released from prison. Consequently, prison-based treatment programs and punishment will have little effect on crime rates in general. There is also evidence from one study that crimes committed by probationers do not contribute significantly to a jurisdiction's crime rate.[12]

- Under certain circumstances, treating offenders can have positive results. These positive results are strongest for programs that provide for long-term aftercare and increase the offender's ability to secure employment (part- or full-time).

- Under certain circumstances, punishing offenders can have positive results.

- Under certain circumstances, treating or punishing offenders can have negative results.

- Change (positive and negative) can also occur and often does occur based on other factors that have nothing to do with treatment (e.g., maturation, random events).

- The vast majority of correctional treatment programs have not been evaluated.

- Most correctional treatment programs are not well administered, target the wrong clientele, and are too small to have any effect on crime rates or public safety.

- It is extremely rare to find a well-administered treatment program that has been evaluated properly and has demonstrated dramatic treatment effects.

- Factors that will undoubtedly reduce the likelihood of maintaining a criminal lifestyle are age, no juvenile crime career, no history of violence, no evidence of drug use or abuse, the ability to secure employment, and the ability to maintain a meaningful marriage or relationship.

- Treatment and punishment will have only moderate effects on crime rates.

Finally, one must take into account the current political climate. Although considerable debate exists among criminologists and correctional administrators regarding the merits of rehabilitation, there is little if any support for such programs among leading politicians. Rather than supporting the funding of more or different treatment programs, the current climate seems to encourage truth-in-sentencing, three-strikes laws, boot camps, chain gangs, lowering of the age for waiving juveniles into adult court, and austere prisons without programs and recreation.

Given this atmosphere, it will take more powerful evidence that treatment reduces rates of recidivism and increases public safety to persuade those who favor a more punitive approach. However, advocates of more and stronger forms of punishment have no conclusive scientific findings to justify their policies either. For this reason alone, the use of rehabilitation and treatment programs that help ensure a more humane and less costly correctional system is warranted and should be expanded. Most important, correctional agencies should become far more accountable (both fiscally and administratively) for such programs and engage in more studies of well-administered programs that better prepare offenders to secure and maintain meaningful employment.

Chapter Resources

DISCUSSION QUESTIONS

1. What are some strategies that communities might consider to reduce crime?
2. To what extent should correctional treatment programs be judged by the recidivism rate of its graduates?
3. What are the strongest predictors of criminal behavior?
4. What are some of the structural factors that affect criminality?
5. What are some of the situational factors that affect criminality?

ADDITIONAL RESOURCES

National Council on Crime and Delinquency, http://www.nccd-crc.org

National Institute of Justice, http://www.ojp.usdoj.gov/nij

Urban Institute, http://www.urban.org

NOTES

1. Hirschi, T., & Gottfredson, M. (1987). Age and the explanation of crime. *American Journal of Sociology, 89,* 552–584; Federal Bureau of Investigation. (1990). *Age-specific arrest rates and race-specific rates for selected offenses.* Washington, DC: U.S. Department of Justice; Flannagan, T., & Maguire, K. (Eds.). (1990). *Sourcebook of criminal justice statistics 1989.* Washington, DC: U.S. Government Printing Office.
2. Braithwaite, J. (1989). *Crime, shame, and reintegration.* Cambridge, England: Cambridge University Press; Crutchfield, R. (1989). Labor stratification and violent crime. *Social Forces, 68,* 489–512; Sampson, R., & Laub, J. (1993). *Crime in the making: Pathways and turning points through life.* Cambridge, MA: Harvard University Press; Shover, N. (1985). *Aging criminals.* Beverly Hills, CA: Sage Publications.
3. Sampson, R. J., & Laub, J. H. (1993). *Crime in the making: Pathways and turning points through life.* Cambridge, MA: Harvard University Press.
4. Gibbens, T. (1987). Borstal boys after 25 years. *British Journal of Criminology, 24,* 49–62; Knight, B., Osborn, S., & West, D. (1977). Early marriage and criminal tendency in males. *British Journal of Criminology, 17,* 348–360; Rand, A. (1987). Transitional life events and desistance from delinquency and crime. In M. Wolfgang, T. Thornberry, & R. Figlio (Eds.), *From boy to man: From delinquency to crime* (pp. 134–162). Chicago, IL: University of Chicago Press.
5. Sampson, R. J., & Laub, J. H. (1993). *Crime in the making: Pathways and turning points through life.* Cambridge, MA: Harvard University Press.
6. Martinson, R. (1974). What works? Questions and answers about prison reform. *The Public Interest, 35,* 22–54.
7. Andrews, D., Zinger, I., Hoge, R. D., Bonta, J., Gendreau, P., & Cullen, F. T. (1990). Does correctional treatment work? A clinically relevant and psychologically informed meta-analysis. *Criminology, 28,* 369–404; Davidson, W., Gottschalk, R., Gensheimer, L., & Mayer, J. (1984). *Interventions with juvenile delinquents: A meta-analysis of treatment efficacy.* Washington, DC: National Institute of Juvenile Justice and Delinquency

Prevention; Garrett, C. (1985). Effects of residential treatment on adjudicated delinquents: A meta-analysis. *Journal of Research in Crime and Delinquency, 22,* 287–308; Gendreau, D., & Ross, P. (1987). Revivification of rehabilitation: Evidence from the 1980s. *Justice Quarterly, 4,* 349–407; Gottschalk, R., Davidson, W. S., Gensheimer, L. K., & Mayer, J. P. (1987). Community-based interventions. In H. Quay (Ed.), *Handbook of juvenile delinquency.* New York, NY: Wiley & Sons; Lipsey, M. W. (1989). *The efficacy of intervention for juvenile delinquency.* Paper presented at the meeting of the American Society of Criminology, Reno, NV; Palmer, T. (1992). *The re-emergence of correctional intervention.* Newbury Park, CA: Sage Publications.

8. Austin, J. (1990). Using early release to relieve prison crowding: A dilemma in public policy. *Crime & Delinquency, 32,* 404–502.

9. Cullen, F. T., Latessa, E. J., Burton, V. S., & Lombardo, L. X. (1993). The correctional orientation of prison wardens: Is the rehabilitative ideal supported? *Criminology, 31,* 69–92.

10. Saylor, W., & Gaes, G. (1997). Training inmates through industrial work participation and vocational and apprenticeship instruction. *Corrections Management Quarterly, 1*(2), 32–43.

11. Saylor, W., & Gaes, G. (1998). *TRIAD drug treatment evaluation project: Six month interim report.* Washington, DC: Federal Bureau of Prisons Office of Research and Evaluation.

12. Geerken, M., & Hayes, H. (1993). Probation and parole: Public risk and the future of incarceration alternatives. *Criminology, 31,* 549–564.

Correctional Academic, Career, and Reentry Education

Steve Steurer

CHAPTER OBJECTIVES

- Provide a rationale for education for the incarcerated. Discuss whether it is a moral imperative because education is valuable for the development of the incarcerated as human beings, or because it is a direct benefit for society in terms of reduced recidivism, community development, and future crime reduction, or for both reasons.

- Provide a guide to practitioners for the development of education programs at the local detention level.

Free and public education up to high school completion has been mandated by law and accepted popularly for American children up to the age of 21. A free and appropriate education has been made mandatory for all students deemed to have a disability covered under the Individuals wih Disabilities Act (IDEA).[1] Legal decisions have confirmed that IDEA is applicable to the incarcerated as well, in juvenile or adult facilities. Free and public education for incarcerated juveniles is normally provided in state and local juvenile facilities. Traditionally, in most states, basic education up to high school completion has been provided in state and federal prisons for many years to adults as well as youth up to 21 years of age. A good number of states and the Federal Bureau of Prisons have actually made education mandatory and/or provided incentives for attendance to incarcerated individuals who have not achieved a certain level determined by law or correctional policy. The State of Indiana has taken this concept even further by guaranteeing a free public education to all its citizens, including postsecondary education. There is little research that reveals the extent to which educational services are provided in county or large city detention facilities or jails.

■ Dearth of Research in Correctional Education

Although federal and state prison systems have generally provided basic education and vocational training as part of inmate programming, local adult detention facilities have a less consistent record. As already noted, there have been no large-scale studies to determine the extent of education programs in county jails, but experts in corrections and education believe many jails provide little or no education for the incarcerated, particularly short-term inmates (those serving less than 1 or 2 months). This is particularly true of county correctional systems with inmate populations of less than 1,000. Large city jails are more likely to provide services because they are run more like small state correctional systems. The National Institute of Corrections defines large jails as more than 1,000 inmates.[2] There are, however, some excellent examples of programs provided through the local corrections department or community colleges, or both (references will include programs from Massachusetts, Maryland, and West Virginia). Although this chapter focuses on jails with a population of less than 1,000 people, many of the recommendations can apply to large jails and prisons as well.

■ General Review of the Status of Correctional Education

Education and corrections research has documented the general deficits of the U.S. prison populations in comparison with adults in the free world. General literacy levels, a lower percentage of high school graduates, and a lack of vocational and career skills have been verified in a number of studies at the national and state levels. The National Assessment of Adult Literacy (NAAL) completed in 2003 included a large inmate sample. The next NAAL survey scheduled for late 2013 will also include incarcerated adults.[3] The take-away points for the correctional sample in the NAAL 2003 study were mixed. It concluded that there are lower levels of educational achievement in prison than in the general community, but there had been some progress since the 1992 National Assessment of Adult Literacy measure. There were significant reductions in illiteracy in general and higher percentages of inmates achieving high school equivalency, but postsecondary completion rates did not increase. A very remarkable finding was that incarcerated blacks were either as literate or more literate than their peers in the community. Blacks who were incarcerated for a few years or more were more literate than their peers. Vocational training was in high demand in the prison population, but more inmates reported being on waiting lists for vocational education than being in programs.[4]

■ Brief History and Content of Correctional Education

Correctional education examples can be found throughout the early history of the United States, but one of the best examples was the Elmira Reformatory in New York in the 1880s, where academic education and employment preparation were emphasized. Although it has been a slow progression, most state prison systems now offer free adult basic education (reading, writing, and computation at the grade school level), English as a second language (ESL) for nonnative speakers, general education development (GED) or high school equivalency, vocational education in areas important for the functioning of the prison or for acquisition of jobs upon release, and reentry preparation in areas needed for success in free society. College-level courses have been taught in many prisons with particular emphasis on career preparation areas such construction, auto repair, and food preparation. In some cases, academic college courses have been offered as well, at the expense of the inmate or paid for by grants or donations. Some inmates have taken advantage of correspondence courses at the college level. Unfortunately, it is an area open to abuse for those who do not have the capacity to check out whether the programs are accredited and accepted by other educational institutions. By far, the largest program in prisons and jails is the GED.

■ Accreditation

The Correctional Education Association (CEA) is the only accrediting body specifically for adult and juvenile correctional education programs at the state, federal, and local levels. Many states have chosen to become CEA accredited. There are more than 60 standards, covering areas such as administration and structure, program content, and staff preparation and credentials. These standards have been met by a large number of small jails, state prisons, and juvenile facilities. The American Correctional Association (ACA), the largest professional organization for correctional staff, recognizes and recommends CEA accreditation for education programs as part of their overall nationally recognized accreditation program.

■ Recent Negative Correctional Education Trends

The highly regarded Texas Windham School System has been seriously threatened with total reorganization in recent legislative sessions and lost 20% of its funds in 2012. Maryland's prison system has experienced cuts in state funds for supplies and teacher training in recent years. In a political fight between the governor and the state superintendent of schools in 2008, the adult education, GED, and correctional education programs were transferred to the department of labor, where academic and vocational education and library program supplies, professional development, and political support were greatly reduced. In Indiana, most vocationally oriented postsecondary education programs were gutted in recent years. In California, prison education programs were cut severely in 2009, with half the teaching staff fired. Unfortunately, informal surveys of state correctional education directors by the CEA from 2008 to 2013 have revealed that no state budgets for inmate education programs have increased.

The federal and state funds for professional development of teachers and bans on travel within and outside states are crippling efforts to train teachers and conduct viable professional conferences. Effectively, correctional teachers are generally unable to keep up with their public school counterparts with new teaching methods, materials, and technological applications.

Ohio had been investing up to $4,000,000 in state money annually to support 15 career-oriented college programs as recently as 5 years ago. The only federal funds for postsecondary education programs were cut 2 years ago, and as a result, Ohio also lost about $1,000,000 in annual federal grants. The state of Virginia has seen significant cuts to staff and programs as well as a complete reorganization of services from a dedicated school system and school board to a smaller agency within the department of corrections.

■ Earlier National-Level Support for Correctional Education

Almost three decades ago, correctional education was experiencing more support for prison education at state and federal levels. First Lady Barbara Bush personally championed adult literacy and made a number of speeches about literacy and correctional education, actually visiting programs and talking to inmate students. There was even a correctional education summit at the White House. The White House worked very closely with ABC-TV on Project Literacy US. Then–ABC President Jim Duffy became personally involved in correctional education. Unfortunately, in the early 1990s, the political trend to "Get Tough on Crime" changed attitudes toward inmate programs, including education. Criminals began to receive much longer sentences for even minor drug crimes. Inmate eligibility for federal vocational and academic education programs was cut or eliminated. Pell grants could no longer be given to incarcerated students. Federal Carl Perkins vocational education and adult education funding for prison programs was severely limited. Many black Americans and other minorities were disproportionately incarcerated because of longer sentences for drug offenses, so these cuts affected them more than other populations.

BOX 10-1

"We must accept the reality that to confine offenders behind walls without trying to change them is an expensive folly with short-term benefits—winning battles while losing the war."

Source: Taylor, J.M 1993. Pell Grants for prisoners. *The Nation*, Vol. 256, No. 3. 25 January.

Postsecondary Education Losses: 1990s to Present

In response to the efforts of Texas Senator Hutchinson to eliminate inmate eligibility for Pell grants, the CEA led an effort to restore college funding. By the late 1990s, the effort resulted in a new and separate program, thanks to Senators Specter, Kennedy, and Harkin, nicknamed "Specter grants." With the huge budget cuts of 2011, funds were cut completely and all federal college funding ended again.

Prospects for Future

Although funding has been reduced, generally research on the positive effects of correctional education continues to be validated. Research demonstrates the effect education can have on crime reduction and how offenders can rebuild their lives to become positive citizens, skilled workers, and good parents. There is bipartisan support for education reentry programs, even though the reentry funding started under President Bush in 2005 was cut significantly in 2012. President Obama and his administration strongly support correctional education under Secretary Arne Duncan and Attorney General Eric Holder. In the private sector, the Vera Institute manages private foundation funds for a few states to develop postsecondary programs with funds donated by the Gates, Sunshine Lady, Ford, and Open Society foundations. The ACA endorses and recommends the CEA adult correctional education standards. The Association of State Correctional Administrators has supported the efforts of the CEA to advance correctional education in its biannual meetings and newsletters. Convincing governors, legislators, the media, and the public is a worthwhile endeavor that can be problematic, particularly during a time of tight budgets. [5]

Making Your Case with the Public

How can one make the case for a correctional education program to the local county board, the state legislature, or the public? The following useful points are taken from an article in *Corrections Today* in August 2010 (*Nine Top Reasons to Increase Correctional Education Programs*).

1. Education is an excellent reentry tool. It is "one of the most productive and important reentry services," according to Gaes.[5]

2. Education has deep roots in American prison history. Since the 1870s, education has grown in importance as an integral part of prison programs. The Elmira Reformatory in New York State first placed emphasis on education and employment preparation.

3. Academic education and vocational education reduce recidivism and support employability after release. There is mounting research evidence, starting with the milestone Three State Study in 2001, demonstrating how education at any level reduces recidivism and improves public safety.[6]

4. Education is much more effective than building prisons in reducing future crime.[7]

5. From a humanistic viewpoint, education is the right thing to do. The United Nations has recommended education for human development.

6. Education is effective as a population control tool. Pairing educational participation with time off sentence and other rewards motivates inmates to become involved, resulting in positive self-image and other positive activities.[8]

7. Education is the foundation for success in other important program areas on postrelease outcomes. Any program that requires the ability to read, write, or do math has much greater potential for inmates who have these skills.

8. The true impact on recidivism may be seriously underestimated.[9] Education is considered a prerequisite for success in other programs that require reading, writing, and necessary quantitative skills. These are all cognitive skills developed through education and are necessary for other rehabilitation programs.

9. Inmates understand the importance of education for their own success. They understand that education is a more important need than housing, employment, drug treatment, or financial assistance and have reported this in a major study.[10]

■ Basic Program Elements

Programs in jails and prisons follow a similar pattern to those offered for adults at the local community college. They normally include basic literacy and life skills, GED or high school equivalency, career or job preparation skills, and basic certification for entry-level jobs such as food safety or construction. Basic literacy includes reading, writing, and math skills at the level of elementary school but taught with adult-oriented materials. Frequently, financial literacy and mathematics for the workplace are taught in conjunction with life skills to help adults with everyday life situations such as shopping, banking, health, parenting, and social situations. In many prisons or jails, noncredit continuing education courses or credit-bearing certificates or college courses are also offered to those who qualify. Although adult basic education, life skills, and GED are offered to students with varying sentence lengths, most other courses enroll students with sentences of a few months or more.

The local community college or literacy council can be very helpful in setting up many of these programs. There are small amounts of federal funds available for these programs, with most funding coming from local or state sources.

■ Educational Assessment

Community colleges or local literacy councils can provide helpful advice and share low-cost or no-cost tools for interviewing students about their educational history and goals. They can also identify low-cost achievement and competency-based tests such as the Test of Adult Basic Education and the Comprehensive Adult Student Assessment System (CASAS). If the jail or prison is lucky enough to have resources for stand-alone or local area networked computers, assessment and instructional materials are available from a number of publishers. These programs, however, can be very costly.

Case management records often provide some information on the educational level of students, but normally they are accessible to educational staff. Case managers are usually willing to share key information to the education department for inmates considering educational programs.

■ Additional Suggestions for Program Planning

The state or county department of labor operates one-stop centers in the community to help people locate information about education and social services. A number of jails have been able to install one-stop centers that are staffed part-time. This is most helpful for finding local market information and social services. Local churches and libraries are often willing to provide volunteers and extension services to jails and information on resources in the community.

■ Trends in Technology

Computer technology offers the promise of reaching and teaching more adults. Although many people on the street carry Smartphones and have some familiarity with computerized applications, inmates have traditionally been forbidden to use the Internet. The issue of gang communication creates real security issues. Stand-alone computers with no connectivity to the Internet through cable or WiFi have been allowed in prisons for many years. Often, school systems and local businesses recycle computers every few years and are willing to donate them to educational facilities.

■ Professional Association Resources

The following national organizations provide information and research on education for the incarcerated: the CEA, ACA, American Jail Association, National Sheriffs' Association, Proliteracy International, National Coalition for Literacy, and National Center for Family Literacy. There are usually state and county adult education and literacy councils that assist anyone interested in setting up educational programs for adults.

Chapter Resources

DISCUSSION QUESTIONS

1. What potential resources are available at the local level for your institution?
2. What motivators might work in your facility to encourage inmate participation in programs?
3. What challenges do you face at your facility in developing education programs?
4. What is the jail or prison policy for inmate use of technology and the Internet?

ADDITIONAL RESOURCES

American Association for Adult and Continuing Education, http://www.aaace.org

American Council on Education, http://www.acenet.edu

Center for Study of Correctional Education, http://www.csusb.edu/coe/csce

Correctional Education Association, http://www.ceanational.org

Education Resources Information Center, http://www.eric.ed.gov

National Institute for Literacy, http://www.nifl.gov

National Institute of Correctional Education, http://www.iup.edu/nice

NOTES

1. U.S. Department of Education. (2010). Office of Civil Rights Free Appropriate Public Education for students with disabilities under section 504 of the Rehabilitation Act of 1973. Retrieved from http://www2.ed.gov/about/offices/list/ocr/docs/edlite-FAPE 504
2. http://nicic.gov/Library/026002
3. National Assessment of Adult Literacy. Retrieved September 4, 2007, from http://nces.ed.gov/NAAL/
4. Education and Correctional Populations. (2003, January). NCJ 195670 Caroline Wolfe Harlow, PhD, BJS statistician. Retrieved from   http://www.ojp.usdoj.gov/bjs/abtract/ecp.htm
5. Steurer, S. J., Linton, J., Nally, J., & Lockwood, S. (2010). The Top-Nine Reasons to Increase Correctional Education Programs. *Corrections Today, 72*(40), 40–43.
6. Steurer, S., Smith, L., & Tracy, A. (2001). Three state recidivism study. Lanham, MD: Correctional Education Association.
7. Bazos, A., & Hausman, J. (2004). *Correctional education as a crime control program.* Los Angeles, CA: UCLA School of Public Policy and Social Research. Retrieved June 28, 2010, from http://www.ceanational.net/PDFs/ed-as-crime-control.pdf
8. McGlone, J. (2002). *Status of mandatory education in state correctional institutions.* Washington, DC: U.S. Department of Education, Office of Vocational and Adult Education.

9. Gaes, G. (2008). *The impact of prison education on post-release outcomes.* New York, NY: John Jay College of Criminal Justice. Retrieved June 28, 2010, from http://www.urban.org/projects/reentry-roundtable/upload/Gaes.pdf

10. Visher, C. A., & Lattimore, P. K. (2007). Major study examines prisoners and their reentry needs. *NIJ Journal, 258*, 32. Washington, DC: National Institute of Justice. Retrieved June 28, 2010, from http://www.ojp.usdoj.gov/nij/journals/258/reentry-needs.html

Correctional Recreation

Suzanne R. Hastings

CHAPTER OBJECTIVES

- Dispel the myths of recreation in a prison environment and describe the evolution of correctional recreation over the years.

- Describe the programs involved in a strong recreational program and why it is important to provide various programs that are geared to that institution's offender population.

- Explain the role recreation plays in the reentry process.

- Describe the challenges faced by correctional recreation employees that others in the same profession but not in the correctional environment do not have to encounter.

istory has proven that incarcerating large numbers of prisoners, in warehouse-like conditions, under poor treatment and with few programs, can result in loss of life or limb. Forty-three citizens of New York State died at the Attica Correctional Facility[1] from September 9 to 13, 1971. What was learned in the aftermath was equally astonishing as the actual disturbance itself. Prisoners were kept locked in small cells, 14–16 hours per day, and movements outside their cells were regulated. Prison administrators throughout the country had continued pledging their dedication to the concept of rehabilitation, while continuing to run prisons constructed in the style and operated in the manner of the 19th-century walled fortresses.[2] Security was the top priority of corrections officials, although most did discuss rehabilitation as well. The inmates that felt such rhetoric about rehabilitation was false rhetoric promises that were viewed as a cruel joke.[3] Several of the recommendations from the Attica uprising involved recreation, that is, #16—Reduce cell time, increase recreation time, and provide better recreation facilities and equipment, and #27—Remove inside recreation walls, making one open yard. For correctional officers, the job involved keeping prisoners in line, ensuring that prisoners obeyed the rules and regulations, and ensuring that the environment was secure in light of the fact that offenders outnumbered the officers. Although prison officials discussed rehabilitation, the Attica officers were not trained to help offenders acquire new skills, reenter society as productive citizens, or problem solve. A New York State Special Commission was appointed to reconstruct the events of that fiery day and to determine why it happened and what could be learned from the incident. The commission recommended that the prison system be restructured with new principles. For example, a serious effort should be made to prepare inmates for release, which does not include cutting them off from contacts in society; and the programs and policies of confinement should focus on enhancing the prisoner's dignity, worth, and confidence.[4] This single event forced the country to revisit its principles regarding confinement and incarceration. As a result, drastic changes had to occur in corrections. One of the changes involved a commitment to developing organized recreation programs. In this chapter, we explore the evolution of correctional recreation dating back to the 1970s, discuss the programs involved in correctional recreation, determine the role recreation plays in the reentry process, and discuss the challenges faced by correctional recreation professionals.

■ Evolution of Correctional Recreation

After the Attica prison riot in the early 1970s, correctional systems made drastic changes to the programs and services offered to offenders. A cultural transformation had to take place in order to go from the law-and-order style of prison management to today's priority of reentry. Correctional recreation has gone through a transformation in itself, going from limited recreation and cell restriction in the 1970s to offenders having access to sports and varied activities in the 1980s. Correctional officers were often assigned the recreation duties of supervising offenders playing sports, cards, and so on. The National Correctional Recreation Association (NCRA) was founded in 1966 by a small group of correctional recreation leaders who were largely custody officers who displayed an interest in sports.[5] After the correctional recreation profession began to flourish, the "Get Tough on Crime" era escalated to the front of the political arena in the 1980s and early 1990s. Politicians felt the only way to get elected and/or reelected was to take the "Get Tough on Crime" approach. Unfortunately, this strategy led to an unprecedented rise in the offender population across the country. In 2006, the prison population grew at a faster rate than in the previous 5 years.[6] In addition to the "Get Tough" legislation, the 1990s produced the "No Frills" era. This era focused on eliminating education and recreation programs that gave the impression that prisons offered expensive programs that hardworking, law-abiding citizens couldn't afford. They often say, "If I don't have tennis courts and softball fields in my backyard, why should inmates have them?"[7] Legislation targeted the existence of equipment and programs that enable a prison's environment to be considered luxurious. They targeted programs such as boxing, karate, weightlifting and/or bodybuilding and any program that an average prisoner would not have experienced if not incarcerated. This was a significant blow to correctional recreation professionals all over the country. Once again, recreation would enter an era of change, and any program implemented from this point would be heavily scrutinized. Other programs eliminated included miniature golf, tennis, high-dollar hobby craft activities, in-cell television viewing, swimming pools, bowling, and so on. Correctional recreation professionals experienced a major setback but have been able to put together programs and services that meet the needs of the offender population, which enables them to acquire the skills needed before their release from prison. This setback actually worked in favor of the reentry movement. After all, recreation professionals want to introduce programs that can be utilized during an offender's period of incarceration, as well as after their release from prison. Some of the "No Frills" programs eliminated would not have been available to the average offender upon their release and could have played a role in recidivism.

On April 9, 2008, the Second Chance Act of 2007 was signed into law. This bill focused on developing strategies that would reduce recidivism and increase public safety by addressing a number of issues for individuals returning home from prison.[8] These issues included mental health, substance abuse, houselessness and homelessness, education and employment, and children and families and led to the recreation profession being included in the reentry process. A large portion of criminal activities take place away from offenders' job sites and during their leisure time. This would suggest that recreation professionals can and should play a vital role in assisting offenders to become law-abiding citizens. Many people who end up behind bars have been labeled as troublemakers, uneducated, and destined for street activities. After being told repeatedly that they will not amount to anything or that they do not have what it takes to be anything, people often become what they are labeled. They give up on their hopes and dreams and succumb to what they hear is their destiny. Once on the streets, they are embraced by gangs, get involved in criminal activities, and have access to large amounts of money. Some feel valued and successful for the first time in their lives and get hooked on that lifestyle. In most cases, this sense of security and abundance is short-lived. And eventually, they get caught and enter the criminal justice system.

As previously mentioned, the correctional recreation profession today is viewed in a much different manner. With local, state, and federal prison populations busting at the seams with no end in sight, along with the dismal economic outlook that has diminished agency budgets, lawmakers have been forced to explore ways to keep people from entering and returning to prison. President George W. Bush announced his Prisoner Reentry Initiative in his 2004 State of the Union address. This policy, from a conservative political leader, was designed to assist offenders and the communities to which they return.[9] When President Barack Obama took office, he made it clear that our strategy of locking people up and throwing away the key was not acceptable and that we must focus on inmates acquiring the needed skills to stay out of prison. The old terminology of "rehabilitation" has now been supplemented with a new concept of "reentry." This concept has forced agencies to focus on programs and services, such as literacy and drug treatment, that reduce recidivism rates and enhance public safety.

■ Correctional Recreation Programs

With the emphasis on providing programs that will assist offenders to make a seamless transition back into the community as law-abiding citizens, correctional recreation, along with other program areas, is attempting to increase activities that involve evidence-based practices and skill attainment. As with most recreation and program-oriented departments, they are dependent on fiscal resources in order to provide a broad range of activities. With today's economic outlook and diminished resources, recreation specialists continue to look for cost-effective alternatives that will offer opportunities for offenders to learn life skills that can and will assist them in becoming better people. Often, diminished government resources mirror what's going on in the community. People, like government agencies, have to explore ways to occupy their leisure time in a cost-effective manner. In other words, the programs in prison should be similar to what is available in an offender's community and should be affordable so offenders can continue that activity once released from prison.

A strong recreation department should offer a wide variety of activities for all offenders so that everyone has a chance to learn how to manage their leisure time in a productive manner. Recreation's peak hours are when the majority of inmates are not at work and when they have free time. This is when most organized activities should be scheduled. Free play or open participation should occur during other periods for those who have time off from work or who work during peak hours. Intramural programs can encompass physical and passive sports or activities. For example, sporting events such as basketball, soccer, flag football, softball, handball, racquetball, volleyball, and so on can be established with additional leagues for the 40-and-over group that cannot quite compete with the younger, more skilled group of offenders. Intramural leagues can also be established for passive types of activities including table tennis, horseshoes, shuffleboard, bocce ball, table games, and so on. These are examples of possible programs, but they are not all-inclusive. Interests, fads, and activities change, and it is imperative that recreation staff offer programs and services that can be continued upon release and that are geared toward that particular population.

Another aspect of a solid recreation department is hobby crafts, better known as arts and crafts. Some offenders are more geared toward the creative activities than the athletic arena. Depending on the department's budget, some facilities provide the materials for the inmates; however, many institutions require the inmates to purchase their own supplies. Some programs offer leather craft, ceramics, painting, sketching, crocheting, and so on. This program can become costly due to equipment maintenance and upkeep. Another program area that taps into the creative side is music. Institutions can provide musical equipment like, guitars, drums, and amplifiers. Offenders who had skills before they entered the system often organize a band and perform for the population. Others join a class and learn how to play an instrument for the first time in their lives. And lastly, a drama program can be offered for those who enjoy this type of activity.

Offender wellness should be a part of all recreational programs. Wellness programs often involve classroom activities in addition to the physical aspect. The idea is to teach offenders how to live a healthy lifestyle. Programs can be implemented that show offenders how to eat healthy, get proper nutrition and exercise, manage stress, and so on. Added benefits include a healthier offender population, which can help lower healthcare costs for the prison system, as well as a decrease in offender misconduct due to an offender's ability to better manage institution stressors. To summarize, you have a healthier and happier offender population that has learned how to properly handle adversity.

It is impotant to discuss passive activities for those offenders who look for programs that do not involve a high degree of physical activity but can help occupy their minds and time. These activities involve table games, such as cards, board games, and dominoes, as well as individual activities like yoga, walking, reading, or being a spectator at a program. Most people do not realize that attending a sporting activity or watching a special program is considered participating in a recreational event. Keep in mind that what a person does in his or her leisure time can be considered a recreational activity.

And finally, there are open play or free play activities. These are all programs that are unorganized and can be done whenever the recreation facilities are open. The open periods of recreation are just as critical for offenders as the scheduled programs and, in some ways, are more important. People, in general, will take the initiative to attend activities that are scheduled for them, but it is more challenging to come up with their own activities outside of a structured environment. Recreation staff should encourage offenders to think about life after release and what will be available to them. In other words, they need to have a recreation release plan similar to their release plan for housing and employment. There has to be some transition from a structured environment such as prison to a free environment such as society.

■ Recreation and Reentry

We briefly discussed the relationship between crime and leisure time, and the need for offenders to establish a recreation release plan. In this section, we focus on life skills that offenders can learn through recreational activities. The Bureau of Prisons responded to the need for better reentry preparation by implementing the Inmate Skills Development (ISD) initiative that focused on building the kinds of skills essential to successfully reintegrating an offender back into society. This initiative involves identifying inmate strengths and weaknesses, using a standardized assessment tool, linking programs used to identify specific deficit areas, and tracking the inmate's progress on his/her individualized plan throughout incarceration.[10] Examples of these skills include daily living, mental health, wellness, interpersonal, academic, cognitive, vocational and career, leisure time, and character, several of which are directly linked to recreational activities. Most obvious are the leisure time skills that assess whether an offender engages in worthwhile recreational activities that lead to positive and effective use of leisure time whether he or she and can effectively manage stress. Other ISD skills linked to recreation include character skills that involve personal responsibility, such as being on time and prepared; cognitive skills that involve personal behavior and overall conduct; interpersonal skills that involve relating effectively to staff and developing favorable peer relationships; and finally, wellness that involves physical well-being, such as developing a healthy lifestyle of good nutrition and a regular exercise regimen.

Recreation plays a vital role in assisting offenders to occupy their free time in an effective and productive manner. Poor social skills can have a detrimental effect on individuals attempting to function in society. In team activities, offenders must communicate effectively with one another and work together toward a common goal if success is to be achieved. If team members are ineffective communicators and cannot work well together, then often, it affects their play during the game. Teamwork also inspires dedication and commitment, and provides team members an opportunity to develop time management skills. Their individual actions affect the entire team. Offenders feel success, often for the first time, which positively affects their self-worth and makes them easier to manage within the institution. Finally, offenders learn about boundaries and how to follow rules and regulations or suffer the consequences of their actions. Reentry is about assisting offenders in acquiring skills that will help them become law-abiding citizens upon release. If they can learn to work with people, communicate successfully, set goals, increase their self-worth, build successful relationships, participate in positive activities, establish a recreation release plan, and abide by rules and regulations, then they increase their chances of successfully transitioning from prison to society. In the end, the offender is in the driver's seat and must make appropriate choices in order to avoid returning to prison. All the tools are available; however, they must make the right choices in order to stay out of prison.

■ Challenges Faced by Correctional Recreation Professionals

All recreation professionals face challenges in their jobs, such as bad weather, budget, and constraints. However, correctional recreation employees face additional challenges not experienced by their peers in the local city recreation department. The biggest challenge to overcome is perception. Recreation staff are often caught in a catch-22 situation with extremists who say "lock the door and throw away the key" versus those who believe offenders should get everything. In the mid-1990s, the political environment focused on removing programs from prisons that the average taxpayer could not afford, like in-cell television viewing, tennis, miniature golf, and weightlifting. Society wanted offenders to do hard time and be punished for their crimes instead of appearing to have access to what the average person in society did not have the opportunity to experience. Recreation professionals not only faced scrutiny from society, but they have also been subjected to ridicule from fellow correctional workers. Corrections officers/workers do not realize that recreation is much more than blowing up basketballs or throwing equipment out on the fields. A correctional recreation employee has all the responsibility of a correctional officer, plus the additional tasks of organizing programs and ensuring that ample equipment is available, that rules are established and followed, and that the facilities are ready for use. Recreation employees supervise more offenders at any given time than any other department in the institution, yet they receive criticism for their high paychecks and for appearing as though they play games all day and babysit offenders.

A second challenge of a correctional recreation professional is the rigid structure of a prison environment. Programs and services have to be scheduled around counts, feeding schedules, work schedules, controlled movements, emergencies, disturbances, and so on. You must possess the ability to switch gears at a moment's notice and be flexible with schedules and activities. More often than not, you will be forced to reschedule programs or alter them in some fashion because of time constraints or setbacks. Another challenge involves security of the institution. Recreation employees must utilize equipment and supplies that do not present a security risk to the institution. Equipment should not contain materials that could be removed easily and utilized as a weapon. Large items have to be bolted down or placed in concrete because they could be used to effectuate an escape, that is, soccer goals, bleachers, basketball poles, horseshoe pegs, and cardio equipment. And the staff must establish an accountability system so that items can be issued to offenders and returned before the end of the day. What is viewed as a useless item in society can easily be turned into a weapon to harm someone or be utilized in an escape attempt. For example, guitar strings can be used to cut through metal bars, or a yoga mat can be used to go over the fence and keep the escapee from being cut by the razor wire. Recreation professionals have the responsibility to provide a wide variety of programs and services that meet the needs of the population, but also to ensure that the environment is safe and secure. It is a challenge that not all individuals can handle effectively.

The final challenge faced by recreation professionals is balancing multiple missions and expectations, that is, security of the institution, their role in reentry, and their role in the management of the institution by keeping offenders busy and out of trouble. With diminishing resources and an emphasis placed on reentry, institutions are looking to provide programs and services that are evidence based. Recreation professionals continue to search for ways to prove that their programs assist offenders in acquiring the skills needed to reenter society. A thorough research project would have to be conducted over a lengthy period to gather credible evidence needed to show the true benefits of recreation. However, there are some data that can be utilized to show skill attainment, for example, institution infractions reports, offender work evaluations, and unit team progress reports. This can provide some form of documentation that will give credibility to your programs. Unfortunately, it takes time and effort to track the information, and you must have documented evidence of poor behavior before and after offenders' enrollment in the program. Most institutions do not have the resources to conduct a full-fledged research project; however, as mentioned, you can utilize existing data to show improvement at the local level. You may need to adopt this approach to justify your program offerings. Recreation professionals must be able to sell their programs to upper management.

■ Conclusion

Correctional recreation has always been a challenging profession, and it takes special people who possess specific skills to work in this environment. Over the course of a career, you will experience many political changes. As discussed in this chapter, and over the course of roughly 30 years, the role of recreation has changed drastically, going from a law-and-order management style in the 1970s, to a programming environment that gave offenders civil rights for the first time in history, to the 1980s with the "Get Tough" initiatives that sent the message "let's lock everybody up for long periods of time," to the "No Frills" era in the 1990s where recreation professionals had to re-create a new model for programs that focused on less luxurious activities for offenders, and finally, to the passing of the Second Chance Act with its goal of reducing prison populations and recidivism rates. Today, many people feel that the United States incarcerates entirely too many people at a cost that the country can no longer afford. It has forced our government leaders to consider alternatives to incarceration and to focus on reentry initiatives that would give offenders the necessary skills to stay out of prison. Although it is yet to be seen, there is evidence that the rate of growth in our prisons is starting to decrease. For example, during 2011, the number of prisoners under the jurisdiction of state and federal correctional authorities declined by 0.9%, from 1,613,803 to 1,598,780, and the number of releases from state and federal prisons (688,385) exceeded the number of admissions (668,800).[11]

Finally, recreation professionals have to create a balance between the political views of the country and the needs of the offenders. A strong program strives to teach offenders skills that can be carried with them upon release and programs that are creative, healthy, and tailored to the needs of the entire population, whether active or passive, young or old.

Chapter Resources

DISCUSSION QUESTIONS

1. Why is it important to provide recreational activities to incarcerated offenders?
2. List three challenges recreation professionals face while working in a prison environment.
3. What role does recreation play in assisting offenders to reenter society once their term of incarceration has been completed?
4. Name two types of legislation that affected correctional institutions, and describe the legislation's effect.
5. Name three types of programs that would be included in a strong, well-rounded recreation department.
6. Name five skills that can be learned and/or obtained by participating in recreational activities.

ADDITIONAL RESOURCES

Aguilar, T. E., & Asmussen, K. (1990). An exploration of recreational participation patterns in a correctional facility. *Journal of Offender Counseling Services Rehabilitation, 14*(1), 67–78.

Arjo, R. L., & Allen, L. R. (1980). Role of leisure time activities in corrections. *Corrections Today, 42*(1), 36–37, 40–41.

Bantam Book. (1971, September). *Attica: The official report of the New York state special commission on Attica.*

Blackburn, E. D. (2011). *Invest in re-entry programs, not in prison cells.* Retrieved from www.oregonlive.com

Chettiar, I., Stamm, A., & ACLU Center for Justice. (2012). *Tough on crime—no longer the American mantra?* Retrieved from www.aclu.org

Clear, T. R., Cole, G. F., & Reisig, M. D. (2008). *American corrections* (8th ed., Chapter 14, pp. 371–373).

Correctional recreation: An overview. Retrieved from www.strengthtech.com

Dallao, M. (1996). Changing the rules of recidivism through recreation. *Corrections Today, 58*(1), 80–101.

Dobie, M. (2004, July/August). *Sports in prison series* Newsday.com

Hormachea, C. Recreation and corrections—it's development, philosophy and future (from Therapeutic Recreation—State of the Art, 1977 by Fain and Fitzhusen). *National Criminal Justice Reference Service,* #NCJ 061110.

Little, S. (1995). Research on recreation in correctional settings. *Parks & Recreation, 30*(2), 20, 22, 24–27.

Lynch, J. P., & Sabol, W. J. (1997). *Did getting tough on crime pay?* The Urban Institute Research of Record. Retrieved from www.urban.org

Mauer, M. (1992, October). State sentencing reforms: Is the "get tough" era coming to a close? *Federal Sentencing Reporter, 15*(1), 50–52.

McDonnell, B. (2011). Improving public safety through prisoner re-entry programs. *The Ripon Forum, 45*(2).

National Correctional Recreation Association. Retrieved from www.ncracentral.com

"No Frills Prison Act", 106th Congress, 1999–2000, Congressional Bill H.R. 370 (106th) found Retrieved from www.govtrack.us/congress/bills/106/hr370

Office of Justice Programs. (n.d.). Faith-Based & Community Initiatives. *Prisoner Reentry*. Retrieved from www.ojp.usdoj.gov

Robertson, B. J. (1997, March/April). Correctional recreation: A time for action. *Parks & Recreation, 55*(1), 20–23, 25.

Robertson, B., & Lesnik, R. (2012). *Introduction to recreation and leisure* (p. 225, Chapter 11). Correctional Recreation.

Telander, R. (1988). Sports behind the walls. *Sports Illustrated, 69,* 82–88.

NOTES

1. *Attica: The official report of the New York state special commission on Attica*—from the Commission's Preface to their official report; published September 1972.
2. *Attica: The official report of the New York state special commission on Attica,* Summary, p. 2; published September 1972.
3. *Attica: The official report of the New York state special commission on Attica,* Summary, p. 4; published September 1972.
4. *Attica: The official report of the New York state special commission on Attica,* Preface, pp. xvi–xviiii.
5. National Correctional Recreation Association (NCRA) pamphlet published in March 1995.
6. Heather Couture, Harrisons, P. M., & Sabol, W. J. (2007, December 5). Office of justice programs. *Bureau of Justice Statistics, NCJ* 219416.
7. Dallao, M. (1996, February). National Correctional Recreation Association (NCRA). *Corrections Today* (the American Correctional Association's monthly publication), *57*(1).
8. *The Second Chance Act.* Justice Center, The Council of State Governments.
9. Prisoner Rentry Initiative. (2007, December). White House website. Retrieved from http://georgewbush-whitehouse.archives.gov/government/fbci/pri.html.
10. Inmate skills development. Department of Justice. Federal Bureau of Prisons. Retrieved from www.bop.gov.
11. Ann Carson, E., & Sabol, W. J. (2012, December 12). Office of justice programs, bureau of justice statistics. *NCJ* 239808.

Religious Programming

Susan Van Baalen

CHAPTER OBJECTIVES

- Explore the role of prison chaplains and understand the challenges of providing religious programs in the correctional environment.

- Illustrate the major programs coordinated by prison chaplains and discuss the available resources for religious programming.

- Describe the general legal framework within which prison religious programs operate.

Religious services departments and programs play an important role in the correctional environment. Programs typically provide three essential services: religious accommodation, spiritual growth and development, and pastoral care.

■ Historical Background

Religion has played an important role in the life of American prisoners since the inception of penitentiaries in this country.[1] Many of the earliest prison facilities in the United States were influenced by the Quaker belief that time away from society—time to meditate on one's sinfulness and transgressions of the law—would change the hearts of offenders.[2] The correctional programs of these institutions sought both to reform the lives of the penitents and to protect society from offenders' aberrant behavior. Study of the Bible and spiritual counseling from local clergy were instituted to help prisoners achieve the goals of penitence and changed behavior. One of the problems with this early Quaker model was that these end goals were not necessarily shared by the offender. In addition, the practice of forced solitude caused many inmates to suffer emotional distress and, in some cases, led to mental illness.

The role of religion in jails and prisons has changed as correctional institutions have continued to realign their mission and goals to societal pressures. Correctional institutions often support religious programming not only as a way to transform individuals but also as a tool to manage inmates more safely and effectively by decreasing crime and antisocial behavior.

■ Religious Accommodation and Freedom Legislation

The First Amendment to the Constitution identifies freedom of religion as a fundamental right of every American citizen. This amendment guarantees the right to embrace the beliefs of one's chosen religion and to unfettered practice of that religion, even behind bars. Religious accommodation is a practice that ensures the prisoner's constitutional right to freedom of religion and is the justification for maintaining a religious services program in a correctional institution, regardless of jurisdiction.

Nevertheless, prison administrators can and do regulate religious practices in prisons to protect against threats to the security and good order of the institution or public safety. What administrators are permitted to regulate has evolved and continues to be affected by the interpretation of new and existing legislation related to religious freedom. During the 1970s and 1980s, the U.S. Supreme Court found some government-imposed limits to religious practice to be appropriate as long as these limits furthered a reasonable penological interest.[3]

The Religious Freedom Restoration Act of 1993 (RFRA) and the Religious Land Use and Institutionalized Persons Act of 2000 (RLUIPA) complement the First Amendment, clarifying the application of the law to persons in the custody of the federal government or state or local institutions. The full intent of these laws is to ensure that the religious rights of all persons confined to long-term care facilities are not abridged or denied.

With the passage of the RFRA, governments were prevented from interfering with individuals' religious observances unless the interference was the least restrictive means of furthering a compelling government interest. Nearly all departments of corrections around the country opposed this legislation, fearing it would require them to succumb to all sorts of religious requests by inmates, stretching staff and budgetary resources, and threatening institution security. Of particular concern were requests from extremist religious movements whose beliefs and practices are greatly offensive to other inmates.

In 1997, the Supreme Court ruled in *Boerne v. Texas* that the RFRA violated the Constitution.[4] As a result, state departments of corrections were free to return to applying the previous standard in determining whether to permit various inmate religious practices. This was pursuant to the Supreme Court's decisions in

O'Lone v. Shabazz and *Turner v. Safley*, which argued that prison regulations that interfered with inmates' religious practices were valid so long as they were reasonably related to legitimate penological objectives.[3]

In response to the Supreme Court's ruling that the RFRA was unconstitutional, many states proposed and enacted laws intended to protect their citizens from encroachments by state and local governments on religious observances. The new state laws required these governments to meet the RFRA standard in justifying laws and actions that interfere with individual religious practices.

RLUIPA prohibits the government from restricting prisoners' religious worship opportunities unless the government can demonstrate that the restriction furthers a compelling government interest and is the least restrictive means of furthering that interest. This act was challenged in *Cutter v. Wilkinson*,[5] a case involving five prisoners from Ohio including a Wiccan, a Satanist, and a member of a racist Christian sect. In this case, the U.S. Supreme Court unanimously ruled that RLUIPA was a permissible accommodation of religion justified by the fact that the government had severely burdened the prisoners' religious rights through the act of incarceration.

These laws (and in at least one case—Alabama—a proposed constitutional amendment) are widely supported by various religious organizations that believe that additional protections are necessary to ensure that religious observance is protected (e.g., allowing Muslim students to wear head scarves to school despite a "no hats" policy and permitting Seventh-Day Adventists and Jews to work shifts that do not conflict with their Sabbath). Religious organizations also argue that the protection of religious freedom provided by RLUIPA or similar state legislation is necessary to prevent corrections officials from denying legitimate, important religious requests, particularly because of the reputed connections between religious beliefs or observance and inmates' successful reintegration into society.

In contrast, many corrections officials oppose these legislative initiatives for the same reasons they opposed the RFRA—they are concerned that inmates will file lawsuits requesting various religious accommodations and prevail. They believe that certain types of accommodations will threaten institution security and place substantial demands on staff and budgetary resources. Although supporters of the proposed legislation argue that in many states the number of lawsuits filed by inmates did not increase following passage of RLUIPA, in some states the number of inmate grievances did increase dramatically. Moreover, many departments of corrections counter that many potential suits were not filed because institutions felt compelled to grant requests that would have been denied before the passage of RFRA and RLUIPA, based on advice from counsel.

The enactment of the RFRA and RLUIPA statutes raised the threshold required for the denial of religious practices in institutions from a threshold of the furtherance of a *reasonable penological* interest to that of a *compelling* government interest—a threshold more favorable toward religious freedom and less favorable toward correctional administrators. Landmark cases upholding the RFRA and RLUIPA standards are yet to be decided, as these laws are only beginning to be challenged in state and federal courts. Nevertheless, it is important for all who work in a correctional environment to know and understand the effect of these laws on religious freedom in prisons. Also, correctional staff should be aware that earlier attempts by state and federal prison administrators and professional correctional organizations to exempt prisons from these laws resulted in an emphatic inclusionary clause for prisons (as opposed to the original draft's silence with respect to application in jails and prisons). A 2005 Supreme Court decision, *Cutter v. Wilkinson*, tested RLUIPA in the courts. In this case, inmates of small and generally unfamiliar religious groups prevailed in their Supreme Court appeal for opportunities to meet for religious worship and programs.[5]

The United States Commission on Civil Rights reports 250 RLUIPA cases litigated in federal courts between 2000 and 2006. Although this appears to be a significant volume of litigation, proper perspective reduces the significance because the 250 suits represent the claims of more than two million incarcerated men and women in hundreds of U.S. prisons and jails. Even more important to the study of correctional management is the fact that the inmate plaintiffs prevailed in only 6% of the cases.[6]

■ Professional Standards

Federal statutes and laws of this country require quality religious programs in prisons and jails. Professional standards such as those established by the American Correctional Association (ACA) require prison administrators to strike the proper balance between providing sufficient and appropriate religious programs and restricting religious practices because of concerns for safety of staff and inmates or the security of the institution. Religious programs are developed within the framework of the pertinent laws and the religious needs of the inmates. As a rule, staff accommodates individual religious practices unless the accommodation will interfere with the security, safety, and orderly operation of the institution.

Inmates may be encouraged to participate in religious programs as a means of preparing for reintegration into the community following release from prison. On the contrary, administrators and other staff must respect the beliefs of inmates who decline to participate in religious programs. All religious programs must be voluntary; inmates should not be required or coerced into participating in religious activities of any kind, nor may those participating in religious programs be granted any preference with respect to housing, job placement, or consideration for parole or early release. To attach rewards or benefits to the practice of religion interferes with the freedom one has not to exercise or hold religious beliefs. Religion must not be used as a tool for manipulation.

Chaplains employed by the government are responsible for working with inmates of all faith groups, administering services for some and accommodating services for all, regardless of religious preference. This requires the management of programs in a fair and consistent manner and the supervision of all contract and volunteer religious service personnel. There may be an inclination on the part of the chaplain to provide more or better services for some groups (e.g., Christians and Jews) while making only a minimal accommodation for new religious movements that may be smaller or less familiar (e.g., Islam, Hinduism, Rastafarianism, or Native American Spirituality).

Because the chaplains or religious coordinators are expected to accommodate inmates' religious beliefs and practices covering a wide spectrum of faith traditions, they necessarily rely on the expertise of community religious leaders to complement the care and services they can provide. Religious service providers (e.g., chaplains, contractors, and volunteers) administer the sacred rites, ordinances, or sacraments of the faith; provide religious education and counseling; assist with the development and provision of religious diets; respond to specific requests for religious objects, apparel, and literature; and coordinate the observance of religious holidays for each faith group.

■ Role of Chaplains

A chaplain may serve as spiritual guide, preacher, teacher, dietitian, counselor, and advocate, often all at the same time. Even volunteer and part-time chaplains must be committed to public safety and security of staff, inmates, and visitors.

The religious effect in the institution depends not on merely what the chaplain does but on the unique pastoral manner in which a chaplain helps inmates and staff deal with the experience of incarceration. In some religious circles and in institutionalized settings like prisons, this careful and tender care of souls is often called pastoral care—the care a religious or spiritual guide provides to believers or those seeking a spiritual transformation. It seems important to note that the term "pastoral care" is a Christian term that has been somewhat generalized within institutions in the United States to describe the qualities of caregiving over a broader spectrum of religions.

Perhaps the gravest problem among religious service providers is that, in their passion for souls, they lose sight of their role as correctional workers. The ACA standards for adult and juvenile detention centers and prisons require that the religious services department be directed by a professional chaplain or religious coordinator.[7] In an ideal world, there would be a chaplaincy corps of full-time trained professional chaplains—but there is hardly any facet of jails and prisons that falls into the category of the "ideal world." In many cases, philosophical differences and budget constraints prevent the use of a professional chaplaincy corps; instead, jurisdictions rely on part-time chaplains or volunteers to ensure that religious accommodation meets the threshold of the law.

The complexity of the multi-faith correctional environment requires a high level of professionalism to ensure that inmates of all faiths have the opportunity for maximum benefit from religious programs. Successful chaplains are generally well-educated and integrated professionals who are trained and experienced in both ministry and correctional management. The integration of ministry and management is essential because of the added dimension and challenges of ministry with an incarcerated congregation.

For many years, a pastor with strong preaching and teaching skills was used to "do church" in the correctional setting; therapeutic and administrative skills were secondary. But penal institutions have changed, making it essential for the religious services provider to have strong administrative and counseling skills as well. This is particularly true where chaplains are part of the prison treatment staff along with social workers, substance abuse counselors, case workers, psychologists, teachers, and medical personnel. Accordingly, clinical training and certification are beneficial qualifications for prison chaplains.

◼ Religious Pluralism

Ideally, the chaplaincy corps would reflect accurately the beliefs of the inmate population. However, time in prison often pushes inmates to new horizons, even with respect to religion. Inmates who came to prison having been raised in one faith, or no faith, may find the loneliness and alienation of the prison setting an opportune time to seek some spiritual grounding. Religious issues or questions raised by inmates whose religious beliefs are outside the chaplain's expertise, training, or ecclesiastical endorsement are referred to qualified spiritual leaders in the community.

Using part-time contract chaplains and volunteers is a reasonable alternative in small jails and prisons where chaplains from various faith traditions are essential to accommodate a wide spectrum of religious beliefs and practices of the inmate population. Contract chaplains are used as spiritual leaders for small groups of inmates whose beliefs are different from those of the full-time professional chaplain. For example, in many institutions, a Catholic priest is contracted to provide the sacraments, religious education, and guidance to Catholic inmates, and an Islamic cleric is contracted to serve as a teacher and spiritual leader for Muslim inmates. These contract chaplains do not function as religious coordinators or chaplains whose commitment is to accommodate all inmates' religious needs. As religious leaders within specific faith traditions, the contractors and volunteers are experts on specific religious subject matter. Accordingly, they need only be recognized by the denominations or faith groups they represent. The role and function of contract chaplains needs to be described in the prison policy, which should also specify the education, training, and other necessary qualifications required of contractors.

◼ Congregate Services

Congregate services—the meeting of several people to worship, study, or pray—should be provided at all correctional institutions unless specific security or safety issues present a legitimate management concern. In these cases, arrangements must be made to provide inmates with the least restrictive alternative means of practicing their religions. The services must not only meet a reasonable professional standard but also demonstrate good correctional management. True spirituality is often discovered and developed through religious study and practice and may help prepare inmates for returning to the community. Inmates who develop or deepen their relationship with a deity and become involved in religious programs have an improved attitude and can draw upon a support group (e.g., a religious congregation) when they leave prison. After inmates are released, congregations and religious organizations frequently assist inmates and their families with jobs, clothes, housing, training, and other practical needs.

Most correctional institutions provide various worship services because of the broad spectrum of religious beliefs the inmates hold. Whichever the case, the diversity can be addressed somewhat if congregate services are designed to appeal to the widest range of persons who share the basic tenets and beliefs of a particular religion. Congregate services are always led by a person with proper credentials. For example, a priest recognized by the Roman Catholic church should conduct mass for Roman Catholic inmates. When there are only a few inmates from a particular religious persuasion, a spiritual advisor can provide assistance to the individual practitioners. If the group is large, then the services of a local minister can be used on a weekly basis. At a minimum, all inmates should have access to spiritual leaders, regular opportunities for worship on weekly and special holy days, access to religious study materials, and, within reason, a religious diet accommodation commensurate with the tenets of their faith.

■ Religious Needs

Religious Programming

The religious coordinator or chaplain develops a religious program that includes more than weekly worship services. Study groups and religious education classes serve a dual purpose in the correctional environment. From a public safety perspective, these programs provide opportunities for personal growth and change that deter the individual from criminal behavior. From a prison management perspective, these programs fill inmates' time that might otherwise be idle (which often leads to negative consequences). Therefore, religious programs, generally offered during inmates' time free from scheduled activities, serve as a management tool protecting against the dangers that can ensue from extended periods of idleness. In 2005, 60,000 inmates (more than 35% of the total prison population) participated in weekly religious programs in Federal Bureau of Prison's chapels.[8] This far exceeds the estimated 20% of American believers who attend church services weekly in the United States.[9]

Development of individual talents should be one objective of religious programs. For example, music education and choir provide an outlet for inmates to express themselves creatively. Special events that bring in choir groups, entertainers, and evangelists usually attract large groups and provide an emotional and spiritual outlet for inmates.

Religious Diets and Holy Days

Inmates of many faiths may request special diets mandated by their religions. It has been the general practice in jails and prisons to ask inmates to document that the requested diet is a basic requirement or tenet of their faith group; they may also be asked to prove their membership in the group. The institution should not be expected to accommodate dietary requests based solely on personal preferences so long as nutritionally adequate meals are provided that do not violate the inmates' religious dietary requirements. However, legitimate requests based on sound religious principles must be accommodated. For this reason, most correctional institutions offer a vegetarian or, at least, a pork-free menu. The broadest interpretation of RFRA and RLUIPA in the courts suggests that requesting inmates to prove their religious affiliation or their religion's requirements for certain dietary accommodations may be too restrictive.

Some religious observances (e.g., Passover) require consumption of particular foods, and some observances require consumption of food at particular times (e.g., Ramadan, during which Muslim inmates must fast during daylight hours). Special accommodations should be made for these occasions. In some instances, particular religious observances include congregate ceremonial meals and days free from work. These requests can be generally accommodated as long as the prison staff is given sufficient notice to make arrangements. The chaplain or spiritual leader is often called upon to explain to staff the significance of the religious observance and the specific accommodations that are required (e.g., completion of all work before sundown of a Jewish holiday).

Religious Literature, Apparel, and Objects

Inmates should have access to religious literature, including the sacred writings or scriptures of their religion. Security, safety, and sanitation concerns may limit the amount of literature inmates may possess in their living areas, but the inmate library or chapel should contain religious literature and make it available to inmates.

Religious clothing and headgear may be permitted as long as it is consistent with the security and good order of the prison. In some correctional facilities, inmates are permitted to wear the religious garb or accessories only while in the chapel and participating in religious worship. Religious items such as a medallion pose only minimal security concerns as long as policy controls are in place to ensure that they are inexpensive and small.

Religious Counseling

Inmates may be provided religious or spiritual counseling from the institution chaplain, community volunteer, or religious leader from the community. Through institution visits, phone calls, and correspondence, religious representatives from the community often minister to inmates who were a part of their church or other religious organization before incarceration.

Special Rites

Special rites are formal religious ceremonies of initiation such as baptism, confession, or individual communion. Special rites should be performed by the appropriate religious leader with proper credentials. The institution should approve special objects or supplies necessary to conduct such rites.

■ Religious Volunteers

A corps of specially selected, trained, and supervised volunteers can greatly enhance the effectiveness of a chaplain. On the contrary, it is important to remember that volunteers generally have their own agendas, and volunteers may not have the clinical skills to counsel inmates. Although volunteers should not be the source of all institution religious programs, they often represent a vital and necessary part of the overall ministry.

The role of the volunteer should be made clear from the beginning. Faith groups that are represented in the inmate population will often provide pastors who are interested in working with inmates from their faith. This will be especially true of smaller groups and nontraditional faiths. For example, Muslim volunteers will work with Muslim inmates, Jehovah's Witness volunteers will work with Jehovah's Witness inmates, and so forth. Volunteers need to understand that they are prohibited from recruiting converts to their faith. They can, however, work with those who seek them out. Volunteers must understand their roles, and the chaplain must ensure that the volunteers operate within appropriate boundaries. Community religious resources are the best sources of volunteers. The chaplain should establish and maintain a good relationship with religious leaders in the community, such as through a community advisory board. Additionally, most states have prison ministry groups and representatives from national groups such as Yokefellows, Prison Fellowship, and Kairos.

ACA standards and sound correctional practice mandate training and orientation of volunteers, including an institution tour. The volunteer should be given materials including a handbook about the institution, its policy on religious practice and confidentiality, information about inmate characteristics and needs, a list of what makes volunteers successful, and a list of "dos and don'ts."

■ Unique Requests for Recognition or Accommodation

Processing religious requests is an important aspect of the chaplain's job. The development of a religious-request review board and a community advisory board can be very helpful. The institution board might include the chaplain, a social worker, the food service director, a legal advisor, a security officer, and an assistant warden. The board should consider several factors in handling requests:

- Whether the requested accommodation is a basic tenet and required of all the religion's members
- Whether the inmate meets the religion's requirements for this practice
- Whether the inmate shows good faith in the discussion of a solution and accommodation

Additionally, it may be helpful to learn what other correctional institutions and the community are doing to accommodate certain practices.

Occasionally, prison administrators are requested to make special provisions for inmates who claim to belong to religions or faiths previously unknown or to make unusual provisions for inmates who adhere to well-known religions (e.g., special dietary requirements for Protestant inmates). Generally it is best to rely on the classic definition of religion: an activity that concerns a person's relationship to a deity, to other people, and to himself or herself. That said, not all requests made in the name of religion will be accommodated. Behavior that threatens or harms others cannot be permitted. Of particular concern in a correctional institution is the creation of a religious organization that includes a hierarchy that would give some inmates authority over others (e.g., one inmate appointing himself the leader, spiritual or otherwise, of a new religion). Also of concern are religions that espouse intolerance or even hatred of persons of particular races or ethnicities, and religions that proclaim the superiority of a particular group. To maintain the security and good order of the correctional institution, such organizations cannot be permitted to practice.

■ Conclusion

The religious programs in correctional institutions should be tailored to the mission and resources of the institutions. Small prisons and those with limited staff and resources may be able to provide only the basic elements, but larger facilities may have the ability to provide well-rounded programs that can affect large numbers of prisoners. Regardless of the extent of religious programming, such programs should be administered in a fair and consistent manner and provide inmates with an adequate opportunity to prepare themselves for return to the community. The chaplain should look to the community for contract chaplains, volunteers, consultation, and support of the inmates' individual faith development.

The responsibilities of institution chaplains have grown over the years, and correctional clergy today are significant members of the management and program team of prisons and jails. The work is important, the opportunities are great, and the challenges are immense.

Chapter Resources

DISCUSSION QUESTIONS

1. What is the role of a prison chaplain?
2. How does a prison chaplain differ from religious providers in the community at large?
3. What are some of the challenges that prison chaplains face?
4. What types of religious programs are often provided to inmates?
5. What have the courts demanded of corrections with respect to the provision of religious programs for inmates?

ADDITIONAL RESOURCES

Cripe, C. A., Pearlman, M. G., & Kosiak, D. (2012). *Legal aspects of corrections management* (3rd ed.). Burlington, MA: Jones & Bartlett Learning.

Dubler, J. (2013). *Down in the chapel: Religious life in an American prison.* New York, NY: Farrar, Straus and Giroux.

Foucault, M. (1995). *Discipline and punish: The birth of the prison* (2nd ed.). New York, NJ: Vintage.

Sullivan, W. F. (2011). *Prison Religion: Faith-based reform and the Constitution* (1st ed.). Princeton, NJ: Princeton University Press.

United States Commission on Civil Rights. (2008). *Enforcing religious freedom in prison.* Washington, DC: Author.

United States Department of Justice, Federal Bureau of Prisons. (2002). *Technical reference manual: Inmate religious beliefs and practices.* Washington, DC: Author. Retrieved from http://static.nicic.gov/Library/017613.pdf

NOTES

1. McKelvey, B. (1977). *American prisons: A history of good intentions.* Glen Ridge, NJ: Patterson Smith.
2. McKelvey, B. (1977). *American prisons: A history of good intentions.* Glen Ridge, NJ: Patterson Smith.
3. *O'Lone v. Shabazz*, 482 U.S. 342 (1987); *Turner v. Safley*, 482 U.S. 78 (1987).
4. *City of Boerne v. Flores*, 521 U.S. 507 (1997).
5. *Cutter v. Wilkinson*, 544 U.S. 709 (2005).
6. United States Commission on Civil Rights. (2008, September). *Enforcing religious freedom in prison.* Retrieved February 19, 2013, from http://www.law.umaryland.edu/marshall/usccr/documents/cr12r274.pdf
7. American Correctional Association. (2000). *Standards for adult correctional institutions* (4th ed., pp. 155–157). College Park, MD: Author.
8. Federal Bureau of Prisons. (2006). *Religious services report, 2005, internal agency document.* Washington, DC: Author.
9. Walsh, A. (1998, Fall). Church, lies, and polling data. *Religion in the News, 1*(2). Retrieved August 22, 2007, from http://www.trincoll.edu/depts/csrpl/RIN% 20Vol.1No.2/Church_lies_polling.htm

Inmate Medical and Mental Health

YOU ARE THE ADMINISTRATOR
■ The Warden's Dilemma with Special-Needs Offenders

The prison's budget was causing major headaches for Warden Kevin Barnello. Although the state had been cutting operational budgets for the past 5 years for all departments, the allocation for the five state prisons had been significantly affected this year. Budget cutbacks were clearly going to hinder overall operations, but now, his new problem was how to fund programs for this growing population of inmates with special needs.

The state penitentiary at Middletown has increased the numbers and types of special-needs offenders every year, and the need to create functional programming for each group is becoming intense. The growing numbers of sex offenders, older and geriatric inmates, prisoners with disabilities, offenders with chronic diseases, the mentally ill, and a huge population of illegal immigrants all require specialized care, sometimes very expensive specialized care. The immediate problem was the looming federal requirement requiring facilities to make all areas accessible for handicapped individuals.

As if things were not bad enough, the recent hiring freeze imposed on all state agencies by the governor created more pressure on the warden. The freeze and funding cutbacks were hitting at the same time that the institution really needed to fund programs that would assist these various groups of special offenders. Barnello knew the right thing to do was to find the money by cutting his budget elsewhere, but after years of "doing more with less" funding, he had no fat left in his budget.

Offenders with unique needs were also becoming a political issue. All U.S. correctional systems have had to assume increased responsibility for many medical, mental health, and social service needs for these specialized populations. State legislators were openly criticizing the governor's inability to provide appropriate access and care for convicted offenders with physical disabilities, and the warden knew it would not be long before other groups became the focus—geriatric inmates, for instance, always generated a soft spot in the public eye.

Barnello's fiscal crisis and pressing responsibilities were reaching the critical stage.

- Why do special-needs offenders create such pressures on correctional managers? Why have these pressures grown in the past 10 years?
- What strategy should be followed: Fund the immediate critical need of disabled prisoner access, or simply focus on institutional basics and not fund special-needs offender support programs? How would you prioritize the needs of these various special-needs groups?
- Should the growing political attention on offenders with unique needs force the warden to cut back on custody and case management positions that supervise the general prison population?
- How should the warden respond to critical media reports of less than stellar programs for special offenders?

Health Care

Robert R. Thompson

CHAPTER OBJECTIVES

- Appreciate the legal basis for standards of medical care in prisons.
- Identify the similarities and differences between community and correctional medicine and be familiar with unique end-of-life issues present in correctional environments.
- Explain the process of intake screening and the importance and exceptions of confidentiality.

Medical practice in the correctional environment shares many similarities with the community at large, but inmates present some unique challenges to healthcare professionals. Thousands of healthcare professionals work inside prisons and jails and do so with care and diligence. It is their responsibility to provide prisoners with appropriate and competent care to the best of their ability, in a fair and ethical manner.

■ The Right to Health Care

Numerous U.S. Supreme Court decisions have established that an inmate's right to health care is essentially the same as the right of a nonincarcerated person. Specifically, in *Estelle v. Gamble*, the Court held that any attempt to withhold or unduly delay medical care constituted cruel and unusual punishment. In the words of the Court, "the public [is] required to care for the prisoner, who cannot by reason of the deprivation of his liberty, care for himself. …We therefore conclude that deliberate indifference to serious medical needs of prisoners constitutes the 'unnecessary and wanton infliction of pain,' proscribed by the Eighth Amendment."[1] Other Supreme Court and lower court decisions have likewise upheld the rights of both prisoners and pretrial detainees to dental care, chronic disease management, prenatal care, mental health counseling, communicable disease screening, acquired immune deficiency syndrome (AIDS) treatment, and medical care during self-imposed starvation (i.e., food strikes).[2] It is noteworthy that an inmate's right to health care in each of the above areas does not address the issue of malpractice or the lack of medical competence; the latter is adjudicated in the courts as a civil matter, and the standard utilized by the courts is that of deliberate indifference.

© auremar/ShutterStock, Inc.

The American Correctional Association, the United States Public Health Service, and the American Medical Association collaborated to form the National Commission on Correctional Health Care (NCCHC), now the primary body that sets standards and accredits correctional facilities. The NCCHC offers technical assistance, educational programs for correctional staff, and clinical guidelines for the health practitioner. The results of these efforts have helped ensure that inmates receive medical, dental, mental health, and addiction treatment in a timely and safe manner by qualified health professionals in essentially the same manner as nonincarcerated persons.

It is important to note that correctional law as it relates to health care is an evolving subject, and the standards of care in the community and in the correctional environment change constantly. The healthcare provider in the prison setting needs to be ever vigilant to this changing landscape to ensure that he or she is meeting the current standards of care while caring for patients.

■ Initial Screening

Good medical care begins with the inmate's arrival at the correctional facility. It is during this all-important interview that the following questions should be addressed:

1. What is the inmate's overall health status?
2. Does he or she have communicable disease risk factors (e.g., tuberculosis [TB] and AIDS) or diseases that might put other inmates or staff members at risk (e.g., hepatitis and sexually transmitted diseases)?
3. Are there obvious signs of mental illness or a history of any severe psychiatric disorders?
4. Are medications (if any) in order, and does the inmate understand how to take them?
5. Has a physical examination been completed to assess any preexisting injuries or deformities?

6. Are there physical or behavioral signs of recent or past alcohol or drug abuse that might suggest impending chemical withdrawal? (Note: Some inmates "self-surrender" to an institution and to have one last "celebration" engage in prolonged drinking. Such inmates are apt to have severe withdrawal and need to be monitored carefully or placed in a detox facility if one is present within the institution.)

7. Are there any other reasons that this inmate might need to be housed separately?

During this initial encounter, the examiner would do well to remember that he or she is a correctional worker as well as a healthcare provider. This may require that the examiner is familiar with the inmate's correctional history and is aware of any behavioral issues that would put prison staff at risk. A review of the inmate's file and awareness of his or her custody status is part of the prison healthcare worker's job description. If restraints are required, they may need to remain in place during the interview, and correctional officers may need to be present. As in all healthcare encounters with prisoners, staff, and other inmates, safety is of foremost importance.

During the arrival interview, the inmate may appear disheveled and unkempt due to a long travel interval from another facility. His or her mental status and level of cooperation may reflect stress due to a long court case, incarceration at another facility, frustration with the justice and legal system, and disappointment over the sentence. He or she may feel insecure in the new facility and be concerned for his or her safety around other inmates. All these things set the tone for the intake encounter and must be taken into account in an evaluation.

Plans for follow-up care should be made if chronic conditions are present. For example, if heart or lung disease is present, arrangements should be made for the inmate to be seen in one of the chronic care clinics as soon as possible after arrival. This is also a good time to ensure that all outside records, X-rays, and tests are available for review. If a contagious disease such as TB is suspected, the inmate must be placed in a negative airflow room (a sealed room in which fresh air is recirculated and air moves out when the door is opened) and appropriate procedures utilized. This may involve placement in an outside medical facility that is equipped for dealing with infectious disease.

In many ways, the initial screening interview sets the stage for the inmate's cooperation with medical personnel and future testing and compliance with medication during the period of incarceration. Trust is the key word. In the end, professional demeanor on the part of the interviewer will overcome hostility and help ensure compliance.

■ Clinics and Sick Call

It is important that the inmate understand the procedure for sick call. This is best accomplished in the inmate orientation session, during which written material is handed out and the inmate has an opportunity to ask questions. Because sick call procedure varies from one institution to another, one cannot assume the inmate is familiar with the processes of a particular facility.

To discourage abuse of sick call, many institutions have instituted nominal inmate co-pay. This has been viewed as successful by many jurisdictions but must be well thought out at each institution so that it is not seen as punitive. Although fee-for-service payments have been demonstrated to reduce inmate abuse of sick call procedures, these fees have also been perceived as preventing genuinely sick inmates from seeking care.

There should be as much continuity and teamwork as possible among the sick call staff so that the same staff regularly care for the same inmates. In that way, potential drug seekers and abusers can be identified more easily. To facilitate this continuity, some outpatient staff may meet as a group for a brief period to review the sick call list for the day and share any information about the inmates that might be helpful. This is also a good opportunity for consultation with each other about particularly vexing problems concerning an inmate.

As in all aspects of correctional medicine, teamwork among the medical disciplines is central to dealing with difficult inmates. Malingering, work avoidance behavior, pseudo-seizures, and drug seeking can best be dealt with by nursing, pharmacy, physical therapy, and mental health staff, and physicians all working together.

The use of the outpatient clinic or sick call is a good opportunity to further patient education. Low back pain, asthma management, and diabetic care are just a few examples of conditions that can be improved through patient education films, question-and-answer sessions, and individual counseling.

■ Confidentiality

All information in the medical record is to be treated with the same confidentiality that exists in community practice. Convicted offenders and pretrial detainees have a right to medical privacy, which means that medical personnel may not share details about an inmate's medical records with other correctional staff. Nonmedical personnel may gain access to protected medical information in the process of doing their jobs, for example, by having conversations with inmates, checking inmates' property, or reviewing inmates' mail. There are, however, several exceptions to this general privacy rule, as outlined in the Health Insurance Portability and Accountability Act (HIPAA). Medical personnel may, on a limited basis, disclose protected health information about an individual to correctional personnel as necessary for

- The provision of health care to such individuals
- The health and safety of an individual or inmate
- The health and safety of correctional officers or others at the institution
- The health and safety of staff members responsible for transporting inmates

Any disclosure of medical information must be based on verified need for personnel to have access to the data; this justification must include the need to ensure the safety, security, and good order of the correctional institution.[3] It is key that all personnel be trained and that every staff member know that it can be a violation of federal law to disclose protected healthcare information if the release is not specifically justified.

■ Medical Emergencies

Inevitably there will be emergencies within the walls or fences of every prison and jail. With the aging inmate population, heart disease, strokes, and peripheral vascular emergencies are increasingly common. In addition to medical emergencies, nonmedical emergencies occur as a result of inmate fights. Staff will also be called to deal with suicide attempts and completions.

Unless the correctional facility has a very well-equipped hospital, and most do not, the main function of staff in such emergencies is to

- Rapidly respond to the scene
- Stabilize the patient
- Transport the patient to a facility equipped to deal with the emergency

Rapid response almost always dictates some radio communication through central control to alert medical staff to the nature of the emergency and the location. Staff should respond as a group and must use good judgment in approaching a "down" inmate, particularly one who is surrounded by other inmates. Such inmates must be dispersed after noting which ones are present. The latter is particularly important if the emergency is due to an assault.

Institutional medical staff who are expected to respond to emergencies should be certified in advanced cardiac life support (ACLS) and in advanced trauma life support (ATLS). All staff should have yearly refreshers and stay current in cardiopulmonary resuscitation (CPR). The use of automated external defibrillators (AEDs) has become widespread; if an institution is so equipped, these should be brought to the scene and appropriate staff trained in their use.

Transporting an injured or unconscious inmate should be done on a stretcher or backboard. If the transfer is to be made to an outside hospital, notification should be made to the facility in advance of the transport.

The receiving medical facility should be notified that an inmate is en route. Because many escape attempts have occurred on medical trips to outside institutions, security remains a high priority. The inmate's history and security/custody classification will dictate the use of restraints and how many correctional personnel are needed for the trip.

As soon as possible after the medical emergency, an incident report should be written by correctional staff and the inmate's medical record should be updated by medical staff to include times and all medications and procedures administered. To keep track of these issues, a recorder is often appointed early in the emergency to note times, medications, and dosages, as well as any inmate patient response to these ministrations. This ensures a complete medical record and is of great assistance if the institutional medical response is questioned later.

■ Medication

Prescription medication is commonplace among prison populations. Most institutions will have a formulary that will dictate which medications within a class may be prescribed. For a new inmate, the use of generic medication equivalents may generate some angst and must be dispensed with a good deal of patient education and reassurance. This is best done by a pharmacist if one is available.

The cost of providing medication for inmates is a major expense for correctional facilities. Many specialized, mandatory drugs are required for care and treatment. State and federal governments spend huge amounts of monetary resources through Medicaid and other aid programs to support citizens who work for the government, retirees from government agencies, and prison inmates. The State of California alone spent $133 million on prison medications[4] in 2002–2003. Prison and jail systems try to save on their pharmaceutical purchases by joining with other agencies to create bulk purchasing power, using generic drugs, and developing procedures for electronic purchases from distant, less expensive providers.

Good record keeping is essential to monitor a specific inmate's appropriate use of medication. In some cases, an inmate may be responsible enough to take the medication without supervision; in other cases, he or she may need direct supervision even to the point of examining the mouth to ensure the medication was swallowed. Various institutions will handle this problem in different ways, and various monitoring mechanisms have been successful in monitoring inmate compliance.

Abuse and Dependency

Opiate abuse is a potential problem during incarceration, just as it is in the community. Many inmates come to incarceration with chronic pain due to injuries and need an effective analgesic. Some inmates, however, have become quite adept at feigning pain; therefore, the best approach to pain management is an inclusive team that meets regularly to discuss to pain control and administration of opiates. All such meetings should be documented in the medical record and a judgment rendered as to whether such medication is habitually necessary and dictated by the medical condition.

In some cases, correctional personnel can be helpful during this assessment. For example, they may have seen an inmate who is allegedly suffering from chronic pain playing vigorously on the ball field and not appearing to be in discomfort. Such an observation should be documented in the record and form the basis for an informed discussion within the committee. In no case should an inmate be denied pain medication without proper documentation in the record or as a punitive gesture.

Inasmuch as drug and alcohol use are widespread in the general population, they are often associated with criminal activity. That is to say that many offenders commit the crime or crimes for which they are incarcerated while either under the influence of alcohol or drugs, or to support the dependency. For this reason, most long-term incarceration facilities have a chemical dependency treatment program. In some cases, the sentencing judge will have predicated the inmate's sentence on the completion of such a program.

Whether a given institution has a complete chemical treatment facility within its walls will depend on its mission, level of custody and security, budget, and trained personnel. In a comprehensive and fully funded program, inmates will have access to a complete initial evaluation, psychological testing and evaluation, lectures, group therapy, and counseling. In many cases, outside self-help groups (such as Alcoholics Anonymous) will be allowed inside the prison to share their personal observations and experiences with the inmates. Without a comprehensive treatment approach for drug and alcohol abuse and follow-up, the inmate recidivism rate is considerably higher.[5]

Preventing drug and alcohol use depends on the vigilance and cooperativeness of the correctional staff. Inmates may ferment fruit and vegetables stolen from the kitchen to make alcohol. Drugs such as cocaine, heroin, and marijuana may come into the institution through mail, visitors, or staff. Only the most intense awareness and monitoring by correctional and medical staff will keep an institution drug free. Random urine monitoring programs, when carried out conscientiously by staff and supported by administration, are effective tools in managing substance abuse within the institution.

■ Infection Control

Communicable diseases are a concern in every confinement situation due to three factors:

1. Confinement lends itself to the spread of infectious organisms, whether airborne or by direct contact.
2. Prior needle drug use, which is high in the prison population, predisposes inmates to certain infectious diseases (e.g., hepatitis).
3. The incidence of human immunodeficiency virus (HIV) is high in certain prison populations (although less than 5% overall).

Each institution needs an infection control manual that is clearly written and communicated to all staff on a regular basis. All people within the walls need to understand the principles of communicability and, most importantly, understand universal precautions, which are outlined by the NCCHC. Such precautions include disposable gloves and CPR masks; all personnel should have immediate access to this equipment.

Public health infection control nurses or equivalent medical staff are invaluable in monitoring TB and other communicable diseases within an institution. It is also important to keep other staff informed about procedures and techniques and to develop educational programs for both inmates and staff. Many inmates come to confinement with misconceptions about the spread of HIV, and such misinformation can lead to institutional unrest. In addition to testing for TB, hepatitis B, and hepatitis C, each institution should develop a policy regarding the routine testing for HIV. This can be a screening test on blood with the Elisa test and appropriate follow-up for positive results. Not all institutions test routinely for HIV. In all cases, pre- and posttest counseling must be done if the testing for the HIV is performed. Strict confidentiality regarding test results must be maintained.

Today's treatment of HIV is expensive, time-consuming, and complex, and it requires vigilance on the part of both the inmate and his or her caregivers. Frequent testing and monitoring of viral blood levels, CD4 counts, and secondary infections nearly always dictate that infected inmates be seen at regular intervals. Compliance with medications, which often have unpleasant side effects, is variable and often poor. This can usually be dealt with by medication adjustments and education, but even with these efforts, sometimes the course of the illness is relentless. All AIDS patients should be monitored carefully for TB.

Medical and correctional staff who have direct contact with inmates should use discretion in obtaining a yearly blood test for HIV for themselves, but all should have a yearly test for TB. Multi-drug-resistant TB has recently become a problem in AIDS patients, especially among those in prison. This is a very serious issue and requires consultation with an infectious disease expert.

■ Unique Medical Situations

In every incarcerated population, medical situations occasionally arise from protests. In these instances, nearly all inmates will relent and respond to the professional, nonjudgmental demeanor of the staff when inmates realize that the particular form of protest they have chosen is not going to be effective. Punitive and abusive behavior on the part of staff can only serve to exacerbate the situation and make inmates more resolved to carry out their protest.

Use of Force

Occasionally, the use of force may be necessary to subdue or restrain an inmate who is a threat or danger to himself or herself, other inmates, or staff. The procedures for this are very familiar to correctional staff and usually prescribed in a manual. Medical staff are not typically involved in the application of restraining force. However, whenever possible, medical staff should be present when force is used and should perform a careful examination of the inmate after the force or restraint has been applied.

Particular attention should be paid to positional asphyxia (restriction of breathing due to positioning) during situations of restraint. Historically, most serious injuries in such emergencies have occurred as a result of airway obstruction. In an older inmate or one with known cardiac risk factors, particular attention should be paid to blood pressure, pulse, and questions of chest discomfort. If instability is suspected, the inmate should be transported to the infirmary and monitored and a physician notified. After the application of force and an exam, medical providers should document their findings carefully and note times and other staff who were present.

Fights or Riots

Disturbances in a prison or jail setting can vary from a fight involving two inmates to a full-blown riot with multiple injuries to staff and inmates. Sometimes fire, explosives, and wounds of various kinds can add to injuries. Medical staff's involvement will vary with the seriousness of the disturbance, and many of the principles that dictate their role will be the same as described above for emergencies. The important general principle is to have a plan to deal with such disturbances (e.g., disaster drills) and to practice the plan at regular intervals. Simple things like triage, proper use of radio frequencies, and transportation of injured persons will be difficult at best under actual disturbance conditions. However, successful medical intervention (and, for that matter, security) is much less likely if no forethought is given to developing and practicing relevant procedures.

Hostage Situations

Hostage taking is fortunately a relatively rare circumstance that may occur and in which medical staff may be asked to play a role. This role will likely be dictated by the manager of the hostage situation, usually the warden or a designed staff member. Again, forethought and planning are part of the educational process of everyone who works in the facility, and medical staff should prepare for their respective roles in emergency management, triage, and transport.

Hunger Strikes

Food strikes may occur among inmates as a group form of protest or by individuals as a protest against some alleged mistreatment or perceived unfairness. Food strikes are best managed by medical staff in a professional and nonjudgmental way. The inmate who declares a food strike is placed in a locked cell, and water to the room is shut off to preclude surreptitious hydration. Food and water should be offered on a continual basis. As the inmate becomes weaker and dehydrated, frequent exams should be done and results recorded with particular attention being paid to skin turgor (tenting) and dryness of mucus membranes. All urine output should be noted and all urine saved for specific gravity determination. After several days of no food or water, blood electrolytes must be drawn and tested on a daily basis to help guard against serious injury. If there has been no progress in resolving the inmate's issues in a reasonable period of time, at some point (medically determined) an intravenous (IV) line is to be infused and IV fluids given to the protesting inmate. All interventions and exams must be documented carefully in the medical record.

■ Eldercare

The aging inmate population across the United States is beginning to take its toll on institutional operations. Because inmates are locked up for longer periods of time and, in many jurisdictions, without the possibility of parole, more offenders age and die in penal institutions. It is projected that by 2030, there will be 33,000 geriatric prisoners in California alone and that one-third of the overall U.S. prison population will be geriatric inmates (those over the age of 55).[6]

The cost of specialized care for the elderly is high. Older inmates require more medical attention, sometimes need special diets, and eventually will be in need of other services that are necessary for geriatric individuals. Indeed, some states have established the equivalent of nursing home facilities that function both as prisons and medical-support programs.[7]

■ End-of-Life Considerations

There are several important end-of-life issues that arise in correctional environments, including in-custody deaths, living wills, hospice care, family visitations, compassionate release, handling the remains, and executions.

In-custody deaths (inmate deaths during imprisonment) are not rare, especially because of recent increases in lifelong sentences. These deaths may be due to natural or unnatural causes, which include suicide, homicide, mysterious surroundings, or death due to work injuries. All in-custody deaths are investigated carefully by a neutral body or commission. Death caused by unnatural causes should require that an autopsy be performed by an outside medical examiner.

At the time of death, the site of the death should be treated as a potential crime scene: The area should be sealed, and no one should move or touch the body after medical staff has declared that death has occurred. A scene investigation and photographs most likely will be taken by correctional staff or the medical examiner. The medical provider's role is to pronounce the death and record relevant physical findings in the medical record. If rigor mortis has occurred, it should be noted, but most likely the outside medical examiner will determine the time of death from other information. Medical staff should personally communicate any information they have to the medical examiner.

In some cases of natural death, the inmate will have a living will. If so, it should be properly drawn and notarized as part of the inmate's medical record. If, for example, the inmate has an incurable terminal disease and does not wish to have supportive care or cardiac resuscitation in the event of cardiac arrest, that information should be communicated to all staff caring for the inmate and should be documented in the inmate's medical record.

Hospice care for terminally ill inmates is not as common as in the community at large, but it does exist in some prisons that have a large percentage of medical cases. This innovative care has allowed other carefully screened and trained inmates to participate as hospice volunteers and sit by the bedside to bring comfort to the dying. In addition, multiple professional staff may be involved, including physicians, nurses, pharmacists, social workers, psychologists, chaplains, and interested correctional staff. This team approach to hospice has been shown to be effective in terminal care management.

Any care of terminally ill inmates will usually involve some communication with their families. Most families, even those estranged from the inmate, need to be informed on a periodic basis, perhaps weekly, of the inmate's status. They may have questions about the inmate's state and care, ranging from the amount of suffering to what will happen with his or her body after death. These are real issues and must be addressed by medical or case management staff members either in person or on the phone. Again, a professional, nonjudgmental manner is the key to good communication with the family. In some cases, a bedside visit within the facility can be arranged after appropriate security and custody clearance. All such visits are generally directly supervised by staff. Many times, a family's anger may be abated by such a visit when they see for themselves the helpful and supportive nature of the medical staff. A frank discussion should also be held with the family about disposition of the body at the time of death. It should be made clear that an autopsy will most likely be performed unless one's religious beliefs oppose it and the coroner accepts this direction. The individual's body will be shipped to the family, or the remains will be cremated and the ashes shipped.

Some states and all federal facilities allow for a compassionate release in the event of terminal illness. Each jurisdiction allowing this has different criteria that must be met to attain a release. In most cases, the inmate will have only a few months to live and must be incapable of reoffending. Inmates must also have some place that is willing to receive them and the means to provide care. Often the sentencing judge and prosecuting attorney are involved in the decision to release the inmate and, depending on the crime, may be reluctant to do so.

■ The Healthcare Professional as a Correctional Officer

Healthcare providers and correctional staff have overlapping functions. Communication between and among all the professional elements within a custody environment is essential to ensure a safe and effective workplace. Occasionally tensions will develop between custody and medical staff over issues of inmate management. These issues invariably pertain to health questions and offender management. If such tensions or disputes arise, they should be resolved in a professional manner in the best interests of both inmate and staff. It is essential for all staff members to realize that everyone in corrections has the same end goal, namely, the secure and humane custody of offenders in a safe environment. If sight of that goal is lost, then the mission is compromised.

One of the best ways to ensure that this tension does not develop between custody and medical staff members is to have training sessions together. All medical, dental, mental, and healthcare staff should be familiar with the principles of security and custody. Correctional staff should be made familiar with basic medical procedures, such as universal precautions in infection control, and be proficient in CPR. When all staff train together in these procedures, a spirit of cooperation and camaraderie may develop to help medical and correctional staff work together to fulfill the mission.

■ Conclusion

The percentage of those incarcerated relative to the general population is rising each year as society makes changes in sentencing laws and demands harsher sentences for offenders. The need for well-trained healthcare professionals is great within the prison system. Physicians, nurses, pharmacists, physical therapists, dentists, and mental health workers are in great demand. Medical practice within a correctional environment offers many exceptional opportunities for professional growth and a challenging, teamwork-driven environment.

As with any institution, there are those who criticize the prison system and the health options and surveillance available to inmates. Although some of these criticisms are valid, others are the product of biased inmate advocacy groups. It is hard to refute such criticism in a general way because there are so many state and federal prisons, and each has its own healthcare delivery system. In addition, county and city jails often contract with the private sector, thus making it even more difficult to evaluate general health care of inmates. Just as in society as a whole, there is not one unifying healthcare system for incarcerated persons. National standards, or a common standard of care such as that developed by the NCCHC and referred to earlier, will eventually serve to make health care more uniform. In the meantime, it is important to remember that access to health care within a correctional facility is a constitutional guarantee, and prisoners are the only segment of our society who have that right.

Chapter Resources

DISCUSSION QUESTIONS

1. Do you believe convicted offenders should have the same standard of medical care as law-abiding citizens in the community?
2. Should inmates have access to medical personnel daily at institutional sick call?
3. What are some problems in the healthcare area in prisons and jails?
4. Should inmates have to pay a small amount of money for seeing healthcare professionals in the correctional environment?
5. What emergency medical situations can arise in a correctional environment, and should these situations be handled by medical professionals?

ADDITIONAL RESOURCES

Faiver, K. L. (1998). *Health care management issues in corrections*. Lanham, MD: American Correctional Association.

Kempker, E. (2003). The graying of American prisons: Addressing the continued increase in geriatric inmates. *Corrections Compendium, 28*(6), 22–26.

Moore, J. (Ed.). (2003). *Management and administration of correctional health care*. Kingston, NJ: Civic Research Institute.

National Commission on Correctional Health Care, http://www.ncchc.org

Robbins, I. (1999, September 22). Managed health care in prisons as cruel and unusual punishment. *Journal of Criminal Law and Criminology, 90*(1), 195–238.

NOTES

1. *Estelle v. Gamble*, 429 U.S. 97 (1976).
2. *Bowring v. Goodwin*, 551 F.2d 44, 48 (4th Cir. 1977); *Lareau v. Manson*, 651 F.2d 96 (2nd Cir. 1981).
3. U.S. Department of Health and Human Services. (2004). Title 45–Public Welfare. *Code of Federal Regulations*. Washington, DC: Government Printing Office. Retrieved August 13, 2007, from http://a257.g.akamaitech.net/7/257/2422/12feb20041500/edocket.access.gpo.gov/cfr_2004/octqtr/45cfr164.512.htm
4. White, S. (2003). *Survey of California department of corrections pharmaceutical expenditures*. Sacramento, CA: Office of the Inspector General. Retrieved August 13, 2007, from http://www.oig.ca.gov/reports/pdf/corrPEsuvery0703.pdf
5. Pelissier, B., Rhodes, W., Saylor, W., Gaes, G., Camp, S. D., Vanyur, S. D., & Wallace, S. (2000). *TRIAD drug treatment evaluation project*. Washington, DC: Federal Bureau of Prisons. Retrieved August 13, 2007, from http://www.bop.gov/news/PDFs/TRIAD/TRIAD_pref.pdf
6. Enders, S., Paterniti, D., & Meyers, F. (2005). An approach to develop effective health care decision making for women in prison. *Journal of Palliative Medicine, 8*(2), 432–439.
7. Stingley, A. (1996, November 30). North Carolina tackled geriatric question early. *The Shreveport Times*.

Mental Health

Sally C. Johnson

CHAPTER OBJECTIVES

- Outline issues inherent to the provision of mental health care in the correctional setting.

- Understand when inmate participation in mental health care and treatment can be required.

- Explore the right to privacy with regard to mental health records.

■ Introduction

Provision of mental health services is a necessary but complex and often inadequately understood part of any correctional operation. Attention to planning and implementation of quality services to address the mental health needs of the inmate population can contribute greatly to the smooth running of a correctional facility; inattention can lead to management problems, negative publicity, and even litigation. Regardless of whether correctional administrators have any training or experience in delivery of mental health care, they will need to familiarize themselves with the needs and demands of mentally ill inmates and applicable standards and guidelines to ensure that adequate care is delivered to their mentally ill offenders.

Over time, the process of caring for the mentally ill in the community has changed dramatically, and these changes have influenced how care is delivered in jails and institutions. With the advent of effective psycho-pharmacology and more focused types of therapies for mental illness, much of the population suffering from illness no longer requires the strict supervision and structure of mental hospitals. Treatment of psychiatric illness, for the most part, is relegated to outpatient settings. Even those patients who are hospitalized are most often quickly released to their home communities with the intent of having them supported by the intermittent supervision offered by community-based mental health care. This process of deinstitutionalizing people with mental illness in the United States began more than a half century ago and created a major decline in the populations of state and county mental hospitals. Years later, however, treating the mentally ill in the community does not always result in successful care. Many of those with mental illness do not follow through with recommended treatment and often are not compliant with taking prescribed medications.

Community resources are limited, and existing support systems may be inadequate to meet the needs of the mentally ill. This can result in mentally ill individuals ending up in the criminal justice system. When symptoms of illness return, the individual's behavior often deteriorates, judgment becomes impaired, and ability to survive independently diminishes. Associated and even minor antisocial behavior can easily result in criminal violations and incarceration. It is not unusual for commitment to a jail or state or federal correctional facility to be seen as an acceptable alternative by the courts. Current data reflect that there are more mentally ill people in penal institutions than in designated community mental institutions. At midyear 2005, more than half of all prison and jail inmates had mental health problems, representing 56% of state prisoners, 45% of federal prisoners, and 64% of jail inmates.[1] Recent estimates indicate that between 5% and 16% of male inmates (and an even higher percentage of female inmates) meet criteria for diagnosis of a major mental disorder.[2]

The *Diagnostic and Statistical Manual of Mental Disorders*, the most commonly used classification system of mental diseases and defects, defines a mental disorder as a "clinically significant behavioral or psychological syndrome or pattern that occurs in an individual and that is associated with present distress or disability." There are more than 300 different psychiatric disorders, any of which may be evident in the inmate population.[3] More severe or major mental disorders include diagnoses such as schizophrenia, major depression, or bipolar disorder. A considerable number of inmates, however, suffer from other disorders or symptoms that may be viewed as less serious or simply as part of their adjustment to incarceration. Many have demonstrated personality dysfunction for years and meet criteria for personality disorder diagnoses, including the commonly discussed disorder of antisocial personality disorder. Personality disorders often present challenges in the institutional setting and remain difficult to treat.

■ Guidelines and Standards

Incarcerated individuals have rights of access to and provision of health care, including mental health care; thus, provision of mental health services is not optional in the correctional environment. Since 1980, through litigation in the courts at state and federal levels, the responsibility for provision of care to those who are denied the ability to access it on their own because of incarceration has been generally defined.[4] Little differentiation exists between the right to assessment and treatment of medical and mental health problems. The current standard requires basic and clinically relevant care. Problems arise when care falls below accepted standards and results in deliberate indifference toward the medical and mental health needs of the incarcerated population. Deliberate indifference can be evidenced by lack of access to care, failure to follow through with care, insufficient provision of staff resources, and poor outcomes due to negligent care.[5] Ensuring that the basic level of services does not fall below acceptable standards requires administrative support for adequate healthcare facilities, staffing, clearly defined program structure, understandable written policy, and ongoing monitoring for quality assurance.

Several correctional and healthcare organizations have established guidelines to define minimum standards for the care and treatment of the mentally ill in correctional settings. These include

- American Correctional Association (ACA)
- American Medical Association (AMA)
- American Public Health Association (APHA)
- American Psychiatric Association (APA)
- The Joint Commission on Accreditation of Healthcare Organizations (JCAHO)
- National Commission on Correctional Health Care (NCCHC)
- National Institute of Corrections (NIC)

Formal reviews and accreditation of correctional mental health programs can be accomplished under the ACA, NCCHC, and JCAHO. These involve site visits, review of written policies and procedures, direct observation, and review of health records and other sources of documentation of care. Institution services are reviewed against standards established by each organization. Although there is considerable overlap of intent in the standards, the degree of fit between standards and a particular program and the degree of detail addressed by the standards varies greatly. For example, ACA standards are broadly focused, addressing all aspects of the correctional operation, and are the least specific in regard to mental health care. Because of this, mental health programs in correctional facilities may want to undergo accreditation review by a more health-oriented accrediting body such as NCCHC or the Joint Commission.

The importance of external review and accreditation should not be underestimated. In addition to providing concrete guidelines for establishing and maintaining quality mental health programs, preparation for the accreditation process forces internal auditing and review. Accreditation visits and reports frequently identify potential problems in service care delivery and in the quality or quantity of services and mandate establishment of a time frame for correction of those deficiencies. Successful accreditation provides support for the correctional system when questions about adequacy of care arise. The accreditation process also promotes integration of the correctional healthcare staff into the larger healthcare community, provides staff support, and gives guidance to the correctional healthcare mission.

■ Access to Care

An adequate care delivery system for mental health services in a correctional environment must address a range of functions and needs within the environment. As early as 1980, in the case of *Ruiz v. Estelle*, the court focused on six issues, attention to which is required to meet minimally adequate standards for mental health care in a correctional environment. These include

- A system to ensure mental health screening for inmates
- Provision of treatment while inmates are in segregation or special housing units

- Training of mental health staff to ensure individualized treatment planning
- Maintenance of an accurate and confidential medical records system
- Presence of an effective suicide prevention program
- Monitoring to ensure appropriate use of psychotropic medication[6]

These issues remain essential in any correctional healthcare program. Together they form a continuum of services designed to meet the demands of the correctional population.

Correctional administrators are responsible for establishing and implementing an adequate mental healthcare delivery system to ensure inmate access to care and care providers. This access is required from the point of arrest to the point of discharge from correctional supervision or oversight. Adequate staff and physical plant resources are crucial to an effective healthcare delivery system and may require vigorous advocacy by administrators. Understandable and realistic policies and procedures with consistent implementation provide the framework for care delivery. These serve as standards against which individual episodes of care can be reviewed as part of a system of continuous performance improvement.

■ Screening

Mental healthcare services begin at the screening stage. Given the volume of patients entering the correctional environment and the fact that the time of entry of these individuals into the system is often difficult to control and frequently occurs outside of usual working hours, it is important that an effective initial screening system be in place. Inmates should be screened promptly upon arrival and before they are placed in a housing situation without direct staff observation. Initial screening is done on an individual basis by trained correctional staff who seek basic information about current or recent medical and mental health problems, care, history of recent hospitalizations, and use of medications. A more detailed follow-up medical and mental health review is then accomplished by designated healthcare providers with training in detecting symptoms of potentially serious mental disorders. Specific inquiry should be made to uncover any thoughts or plans of harm to self or others. Individuals entering the criminal justice system are often angry, upset, frightened, anxious, or confused and may have difficulty providing information or present as uncooperative. It is important that staff persist in obtaining necessary information to screen incoming inmates adequately.

The primary goal of screening is to identify emergent and urgent problems and determine which inmates might require more extensive assessment and intervention before placement into the general inmate population. This can be facilitated by staff members taking the time to identify themselves and their roles and explain the purpose of these interviews. The inmate's general presentation and understanding of the situation should be assessed. Staff members should provide correct orientation as to place, time, and situation and reassure and educate individuals if necessary. The initial screening questions should be standardized for each inmate, with further exploration and data collection pursued where indicated. Responses should be documented on a screening intake form, which should then be placed in the inmate's correctional health record. Documentation of necessary referrals should be included. Proper mental health intake screening will determine the type and immediacy of need for other mental health services.

Inmates requiring further assessment or evaluation of their mental health need to be housed in an area with staff availability and observation appropriate to their needs. Further assessment and evaluation should be assigned to specific staff members and should be accomplished within reasonable and specified time frames. Normally this will include additional interviews, record collection and review, physical examination, laboratory studies, drug screening, continued observation, and occasionally psychological testing. Differential diagnoses (a list of possible problems) or a working diagnosis should be established to allow initiation of treatment planning until the diagnostic picture becomes clear.

■ Treatment and Follow-Up Care

Treatment needs arising within the correctional environment can be met in various settings. Inmates are frequently moved from one level and location of treatment to another during their period of incarceration.

- Outpatient—inmates who are housed in general population but receive mental health services at the medical clinic or on-site in their housing units
- Inpatient—inmates are admitted to a hospital facility in the correctional system or in the community
- Transitional or intermediate—inmates with similar problems may be housed together in a specific area of a general population housing unit or in a separate, specially designated program-related area

General mental health outpatient services involve counseling, consultation, medication management, and continued screening to identify changes in treatment needs. Much of the counseling at this level is supportive. It can provide a cost-effective mental health intervention that may prevent escalation to a higher level of care. The frequency of outpatient visits generally varies from weekly to every 90 days or more.

Psychiatric inpatient hospital services are often established on-site in correctional facilities to avoid the need for movement into the community of individuals, who could pose significant threats. Some systems, however, due to size, financial resources, or unavailability of staff, must continue to use community-based hospitals, often psychiatric units of general hospitals or state mental health hospital facilities. Admission in either case may be voluntary or involuntary. Each inmate patient must be reviewed for competency to consent to psychiatric hospitalization.[7] Those not competent to give voluntary informed consent must undergo a formal administrative or judicial review concerning need for hospitalization. Reasons for admission to inpatient psychiatric hospitalization most often include

- Presence of severe or disruptive psychiatric symptoms
- Inability of the system to handle the inmate in a less restrictive environment
- Need for a more complex or comprehensive assessment than is available in the outpatient setting
- Court orders for inpatient evaluation or commitment
- Assessed risk of imminent danger to self or others

In recent years, in part due to limited resources, improved screening, and efforts to manage rising costs, the concept of transitional, intermediate, or habilitative care has gained attention.[8] Inmates who have known chronic mental disorders are prone to relapse, have significant behavioral problems, or are unable to integrate well into the general prison population often benefit from more attention and structured intervention. Efforts are made to stabilize symptoms during a 3- to 6-month period of less intensive treatment in a sheltered environment. Treatment is aimed at symptom reduction and management, improving coping skills, and helping each inmate to better adapt to the general prison environment. The overall goal of treatment is reintegration into a regular prison population or preparation for release to the outside community.

All mental health treatment interventions are related directly to diagnoses or symptom management. Treatment may be delivered or coordinated by various members of the mental healthcare treatment team. Clear documentation of an individualized treatment plan should be kept in the inmate's health record. This helps available staff to efficiently direct interventions toward accomplishment of the inmate patients' goals. **Table 14-1** provides a simplified outline of typical treatment interventions across the spectrum of psychopathology likely seen in a correctional setting.

Because of the relapsing nature of some mental disorders and the chronicity of others, discharge planning and follow-up care are crucial both when returning inmates to general population and when releasing them to the community. The cornerstone of successful discharge planning remains sound diagnostic assessment.

TABLE 14-1 Generalized Classification of Mental Disorders

Category	Symptom Presentation	Treatment	Typical Settings	Provider
Psychosis	Hallucinations Delusions Bizarre behavior	Medication Supportive treatments	Hospital Outpatient Transitional care	MD Psychologist
Mood disorders	Increased or decreased mood Sleep disturbance Appetite disturbance	Medication Counseling	Hospital Outpatient Transitional care	MD Psychologist
Situational problems	Anxiety Mild depression	Counseling Environment support	Outpatient	MD Counselor Psychologist
Substance abuse	Drug-seeking behavior Sleep disturbances Anxiety	Education Relapse prevention		Social worker Counselor
Developmental disability Organicity	Adjustment difficulties Viewed as vulnerable	Assisted living Supportive counseling	Transitional care	MD Social worker Unit team
Sexual offenders	Sexual offense by history	Education Relapse prevention	Outpatient	MD Psychologist Counselor
Personality disorders	Problem behaviors	Counseling Environment support	Outpatient	Unit team Psychologist MD

Assessment of dangerousness to self and others should routinely occur at each visit, before any change in housing or security status and before release to the community. Ensuring adequate and cost-effective continued treatment is a reasonable goal. Education about the anticipated course of illnesses and treatment needs while inmates are still incarcerated may increase the likelihood that they continue treatment outside the hospital/prison setting. Exploration of necessary follow-up resources that can meet the inmate's needs and exchange of pertinent information between correctional and future community providers should occur before release of an inmate with known mental health problems.

■ Crisis Intervention

The need for crisis intervention or suicide prevention may arise with inmates at any level of treatment, as well as among those not yet identified as in need of treatment. Crisis intervention includes short-term interventions aimed at reducing acute mental distress. Crises may be precipitated by problems ranging from acute anxiety or anger to those associated with psychotic decompensation. Frequently, the crisis presents as suicidal ideation, a suicide attempt, or externally directed aggression. All correctional staff need to be familiar with suicide risk assessment and prevention. Sound correctional management requires that an adequate suicide prevention program be in place in the correctional environment. Suicide prevention programs include adequate training of staff in the identification of signs and symptoms of suicide risk and availability of safe environments in which a suicidal inmate can be observed and housed. The observation requirement can be costly and time intensive. Some systems, such as the Federal Bureau of Prisons, have tried to utilize inmate companion or peer watcher programs to assist in observation. Others have turned to modification of the housing environment and use of audiovisual monitoring to ensure that inmates remain safe while their treatment needs are addressed.

■ Issues Arising from Confinement

Mental health problems and the types of services needed to address these problems must exist throughout all phases of the criminal justice operation. Some individuals enter the criminal justice system while mentally ill, whereas others develop new symptoms or illness once in custody. The stress of being in the criminal justice system itself can create or exacerbate symptoms or illness. Known stressors include involvement in the legal system, separation from existing community support systems, peer problems within the facility, and internal stressors associated with loss of control and individual decision making. Incarceration frequently disrupts sleep and eating routines, and access to anxiety-reducing activities such as television, exercise, spontaneous socialization, and smoking may be severely limited. Stress can also result from a lack of familiarity with the legal or criminal justice system, fear of the future, and the position of dependence, and loss of control that comes with being an inmate. A well-functioning mental health service is crucial to understanding and addressing the effect of these issues.

■ Legal Requirements

Hospitalization in a psychiatric facility, even in a correctional environment, is voluntary unless the level of impairment is so severe that inmates present a clear risk of harm to themselves or others or could benefit from care in a hospital. Legal provisions exist to protect those inmates who are unable to function in a general population because of mental illness. Each state and the federal government, by statute, direct how an individual can be involuntarily hospitalized for psychiatric care. Involuntary hospitalization, also known as civil commitment, in a prison facility parallels the process outlined by statute in the community. This involves attention to due process, legal representation, and judicial decision making. Voluntary psychiatric hospital admission must be agreed to by a competent inmate. The hospital record should contain documentation of the informed consent to hospitalization and assessment of competency to give consent.

It is important to note that psychiatric hospitalization alone, whether voluntary or involuntary, does not necessarily grant the care provider authority to treat.[9] Treatments, as well as the absence of treatment, carry varying degrees of risks and benefits. Before any psychiatric treatment, the inmate must give informed consent to the specific treatment, unless the situation has been deemed an emergency or treatment has been authorized by the court. Informed consent requires that the care provider give sufficient, understandable information regarding the proposed treatment to an inmate patient capable of understanding the information. It also requires discussion of treatment alternatives including the option of no treatment. The risks and benefits of any proposed treatment must be discussed thoroughly with the patient. Any common or severe potential side effects must be reviewed. Patients accepting voluntary treatment must be made aware that they may elect to discontinue the treatment at any time simply by withdrawing their consent.

■ Privacy

Correctional healthcare providers are constantly confronted with issues of patient privacy and confidentiality of health information in the correctional environment. Patients in prison, like those outside prison, come to their healthcare providers with the expectation that the information they share will be kept confidential. Although medical and mental health information can be shared among healthcare providers on a need-to-know basis, there are strict limits on other release of healthcare information. Records must be kept secured, preferably on the treatment units, with access limited to healthcare providers involved in the patient's care. Internal policy should define the members of the healthcare team. Patients should be advised as to the limits of confidentiality that may apply in special situations such as court-ordered forensic evaluations or injury assessment exams. Inmates have the right to obtain copies of their records and to review their healthcare records under observation unless their healthcare providers deem such reviews would be detrimental to the inmates' health.

■ Dual Roles of Staff

At times, clinical staff may feel caught between their roles as providers and correctional workers. Administrators must ensure that this issue is discussed with staff. It is also important that these dual roles be explained to the inmate patients at the onset of evaluation or treatment. Inmate patients should be advised that any information that affects the security of the institution; requires intervention to prevent harm to the patient, other inmates, or staff; or concerns situations where serious damage to property will occur will not be kept confidential.

■ Special Treatment Procedures

The use of special treatment procedures, such as seclusion or restraint with the mentally ill, requires close attention in a correctional environment. Both interventions are used at times for correctional reasons unrelated to psychiatric issues, but because they may also be used as part of the spectrum of treatment interventions for acutely disturbed psychiatric patients, all uses must be carefully reviewed. A consistently monitored system should be established to ensure that special treatment procedures are used only when necessary, that justification for use is clearly documented, and that the inmate's physical and psychological needs are assessed before, during, and after use. The goal should be to keep inmate patients in these most restrictive situations for the minimum amount of time to ensure their safe management in the correctional system. Guidelines for the psychiatric use of seclusion and restraint have been available to practitioners since 1985, and current accreditation standards continue to focus attention on this high-risk area.[10] Use of these special treatment procedures is generally restricted to cases in which inmates pose an imminent risk of harm to themselves or others or serious threat of extreme damage to property or the orderly running of the institution.

Inmates in seclusion require enhanced staff observation and monitoring, including continuous observation if the inmate is identified as suicidal. Inmates in restraints must be checked by medical personnel regularly to ensure that they are medically stable and circulation has not been compromised. It is the responsibility of correctional staff to ensure that toileting, meals, and repositioning are accomplished as necessary. Healthcare providers and correctional staff share responsibility to ensure appropriate, safe use of seclusion and restraint.[11]

■ Medications

Medication prescription is a frequent, costly, and potentially high-risk function in the correctional environment. Appropriate use of psychiatric medications can be defined as using the right medication at the right dosage for the right period of time. Pharmacotherapy is a mainstay of current mental health treatment but can present unique problems in a correctional environment. Some inmates will be medication seeking and prone to abuse prescribed medication. These may include chronic pain patients, insomniacs, and substance abusers without access to their drug of choice. Other inmates may want to obtain medications to sell or trade for profit or specific goods or services. Establishing clear and widely understood prescription guidelines is useful in managing the use of psychiatric medications, controlling costs, and preventing abuse:

- Medication prescription in general should be kept to a minimum except for the treatment of clearly documented medical or psychiatric conditions. All prescriptions should be time limited, and the need for continuing a particular medication should be reassessed at each visit.
- Sleep medication should be avoided except in acute situations and limited to three days without further review. The cause of the sleep disturbance should be sought, taking care to uncover any underlying depression. Alternative nonpharmacologic interventions should be encouraged.
- Medication compliance should be followed closely. Noncompliance that persists should result in documenting treatment refusal, clarifying the reason behind the refusal, and discontinuing the prescription. Mouth checks and blood and urine screens should be used to encourage compliance, limit misuse or redistribution of medications among inmates, and ensure adequate dosing.
- Cost and ease of use as determined by route and dosing frequency should be considered in each case as it may influence compliance and assist with staff workload management.
- Polypharmacy, the use of multiple medications from the same class or from similar classes, should be avoided.
- Consistency of prescriber may help to decrease medication-seeking behavior. Except in emergency situations, a single prescriber should manage any one inmate's medications.
- Close attention needs to be paid to possible side effects of medications prescribed and to the possibility of drug interactions. It is not uncommon for inmate patients to overdose on or use drugs in nonconventional ways. Any adverse reactions should be documented, reported as required, and reviewed through appropriate channels.

▪ Personality Disorders and Malingering

In any correctional healthcare setting, the label of antisocial personality disorder is frequently heard. Antisocial personality disorder is a diagnosis based almost exclusively on historical information. Criteria to support the diagnosis include a pattern of disregard for others demonstrated by breaking the law and lying, as well as impulsive, irresponsible, and aggressive behavior. It is important to note that not every incarcerated individual meets the criteria for this diagnosis, although the incidence is increased in the incarcerated population. Inmates with other mental disorders can also demonstrate features of this personality disorder diagnosis. Antisocial personality disorder is difficult to treat. Despite its inclusion in psychiatric classification systems, this diagnosis is most often not viewed as a severe mental disease or defect for legal purposes.

Malingering is a conscious behavior that involves falsely claiming and/or misrepresenting symptoms of an illness. People may malinger to avoid the consequences of being held responsible for their behavior and often believe doing so will improve their situation. Staff in correctional treatment settings should not be too quick to label an inmate patient as malingering. Doing so can prevent a psychiatrically disturbed inmate from receiving necessary assessment and care. Malingering should always be a diagnosis of exclusion, made only after true psychopathology is ruled out. A previous diagnosis of malingering does not rule out the presence of current mental illness or medical problems.

■ Integration of Mental Health and Medical Care

The success of any care delivery system for mental health services is integrally related to the adequacy of the general medical services available to the correctional population. It is not uncommon for medical illnesses to present with psychiatric symptoms. Anxiety, disorientation, confusion, and hallucinations can herald the onset of or unmask the existence of physical illness or disease. A significant number of psychiatric patients in the correctional environment also have concurrent medical illnesses. At times, staff get caught up in managing individual symptoms and miss the bigger picture. Each inmate entering the correctional system should have had a complete physical examination and at least minimum laboratory studies at the time of admission. Each inpatient admission to a psychiatric hospital facility within the correctional environment requires a current physical exam, review of medical history, and infectious disease screening. More extensive laboratory studies to rule out organic causes of a symptom picture are often indicated. These studies can serve as a baseline against which potential side effects from medication treatment can be assessed. Screening for infectious diseases (including TB, HIV, hepatitis, and syphilis) should be conducted on a routine basis.

■ Conclusion

Staffing correctional healthcare and mental healthcare programs can be a difficult task. Few clinicians and other providers are routinely trained during their professional education to work in correctional environments. Most enter the field by chance and ultimately come to view it as either a challenge or a curse. In the correctional environment, provision of adequate medical and mental health care constantly competes with maintaining adequate security. Security demands can put limitations on how efficiently or effectively evaluations can be done and treatment can be delivered. Salaries for clinicians may lag behind community levels, leading to low morale and preventing successful recruiting.

Ironically, despite these barriers, many clinicians are realizing that the correctional environment may be one of the last public strongholds for adequate care of seriously and chronically mentally ill patients. The structure of the environment, the absence of third-party payers, and the effect of externally imposed motivation to change create a unique setting for the provision of mental health care. The correctional mental healthcare environment raises interesting questions about clinician–patient relationships, adequate data collection, personal responsibility for behavior, and the roles of genetics, economics, and education in the onset and continuation of illness. The experiences of correctional healthcare clinicians potentially have much to offer to the broader field of mental health care.

Chapter Resources

DISCUSSION QUESTIONS

1. Why must mental health practitioners have an offender's approval to proceed with mental health care?
2. What is the role of inmate screening, and who does this process serve to protect?
3. Why is it important that staff members receive training in the recognition of mental illness?
4. How is the correctional environment unique in the field of mental health care?
5. What role should medication play in mental health care in prisons and jails?

ADDITIONAL RESOURCES

American Psychiatric Association. (2000). *Psychiatric services in jails and prisons* (2nd ed.). Washington, DC: Author.

APA. (2000). *Guidelines for psychiatric services in jails and prisons* (2nd ed.). Washington, DC: Author.

APHA Task Force on Correctional Health Care Standards. (2003). *Standards for health services in correctional institutions.* Washington, DC: APHA.

Fagan, T. J., & Ax, R. K. (Eds.). (2011). *Correctional mental health, from theory to best practice.* Los Angeles, CA: Sage.

Hills, H., Siegfried, C., & A. Ickowitz. (2004). *Effective prison mental health services: Guidelines to expand and improve treatment.* Washington, DC: Department of Justice, National Institute of Corrections.

The Joint Commission Behavioral Health. (2012). *Comprehensive accreditation manual for behavioral healthcare (CAMBHC).* Washington, DC: Author.

Moore, J. (2003). *Management and administration of correctional health care.* Kingston, NJ: Civic Research Institute.

National Commission on Correctional Health Care. (2008). *Standards for mental health services in correctional facilities.* Chicago, IL: Author.

Perlin, M. L., & Dluqacz, H. A. (2008). *Mental health issues in jails and prisons, cases and materials.* Durham, NC: Carolina Academic Press.

Ruiz, A., Dvoskin, J., Scott, C., & Metzner, J. (Eds.). (2010). *Manual of forms and guidelines for correctional mental health.* Arlington, VA: American Psychiatric Publishing.

Scott, C. L. (Ed.). (2010). *Handbook of correctional mental health* (2nd ed.). Washington, DC: American Psychiatric Publishing.

Simon, R., & Metzner, J. (Eds.). *Correctional psychiatry in American Psychiatric Association textbook of forensic psychiatry* (2nd ed., pp. 395–411). Washington, DC: American Psychiatric Association.

NOTES

1. Bureau of Justice Statistics. (2006). *Special report: Mental health problems of prison and jail inmates.* Washington, DC: US Department of Justice, Office of Justice Programs, NCJ213600.

2. American Psychiatric Association. (2000). *Diagnostic and statistical manual of mental disorders* (4th ed.). Washington, DC: Author.

3. American Psychiatric Association. (2000). *Diagnostic and statistical manual of mental disorders* (4th ed.). Washington, DC: Author.

4. *Estelle v. Gamble,* 429 U.S. 97, 98 (1976); *Bowring v. Godwin,* 551 F.2d 44 (4th Cir. 1977); *Farmer v. Brennan,* 51 U.S. 85, 832 (1994); *Ruark v. Drury,* 21 F.3d. 231, 216 (8th Cir. 1997).

5. Shanski, R. (1989, November). *Identifying and correcting constitutional violations in correctional settings: The role of physician experts.* Paper presented at the annual meeting of the American Public Health Association, Chicago.

6. *Ruiz v. Estelle,* 53 F.Supp. 1265 (S.D. Texas 1980).

7. *Zinermon v. Burch,* no. 87-1965 (US, February 27, 1990); *Vitek v. Jones,* 445 U.S. 480 (1980).

8. Condelli, W., Dvoskin, J. A., & Holanchock, H. (1994). Intermediate care programs for inmates with psychiatric disorders. *Bulletin of the American Academy of Psychiatry Law, 22*(1), 63–70.

9. *Washington v. Harper,* 110 S.Ct. 1028 (1990).

10. Condelli, W., Dvoskin, J. A., & Holanchock, H. (1994). Intermediate care programs for inmates with psychiatric disorders. *Bulletin of the American Academy of Psychiatry Law, 22*(1), 63–70.

11. American Psychiatric Association. (1985). *Task Force Report 22: Seclusion and restraint: The psychiatric uses.* Washington, DC: Author.

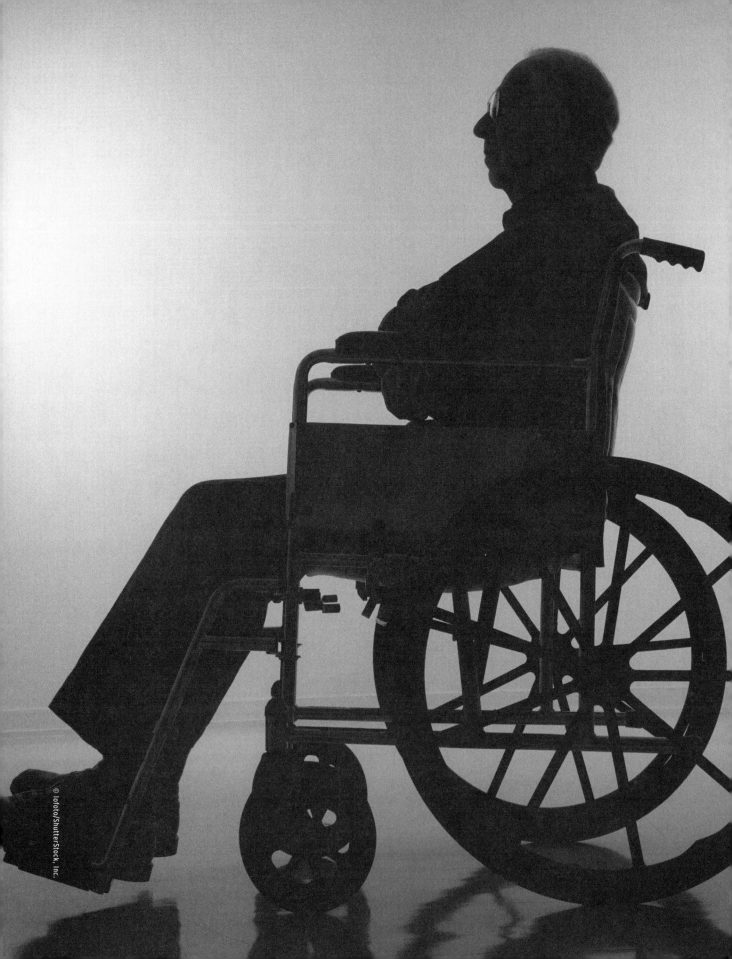

Offenders with Special Needs

Judy C. Anderson

CHAPTER OBJECTIVES

- Describe the variety and prevalence of physical and mental health issues present in a prison population.

- Outline the challenges posed by inmates with disabilities or special needs.

- Identify some of the measures that institutions must take to manage inmates with special needs effectively.

S pecial-needs offenders are those incarcerated men and women with unusual or unique requirements stemming from their physical or mental age or other disabilities such as physical impairment, terminal illness, chronic medical condition, mental illness, and mental challenges. Special needs can encompass many types of conditions, and practitioners have had to find ways of handling such offenders. These approaches have ranged from complete lack of acknowledgment to the provision of specialized services and units.

At the American Correctional Association's 141st Congress of Corrections in Kissimmee, Florida, the Delegate Assembly affirmed several of its existing policies that were revised, or amended in some cases, and approved for continuation in August 2011; two of these policies address special-needs offenders. They are

- Public correctional policy on offenders with special needs
- Public correctional policy on correctional health care

The former identifies offenders with special needs as the following:

- Offenders with psychological needs, developmental disabilities, psychiatric disorders, behavioral disorders, disabling conditions, neurological impairments, or substance abuse disorders
- Offenders who have acute or chronic medical conditions, are physically disabled, or are terminally ill
- Older offenders
- Offenders with social and/or educational deficiencies, learning disabilities, or language barriers
- Offenders with special security or supervision needs
- Sex offenders
- Female offenders[1]

The latter policy establishes guidelines for providing appropriate classification, programs, and housing assignments for these identified groups of offenders.[2]

For purposes of this discussion, offenders with special security or supervision needs, sex offenders, and female offenders will be omitted as they are addressed in other chapters.

■ Special-Needs Classification

The Americans with Disabilities Act (ADA), passed by Congress in 1990, defines a disabled person as one who has "a physical or mental impairment that substantially limits one or more major life activities, has a record of such an impairment, or is regarded as having such an impairment." This definition covers all persons, including inmates. Physical impairments are defined as severe mobility, visual, hearing, and speech limitations. People with mobility impairments include those who use wheelchairs or ambulate with assistive devices such as walkers, crutches, or canes. Chronic medical conditions that usually result in hospitalizations or medical segregation include[3]

- Cardiovascular conditions
- End-stage renal disease
- Respiratory conditions
- Seizure disorders
- Tuberculosis
- Acquired immune deficiency syndrome (AIDS)

Mentally ill inmates include those with any diagnosed disorder defined in the *Diagnostic and Statistical Manual of Mental Disorders*, published by the American Psychiatric Association. Mental illness causes severe disturbances in thought, emotions, and ability to cope with the demands of daily life. The co-occurring disorders (CODs) of substance abuse and mental disorders have become an increasing diagnosis, especially among female offenders.[4] Mental illness, like other illnesses, can be acute, chronic, or under control and in remission. Mental health services can include intake screening, crisis intervention, inpatient admission, long-term therapy, outpatient treatment, and reentry services.

A developmental disability is defined as having less than normal intellectual competence, characterized by an intelligence quotient (IQ) of 70 or less. A developmental disability usually results in impairments in adaptive behaviors such as personal independence and social responsibility.[5]

Terminally ill offenders are usually defined as having a fatal disease and less than 6–12 months to live.

Geriatric offenders are frequently categorized as those offenders over the age of 65; however, preventive health care dictates that an earlier age should be used as a guideline. Many correctional systems have adopted 50 years of age as the defining age for geriatric offenders based on their socioeconomic status, access to medical care, and lifestyle.[6]

■ Prevalence

The number of older offenders is rising because of longer and mandatory sentencing. A 2006 Bureau of Justice Statistics special report noted that at midyear 2005, more than 50% of state and federal inmates suffered from a mental health problem. Moreover, many of these offenders also suffered from substance dependence or abuse (42% of state inmates, nearly 30% of federal inmates, and nearly 50% of jail inmates).[7]

The American Civil Liberties Union reports that elderly inmates are the fastest growing segment of the prison population, and that is true, in part, because of tougher sentencing laws[8] coupled with inmates who committed crimes at a younger age who are now "aging in place."

It is estimated that offenders with a developmental disability are overrepresented in the entire correctional system, especially in prison. A 1998 study suggested that the number of developmentally disabled persons is two to three times greater in prison than in the community. It should be noted that many offenders in custody are considered to have borderline disabilities, thus increasing the absolute numbers.[9]

Bruce Sieleni, MD, staff psychiatrist with the Iowa Department of Corrections, reports that approximately 40% of that state's prison population may have a mental illness.[10] Based on the changes in the community mental health system, many who have mental illness have become incarcerated. It has been such that corrections has also become the main provider of mental health services.

■ Identifying Those with Special Needs

During intake (the process of evaluating inmates as they enter the correctional system) any special needs must be identified as soon as possible in order to provide appropriate services, both during intake and throughout the period of incarceration. Intake is often conducted at a separate facility or unit in a reception and diagnostic center.

Within the first few hours of admittance, a medical examination or at least a medical screening should be conducted. Although a thorough medical examination is preferable, it may be impossible to provide if intake volume is high. The medical screening, which serves as a minitriage, should identify any medical or mental health concerns that need immediate attention; these cases should be assessed immediately by appropriate medical/mental staff.

■ Protocols for Care

Each correctional facility should develop written policies and procedures that are consistent with the ADA. When evaluating services, the institution must ascertain if there are policies, procedures, and practices that would prevent inmates with disabilities from participating. If there are, then reasonable modifications might be indicated to avoid potential discrimination. For example, library or law books might be brought to a wheelchair-bound inmate if the library is located in a building without wheelchair access. The ADA does provide for exclusion from a program if a disabled inmate presents a direct threat to the health and safety of others. For instance, a mentally ill inmate who hears a voice telling him or her to kill another person would need not be included in general population activities. The effect, if any, on corrections from the ADA Amendments of 2008 is still being explored/determined.

■ Segregation or Mainstreaming?

After acknowledging that special-needs offenders may be in the prison population, the first major task is to decide how to handle these groups of inmates—should they be segregated or mainstreamed? Reasons cited for separating special-needs offenders from the general population include

- *Cost containment.* It is a more efficient use of funding if special-needs inmates are housed and treated as a group.
- *Managed care.* More effective care can be focused on a specialized unit.
- *Concentration of resources.* Relevant staff and resources can be more concentrated if special-needs inmates are housed in one location.

Mainstreaming (the integration of a person with a disability into the normal prison population) is a basic premise of the ADA, which requires that disabled inmates have complete access to prison programs and services. However, as previously noted, the ADA does allow correctional administrators to exclude or remove an offender with a disability from the general population if he or she is a direct threat to the health and safety of others.

Consequently, a combination of mainstreaming and segregation (with emphasis on the former) should provide services for inmates with disabilities as well as follow the law outlined in the ADA. This approach would also be consistent with the way persons with disabilities are handled outside correctional facilities. For example, a disabled person who can no longer live alone safely may hire an aide to come into his or her home, move in with someone else, or move to an assisted living, intermediate, or long-term care facility. Changes in status typically represent a progression rather than a jump, for example, from independent living to long-term care, or could involve movement back and forth among various levels of assistance. Within the correctional system, options mirror those found in the community.[11]

Facilities should emphasize mainstreaming and segregate as a last resort, except for the severely mentally ill and the acutely ill. Even then, services should be provided so that persons with disabilities or illnesses have an equal opportunity to benefit from programming.

Because of budgetary constraints, clustering of inmates with special-needs offenders appears to be an option that many correctional systems are adapting. Consequently, these inmates will be housed in the same facility/complex.

■ Access and Communication

Program access, which usually refers to architectural or design barriers, is also a significant concern when dealing with special-needs inmates. Inaccessibility of facilities is not justification for denying programs, services, or activities. Although the ADA does require accessibility in new construction and alterations to existing buildings, it does not require that all existing facilities be modified to the new standard. Alternate methods of program delivery can satisfy the law's requirements in many cases if the program, service, or activity can be brought to the offender.

Universal design should be considered for all new construction so that ADA and applicable standards for persons with disabilities can be met. Universal design means that the construction is built to meet ADA standards so that structural changes will not be needed later so that the inmate can age in the same location. For the community, universal design means that the building design employs features that let the space grow and contract with changes in needs and lifestyles. Examples of universal design include wider doors, ramps instead of stairs, higher commode seats, flapper levers on sinks instead of knobs, and heavier building material so that grab bars or railings might be installed later if needed. Universal design allows far greater flexibility in all aspects of programming in the present and the future. Although universal design is initially more expensive, it costs less over time as modifications are easier and not as expensive to implement.

Communication is a factor in program access. Communication with special-needs offenders should be as effective as it is with other inmates. Examples of ways to enhance communications include auxiliary aids for inmates who are deaf or have hearing or speech impairments include telecommunication devices for the deaf (TDDs), communication boards, and assistive listening devices. Written notes could also be effective for short or routine communications. Certified sign language interpreters should be accessible on either a volunteer or a contract basis. Staff members could also be trained as interpreters.

Audiotapes and books in Braille should be available for inmates with vision impairments. Signs in Braille throughout the facility would enhance communications and eliminate confusion. Other adaptations could be large-print memoranda, talking directly to the offender at eye level (if not a security risk), and lowering pitch rather than talking louder.

Program and Activity Availability

Whether an inmate is assigned to a specialized unit or a modified living space in the general population, programs, services, and activities must be available. Again, the program, service, or activity may need to be brought to the inmate rather than the inmate going to the specific location. For instance, certain prison industry tasks, such as folding or packaging items, might be performed on the unit rather than at the prison industries location. If other inmates are offered work assignments involving pay or the possibility of sentence reduction, then the same must be available to inmates with special needs. If boot camps and work release programs are offered, modified or alternate programs should be designed for special-needs offenders. If the education area is inaccessible, then a tutor could come to the living unit. Staff must learn to think "outside the box," while still keeping security foremost in the design of individualized programs. Staff should also consider involving special-needs inmates in the design process, as these inmates best know their own capabilities.

Partnerships with other federal, state, and local agencies should be developed to provide better and more suitable programs and activities. Because reentry starts the day the person comes into the institution, correctional agencies need to be proactive to ensure an inmate's successful return to the community.

Depending on the severity of their illness, mentally ill inmates may require segregation in a specialized unit. Where the unit is under the auspices of medical, psychiatric, or corrections professionals, the institution should provide a liaison to ensure that sound correctional practices are followed. Frequently, a medical or human services professional and a correctional staff member will manage the unit together.

The major focus in such units is therapy, whether medical, psychological, or a combination of both. The emphasis is on returning the inmate to a state of wellness. As inmates progress, they may be returned to the general population either by participating in programs and work activities or by moving to a unit that provides transitional care.

Developmentally disabled inmates may also require placement in a specialized unit. Again, specialized staff will provide programming in concert with correctional staff. Because a major focus must be on the ability to function independently, daily living or survival skills will be central, resulting in activities that may seem out of place in a correctional environment. Such activities might include cooking, shopping, or doing laundry.

On the basis of the level of functioning, inmates might stay in specialized units until their release from the correctional facility. As with all special-needs offenders, continuity of services must be provided as the inmates move back into the community. Partnerships with community agencies for mentally ill offenders will provide needed services in the institution as well as a seamless delivery of services for offenders transitioning into the community.

■ Classification Considerations

During classification, the dangerousness and mental stability of inmates are evaluated, and usually, persons with similar characteristics are sent to similar locations. Most classification systems consider risk factors such as prior and current convictions, escapes or attempted escapes, length of sentence, and institutional adjustment. Age, educational level, history of substance abuse, and history of violence may also be considered.

A provision for override allows staff to factor in information such as medical and mental health conditions and to change the custody and security levels of the inmate to accommodate these conditions. These override decisions should be made on a case-by-case basis and should place the inmate in the least restrictive custody possible. For example, inmates in wheelchairs should not automatically be placed in a medical unit but should be placed where they could best function, such as a regular housing unit on the ground floor with full access to all programs and services in the facility. An inmate who is suicidal or psychotic should be placed in an appropriate specialized unit for treatment until it is determined that he or she can return to general population or a step-down unit. Classification decisions must not be made solely on the basis of a disability or special need, but it should be among the many factors considered.

■ Housing Accommodation

Many special-needs offenders will need special housing and programming. Inmates with mental illnesses, like those with acute medical concerns, may need to be admitted to a specialized unit and the intake process completed there or deferred until a later time. Special-needs inmates retained in intake should be housed on the ground level near the officers' station or in a monitored observation cell. Some type of identification (such as red reflective tape) should be placed on the cell door or at eye level and about a foot from the floor to denote that assistance is required should the facility need to be evacuated. Medical or human services staff should be assigned to monitor these inmates and provide necessary services.

Alternate types of aids may need to be provided. For example, a white cane used by an inmate with a visual impairment is considered a weapon in a correctional facility and could be replaced with a collapsible one if it is consistent with the security level of the facility. To provide for individuals with physical limitations, the institutions should ensure that wheelchairs are accessible throughout the unit or have an alternate plan for providing various services.

■ Special Facilities

Physical plant modifications will probably be necessary for older construction. Modifications include lowered storage lockers, booster seats on commodes, handheld shower heads, bath chairs, and tables that allow a person in a wheelchair to roll close to the table. Blackboards can be hung vertically instead of horizontally to allow accessibility by inmates in wheelchairs. Lower water coolers, bulletin boards, and door levers, in addition to telephones with volume controls, specialized door closure systems or automatic doors, and roll-in showers help provide independence as well as accessibility. Air-conditioning may also be needed because many special-needs inmates are on psychotropic medications, and overheating can cause medical complications.

For the visually impaired, colors need to be distinct so that a person can tell the difference between the wall and the floor, the steps and the riser, and the wall and the door. Rooms, cubicles, and beds should be marked with reflective tape to denote assistance is needed for evacuation.

Scheduling can also improve access. A separate meal shift can be established for special-needs inmates who either need more time or assistance to eat or who need to be segregated from the rest of the population to prevent victimization. The same rationale should hold true for the amount of time allowed for moving from one location to another, such as from a living unit to a work location or to medical services, or for completing a task such as cleaning a living area.

Before locking up a special-needs inmate, medical staff should be consulted about what, if any, requirements must be met. These requirements may range from no restrictions to an order for no placement in a segregation unit. If no segregation is ordered, alternate arrangements such as placing a deadlock on the present cell with appropriate, documented visual checks should suffice.

■ Special Support

Assistance may be required to complete activities of daily living or, in some instances, the task will have to be completed by other inmates or staff. Other inmates can work as caregivers or assistants. These jobs should have clear descriptions specifying that caregivers do not have authority over the special-needs inmates. Inmate caregivers should be chosen as carefully as staff. Training should be provided before beginning work with special-needs offenders and should be offered on a scheduled basis. All inmates who assist should be directed by staff and should consult with specified staff on a daily basis.

■ Hospice and Palliative Care

Just as hospice and palliative services are becoming more common in the community, the same is happening in the correctional system. Usually, terminally ill inmates are placed in a facility with the highest level of medical care available. Treatment of the terminally ill concentrates on palliative care—keeping the patient comfortable and pain-free—instead of curing the disease.

Hospice programs utilizing other offenders as aides focus on providing spiritual, emotional, and supportive care to the persons receiving end-of-life care. Careful screening, training, and monitoring of hospice workers are vital to the success of the program. This interdisciplinary program involves commitment and support from all levels of the institution to be effective. As with staff working with specialized programming, the inmate workers should be provided postincident debriefing/counseling. It is difficult for all involved in the care and subsequent death of another person.

■ Reentry

Reentry to the community begins the day the offender enters the correctional system. Efforts should focus on returning a productive person to the community. This is difficult to accomplish for any offender and will probably be more difficult for a special-needs offender. The focus for the special-needs population is ensuring that their needs are met adequately.

As outlined in the National Institute of Corrections' *Effective Prison Mental Health Services*, discharge planning should center on housing, medical and mental health services, employment, family support, and enrollment or reinstatement of benefits including Medicare, Medicaid, and veterans' benefits.[12] Whenever possible, community agencies should serve as partners to provide services during incarceration and then become the primary service provider upon release. Detailed planning for provision of services should start at least 6–8 months before the special-needs offender is released. Multiagency staffing is very productive and results in better reentry for the inmate as appropriate links and services are secured before release.

■ Staff Development

Education, training, and staff development are integral parts of corrections. The National Congress on Penitentiary and Reformatory Discipline held in Cincinnati, Ohio, in 1870 adopted a Declaration of Principles that proclaimed that "special training as well as high quality of head and heart, is required to make a good prison or reformatory officer."[13] Although preemployment and annual training are required for correctional staff, little training focuses on working with special-needs offenders. In order to work effectively with this group, all involved staff should be provided with relevant training and development. Training components should include but not be limited to the following areas as they relate to special needs:

- Familiarization and sensitization techniques
- Educational and medical information on various special needs
- Techniques, tips, and strategies for managing special-needs inmates more effectively

The professionally trained staff who work with special-needs offenders (particularly with persons with mental illness) have mandated training hours in order to maintain licensure and certification in addition to the agency, accreditation, and statutory requirements that all correctional staff must meet. These professionally trained staff are a good source for providing training for the other correctional staff. Security staff should be able to learn techniques for managing special-needs inmates, such as using belly chains instead of handcuffing behind the back for heart patients, transferring an inmate from a wheelchair to a bed, and communicating with inmates with hearing or sight impairments.

Other resources for training include state agencies, medical facilities, advocacy and special interest groups, and other providers of services. Additionally, training plans from other correctional facilities might be available through the National Institute of Corrections' Resource Library or from the facilities themselves. Staff should be encouraged to participate in professional and special interest groups in the community for education and professional growth as well as for networking opportunities.

Correctional staff should also inform the community about special-needs offenders. Contacts and partnerships should be developed with the appropriate groups to provide services during incarceration and after reentry and to ensure that information is provided to both inmates and service providers. Intake forms in corrections should be revised to collect the information required by community service providers, especially those managed by state and federal agencies.

■ Tips for Working with Special-Needs Offenders

- Move more slowly than normal. Sudden movements can frighten special-needs inmates or make them think they are being attacked.
- Talk directly to the inmates. Those with hearing or speech disabilities may need to read lips.
- Address conversation to the inmates. Do not talk around them as though they are children or invisible.
- Talk at face level. If a longer conversation is indicated, either sit or stoop down to eye level with inmates in wheelchairs.
- Speak clearly, in a low tone. Do not talk loudly or in a shrill voice.
- Use terms that the inmates can understand.
- Simplify instructions. Give one direction at a time to avoid confusion. Sometimes it helps to put instructions in writing.

- Establish and maintain a familiar routine. Do things in the same sequence—get up, straighten cell, have breakfast, go to pill line, and so on.
- Talk in positive terms. Talk about what can be done, not what cannot be done.
- Be patient. Allow extra time to complete tasks.
- Be flexible and creative when providing programs, services, and activities.
- Use large type so that the font is easier to read.
- Utilize the public address system for announcing changes and to read memoranda concerning changes.
- Ensure that inmates eat properly. Poor nutrition can lead to other problems.

■ Conclusion

The growing number of special-needs inmates and the regulations outlined in the ADA are having a great effect on the U.S. correctional system. In addition to making physical plant modifications or building new construction, correctional administrators will need to lead their staffs and facilities toward compliance with all provisions relevant to federal and state laws and ADA and American Correctional Association standards. Policies, procedures, and practices may need to be altered to provide appropriate programs, services, and activities to special-needs offenders.

Resources are available through local, state, and federal organizations and agencies. Staff should partner with local providers so that necessary services can be offered to special-needs persons while incarcerated and upon reentry. Line staff must be selected carefully, as not everyone is suited for working with special-needs offenders. These staff members must be provided the specialized training required to provide care for these inmates. A successful correctional program for special-needs offenders takes commitment from all levels—administrative, program services, and security—as well as the community at large.

Chapter Resources

DISCUSSION QUESTIONS

1. What types of physical and mental disabilities are present in the inmate population and to what extent?
2. In general terms, what does the ADA require in terms of managing special-needs offenders?
3. What measures can be taken to effectively manage inmates with special needs?
4. What are the advantages and disadvantages of separating or mainstreaming special-needs offenders?
5. What issues arise when special-needs offenders face reentry into the community?

ADDITIONAL RESOURCES

American Correctional Association. (2003). *Standards for adult correctional institutions* (4th ed.). Lanham, MD: Author.

Anno, B., Graham, C., Lawrence, J. E., & Shansky, R. (2004). *Correctional health care: Addressing the needs of elderly, chronically ill, and terminally ill inmates.* Washington, DC: National Institute of Corrections.

Hills, H., Siegfried, C., & Ickowitz, A. (2004). *Effective prison mental health services: Guidelines to expand and improve treatment.* Washington, DC: National Institute of Corrections.

NOTES

1. American Correctional Association. (n.d.). *Policies and resolutions.* Retrieved September 2011, from http://www.aca.org/
2. American Correctional Association. (n.d.). *Policies and resolutions.* Retrieved September 2011, from http://www.aca.org/
3. Anno, B. (1991). *Prison health care: Guidelines for the management of an adequate delivery system.* Washington, DC: National Institute of Corrections.
4. Schoeneberger, M. (2006). *Prison treatment for the female offender with co-occurring disorders: What is and what could be?* Workshop at 130th Congress of Corrections, Charlotte, NC.
5. Rubin, P., & McCampbell, S. (1995). *The Americans with disabilities act and criminal justice: Mental disabilities and corrections.* Research in Action. Washington, DC: National Institute of Justice.
6. Morton, J. (1992). *An administrative overview of the older offender.* Washington, DC: National Institute of Corrections.
7. GRACE Project. (2001). *Incarceration of the terminally ill: Current practices in the United States.* Alexandria, VA: Volunteers of America.
8. *Assisted Living News.* (n.d.). Retrieved January 10, 2012, from http://allassistedlivinghomes.com/assisted-living-news
9. Gardner, W., Gracber, J., & Machkovitz, S. (1998). Treatment of offenders with mental retardation. In R. Wellstein (Ed.), *Treatment of offenders with mental disorders.* New York, NY: Guilford Press.

10. Sieleni, B. (2011, December). Addressing the mental health crisis in corrections. *Corrections Today*, 10–12.
11. Anno, B., Graham, C., Lawrence, J. E., & Shansky, R. (2004). *Correctional health care: Addressing the needs of elderly, chronically ill, and terminally ill inmates*. Washington, DC: National Institute of Corrections.
12. Hills, H., Siegfried, C., & Ickowitz, A. (2004). *Effective prison mental health services: Guidelines to expand and improve treatment*. Washington, DC: National Institute of Corrections.
13. American Correctional Association. (n.d.). *Declaration of principles*. Retrieved September 17, 2007, from http://www.aca.org/pastpresentfuture/principles.asp

Offenders with Specialized Needs

PART VI

YOU ARE THE ADMINISTRATOR
■ Legal Oversight

Inmate Phil McKenzie was determined to get out of the segregation unit of the prison at all costs. He cut his arms and legs and tried to hang himself with the tube from his breathing machine (provided to address his sleep apnea). When that didn't work, he broke off a sharp piece of metal from the machine, which he first used to slice his neck and then swallowed, in hopes of causing internal bleeding. Corrections staff managed to save McKenzie and released him from isolation to get him much-needed medical and mental health treatment. McKenzie had a long history of depression, and when he returned to segregation 5 weeks later, he hanged himself, thereby becoming the 13th inmate in the state to commit suicide in less than 2½ years.

Inmate advocates have filed suit in federal court, claiming that McKenzie and 18 other inmates who committed suicide or attempted suicide were driven to harm themselves by the conditions they endured in isolation units in prisons around the country. Most states operate segregation units, though some have recently reacted to lawsuits by no longer putting mentally ill inmates in such units. Others have implemented more frequent monitoring of the inmates, increased training of staff, and removed fixtures that could be used for hangings.

Around the country, department of corrections staff are struggling with how to treat violent inmates who are out of control and need to be segregated from others for their own safety, as well as the safety of other inmates and staff. However, for the mentally ill inmates who fall into this category, placement in segregation (which often results in being locked in a cell for 23 hours a day with just 1 hour for shower and recreation in an outdoor cage) can amount to a death sentence.

The expert retained by the state to examine Mckenzie's case concluded that "confining suicidal inmates to their cell for 24 hours a day only enhances isolation and is antitherapeutic." The department of corrections vowed to adopt all of the resulting recommendations, including better inmate assessments, better supervision and monitoring of inmates, and better officer training.

- How can prison and jail administrators deal with mentally ill and special-needs offenders?
- Are segregation units ethical and safe for mentally ill inmates?
- How can specialized inmate programming help offenders like McKenzie?
- What standard should the courts employ to determine cases like this one?

Source: P. Belluck, "Mentally Ill Inmates at Risk in Isolation, Lawsuit Says," *New York Times*, March 9, 2007, available at http://www.nytimes.com/2007/03/09/us/09prison.html?ex=1331096400&en=7b9093960e12d25d&ei=5124&partner=permalink&exprod=permalink, accessed October 10, 2007.

Women Offenders

Joann B. Morton and Samantha Hauptman

CHAPTER OBJECTIVES

- Provide an historical overview of the treatment of women in correctional institutions.

- Describe extent of female crime, characteristics of incarcerated women, and how they differ from male offenders.

- Identify some innovative programs and best practices to improve services for women offenders as well as sources for more information.

■ Introduction

Women offenders are vastly outnumbered by male offenders and are typically ignored by most governmental policy makers and correctional administrators. Although women offenders share many substantive issues with male offenders, they have a number of unique needs and problems that are not the same as those of their male counterparts. This requires that prisons for women be different in form and substance from facilities for males.

Meeting the needs of women offenders can be achieved by implementing what are known as "gender-responsive" programs and services. Being gender responsive means implementing policies, programs, and procedures developed specifically to meet the needs, problems, and strengths of women offenders, not just superimposing programs designed for men on women's facilities. Implementing gender-responsive programs and services strengthens the management and security of women's correctional facilities and, if operated in compliance with research-based principles, should also improve the chances of women leading more successful, crime-free lives upon release.

■ History of the Treatment of Women in Correctional Facilities

Although the number of female offenders has increased over time, most correctional systems continue to operate several facilities for men and one or two for women. These facilities are typically smaller and more complex than male facilities, because they house all levels of custody and include the full array of functions from intake to release incorporated throughout the male system.

The treatment of women offenders has evolved over time and continues to evolve today. Attitudes toward and beliefs about women offenders are a direct reflection of how society views women in general and change as modifications take place in the larger society. These changes are slow and not uniform across the country. For example, a basic thing such as complete separation of male and female inmates is still a problem in some jurisdictions, particularly in local jails, and can result in abuse and less programming and services for women.

From colonial times until the mid-1800s, few women broke the law. Those who did were considered "fallen women" and thought to be beyond help. Because few in power cared what happened to them, women were thrown in the same cells with men, where they were regularly victimized and suffered a host of indignities.

Following the Civil War, interest in the plight of the less fortunate, including female offenders, grew, particularly in the northeastern part of the United States. Reformers, most of whom were upper-class women, began to believe it was their moral duty to save female offenders. Lobbying by reformers, fueled by a series of scandals involving sexual and other abuses of incarcerated women, increased the demand for separate prisons for women. In 1870, the National Congress on Penitentiary and Reformatory Discipline (which later became the American Correctional Association [ACA]) endorsed the concept of separate facilities for women, and the first facilities for women opened in Indiana (1873), Massachusetts (1877), and New York (1901).[1] Even with the implementation of separate housing, women continued to receive inadequate care with regard to health needs, offense, age, gender, and other factors. Also, women were not given opportunities to develop skills to help them obtain the jobs that were available for them in the community upon release.

Reformers then began to call for more humane institutions better designed and programmed to meet the roles of women at the time. Because women were believed to be the keepers of family values whose sphere of influence was the home, the reformatory model emphasized a more home-like environment or domestic atmosphere called the "cottage plan" or "cottage system." The goal of programs in these facilities was reformation, not punishment. Even with a nationwide push for this approach, by 1933, only 17 states had, for the most part, adopted the women's reformatory model as the basic design for their female facilities and programs.[1] Some states continued to keep women, particularly minority women, in male facilities until modern times.[2]

By the 1940s, many of innovations established under the reformatory movement were abandoned, and women offenders were forgotten by the criminal justice system. This changed with the growth of the civil and women's rights movements of the 1960s and 1970s, when deplorable conditions in prisons in general and women's facilities in particular gained national attention. In addition to poor conditions of confinement in women's facilities, there were serious disparities between the programs provided for men and those available for women. Several federal lawsuits and threats of court intervention finally spurred a number of changes in women's institutions.

Not all of these changes were positive because many confused the concept of *comparable* or *equal* programming as meaning that women's facilities should be the *same* as male institutions.[3] This resulted in many facilities for women becoming more custody oriented.[4] As the number of women in prison grew, primarily as a result of the war on drugs and the "get tough" changes in federal and state laws, there was tremendous pressure to treat women the same as men. This treatment in many cases made women more hostile and more difficult to manage.[5] Some carried the concept of sameness to extremes, like the Arizona sheriff who declared he was an "equal opportunity incarcerator" and established a "volunteer" chain gang for women (p. 10).[6]

In response to these excesses, the ACA in 1986 passed its Public Correctional Policy on Female Offender Services, which called on correctional agencies to provide programs that were "equivalent" to ones for males and also to offer additional services to "meet the unique needs" women.[7] The current ACA Public Policies for Corrections are available online at https://www.aca.org/government/policyresolution/.

In the 1990s, the Prisons Division of the National Institute of Corrections (NIC) began funding grants to develop a research-based set of policies and practices designed around the specific needs of women offenders to provide a foundation for improved gender-responsive services. In 2003, a landmark study titled *Gender-Responsive Strategies: Research, Practice and Guiding Principles for Women Offenders* was completed by Barbara Bloom, Barbara Owen, and Stephanie Covington (available online at http://nicic.gov/library/018017).[8] This study provides a comprehensive research and policy base for implementing programs for women that meet their specific needs.

By 2013, a number of states including Rhode Island, Washington, and Connecticut had begun implementing gender-responsive programming, and the NIC launched a new program called Gender Informed Practice Assessment (GIPA) to help correctional systems examine their understanding of gender-responsive programming. GIPA is a tool that aids in the assessment of "correctional environments and practices for women in prison settings" and assists systems in strategic planning, training development, and program gap analysis (p. 2).[9]

Correctional administrators now have a strong research base and specific tools to help them implement gender-responsive policies, programs, and practices for women offenders. Time will tell whether they will make the commitment of resolve and resources necessary to make gender-responsive programs a reality nationwide and whether those who follow them will continue the effort.

■ Profiling Female Offenders

According to the Uniform Crime Report, of the 12,408,899 people arrested in 2011, some 25.9% were females.[10] This was an increase over 2000, when of the 9,116,967 people arrested, 2,020,780 or 22% were women or girls.[11]

The number of women convicted of a crime and sentenced to prison remains much smaller than the number of incarcerated males. For example, according to the National Bureau of Justice Statistics, men are incarcerated at a rate 14 times higher than women. In 2011, women made up only 6.7% of the state and federal prisoner population[12] compared to 6.9% in 2003.[13] Their actual numbers, however, grew from 97,491 in 2002 to 111,387 in 2011. Because most states have one or two small facilities for women, even a few additional offenders can create severe overcrowding.

The population of incarcerated women varies by state and can move up or down dramatically with the addition of only a few admissions or releases. In eight states, South Dakota, Idaho, Kentucky, Montana, West Virginia, Wyoming, Alaska, and North Dakota, at least 10% of the prison population was female. Rhode Island, North Dakota, California, and New Hampshire had the greatest decline in women in the population between 2010 and 2011, declining between 15% and 24%. In Kentucky, Alaska, and Tennessee, the population of women increased by at least 14%.[12]

On the basis of arrest and incarceration data, men are more likely to commit violent crime than are women. Men incarcerated for violent crime tend to victimize strangers. Women who commit violent crimes tend to kill or assault family members, husbands, children, or close acquaintances, usually boyfriends. This difference causes the community to view violent men as more dangerous than violent women. But the societal expectations of the proper role of women create more sensationalism and loathing of violent female offenders, particularly those who kill their children.

The involvement in abuse of both illegal and prescription drugs accounts for much of the rise in the number of women in the prison population. This increase in female criminality appears to be more closely tied to changes in government drug enforcement and incarceration policies rather than on any modification of behavior among women in society.[3]

Men and women offenders' demographic characteristics vary considerably. For example, male offenders tend to be younger than female offenders, they have someone to return to upon release, their children stay with the children's mother, they have less history of sexual or physical abuse particularly as adults, and they have fewer medical/mental health problems.

The demographic characteristics of incarcerated women have stayed relatively constant over the past 40 or so years and are summarized by Morton[3] as follows:

- Average 30 years of age and are more likely to be a minority (black or Hispanic) than white
- Grew up in a dysfunctional family and typically do not have a spouse to return to upon release
- Have children who have been displaced either before or during their mother's incarceration and who will be living with a family member, most likely the offender's mother
- Have a high school degree but limited vocational training and spotty work history, typically at minimum wage service jobs
- Have a history of sexual and/or physical abuse, often as both children and adults
- Have significant drug abuse problems and use drugs to self-medicate from the pain of trauma
- Have multiple medical problems, and many have significant mental health disorders.

Particular attention must be paid to women offenders' history of abuse. Trauma, much of which occurs in the home, is no excuse for criminal behavior, but it does put victims at risk for self-destructive behavior. Women who have been victimized are also at risk for further victimization. Female offenders' extensive history of physical and sexual abuse requires that trauma therapy become a critical component in progressive gender-responsive programming.

■ Mothers in Prison

One of the most obvious differences between male and female inmates is the woman's role as a mother. The concerns and problems surrounding child custody and related family matters have a high priority among women inmates, particularly those with minor children. Even if her relationships with her children were not ideal when she was in the community, in prison, she will miss her children and worry about what is happening to them.[3]

Giving attention to the issue of mothers in prison is important, as 62% of women in state prison report being a parent and 41% report having more than one minor child. This accounts for approximately 131,000 children. About 61% of women report living with their children immediately prior to incarceration.[14] It is also of concern because many children do suffer "poor emotional health and well-being and lack of physical care and custody" while their mothers are in prison (p. 472).[15] Such problems put these children at risk of second-generational criminal behavior.

Cognizant of the mother–child relationship issues, most corrections facilities provide for children's visitation. However, given the dysfunctional family environment experienced by many women in prison, programs on parenting and other aspects of working with children are needed. One such program is a cooperative effort between specific correctional facilities and the Girl Scouts of America called "Girl Scouts Beyond Bars." This program is available in some jurisdictions and is particularly helpful in teaching offenders parenting and developing positive relationships with children. The girls meet once a month with their mothers and the other weeks with their troop. The mothers meet weekly to learn about parenting and developing activities to do with their children.

Pregnant women present another set of problems that need to be addressed. Some jurisdictions struggle to provide even the basic prenatal, delivery, and postpartum medical care that is essential for the health of the mother and baby. The provision of care is exacerbated by the fact that many women received no medical care in the community prior to coming to prison. Also, many women have high-risk pregnancies because of the abuse they have experienced, drug use, or other lifestyle issues. Questions also arise about how to provide a safe environment during the final stages of pregnancy and whether the mother can keep her baby in prison.

To address the question of prenatal and postpartum environment, the Federal Bureau of Prisons established a program for expectant mothers known as MINT (Mothers and Infants in Transition). In this program, selected mothers in minimum security status can transfer to a community-based facility 2 months prior to delivery. It allows women to be in a supportive environment during the latter stages of their pregnancy, and they can stay approximately 3 months following the delivery of their child for postpartum adjustment. They cannot keep the babies with them but are encouraged to maintain contact with them until release.[16]

The New York Department of Corrections has been a leader in allowing newborn babies to stay with their mothers. The New York Reformatory for Women at Bedford Hill has housed a nursery since 1901.[1] In that program, women who give birth while in prison, subject to security clearance, can keep their babies with them for 1 year. The babies live in the cells with their mothers, who are responsible for their care. Parenting and other skills are taught to mothers, and they have the satisfaction of knowing their child is safe and cared for during this period. It allows the mother and child to bond and works best if the mother and child can be released together.

Over the years, other states established similar programs but abolished them depending on agency leadership and resources. Some states even passed legislation prohibiting babies from being kept in prison. According to Maureen Buell of the NIC, seven states, West Virginia, Nebraska, Washington, Ohio, Indiana, Massachusetts, and Illinois, in addition to New York, had nurseries in their women's facilities in 2013.

■ Sexual Misconduct

Concerned about charges of widespread sexual abuse in jails and prisons nationwide, Congress passed the far-reaching Prison Rape Elimination Act (PREA) of 2003 (available online at http://nicic.gov/prea). PREA addresses the problems of sexual abuse (including sexual assault and rape) of anyone incarcerated in federal, state, or local facilities and covers acts by inmates, staff, volunteers, or any other person who might come into contact with the offender. Staff or others who violate PREA or similar state statutes face dismissal, fines, or imprisonment, and can be required to register as sex offenders. Civil charges can also be brought, and a staff member or other individual can be required to personally pay punitive damages directly to the inmate. Correctional agencies are required to report data relative to sexual assaults, and prosecution of those accused of sexual assault is becoming more common. Correctional agencies can also be found liable for failing to train and properly supervise staff and for not conducting comprehensive background checks.

This legislation is particularly important for women's institutions because sexual assault and rape of female offenders have been long-standing problems throughout the country.[17] In fact, women are more likely than males to be victims of sexual assault by both other inmates and staff.[18] To combat this problem, the NIC has designed and implemented a training program to address sexual assault specifically in women's facilities and encourages all staff working with female offenders to participate in such courses.

■ Developing Gender-Responsive Programming

To properly develop appropriate gender-responsive services for women offenders, it is essential to understand the concept of gender, its effect on society's views of masculinity and femininity, and how it governs what are seen as appropriate roles for men and women in today's society. These roles have certainly changed over time and continue to evolve much more rapidly today than they did in the past. For example, only a few years ago, the idea of women serving as wardens or correctional officers in male correctional facilities was considered unthinkable. Now women working in these capacities are commonplace.

There is little doubt that women offenders differ significantly from male offenders in both their personal histories and their pathways to crime.[19] These differences are especially evident in their gender-based experiences relating to socioeconomic status, domestic violence, sexual abuse, education, and employment, and in frequently having sole responsibility for dependent children.[20] To implement gender-responsive programming, correctional systems must take a holistic approach. They must create an environment in which carefully selected staff implement programs with content based on the reality of women offender's lives and attempt to precisely address their unique strengths and challenges.[21] Programs should also be systemwide, including community corrections, and must have strong support from top policy makers and administrators.

Changing a correctional organization is difficult, but in 2002, New Mexico began a new women-centered approach to its programming for offenders returning to the community that appears to meet many of the requirements for a successful transformation. Governor Bill Richardson made "effective management of female offenders" (p. 64)[22] a priority at the New Mexico Corrections Department and supported a gender-responsive approach that made an "effort to find sustainable and effective ways [to] keep women out of the prison system and from returning to prison" (p. 64).[22] Carr[22] summarized the approach that includes several components designed to improve women's lives and aid them in successfully reentering the community and reuniting with their families, including:

- Gender-specific case management/programming
- A four-phase therapeutic community residential program focusing on female-specific issues and relapse planning
- A long-term transitional program building employment and social skills
- Reentry planning that both works with the offender to find community resources and services and helps develop a feasible parole plan
- Community work release that also provides job skills training and, in some cases, continued postrelease employment

- Visitation initiatives such as therapeutic visits, overnight visits for incarcerated mothers, telecast family reunification opportunities, and even providing gas cards to facilitate family visits
- Access to the New Mexico Women's Recovery Academy (http://www.cecintl.com/facilities_rr_nm_002.html) for women reentering the community with a variety of needs such as education, job training, victim treatment, and substance abuse and mental illness support and counseling services. There is also a halfway house for women who may need additional help transitioning into the community.

This and other efforts to implement gender-responsive programs for female offenders, if successful, will benefit the offenders, their families, staff who work with them, and the community at large.

■ Conclusion

Correctional agencies today face many challenges, not the least of which is developing and implementing gender-responsive services for women offenders at all levels of the criminal justice system. Real changes are being made slowly around the country as a more research-based approach is finding both success and support in the field. Change in corrections is, however, notoriously slow, and it will take a systemic approach to implementing gender-responsive policies, programs, practices, and services at all levels of the criminal justice system. Ultimately, effectively addressing the specific needs of women offenders must consider "a gender-responsive approach [including] comprehensive services that take into account the content and context of women's lives . . . [with programming that reflects] the larger social issues of poverty, abuse, and race and gender inequalities, as well as individual factors that impact women" (p. 17).[21] It is not enough to provide women offenders with the tools they need to be successful; we must also provide them with "a sustained continuum of treatment, recovery, and support services" (p. 17)[21] that can effectively keep them from coming into and from staying out of prison.

Chapter Resources

DISCUSSION QUESTIONS

1. Describe how attitudes toward women in general have influenced treatment of women offenders over time.
2. Discuss the differences in criminality between male and female offenders.
3. List the seven characteristics of women offenders and how they might influence programs for incarcerated women.
4. Define what is meant by "gender-responsive" programs and services for women offenders.
5. Identify what is required to provide gender-responsive programming and give an example of how one state has done it.

ADDITIONAL RESOURCES

GOVERNMENT

The NIC has a number of initiatives directed toward expanding gender-responsive services. In addition to the GIPA, the NIC provides several training and technical assistance programs. Accessible through the NIC Learning Center (http://nic.learn.com/learncenter.asp?id=178409&sessionid=3-43FE93BF-0A40-402C-9EA9-13227BCD6978&page=1), there are a variety of comprehensive e-courses, webinars, virtual instructor–led training, and even classroom training sessions on a variety of subjects available to corrections professionals, including PREA and working with women offenders. These resources provide the most current information available and enable the wide dissemination of information that can enhance existing programs or aid in the development of new ones.

More recently, new federal initiatives focusing more on gender-responsive programming and recognizing the unique needs of women offenders are available on the Internet. The NIC has partnered with the Bureau of Justice Assistance to establish the National Resource Center on Justice-Involved Women (see http://cjinvolvedwomen.org/), which serves as a resource for a variety of professionals who work with women offenders in the criminal justice system. Resources include technical assistance; conferences, training, and meeting announcements; webinars; presentation links; guidebooks; reports and statistics; links to Internet resources; and a variety of other sources of current and innovative gender-responsive materials.

Another resource that links to effective gender-responsive resources is the Center for Effective Public Policy (http://www.cepp.com/women-offenders), which provides links to "Noteworthy Projects" and current gender-responsive products and resources. Some state agencies also have program descriptions on their websites. Check yours and surrounding states.

ASSOCIATIONS

The American Correctional Association (www.aca.org) provides model policies and accreditation standards for correctional programs nationwide including a policy on women offenders and some standards specific to women and girls. It also sponsors national conferences twice a year to address the latest trends and programs for offenders and is a link to other related organizations.

The Association of Programs for Female Offenders (www.apfonews.org), an affiliate of ACA, is an organization for those working with or interested in adult and juvenile female offenders to network and addresses the needs of their clients. It cosponsors with a different state biennially a national conference devoted specifically to programming for women and girls in the correctional system.

Women's Prison Association (www.wpaonline.org) is the oldest service and advocacy group in the United States. It operates a number of programs for women offenders in the New York City area.

COLLEGES AND UNIVERSITIES

University and college faculty are the source of much of the study and development that has been done on gender-responsive services for women offenders. In addition to the sources listed below, for example, see the work done at the University of Cincinnati by Dr. Patricia Voorhis and her associates on needs and risk assessment tools based on studies of women offenders.

REFERENCES

1. Hawkes, M. Q. (1994). *Excellent effect: The Edna Mahan story*. Lanham, MD: American Correctional Association.
2. Freedman, E. B. (1981). *Their sisters' keepers: Women's prison reform in America, 1830–1930*. Ann Arbor, MI: The University of Michigan Press.
3. Morton, J. B. (2004). *Working with women offenders in correctional institutions*. Lanham, MD: American Correctional Association.
4. Strickland, K. (1976). *Correctional institutions for women in the U.S.* Lexington, MA: Lexington Books.
5. Kruttschnitt, C., Gartner, R., & Miller, A. (2000). Doing her own time? Women's responses to prison in the context of the old and the new penology. *Criminology, 38*(3), 681–717.
6. Sharp, S. (2003). *The incarcerated woman: Rehabilitative programming in women's prisons*. Upper Saddle River, NJ: Prentice Hall.
7. Morton, J. B. (1991). *Public policy for corrections* (2nd ed.). Lanham, MD: American Correctional Association.
8. Bloom, B., Owen, B., & Covington, S. (2003). *Gender-responsive strategies: Research, practice and guiding principles for women offenders*. Washington, DC: U.S. Department of Justice, National Institute of Corrections, NIC 018017.
9. Buell, M. (2010). *NIC's women offender initiative: New research in action*. Retrieved from https://www.aca.org/research/pdf/ResearchNotes_Dec2010.pdf
10. U.S. Federal Bureau of Investigation. (2012). *Crime in the United States: Uniform crime reports, 2011*. Washington, DC: U.S. Department of Justice.
11. U.S. Federal Bureau of Investigation. (2001). *Crime in the United States: Uniform crime reports, 2000*. Washington, DC: U.S. Department of Justice.
12. Carson, E. A., & Sabol, W. J. (2012). *Prisoners in 2011*. Washington, DC: U.S. Department of Justice, Bureau of Justice Statistics.
13. Harrison, P. M., & Karberg, J. C. (2003). *Prisoners and jail inmates at mid-year 2002*. Washington, DC: U.S. Department of Justice, Bureau of Justice Statistics.
14. Glaze, L. E., & Maruschack, L. M. (2008). *Parents in prison and their minor children*. Bureau of Justice Statistics Special Report, NCJ 222984. Retrieved from http://bjs.ojp.usdoj.gov/content/pub/pdf/pptmc.pdf
15. Seymour, C. (1998). Children with parents in prison: Child welfare policy, program, and practice issues. *Child Welfare, 77*(5), 469–493.

16. Gaseau, M. (Ed.). (2000). Mother and child bonding behind bars. *The Corrections Connections News Letter.* Retrieved from http://www.corrections.com/news/feature/index.html

17. Human Rights Watch, Women's Rights Project. (1996). *All too familiar: Sexual abuse of women in the U.S. state prisons.* New York, NY: Human Rights Watch.

18. Beck, A., & Guerino, P. (2011). *Sexual victimization reported by adult correctional authorities, 2007–2008.* Washington, DC: U.S. Department of Justice, National Institute of Corrections, NCJ 231172.

19. Belknap, J. (2007). *The invisible woman: Gender, crime, and justice* (3rd ed.). Belmont, CA: Thompson Wadsworth.

20. Bloom, B., Owen, B., & Covington, S. (2004). Women offenders and the gendered effects of public policy. *Review of Policy Research, 21*(1), 31–48.

21. Covington, S., & Bloom, B. E. (2006). Gender-responsive treatment and services in correctional settings. *Women and Therapy, 29*(3/4), 9–33.

22. Carr, H. (2007). A woman-centered approach for female offenders in New Mexico. *Corrections Today, 69*(4), 64–66.

Sex Offenders

Gilbert L. Ingram and Peter M. Carlson

CHAPTER 17

CHAPTER OBJECTIVES

- Provide examples of different types of sex offenders.
- Explain why the identification of sex offenders is often a difficult task.
- Outline components of a viable sex offender treatment program.

Any thought of living near or working with a sex offender represents a nightmare to many in American society. Sex offenders have molested, raped, or otherwise victimized women, girls, men, or boys and are part of the dark underside of society that many do not comprehend or even want to acknowledge. Whenever a horrible sexually related crime is reported, the public outcry may be deafening. The usual response to sexual atrocities is to demand harsh justice in the form of a court sanction that involves significant prison time. In short, society typically loathes the sex offender more than other social outcasts who have been convicted of any one of a multitude of equally outrageous crimes.

The difficulties inherent in dealing with sex offenders are then passed on to the correctional setting. Because of fear of failure, lack of resources, or lack of commitment, some managers avoid the issue by not officially acknowledging sex offenders as a group requiring special attention. This tactic is shortsighted, unprofessional, and even unethical. It should never be an option.

■ Magnitude of the Problem

Sex offenders have attracted tremendous negative publicity during the past few years. Highly visible sex crimes have always generated an inordinate amount of public interest, but the recent intense media attention has created a public rage unprecedented in correctional history. Because sex offenders have no visible supporters, politicians feel free to clamp down hard, calling for longer sentences and lifelong public identification after release from prison.

Some people say the prevalence of sex offenses is growing, but valid data are not available. Many factors contribute to the lack of highly reliable data:

1. Embarrassment, fear, or self-blame on the part of victims deter many from ever reporting these acts.
2. Authorities, unless compelled to act or under unusual circumstances, frequently overlook sexual behavior that the public seems to condone. (Some sexual acts technically violate the law but are considered acceptable behavior when they take place between consenting adults in private settings.)
3. Even if arrested, a large number of sex offenders are not legally convicted after arrest or plead guilty to a lesser charge.
4. Only convicted sex offenders appear in sex crime statistics.

The collection of reliable data has been even more complicated in recent years. For example, the public spotlight on abuse by family members and a generally more supportive environment for reporting victimization have encouraged more people to step forward. In addition, the definition of sexual offenses remains a continuing problem; behavior deemed unacceptable in one state may be acceptable in another. However, there are enough statistics available to conclude that the problem is fairly extensive. In 2010, the latest data available from the FBI indicated that there were 84,767 forcible rapes reported in the United States,[1] and the National Center for Missing and Exploited Children reported that as of 2011, there were 739,853 registered sex offenders.[2]

Although there is a lack of agreement among researchers, a review of data does not reflect that this group recidivates at a greater rate than criminals who have served time for other offenses. However, data generally indicate that certain categories of sex offenders are more likely than other types of criminals to repeat their offenses (see **Table 17-1**). Recidivism varies among different types of sex offenders, but it is often related to specific characteristics of the offender and the offense. For example, federal studies confirm that rapists were 10.5 times more likely to be rearrested for rape than were other released prisoners.[3] A study of 54 rapists who were released before 1983 found that after 4 years, 28% had new sex offense convictions and 43% had a conviction for a violent offense. Studies of child molesters reveal relatively equal rates of reoffending. Extrafamilial molesters were followed up for an average of 6 years; during this period, 31% had a reconviction for a second sexual offense.[4] This is only a sampling of many generally accepted studies that

TABLE 17-1 **Characteristics of Sexual Offender Recidivists**

Multiple victims
Diverse victims
Victims were strangers
Juvenile sexual offenses
Multiple paraphilias
History of abuse and neglect
Long-term separations from parents
Negative relationships with their mothers
Diagnosed antisocial personality disorder
Unemployed
Substance abuse problems
Chaotic, antisocial lifestyles

Source: Center for Sex Offender Management, U.S. Department of Justice, Recidivism of Sex Offenders, available at http://www.csom.org/pubs/recidsexof.html.

confirm that deviant sex behavior is a large and continuing problem in this country. It is easy to appreciate the reluctance of some public administrators to take responsibility for managing a very unpopular group whose aberrant behavior is extremely difficult to change.

Even though successful treatment is possible, many sex offenders do repeat their inappropriate behavior after release from custody.[5] However, correctional administrators must keep in mind the greater public good. Many sex offenders may be deterred with proper intervention. Further more, it is good management practice to involve all offenders in a meaningful activity to facilitate better control of the institution and to allow better use of public resources. Because nearly all offenders will be returning to their communities, one very good reason to promote intervention for this group of offenders is that they will be someone's neighbor again in the future.

■ Basic Approach to Sex Offender Management

Each correctional situation is different, and there is no single formula for successful management. Consequently, many programs producing good results in one institution have failed completely when attempts were made to replicate them elsewhere. Differences in administrator personalities and levels of motivation as well as insufficient resources often make duplication impossible. However, certain basic management practices produce successful sex offender programs at the local, state, and federal levels. In discussing these approaches, this chapter focuses on male offenders because they are the largest concern for correctional officials. Nonetheless, it must be kept in mind that instances of sex offenses by women have been increasing.

Institutions must focus on correctly identifying sex offenders as soon as possible after incarceration. For this to occur, an efficient classification and designation process must be in place. During classification, there is no need to try to uncover the underlying psychological reasons for offenders' inappropriate sexual behavior; this information will play an integral part later during treatment.

Immediately after classification, the offender should be separated from the general population as much as possible. At a minimum, a separate area for special treatment is necessary, and if possible, a separate housing area can minimize the many adjustment problems that sex offenders typically encounter. A special housing unit for sex offenders should be placed in an institution with a progressive, open-minded administration that can handle difficult cases easily. Inmate participation in other institution-wide activities outside the special unit seems to work well in this situation.

■ Classification

Early identification of sex offenders is not always an easy task. Sex criminals are usually reluctant to be candid about their activities, and they attempt to hide or alter facts in their favor. Official records are not necessarily the solution for classification purposes, because details of the commitment offense are frequently affected by lengthy legal maneuvers and sometimes not available to classification staff when the records are needed. Also, many offenders are incarcerated for apparent nonsexual activities such as breaking and entering or assault when their intent may have been the sex offense of rape.

Classification staff need be sensitive to these possibilities and convince inmates that a complete reporting of their activities is in their best interests. This is a formidable task but is attainable if interviewers are trained to deal with sex offenders. Offense details frequently help staff identify this target group, and self-reports from those already motivated to seek help also are useful. Ideally, once inmates are made aware of the existence of a good sex offender treatment program in the correctional system, those who recognize their deviance as a problem will cooperate during classification.

Classification staff should record the information they collect on a standard checklist or inventory.[6] Many checklists provide a structured format to ensure that all relevant areas of inquiry have been assessed. If the identification of sexually deviant behavior remains in doubt after the initial interview process, additional attempts to obtain background information should be made, and a follow-up interview should be scheduled. If reluctant inmates learn more about the treatment program or have more time to talk, they may be less guarded in their responses.

Trained staff should use their knowledge about typical sex offender profiles. For instance, they should remember that almost all sex offenders have engaged in many minor transgressions before the current incarceration and that their current offense is part of an unhealthy cycle of behavior.[7] To gain cooperation during the interviews, staff should tell inmates that many people have been involved in all sorts of sex acts as they matured and that they should not be concerned, because the interviewer has heard just about everything. Staff should not condone such behavior but simply acknowledge its occurrence to elicit more information from the suspected sex offender.

Sex offenders will not necessarily have histories of physical aggression or attacks. In fact, most sex offenses do not involve forceful acts, and most sex offenders do not fit the image of the dangerous psychopath. Many, but not all, appear to be psychologically or emotionally impaired, neurotic, psychotic, or even brain-damaged. A trained professional will be able to make these kinds of determinations.

Intelligence level, age, and income level are not very helpful in identification at this early stage of classification. Even though many sex offenders are young and have somewhat low intelligence, the same can be said of inmates in general. Similarly, most sex offenders exhibited their inappropriate behavior at an early age and most come from poor family backgrounds, but the same can be said of other offenders.

■ Staff Issues

After classification has been completed and transfer to the treatment unit has been accomplished, the offender will be handled almost exclusively by staff who specialize in dealing with sex offenders. The most essential step in developing and running a useful program for sex offenders is having trained staff who have the right attitude toward these inmates. Staff should not be people who view sex offenders as horrible persons who deserve the worst punishment that the institution can create for them. On the other hand, staff should also not be people who consider sex offenders to be victims of poorly conceived social laws, innocent by-products of dysfunctional families, or youngsters guilty only of normal youthful experimentation.

Staff members should be realistic and mature. They should be people who view the sex offense as illegal and inappropriate but believe the offender is capable of changing with proper motivation and assistance.

People who are uncomfortable with the topic of sex or show too much interest in the area may not be right for this job.

It is best to hire professionally trained specialists. If this is not possible for all staff positions, additional personnel should be chosen carefully. Enough personnel should be available to give significant individual attention to each program participant. After staff are selected, they should be trained. They should learn about sex offenders in general, sexual behavior in all of its ramifications, and, of course, the particular treatment approach that will be followed. Staff should also be sensitized to the need for confidentiality and to the possible negative feelings that other staff who work in other areas of the institution may exhibit.

Staff must work well as a team. Total communication and cooperation are needed to monitor progress and to make important decisions about readiness for additional programs, privileges, and reentry to the community. Staff need to encourage positive behavior while also being able to react quickly, decisively, and appropriately to offender setbacks. Demonstrating acceptance but not approval of inmate transgressions is a very challenging balancing act, but it has been accomplished successfully in correctional environments.

Recruitment and financial limitations may make staff selection more difficult. The quality and quantity of professional treatment staff and resources available to administrators varies considerably in different locations. If professionals trained in sex offender treatment (usually psychologists and, less frequently, psychiatrists) cannot be hired, it may be best to defer implementation of the program. Attempting to run such a demanding program is difficult under the best of circumstances; if the right professionals are not present to train correctional staff or to provide specialized treatment, the program may fail. In most instances, a failing program is worse than no program and may cause significant legal liability.

That said, too often administrators have used a lack of human resources to justify not implementing programs when, in fact, they have not spent sufficient time or effort in seeking professional staff. The marketplace for suitable candidates is looking better as competition and cutbacks increase in the general medical area and recent advances in treatment techniques for sex offenders produce more trained personnel interested in employment.

■ Evaluating and Admitting Sex Offenders

After arrival at the special treatment unit, all sex offenders identified through classification or by the courts as suitable candidates for treatment should be given a full explanation of the program requirements. An excellent example of a comprehensive handout for sex offenders is used by the Federal Bureau of Prisons.[8] Candidates are told that they will need at least enough time to complete all program requirements before release and that they should be able to complete these within a reasonable period.

After offenders understand everything they need to know about the program, particularly their responsibilities in it, they are asked to volunteer for participation. This willing acceptance is necessary because sex offenders often become resistive during treatment; they have had a great deal of immediate gratification from their sexual behavior. Because the program demands intensive work from offenders, successful treatment will not occur if they do not wish to take part.

In determining offender suitability for the program, staff must remember that full participation is not possible if severe mental illness or basic deficiencies in areas such as reading and writing are present. These needs should be addressed before the offender is formally admitted to the treatment unit. Those offenders who are seeking admission for reasons other than treatment of sexual deviancy should not be accepted; inmates hoping for a diversion from routine prison life or seeking an earlier release opportunity should be screened out.

The evaluation phase of the program continues after the offender is officially admitted. Because every sex offender has a unique set of problems that needs to be addressed, it is vital to program success that the offender complete very extensive questionnaires pertaining to family background, education, social history, and sexual behavior. This information will help staff develop a workable plan for treatment and release into the community.

Extensive psychological testing is also necessary at this stage. These tests may vary according to staff preferences, expertise, and availability, but a basic assessment of personality, cognitive abilities, social attitudes, and sexual thoughts is necessary. If competent staff are present, and the cooperation of all concerned has been obtained (including, e.g., top management's commitment to support and defend the use of a potentially controversial treatment tool), an assessment of the participant's sexual response to deviant and nondeviant themes is conducted. This assessment is accomplished by the use of penile plethysmography initially and at regular intervals during treatment. The plethysmograph is a widely accepted instrument consisting of a small penile transducer (a circular gauge similar to a rubber band) that measures sexual arousal based on an offender's erectile response to certain sexual stimuli. The information is not only useful in determining the proper course of treatment but also is frequently used during the actual treatment to condition appropriate sexual responses.

All of the information gained during the evaluation period is used by staff to formulate an overall treatment plan for each offender. This plan may be modified at any time as more information becomes available.

■ Treatment Program

Sex offender treatment programs throughout North America today use a combination of cognitive behavioral treatment and relapse prevention strategies. Programs typically include both individual and group therapy and focus on cognitive restructuring—helping the offender reconsider issues that surround sexual deviancy. Offenders are taught to be more aware of the victims of their offenses, are given empathy training, and learn about the sexual abuse cycle. Most programs include anger management training, relapse prevention, and how to improve social and interpersonal skill development. The programs emphasize changing deviant sexual arousal patterns.[9]

Teaching the offender to engage in meaningful social interactions, healthy recreation, and other self-improvement activities should be a high priority for staff. Like all inmates, sex offenders must be actively engaged in productive activities. Although the basic premise of treatment—which must be accepted by participants—is that there is no cure for their problem, offenders should be encouraged that with their full participation and motivation, staff can teach them to control their deviant behavior.[10] Further more, participants should accept that their deviant sexual behavior is totally inappropriate and unjustified. Holding sex offenders accountable for their behavior, past and present, is critical.

A comprehensive program for every sex offender includes specialized treatment activities in addition to the self-improvement and work activities assigned to all inmates. Naturally, treatment takes priority initially, occupying most of the offender's time during the intensive part of the sex offender program. However, treatment activities alone are insufficient for rehabilitation. Full programming is as essential to good institutional management as it is to good treatment.

Once a treatment plan is in place, the offender is assigned a staff member who serves as the lead therapist, providing individual counseling and coordination of the total treatment plan. Individual therapy is used to explore the dynamics of sex offenders' behavior, the difficulties they continue to have in relationships, and other issues raised in group therapies. As treatment progresses, discussions move to offenders' adjustment to the treatment program and finally to release planning. In addition to individual sessions at least once per week, various group therapy programs are essential.

Throughout the treatment program, offenders meet in group sessions aimed at resolving their long-standing difficulties and gaining understanding about their behavior. Regardless of the number of required therapy groups, one central group continues to focus on the basic deviant behavior, including a thorough discussion of inmates' offenses, victims, background, and present sexual thoughts and acts. The principal goal of this group is to examine how the offenders' behaviors, feelings, and thought processes led to their inappropriate sexual activity. The individual sessions complement this group work and add to this intensive self-examination. Many offenders must deal with extremely sensitive issues in private sessions before they can explore them in the group setting.

Several other key groups are significant components of a complete treatment effort. One such group deals with abuse and its ramifications in the offenders' lives. Most sex offenders were abused themselves as youngsters, frequently in a sexual way, but also physically or emotionally. In this group, offenders gain an understanding of how this abuse affected them and prepare for a later group designed to help them develop empathy for victims. Other groups might address anger management, social skills, sex education, and substance abuse, areas that cause difficulty for many sex offenders and are frequently factors in their sexually deviant behavior.

The final mandatory part of group treatment is relapse prevention training. Offenders have to accept the fact that the probability of offending again is very high if proactive steps are not taken. This group teaches offenders to recognize risk factors associated with deviant sexual behavior, to anticipate and modify risky situations, and to cope successfully with their postrelease environment.

■ Transition to the Community

A comprehensive treatment program must include a plan for reentry. Regardless of the offenders' level of program involvement, their success in completing the treatment goals, or the development of a realistic relapse prevention plan, staff must attend to another important task: ensuring offenders' successful reentry.

Presumably, after successful program completion, offenders can anticipate and know how to cope with the challenges of life outside the institution. Knowing that they will need help from many others to maintain a nondeviant lifestyle, offenders must seek out socially approved support groups, positive recreational activities, and other forms of community assistance. However, staff responsibility goes beyond helping offenders with these preparations and should include informing the relevant local authorities when and where the offenders will be released. Until recently, ensuring that all contacts required by law had been made was relatively simple—notifying the courts and probation authorities usually satisfied all concerned. Today, however, staff also need to contact local law enforcement.

In addition, staff must ensure that all sex offenders in their institutions are aware of required registration with the National Sex Offender Public Registry and the anticipated increased public attention that may result. This project, coordinated by the Department of Justice, is a cooperative effort between the state agencies hosting public sexual offender registries and the federal government and allows users to search for information about sex offenders.

Sex offender registration and community notification policies vary across the United States and are still debated in terms of their utility. These requirements, although appreciated by the public, have had little effect on reducing sex offender recidivism. Such mandates do impose social, psychological, and financial effects on offenders.[11]

■ Conclusion

Although successful techniques for treating sex offenders continue to be developed, dealing with sexual deviance will remain problematic for both staff and offenders. Increased public attention only exacerbates an already difficult task, in that no treatment program can promise that an offense will not recur. Fortunately, a realistic treatment effort can prepare the offenders to control their behavior and thereby better protect the community. Sex offenders who take responsibility for their behavior, discuss their past offenses openly, understand why their deviant acts were wrong, exhibit genuine remorse, and actively work in the treatment programs to acquire relapse prevention skills will undoubtedly pose less of a danger to the community than they did before their arrival at the institution.

Chapter Resources

DISCUSSION QUESTIONS

1. Do sex offenders require specialized treatment in correctional institutions?
2. Should individuals who have been convicted of sex offenses and have refused institutional treatment for these offenses be confined by the government after their sentences have been completed?
3. Should taxpayers pay for expensive sex offender rehabilitation programs?
4. Could you work with and provide supportive programming for sex offenders?
5. What unique problems do sex offenders pose in correctional settings?

ADDITIONAL RESOURCES

Center for Sex Offender Management (CSOM), http://www.csom.org/

The goal is to enhance public safety by preventing further victimization by improving the management of adult and juvenile sex offenders in the community. The Center for Sex Offender Management is sponsored by the Office of Justice Programs (OJP), Department of Justice, in collaboration with the National Institute of Corrections, State Justice Institute, and the American Probation and Parole Association. CSOM is administered through a cooperative agreement between OJP and the Center for Effective Public Policy.

The Association for the Treatment of Sexual Abusers, http://www.atsa.com

Dru Sjodin National Sex Offender Public Registry, coordinated by the U.S. Department of Justice, http://www.nsopr.gov/

International Association for the Treatment of Sexual Offenders (IATSO), http://www.iatso.org/

It is an international nonprofit organization committed to the promotion of research and treatment for sexual offenders. It promotes conferences on the treatment of sexual offenders and created the IATSO Standards of Care for the Treatment of Adult Sexual Offenders available at http://www.iatso .org/index.php/standards-of-care

NOTES

1. Federal Bureau of Investigation. (2010). *Crime in the United States.* Retrieved from http://www.fbi.gov/ucr/
2. National Center for Missing and Exploited Children. (2011, July). Retrieved from http://www.missingkids .com/en_US/documents/sex-offender-map.pdf
3. Chaiken, J. *Sex offenses and offenders: An analysis of data on rape and sexual assault, Bureau of Justice Statistics.* Retrieved from http://www.ojp.usdoj.gov/bjs/pub/ascii/soo.txt
4. National Center for Missing and Exploited Children. (2006). Retrieved from http://www.missingkids.com/ en_US/documents/sex-offender-map.pdf; Rice, M., Harris, G., & Quinsey, V. (1991). Sexual recidivism among child molesters released from a maximum security institution. *Journal of Consulting and Clinical Psychology, 59,* 381–386.

5. American Correctional Association. (1996). *A directory of programs that work* (pp. 124–136). Lanham, MD: Author.

6. Borum, R. (1996). Improving the clinical practice of violence risk assessment. *American Psychologist, 51*(9), 945–956.

7. Bays, L., Freeman-Longo, R., & Hildebran, D. (1990). *How can I stop? Breaking my deviant cycle* (pp. 19–48). Brandon, VT: Safer Society Press.

8. Federal Bureau of Prisons. (1996). *Program participation package* (pp. 1–36). Butner, NC: Federal Correctional Institution.

9. American Probation and Parole Association, the Center for Effective Public Management. (2001, August). *Myths and facts about sex offenders* (p. 7).

10. Bays, L., & Freeman-Longo, R. (1989). *Why did I do it again? Understanding my cycle of problem behaviors* (p. 72). Brandon, VT: Safer Society Press.

11. Tewksbury, R., Mustaine, E. E., & Payne, B. K. (2011). Community corrections professionals' views of sex offenders, sex offender registration and community notification and residency restrictions. *Federal Probation, 75*(3), 45–50.

Drug Treatment

James A. Inciardi, James E. Rivers, and Duane C. McBride

CHAPTER OBJECTIVES

- Explain why detoxification is a necessary component of effective drug treatment.
- Outline how methadone maintenance assists patients.
- Describe the benefits of residential-based drug treatment programs.

There are several major modalities of substance abuse and addiction treatment available for prison and jail inmates:

- Chemical detoxification
- Methadone maintenance
- Drug-free outpatient treatment
- Self-help groups
- Residential therapeutic communities

Each modality has its own view of substance abuse and addiction, and each affects the patient in different ways.

■ Chemical Detoxification

Designed for persons dependent on narcotic drugs, chemical detoxification programs typically involve inpatient settings and last between 1 and 3 weeks. The rationale for using detoxification as a treatment approach rests on two basic principles:

1. **The concept of addiction.** Addiction is viewed as drug craving accompanied by physical dependence that motivates continued usage. Addiction results in a tolerance to the drug's effects and a syndrome of identifiable physical and psychological symptoms when the drug is withdrawn abruptly.

2. **The concept of withdrawal.** Negative aspects of the abstinence syndrome discourage many addicts from attempting withdrawal. This makes addicts more likely to continue using drugs.

Given these principles, the aim of chemical detoxification is the elimination of physiological dependence through a medically supervised procedure.

Methadone, a synthetic narcotic that produces many of the same effects as morphine or heroin, is the drug of choice for detoxification from heroin addiction. Generally, a starting dose of the drug is reduced gradually in small increments until the body adjusts to the drug-free state. Although many detoxification programs address only the addict's physical dependence, some provide individual or group counseling in an attempt to address the problems associated with drug abuse, whereas a few refer clients to other longer term treatments. For drug-involved offenders in prisons and jails, the mechanism of detoxification varies by the client's major drug of addiction. For opiate users, methadone or clonidine is preferred; for cocaine users, desipramine has been used to ameliorate withdrawal symptoms.[1] Almost all narcotic addicts and many cocaine users have been in a chemical detoxification program at least once. Studies document, however, that in the absence of supportive psychotherapeutic services and community follow-up care, virtually all addicts relapse.

In all detoxification programs, success depends on the following established protocols for drug administration and withdrawal. Research shows increasing rates of program completion, yet many clinicians feel that mere detoxification from a substance is not drug abuse treatment because it does not help people stay off drugs.[2]

From this perspective, for detoxification to be successful, it must be the initial step in a comprehensive treatment process.[3] Thus, detoxification is a temporary regimen that gives addicts the opportunity to reduce their drug intake; for many, this means that the criminal activity associated with their drug taking and drug seeking is interrupted. Finally, given the association between injection drug use and the human immunodeficiency virus (HIV) and acquired immune deficiency syndrome (AIDS), detoxification also provides counseling to reduce HIV/AIDS-related risk behaviors.

■ Methadone Maintenance

Methadone maintenance uses methadone as a substitute drug that prevents symptoms of withdrawal from morphine or heroin. More importantly, however, methadone is orally effective, making intravenous use unnecessary. In addition, it is longer acting than heroin, with one oral dose lasting up to 24 hours. These properties have made methadone useful in the management of chronic addiction.[4] During the first phase of methadone treatment, the patient is detoxified from heroin on dosages of methadone sufficient to prevent withdrawal without either euphoria or sedation. During the maintenance phase, the patient is stabilized on a dose of methadone high enough to eliminate the craving for heroin. Although this process would appear to substitute one narcotic for another, the rationale behind methadone maintenance is to stabilize the patient on a less debilitating drug and make counseling and other treatment services available.

Studies have demonstrated that methadone maintenance patients have favorable outcomes in a number of areas. However, they also indicate that few patients remain drug free after treatment. More specifically, a number of investigations have found that individuals on methadone maintenance continued to use high levels of such nonopiate drugs as cocaine and marijuana.[5] On the other hand, much of the research has concluded that those on methadone maintenance have been more likely to reduce their criminal activity, become employed, and generally improve in psychosocial functioning.[6] Well-designed programs tend to be integrated with other forms of treatment and social services.[7]

As such, methadone maintenance is effective for blocking heroin dependency. However, methadone is also a primary drug of abuse among some narcotic addicts, resulting in a small street market for the drug. Most illegal methadone is diverted from legitimate maintenance programs by methadone patients. Hence, illegal supplies of the drug are typically available only where such programs exist.

The role of methadone in prison settings is complex, and only a few such programs are available for incarcerated populations. The difficulties seem twofold. First, there is a major security concern. Prison officials are uncomfortable with the general distribution of methadone to potentially large numbers of their inmates. Moreover, many feel that treatment should be "drug free" and that methadone simply continues drug dependence.

One of the few methadone maintenance programs in a jail is the Key Extended Entry Program (KEEP) at New York City's Rikers Island correctional facility. KEEP's client population includes those awaiting trial and sentenced prisoners, with some 3,000 receiving treatment each year. The program meets all federal guidelines. An evaluation of KEEP found that those in the program were more likely to continue treatment after leaving jail than those in other types of drug treatment.[8]

Perhaps the major argument for methadone maintenance in a jail setting is that, unlike stays in state and federal prisons, jail stays tend to be short. In KEEP, for example, the treatment period is only 45 days. As such, a strong case can be made for offering methadone maintenance as a means for continuing or initiating treatment for those returning to the street relatively soon.

■ Drug-Free Outpatient Treatment

Drug-free outpatient treatment encompasses a variety of nonresidential programs that do not employ methadone or other pharmacotherapeutic agents. Most have a mental health perspective. Primary services include individual and group therapy, and some programs offer family therapy and relapse prevention support. An increasing number of drug-free outpatient treatment programs are including case management services as an adjunct to counseling. The basic case management approach is to assist clients in obtaining needed services in a timely and coordinated manner. The key components of the approach are assessing, planning, linking, monitoring, and advocating for clients within the existing nexus of treatment and social services.

Evaluating the effectiveness of drug-free outpatient treatment is difficult because programs vary widely—from drop-in centers to highly structured arrangements that offer counseling or psychotherapy. A number of studies have found that outpatient treatment has been moderately successful in reducing daily drug use and criminal activity. However, the approach appears to be inappropriate for the most troubled and the antisocial users.

The number of rigorously designed studies of corrections-based outpatient programs is quite small.[9] One of the few examples involves a relatively well-funded and designed program known as "Passages"—a 12-week nonresidential program for women incarcerated in the Wisconsin correctional system.[10] Although the treatment staff and correctional administrators agreed that the program improved clients' self-esteem and their ability to deal with important issues, evidence of subsequent reduced drug use and criminal activity was not reported.

■ Self-Help Groups

Self-help groups, also known as 12-step programs, are composed of individuals who meet regularly to stabilize and facilitate their recovery from substance abuse. The best known is Alcoholics Anonymous (AA), in which sobriety is based on fellowship and adhering to the 12 steps of recovery, which include belief in a greater power or being, prayer or meditation, and admission of wrongdoing. The steps move group members from a statement of powerlessness over drugs and alcohol to a resolution that members will carry the message of help to others and will practice the AA principles in all affairs. In addition to AA, other popular self-help groups are Narcotics Anonymous, Cocaine Anonymous, and Overeaters Anonymous. All these organizations not only operate as stand-alone fellowship programs but are also used as adjuncts to other modalities. Although few evaluation studies of self-help groups have been carried out, the weight of clinical and observational data suggest that they are crucial to recovery.

Research has failed to demonstrate that anonymous fellowship meetings by themselves are effective with heavy drug users.[11] Furthermore, there are few known evaluations of prison-based self-help programs, for a variety of reasons:

- Prison administrators and treatment professionals tend to prefer other types of programs.
- The model contains variables that are extremely difficult to operationalize and measure.
- Members and leaders often view scientific studies of their groups as intrusive threats to anonymity and therapeutic processes.
- Evaluation research funding is more often available for innovative programming than for such well-established services.[12]

Nevertheless, self-help programs are widespread in correctional settings. There is a widely shared belief that they work. The meetings are organized and run by volunteers at no cost to the prison authorities, and the meetings appear to help inmates make the transition from correctional to community-based settings.[13]

■ Residential Therapeutic Communities

The therapeutic community (TC) is a total treatment environment in which the primary clinical staff are typically former substance abusers—"recovering addicts"—who themselves were rehabilitated in TCs. The treatment perspective of the TC is that drug abuse is a disorder of the whole person—that the problem is the person and not the drug—and that addiction is a symptom and not the essence of the disorder. In the TC's view of recovery, the primary goal is to change the negative patterns of behavior, thinking, and feeling that predispose a person to drug use. As such, the overall goal is a responsible, drug-free lifestyle. Recovery through the TC process depends on positive and negative pressures to change. This pressure is brought about through a self-help process in which relationships of mutual responsibility to every resident in the program are built. In addition to individual and group counseling, the TC process has a system of explicit rewards that reinforce the value of earned achievement. As such, privileges are earned. In addition, TCs have their own rules and regulations that guide the behavior of residents and the management of their facilities. Their purposes are to maintain the safety and health of the community and to train and teach residents through the use of discipline. There are numerous TC rules and regulations, the most conspicuous of which are total prohibitions against violence, theft, and drug use. Violation of these cardinal rules typically results in immediate expulsion from a TC. TCs have been in existence for decades, and their successes have been well documented.

Hillsborough County Sheriff's Office Substance Abuse Treatment Program

The Hillsborough County jail program in Tampa, Florida, was established in 1988 to address the short-term treatment needs of pretrial jail inmates.[14] The program provides services for 60 inmates—48 males in a direct supervision pod and 12 females housed in a unit with women who are not in treatment. In a treatment milieu emphasizing recovery, cooperation, and interdependence, treatment is provided in groups of 8–12 inmates using a cognitive–behavioral, skills-based approach that focuses on relapse prevention. The goals of the program are to encourage long-term abstinence and to involve participants in ongoing treatment services after release from jail. Aftercare is accomplished through linkages with the local programs.

The evaluation of the program examined 535 admissions from June 1988 through January 1991 and 422 untreated "controls" who requested treatment but were not admitted either because of a lack of space or because they were released from jail prior to treatment entry. At 2 months after release from jail, 16% in the treatment group and 33% in the control group had been rearrested; at 6 months, 46% in the treatment group and 58% in the control group had been rearrested. During the year after release, those in the treatment group had a mean elapsed duration of 221 days prior to rearrest, as compared with 180 days for those in the control group.

Stay 'N Out TC

The Stay 'N Out TC in New York's Arthur Kill Correctional Facility was established in 1974 and follows the traditional TC model.[15] Treatment occurs in prison, and no aftercare services are provided. A follow-up study compared a group of several clients with a no-treatment control group on the following major variables: arrest and parole outcome.[16] For both men and women, the lowest proportion arrested were those in the TC group.

Cornerstone

Cornerstone, founded in 1976 on the grounds of the Oregon State Hospital, is a prerelease TC program with a 6-month aftercare program. Clients are referred from the state's three prisons. In a 3-year follow-up study, 144 Cornerstone residents who graduated between 1976 and 1979 were compared with three other groups—inmates who dropped out of Cornerstone within 30 days of entry; all Oregon parolees with a history of alcohol or drug abuse who were released during 1974; and a similar population released in Michigan at the same time.[17] The Cornerstone dropouts had the highest rates of recidivism, with 74% returning to prison within 3 years after release. The Michigan group had between 45% and 50% who returned, and the Oregon parolees, 37%. The Cornerstone graduates had the lowest rate of recidivism, with 29% returning to prison within 3 years after release.

KEY and CREST Outreach Center

Delaware's KEY/CREST program is a three-stage continuum of treatment that begins in the institution and extends to community-based aftercare. Treatment begins in the KEY, a prison-based TC for male inmates established in 1988 and located at the Multi-Purpose Criminal Justice Facility in Wilmington, Delaware.

During the closing months of 1990, CREST Outreach Center was established, also in Wilmington, under a 5-year National Institute on Drug Abuse treatment demonstrations grant as the nation's first work release TC. CREST is a transitional facility with a 6-month residential program that continues the basic TC treatment approach combined with work release. After 6 months at CREST, clients proceed to community-based aftercare.[18] Follow-up studies have demonstrated this treatment continuum to be highly effective in that those who have received the full continuum of treatment are three times more likely to be drug free and almost twice as likely to be arrest-free 18 months after release than the no-treatment controls.[19] This suggests that an integrated continuum of treatment may be a highly promising approach.

Federal Bureau of Prisons' Residential Drug Abuse Treatment Program

The Federal Bureau of Prisons' Residential Drug Abuse Treatment Program attempts to identify, confront, and alter the attitudes, values, and thought patterns that led to criminal behavior and drug or alcohol abuse. The program consists of three stages. First, there is a unit-based treatment within the confines of a prison where prisoners live together and undergo therapy (generally for 9–12 months). Second, following completion of the residential portion, inmates continue treatment for up to 12 months while in the general population of the prison through monthly group meetings with the drug abuse program staff. Third, if transferred to community-based facilities prior to release from custody, inmates who completed the residential portion (and the institutional transition portion, if time allows) participate in regularly scheduled group, individual, and family counseling sessions.

The Federal Bureau of Prisons (BOP) conducted a rigorous analysis of its Residential Drug Abuse Treatment Program using a comparison group of inmates who were matched with the inmates who participated in the program on a variety of important background characteristics. The BOP concluded that the program is highly effective. Inmates who participated in the program were significantly less likely to recidivate and significantly less likely to relapse to drug use, for as long as 3 years after release from prison. The large sample size (1,800 offenders), the research methodology, and the multisite sample make these outcomes particularly noteworthy.[20]

Although TCs and residential treatment programs are the most visible drug abuse treatment programs in prison settings, there are numerous other types, many of which are grounded in individual and group counseling and 12-step approaches. However, there is limited information about these programs in the substance abuse literature.

■ Conclusion

A legacy of the "war on drugs" has been a criminal justice system that is drug driven in many respects. In the legislative sector, new laws have been created to deter drug use and increase penalties for drug-related crime. In the police sector, drug enforcement initiatives have been expanded, which, in turn, has increased the number of arrests for drug-related crimes. In the judicial sector, the increased flow of drug cases has resulted in overcrowded dockets and courtrooms and the creation of new drug courts, special dispositional alternatives for drug offenders, and higher conviction and incarceration rates. In the correctional sector, there has been the further crowding of already overpopulated jails and penitentiaries.

In response to this situation, criminal justice systems throughout the United States have been structuring and implementing treatment programs at every level—for arrestees (those released before trial), those on probation, jail and prison inmates, parolees, and those individuals under other forms of postrelease surveillance. Although some highly visible programs have been highlighted in the literature, little is known about what is being accomplished in most jurisdictions.

Although it is generally agreed that criminal justice systems throughout the United States are overwhelmed with drug users, little is known about the actual health services and treatment needs of drug-involved offenders. It is important that treatment needs assessments be conducted to determine what services and how many treatment slots are needed by criminal justice clients at all levels. In addition, only minimal attention has focused on the issue of comorbidity, which might apply to those inmates with dual diagnoses. Additional research is also needed to determine the number and types of treatment services available to probation departments, diversion programs, and other criminal justice entities and how effective these services are, alone or in combination.

Chapter Resources

DISCUSSION QUESTIONS

1. How is drug addiction defined?
2. Are drug programs effective when operating inside prisons or jails?
3. Should taxpayers fund drug treatment programs?
4. What are they key components of a successful correctional drug treatment program?
5. Why is methadone considered problematic in the prison environment?

ADDITIONAL RESOURCES

Anglin, M., Prendergast, M., & Farabee, D. (1998). *The effectiveness of coerced treatment for drug abusing offenders.* Paper presented at the Office of National Drug Control Policy's Conference of Scholars and Policy Makers, Washington, DC. Retrieved from http://www.ncjrs.gov/ondcppubs/treat/consensus/anglin.pdf

Inciardi, J., Martin, S., & Butzin, C. (2004). Five year outcomes of therapeutic community treatment of drug-involved offenders after release from prison. *Crime & Delinquency, 50,* 88–107.

Sims, B. (2005). *Substance abuse treatment with correctional clients: Practical implications for institutional and community settings.* Binghamton, NY: Haworth Press, Inc.

Wallace, B. (2005). *Making mandated addiction treatment work.* Blue Ridge Summit, PA: Jason Aronson Publishers.

NOTES

1. Gerstein, D., & Harwood, H. (Eds.). (1990). *Treating drug problems* (Vol. 1). Washington, DC: National Academies Press; Mattick, R., & Hall, W. (1996). Are detoxification programmes effective? *The Lancet, 347,* 97–100.
2. Mattick, R. P., & Hall, W. Are detoxification programmes effective?
3. Gerstein and Harwood, eds., *Treating drug problems* (pp. 174–176); McBride, D., & VanderWaal, C. (1997). An evaluation of a day reporting center for pre-trial drug-using offenders. *Journal of Drug Issues, 27,* 377–397; Magura, S., Rosenblum, A., Lewis, C., & Joseph, H. (1993). The effectiveness of in-jail methadone maintenance. *Journal of Drug Issues, 93,* 75–99.
4. Dole, V., & Nyswander, M. (1965). A medical treatment for diacetylmorphine (heroin) addiction: A clinical trial with methadone hydrochloride. *Journal of the American Medical Association, 193,* 80–84.
5. Chambers, C., Taylor, W., & Moffett, A. (1972). The incidence of cocaine abuse among methadone maintenance patients. *International Journal of the Addictions, 7,* 427–441.
6. Ball, J., & Ross, A. (1991). *The effectiveness of methadone maintenance* (p. 202). New York, NY: Springer-Verlag.
7. Ibid., p. 162.

8. Magura, S., Rosenblum, A., Lewis, C., & Joseph, H. The effectiveness of in-jail methadone maintenance (pp. 75–99).

9. Peters, R. (1993). Drug treatment in jails and detention settings. In J. Inciardi (Ed.), *Drug treatment and criminal justice* (pp. 44–80). Newbury Park, CA: Sage Publications; Wellish, J., Anglin, D., & Pendergast, M. (1993). Treatment strategies for drug abusing women offenders. In J. Inciardi (Ed.), *Drug treatment and criminal justice* (pp. 5–29). Newbury Park, CA: Sage Publications.

10. Falkin, G., Wayson, B. L., Wexler, H. K., & Lipton, D. S. (1991). *Treating prisoners for drug abuse: An implementation study of six prison programs.* New York, NY: Narcotic and Drug Research, Inc.

11. Falkin, G., Wayson, B. L., Wexler, H. K., & Lipton, D. S. *Treating prisoners for drug abuse: An implementation study of six prison programs*; Wellish, J., Anglin, D., & Pendergast, M. Treatment strategies for drug-abusing women offenders (pp. 6–9).

12. Brown, B. (1992). Program models. In C. Leukefeld & F. Tims (Eds.), *Drug abuse treatment in prisons and jails* (pp. 31–37). NIDA Research Monograph, no. 118. Rockville, MD: National Institute on Drug Abuse.

13. Peters, R. Drug treatment in jails and detention settings (p. 65); Brown, B. Program models (p. 35).

14. Peters, R. Drug treatment in jails and detention settings (p. 55).

15. Wexler, H., & Williams, R. (1996). The stay 'n out therapeutic community: Prison treatment for substance abusers. *Journal of Psychoactive Drugs, 18*, 221–229.

16. Wexler, H., Falkin, G. P., Lipton, D. S., & Rosenblum, A. B. (1990). Outcome evaluation of a prison therapeutic community for substance abuse treatment. *Criminal Justice and Behavior, 17*, 71–92.

17. Field, G. (1985). The cornerstone program: A client outcome study. *Federal Probation*, 50–55.

18. Hooper, R., Lockwood, D., & Inciardi, J. (1993). Treatment techniques in corrections-based therapeutic communities. *The Prison Journal, 73*, 290–306; Inciardi, J. (1996). Prison therapeutic communities. In J. Inciardi (Ed.), *Examining the justice process* (pp. 397–409). Fort Worth, TX: Harcourt Brace.

19. Inciardi, J., Martin, S. S., Butzin, C. F., Hooper, R. M., & Harrison, L. D. (1997). An effective model of prison-based treatment for drug-involved offenders. *Journal of Drug Issues, 27*, 261–278.

20. Pelissier, B., Rhodes, W., Saylor, W., Gaes, G., Camp, S. D., Vanyur, S. D., & Wallace, S. (2001). TRIAD drug treatment evaluation project. *Federal Probation, 65*(3), 3–7.

Staff Management

YOU ARE THE ADMINISTRATOR

■ Lessons from Abu Ghraib

The mistreatment of Iraqi prisoners held in Abu Ghraib prison in Baghdad was terrible for American military leaders and those responsible for the oversight of American intelligence. The situation at Abu Ghraib involved American soldiers abusing and humiliating Iraqi prisoners, and the media seemed to delight in presenting American hypocrisy—the forces of good caught in an evil act within the military prison.

Questions that arise from such an even are appropriately asked of those in change of the institution. How could daily activities, as alleged by some, be happening without the knowledge of the supervisory personnel? Senior administrators should be aware of abusive behavior and stop it when it occurs. The leadership structure of a prison or jail facility must know what is going on within the walls and fences of the institution and hold all personnel to a high standard of behavior.

When institutional leadership fails, as Abu Ghraib demonstrates, extremely bad things can happen.

- How can prison and jail administrators stay in touch with the ongoing issues in their facilities?
- How can negative behavior by staff be prevented?
- Should senior personnel be held accountable for the behavior of junior staff?
- What key lessons about staff management can be learned from the Abu Ghraib scandal?

Source: "Abuse of Iraqi POWs by GIs Probed," CBS News, April 28, 2004, available at http://www.cbsnews .com/stories/2004/04/27/60II/main614063.shtml, accessed March 7, 2007.

Governing: Personnel Management

Robert L. Wright

CHAPTER OBJECTIVES

- Outline the desired characteristics of correctional staff.
- Explain leadership selection in a healthy and effective organization.
- Explore the role of professionalism in running a penal institution.

With most correctional facilities spending at least 80% of their appropriated funds on personnel services for staff salaries and other payroll expenses, most prison administrators recognize that staff are the heart of their programs.[1] Staff are involved in every aspect of a correctional setting. They serve as ambassadors, peacekeepers, and role models. They lead, supervise, and control the activities of the men and women who serve time. Staff ensure that a facility is safe, humane, and efficient—a place where meaningful change can occur.

■ Staff Opportunity

People who have been successful in corrections are honest, hardworking, and dependable. Their performance at previous jobs has been above average or better. They are valued members of their communities, participating in local organizations and helping to build strong, wholesome places to raise families. Corrections work provides an excellent career opportunity for people who have these distinguishing qualities.

Corrections has been one of the leading growth industries in the United States, and corrections continues to be a field where an employee may begin at the entry level—as a correctional officer, budget technician, teacher, recreation leader, or counselor, for example—and end up as a top-level administrator. With the growth in the industry, opportunities abound. The only limiting factors may be the employee's interest, education, and initiative. Many administrators recognize that the best wardens and superintendents have risen through the ranks and supplemented their correctional experience with criminal justice or human services education and specialized correctional education. Often, this education is offered by the American Correctional Association (ACA), the National Institute of Corrections (NIC), and local criminal justice academies. As correctional leaders recruit, train, and promote new employees, they recognize that they are preparing the next generation of correctional leaders.

■ Correctional Standards and Laws

The ACA publishes *Standards for Adult Correctional Institutions*, which establishes expectations for correctional administration and personnel management in at least 10 areas of critical importance:

1. Written policy and procedures
2. Staffing
3. Affirmative action and diversity
4. Selection
5. Probation
6. Physical fitness
7. Compensation and benefits
8. Ethics
9. Personnel records
10. Employee counseling

Other standards address staff training and the minimum guidelines for adult correctional facilities.

Correctional professionals regard the development of these standards as the most significant accomplishment made during the 20th century in corrections. Correctional administrators are encouraged to become fully conversant in these guidelines in their respective areas. Personnel and training are 2 of the 32 areas of correctional administration addressed by the 463 standards for adult correctional facilities.

Correctional administrators must also understand the law and statutes of their area; there are statutes, administrative codes, executive orders, court decisions, and personnel and civil service merit system rules that are specific to each jurisdiction. A working knowledge of these laws is central to enlightened, effective management. Legal counsel and personnel specialists should guide correctional leaders in the specifics of these legal concerns.

■ Workplace Behavior and Professionalism

There are other areas that corrections leaders must understand as well. Some wardens and superintendents recognize that certain staff might focus on the technical aspects of the business (such as shakedowns, searches, and counts), while paying less attention to issues concerning workplace behavior and professionalism. However, staff members must also pay attention to current expectations about workplace behavior and professionalism. Individual employees may be subject matter experts or may have made significant contributions, but if they lack self-discipline, disregard published departmental expectations, or neglect to treat fellow employees with dignity and respect, their corrections careers may be short-lived.

Each correctional employee should be informed of the department's or agency's expectations. Employees at all levels should expect from and provide to each other:

- Decent, civil speech, without profanity
- Common courtesy
- Respectful conduct
- Cooperation and teamwork

These simple expectations are important. Where they are observed, all employees can expect a relatively pleasant, professional, and fair workplace. That workplace will be free from harassment, rude behavior, retaliation, disparate treatment, intimidation, and discrimination. Illegal discrimination includes any discrimination based on age, sex, marital status, race, religious or political beliefs, creed, color, or national origin, as well as the presence of any sensory, mental, or physical disability.

To encourage helpful, healthy working relationships, it is essential for correctional management to articulate these expectations about professionalism. And agency managers, without exception, must not only talk about the desired behavior but also model it in every interaction. These understandings should be included in an employee handbook that is presented to each employee, emphasized during recruitment and selection interviews, discussed and modeled in new-employee orientation, and reviewed in annual in-service training.

Meeting the important objectives of professionalism and teamwork—with correctional employees conducting themselves in a manner that is courteous, respectful, and businesslike—is essential for the agency and its mission. These minimum expectations are also essential for ensuring that correctional employees meet their personal and career goals.

Correctional staff must manage the lives of others—individuals who, when left on their own, may be out of control. To achieve good results with others, correctional staff must first manage themselves. As agents of the city, county, state, or federal government, employees can expect that there will be inquiries about performance. Everything correctional staff do is subject to scrutiny. The correctional agency must have well-established procedures—published and available to all staff—that outline the agency's practices for conducting business and handling inquiries into allegations about staff performance and conduct. These reviews of employee conduct must ensure that staff have an opportunity to review allegations. The agency conducts an investigation, the results are shared with the employee, and the employee has a hearing and opportunity to respond.

When employees conduct their day-to-day business in accordance with agency policy, administrative codes, and the law, they have the full support of the agency and the attorney general and other jurisdictional legal counsel. When staff at any level operate outside the published agency guidelines, they are on their own, individually responsible for their behavior and decisions.

Employees should always:

- Be mindful—while at work, stick to business.
- Be polite—work with others with courtesy and respect.
- Respect procedures and follow them.
- Respect honesty and deal factually with fellow employees and supervisors.
- Avoid gossip—staff should not pass along any information that is not factual.
- Contribute to a healthy workplace.
- Let things go—no one in public sector employment has any authority or license to participate in retaliation or intimidation behavior intended to frighten, belittle, discourage, threaten, menace, harm, get even, or "pay back."
- Honor coworkers and expect the best.
- Understand sexual harassment—harassment is behavior that is unwelcomed by another; it is not determined by the intentions of the instigator but by the recipient.
- Respect the rights, feelings, and opinions of others—rude behavior is unacceptable.

All employees in the corrections agency need to understand that there is no higher priority than the workplace behavior of employees. Every employee must remember that each employee is responsible for the healthfulness of the corrections workplace. Fellow employees must be respected, and concerns must be conveyed factually and with courtesy, never in a derogatory or mean-spirited way.

Correctional staff are challenged to be professional—to be honest, hardworking public servants dedicated to the public good. The public constantly evaluates correctional staff at all levels. The correctional employer and the agency should welcome inquiry and inspection. Whenever correctional staff have disagreements, they should remember their role as peacemakers. Employees should go directly to the individual with whom they have a concern and discuss the issue, seeking resolution. If that fails to resolve the situation, they are encouraged to seek assistance from their supervisor. There is enough negative activity in the corrections workplace that has been generated through the lives of the inmates serving time. It is destructive for corrections employees to be sidetracked or manipulated into negative behavior.

■ Leadership Development

Quality institutions with effective, determined, and inspired leaders that meet challenges effectively and professionally will foster many future leaders—unit supervisors, program managers, lieutenants, assistant superintendents, and superintendents.

Some of the most successful superintendents and wardens have learned from an effective, progressive leader. They have had the opportunity to observe the organization and the leader up close. Approaches and issues have been discussed, with the rationale for decisions examined and alternatives reviewed. Astute, attentive, aspiring corrections executives are able to build on and apply the lessons that they learn from their organization. Interaction with their peers provides opportunities for them to work together effectively. As these individuals participate in the business of the organization, modeling the behavior of the leaders, they are also providing opportunities for evaluation of their own leadership qualities and integrity.

Healthy and effective organizations will foster healthy and effective leaders. Correctional administrators should expect surprises among the talent pool in the effective and healthy organization and select leaders solely on the basis of merit. It is not beneficial to attempt to identify future leaders too early. Rather than expend special training resources on only selected individuals, it is best to create a rewarding and rich environment where excellence is the order of the day, performance is evaluated, competition is healthy, and the level of performance of all employees is raised. In the healthy organization, people understand that any entry-level employee could end up running the place. The only limit is their interest, their education and experience, and their ability to apply their knowledge effectively and work with others.

These views represent the opinions of wardens who have served in healthy and effective organizations run by enlightened leaders. Truly great leaders often credit their work in a vital organization as the key to their success. There are few satisfactory substitutes for strong mentoring. However, many forums exist that are designed to assist and prepare future leaders. The ACA and NIC offer training, and professional corrections associations meetings can provide substantial opportunities for corrections practitioners to meet and share strategies and experiences. Also, the opportunity to read and study the accounts of correctional leaders can stimulate the insight, reflection, and assessments critical to the development of effective correctional leaders.

■ Setting the Tone

It has been said that corrections management is an art, not a science. Some people have degrees and substantial credentials, but they can lack common sense and the ability to understand key issues and significantly influence the organization. An effective corrections manager is never satisfied with the status quo. Goals and expectations are set and communicated, and the organization moves toward those goals. In large part, the effectiveness of the organization depends on the example that the leaders set. There is a direct correlation between the expectation of the leader and the results. When leaders or managers tolerate mediocrity, the result is mediocrity. When excellence and professionalism are the expectations, the momentum of the organization increases, and employees perceive the ways they may serve as helpful contributors.

Corrections is a people business. The staff of any correctional organization are common people; working together, they can achieve an exceptional result. Honest, hardworking, and dependable, they follow instructions and treat others with dignity and respect. They show integrity and compassion, and they are effective team members. All staff must understand that they must follow agency guidelines and be consistent in performing their duties and enforcing rules. There is no room for free agents or mavericks; they create chaos and make the facility a dangerous place for others to work. When dealing with inmates, staff must remember to be firm, fair, and consistent. Staff should not show favoritism toward certain inmates and should hold inmates accountable for their actions. Staff in a healthy corrections organization realize that one of the greatest opportunities they have is to serve as an example and influence the inmates in their care by their professionalism.

Leaders must inform staff at all levels of the agency's position concerning rehabilitation. For example, they should remind staff that there is no quick fix for crime. Although the agency provides opportunities for those in custody to make wholesome use of their time, staff should recognize that if change occurs, it comes from within the mind and heart of the individual. Change is possible, and many correctional employees are motivated by the hope that change will occur. A healthy institution is filled with hope, meaningful work and education opportunities, and significant self-help and leisure activities that challenge and motivate inmates.

Staff should understand that they set the tone in the facility. They establish the community and the quality of life. When staff understand their effect, facilities can offer life-enriching experiences for inmates serving time and a healthy and safe place for people to live, where staff are proud and honored to serve. Lives are affected positively while the interests of the public are served. Employees are truly role models—for other staff members and for the inmates of a prison or jail.

■ Corrective and Disciplinary Action

In a strong, successful organization, staff are selected on the basis of merit and everyone continues to learn. Therefore, it is in the agency's best interest to provide training and assistance to help all employees be successful—to help them handle the challenges of corrections. The agency has a duty to outline what each position requires, prepare staff for changing roles, develop operational procedures, and show employees how to follow those procedures. This means senior management must provide appropriate opportunities for staff to become informed and proficient.

Training and orientation in a correctional institution should cover rules and regulations and their rationale—not only for the inmates but also for the staff. Training should also cover the consequences of not following rules and regulations. Every organization must have discipline to achieve its objectives. Supervisors, to be effective, must know the rules and administer them fairly.

The communication between supervisor and subordinate is critical. Supervisors must be mindful that agencies must train and improve staff. Positive reinforcement helps develop personnel, but when an order or rule is disobeyed, supervisors cannot ignore it. It is critical that any corrective or disciplinary action is conducted in private. It is embarrassing for anyone to be corrected in a public setting, and it makes for a much more positive encounter if these discussions are handled in an office that affords a confidential conversation. In nearly every situation, public employees have considerable rights to privacy.

The most common method of correcting unacceptable behavior is a simple warning. A minor disciplinary action such as a warning must be instructional and constructive. It must help the employee understand the importance of and reason for the corrective procedure being followed and the logic behind the facility's roles about how a task should be performed. Employees must understand that consistency—having all staff carry out their duties and procedures in a uniform manner—is essential for the institution.

Effective supervisors are thorough and thoughtful in addressing performance issues. When an event occurs, they find out what happened; who was involved; and where, when, and why it occurred. They address the issue with the employee privately in a calm and factual manner, without anger or debasing remarks. The warning should present the facts and be appropriate for the individual and the situation. It is often helpful to try to find out why the employee took the action in question. For example, asking, "I see you did it this way. Is there a reason for that?" The answer can help establish the motivation of the staff member. Once the employee realizes and admits to the error and understands how to behave in the future, the warning process should be ended gracefully.

It is generally not helpful to threaten a staff member about what would happen if future mistakes were made. The supervisor should instead make sure that the employee understands that the "air is clear" and the situation is history. There are few situations for a supervisor that require more tact, good judgment, common sense, and fairness than the handling of corrective action with a staff member. Every supervisor must understand that the objective of corrective action is to help the employee be successful. Often, the manner in which corrective action is handled matters more than what particular issues are addressed.

Warnings, well intended as they may be, are not always enough. When repeated rule or procedural violations occur, a supervisor should follow up with the staff member. In these situations, the supervisor should follow the same guidelines as in preparing for a warning but also document in writing the facts of the situation, the conversation with the employee, and the expectations for the staff member. It is helpful to have the employee sign this document to acknowledge that the facts are correct. This written document can be used in a memorandum of instruction or a letter of reprimand in the future.

The document should be reviewed with and presented to the staff member in private, and a copy should be provided to the individual. If performance issues persist, it will become necessary to take progressive corrective or disciplinary action.

Normally, corrective or disciplinary action for successive infractions will follow a progression in the disciplinary process:

1. Verbal instruction
2. Verbal warning
3. Written memo of instruction
4. Letter of reprimand
5. Disciplinary reduction in pay
6. Disciplinary suspension without pay
7. Demotion
8. Discharge from employment

Warnings and letters of reprimand are generally understood to be corrective action. Disciplinary action, on the other hand, is more severe and formal. Corrective action is usually taken by the supervisor, and disciplinary action is taken by the agency.

There are events or incidents that result in or require immediate separation from service and for which the principle of progressive discipline is not necessary. These include:

- Conviction in a civil court for domestic violence
- Crimes of moral turpitude (rape, child molestation)
- Reporting to work under the influence of alcohol or drugs
- Trafficking institutional contraband
- Sexual or inappropriate relationships with inmates
- Establishing personal relationships with families of inmates
- Bringing weapons into the institution

These and similar offenses can be expected to result in the employee's immediate suspension from duty, an investigation of the allegations, and a hearing as prescribed by the policy of the agency.

■ Conclusion

The chief executive officer, the warden or jail administrator, should strive to create a correctional facility where staff are recognized as the greatest asset, dignity and respect prevail, employees are valued and allowed to grow, and inmates and staff have a wholesome place to live and work. These personnel management duties cannot be outsourced. They are the central business of the agency, and they require the personal direction of the agency's top administrator. Strong central leaders will positively influence the people who live and work in these prison communities.

Chapter Resources

DISCUSSION QUESTIONS

1. Why is senior management expected to deal carefully with unacceptable staff behavior in a corrective manner?
2. Do you believe that the concept of progressive discipline is helpful to the institution?
3. Is progressive discipline helpful to the individual?
4. How are employees in a correctional facility role models?
5. What forms of disciplinary action are available to management?

ADDITIONAL RESOURCES

Berman, E., Bowman, J. S., West, J. P., & Van Wart, M. R. (2001). *Human resource management in public service. Paradoxes, processes, and problems.* Thousand Oaks, CA: Sage Publications.

Block, P. (1987). *The empowered manager: Positive political skills at work.* San Francisco, CA: Jossey-Bass.

Fisher, R., Ury, W., & Patton, B. (1991). *Getting to yes: Negotiating agreement without giving in* (2nd ed.). Boston, MA: Houghton Mifflin.

Patenaude, A. L. (2004). No promises, but I'm willing to listen and tell what I hear: Conducting qualitative research among prison inmates and staff. *The Prison Journal, 84*(4 suppl), 69S–91S.

The Society for Human Resources Management, http://www.shrm.org/hrlinks/

Wright, K. (1994). *Effective prison leadership.* Binghamton, NY: William Neil Publishing.

NOTE

1. American Correctional Association. (2005). *The 2005 directory of juvenile and adult correctional departments, institutions and other agencies.* College Park, MD: Author.

A Day in the Life of the Warden

James A. Meko

CHAPTER 20

CHAPTER OBJECTIVES

- Identify personal skills the warden needs to be successful on the job.

- Name four areas of institutional operations, in particular, that require the warden's close attention. Explain why.

- Describe what most staff and inmates look for in an effective warden.

- Explain what makes communication effective, and recognize how effective communication is important to a successful warden. Give examples.

- Discuss what we learned about American correctional leadership at Iraq's Abu Ghraib Prison.

"Prison executives face unprecedented challenges today. Inmate populations continue to soar, while state and federal budgets face severe shortfalls. External scrutiny by the press, the courts, and legislative and executive budget analysts is increasingly intense. In some areas, unions are gaining strength and demanding different working conditions. The workforce is changing. More women and minorities are entering prison service which, in itself, is good, but creates a new set of organizational circumstances. . . . Within this morass of internal and external changes, prison executives must somehow attempt to maintain stable, coherent, and predictable institutions, where inmates and staff are relatively safe, conditions are humane, facilities are sanitary, and opportunities for meaningful work are available. The challenge is great. To meet these demands, contemporary prison leaders must be highly motivated to achieve excellence, excited about what they do, passionate about mastery of their craft, and sufficiently energetic to get the job done. Passive acceptance of responsibility will not lead to success. Rather, leaders must create an institutional vision of greatness and commit themselves to its accomplishment. They must give their hearts, not just their minds nor just their time. Prison leaders must commit that element of human character from whence fervor, inspiration, and dedication flow.

These are high-sounding words—abstract and lofty. Few people working in prisons would argue with them, but when the Governor is calling, the inmates are threatening a food strike, and the safety supervisor has just informed you that the backup generator is insufficient should the facility experience a total power outage, you hardly have time for such lofty thoughts. Welcome to the world of prison administration!"

Reprinted with permission from Kevin N. Wright, *Effective Prison Leadership*, pp. 1–2, © 1994, William Neil Publishing.

There are few mundane workdays for a chief executive officer (CEO) of a jail or prison. Even on slow days, these CEOs must be ready for emergencies or unusual events. Accordingly, it is difficult to describe a typical day for senior administrators of today's jails and prisons.

The effective CEO must either have or actively develop specific "soft" personal skills to be effective on the job. These include a positive work ethic, the ability to screen information to identify problems as well as opportunities, very good oral and written communication skills, and the ability to interact positively with racially and socially diverse staff and inmates. Additionally, the ability to analyze complex situations and to make timely, effective decisions are also necessary to be effective.

A prison or jail CEO must be able to quickly respond to challenges that arise both inside and outside an institution. The best warden is a leader, not just a manager. He or she is proactive, anticipating and preparing for most correctional situations. An institution leader who is reactive is often overwhelmed by circumstances and, therefore, slow to respond. Each day, strong leaders accomplish tasks that reflect their values and those of the people they serve.

A warden's day is not always limited to normal work hours, Monday through Friday. A proactive warden is available to staff at all hours, night and day. Such access to staff ensures that the CEO is always aware of important developments at the institution. The proactive warden ensures that communication moves along the chain of command in both directions. A lieutenant or department head should not hesitate to call senior staff on a question related to an important issue at any time, day or night.

Before arriving at the institution on a normal day, the warden should review the local newspaper and television and radio broadcasts in preparation for discussing with staff any significant outside events that could influence the institution. Examples of such events include legislation affecting staff or inmates, a local politician's negative remarks about the facility, or an incident at another lockup that could affect local operations. Once in the institution, the CEO will start the day by reviewing the shift commanders' logs of the previous day's or weekend's activities.

These logs typically summarize events in the institution and identify both the staff and the inmates involved in any incident. The warden must be satisfied that these occurrences were handled appropriately. If they were not, immediate corrective action should be taken. See **Table 20-1** for an average workday for a warden.

■ Early Morning

A normal institution day often begins with a meeting involving the warden, the associate wardens, the warden's executive assistant, the head of institution security, and any other individual the CEO would like to have attend. Generally, the security chief reviews significant events that have occurred during the preceding day or weekend, and each participant is free to contribute new items or discuss plans for the day.

This meeting is important for several reasons. First, it keeps vital lines of communication open. Honest feedback, in both directions, ensures high-quality institutional operations. Such feedback also ensures that key players understand what is important to the warden and the agency and empowers them to act accordingly. Second, the meeting enables the warden to give direction to one or all members of the group with the benefit

TABLE 20-1 Warden's Workday Timetable

7:40 A.M.	Arrive at the institution; clock in and clear security (metal detector and search of personal items). Meet and greet departing midnight shift correctional staff and arriving day shift staff. Review daily shift logs.
8:15 A.M.	Meet with deputy wardens and duty officer to discuss weekend events and activities (meeting occurs on Mondays only).
9:00 A.M.	Review and sign detention orders, inmate correspondence, e-mails, inmate grievances and appeals, and institutional policy and procedures.
10:30 A.M.	Visit and observe inmate work areas, correctional industries, education and vocational training, housing units, maintenance shop, and so on.
11:30 A.M.	Observe lunch meal in the dining hall. Answer questions from inmates during mainline. Walk the yard and observe outside recreation areas, be approachable, and manage by walking around. Experience will teach you that more inmates will approach you if you are alone rather than having other staff with you. Visit and tour the minimum security unit (MSU) (camp) outside the secure perimeter, talk to the inmates and staff at MSU, and observe operations of road crews coming and going. These inmates work with the department of transportation (DOT). Minimum security inmates are assigned to work with the DOT in cutting brush, picking up litter, and so on along the highways.
1:30 P.M.	Back to the office, return phone calls, sign personnel actions, and review litigation.
2:00 P.M.	Meet with business manager and sign purchase requests, review cost center spending, and review staff and inmate canteen budgets and spending.
2:45 P.M.	Meet with internal affairs, review investigations regarding staff misconduct, and review inmate investigations and confidential informant information.
3:15 P.M.	Call the boss (central office deputy commissioner) and apprise him or her of personnel disciplinary actions, staff grievances, and high-profile inmate cases.
4:00 P.M.	Close-out meeting with deputy warden programs, chief of security, and deputy warden of operations (this meeting occurs daily, Tuesday through Friday) to discuss the day's activities, security concerns, inmates of greatest concerns, and population issues.
4:30 P.M.	Clock out and leave.

that all hear the direction and are able to question the rationale for the direction. Such a system promotes mutual respect, shared values, and camaraderie.

For instance, to ensure a safe and sanitary institution, many wardens are proponents of the "broken windows" theory first put forth in 1982 by criminologists James Q. Wilson and George L. Kelling.[1] They argue that in community police work, minor violations create a disorderly environment and actually encourage more serious crime. If the authorities take care of small offenses like public urination, aggressive panhandling, and graffiti, there will be a decrease in more serious offenses. The same approach should be used in the prison community. If staff at all levels do not tolerate littering, defacing property, or having dirty, cluttered cells, they establish themselves as "in charge," the institution is clean and orderly, and inmates are less likely to engage in more offensive behavior. In short, everyone recognizes that there is a sense of orderliness within the facility.

The morning meetings with key staff enable the warden to share such strategies with decision makers at the institution and to ensure that all are "on board." These meetings should never be longer than 1 hour, because each principal is responsible for a vital area of institutional operations; they best serve the agency on the job and not in a meeting. At the close of the meeting, individual members should feel free to seek some private time with the CEO to discuss significant personnel issues not related to the group.

Wardens should never forget that discussions about sensitive issues such as discipline, personnel, tactics, and strategy should be discussed with staff on a "need-to-know" basis. This means that only individuals with a real need to know should be told specific sensitive information.

The departure of the group gives the warden time to review incoming mail, identify individuals to prepare responses, and establish suspense dates when the response is due. Staff who prepare mail responses must be aware of the importance of and pay special attention to particular individuals, such as those at the agency's headquarters, key legislators, judges, local officials, or local media representatives. The effective warden maintains a personal and continuing dialogue with all these individuals to keep them informed of noteworthy developments at the institution. This demonstrates respect for them and shows them that the leader is professional and responsive.

Mail reviewed or signed by the warden should be routed through the appropriate associate warden and department head for two reasons. First, it keeps them in the loop and ensures that they will feel a sense of ownership of the finished product. Second, it prepares each for positions of increased responsibility in the future.

■ Midmorning

Time must routinely be set aside to meet with key staff on important matters such as budget, personnel, facilities, industries, and strategic planning. It is important, however, that meetings do not consume all of the CEO's time. The prison or jail administrator should establish guidelines for staff conducting meetings so that time is not wasted on extraneous, irrelevant issues. These guidelines should require a well-thought-out agenda shared with participants in advance and tied to articulated meeting objectives, specify the preparation required of participants, establish a time limit, state that discussion will be encouraged and dissent tolerated, require that data presented be accompanied by visual aids to facilitate the presentation, and state that no one will be permitted to monopolize the agenda. The individual chairing the meeting should ensure that each person's participation is monitored in a firm and dispassionately fair manner. These guidelines will ensure that the warden will have the time necessary to manage the institution by walking around.

Management by walking around (MBWA), first identified by Tom Peters and Nancy Austin,[2] is a trait of administrators who are in touch with both staff and inmates. These senior managers know what is happening in their institutions. Such a philosophy encourages the warden to visit all areas of the facility, ask questions, listen to answers, assess the morale of both staff and inmates, and identify problems to be resolved.

Successful prison leaders visit special housing units, the food preparation area, and the health services unit and staff training venues at least once a week to assess the quality of operations in each area, measure staff performance, and listen to staff and inmate concerns. Other areas of the confinement facility should be visited on a regular basis, but not as frequently. Experience has shown that problems in these four underscored areas are good predictors of more serious difficulties.

While touring a jail or prison, administrators must really see what is happening. One must ensure that staff are communicating with inmates—not dictating to or haphazardly confronting inmates. If staff are permitted to aggressively deal with inmates routinely, they quickly develop a confrontation mentality when speaking with inmates. Frank and direct communication demonstrates respect and tolerance. A domination mentality begets fear, intimidation, and hostility. Truly exemplary staff members care and control, exerting both compassion and authority as needed.

A warden must insist that staff be responsive to legitimate inmate concerns and complaints. Showers without hot water, heating systems that do not work, stopped-up plumbing, and poorly prepared food are small nuisances for inmates. But if these little problems are ignored, they can quickly become the basis of negative, collective inmate hostility. A warden who permits such inmate complaints to be ignored by staff will undoubtedly face major problems.

While walking and talking, the prison administrator must ensure that agency policies are being followed and that, even more important, basic standards of propriety and decency are being respected by staff. With the growing numbers of young and inexperienced staff members, it is often the warden's responsibility to ensure that these staff members know what is expected of them as well as why something is being done. For example, security concerns dictate that inmates be strip-searched upon arrival at a secure institution. However, an inmate's personal dignity can be respected in a search; the search should be performed in an area that protects an inmate's privacy. Such tours also enable the warden to establish and maintain multiple channels of communication.

In this way, the warden can take the pulse of the facility; firsthand knowledge of operations is an absolute necessity. It is a big mistake for a prison CEO to sit in his or her office and wait for subordinate staff to bring in news about what is happening. Too often, what the warden hears is what the reporting staff member thinks the warden wants to hear or what makes the staff member look good. Multiple channels of communication provide multiple sources of information to be analyzed and evaluated.

■ Early Afternoon

The afternoon begins with a daily stint "standing mainline" for the lunch meal. A proactive warden requires associate wardens and department heads to attend the serving of one meal each day. This provides additional opportunity to interact with the inmate population and staff; questions or concerns can be responded to, or written down and responded to later. This is yet another opportunity to assess the atmosphere of the correctional facility. Positive interaction between senior staff members and inmates in the dining room is a very visible way for senior staff to demonstrate care, compassion, and fair management for inmates, as well as the importance of responsiveness to legitimate inmate concerns.

The CEO thus sends an important message to all inmates: Those who administer the institution are approachable and responsive. Never does the warden want to send the message that he or she talks to only certain inmate leaders or specific inmate groups; inmates must not be given the message that they must deal through other offenders to get things done.

It is equally important to ensure that all associate wardens and the warden are not in the dining room simultaneously. One of the senior staff members should always be outside the security envelope of the institution in the event of a hostage taking.

It is also good practice to regularly eat a meal in the inmate dining room. This allows senior administrators to evaluate the food, demonstrate concern for inmate welfare, and show confidence in the food service staff. Another good practice is to carry a food thermometer to test the temperature of food items on the serving line. This keeps staff "on their toes" and shows inmates that administrators care about what inmates are served.

After mainline, it is worthwhile to visit the staff dining room to relax, visit with staff, field questions, and assess morale.

■ Midafternoon

After returning to the office to check on and return phone calls, it is probably meeting time for the CEO. Meeting with various department heads enables the warden to monitor areas of facility operations. This can also be the time for "close outs" with agency auditors who have been in the institution assessing the quality of some specific operation (business office, personnel, case management, etc.). These should be looked upon as learning opportunities. When audit teams critique a department's operation, it is important that staff not be defensive or challenge an auditor's integrity. This is a perfect time to learn about necessary changes and evaluate the performance of individual staff members.

At this time of day, a CEO might also greet tour groups as they enter or leave the facility. These encounters provide the CEO with a great opportunity to personally offer insight into facility operations and present the agency in the best light possible. Such tour groups are often composed of college students, members of the media, or local citizens.

■ Late Afternoon

Before calling it a day, a CEO must set aside time for staff development. The proactive leader sees staff development as a personal responsibility. This entails meeting with new and existing employees to outline the agency's, as well as the warden's, standards for behavior and treatment of inmates. No training or inadequate training sets the stage for problems both in the institution and in the court. It is important to personally visit staff training as it occurs to assess its quality and to interact with participants and teachers. The effective CEO conducts annual refresher sessions on subjects such as staff integrity and career planning, and meets with employees at all-staff assemblies to present issues of the day and changes in operations that are anticipated. Staff respect CEOs who not only lecture but also participate as students in required agency training. An institution leader must also make time to meet with individual staff members who need career advice and seek mentoring.

It is important to "check out" with the associate wardens before leaving the institution to determine whether there are any new developments that require the warden's attention. It is extremely beneficial to keep the associate wardens informed and to provide them with daily feedback about their performance. Administrators must carefully evaluate all the information staff provide in light of information received from personal observations and other sources.

Managing the senior leadership team of an institution is a subject that requires a volume unto itself. Suffice it to say that the CEO must never permit a situation to develop in which teamwork is adversely affected by unhealthy competition between associate wardens. Such an atmosphere is dangerous and debilitating. In a jail or prison setting, all associate wardens must be capable of serving in place of the warden for short periods of time. Given that requirement, each should be treated and informed with the knowledge that he or she may have to cover for the CEO tomorrow.

True leadership mandates that the institution warden give the associate wardens the necessary experiences and chances for personal development to assist them in achieving their career goals. This must include education, outside management courses, daily decision making, and agency training. In this manner, the leadership team at the institution builds on its strengths and overcomes its limitations.

On the way home or on the way to work, the warden should consider stopping by the gym to work out. Stresses of the day have less impact if one is able to exercise vigorously for a period of time. The warden must endeavor to maintain balance in life. Once at home, the prison or jail administrator should try to forget the day's events and focus on loved ones. One should never let a job be all-consuming. Whenever possible, the warden should be involved in community activities such as youth groups, church groups, or civic organizations. This helps the administrator maintain a positive perspective and make contributions to the community outside the job.

■ Conclusion

Correctional management is complex and demands a high level of energy, fairness, and integrity. Leadership of an institutional community requires a leader in the largest sense of the word; a warden must really be all things to all people. Wardens serve and protect the staff and inmates of the institution as well as the people in the community.

In closing, one should consider an extremely poor example of correctional leadership that occurred in Iraq in 2003 and 2004 at the Abu Ghraib prison under the jurisdiction of American forces. There, Iraqi prisoners were tortured and humiliated by their keepers. As leaders, we can learn from bad experiences too.

In testimony before the U.S. Senate Armed Services Committee in May 2004, the chief Army investigator, Major General Antonio Taguba, was asked by Senator John Warner to explain, in simple soldiers' language, how prisoner abuse arose. In frank, direct terms, the General responded:

> "Failure of leadership, sir, from the brigade commander on down. Lack of discipline, no training whatsoever, and no supervision. Supervisory omission was rampant. Those are my comments."[4]

The effective leader of a penal facility must be a leader who is involved and who prevents such things from happening. The leader must be able to establish and maintain good relationships with people at all levels. Staff and inmates want neither a tyrant nor a pushover as their warden. They want a fair, firm, and consistent administrator who creates a positive interpersonal working environment. Everyone wants an individual who is friendly and cheerful, who listens more than he or she speaks, who keeps an open mind, and who is calm and considerate. A successful warden is one who is involved, who praises as well as criticizes, who avoids discouraging comments and gossip, who is sensitive and considerate regarding others' shortcomings, and who holds others in high esteem.

To serve as a warden is indeed a high calling.

Chapter Resources

REVIEW QUESTIONS

1. How does "the broken windows theory" apply to prison/jail management?
2. In what ways does "management by walking around" (MBWA) make a prison environment better?
3. Why is quality staff training so important in prison/jail operations?
4. You have been named "Warden of the Year" by the American Correctional Association for your work in prison/jail. Prepare an outline of your acceptance speech citing the secrets to your success.

DISCUSSION QUESTIONS

1. What is a confrontation mentality in inmate management? Why should it be avoided?
2. Give some examples of effective leadership skills in correctional environments.
3. What is meant by maintaining balance in one's life? Give examples.
4. Think about proactive versus reactive leadership. Which approach do you prefer? Why?
5. Why should you never have the warden and all associate wardens together in one area inside the institution security envelope at one time?

ADDITIONAL RESOURCES

Buice, E. (2002, April). Going the extra mile with the media. *Law and Order, 50*(4), 16.

Giuliani, R. W. (2002). *Leadership.* New York, NY: Miramax Books.

Kokkelenberg, L. D. (2001, February 14). Real leadership is more than just a walk in the park. *Law Enforcement News* (p. 9).

Seiter, R. P. (2011). *Correctional administration: Integrating theory and practice* (2nd ed.). Upper Saddle River, NJ: Prentice Hall.

Wayne, W. (2004). *Bennett and Karen Hess management and supervision in law enforcement.* Belmont, CA: Wadsworth/Thompson Learning.

NOTES

1. Wright, K. N. (1994). *Effective prison leadership* (pp. 1–2). Binghamton, NY: William Neil Publishing. Reprinted with permission.
2. Wilson, J., & Kelling, G. (1989). Broken windows. In R. Dunham & G. Alpert (Eds.), *Critical issues in policing* (pp. 208–218). Prospect Heights, IL: Waveland Press.
3. Peters, T., & Austin, N. (1985). *A passion for excellence* (p. 123). New York, NY: Random House.
4. U.S. Senate Armed Services Committee. (2004, May 11). *Hearings on Iraqi prisoner abuse.* Transcribed by Media Millwork Incorporated.

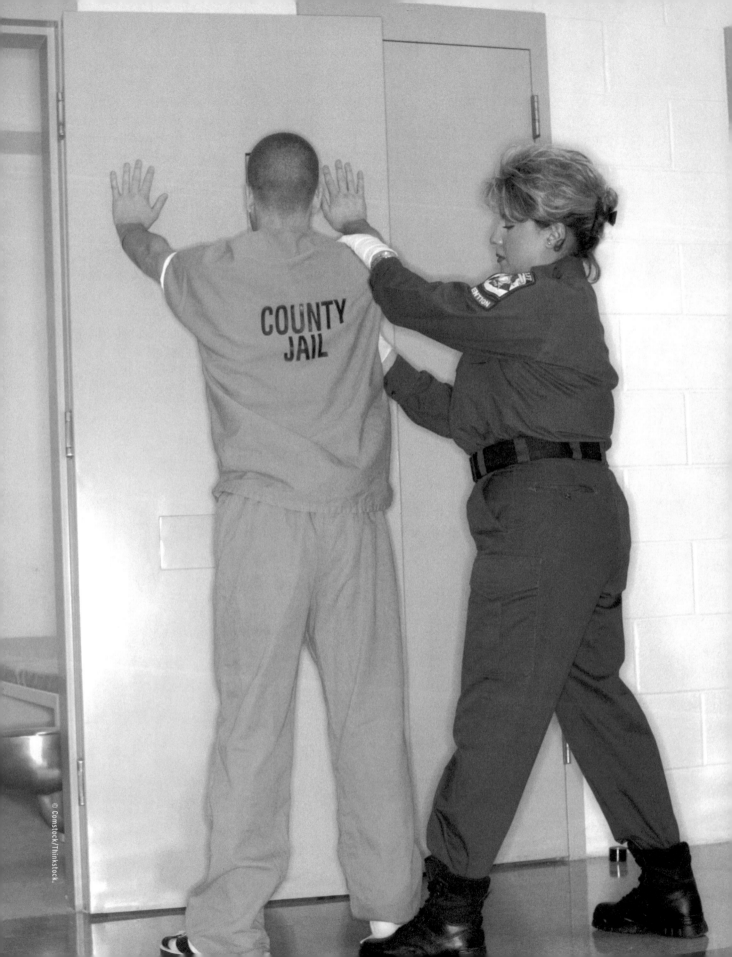

The World of a Correctional Officer

Brandon Howard

CHAPTER OBJECTIVES

- Identify the basic role and functions of a correctional officer.

- Obtain a general overview of a correctional officer's role in the institutional schedule, particularly in terms of individual post assignments.

- Identify fundamentals of officer–inmate interaction, along with common approaches and the definition of inmate "manipulation."

- Forms of officer misconduct and issues facing correctional officers at work and home.

- Routes to advancement and promotion through training.

The day-to-day activities of a correctional officer, while often routine, are far from boring. Unpredictability is a hallmark of the profession; some days might be quietly peaceful, whereas the next might be rife with nonstop activity. Correctional officers therefore learn to expect the unexpected and prepare for the worst-case scenario at all times. Regardless of how the day is divided, a correctional institution is a facility that demands 24-hour staffing. Shift hours can differ, with some facilities employing a system of three 13-hour shifts and others keeping to a more traditional 8-hour shift. The daily activities of a correctional officer vary considerably, depending on several factors; these include but are not limited to the security level of the institution, the shift, and the post that the officer works.

■ Definition, Posts, and Duties

A correctional or prison officer is defined by the Bureau of Labor as being "responsible for overseeing individuals who have been arrested ... or who have been sentenced to serve time in a jail, reformatory or prison."[1] Essentially, the most basic function of a correctional officer is to maintain the safety and security of the institution so that the public at large remains safe. To this end, correctional officers are entrusted with a very old and important function: the management of outcast individuals that society has deemed dangerous and threatening. Typically, a college degree is recommended but not required; candidates need to have completed high school or possess a general equivalency diploma. Individual training programs differ considerably as correctional officers serve at the federal, state, and county levels at facilities requiring 24-hour staffing. Most training programs will cover inmate interaction, official document composition and report writing, basic self-defense and weapons retention, and finally, firearms qualification on pistols, semi-automatic rifles, and shotguns.

Regardless of the facility or shift, most correctional officers' days begin at roll call. This often occurs approximately 15 minutes before officers can clock in and entails a general debriefing by the shift supervisor of anything that might have happened on the previous shift that warrants discussion: this can be the number of fights/injuries that have occurred, discovery of dangerous contraband, or incoming/outgoing inmate transfers. It is during roll call that officers will find out where they are working that day. Most facilities keep officers on fairly consistent weekly post assignments, but this is rarely definite and is influenced by the number of officers working overtime from other shifts and institutional need. Some officers serve in a relief capacity, filling in on regular posts on others' off-days, and are rarely assured of where they will be working during that shift until they look at the roster. Once roll call is concluded, officers can begin checking out the gear they require, usually from the institutional control center. Items that most officers carry include flashlights for cell searches and counts, handcuffs, oleoresin capsicum (OC) or "pepper spray," and personal radios for communication.

After correctional officers ("C/Os," as they are usually addressed by inmates) begin clocking in, they head out to their post assignments. Every shift has certain key posts in common, such as living or housing unit posts, perimeter patrols, tower security, control center, yard patrol, and the special housing unit (SHU). For the purposes of this chapter, the three posts considered will be living units/dorms, yard/tower, and SHU. Although post assignments vary in function, all officers spend the first few minutes on paperwork. This is in the form of post orders and logbooks, the former being a written guideline of what duties are expected at that specific post and the latter a record of the events of the day. Post orders are based on institutional policies and may vary from facility to facility.

Once the post orders and logbook have been signed, the officer inventories all the equipment that has been handed to him from the previous shift officer. This often consists of keys, which are checked individually to ensure that all are in proper working order and accounted for. The relieving officer is also expected to check the logbook for the previous shift to get an idea of what kinds of activities occurred on the previous shift. A general security check of the unit usually follows, during which the officer will check the state of the fire extinguishers and emergency equipment, unit cleanliness, and whether all doors are secure and locked. Most shifts will have the inmates on lockdown status, that is, confined to their cells, so that the relief shift can perform their initial security check without interference. When this has been completed, the shift's daily activities will commence.

The first or day shift is by far the busiest in terms of activity and therefore carries the largest complement of officers. Administrative personnel such as inmate caseworkers, unit administrators, and deputy wardens are also conducting their daily activities, adding to the bustle. For living unit officers, the day will usually consist of conducting unit security checks (usually a minimum of two per hour), cell searches, maintaining an orderly and clean unit appearance by managing inmates assigned to janitorial duties, and finally, counting. This sounds simple enough, but it is often compounded with numerous requests from administrative personnel, such as locating inmates at work assignments and classes and with classification procedures. Correctional officers follow a specific chain of command, so directives and tasks that are issued through the captain make their way through a lieutenant, then a sergeant each day. Officers serving in a living unit will answer to a sergeant or lieutenant in charge of that unit.

Officers assigned to the yard post will maintain a visible presence on the recreation yard, which is often during the daylight hours. These individuals are most often designated as first responders in the event of a fight, fire, or assault because they have freedom of mobility in patrolling the grounds. Yard officers are generally responsible for conducting random pat-downs of inmates on the yard, investigating suspicious activity, escorting inmates to secure areas, and running errands that might arise. A typical day may see a total of five yard officers assigned to monitor a yard the size of a football field containing, at any given time, approximately 80–100 inmates. This disadvantage is somewhat offset by the presence of security towers, each manned by an officer whose duty is to look for suspicious or potentially dangerous activity that could occur. How this is determined is usually peculiar to the institution itself, as officers are familiar with the idiosyncratic behavior of the inmates in their charge. This includes groups of inmates who are always together, if they appear to be passing items between themselves and if they appear to be on the lookout for officers.

Another post deserving special mention is the special housing unit (SHU). Commonly (and inaccurately) referred to as "the hole" or "solitary," this prison-within-a-prison is where inmates are placed for disciplinary action or where incorrigible inmates serve their sentences. Instead of having double bunks, cells in SHU are designed for a single occupant and are quite bare, usually containing a concrete bed and desk along with a sink and a toilet built into the wall. The inmates are given a mattress and pillow along with bed linens and toiletries but little else, save for some books, magazines, and writing paper for letters. Most inmates are confined to SHU cells for 23 hours a day, with an hour of recreation time in a bullpen and three showers a week. The punitive aspect of SHU is essentially iron boredom, depriving the inmate of contact with friends on the yard and access to television/recreation, and limiting them to three institutional meals a day with no access to the inmate canteen. Officers assigned to SHU are usually more experienced and exhibit a high tolerance for stress, as there can be constant noise of yelling, door kicking, and other abrasive behavior from inmates. A good deal of administrative work is expected of the officers at this post as well, because officers must preside over the intake procedures of new inmates, inventory their personal property when it arrives, and fill out the appropriate paperwork. SHU usually carries a minimum of four officers, is supervised by a sergeant or lieutenant, and operates largely independent of the institutional routine, except whenever inmates are admitted to or released from SHU.

■ Interacting with Inmates

Despite the differences between these posts, all have a common factor: interacting with inmates. Officers are to hold inmates to the standards of appearance that are expected of them: presentable dress, visible ID at all times, and an orderly and professional manner. Most initial training covers officer–inmate interaction quite thoroughly, using various techniques. Officers are taught not to be disrespectful to inmates in their confrontations and to maintain their professional demeanor: no swearing, name calling, or aggressive vocalizations. A common interaction model for conflict resolution is "motivational interviewing," a clinical approach that employs nonconfrontational dialogue to deescalate and defuse potentially volatile situations.[3] Officers are trained on various sensitive topics that affect inmate interaction, including racism, gang behavior, and mental disorders among inmates. Race is an ever-present issue in prison and runs hand-in-hand with gang activity at times. Inmates show a distinct tendency to self-segregate, with individuals from certain ethnic groups tending to sit at the same tables and hang out together. Recognizing suicidal tendencies such as self-harm, giving away possessions, and withdrawing from life is essential to officers because prison suicide rates are higher than those in the general population.[4]

Correctional officers are expected to maintain a firm, fair, and consistent daily interface in inmate interactions. It is often been said that correctional officers are not to punish but to enforce, similar to the way a patrol officer might issue a speeding ticket. To this end, the job can become very stressful whenever an officer takes aspects of the job personally. Officers encounter confrontational, angry, and even physically aggressive behavior on a daily basis and yet are expected to maintain a businesslike professionalism at all times. It is this aspect of the job that many people tend to fail at, not having the ability to be both disciplinary and yet somewhat personable. In fact, the position of correctional officer is one of the few entry-level jobs where new hires are expected to supervise others on a daily basis. Officers at the beginning of their careers are obviously at the most vulnerable point as they are unsure of how to present themselves. Being too assertive is one extreme; the other is timidity and failing to enforce the rules. Both of these approaches typically fail as the inmates do not respect the officer and instead manipulate or subvert him or her.

This is why the first impression is crucial. Every new officer feels apprehension on the first day, if not outright fear. Being a single officer among 100 inmates in a living unit feels a lot like having a large crosshair on you at all times. Officer trainees are taught to come in firm, though fair, because they can always lighten up on the inmates later. Conversely, it is very hard to initially present yourself as a lax officer and then assert your authority later. Most institutions have a myriad of rules, usually distinguishing between minor and major infractions. An example of a minor infraction might be an inmate not having his shirt tucked in or wearing a cap indoors. Although technically a punishable offense according to policy, it is ultimately up to the officer what is to be done. The officer can take the hard line and write up the inmate or just let it go. Prisons typically base their rule system on the "Broken Window theory," the idea being that if conditions are not corrected early on, then they can become more serious problems.[5] In the above example, if the officer were to let the inmate off entirely, other inmates will take notice and stop dressing appropriately. If they notice that the officer tolerates this behavior, then they will begin pushing the envelope to see what else they can get away with. At this point, the officer has lost the respect of the inmates and is being manipulated and may not even be aware of it.

On the flip side, if the officer were to write up the inmate and not give him a chance to explain himself, the other inmates in the unit will notice and adjust their behavior accordingly. The hard-line approach typically works in the short term, as inmates are wary of trying to get anything past an authoritative officer. As time goes on, officers who are quick to punish even minor offenses lose respect among inmates, because they feel they have nothing to lose and work harder to find ways to subvert and annoy the officer. This is fairly easy to accomplish because, as it is often explained to officers in training, inmates have 24 hours a day and 7 days a week to plot, whereas officers have only 40 hours, essentially the difference between a lifestyle and a job. With the odds so heavily in the inmates' favor, officers must pick their battles. A middle path is advisable—instead of writing up or letting the inmate off the hook, an officer should issue the inmate a warning and note it in a logbook, with the understanding that a repeat offense will result in disciplinary action. This gives the offender the opportunity to save face in front of other inmates without the officer backing down.

Although over-empathizing with inmates is discouraged at all costs, officers are expected to display a degree of humanity. Working side by side with individuals on a day-to-day basis over long periods of time necessitates respect and understanding. Officers may supervise some inmates with life sentences for the entirety of their careers and will undoubtedly come to know them quite well. Because they occupy a similar place in the prison hierarchy, officers and inmates do not always share a mutual antipathy. Inmates tend to understand that officers, unless they are acting out of bounds, merely enforce rules and directives issued to them through supervisors. Because officers and inmates work so close together at times, it is officers who learn more about the personal lives and activities of inmates than anyone else in the facility. It should be noted and strongly emphasized that it is not an official duty of officers to provide mental health advice to inmates. However, psychological insight is a valuable advantage to officers. This comes about through daily interaction, which is why "a well-trained and conscientious correctional officer is more likely to be responsible for diffusing a potential problem than is any member of the mental health staff."[6]

Once an officer has found his or her stride, the days become regular and a routine is found. Inmates know what a particular officer expects of them, and officers find that their jobs become easier as a result. In fact, the inmates will usually assist the officer in some ways, such as explaining to new arrivals what the particular officer expects from inmates. After a while, the job seems mundane. Corrections work has been referred to as being "like an adult daycare"—an appropriate enough simile at times. However, routine can be the enemy of officers because it encourages complacency and makes officers more vulnerable to manipulation. Inmate manipulation in this context is an attempt by an inmate to obtain special privileges by playing on an officer's sympathy or behavior. This can happen so subtly that it is often impossible to detect. Inmates are very alert to officer habits and use this to their advantage. Manipulation usually begins innocently enough, sometimes with just a request for an extra cup of juice at dinner. This escalates quickly and is a prime example of the psychologically persuasive "foot-in-the-door" technique.[7] Once an officer begins making allowances in behavior for one inmate, other staff and inmates quickly notice the special treatment. This makes the work harder on the officer in the long run because it destroys credibility. The tenuous bond of trust between officer and inmate is only as good as the officer's actions—in prison, credibility or "face" is as essential for the officer as it is for the inmate in establishing a good rapport.

When inmates become disorderly, the behavior has to be corrected immediately, with the response depending on the severity of the situation. If an inmate quietly disagrees with an officer, he is usually told in a professional but firm manner that he is out of place. But should an inmate yell at an officer in front of other inmates, then he is taken to SHU immediately for creating an aggressive demonstration, as such activity might compromise the harmony within the living unit. A fight or assault is dealt with in the same manner: after the officer has announced it via radio, then first responders arrive to subdue and escort the inmates to the medical department for examination. If there are no injuries severe enough to warrant a trip to an outside hospital, then the inmates are cleaned, treated, and taken to SHU, where they are strip-searched and undergo an OC decontamination. Officers are discouraged from trying to break up a fight by themselves because there is greater chance for injury. The use of force is clearly defined by state policy, and officers are subject to disciplinary action if force is deemed excessive. The classic image of a prison guard with a wooden baton is now hopelessly out of date—modern correctional officers report to post armed with nothing more than a personal radio, flashlight, and, increasingly, OC spray. When it comes to physical confrontation, officers are to be practical and not do anything to jeopardize the safety and security of the institution, including acting like a hero and charging in without backup.

Of special note is the phenomenon of prison rape. Even until recently, this was considered a semi-taboo subject. It was not until the 2003 passage of the Prison Rape Elimination Act (PREA) that this topic was finally given appropriate acknowledgment in both the psychiatric and legislative realms.[8] Because of PREA, incidents of prison rape were given higher recognition and measures were taken to curtail future occurrences, with a "zero tolerance" mentality. For the officer, this entails a special protocol, different from that of a fight or other assault, in the event of a rape. If an officer is informed that a rape may have occurred, he contacts the supervisor, who has the inmates involved immediately isolated for protective custody. Any involved inmates are usually placed in SHU pending an internal affairs investigation. Clothes are surrendered as evidence if they contain blood or other bodily fluids. Once the passive and active roles have been established, the victim is not allowed to shower, eat, or drink until a sexual assault forensic evidence (SAFE) kit has been administered. In a state facility, this is usually done by the state police and internal affairs unit of the prison. After the veracity of the incident is determined, action is taken that includes criminal charges against the aggressor(s), in addition to sanctions such as good time loss and assignment to SHU for a prolonged period.

■ Issues, Training, and Advancement

Correctional officers face various challenges each day, both at work and when they leave. Under the same scrutiny as inmates, officers have to account for their behavior when they fail to follow policy. Misconduct can be passive or active. Being forgetful is easy and happens to everyone at some point in their careers. This can include not signing the logbook or post orders, forgetting to conduct an inventory of a new arrival's personal property, or misplacing a set of keys. Although these can be serious, isolated incidents usually do not warrant concern. It is when an officer purposefully displays negligent behavior on a consistent basis that there is greater chance for trouble. This most often manifests in subtle, seemingly innocent offenses.

A good example of this is when an officer falsifies walkthroughs of their unit. Although it can be tempting to forgo a security check, culpability will rest squarely with the officer if something goes awry. A good example might be the following: an officer conducts a walkthrough of Dorm A at 6:05 P.M. and notes nothing unusual. When he gets back to the control station, he begins to read or calls an officer on another post to talk. Minutes pass, and soon it is time for another security check, but the officer does not want to get up and bother, so he skips it but writes one down anyway. The next time he conducts a walkthrough, it is 8:01 P.M., and he finds an inmate dead of a heart attack in his cell. There is nothing that could save the officer at this point, particularly if it is a new institution that has extensive camera coverage. Because the post orders clearly state that a *minimum* of two security walkthroughs per hour are to be conducted and the officer has falsified his logbook, he has violated policy. This can warrant dismissal, not to mention possible legal repercussions, and underscores the vigilance and dedication necessary for correctional work. It can be boring at times, but it is better adhere to routine than to end up in court, facing life on the other side of the fence. Bearing this in mind, officers will do well to remember that policy and procedure, while seeming like so much government red tape, is not a binding tie but a lifeline in the labyrinth.

More serious than simply neglecting to perform their duties are officers who engage in professional misconduct with inmates. This includes giving sensitive information to inmates, bringing in contraband from outside, and committing sexual offenses with inmates. These are unpleasant but vital issues to discuss, not just for new hires. Most institutions conduct an annual in-service training to refresh officers on their job duties and discuss incidents that occurred during the previous year. Professional misconduct, particularly sexual in nature, is always covered during this process, along with introducing contraband. Contraband is any substance or device deemed a threat to the security of the institution and includes drugs, weapons, cell phones, and books or magazines of a subversive nature. The definition of contraband is not always obvious to the officer but is usually defined by policy. Various psychological reasons are posited for why officers would betray their ethics so blatantly: money, depression, and lack of satisfaction in home life. This depressing phenomenon is by no means uncommon and is all the more unfortunate for the high-profile damage it does to correctional employees in the public eye. Officers acting inappropriately with inmates do not realize that they are not merely acting selfishly but are actively endangering the lives of everyone they work with, as well as the public they have been tasked with defending. This ripple effect extends to family and friends in the community and is particularly hard on officers with spouses and children.

Corrections employees are told to "leave the job at the door." Do not take any of the day's events home with you, and start the next day fresh. This bit of wisdom holds true consistently and helps to combat burnout. The same is true of personal problems; do not bring them to work lest they compromise performance. Although this is true with any job, it is especially important in corrections, where there is responsibility for others. If officers bring their issues to work and take them out on inmates, they lose respect. Inmates have problems just like anyone else, perhaps more so because many have families and children on the outside, and they are not able to provide for them. Stress is a disease common to both inmate and officer, and both should make great efforts to keep their personal lives out of any interaction. This is especially true in regard to casual conversation: officers are repeatedly told not to discuss personal matters in front of inmates. Though obvious, this is harder than it sounds, and most new officers simply are not aware of how observant inmates are. Although it may not seem like a big deal that an inmate learns an officer's hometown, it would take little more to learn the officer's address during a weekly phone call home. It is for this reason that officers rarely carry into the facility wallets, driver's licenses, financial information, or any kind of document that may display any personal financial or geographical information. The same token applies to inmate interactions—it is okay to share a joke here and there, but an officer and an inmate should always remember their respective roles. Inmates are not potential friends, and treating them as such is a conflict of interest. This especially applies to inmates an officer may have known in private life, which is a relatively common circumstance in state facilities. Again, the absolute need for separation of personal and occupational lives is essential here—an officer should *never* get too close to an inmate, regardless of intentions.

However ideal, this is not always possible because, like those who have any other job, correctional officers are human. Officers have to tolerate a lot of negativity, from both inmates and other officers. Supervisors can be another source of tension, as they are under pressure to run shifts as efficiently as possible while keeping the lowest possible staff complement for financial reasons. Additionally, the turnover rate in corrections can be high at times, and it is time-consuming to replace an officer because most training programs take a minimum of 3–4 weeks. When this occurs, it becomes harder for officers to obtain days off and the overtime rate begins to climb. Overtime in a prison setting is especially grueling because a call-in warrants a double shift: for an 8-hour workday, this means a 16-hour shift. When overtime becomes rampant, then officers might call in sick just to get some time off, complicating the low staff problem. After a while of this vicious cycle, many people simply burn out on the job and quit. It should be stressed at this point that being a correctional officer is not a 9-to-5 job but a 24-hour obligation. Officers are constantly on call in case of emergencies and are expected to report to work if called, even on off-days. This can be a daunting commitment and strains an officer's personal life, especially for institutions that employ an alternating shift or off-day schedule. Having to work odd and long hours on short notice results in poor sleep and decreased performance, something inmates will not hesitate to take advantage of. It also makes it difficult for officers to get habituated to a single shift and develop closer relationships with their coworkers.

A typical result of accumulated stress at work is compassion fatigue, a psychological disorder commonly seen in nurses, emergency medical technicians (EMTs), and caregivers. Compassion fatigue resembles post-traumatic stress disorder in that the afflicted typically begins to withdraw emotionally because of prolonged exposure to traumatic or painful emotional experiences.[9] For correctional officers, this occurs because of the high demands placed on their emotions. Most inmates strive to gain officer sympathy, either for manipulative purposes or because of genuine loneliness. Officers, although encouraged to refrain from learning about inmate crimes, inadvertently do so by overhearing conversations or from the local news. In addition, officers have to contend with mentally unstable inmates, attempted suicides, and violent assaults or even homicides.

Family problems can exacerbate an already overextended individual, making emotional connections even more difficult. After a while, some officers lose the ability to feel compassion both at work and at home. The effect this has on the officer's home life, much less on their work performance, is not difficult to imagine.

Training helps to combat many of the aforementioned issues. As mentioned previously, most correctional facilities dedicate several months out of each year for refresher courses and officer retraining. This is essentially a review of the initial training that officer candidates undergo during the hiring process. During this time, issues common to officers are discussed, along with possible solutions or avenues of support. Training serves to remind officers that each one of them bears a part of the burden and that they are not alone. Team mentality is one of the hallmarks of corrections work. Being outnumbered and sharing a common purpose fosters a necessary dependency on each other, which is why many facilities emphasize team-building exercises. Officers can participate in many supplemental training and certification classes throughout their careers. Certifications may be obtained for OC spray, the X-26 Tazer, pepper ball, and/or other less than lethal weapons, riot shield, and defensive tactics. Depending on the hours of training involved, officers may obtain instructor or "train the trainer" certifications and assist in teaching others at the institution.

Beyond simple certifications, officers have the option to participate in voluntary extracurricular organizations. The number and functions of these groups vary depending on facility, but some of the most common are the Hostage Negotiation Team (HNT), K-9 unit, and Special Response Team (SRT)/Corrections Emergency Response Team (CERT). For officers interested in the HNT, specialized training includes psychological persuasion techniques and counseling. Officers must be willing to lose and retain control of their emotions, because they most likely know the inmates involved and must use that knowledge during their negotiations. HNT is typically divided into multiple teams, each headed by a team leader and an assistant team leader.[10] The SRT/CERT organization is more paramilitary, in keeping with its dominant function.

Correctional special operations teams are the corrections equivalent of police Special Weapons and Tactics (SWAT) teams, responsible for tactical entry during substantial breaches of security such as riots, mass cell searches, inmate protests, and other disturbances.[11] Officers volunteering for this assignment are given more intense physical training on additional weapons such as a 40-mm projectile launcher, baton use, and formation marching in riot gear. Similar to the HNT, special operations teams are organized into teams, with each team organized by squad. Squads typically comprise 4–6 officers and are headed by a squad leader and assistant squad leader. Each officer on the team may perform a distinct function, such as firearms, shield operation, blueprint reading, rappelling, and medic skills. Finally, the K-9 unit is the team responsible for contraband detections and the recovery of escaped inmates through the use of tracking dogs, usually bloodhounds or German shepherds.[12] Officers involved with K-9 activities must also be physically fit and enjoy working with dogs. Training also includes other person-tracking techniques such as compass navigation and map reading, stealthy movement, and night tracking.

It needs to be mentioned that officers participating in any of these teams are usually issued a pager because they need to be constantly on call in case of activation. Although this is true of all officers, those assigned to special teams can also be activated for other community mishaps, such as natural disasters, or to augment local search-and-rescue teams. Participants may also be paged at odd hours for spontaneous training exercises. Most institutions insist that each team train a minimum of 8 hours per month. Officers interested in applying for any of these organizations, after successfully passing a physical and interview process, spend at least a week at a training facility for initial instruction. Once officers are on the team of their choice, they are usually sent for additional training several times throughout the year to acquire new skills. This is a bigger commitment than it sounds, as most volunteer groups offer no monetary incentives for joining. Thus, officers participating in additional training are highly motivated and career oriented. The effort is not without reward, however, as officers typically find it easier to get a promotion because they have the appreciation of their supervisors.

Promotion as an officer typically takes three paths: security, administrative, and related fields. Although this is not set in stone, officers rarely promote to other areas of the facility unless they have highly specialized skills or degrees, such as maintenance or education. Because officers begin their careers in security, most tend to seek promotion in this fashion. Depending on the level of government at which one serves, the next step up for an officer is usually sergeant. Some state correctional departments have multiple officer ranks, such as senior officer, but for the sake of simplicity, these will not be discussed because they ultimately amount to a slight increase in pay and responsibility. To apply for sergeant, officers must have at least 1 year of experience as an officer—in practice, officers may have several years and multiple interviews before they promote. Sergeants are typically the first-line supervisor for officers to report to and supervise certain areas of the institution, such as SHU or the control center. Sergeants who have a year of supervisory experience may then apply for lieutenant although, again, in practice this takes several years. Lieutenants are the intermediate supervisor between captains and sergeants and serve to facilitate directives from the former to latter. Lieutenants are also responsible for the operation of the shift on the captain's days off and handle a great deal of the administrative tasks during the shift, such as clerking duties. To become captain, 3–5 years of supervisory experience is necessary. This is usually the highest post that an officer can promote to without a college degree and is also the highest post in the security branch. Captains oversee the day to day operations of the shift and communicate administrative orders from the deputy wardens to those on their shift. Depending on the educational requirements of the agency, captains can be promoted to higher-level administrative positions, such as unit administrators or even deputy wardens. However, nearly all agencies tend to require formal education for the position of warden.

Promotion through the administrative route follows a similar pattern. The majority of administrative positions, say for office support personnel, require a 4-year degree though the field usually does not matter. Entry-level administrative positions often begin with the classification officer or "caseworker," who is responsible for determining inmate custody and security levels. This is based on various contributing factors like criminal history and the number of disciplinary violations accumulated over the previous year. Caseworkers manage a caseload of inmates and act as a liaison between the inmate and the outside world at times by arranging outside calls, special visits, and funeral trips for inmates. They report to administrative unit leaders who are charged with the oversight and management of inmate housing units, with each unit having its own caseworker. Classification officers most often promote to the unit administrator position, where they work with the shift captain to enforce discipline. Unit administrators are also responsible for the daily routine of their units by managing inmate bed assignment requests, determining meeting schedules for facility-sanctioned inmate groups, and overseeing classification procedures with caseworkers. Unit administrators may advance to deputy warden, the second highest position in the facility. Typically, there are three deputy wardens overseeing areas such as security, programs, and operations. Deputy wardens handle the affairs of their departments and assist the warden with implementing institutional policy and determining changes to it as necessary.

Finally, promotion can be pursued outside the facility setting, which opens various potential career avenues. One of the most popular corrections positions outside the facility is the probation/parole department. Although this department often has a representative at the institutional level, probation/parole officers are typically located in offices in cities and county seats. Newly paroled inmates report to them upon release to determine the conditions and obligations of parole. This usually means finding gainful employment, obeying a curfew, and keeping scheduled visits to determine progress. Correctional officers with 4-year degrees make prime candidates because they have the requisite education as well as experience with offenders. Some officers seek advancement in other areas of corrections like officer training and become training instructors and coordinators. These individuals are responsible for the initial training officers receive and conduct classes regarding other training incentives annually.

■ Conclusion

One of the first things taught to officer trainees is the obsolescence of the term "prison guard." This implies a rather simple duty: the protection of property. Nothing could be further from the truth as it fails to describe the difficult path that officers must walk each day. Correctional officers do far more than merely watch fences; they are expected to project authority on those who do not respect it, impose order among chaos, and handle routine and the unexpected with equal dexterity. At times, being a correctional officer is a study in extremes, for example, between compassion and firmness. In this way, the job is not dissimilar to police officers in their efforts to maintain balance and harmony within a community. This is achieved through consistency, vigilance, fairness, and dedication. To be successful as a correctional officer, one must possess each of these traits in abundance.

Although it can at times be trying, a career in corrections lays a solid foundation for the future. Individuals mature rapidly when forced to account not only for themselves but for others. The training received in managing not only the activities but the daily lives of inmates imparts a great sense of managerial responsibility from the outset, something that few jobs can offer to entry-level employees. Many other positions, such as restaurant manager, achieve this only after years of service—in corrections, this is the norm rather than the exception. What makes corrections a great career is that leadership is not required from an officer's first day but comes to be expected through experience. Many people of different personality types find success in this field if they are dedicated, committed, and punctual. (It has been said, jokingly, that 99% of effort is simply showing up.) Correctional work is also a field that almost guarantees constant employment—correctional officers usually do not have to worry about downsizing, for instance. In these troubled economic times, this is a rare state of affairs.

Correctional officers have an opportunity to serve and protect the public in a unique capacity. The opportunities for personal growth through experience and training bestow strong qualities of leadership and responsibility that benefit officers both in the workplace and at home. Yet perhaps one of the strangest complaints about the job is the intangibility of it. Unlike a construction worker or a custodian, a correctional officer rarely sees a physical product of the day's efforts. At the end of a shift on a good day, the institution looks the same as it did when the officer clocked in. Praise for work well done can go unnoticed at times due to daily business and unexpected occurrences. In this environment, it is easy to lose sight of the ultimate goal—to ensure that your coworkers go home safe and every inmate is safe and accounted for. For correctional officers, each routine day is, in fact, a victory.

Chapter Resources

DISCUSSION QUESTIONS

1. What is "compassion fatigue," and how does it affect an officer's professional and personal lives?
2. What are potential career advancement paths in corrections for officers?
3. Give one example of both passive and active officer misconduct and why each is detrimental to the security of the institution.
4. Name three volunteer extracurricular organizations that officers might join.
5. What is the PREA, and why is it important in corrections?

ADDITIONAL RESOURCES

Bureau of Labor Statistics Occupational Outlook Handbook: Correctional Officer, http://www.bls.gov/ooh/Protective-Service/Correctional-officers.htm

Corrections.com, http://www.corrections.com

Federal Bureau of Prisons Career Opportunities: Correctional Officer, http://www.bop.gov/jobs/job_descriptions/correctional_officer.jsp

National Institute of Corrections, http://nicic.gov

NOTES

1. United States Department of Labor. (2012, April 26). What do correctional officers do? *Bureau of Labor Statistics: Occupational Outlook Handbook*. Retrieved from http://www.bls.gov/ooh/Protective-Service/Correctional-officers.htm
2. Cooper, L. (2012). Combined motivational interviewing and cognitive-behavioral therapy with older adult drug and alcohol abusers. *Health & Social Work, 37*(3), 173–179.
3. Mumola, C. J., & United States Department of Justice. (2005). Bureau of justice statistics special report. *Suicide and homicide in state prisons and local jails*. Retrieved from http://www.bjs.gov/content/pub/pdf/shsplj.pdf
4. Wilson, J., & Kelling, G. (March 1982). Broken windows: The police and neighborhood safety. *Atlantic Monthly*.
5. Dvoskin, J. A., & Spiers, E. M. (2004). On the role of correctional officers in prison mental health. *Psychiatric Quarterly, 75*(1), 41–59.
6. Rodafinos, A. S., Vucevic, A., & Iderdis, G. D. (2005). The effectiveness of compliance techniques: Foot in the door versus door in the face. *Journal of Social Psychology, 145*(2), 237–239.
7. United State Department of Justice. PREA/Offender Sexual Abuse. *National Institute of Corrections*. Retrieved from http://nicic.gov/PREA
8. Janik, J. (1995). Overwhelmed corrections workers can seek therapy. *Corrections Today, 57*(7), 162–163.
9. Oklahoma State Government. Department of Corrections. (2012). *Hostage situations*. Retrieved from http://www.doc.state.ok.us/offtech/op050401.pdf

10. Correctional Emergency Response Team. (2013). *Online criminology and criminal justice*. Portland State University. Retrieved from http://online.ccj.pdx.edu/ccj-careers-resources/criminal-justice-resources/research/correctional-emergency-response-team/

11. K-9 Unit. Kansas Department of Corrections. (n.d.). Retrieved from http://www.doc.ks.gov/facilities/hcf/k-9-unit

Labor Relations in Corrections

Michael H. Jaime and Armand R. Burruel

CHAPTER
22

CHAPTER OBJECTIVES

- Give examples of recent collective bargaining agreements (CBAs) that affect a jurisdiction's general fund.

- Give examples of typical and unusual provisions found in CBAs covering the corrections jurisdictions.

- Explain why the preparation for, the process, and the conclusion of bargaining toward a master agreement in a corrections jurisdiction can be prolonged.

- Describe the components of a sound management and supervisor learning program on labor relations.

- Discuss the tensions that develop between labor and management in corrections when a protracted decline in public sector funding exists for more than a few years.

Among the many demands that prison and jail administrators face, many related to inmate conditions of confinement and population management, one of the most difficult involves the interaction between management and labor organizations. This complex interaction is referred to as labor–management relations (LMR). The U.S. economy downturn starting in 2005 through 2011 complicates LMR at all levels of public sector governments. Corrections administrators must become involved in the plethora of LMR activities. They must learn the vocabulary of LMR: grievance, unfair labor practice (ULP), job steward, collective bargaining agreements (CBAs), mediation, arbitration, and so forth. But LMR need not be daunting. Every organization has a management professional who knows how to deal with LMR. Administrators should remain calm and handle any LMR matter professionally, not personally. If supervisors can avoid personalizing the process, they will minimize their chance of losing control.[1]

■ Brief History

In 1935, Congress adopted the Wagner Act, or the National Labor Relations Act (NLRA), which formally recognized employees' rights to form and join labor organizations and to participate in collective bargaining. The NLRA thrust upon the nation new rules that would be codified in later years—in whole and in part—by federal, state, and local jurisdictions. These rules provided rights to employees and labor organizations to organize, bargain collectively, and represent members before management and created definitions of ULPs.

In 1947, Congress further amended the NLRA with the Taft-Hartley Act. The various amendments prohibited unions and labor organizations from engaging in certain activities. Further acts and amendments established other prohibitions and directions for labor and management.[2] The National Labor Relations Board (NLRB) administers the NLRA and adjudicates complaints of violations of the NLRA.

States adopted their own laws governing collective bargaining. For example, in 1967, New York State adopted the Taylor Law, which was used as a model by other states. This legislation granted public sector employees of New York State the right to organize and to be represented by employee organizations of their choice, required public employers to negotiate and enter into agreements with public employee organizations regarding their employees' terms and conditions of employment, established impasse procedures for the resolution of collective bargaining disputes, defined and prohibited improper practices by public employers and public employee organizations, prohibited strikes by public employees, and established a state agency to administer the Taylor Law. The agency is called the Public Employment Relations Board (PERB).[3]

In 1977, California passed the State Employer Employee Relations Act, later to be called the Ralph C. Dills Act. The Dills Act is a comprehensive labor law that governs the collective bargaining process of California's state employees. The Dills Act, like New York's Taylor Law, provided employees the right to organize and be represented, required the governor or a designated representative to meet and confer in good faith on matters within the scope of representation, provided for a mediation process (impasse process) in the event the parties fail to reach an agreement, defined unlawful practices for the state or an employee organization to engage in unfair labor practice (ULP), and established a state agency, the public employment relations board (PERB), which would be responsible for the administration of the Dills Act.[4]

Collective bargaining laws for public sector employees in state and local governments such as these have empowered corrections employees to form and join the labor organization of their choice, through an election process, and to select the organization that would be their exclusive representative in labor matters before management. The collective bargaining laws in any given state are likely to demonstrate how state-level politics respond to pressures and influences from different labor unions. Politics greatly influence the key elements found in the differing sets of collective bargaining laws.

In 2011, the National Labor Relations Board (NLRB) and the U.S. Department of Labor demonstrated that they are not insulated from major political influences.[5] Their collaboration to propose speculative and politically charged federal regulations is a classic example of political and economic influences. The proposed regulations in question appear to change the relationships between employees, labor unions, and employers. The effort to propose changes to the status quo by that part of the executive branch of the federal government should be considered first as a disruption to existing relationships, putting into question the validity of current precedent decisions by the NLRB and federal courts that are relied upon by the three parties. This disruption is likely to force the three parties to spend substantial funds for attorney talent to translate and advocate the effect of any of the new regulations that may be adopted. The NLRB should be considered a federal administrative agency with judicial authorities whose actions typically favor a labor union–oriented work environment in America's private sector businesses. Its regulatory powers and judgment is at times palpably political, as examined in the above noted article.

The notions of fairness, equity, and protection of the rights of the parties under collective bargaining laws should be considered politically flexible. A closer study of private sector businesses or public sector government work environments will reveal that, depending on who is seated on the labor relations board(s), will determine when and how much flexibility will be applied to the current or proposed regulations. The three parties—employees, labor unions, and employers—need to be on regular watch for such changes in order to understand how they will, respectively, be required to conduct LMR.

■ Issues That Are Driven by the Union

Corrections administrators should research issues important to the respective labor organizations. These issues may vary from area to area; however, there are four basic vehicles used by the union to deliver messages to management.

1. Master bargaining table issues or local bargaining issues
2. Grievances
3. Unfair labor practice (ULP) charges
4. Issues of importance that are discussed by the union with management on a regular basis

Bargaining Issues

The concept of management meeting with employee organizations that have achieved "exclusive representative" status is well established in law and is a routine practice in most jurisdictions of state government and in the federal government. The basic and most important right in any collective bargaining law is the exclusive representative's ability to negotiate terms and conditions of employment through the "meet and confer" process on behalf of the rank and file. "Meet and confer" is a term commonly used and essentially means to bargain. Management and the exclusive representative are obligated to personally meet and confer promptly, for a reasonable period of time, upon request by either side, to exchange information, opinions, and proposals, and to endeavor to reach agreement. "Master agreement" is a term describing the main collective bargaining agreement (CBA) or contract to which other later agreements or subordinate agreements may append.

Depending on the provisions of each jurisdiction's bargaining law, items outside the master agreement, such as a management change in policy or practice that is to occur after the master agreement is settled, may have to be negotiated with the employee organization. This commonly requires that management provide a written notice to the exclusive representative and allow time for a written response stating an intention to negotiate the item that is subject to the change in policy or practice. Generally speaking, the effect of the change that is being made—not the decision to make the change—is subject to negotiations.

However, depending on each jurisdiction's collective bargaining law, in the absence of a master agreement that provides controlling language, one may be obligated to bargain with the exclusive representative over the decision to make the change, not just the effect of the change.

Grievances

A grievance is a dispute between the employee organization and the employer or a dispute of one or more employees against the employer involving the interpretation, application, or enforcement of the master agreement. The grievance process, more than likely, will be specified in the CBA. Jurisdictions that do not have such an agreement may have a grievance or a complaint process spelled out in some form of law. The exclusive representative will use the grievance process to challenge management's administration of the CBA. If not satisfied with management's response to the grievance, the union may, subject to the CBA provisions, ultimately elevate the grievance to a binding arbitration process. It is at this step in the grievance process that management and the union must abide by the final decision made by the arbitrator, a neutral third party. Normally, only "contract grievances" have the potential to be arbitrated. Once a grievance has been properly filed, management should promptly review the practice that is creating the concern. It is highly unlikely that a well-drawn CBA does not have a grievance and arbitration procedure.

Unfair Labor Practice Charges

ULPs are actions or decisions that directly or indirectly interfere with the organizational rights of employees, employee organizations, or the employer. Actions or decisions that may be unlawful for the employer to engage in include imposing or threatening to impose reprisals on employees; discriminating or threatening to discriminate against employees; otherwise interfering with, restraining, or coercing employees because of the exercise of their guaranteed rights under a collective bargaining law; or refusing to meet and confer in good faith with a recognized employee organization.

Management may not dominate or interfere with the formation or administration of any employee organization, contribute financial or other support to it, or in any way encourage employees to join any organization instead of another; or refuse to participate in the mediation procedure.

Actions or decisions that may be unlawful for the union to engage in include causing or attempting to cause the employer to violate a collective bargaining law; imposing or threatening to impose reprisals on employees, discriminating or threatening to discriminate against employees, or otherwise interfering with, restraining, or coercing employees because of their guaranteed rights under a collective bargaining law; refusing or failing to meet and confer in good faith with the employer; or refusing to participate in the mediation process.[6] ULPs are adjudicated before the administrative body that is empowered by legislation to oversee the appropriate administration of the collective bargaining law. For instance, under the NLRA, private sector ULP charges are brought before the NLRB.

Issues of Importance

Employee organizations or their representatives frequently bring up other matters of concern to the organization and the membership in other forums. These forums may include an informal or formal meeting with the agency director, warden, or other jail or prison administrator. Although the issue being referenced by the employee organization may be a topic currently in negotiations; may have been negotiated; or may be a topic of a grievance, arbitration, or ULP case, the union nonetheless may take every available opportunity to redirect its efforts in dealing with the issue. All management staff must be aware of what is important to the corrections organization. If the issue appears to be significant to the union, it would be helpful for the manager to communicate this to the labor relations or employee relations office and the administration. It is best to coordinate a uniform response to the employee organization when dealing with matters of policy or significant practice that concern the employee organization.

As stated earlier, each corrections organization generally has a professional or group of professionals who are trained in dealing with labor organizations and labor issues. Typically, in any prison or jail operation, this will be the employee relations or labor relations office. In an effective corrections organization, the labor relations office provides resources to its departmental management staff. Investing administrative resources (time, staff, and training) will help create a coordinated program effort that will meet the challenges presented by the labor organization. Typically, a labor relations office or program in any governmental entity will be charged with representing management in all areas of LMR, including contract negotiations and administration, resolution of employee grievances and complaints, arbitration cases, ULP charges, and related court litigation.

Training is key to the success of an effective labor relations program. Training should be conducted in areas such as contract administration, grievance handling, supervisor conduct with the union, the bargaining process, and basic interaction with job stewards or union representatives. For example, in the California Department of Corrections and Rehabilitation (CDCR), training in labor relations is offered to supervisors and managers on labor relations topics at basic and advanced levels of learning. There is also a management development training module on how to negotiate.

In basic labor relations for supervisors, first-line supervisors learn why the agency has collective bargaining with employee organizations, how to interact with the job steward, how to investigate and respond to a first-line grievance, how to identify the basic properties of ULPs, and how to avoid ULPs. The advanced labor relations training for supervisors instructs second-line supervisors on the detailed background of and case law concerning the negotiation process. Second-line supervisors are given instructions on how to bargain, what makes a management bargaining team, the importance of note taking at a bargaining table, and how to implement a bargaining agreement. When second-line supervisors are promoted to the management ranks, they must attend a management development and training program. This includes a hands-on course on how to conduct local bargaining. Participants hear lectures on the negotiations process and become involved in a mock bargaining scenario. This training scenario allows the participants an opportunity to respond to hypothetical union proposals on staffing, health, and safety issues, as well as other routine issues that regularly confront correctional managers.

Training sessions such as these will not make the average supervisor or manager a highly skilled labor relations professional. However, such training courses allow supervisory and management staff to become familiar with the labor relations area, to gain confidence in how to effectively address the issues presented by employee organizations, and to help remove the mystique surrounding labor relations.

Working with an employee organization representative on various issues does not mean always reaching agreements and concessions. It does require treating the representative with integrity and respect. It is always beneficial for management to resolve problems at the lowest level. Management, working with the representative as a problem-solving team, should make grievance handling a positive experience rather than one filled with conflict and hostility. Whether the representative becomes a link or a barrier between management and employees depends on the way management deals with day-to-day situations.

"A steward can be a good ally, or a bad adversary, [and] the choice is generally made by the supervisor."[7] Taking care of problems is key to effective relations with the labor organization. No matter how large or small, an issue can be equally important to the union. A small, unattended problem can eventually blow up into a huge administrative nightmare. By dealing with issues promptly and professionally as they are brought forward, prison and jail administrators will be communicating a very important message to the union: Management is responsive and responsible. Administrators should not worry if the response they must provide is negative. "No" is a valid answer. Sometimes, management's response to the union will be affirmative. Management must know how to separate frivolous issues from bona fide ones.

Management's response should be deliberate and well thought out. It should initiate a course of action to take care of the problem. Stay away from the "you can trust me" approach; this will lead to the "you can't trust me at all" syndrome. If a management official loses credibility on one issue, it can affect all subsequent discussions about problems.

As mentioned earlier, grievances in a specific department should indicate the problem areas being encountered in the interpretation of the bargaining agreement. When in doubt about how to respond appropriately to any union concern or grievance, managers should contact the employee relations or labor relations office.

■ Developing the Management Team

Communication helps keep the management team cohesive and effective. Corrections administrators should share both routine and unusual occurrences involving the union with the department's labor relations staff. Administrators are not expected to know everything about LMR. If managers have questions, they should contact professionals who will be able to help. LMR training programs for administrators, managers, and supervisors develop understanding, clarify expectations, and improve the abilities and confidence in the management team members to effectively address the labor organization while representing management's interests.

The management team consists of all administrators, managers, and supervisors in the correctional facility or agency. Management staff involved in any specific issue may vary depending on the issue. For example, during master table negotiations, the management team is typically led by the agency director, who is the decision maker. Wardens, other corrections administrators, and labor relations, personnel, and other administrative staff may participate as the main body of the negotiating team. It is not advisable to include top decision makers directly at the bargaining table. Similarly, at the local level, the warden or other senior administrator serves as the decision maker, and institution administrators and custody management and administrative staff will typically make up the main body of management's bargaining team that develops and researches proposals. Again, if the management team members have received appropriate training, their familiarity with the labor relations process will make them stronger management team members.

■ Ethics and Labor Relations

Ethics refers to standards of conduct—standards that indicate how one should behave based on moral duties and virtues, which themselves are derived from principles of right and wrong.[8] "Labor relations ethics" may initially appear to be an oxymoron. Take away the term "labor relations" and substitute the term "management decision making." The same principles used in evaluating all ethical behavior can be applied to ethics in the labor relations process. Ethical behavior in this process involves six pillars of character: trustworthiness, loyalty, respect, responsibility, fairness, and caring. Michael Josephson (see http://josephsoninstitute.org/michael/), explains the meaning of each ethical value and demonstrates applications in various environments.[9]

An ethical decision making model for the CDCR has been developed and in use for the past 10 years.[10] The key element of learning, using focused questions, includes

- Thinking ahead—Realize that all actions, words, and attitudes reflect choices and that we are morally responsible for the consequences.
- Clarify goals—What are my short-term and long-term goals? Balance against immediate "wants" and "needs."
- Gather facts—Demand adequate information in order to determine what you know and what you need to know. Identify stakeholders. Check for credibility, consider all perspectives.
- Consider the consequences—Filter your choices through the six pillars of character.

- Determine ethical and moral issues—Who is affected, and can the decision be justified on ethical grounds? What are the benefits and harm of the decision?
- Determine fiscal effect—What is the effect on your employer? What is the effect on you?
- Decide—If the choice is not clear, review again and ask, "What would my ethical role model do?"
- Monitor and adjust—Did the decision produce the desired results?

■ Politics in Public Sector Labor Relations

As money makes political access a reality for various organizations, so too, do public sector labor unions use money to influence their access to the different strata of politics. The correctional environment is not different in this regard. Political oversight of correctional facilities, whether at the federal, state, or local level, brings opportunities for politically sensitive public sector labor organizations. Some public sector labor unions have successfully increased dues by a membership vote. Some of the dues increases were plainly advertised for the purpose of influencing voters (political action funds) during elections for local and state offices, and for continuing to influence elected officials through current access and future election support.

This reality of political access must be kept in mind by correctional workers, whether line workers, supervisors, or managers. Labor union political awareness increases for various reasons, not least of which is based on the regular access by labor unions, or employee associations, to executive management and elected officials and drawing attention to the many operating practices of the correctional organization. A May 2006 report, Dr. Joan Petersilia, of the UC Irvine California Policy Research Center, details the California corrections environment, including political and economic vectors, with a summary of the political actions and influences exercised by the corrections labor union. A summary report is provided by Dr. Petersilia, under the UC Irvine Center for Evidence-Based Corrections, on the political and social environment of California corrections, with a minor reference to correctional unions (see http://ucicorrections.seweb.uci.edu/pdf/CASentencingReformNeededLAT.pdf).

In this latter report, Dr. Petersilia offers a long view of the complex vectors, both political and economic, found in the CDCR. Similar reports on the CDCR by the UC Irvine Center's research professionals provide excellent sources for deeper study and information.

Another forum for review and criticism is given by the California Bureau of State Audits (BSA) in its report "California Department of Corrections and Rehabilitation: It Fails to Track and Use Data That Would Allow It to More Effectively Monitor and Manage Its Operations" September 2009 Report 2009-107 (see http://www.bsa.ca.gov/pdfs/rep).[11] This report says that spending by such a large state agency is showing a greater increase compared to the decreasing inmate population (by 1% of total during the previous 12-month period); that out-of-state inmate housing is less expensive than some in-state inmate housing; and that other funds dedicated to support inmate population management do not translate into adult offender rehabilitation (or lower recidivism rates). The California BSA has historical files and online reports from earlier years on corrections. The California Little Hoover Commission is another source for independent reports on the business policies and practices of California corrections.[12]

A large part of any corrections agency's annual spending per inmate is a combination of salaries for correctional personnel and for the medical and mental healthcare personnel and contracts for services required by existing law or by a federal court that is overseeing the healthcare delivery system, such as is the case in California corrections.

Economic Influence on Public Sector Labor Relations

Politics at federal, state, and local levels is the context within which any labor agreement is worked, warped, fashioned, and sold to elected officials, their appointees in executive-level positions, and to union membership who decide to accept or reject a labor contract's contents and terms. A key element in the outcome of the contract is money and usually with a big "More!" Historically, this statement of "More!" is attributed to Samuel Gompers, a key figure in private sector labor relations, when the print media asked him what he was after for the rank-and-file workers. This honest and demanding statement has been said in many different ways by public sector labor unions, including those representing corrections workers. Labor unions also seek "More!" concessions from the public sector employer in improvements in working conditions, policies, and practices, and in longer delays before making a policy decision that might affect employees.

When a CBA is finalized by the parties and ratified by the legislature, the labor union is trusting that the governor's office will ensure that the executive and field managers of the state agencies affected by the CBA will do their parts to uphold the provisions of the CBA, and that the legislature will stand by their approvals of the monies addressed in the CBA. This trust is shallow and fragile and develops in the officials of the labor unions based on their experiences across the states. Again, the experiences demonstrate to the covered employees and labor union officials that errors, omissions, and occasional outright refusals by a manager (or two) appear to cause a violation of the trust if not an outright abridgment of a contract provision. It is one thing for a state governor's executive appointee (at the direction of the governor with the support of key legislators) responsible for negotiating the CBA to bind the state, taxpayers, elected officials, and future tax revenues into a binding contract, and it is another thing to ensure compliance with the provisions of the CBA.

During the U.S. Chamber of Commerce (the Chamber) "Jobs and the Economy" presentation on August 31, 2011, by Randy Johnson, Senior Vice President of Labor, Immigration, and Employee Benefits, and by Martin Regalia, Senior Vice President and Chief Economist, it referenced the Chamber's recent reports that more than $1 trillion in wages and $1.5 trillion in benefits are being paid out in the private sector United States. Their report also referred to the Depew Survey on employee satisfaction working for companies in America. The Depew Survey reported that employees responded in the high 80% satisfaction rating. These two items are mentioned as context for considering public sector economic effect on employment and dealing with labor union involvement in public sector economics. During their presentation, Mr. Regalia provided a summary of the American economic stalemate; that is, economic growth is based on the choice by private sector companies that discover they cannot keep up with buyer demands for their goods or services, even with productivity improvements. The company owners are then more likely to decide to hire more people to meet the demand rather than risk losing their customers. This increased hiring over current employment ranks is considered economic growth. He further noted that private sector employers believe the rules of the game in the economy have changed in the form of federal regulations on businesses, causing more uncertainty among private sector companies and a reluctance to invest in expansion. These pointers are helpful when considering the challenges of making tax revenue assumptions and finding the actual tax revenue for state and local governments. Reports by the U.S. Department of Commerce and the Congressional Budget Office note the actual reduction in tax revenues and increased spending for the federal government and some states from 2005 through 2011.[13,14] This tax revenue reduction and increased spending directly affects the ability of public sector governments to fulfill the fiduciary obligations found in their CBAs. This matter has been covered in nearly every major newspaper in the United States, multiple times during the past decade or so.

Economic changes in the United States affect many segments of society, and the local and state correctional systems are not immune from economic changes and related effects. The review of economic changes between June 2004 and June 2011 can provide readers with a few insights on the lag and serious effects of political delays in making decisions about a balanced budget for the respective governmental sector CBAs.

Home buying is frequently referred to as an indicator of economic vibrancy for public sector funding. In 2004, housing prices begin to peak in major cities in the United States. During 2005, housing prices began to turn downward based on the number of new homes left unsold, an increase in defaults on home loan payments, and the lack of serious buyers available for resale homes. Between 2004 and 2007, congressional pressures on Fannie Mae and Freddie Mac lending organizations increased, focusing on lending policies and practices that they believed would help low-income to middle-income persons or households to purchase or refinance their existing homes.

Starting in 2006 and 2007, many state corrections labor contracts were expiring, with little or no interest on the part of the labor unions to negotiate any give-backs, and low interest by governors to seriously negotiate a successor agreement. "Roll-over" CBAs are common during constrained economic times. California, New York, Illinois, and other states with collective bargaining for state government employees continued their practices of allowing expired CBAs to not affect the basic provisions of pay, benefits, or working conditions of those employees covered by the expired CBAs. The extent of this allowance for continuing provisions is a key phenomenon of politics in state government. Few elected officials relish the negative press that comes when, or if, a political official sponsors any form of take-back from those employees covered by CBAs. Wisconsin's state government changed its public sector collective bargaining landscape during the 2010–2011 legislative session. They changed their set of applicable laws to restrict the type of bargaining that public sector employees may engage. The television, print, and electronic media covered the mostly negative reactions by the Wisconsin public. There were multiday demonstrations by masses of people that disrupted the state capitol operations.

In 2008, Public Law 110-343, through the enactment of the Emergency Economic Stabilization Act of 2008, provided the Troubled Asset Relief Program (TARP), a program of the U.S. government to purchase assets and equity from financial institutions to strengthen the financial sector. President George W. Bush signed the Act into law on October 3, 2008. It was a component of the federal government's measures in 2008 to address the subprime mortgage crisis. This act uses taxpayer funds in an attempt to address the substantial stress on the financial sector. The successor administration, under President Barack Obama, amplified these spending efforts. The debate continues about which generation of taxpayers will be paying off portions of the tremendous debt.

In 2009, state budgets began showing greater gaps between spending and tax revenues. In California, the multi-billion-dollar budget gap identified in 2007 was not closed after 2 years of closed sessions and open debate between the legislature and the governor's office. There were small results in any substantive spending reductions during this time. California is not the only state that suffered under this political stalemate. During 2010, delayed and reduced tax revenues for most states further aggravated the economic relationships between the employer and employees represented by labor unions.

In 2009 and 2011, while new governors arrived after state elections, along with new judges and new county and city officials, few political and economic observers held out any hope for balanced budgets from many of the states. A few of the smaller states, without collective bargaining, appeared to be closing their financial gaps as early as mid-2011.

Labor unions, whether private sector or public sector, must rely on the sources of money their employer can identify and secure. The money sources in the public sector must rely on the private sector economic growth and stability mentioned earlier. The public sector selling of bonds to raise money, or taking loans from larger public entities, remains a taxpayer gambit. Who elected whom to do what with tax money? Newspaper articles on the federal economic policy and situation (see an example at "The Economy Is Worse Than You Think," by Martin Feldstein, *The Wall Street Journal*, June 10, 2011; Dr. Feldstein is a professor at Harvard and a member of *The Wall Street Journal*'s board of contributors) provide more details and analyses of the severe financial problems faced by public sector governments. Although there are experienced economists who might argue with some of points in the noted article, the fact remains that private sector economic downturn means dire consequences to taxpayer-funded CBAs.

Elected officials often receive direct support from labor unions based on how they answer this kind of background question: Are you willing to provide a personal audience to the labor union, listen fully to their interests and concerns, and, where it is in the interest of sound LMR, vote in support of the labor union's petitions and CBAs? Arguments should be made about the framing of this question posed to elected officials by labor unions, but although the wording may be changed by one or more experienced labor relations experts, the emphasis remains the same.

In "right to work" states, where there is a restricted or nonexisting right for public sector employees to organize for collective bargaining purposes, employee associations may still form under other protections found in federal or the respective state laws. The associating practices of persons with a shared community of interest can, theoretically, also lead to a powerful money engine that may potentially be used for political access. However, these types of associations typically present a less compelling political voice in comparison with those associations found in collective bargaining states.

These differences based on the political fabric and will of associations and labor unions are all the more reasons for corrections administrators, managers, and supervisors to pay attention to the earlier mentioned principles of effective management practices, including the call for ethical decision making.

■ Conclusion

Labor relations issues in any correctional environment are typically affected by the perceptions of both parties. It is critical for management to deal with all LMR issues in a professional, honest, and straightforward manner. Emotions should never enter the decision-making process; once an issue becomes personal, it will be extremely difficult to resolve. All prison and jail administrators have available to them a professional, peer network within the local agency and across jurisdictions. When a particularly tough issue arises, administrators should call other administrators, jail commanders, or wardens and find out how they have handled similar issues. When in doubt, request assistance from labor relations staff.

Although LMR can be contentious, both sides should remember that they are working for the same agency and share the goal of operating safe and effective correctional facilities.

Chapter Resources

DISCUSSION QUESTIONS

1. Should management decision making be part of the meet-and-confer obligation?
2. Should public sector labor unions have limitations on how much political access they can exercise on matters related to corrections administration?
3. Should supervisors or managers in a corrections jurisdiction have collective bargaining rights?
4. If ethics and ethical decision making is important to the corrections environment, what should an ethical relationship look like between a corrections labor organization and a corrections administration?
5. How does a corrections administration ensure its ability to manage operations and ensure public safety and public service in a political environment with severe financial constraints?
6. What would be the effects of a federal receivership on a state or local government's CBA and LMR?
7. What might be the likely "give" and "take" as labor and management bargain toward a successor CBA when the constrained economic environment presses upon their relationship?

ADDITIONAL RESOURCES

An article demonstrating that the NLRB and the U.S. Department of Labor are not insulated from major political influences, www.martindale.com/labor-employment-law/article_Crowell-Moring-LLP_1310800.html

Josephson, M. *Making ethical decisions*. Retrieved from http://josephsoninstitute.org/michael/

Report by Dr. Petersilia, under the UC Irvine Center for Evidence-Based Corrections, on the political and social environment of California corrections, with a minor reference to correctional unions. Retrieved from http://ucicorrections.seweb.uci.edu/pdf/CASentencingReformNeededLAT.pdf

California Department of Corrections and Rehabilitation. (2009, September) *It fails to track and use data that would allow it to more effectively monitor and manage its operations*. Report 2009-107.1. Retrieved from http://www.bsa.ca.gov/pdfs/rep

California Little Hoover Commission, www.lhc.ca.gov/reports/reports.html

Reports by the U.S. Department of Commerce and the Congressional Budget Office, http://www.esa.doc.gov/about-economic-indicators

NOTES

1. California Department of Corrections, Basic Supervision Lesson Plan, Labor Relations.
2. Kahn, L. The law of labor relations—an overview. In L. G. Kahn (Ed.), *Primer of labor relations* (25th ed.). Washington, DC: The Bureau of National Affairs, Inc.
3. New York State, Governor's Office of Employee Relations. *NYS—Public Employees Fair Employment Act, The Taylor Law*. Retrieved from http://www.goer.state.ny.us/About/taylor.html
4. State of California Government Code, sec. 3512–3524.

5. Gies, T. P., Grant, G. D., Pagano, J. W., Repash, P. F., & Romeo, M. A. (2011). The NLRB and USDOL Issue Controversial Proposed Regulations to Aid Union Organizing. Retrieved from http://www.martindale.com/labor-employment-law/article_Crowell-moring-lip_1310800.htm

6. California Department of Corrections, Basic Supervision Lesson Plan, Labor Relations.

7. Ibid, p. 32.

8. Josephson, M. (1996). *Making ethical decisions* (4th ed., p. 2). Marina del Rey, CA: Josephson Institute of Ethics.

9. Josephson, M. *Making ethical decisions*, 9–17. California Department of Corrections and Rehabilitation Ethical Decision Making Model, 2004, sponsored by the Ombudsman's Office.

10. Petersilia, J. (2006, May). *Understanding California corrections*, a CPRC Report (pp. 17–28). California Policy Research Center, University of California.

11. California Department of Corrections, Basic Supervision Lesson Plan, Labor Relations.

12. Little Hoover Commission. The Commission's On-line Report Library. Retrieved from http://lhc.ca.gov/reports/reports.html

13. Economics & Statistics Administration, United States Department of Commerce. About Economic Indicators. Retrieved from http://www.esa.gov/about-economic-indicators

14. Congressional Budget Office. Publications by Topic. Retrieved from http://www.cbo.gov/topics

Changing Diversity of Correctional Officers

CHAPTER 23

Peter M. Carlson and Lindsey Battles

CHAPTER OBJECTIVES

- Explore the position of correctional officers today and explain how the role of correctional officers has evolved over time.

- Describe the importance of a diverse workforce and explain why women have typically had a difficult time being accepted in correctional positions in male facilities.

- Discuss the performance level of female correctional officers in varying corrections environments.

■ The Role of the Correctional Officer

Correctional officers generally make up the majority of the staff of a penal facility and are charged with directly supervising prisoners. Often, staff begin their careers in corrections as correctional officers. Many state systems and the Federal Bureau of Prisons frequently promote officers to other departments and jobs.

Correctional officers, also known as guards or detention officers, have various shifts and responsibilities in the facilities. In general, correctional officers provide oversight for individuals who have been arrested and are awaiting trial or those who have been convicted of criminal activity and sentenced to a period of confinement. Correctional officers are primarily responsible for supervising inmates, maintaining order and discipline, and serving as informal counselors and mentors. They also oversee and control inmate housing areas, common areas throughout the institution, work areas, and the dining room. Officers provide account-ability to institutions as the individuals responsible for enforcing rules and preventing disturbances, assaults, and escapes. Officers count the inmate population at specific times during every 24-hour period. They assist in transporting prisoners to medical or other correctional facilities and provide perimeter as well as general security.

Salaries for these security positions have improved greatly since 2000. According to data released by the Federal Bureau of Labor Statistics, full-time bailiffs, correctional workers, and jailers are earning over $100 more a week in 2010 than they were earning in 2000.[1] Data from the Bureau of Labor Statistics also note that the median annual wages across the United States of correctional officers and jailers were $39,040 in May 2010, where the lowest 10% earned less than $26,040 annually and the highest 10% earned more than $67,250 annually. Additionally, in May 2010, the median annual wage of public sector federal correctional officers and jailers was $54,310.[2] Federal salaries were slightly higher in areas where prevailing local pay levels were higher. In some states, security staff who choose to stay in the correctional officer position can earn more than $65,000, taking into account the wide range of median annual earnings; senior correctional captains in New Jersey, for example, can earn up to $109,000.[3]

■ Cultural Diversity and Demographics

In the past, prisons were in rural areas and security staff were usually hired locally. This industry tradition-ally pulled white, non-Hispanic males from the workforce pool.[4] Women and minorities were seen as a threat to the cohesiveness of the correctional workforce, and as a result, those officers were often victims of discrimination or abuse. Many African American, Hispanic, and women staff reported that Caucasian, male coworkers were very slow to accept them and were viewed as too supportive of the prisoners or not trust-worthy.[5] However, the demographics of correctional employees in the United States have changed drastically over the past 20 years, a shift that has paralleled the transformation that has occurred in other workplaces.

The workforce pool in the United States has been changing even in the past 10 years. Census data from 2010 identified multiple states with "majority-minority" populations. According to the most recent *Overview of Race and Hispanic Origin* brief, more than half of the growth in the total population of the United States between 2000 and 2010 was due to an increase in the Hispanic population. Additionally, it was reported that the Asian population grew faster than any other major race group between 2000 and 2010.[6]

Today, minorities and women are an integral part of the correctional workforce, as both correctional officers and senior managers. **Figure 23-1** illustrates the overall rise in the percentages of non-Caucasian bailiffs, correctional officers, and jailers. There is a noticeable drop in the number of black or African American employees in 2004, with a corresponding increase in the number of Asian and Hispanic or Latino ethnicity employees. Since 2004, the number of Asian and Hispanic or Latino ethnicity employees had dropped, but the numbers began to rise again in 2008 and are continuing to increase. The number of black and African American employees, on the contrary, has leveled off around 22% of the total employed.

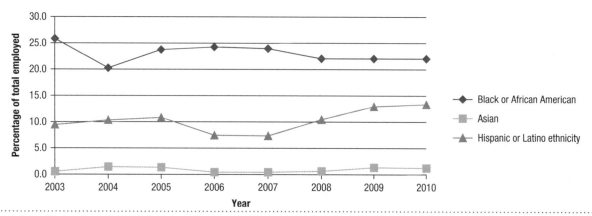

FIGURE 23-1 Employed people by detailed occupation, race, and Hispanic or Latino ethnicity

Source: Current Population Survey, U.S. Bureau of Labor Statistics, Labor Force Characteristics by Race and Ethnicity (2003–2010).

Administrators have tried to include people of all races and both genders and have become convinced that institutional management depends on the ability to relate to and communicate with inmates. Positive control and accountability in a penal facility cannot be viewed as the ability to respond to negative behavior with force. A well-run institution is clearly one that has open communication—not tension—among staff members and between staff and prisoners.

Major riots and disturbances have often resulted from a lack of understanding and open communication. One of the most notorious rampages in correctional history was the riot at the New York State Correctional Facility in Attica in 1971. This revolt occurred for many reasons, but the commission that investigated the disturbance concluded that the predominantly Caucasian and rural correctional force could not understand or adequately relate to the African American and Puerto Rican inmates who were young and unwilling to accept the authoritarian attitude of the correctional staff.[7]

Attica and similar riots have provided some hard-learned insight into managing prisoners. Administrators have learned that fairness and reasonable treatment are critical factors in any well-operated prison or jail and that staff members must be able to relate to the inmate population. The staff must "look like" the inmates; the ideal is to have the same proportions of Caucasians, African Americans, Hispanics, and Asians in staff and inmate ranks. This rule is a logical part of good institutional management. It makes sense to have a staff that can more easily relate to all inmates. With the continuing growth of inmate populations and the number of newly constructed correctional facilities, prisons and jails must adapt to the changes in the job market because they need more employees.

■ Female Correctional Officers

Stereotyping of occupational roles by sex has deep roots in American culture, including a "sex-linked ethos" in which specific occupational groupings are associated with one sex or the other.[8] The culture and ideologies surrounding the qualifications and pursuit of these employment roles tend to define both the qualified labor pool from which the occupations draw and the sought-after qualities and attributes of the people in that pool. Although the number of women in the general labor force has expanded greatly in recent years, women have not been assimilated fully into professional, technical, or management roles, despite the fact that they have performed extremely well in all occupational areas.

Inside the criminal justice arena, the Joint Commission on Correctional Manpower and Training noted in 1969 that while women made up 40% of the general workforce, they accounted for only 12% of the correctional workforce.[9] Women have been associated with prison work from its earliest days, but historically they have been employed for tasks associated with clerical duties, teaching roles, support services, or guarding female offenders. It was not until the 1970s that women correctional officers were placed in prisons with male inmates.[10]

In 1985, women accounted for approximately 13% of correctional officers in prisons; by 2002, that number had increased to 22.7%.[11] The proportion of women as correctional officers has continued to increase, but they are still underrepresented. Although this larger proportion is significant, it is still not as high as the proportion of women in the workforce in general. **Figure 23-2** illustrates the increasing trend of women employed. There were drops in the number of women employed in 2001, 2002, and 2008, but there were also drops in overall employment and the number of men employed these same years, suggesting that there could have been outside factors that affected employment. However, even after these drops in women's employment, there were more women working in corrections in 2010 than in 2000. Also, women as a percent of the total employed, found in the same data set, has increased from its 2000 percentage.

Explanations for the historical and contemporary employment bias in corrections cover a broad spectrum of arguments. Many males dispute the ability of women to maintain order and control in an adult men's prison environment. The conviction that prison tasks are "men's work" has been based in the belief that physical strength, as well as bravery, are requisites that women lack. Men have argued that the isolation and harsh working conditions of prison life are factors working against the entrance of women into corrections; others share the concern that the use of female officers violates the right of privacy of male offenders. Still other male officers and administrators believe that women create management problems by becoming romantically entangled with inmates or staff members.[12]

Resistance to the employment of women as correctional officers goes beyond simple personal bias. This attitude is often embedded in the organizational structure and culture of the prison. As new employees are placed in the correctional environment, they must quickly accept the customs, traditions, values, and other criteria of conduct that are part of the institution's environment if they are to assimilate successfully into their new work culture.

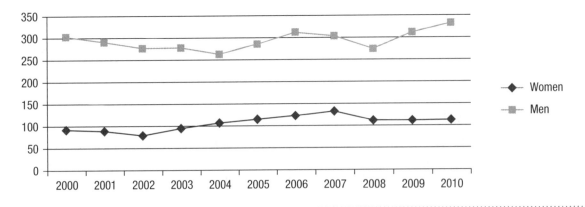

FIGURE 23-2 Employed full-time wage and salary bailiffs, correctional officers, and jailers by sex

Source: Data provided by Current Population Survey, US Bureau of Labor Statistics upon request. Data was revised back to 2000 by BLS to meet classification changes of 2003 and to provide a comparable series from 2000–2010.

Employees' expectations and internal belief systems often determine how much success they have at work. Researchers note that both sexes behave differently in work organizations because men have more real power and greater promotional opportunity.[13] Individuals of both sexes, when placed in situations in which they are powerless and have limited promotion potential, respond by lowering their goals and developing differing patterns of behavior in comparison with those who see greater potential for opportunity and power. Researchers have found that women in law enforcement lack the aggressive social skills that men bring to the job: Women traditionally have had less experience with the aggressive behavior associated with organized sports and less experience with teamwork or asserting authority.[14] These skills have to be learned on the job and require new patterns of behavior and new body language, including facial expressions that project authority rather than a pleasant demeanor or subservience.

Women in corrections report that even when they have the skills and commitment to the work, they are often at a major disadvantage. A glass ceiling, defined as an actual or perceived obstacle to organizational advancement for women or other minorities, is partially created by not including women employees in informal social circles, not providing mentoring assistance on the job, and holding women to a different standard of behavior. Paternalism or efforts to protect women often prevent them from working all posts in normal institution roster assignments; this places women at an experiential disadvantage and creates a competitive edge for others at the time of promotion consideration.

Numerous studies have reported great hostility and resistance from male staff when women have attempted to enter the correctional workforce as equals.[15] Criminal justice occupations have been often associated with machismo and masculinity, and the presence of women seems to throw doubt on this association. Some believe the jobs become devalued when women take them.

Additionally, the problem of sexual harassment affects the workplace in very negative ways. Harassment includes behaviors such as swearing, touching, intimidation, or even inappropriate humor. This type of conduct is often prevalent in work environments dominated by men and creates additional stress for women. In the prison and jail setting, men staff and inmates can present challenges even to the most competent women and establish an atmosphere that demeans and blocks women staff from achieving their potential. In its most favorable light, sexist and demeaning behavior creates an unpleasant work environment; at worst, such attitudes and behavior lead to high turnover rates and diminish the ranks of skilled women employees in the correctional facility. Some male staff members fervently believe that female employees working as correctional officers jeopardize the safety of male officers by being more susceptible to rape. Male staff members believe that this requires them to place themselves in danger by having to respond to such explosive situations.[16] This concern seems to confirm the belief that the security of the institution, and therefore men's safety, is placed at risk by women's presence.

Female Performance

Women in correctional uniform have performed very well in male and female facilities at all security levels. Although women have had difficulty finding peer acceptance as correctional officers in prisons, they have adapted reasonably well to this work environment. In the jail setting, studies have found mixed results. As predicted, women officers were perceived as being less effective in breaking up fighting inmates or controlling larger, more aggressive inmates. However, male staff members believe that female officers were very impressive in calming angry inmates and inmates who are mentally or emotionally disturbed.[17] Studies have found that inmates and male staff members have reacted positively to the presence of women personnel; men have controlled their language, acted more politely toward women officers, and exercised more care with their appearance.

Some evidence indicates that women working in male prisons conduct themselves differently as they perform the responsibilities of a correctional officer. Research has noted that some women adopt a more service-oriented demeanor than their male counterparts and take on a less confrontational style of dealing with offenders.[18] Many believe this style is an asset in the prison and jail setting.

A 1983 study of correctional officers in the California Department of Corrections found that male and female staff performed their jobs equally well. However, major differences were noted among the three job groups sampled: male officers, female officers, and male inmates. Both groups of men felt that women were less effective in tasks requiring physical strength and in violent emergency situations. Female officers scored well in all other tasks evaluated, including supervisory performance evaluations, number of commendations and reprimands, and use of sick leave.[19] In general, female officers were found to have established a great deal of self-confidence on the job.

Female officers in the Federal Bureau of Prisons fared well in a more recent study.[20] Both studies of female correctional officers noted many reports of hostility from male staff and male inmates and examples of sexual harassment of female staff. This study found no difference in job satisfaction between male and female officers.

Many male correctional officers in high-security U.S. penitentiaries expressed their surprise at how effective female officers have become at their jobs—particularly in the cellblocks. Men working in this environment highlight women's ability to relate positively to male offenders. This skill becomes especially useful during tense situations, and many examples have been cited of female officers calming angry inmates. The majority of male staff, while initially opposed to hiring female officers in federal penitentiaries, changed their opinions after observing women on the job.[21]

Women have been integrated successfully into employment at prisons and jails for men offenders in the past 25 years. Although this public policy shift has not been easily accepted by the staff—mostly men—many institution administrators and line staff members believe women have helped increase the level of fairness and the quality of operations.

■ Conclusion

Equal employment opportunity and workplace diversity are important features of American society and institution administration. Caucasian male correctional officers have had to adjust to the changing workforce. The new personnel have brought many outstanding skills and abilities to the correctional environment, and institutional operations have benefited from this diversity. Minorities and women have become successful correctional officers, supervisors, and senior administrators in all areas of the American criminal justice system.

Chapter Resources

DISCUSSION QUESTIONS

1. Now that the correctional workforce is more diverse, how have women performed in this unique career environment?

2. Do you believe the physical size of correctional personnel is an important factor when hiring new staff?

3. What are the benefits of a racially diverse correctional staff to prison management?

4. What are the benefits of a culturally diverse correctional staff to prison management?

5. Should male correctional facilities employee female correctional officers and vice versa?

ADDITIONAL RESOURCES

Camp, S., Saylor, W., & Wright, K. (2000). *Racial diversity of correctional workers and inmates: Organizational commitment, teamwork and worker efficacy in prisons.* Washington, DC: Federal Bureau of Prisons, Office of Research and Evaluation. Retrieved from http://www.bop.gov/news/research_projects/published_reports/equity_diversity/oreprcamp_jq2.pdf

Ellis, T., Tedstone, C., & Curry, D. (2004, December). *Improving race relations in prisons. What works?* Home Office: Online Report. Retrieved from http://www.monitoring-group.co.uk/News%20and%20Campaigns/research%20material/Prisons/racism_in_prisons_what_works.pdf

Scarborough, K., & Collins, P. (2002). *Women in public and private law enforcement.* Boston, MA: Butterworth Heinemann.

NOTES

1. U.S. Bureau of Labor Statistics, Current Population Survey. (2000–2010). *Median usual weekly earning of full-time wage and salary workers, by detailed occupation and sex.* Washington, DC: Author. Comparable series provided by Eleni T. Sherman of the Bureau of Labor Statistics on November 2, 2012.

2. Bureau of Labor Statistics, U.S. Department of Labor. (2012). *Occupational outlook handbook*, 2012–2013 edition. Retrieved from http://www.bls.gov/ooh/protective-service/correctional-officers.htm

3. Anonymous. (2007, May/June). Correctional officers: Hiring requirements and wages. *Corrections Compendium, 32*(3), 12, 16.

4. American Correctional Association (ACA) and Workforce Associates, Inc. (2004). *A 21st century workforce for America's correctional profession.* Indianapolis, IN: Workforce Associates, Inc. Retrieved from http://www.aca.org/news/pdfs/copy ACA Report Discovery Final 26 Jul 04 04.pdf

5. Irwin, J. (1977). The changing social structure of the men's correctional prison. In D. Greenberg (Ed.), *Corrections and punishment.* Beverly Hills, CA: Sage Publications.

6. Humes, K. R., Jones, N. A., Ramirez, R. R., U.S. Department of Commerce, Economic Statistics Administration, and U.S. Census Bureau. (2011). *Overview of race and Hispanic origin: 2010* (C2010BR-02). Washington, DC: U.S. Department of Commerce. Retrieved from http://www.census.gov/prod/cen2010/briefs/c2010br-02.pdf

7. New York State Special Commission on Attica. (1972). *Attica: The official report of the New York State Commission.* New York, NY: Bantam Books.

8. Kanter, R. (1977). *Men and women of the corporation*. New York, NY: Basic Books.

9. Kehoe, C. (2004, August). Addressing the challenges of the correctional work force. *Corrections Today, 66*(5). Retrieved from http://www.aca.org/pastpresentfuture/archivemessages.asp

10. Pollock, J. (1986). *Sex and supervision: Guarding male and female inmates*. New York, NY: Greenwood Press.

11. Camp and Camp. (2003). *The Corrections Yearbook*, p. 157.

12. Feinman, C. (1986). *Women in the criminal justice system*. New York, NY: Praeger Publishing.

13. Kanter, R. (1977). *Men and women of the corporation*. New York, NY: Basic Books.

14. Martin, S. (1980). *Breaking and entering: Policewomen on patrol*. Berkeley, CA: University of California Press.

15. Carlson, P. (1996). *Assignment of female correctional officers to United States penitentiaries: Implementation in the federal bureau of prisons* (p. 12). Doctoral dissertation, University Microfilm International. Ann Arbor, MI: UMI #9705080.

16. Ingram, G. (1981). The role of women in male federal correctional institutions. In *Proceedings of the 110th Congress of Corrections*. San Diego, CA: American Correctional Association.

17. Kissel, P., & Seidel, J. (1980). *The management and impact of female corrections officers at jail facilities housing male inmates*. Boulder, CO: National Institute of Corrections.

18. Alpert, G. (1984, November). The needs of the judiciary and misapplication of social research. *Criminology, 22*, 441–456.

19. Holeman, H., & Krepps-Hess, B. (1983). *Women correctional officers in the California Department of Corrections*. Sacramento, CA: California Department of Corrections Research Unit.

20. Wright, K., & Saylor, W. (1991). Male and female employees' perceptions of prison work: Is there a difference? *Justice Quarterly, 8*(4), 505–524.

21. Carlson, P. (1996). *Assignment of female correctional officers to United States penitentiaries: implementation in the federal bureau of prisons* (pp. 162–163). Doctoral dissertation, University Microfilm International. Ann Arbor, MI: UMI #9705080.

Developing Human Resources

YOU ARE THE ADMINISTRATOR

■ Emergency in Segregation—A Need for Leadership

The emergency body alarm was sounded in the segregation unit at 9:20 A.M., and nearly 20 staff members responded swiftly to the crisis; one of the responding staff was the new institutional Director of Security, Steven Conklin. As he arrived on the scene in the maximum security penitentiary, Conklin observed an inmate armed with what appeared to be a large homemade knife. The weapon was being brandished toward a group of correctional officers, effectively keeping them at a safe distance.

Conklin saw the officer-in-charge of the unit, Sergeant Mazalla, begin to unroll a fire hose from the closest fire box, and several officers were preparing to turn the hose on the inmate to pin him down. Conklin flashed back in his mind to the security conference he attended 2 months prior, where the state prison security chief had warned all attendees that it was unacceptable to use fire equipment for inmate control needs, and he wanted the practice to stop. He said institution leaders had to crack down on this practice. Unfortunately, Conklin had only been on his new assignment for 5 days and had not yet discussed this change with his correctional lieutenants and sergeants.

Conklin yelled to Sergeant Mazalla to stop and waved him over to talk. Mazalla was angry both at the situation in segregation and at the interruption to his planned response. The armed inmate was screaming at staff, and the officers involved were growing upset at the lack of response to the threats. Conklin told Mazalla that he did not want the fire hose used in this situation because he felt it was a misuse of fire equipment. Mazalla was incredulous, and his verbal response was less than politically correct: "Why the he** can't we use the hose? We've always used water to control an armed inmate!" Conklin did not wish to discuss the issue in front of a large number of staff, and he was really feeling pressed to deal with the situation. He quickly responded that he simply did not want the hose used, and Mazalla yelled, "Then maybe you'll go take the damn shank away from the inmate!" Conklin immediately jumped back at Mazalla, and the argument escalated.

As this verbal altercation was taking place, another officer who knew the inmate began talking to him, and after a few moments, the officers could see the anger of the inmate begin to dissipate. The inmate dropped the knife and agreed to allow the officer whom he knew to place him in cuffs. He was moved back into a cell and secured. This solution to a crisis situation resulted from a line staff member taking the initiative, while his supervisors loudly argued about the use of the fire hose.

- Was Director Conklin doing the right thing by stopping the use of fire equipment? How did he handle the situation?
- Why did the leaders at the scene allow themselves to be diverted from the emergency situation?
- How would you have dealt with the situation?

Organization and Management of the Prison

Peter M. Carlson and
John J. Dilulio, Jr.

CHAPTER OBJECTIVES

- Outline three key factors that contribute to excellence in penal management and leadership, and identify the basics of a well-run prison or jail.

- Differentiate between management and leadership.

- Name three primary means of establishing measurement and accountability in a government agency.

◼ Introduction

The world of prison and jail management has long been unfairly considered a backwater of public administration, organizational theory, and management behavior. Although the academic centers of the nation have been preparing future gurus of business—tomorrow's leaders of city, state, and federal government and assorted other public administrative functions—few have taken on the complex task of developing prison and jail administrators. Almost all of today's penal leaders have entered the field in an entry-level position and earned their way to top management roles. Programs in correctional leadership must be expected to keep up with the national increase in prisons and jails.

Leaders of state and federal correctional systems, chief executive officers (CEOs) of major institutions, and all those who work in developmental assignments under these senior leaders are responsible for millions of dollars' worth of buildings and equipment, thousands of staff members, and many thousands of inmates in each facility or jurisdiction. The field of corrections is a demanding environment in which the leaders and managers of institutions must be bright and capable of governing thousands of staff and inmates. The challenges of prison and jail management have never been greater, with expanding inmate populations, legal complications, more aggressive and dangerous inmates, politicians who want to micromanage institutions, and staff issues that are complex and unending.

The need to manage correctional facilities effectively—to focus staff on the basics of operating safe, secure, and humane institutions—has never been more critical. Prison and jail professionals are responsible for public safety and performing a public service of great significance, but other institutional management tasks are very important as well. A warden must constantly work to ensure staff safety, staff integrity, proper stewardship of government financial resources, and a safe environment for inmates. Corrections leaders are accountable to all constituents: the public, elected representatives, the judiciary, superiors in government, staff, and inmates. Management and leadership skills are essential in this role.

◼ Decentralized Organization

In the United States, prisons and jails are decentralized. The federal government, each state, and most counties and cities operate individual correctional networks. Each system tends to operate independently with little or no linkage among agencies. Federal corrections are primarily the responsibility of the Federal Bureau of Prisons (BOP), but other federal agencies are responsible for immigration detention facilities and military prisons. Adult prisons are also operated by private corrections companies that contract to house state and federal offenders. Because so many jurisdictions are involved in prison and jail administration, the administration of justice in the United States is a mixture of various organizational systems and management structures.

Besides the obvious impediment to open communication created by the fragmentation within justice administration, this separation has greatly hindered interagency cooperation in the development of meaningful policy. For instance, many institution administration professionals have accepted that they simply have to receive and process the people the police, prosecutors, and courts send their way. The political process often precludes correctional experts from providing any meaningful input to justice policy-setting circles. Correctional professionals, as a result, have become very myopic, often unable to see beyond the boundaries of their own agencies.

Correctional organization, or disorganization, in various U.S. jurisdictions has created a disarray of services and programs. This complicates any concerted effort to improve corrections systemically. It is nearly impossible to shift financial or other resources among federal, state, and local jurisdictions; to establish common goals and coordinated policy; and to share exceptional procedures and programs between institutions in adjoining states or even among facilities within a single county or city. Simply put, agencies operate independently according to the philosophy of their jurisdiction's governing body—the sheriff, mayor, commissioner of corrections, governor, or federal government.

Oversight

General oversight and control of correctional agencies varies throughout the United States. Some jurisdictions combine penal management with other public service organizations such as law enforcement or mental health departments. Other jurisdictions operate independent agencies ranging from very small city jails up to huge, centralized prison systems. An increasing number of state correctional organizations have evolved into separate departments with the CEO selected by the state's governor. In 2007, 32 states had separate departments of corrections reporting to the governor; 11 had departments reporting to boards or commissions; 5 operated under a department of public safety umbrella; and 1 fell under a social services umbrella. Twenty-four of the separate departments have been organized in this manner since 1979.[1]

Clearly, vast differences within the field are created by these separate jurisdictions. Institutions differ with respect to mission; types and amounts of funding; the numbers of staff in roles as psychologists, counselors, case managers, teachers, and so on; and the types of inmate populations served. But these agencies have one unifying characteristic—they each serve the people by confining individuals who have violated the law. Because the laws that govern conduct are established by the political authority of a specific community, city, county, state, or federal jurisdiction, the system of justice administration also varies.

■ Multiple Missions

Prisons and jails are generally expected to accomplish several often conflicting goals in dealing with law violators. They are asked to punish, incapacitate, and rehabilitate offenders, as well as deter others from violating society's rules and regulations. The organization and structure of a penal facility is affected significantly by these different goals. Many people believe that the conditions necessary to reform or rehabilitate an inmate conflict with the conditions necessary to punish offenders. Confronted by these contradictory pressures, correctional administrators often try to walk a fine line between opposing missions.

Criminologist Donald Cressey has said that correctional institutions can be placed on a continuum of organizational structures, ranging from a maximum security, old-line penitentiary surrounded by gun towers to a minimum security, program-oriented, unfenced facility.[2] At one extreme is the highly controlled, custody-oriented prison, and on the opposite end is the relaxed, unstructured institution focused on treatment and rehabilitation. However, most prisons and jails attempt to achieve both custody and resocialization goals.

■ Organizational Theory

Organizational theory conceptualizes how authority is distributed within an organization and how it is used to accomplish the agency's mission and goals. A correctional setting's organization is extremely important to staff and inmates. Although a public organization may seem impersonal and monolithic, in reality each public entity is a complex mixture of people, personalities, programs, rules, and behaviors. Every organization is composed of people who act individually and collectively to create a culture. These individuals are affected each day by the organizational structure within which they work; hence, the system of management and control of individual staff members is a key variable in work productivity, morale, and overall agency efficiency.

In the theory and practice of public organization, particularly in correctional administration, efficiency is the point around which everything turns. Many management experts have discussed how best to develop private business or government to produce the most efficient operations. In the 1930s, business executives James Mooney and Alan Reiley noted several important principles of organizational structure:[3]

- *Unity of command*: Work is coordinated through a hierarchy of leaders; every staff member has only one supervisor with a goal of strong executive leadership.
- *Scalar principle*: A vertical structure outlines different responsibilities throughout the hierarchy.
- *Separation among departments:* Distinct responsibilities are outlined for different roles and divisions.

- *Relationship between line and staff roles:* Line command flows through the direct chain of command, whereas related staff support offices (personnel and financial management) provide advice and assistance to the chief executive/warden.

This set of principles is an effective means of considering how a penal facility can and should be organized.

■ Correctional Models of Management

Within corrections, three different organizational models exist: an authoritarian model, a bureaucratic model, and a participative model.

The authoritarian model is generally characterized by the presence of a strong leader, very firm control of the prison environment, and the harsh discipline of inmates (or staff) who do not acquiesce to the central authority. This style of institution was prevalent in the United States from colonial days through the mid-1900s.[4] This highly centralized style creates a regimented workplace with consistent application of rules for all. It funnels all decision making to the central power figure, even though some decisions could be better made at a lower level. This model denies all other staff the experience of making decisions and can create an arbitrary and capricious system that may easily become corrupt.

The bureaucratic model also revolves around a strict hierarchical system but is not focused on one dominating personality. Organization control flows through the hierarchy with a strict chain of command and a formal process of communication. Rules and regulations for the correctional institution are written and specific. The facility has a clear set of standard operating procedures. The practical benefit of this model is that a correctional system or institution is not overly dependent on one or two people and can easily promote or substitute personnel. Additionally, the policy parameters stressed in this management structure are clear for all parties, and staff can be held accountable if they do not comply with the written expectations. On the negative side, written rules do not guarantee consistent enforcement, and they are not helpful in every situation. Bureaucratic processes are slow to respond to change and do not encourage staff to demonstrate new initiative at any level of the organization.

The participative model of management is much more open and democratic than the first two models, although it is not as effective in dealing with fast-moving crisis situations. This method allows and is dependent on staff input about how the organization should be run. In a few experiments, inmates have given feedback as well. The assumption inherent in this model is that agency and correctional goals are more efficiently accomplished when all staff have participated in reaching a consensus on how to proceed. The participative style gives staff an increased sense of ownership in planning and operations, often resulting in better attitudes toward and support of routine events and new initiatives. Unfortunately, formal and open discussions and negotiations—collective participation in institutional operations—can be time-consuming.

The authoritarian and bureaucratic organizational structures are much more prevalent in correctional administration. These models, unfortunately, do not lend themselves to change; the built-in resistance to new ideas is self-defeating. Yet few successful administrators champion the looseness and lack of structure that can be associated with participatory management.

Many successful agencies have adapted the bureaucratic model to include elements of the participatory style. These correctional leaders decentralize as much of the daily decision making as they can and seek participation from all staff in many avenues. The involvement of midlevel managers and line staff in specific work groups or in overall strategic planning can be extremely beneficial. Staff generally enjoy such activity and, as the individuals closest to the work arena, can make significant contributions. Such forms of representative democracy in the correctional workplace are considered quite effective.

Management Structure

As prescribed by organizational theory, the prevailing management structure in correctional facilities in the United States is hierarchical, centralized, and paramilitary. The bureaucracy of institution management is very controlling and often inflexible, yet it is the most efficient and functional structure for the coordination and control of hundreds of staff members and thousands of prisoners. The critical and dangerous task of running prisons requires uniformity within each specific facility (fairness and equity—the perception that all inmates receive the same treatment) and precision of control (see **Figure 24-1**).

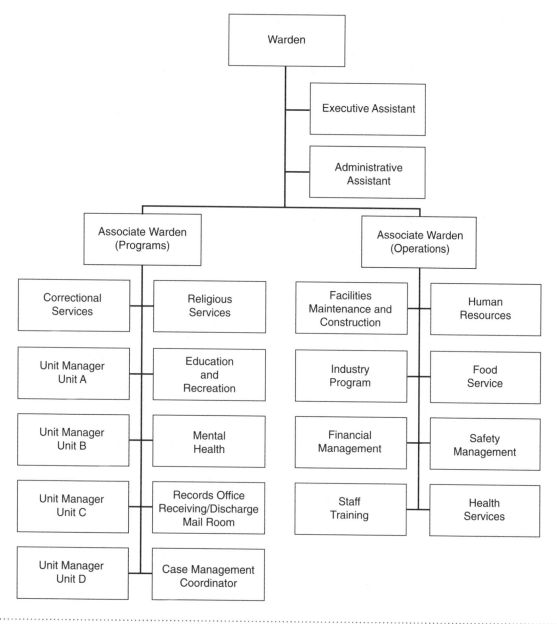

FIGURE 24-1 A typical adult institution organizational chart

Source: Federal Bureau of Prisons.

CHIEF EXECUTIVE OFFICER. This is the individual responsible for the crucial responsibilities within the jail or prison and may be called warden, superintendent, or administrator. This individual holds the highest executive position and is accountable for all aspects of institution life. The senior administrator establishes policy for the facility and is responsible for personnel, property, programs, and activities. This staff member is also charged with handling the external world of the facility: the public, the media, the politicians, and the courts.

ASSOCIATE WARDEN. Several deputy or associate wardens (AWs) usually head the various organizational structures in large-scale institutions and report to the warden. Often, there is one AW who oversees custody, another who supervises operations, and a third who handles programs. The custody AW is responsible for all security matters and supervises all correctional officers. The operations AW is accountable for all support services within the facility: food and medical service, facilities maintenance and construction, human resource management, and financial management. The programs AW usually heads classification, unit and case management, religious services, mental health programs, education, recreation, and records functions. If a prison has a large industrial operation, there may also be an AW responsible for this production area.

DEPARTMENT HEADS. These are generally veteran employees who are experienced in the tasks and skills required within each functional area of the institution. For example, department heads are assigned to areas such as health services, food services, correctional services, or the records office.

OTHER SUPERVISORS. Other lower-level supervisors may include assistant department heads or first-line supervisors.

LINE STAFF. Line staff are the individuals who are responsible for the correctional facility on a day-to-day basis. Individuals such as correctional officers or case managers, for example, have face-to-face contact with inmates and are in charge of inmates' daily care.

Decentralized Management

In bureaucratic style, significant decisions within a centralized power structure are made by relatively few individuals, and these decisions are generally consistent and in accordance with the need to operate the penal institution in a safe and secure manner. However, there are also several disadvantages. Department heads and line staff are not empowered and may feel very little ownership of any aspect of institution operations. Additionally, the very bureaucratic process of referring all decisions to senior staff can add great delays, and high-level administrators may not be as familiar with a situation as lower-level staff. If these decisions are not made locally (i.e., the authority rests in a headquarters office rather than the field facility), these negative factors can be greatly magnified.

One of the best examples of the successful decentralization of correctional management is unit management—the process of dividing and distributing authority and responsibility to administrative personnel—often enhances the effectiveness of administrative operations. When decision-making responsibilities are delegated to staff, staff members gain greater expertise in and ownership of problems and solutions. Critics of decentralized management in the correctional setting believe that dispersing authority and responsibility lessens accountability and does not promote consistent decisions. Decentralizing the process is often considered more expensive, because the process involves training more staff about key issues.

One of the best examples of the successful decentralization of correctional management is unit management, which can be found in many state and all federal institutions. In this model, classification and inmate management authority is delegated to a team of staff members who work in close association with an assigned number of inmates. These staff members (representatives of case management, education, and psychology departments) have offices in the inmate living units and are fully responsible for the day-to-day aspects of the inmates' lives. For example, the unit teams classify inmates for security level and custody needs, make work and program assignments, and handle disciplinary matters for their prisoner caseloads. The staff members report to a department head (referred to as a unit manager) and are held accountable for the overall operation of the unit and management of the inmates.

■ Leadership and Innovation

Correctional institutions work best when administrators stick to the basics of inmate care and custody, as exemplified by wardens who, despite all the competing demands on their time and attention, leave behind the purely administrative tasks and paperwork and practice "management by walking around." The field's most successful executives and managers do not get into routine ways of doing things; rather, they are open to both human resource and technical innovations. Prison and jail leaders who last long enough to innovate are almost invariably individuals who, whatever their personality or ideology, operate as pragmatic professionals and political realists.

Successful prison and jail administrators know from experience that they operate in the context of multiple and competing public objectives (punish, rehabilitate, deter, and incapacitate), ever-shifting legislative priorities, small to sweeping judicial interventions, and always incomplete (and often crisis-driven) media renderings of their work. But they wisely seek neither to master nor to withdraw from external demands and pressures. Instead, they and their staffs are responsive to reasonable external demands and pressures, and they engage in the civic life of the surrounding community.

The overarching challenge facing contemporary prison and jail administrators is to remain focused on specific safety, program, and other operational goals and activities. Corrections executives and managers have more or less direct control over these aspects of institutional life. Therefore they shoulder legal, moral, fiscal, and administrative responsibility for these areas, regardless of how the legislative, judicial, community relations, or media winds blow.

Present-day institutional corrections leadership is neither an art nor a science but a craft. Fortunately, the field of institutional corrections, for all its problems, for all its real or perceived failures, has been blessed with a truly extraordinary number and variety of superb craftspeople.

Still, have even the best prison and jail administrators kept pace with their peers—superior public sector entrepreneurs in other arenas of government? The field's present and aspiring leaders must answer this question for and among themselves with respect to at least three sets of issues: boundary spanning, performance management, and public communications.

Boundary Spanning

As Donald F. Kettl has definitively argued, most of contemporary governance and administrative politics involve government by proxy; in other words, no taxpayer-supported bureaucracy operates entirely independently. Rather, a public institution's administration involves working in partnership with other entities, including government agencies, private firms, and nonprofit organizations.[5] Even within prison and jail administration, which some unknowing public management specialists still cite as the paradigm of traditional or direct public administration, government by proxy is commonplace, with all its attendant administrative complications and possibilities. For example, prison and jail administrators interact constantly with the courts and other law enforcement agencies, including those representing other jurisdictions or levels of government. They deal with government safety or health inspectors, hire for-profit and nonprofit consultants, and increasingly contract for one or more basic or auxiliary services, from food services to physical plant maintenance.

In fact, in institutional corrections, the list of daily and long-term planning functions performed as government by proxy is getting longer all the time. Thus, the work of contemporary prison and jail administrators, like that of most contemporary public sector executives and managers, requires what Kettl terms "boundary spanning," which includes three crucial capacities:

1. The capacity to work productively in a bureaucratic hierarchy and across divisions
2. The capacity to establish constructive professional and administrative ties to other public sector organizations that can affect everything from the agency's daily internal operations to its vulnerability to legal action or its level of legislative support
3. The capacity to enter into cost-effective relationships or contracts with both nonprofit and for-profit service providers

Prison and jail administrators must begin to think strategically about organizational boundary spanning. Accordingly, they need to develop innovative and forward-looking preservice and in-service training and staff development programs.

The steps toward boundary spanning follow those outlined by Jameson W. Doig and Erwin C. Hargrove in *Leadership and Innovation*:[6]

1. Identify new missions and programs for the organization
2. Develop and nourish external constituencies to support the new goals and programs
3. Create internal constituencies that support the new goals through changes in recruitment systems and key appointments
4. Enhance the organization's technical expertise
5. Motivate and provide training for members of the organization that transcends standard or accepted training goals
6. Systematically scan organizational routines and points of internal and external pressure in order to identify areas of vulnerability to mismanagement, corruption, the loss of leaders' positions, and blows to organizational reputation

Prison and jail system administrators who have already taken these preliminary steps to limit vulnerability to mismanagement and corruption should forge ahead with boundary-spanning retooling of their training and staff development programs.

Performance Management

The U.S. Department of Justice has determined several main goals of performance-based management in corrections, each with its own indicators:

- Security—security procedures, drug use, significant incidents, community exposure, freedom of movement, staffing adequacy
- Justice—staff fairness, limited use of force, grievances (number and type, the grievance process), the discipline process, legal resources and access, justice delays
- Safety—safety of inmates, safety of staff, dangerousness of inmates, safety of environment, staffing adequacy
- Conditions—space in living areas, social density and privacy, internal freedom of movement, facilities and maintenance, sanitation, noise, food, commissary, visitation, community access
- Order—inmate misconduct, staff use of force, perceived control, strictness of enforcement
- Management—job satisfaction, stress and burnout, staff turnover, staff and management relations, staff experience, education, training, salary and overtime, staffing efficiency
- Health—stress and illness, health care, dental care, counseling, staffing for programs and services
- Activity—work and industry, education and training, recreation, religious activities

Yet neither the BOP nor any other institutional corrections agency has developed performance-based management systems designed to serve both internal administrative and external constituency-building needs. As Kettl explains:

> The biggest difficulty in thinking through the problems of performance-based management is that reformers and managers far too often consider it simply as a problem of measurement. Committing the government to performance-based management, of course, requires that officials identify and measure results. The more fundamental question, however, is what to do with these measures. Performance-based management is most fundamentally about communication, not measurement. Moreover, this communication occurs within a broader political process, in which players have a wide array of different incentives. Performance-based management will have meaning only to the degree to which it shapes and improves incentives. How does what [executives and managers] know about results shape decisions about what programs they adopt? And how does the process of measuring results affect the behavior of political institutions?
>
> *Source:* D. Kettl, "Building Lasting Reform," in *Inside the Reinvention Machine: Assessing Governmental Reform*, J. Dilulio, Jr. and D. Kettl, eds. (Washington, DC: The Brookings Institution, 1994).

Public Communications

Improvements in correctional institution performance can only occur if practitioners of the correctional administration improve public communications about what they actually do and how they do it, subject to legal and other constraints. In particular, institutional corrections may be the only area of public sector life in which academics, analysts, activists, journalists, judges, lawyers, and lobbyists have turned the field's practitioners into little more than bit players in defining their clients, budgetary and organizational needs, and the likely social costs and consequences of alternative ways of performing their functions.

Prison and jail wardens and superintendents must actively enter these public debates; they are the practitioners and experts in the field. Even fundamental factual matters such as what the criminal records and physical health, mental health, and employment histories of most prisoners look like—the stuff of rap sheets, presentencing investigation reports, and reception and diagnostic admissions forms—are now largely defined by contending camps of nonpractitioner (or ex-practitioner) reformers and experts. The seeming lack of interest and involvement in these issues by current correctional facility administrators is puzzling.

Presumably, prison and jail administrators know a great deal about the official criminal records and troubled life histories of the confined populations they manage and have an organizational stake in sharing their best, most objective understanding of who their day-to-day clients are. They should also be keenly aware of the demands and challenges that they, as institution administrators, face in providing care and custody to large, transient populations of troubled and troublesome persons. Presumably, they have ideas about which, if any, subpopulations of inmates should be sentenced or treated differently to better serve the public. However, the poor state of public communications about the fundamentals of institutional corrections—the relative silence—is rather deafening. For the field's present and aspiring entrepreneurs in government, this silence is professionally and organizationally self-defeating and ought not to persist.

■ Management Versus Leadership—An Unfair Dichotomy

Many exceptional researchers and authors distinguish between leadership and management. Warren Bennis describes the differences between leaders and managers as the differences between those who master the context and those who surrender to it. He believes that the manager focuses on systems and structure, whereas the leader stresses the people in the business. Bennis believes that managers are more "blue collar" and heavily involved in the practical details of organizational life, whereas leaders are more engaged in the loftier calling of organizational directing.[7]

Tom Peters and Robert Waterman are a little kinder toward management, although they also stress that leaders go beyond the daily grind of basic decision making. Their research reveals that successful people learn from their mistakes, think globally, encourage innovation, and master new knowledge.[8]

Other observers of leadership roles in prisons have softened the line between management and leadership. Kevin Wright describes the merging roles of managers and leaders.[9] Although he describes many farsighted responsibilities of leaders, he puts them in the context of day-to-day management activities. A warden must watch the bottom line of the budget but also be able to articulate the necessity of accomplishing longer-term goals. Prison and jail administration requires unique individuals with exceptional people skills. Penology demands institution experience and leadership abilities.

As Chester Barnard said, "It is important to observe … that not all work done by persons who occupy executive positions is in connection with the executive functions."[10] In other words, if the warden or superintendent of an institution stops to listen to a complaint from an inmate or staff member, this is not expressly an executive task. As Barnard notes, nearly all high-ranking executives do a considerable amount of nonexecutive work, and this effort is sometimes more valuable than the executive function. The hands-on managerial tasks are generally associated with maintaining an organization and ensuring that systems of cooperative effort are emphasized and enforced.

It is critical for today's prison and jail CEOs to successfully combine the reality of management in the trenches with the ability to lead others toward the future. A warden must stay in close touch with the daily responsibilities of institution management yet set a tone that defines what the facility is and where it is headed. Separating management from leadership requires an artificial division that does not reflect the reality of organizational behavior. Hans Toch notes that penology deals with policy and administration, process, and procedures.[11] Daily oversight is necessary; a warden's job is very much a hands-on experience.

Many factors determine the quality of prison administration, but the most important is management practice. Strong prison and jail governance is key to the attainment of effective and efficient operations, but a CEO with a strong, involved management style may possess many intrinsic leadership qualities.[12] The skills must be merged. The effective, reality-driven manager must model other characteristics of a leader. He or she must be able to empower and delegate to capable staff; demonstrate sensitivity, diplomacy, and vision; and show a willingness to take responsible risks.

■ The Challenge for Institutional Leadership

All wardens or senior-level leaders in any correctional environment want to be known for running a high-quality operation and getting positive results. But what are positive results in a prison or jail environment? An effective prison or jail operation is generally considered to be an institution that is safe, secure, clean, and responsive to the needs of its staff, inmates, and external constituencies. Yet if we gathered a group of correctional leaders and asked them to define these qualities, there would be some disagreement. Which factors are the most important? How do we operationally define successful attainment of each factor? How should staff go about trying to reach each goal, and how do we know when the goal has been attained?

Wardens and senior administrators must establish a vision of a successful correctional operation. They must delineate institutional goals, train staff to ensure that all personnel are aware of the desired outcomes, implement programs in support of the goals, establish a system of feedback on progress toward the goals, and create a means of reinforcing successful accomplishment and good performance. Once this process is in place, accountability and tracking institutional operations become key.

■ Delegation

Management is often defined as the art of getting things done through other people. A leader must delegate the responsibility for specific tasks to qualified individuals while remaining ultimately responsible for these functions. Today, delegation is often referred to as the act of empowering staff. The senior staff member must give the employee not only responsibility for the task but also the authority and the resources to accomplish it. This can be a frightening concept in a prison or jail, where so many things can go wrong, and some errors have extreme consequences. Yet delegation is necessary if a major facility is going to operate effectively 24 hours a day. Staff must be able to take responsibility for work in the facility. Failure to delegate operational supervision to competent staff will guarantee personal burnout, damage the development of subordinate staff, reduce productivity, and harm overall morale.

Delegation is critical at all levels of correctional institutions. Although the responsibilities of correctional management are more complex than those in many other lines of work, leadership and management in all organizations requires the sharing of responsibilities. Once leaders do delegate tasks, they must learn how to provide oversight and establish accountability.

Even though delegation is so essential to leadership and management, it is often a difficult skill to develop. Richard Phillips and Charles McConnell believe that there are three primary barriers to effective delegation: old habits, lack of faith in subordinates, and the perceived lack of adequate time to train staff.[13] Traditional, comfortable work patterns can be difficult to change. To overcome this inertia, leaders must develop an awareness of this shortfall and practice new behaviors. Leaders must first surround themselves with a quality staff and then mentor them until the leaders become more confident in the staff's skills. These solutions require time; leaders more naturally assume that the job will be done better if they do it themselves. Unfortunately, this assumption is not always true. True leaders invest time in training and supporting others for the sake of personal sanity and for the future of the organization.

■ Measures of Success

Within the parameters of leadership and institution management, the most important factor in creating successful operations is the establishment of accountability. A superior manager creates high-performance expectations, delegates the task, and follows up to evaluate results. Staff cannot and will not be able to comply with a superior's expectations if they are not communicated clearly. Senior managers and executives must share their ideas and concerns with staff. Once the information and desired expectations are placed on the table, it is important to set procedures in place to ensure compliance.

Paul Light highlights three primary avenues to accountability in a government agency:[14]

1. Compliance accountability seeks to measure conformity with written rules and regulations that are defined clearly. Auditing for compliance essentially looks for occurrences of noncompliance and corrects the situation, if possible; staff who erred are corrected with negative sanctions.

2. Performance accountability uses incentives to encourage staff performance. This positive program seeks to encourage appropriate and voluntary compliance with policy at the inception of a task.

3. Capacity-based accountability requires an organization to place necessary resources in positions that are required for a task. Staff, money, and technology must be available for the work to be accomplished in an effective manner.

The proper stewardship of resources is a fundamental responsibility of all correctional agency managers and staff. For example, the federal government, in an effort to support results-oriented management, implemented the Government Performance and Results Act. This act requires all federal agencies to develop strategic plans, set performance goals, and report annually on actual performance compared to goals. These plans and goals must be integrated into several areas:

- Budget processes
- Operational management of agencies and programs

- Accountability reporting to the public on performance results
- The integrity, efficiency, and effectiveness with which these goals are achieved[15]

Management accountability is defined as the expectation that agency leaders will take responsibility for the quality and timeliness of program performance, control costs, and mitigate adverse aspects of agency operations. Leaders must ensure that programs are managed with integrity and in compliance with applicable law. Management controls—organization, policies, and procedures—are tools to help program and financial managers achieve results and safeguard the integrity of their programs.

Although there is no single best method to ensure accountability, in government the preferred method is compliance accountability. Auditing generally involves teams of personnel, internal or external to the agency, reviewing processes and procedures in order to compare actual performance with the expectations established by policy.

Historically, accountability in bureaucratic organizations has meant limiting staff discretion by utilizing carefully developed rules and regulations. Prison and jail employees in many situations and certain jurisdictions are treated as untrustworthy adolescents. The command and authority of large-scale organizations are generally very hierarchical, and every staff member's role and responsibility are delineated clearly. If all significant decisions are made by a limited number of senior executives, staff quit caring and pass all decisions up the ladder. Independence and creativity do not mesh well with this system. Ironically, in this inflexible accountability structure, the very mechanisms intended to ensure quality sometimes reduce quality. Innovative employee behavior and risk taking can be lost when administrative control is too tight. Yet in corrections, the desire for tight administrative control is understandable. Prisoners of the state are not confined for conforming to laws. Many inmates are very willing to ignore a rule, policy, or general expectations of polite society. In short, they need external control. In order to ensure consistent application of institutional standards of behavior and develop a fair and standard way of operating, staff must know and follow correctional policy.

■ Creating Accountability

In prison and jail environments, the first step is to ensure that all staff clearly comprehend the agency's mission. The guiding vision must be established for all. If security and safety are to be primary goals, leaders must spell this out for staff. All personnel must grasp the purpose of the organization. Once this is established, the chief executive must establish the standards for operation that will support the organizational purpose. There are several important means of creating standards for institutional operation and ensuring compliance with them.

Policy

All prison and jail facilities must have written policy and procedures. These documents should establish the philosophy of operation for each program area, identify the outcomes expected, and define what is required of staff and inmates. Policy must accurately reflect current expectations and be expressed in measurable terms. In the prison and jail setting, control of a facility is organized around rules, and consistency is maintained by ensuring that all staff enforce rules in an impartial manner. This requires extensive staff training so that all staff understand policy requirements. Ongoing monitoring by first-line supervisors ensures that policies are applied correctly.

Training

It is not enough to plan, write, and publish policy in a business or government setting. Individuals who are expected to comply with rules and regulations, and those expected to enforce policy, must receive appropriate training in the process, program, or procedure. In-service training is extremely important to ensure that all personnel are fully informed of the strategy, whether it is a new process or a change in the current practice. In general, staff at all levels of the correctional agency will fare better with policy if senior managers take the time to explain why it is important and seek staff input.

Compliance Audits

For policies to have meaning, organizational leaders must assess compliance with written policy directives. Program audits are the best means of assessing staff operations. These routine reviews enable senior management to gauge program performance, determine the degree of risk, test the adequacy of internal control, and make midstream adjustments to operations to help achieve the desired results. It adds validity to the process if the reviewers know the program area but are organizationally independent.

Another aspect of auditing that can be very helpful is the requirement that program staff perform an internal review of their operations at scheduled intervals. Honest self-monitoring is truly the best means of keeping an organization on track and effective.

Benchmarking

It is always useful to compare one's operation to other similar programs. Key data points of institution management are identified easily (i.e., number of escapes, homicides, suicides, assaults, disciplinary reports, inmate grievances). Once this information is gathered, it is easy to compare data longitudinally at the same facility or for the same periods in similar institutions. Such benchmarking can provide managers with helpful data. For instance, does a positive "hit rate" of 13% of all urinalyses indicate an unusually high use of illegal and contraband substances? By comparing this percentage with the percentage at that institution 1 year earlier or with the percentage at another facility of similar security, leaders can better answer that question.

Accreditation

The American Correctional Association (ACA) has established standards for adult correctional institutions and separate standards for adult detention facilities. The ACA will, for an established fee, help correctional jurisdictions develop a local accreditation process and then provide a team of auditors to assess compliance with the nationwide standards on a preestablished schedule every 3 years. This excellent system provides external oversight of local implementation of nationally recognized standards. Such feedback can be very helpful in assessing institution operations, defending against legal challenges, and providing ongoing comparisons of significant aspects of facility management for line staff and senior managers.

Identification of Corruption

All correctional jurisdictions must have an internal affairs office to ensure that agency resources are used in a way that is consistent with the mission and that government resources are protected from waste, fraud, and abuse. Staff and inmates must be accountable for their behavior and should understand clearly the expected standard of conduct. A crucial piece of management accountability is the obligation to ensure that institution operations are conducted with integrity and in compliance with the law. Inmate and staff allegations of impropriety must be investigated promptly, and all individuals held accountable for their actions. Federal agencies are subject to the Inspector General Act and the Chief Financial Officers Act; state and local jurisdictions generally have similar watchdog legislation that puts teeth into management control.

Strategic Planning

Core values are critical to an organization, and they are rooted firmly in the mission of the agency. A warden must have a well-developed and well-publicized vision of what an organization is and what it is striving to become. Effective leadership does not require a sheriff, warden, or senior administrator who is highly charismatic and larger than life, whether feared or revered. Indeed, some of the great leaders in the private world of business avoid the limelight, focus on creating an organization that handles basic functions well, and keep their eyes on goals to which staff are deeply committed.[16]

Staff at all levels must be involved in this process of preparing the institution for tomorrow's trials and tribulations. Once a strategic plan is developed, it should serve as a guideline for moving the facility through the future issues that develop. One word of caution: Management accountability depends partly on the chief executive's ability to select appropriate organizational responses to new challenges and to ensure that staff stay on track with well-conceived goals. Planning commitments are very powerful; leaders can approve actions or plans that, although helpful in the short run, create lasting constraints on the organization. The best managers know when to make commitments . . . and when to break them.[17]

■ Large-Scale Management Structures

Governments often have huge bureaucracies to ensure that personnel do what they are paid to do. In the past, this has meant many people supervising other people performing routine tasks in a mediocre manner. Government leaders have expended great effort in reinventing how government employees lead and manage, and this has led to some recognition that less can be more.[18] It is important to create an atmosphere where staff believe in what they are doing, have input to how work is structured, and are permitted to exercise judgment in day-to-day tasks. Although some prison and jail managers argue that top-down management is better management, this is not necessarily true. These opposing philosophies are not incompatible. Although it is critical to have policy that establishes broad parameters and requires ethical enforcement, it is not necessary to require mindless compliance with little room for individual innovation. Government reformers are absolutely correct in their quest to put common sense back into government and to encourage individual enthusiasm. Too much emphasis on policy compliance can drive innovation out of an organization, but a sense of reasonableness should prevail. The establishment of management accountability is the heart and soul of being a high-quality leader in the fast-paced correctional environment.

■ Conclusion

Prisons and jails throughout the United States operate under many organizational and management structures—some clearly more effective than others. The more progressive systems have integrated their operations into cohesive systems that work effectively to meet the societal goals of confining inmates and preparing them for their eventual release back to their communities. In these few systems, the courts and corrections, parole, and probation staff seamlessly work with felons and then pass them from one stage of the correctional process to the next in a goal-focused manner. Unfortunately, most systems do not operate this way. In these institutions, the agencies work on their own disparate goals and typically are involved with prisoners only from their isolated perspectives. They then pass inmates on with little continuity of care and no ownership in the success, or failure, of the overall process. This disorganization affects many correctional systems and is the biggest weakness in the system of justice administration in the United States.

Chapter Resources

DISCUSSION QUESTIONS

1. Do you believe there is a difference between leadership and management?
2. Explain the importance of accountability and performance measurement in the correctional environment.
3. Is there a unique requirement in prisons and jails for this type of assessment that is different from other types of government, nonprofit, or for-profit organizations?
4. How does a correctional leader establish an organizational culture of accountability and integrity?
5. Why is that culture important to prison and jail operations?

ADDITIONAL RESOURCES

DiIulio, J., Kettl, D., & Garvey, G. (1993). *Improving government performance.* Washington, DC: Brookings Institute Press.

Freeman, R. (1999). *Correctional organization and management: Public policy challenges, behavior, and structure.* Philadelphia, PA: Elsevier Science and Technology Books.

Gaes, G., Camp, S., Nelson, J., & Saylor, W. (2004). *Measuring prison performance: Government privatization and accountability.* Walnut Creek, CA: Alta Mira Press.

Mears, D. (2010). *American criminal justice policy: An evaluation approach to increasing accountability and effectiveness.* Cambridge, England: Cambridge University Press.

Phillips, R., & McConnell, C. (2005). *The effective corrections manager: Correctional supervision for the future.* Sudbury, MA: Jones & Bartlett.

Wilson, W. (1886). *The study of administration.* Retrieved August 30, 2007, from http://teachingamericanhistory.org/library/index.asp?document=465

NOTES

1. Riveland, C. (1997). The correctional leader and public policy skills. *Corrections Management Quarterly, 1*(3), 22–25.
2. Cressey, D. (1965). Prison organizations. In J. March (Ed.), *Handbook of organizations.* New York, NY: Rand McNally.
3. Mooney, J., & Reiley, A. (1939). *The principles of organization.* New York, NY: Harper and Row.
4. Barak-Glantz, I. (1986). Toward a conceptual scheme of prison management styles. *The Prison Journal, 61,* 42–60.
5. Kettl, D. (1988). *Government by proxy: (Mis)Managing federal programs* (p. 50). Washington, DC: Congressional Quarterly Press.
6. Doig, J. W., & Hargrove, E. C. (Eds.). (1990). *Leadership and innovation: Entrepreneurs in government.* Baltimore, MD: The Johns Hopkins University Press.
7. Bennis, W. (1989). *On becoming a leader* (p. 37). New York, NY: Addison-Wesley Publishing.

8. Peters, T., & Waterman, R. (1982). *In search of excellence: Lessons from America's best-run companies* (p. 118). New York, NY: Warner Books.

9. Wright, K. (1994). *Effective prison leadership* (p. 3). Binghamton, NY: William Neil Publishing.

10. Barnard, C. (1989). The executive functions. In J. Ott (Ed.), *Classic readings in organizational behavior* (pp. 265–275). Belmont, CA: Wadsworth Publishing Company.

11. Toch, H. (1997). *Corrections: A humanistic approach* (p. xiv). Guilderland, NY: Harrow and Heston Publishers.

12. DiIulio, J., Jr. (1987). *Governing prisons: A comparative study of correctional management* (pp. 6–7). New York, NY: The Free Press.

13. Phillips, R., & McConnell, C. (1996). *The effective corrections manager* (p. 60). Gaithersburg, MD: Aspen Publishers, Inc.

14. Light, P. (1992). *Monitoring government: Inspectors general and the search for accountability* (p. 3). Washington, DC: The Brookings Institution.

15. United States Government, Office of Management and Budget. (1995). *Government Performance and Review Act, revised June 1995*. Washington, DC: U.S. Government Printing Office.

16. Collins, J., & Porras, J. (1997). *Built to last: Successful habits of visionary companies* (p. 8). New York, NY: HarperCollins Publishers.

17. Sull, D. (2003, June). Managing by commitments. *Harvard Business Review,* pp. 82–91.

18. Gore, A. (1996). *The best-kept secrets in government* (pp. 15–16). Washington, DC: U.S. Government Printing Office.

Recruitment and Selection in a Correctional Environment

CHAPTER 25

Stephanie R. Appel

CHAPTER OBJECTIVES

- Define the recruitment process for correctional facilities and describe the key factors that affect it.

- Identify the methods of internal and external recruitment.

- Explain how and why prisons and jails recruit specific groups such as women, veterans, and minorities and the mechanisms for recruitment.

- Define the selection process for a correctional environment.

The process of staffing a correctional environment is one of the most critical tasks that any organization faces. Putting the right people in the right positions at the right time is key, especially in larger prison and jail facilities where this complex and continuing process requires extensive and ongoing planning efforts to ensure that the mission, vision, and values are achieved. Prison and jail administrators recognize that staff recruitment, selection, and retention are essential because of the ongoing, rapid growth of the inmate population. Turnover rates are high and escalating, averaging from 16.6% to as high as 43% in some facilities, and result in a cost of nearly $20,000 associated with each new correctional officer hired.[1] Often, prisons and jails spend time, money, and effort on recruitment and selection processes and end up settling for filling a position just to have a "warm body" to achieve mandated staffing levels. Successful prison and jail administrators need to recognize the importance of using both internal and external resources for recruitment to meet critical staffing needs and to ensure that the best possible candidates are selected for vacant positions.

In order to create a successful recruitment plan, you must start with the two initial steps: recruitment (the process of finding qualified people and encouraging them to apply to work with the agency) and selection (the process of choosing among those applicants who do apply for the position).[2] These two steps are the foundation on which to develop a successful staffing plan. Depending on the state and jail/facility, selection and screening criteria may vary according to local regulations and statutes.

■ Recruitment Process

To maintain the ideal staffing levels of a facility at all times, your recruitment process should ensure that for every vacant position in the organization, there are a consistent number of qualified applicants to fill vacancies at all times. These applicants should come from a diverse group of potential employees representing all genders, educational levels, disabilities, and race. Quite often, this proves to be difficult for facilities because of facility or office location, demographics, budgetary effects, and so on.

Organizational Factors

Staffing a prison or jail is a unique and difficult task as each position has the utmost responsibility of ensuring safety and security at all times. This typically requires all staff in the facility to participate in basic correctional skills training, regardless of their field of specialty. An employee who works in a prison or jail is a correctional worker first and a specialist second (such as maintenance, mental health, and food service workers) because all staff could be required at any time to perform security tasks during an emergency or severe staffing shortage. These additional roles and responsibilities, combined with the unique skill sets of jail and prison employees, should be recognized throughout the recruitment process in order to effectively staff a facility.

Often, the reputation of a facility determines if an agency is successful with its recruitment. The image the facility presents throughout the community can be the key factor to successfully recruit new applicants. Specifically, having good public relations with positive stories combined with public appreciation and positive community knowledge of the facility can have a huge positive effect on recruitment. Because potential applicants hear about the facility and job openings from friends and locals in the community, having a positive image can go a long way toward having a successful recruitment program. Consequently, social attitudes about the facility or the type of work associated with the field of corrections may also affect the supply of applicants. If the job is unappealing and undesirable based on public perception, then applicants likely will shun the job, regardless of the benefit package associated with it.[3]

Employment Branding

Making your prison/jail the "employer of choice" in the community is essential to a successful recruitment plan. In years past, prisons and jails had a reputation of hiring people who could not find another job or those who were appointed for political reasons. Furthermore, there is a negative image of working in a jail or prison that has developed as being an environment full of corruption. However, correctional administrators have worked hard to dispose of this public negative mindset and to promote the correctional environment as a professional environment. This is often demonstrated through a set of ethical and professional standards and publicizing the positives of the environment.[4]

By having a successful employment brand, you will create an image that makes those members of the community want to work for your facility and stay working for the facility. To be successful for your recruitment branding, you should do the following:[5]

- Create a positive image of your organization
- Encourage the best potential candidates to apply for the job
- Give employees a sense of pride in the facility
- Reinforce the public's image of the organization[6]

Employment branding can be implemented through various mechanisms such as websites, media campaigns, job fairs, community events, brochures, and so on.

Environmental Factors

Finding a supply of qualified applicants to best meet your facility's needs can be a tricky task depending on the current labor markets in the area. If the supply is limited, agencies might be forced to conduct regional or national searches in order to find qualified applicants. Recruitment may be no problem in areas where jobs are scarce and employment is limited—typically in rural areas. However, closer to urban areas, where there is a competing job market, prisons and jails have a hard time finding qualified staff and are faced with higher turnover rates.

Additionally, trends in the economic markets can affect the number of applicants with the desired skill set. As technology evolves and the agencies develop new missions, and as new initiatives are implemented—that is, Prison Rape Elimination Act (PREA) requirements, reentry initiatives, and so on—your recruitment plan might have to be revised to attract the desired candidates based on these agency needs. With these initiatives being implemented and the ongoing technological changes, organizations might require revisions to their job postings to include additional experience and education as desired based on the agency's needs.

Management Factors

In order to have a successful, ongoing recruitment program, the human resources office must have buy-in from all management staff in the facility. A plan must be developed that is designed to meet all legal and personnel needs, this includes drafting and placing advertisements through various sources, contacting schools and universities, establishing a protocol for equal employment opportunities, and establishing a budget for recruitment purposes.[7]

Prison and jail administrators typically feel that they never have enough staff members or a large enough applicant pool. In addition, with financial and budgetary concerns in recent years, government agencies have been quick to cut agency budgets in the correctional environment to include reductions in staffing levels. This can require a change in recruitment and staffing skill sets while strengthening the communication and working relationship between programs and security staff and developing a unit team with a diverse group of employees. It is key for management to implement and promote this type of team concept and to work with human resources to ensure that this skill set is looked at from a recruitment and selection perspective. No longer are employees hired to work with the same group and team during their entire careers. Managers should expect that new employees will be part of a full range of tasks and teams in a correctional environment.[8]

Recruitment can come from two different areas: within the organization and outside the organization. Typically, the ideal staffing pattern would consist of a balance of internal and external employees within an organization to bring in fresh ideas from outside while mentoring and developing new staff for strategic planning purposes.

Within the Organization

Recruitment of current employees within a facility might be the best source of applicants for those positions above entry level. Most facilities and agencies have a promotional process or career ladder program implemented to encourage current employees to continue their education, training, and career development. These internal recruitment programs are beneficial, both financially and to increase morale and motivation, for existing staff. The hiring manager is familiar with the employee already and knows his or her performance level and skill set. By hiring within the organization, there are fewer on-boarding and initial training requirements.

On the other hand, the disadvantages of recruitment within the organization are that if other employees do not get selected for the position, they might get frustrated, lose motivation, or eventually quit. Additionally, by only selecting to recruit within the organization, you might not get the most qualified candidate with a complete skill set to bring to the table.

Outside the Organization

Recruitment of qualified applicants outside the prison or jail can be one of the most difficult tasks your facility may face. Often, there is a shortage of qualified applicants to fill essential positions, such as security, medical, mental health, and maintenance. Typically, prisons and jails experience a high turnover with these positions because of competition with the private sector. Additionally, prisons and jails are seen as high-stress working environments, which can affect successful recruitment. For example, the Kentucky Department of Corrections averages a 28% turnover rate each year. However, in recent years, specific facilities in Kentucky have seen a turnover rate greater than 45% in security staff. Because of this high ongoing vacancy rate, prisons and jails must develop and implement a solid and ongoing recruitment plan to meet the essential needs of the facility.

ADVERTISING. Advertising may range from a simple job vacancy posting on a board in the break room to a full nationwide media campaign. To develop your recruitment plan, you must look at the skill set of the position you are trying to fill. For example, in 2004, the Kentucky Department of Corrections was experiencing a huge shortage of correctional and medical staff in the Louisville, Kentucky area. Current recruitment efforts of advertising in local newspapers were coming up short. Turnover was at an all-time high. The department developed and implemented a 3-month, intensive recruitment plan targeted at untapped resources in the area. Additionally, the department was looking to increase the diverse workforce and strived to achieve this goal during the recruitment process.

To implement this plan, the department first established a budget for the 3-month recruitment event to include all media outlets possible. Because budgets were limited, the department had to be creative in its endeavors by finding no-cost places such as the YMCA, local middle schools, and community centers where it could hold corrections-specific employment events. The department enlisted the help of various popular public figures who were willing to donate their time to help with the recruitment process. For example, a former councilwoman in Louisville donated her time to record advertisements for targeted radio stations throughout the city as well as to participate in local segments on television stations to air weeks before the recruitment events. These endeavors proved to be successful; through the first recruitment event, there were more than 800 applicants who showed up specifically to apply for employment at the local prison.

Recruitment efforts can take the following forms:

- *Telephone calls*: Call previous applicants or retired staff from the facility to see whether they know of any potential applicants or to inform them of vacant positions.

- *Mailings*: Send out letters/flyers to local businesses, libraries, employment offices, former employees, or retired employees to solicit potential applicants.

- *Recruitment posters*: Display posters in parks, banks, unemployment offices, veterans centers, community centers, schools and universities, churches, real estate agencies, and so on.

- *Radio*: Advertise on local stations for prison-specific job recruitment events. Contact radio stations in the area to obtain information on their listener demographics.

- *Open houses*: Have open houses at your jails and prisons. The general public is not always familiar with the environment of your facilities, and there is a general anxiety and fear associated with the prison environment. By hosting an open house at your facility, potential applicants can get a firsthand look at the daily operations, which might eliminate fears. To have a successful open house, publicizing it through the media and various other mechanisms (flyers, posters, radio, etc.) is key. Staff working during the open house should be professional and give as favorable an impression of the prison/jail as possible.

- *Television*: Contact local cable channels or develop public service announcements (PSAS) or cable bulletin boards for new job openings at the facility.

- *Referral programs*: Sponsor a "get a new employee" campaign where a reward is granted to each existing employee whose referral leads to the successful hire of a new employee. Many employers can offer these incentives by offering special prizes during break periods, advertising the vacant positions during staff meetings and roll calls, and listing referring employees in prison newsletters.

- *Local layoffs*: Monitor local newspapers for factory closings and jobs losses in the area. Contact the closing businesses and agencies to set up recruitment booths and distribute flyers. These events can prove to be successful because these applicants come with a deep skill set.

- *Internships/summer employment*: Enlist local universities and technical colleges to recruit interns. Send employees to local campuses to promote what the prison or jail has to offer. Run advertisements in student newspapers. Internships can be a great way to assess the potential capabilities of the student and to give the student a firsthand perspective of the facility environment.

- *Professional associations*: Enlist the help of professional associations such as the American Correctional Association (ACA) to recruit and solicit names of potential applicants for hard-to-fill positions. Most professional associations have some type of employment referral/job posting service through the Internet, e-mail, or resume banks.

- *Job fairs*: Set up a booth at a job fair that is sponsored by a professional or community organization. Always send your best recruitment staff to these events, and if possible, send professional security staff in uniform to offer firsthand knowledge of the specifics of working in a correctional environment. Job fairs can be very competitive; therefore, its essential to have an attractive booth to make a strong impression.

- *Internet*: Most employers now have a website with employment information and/or an online application process.
- *Social media*: This form of recruitment is rapidly evolving with sources such as Facebook, careerbuilder.com, monster.com, and LinkedIn. This popular method is cheap and reaches a large, diverse group of people.[9]

As you can see, recruitment can be a time-consuming and daunting process. For organizations to get out and find the best candidates, they must search for them using various methods as outlined above. When developing advertisements make sure you are advertising as if you are selling a product, because you are essentially selling someone on the facility. Ensure that your ads have a favorable and positive impression, and specify the minimum requirements for the positions and any skills or training that might be required.

The disadvantage of recruiting outside the organization is the cost associated with the recruitment process. It can prove costly to advertise using various media outlets, such as television, radio, and newspapers. Therefore, it is essential to develop a budget with your finance department prior to developing a recruitment plan for your agency.

■ Recruitment of Specific Groups

Many prisons and jails strive (and are required by law in some areas) to achieve a diverse workforce to meet affirmative action requirements as well as to meet the evolving needs of the inmate population. Specifically, prisons and jails are striving to recruit such groups as women, minorities, and veterans to diversify their workforce. Often, agencies will target women and/or minorities by posting job notices in professional organizations such as the National Society of Hispanic MBAs, the National Association of Blacks in Criminal Justice, and various sites found though the ACA.

Jails and prisons should strive to hire as diverse a workforce as possible in order to be representative of the inmate population demographics. This diversification should be done in compliance with applicable equal employment opportunities. Recruitment factors such as using more female, disabled, and multilingual applicants have become more prevalent in hiring in the correctional environment.

■ Veteran Hiring

Many employers are developing or enhancing a veterans-hiring initiative for their facilities. To recruit from this group, do the following:

- Design a strategy for a veterans-hiring initiative.
- Create an educated and welcoming environment for veterans transitioning to the workforce.
- Actively recruit both the veteran and his or her spouse.
- Promote an inclusive workplace to retain veterans.[10]

Getting involved actively with a local national guard group and promoting a program like Employer Support of the Guard and Reserve (ESGR) has proven to be successful in hiring in the prison/jail setting. For example, sending a weekly job posting of vacant positions to the ESGR can actively recruit those veterans who need jobs upon returning home from deployment and be a win–win partnership. Additionally, many states are mandating a "veterans preference" status to veterans that treats being a veteran as a preferred qualification or giving preference to a veteran applicant who has a service-connected disability rating by treating the veteran's disabled status as a second preferred qualification.

■ EEO and ADA Considerations

Institutions should take voluntary and positive steps to provide equal employment opportunities for all individuals. This begins, of course, with the applicants themselves. The goal is to recruit, hire, retain, and promote a diverse workforce in all employment categories and job classifications. Working to ensure a diverse workforce at all levels helps branding in the community, recruiting in general, and avoiding expensive lawsuits and bad publicity.

Several federal laws apply to the hiring process:

- The Civil Rights Act of 1964
- The Age Discrimination and Employment Act of 1967
- The Pregnancy Discrimination Act of 1978
- The Americans with Disabilities Act of 1990
- Genetic Information Nondiscrimination Act of 2008[11]

Combined, these federal laws prohibit discrimination based on the following:

- Race
- Color
- Religion
- Sex
- Pregnancy
- National origin
- Individuals age over 40 and older
- Veterans
- Qualified individual with a disability
- Genetic information

In short, prisons and jails cannot discriminate against any of these protected classes at any step of the hiring process, from the very beginning of the application process to the final job offer. Furthermore, discrimination includes "disparate impact" against a protected class in general. The Supreme Court defined disparate impact as "practices that are fair in form, but discriminatory in operation." *Griggs v. Duke Power Co.*[12] The use of criminal background checks is being debated now as whether it has a disparate impact against certain minorities.

In fact, the Equal Employment Opportunities Commission specifically highlighted the hiring process (and disparate impact) as part of its 2013 Strategic Enforcement Plan:[13]

Eliminating Barriers in Recruitment and Hiring: The EEOC will target class-based intentional recruitment and hiring discrimination and facially neutral recruitment and hiring practices that adversely impact particular groups. Racial, ethnic, and religious groups, older workers, women, and people with disabilities continue to confront discriminatory policies and practices at the recruitment and hiring stages. These include exclusionary policies and practices, the channeling/steering of individuals into specific jobs due to their status in a particular group, restrictive application processes, and the use of screening tools (e.g., pre-employment tests, background checks, date-of-birth inquiries). Because of the EEOC's access to data, documents, and potential evidence of discrimination in recruitment and hiring, the EEOC is better situation to address these issues than individuals or private attorneys, who have difficulties obtaining such information.[5]

The greatest issue for the prison or jail is the screening tool, and the EEOC is clearly defining its expectations versus the unique needs of jails and prisons. That being said, facilities at the very least should be consistent with background checks and not assume, for example, mere youthful indiscretion for certain classifications.

State and local governments may place additional and stricter requirements on employers. For example, Kentucky law also forbids discrimination against status as a smoker for all employers, and political affiliation, sexual orientation, and gender identity for state employers. See Kentucky Revised Statute 18A.140 and Kentucky Governor's Executive Order 2008-473.[14, 15]

No part of the hiring process should indicate any bias to discourage individuals from applying. This includes the initial advertisements (e.g., "we are looking for a few good men") and general recruiting (e.g., focusing efforts on a particular class of individuals).

Finally, the Americans with Disabilities Act adds further duties such as (1) providing job applicants who have a qualified disability a reasonable accommodation to apply for the position and (2) inquiring about disability before offering employment (inquiries about other).[16]

■ Cost of Recruitment

Financial budgets with regard to recruitment must be watched over both the short and long run to measure and evaluate a successful recruitment program. For example, short-term recruitment plans (such as radio and television ads) might be more costly than planned efforts (job fairs); however, these activities may pay off in the long run by providing a ready group of applicants to fill vacant positions. You must take into account the expenses like advertising, materials, and training costs, as well as the cost of coworkers and managers to implement the plan and the time it takes to fill a specific position in your prison or jail. Additionally, by gathering and reviewing recruitment data, you might discover that although radio advertisements generate many phone calls, only a few applicants actually qualify for the position. Each facility will need to conduct a budget analysis on how much can be allotted to the program to find the best possible candidates for all current and future vacancy needs. Furthermore, managers should monitor recruiting efforts on a daily basis and evaluate the progress of the program. Depending on how urgently the positions need to be filled will determine whether recruitment needs to be stepped up or modified.

Administrators should require an annual audit of recruitment successes and failures and develop a plan for the following year. This plan should include turnover rate versus costs of recruitment mechanisms, a survey of the facility to ensure that recruitment needs are being met, and areas where improvements are needed.

■ Selection Process

Upon successful implementation of your prison or jail's recruitment plan, the next step is the selection process. This is of utmost importance to your agency in order to select the best applicant for the specific vacancy. The selection process can involve numerous selection methods, including the application process, reference checks, background checks, physical examination, drug screening, and written tests. Specific rules and regulations vary by jail, prison, and state.

However, best practices for selection can be outlined as follows:

Step 1: Create a file for documentation: This first step helps to keep the interview panel and human resources organized and is an essential step for keeping in compliance with an open records request.

Step 2: Review the position description: All agencies should have updated descriptions for all positions on file at all times. An interview panel should review the position descriptions to ensure a consistent approach to determine the knowledge, skills, and abilities needed in order to select the best applicant for the position.

Step 3: Request to fill the position: The hiring manager should consult with human resources to determine the appropriate method to fill the position and whether the recruitment for the vacancy will be done internally or externally.

Step 4: Develop a screening criteria: This is an essential step in the selection process. In this step, the knowledge, skills, and abilities necessary to perform the essential functions of the position should be outlined. This should be consistent with the position description currently on file. There should be a minimum education level (for correctional officers, typically a high school diploma or a general equivalency degree) and a minimum requirement of job experience. The institution should be very cautious when reviewing the depth of the work history.

Step 5: Prepare standard questions: Prepare questions to assess candidates' skills, abilities, and past work performance in relation to the open position. Questions should be consistent for all candidates, and interviews should include (1) follow-up questions to have candidates expand on or clarify answers to previous questions; (2) questions pertinent to candidates' application and resume.

Step 6: Assign a selection panel: Traditionally, the selection panel should include a lead member and at least two additional people. The hiring manager should serve as the lead and is responsible for ensuring accurate completion of documentation related to the selection process for the position being filled. Panel members should be diverse and remain consistent throughout the interview process. Furthermore, panel members should not be involved in recommending or approving family members for positions in the agency. Before the interview process, panel members should discuss how they will ask questions, compare notes, and determine the method for evaluation of the candidate's knowledge, skills, and abilities. Finally, panel members should keep information discussed during the selection process strictly confidential.

Step 7: Screen candidates for consideration for interview: After the recruitment process is completed and all applications are received, the hiring mangers should use a set of criteria for evaluating applications and resumes and identify those candidates who meet the established minimum criteria for further consideration.

Step 8: Evaluation and selection: The interview panel should review, compare, and discuss the interviewed candidates' information. Each candidate should be evaluated on the same criteria. Appropriate consideration may be given to items such as conduct, record of performance, seniority, performance evaluations, and qualifications. Additionally, outside factors may be looked at for working in a prison environment such as whether the candidate can make independent decisions, has integrity, understands human nature, and can use good judgment. These characteristics should be explored during the interview process as well as through reference and background checks before making an offer of employment to the candidate. It is better to discover these traits before employment rather than discover negative factors after the employee is hired.

The interview process presents unique issues. Anyone conducting an interview should be trained on how to present their questions to applicants. For example, it is inappropriate to ask female applicants about child care arrangements (not relevant for males or females, but more commonly asked of females); to discuss membership in organizations that indicate the protected class of its members (as opposed to relevant professional organizations); or to talk about the birthplace of applicant, parents, spouse, or other relatives (as opposed to verifying eligibility for employment in the United States if hired).

■ Conclusion

A successful recruitment program is an ongoing process. Prisons and jails should always be on the lookout for potential applicants, even if current vacant positions do not exist. Prisons and jails should keep an updated database of potential, qualified applicants at all times. There should always be a continual presence at local job fairs and events, not only to recruit potential staff, but to continue with the ongoing positive public image of the facility.

Chapter Resources

DISCUSSION QUESTIONS

1. What are various forms of recruitment efforts?
2. Why should prisons and jails strive for a diverse workforce?
3. What is "disparate impact," and what steps can you take to avoid it?
4. What factors should you consider when assigning staff to a selection panel?
5. Why is a successful employment branding program essential to the success of a recruitment operation?

ADDITIONAL RESOURCES

Atherton, E. E., & Phillips, R. L. (2007). *Guidelines for the development of a security program*, 3rd ed. Alexandria, VA: American Correctional Association.

Brown, J. N., & Swain, A. (2009). *The professional recruiter's handbook: Delivering excellence in recruitment practice.* Philadelphia, PA: Kogan Page Limited.

Doverspike, D., & Tuel, R. C. (2000). *The difficult hire: Seven recruitment and selection principles for hard to fill positions.* Manassas Park, VA: Impact Publications.

Falcone, P. (2002). *The hiring and firing questions and answers book.* New York, NY: AMACOM, American Management Association.

International Public Management Association for Human Resources, http://www.ipma-hr.org/

National Institute of Corrections, http://nicic.gov/

The Society for Human Resources Management, http://www.shrm/org

NOTES

1. MTC Institute. (2004). *Correctional officers: Strategies to improve retention.* Centerville, UT: MTC Institute.
2. French, W. L. (1994). *Human resources management.* Boston, MA: Houghton Mifflin Company.
3. French, W. L. (1994). *Human resources management.* Boston, MA: Houghton Mifflin Company.
4. Management, S. S. (2008). *Module to: Workforce planning and employment.* 2-149.
5. Management, S. S. (2008). *Module to: Workforce planning and employment.* 2-149.
6. Management, S. S. (2008). *Module to: Workforce planning and employment.* 2-149.
7. French, W. L. (1994). *Human resources management.* Boston, MA: Houghton Mifflin Company.
8. French, W. L. (1994). *Human resources management.* Boston, MA: Houghton Mifflin Company.
9. SHRM Online Staff. (2013). Survey: LinkedIn remains most popular site for finding candidates. *Society for Human Resources Management On-Line Journal.*
10. Management, S. S. (2008). *Module to: Workforce planning and employment.* 2-149.
11. Management, S. S. (2008). *Module to: Workforce planning and employment.* 2-149.
12. *Griggs v. Duke Power Co.,* 401 U.S. 424, 431-432 (1971).
13. U.S. Equal Employment Opportunity Commission. (n.d.). *Prohibited employment policies/practices.* http://www.eeoc.gov/index.cfm
14. Beshear, S. (2008). *Kentucky Governor's Executive Order 2008-473.* Frankfort, KY: Kentucky State Government.
15. Kentucky Revised Statutes. (2010). *KRS 18A.140 Prohibition against discrimination and political activities.* Frankfort, KY: Kentucky Legislative Commission.
16. EEOC. (n.d.). http://www.eeoc.gov/laws/practices/index.cfm

Leadership: Executive Excellence

Harley G. Lappin

CHAPTER OBJECTIVES

- Explain the importance of leadership in the field of corrections.
- Outline the fundamental principles of an effective organization.
- Describe the concept of forward thinking and several of the relevant future trends.

■ Introduction

The United States currently imprisons more people for longer periods than at any other time in its history. According to the Bureau of Justice Statistics, at year-end 2011, the total number of prisoners under the authority of federal and state correctional jurisdictions exceeded 1.5 million persons.[1] The number of inmates returning to the community also has increased substantially over the years. The rates of incarceration and releases to the community reinforce the necessity for effective leadership of correctional systems, which is critical to an agency's operations and to achieving its mission of enhancing public safety.

Leadership in the field of corrections starts with the recognition that there are two core purposes of correctional systems:

1. To protect society by incapacitating criminals (preventing escapes and providing a safe, secure, humane environment within the prison for all staff and inmates)

2. To reduce recidivism (the rate at which inmates who have served their sentences commit new crimes and are returned to the corrections system)

The rate of recidivism is nationally very high for all types of offenses and is influenced by many factors, including employment opportunities, family support, and peer group influence.[2] Correctional systems can help, but sound leadership is required across agency levels (from direct line supervisors to the agency's executive staff) to accomplish both components of corrections' core purpose.

■ A Context to Leading: Fundamentals

Since 2003, the Federal Bureau of Prisons (BOP) has made a concerted effort to reinvigorate staff focus on its core principles and values. There is no question that establishing and maintaining core ideologies is fundamental to the success of the BOP. The heart of the BOP's continuity has been its core ideologies; they are integral to both the agency's expectations for its workforce and its interaction with the outside environment.

The emphasis on core values has been particularly critical because the agency has had to undergo myriad major changes to reduce costs and live within its budget. BOP leaders have sought to maintain the essence of its operations while at the same time making substantial improvements and gaining efficiencies. Experience has demonstrated that the following principles are necessary to effectively lead an agency and position it to succeed under future leaders:

- Leaders must enable staff to think for themselves and develop and communicate their own innovative ideas.

- Organizational processes must be in place that can be learned by and communicated to others within the agency so that the organization can function regardless of its designated leader.

- An organization must adhere to a firm core ideology and still be able to adapt to environmental changes; it must be visionary and still have exceptional daily execution of the "nuts and bolts."

Core ideologies have allowed the agency to maintain consistency, even when faced with shifting political currents and other external demands. They have facilitated the management of the significant expansion of the federal inmate population and the BOP's transformation into the largest correctional system in the United States with a current total population of almost 219,000 inmates.[3] For the prison system, core values have kept resources applied to what is essential and have anchored the agency's national strategic plans. They make it easy for staff to understand the importance of what they do on a daily basis and understand how practices may change even though core values do not.

The following ideas reflect the importance of core ideologies to the successful accomplishment of the BOP's mission:

1. A safe environment for both staff and inmates
2. Secure institutions to confine offenders and protect the public
3. Skills-building programs to offer inmates the opportunity to prepare to live crime-free lives upon release
4. Service and stewardship to the public and a continued tradition of excellence
5. Staff who are ethical, professional, well trained, and diverse

The first three ideas are specified in the BOP's mission. The fourth concept (service and stewardship) is a requirement based on the agency's role as a steward of the public's trust and taxpayer funds. And finally, the fifth item recognizes the BOP's most important resource and the qualities it desires in its workforce—without quality staff, nothing else is possible.

Although laws establish minimum standards of care to which all inmates are entitled, the BOP has always worked to achieve the highest of standards: to manage inmates effectively, to establish and maintain its reputation of excellence and outstanding public service, and to continue its leadership role in the field of corrections. Staff are largely the reason for this success because of three qualities that consistently have been present in those individuals who have attained significant professional and personal success: excellence, respect, and integrity. Striving for excellence and having respect for oneself and others are not only key to achieving success both in and out of work but also very important values, particularly for those who work in institutions, to model to the inmate population.

The current environment requires having the most capable, qualified, talented, hardworking, committed, professional leaders possible. Leading is an enormous responsibility that carries with it high expectations. Individuals selected for advancement are acknowledged, formally, through the promotion itself, and informally, through the recognition of their hard work, dedication, and professionalism. And although they have already demonstrated their commitment to excellence on some level, with advancement their responsibilities expand significantly, as do the BOP's expectations of them.

No single individual has a magic formula for leading or managing, and one's philosophy should evolve with experience; however, review of the BOP's history indicates that leaders tend to be far more successful than others if they have certain qualities:

- Integrity—high integrity and ethics; conduct on and off the job must be beyond reproach
- Effective communication—ability to establish and communicate high performance standards and expectations, listen and communicate effectively with staff, have a positive attitude, and be a good role model
- Respect—recognition that each employee is an individual and that expectations may not be the same for everyone
- Self-awareness—knowing oneself and being aware of one's strengths and weaknesses
- Resourcefulness—ability to recognize and use wisely the extensive expertise and resources available, which are designed to help prison facilities succeed, and appropriately acknowledge assistance received
- Ability to analyze—ability to assess a given situation using skills of the head (technical knowledge, delegation, strategic thinking) and skills of the heart (interpersonal relations, emotional intelligence, humility, acting as a team player) and knowing when these skills apply
- Loyalty—unwavering loyalty to the agency while effectively balancing doing what is right for staff and what is in the best interest of the agency

- Understanding of the big picture—an understanding of the climate and culture of the location and external factors that affect the agency (e.g., legislation, prosecutorial initiatives); knowledge of the agency's history and of lessons learned
- Problem-solving capabilities—the ability to zero in on causes and on what is important and to overcome obstacles; the ability to make informed, sound decisions, even under stress, including the tough ones

In addition, effective leaders must have a desire to continue growing and learning. If corrections professionals wish to expand their scope of impact by pursuing higher-level leadership roles, then their performance and conduct must be exemplary, and these individuals must continue to enhance those skills necessary to succeed (e.g., by taking advantage of mentoring opportunities). No one is above learning, and each person is responsible for expanding his or her own horizons. It is critical that a corrections professional keep learning and stay on top of developments in the field. Stagnation is extremely counterproductive, because the agency, with or without a particular individual, will continue to adapt to its environment to ensure readiness to meet future demands. Thus, an individual must commit to ongoing professional development for himself or herself and for the agency.

Integrity

Staff integrity is a key to accomplishing the BOP's mission and dealing with its very broad range of constituents effectively, including:

- Inmates and their families
- Government and court officials
- Law enforcement
- The public
- Advocacy groups
- Oversight entities
- The media

Integrity affects the agency's credibility; the level of trust and confidence garnered from its constituency groups depend on it. It affects how the BOP's message is received and the support that is returned. At the most basic level, integrity affects the agency's ability to secure funding and select sites for prisons.

As stewards of the taxpayers' trust, corrections professionals should not expect notice or praise from their constituents when they do the right thing, conduct themselves professionally, or excel at performing their duties. Doing the right thing is expected—in fact, it is what all correctional staff, management, and line staff alike should expect of themselves, and those wishing to lead must model that, first for their peers, then for their staff.

Michael Josephson and the Government Ethics Center Commission (part of the California-based Josephson Institute of Ethics) offer five principles designed as a guide to public service ethics.[4]

1. Public office is a trust; use it only to advance public interests, not personal gain.
2. Make decisions on the merits, free from partiality, prejudice, or conflicts of interest.
3. Conduct government "openly, efficiently, equitably, and honorably" so that the public can make informed judgments and hold public officials accountable.
4. Honor and respect democratic principles; observe the letter and spirit of laws.
5. Safeguard public confidence in the integrity of government by avoiding appearances of impropriety and conduct unbefitting a public official.

It is important to remember that the public views each BOP staff member as representing the agency, and corrections systems go as their staff go. Corrections professionals must conduct themselves in a manner consistent with the highest of ideals in all aspects of their lives. Leaders must model this behavior and demand it of their staff.

Understanding the Big Picture

Effective leadership requires a solid understanding of the larger context within which the agency operates. A leader must keep in mind that his or her institution is one small part of the agency, which in turn, in the case of the BOP or state departments of corrections, is just a small part of government. That larger context and factors external to the agency can directly or indirectly affect the correctional system: Using the budget as an example, if more is funneled to one department, less is available to the others, because the government (whether federal, state, or local) must live within certain total overall dollar limits.

As a large correctional system, the BOP deals with a variety of complicated issues and subpopulations that by necessity require a broad range of programs and services. Several challenges have driven much of the agency's decision making and planning over the past few years. But to grasp the enormity of these challenges and their impact, leaders must first look closely at the agency's history over the last several decades.

The BOP's inmate population growth was gradual through its early history until the late 1980s, when the Comprehensive Crime Control Act became effective. This legislation abolished federal parole and established sentencing guidelines. Several other major factors have affected the federal prison system, including legislation establishing mandatory minimum drug and firearms sentences; the National Capital Revitalization and Self-Government Improvement Act of 1997 (which required the BOP to absorb the entire felony population of Washington, DC); and prosecutorial initiatives targeting gangs, firearms, immigration, and drug offenses.

The events of September 11, 2001, resulted in a pronounced shift in this nation's resource allocation to those departments or agencies responsible for homeland security and counterterrorism activities (and later to the military in support of the war in Iraq). The end result to other domestic agencies, including the federal prison system, was several years of very tight budgetary constraints, further exacerbated by the country's response to the various natural disasters that followed, most notably Hurricane Katrina. Again, if one department receives more, less is available to the others from the finite budget, so the BOP has had to manage growth and crowding during this period of diminishing resources.

Extensive restructuring and streamlining initiatives had to be implemented to reduce costs and allow the agency to live within its means. Cost-reduction initiatives cut across all agency levels, including:

- Closing four independent prison camps that were determined to be too costly to update and operate
- Discontinuing the intensive confinement program that had proven to be no more effective than regular camps at reducing recidivism (even though they were more labor intensive)
- Creating centralized designation, sentence computation, and classification processes
- Implementing a medical classification system (modifying how medical services are provided by identifying institution care levels based on availability of resources and designating inmates to those matching their specific medical needs)
- Consolidating two training sites

Some initiatives are still ongoing, including mission changes at a limited number of institutions (e.g., security levels) to better manage the inmate population and a restructuring of Federal Prison Industries, otherwise known as UNICOR.

These initiatives resulted in displacement of a large number of staff as positions were abolished, but it was extremely important for the agency to retain its highly skilled, trained, and experienced workforce.

A vacancy clearinghouse process was established to help place displaced staff; the majority of displaced staff chose to remain with the BOP.

Since beginning the streamlining process, the result of these changes has been the elimination of thousands of positions and a cost avoidance of tens of millions of dollars, all accomplished without compromising the safety and security of the BOP's institutions. The flexibility, creativity, and dedication of BOP staff have contributed significantly to these achievements. By establishing and promoting a staff feedback mechanism on the agency's Intranet, the agency's executive staff was able to solicit staff input that identified many areas of potential cost savings. There is no question that open, two-way communication has been key to the success of these initiatives.

To optimally achieve the core purpose of corrections, leaders must ensure that the BOP continually refines its processes and services. For example, in each of the past several years, the agency has released an average of more than 40,000 federal inmates per year back to U.S. communities.[5] Most inmates who go to prison also leave prison and return to the community. Consequently, BOP leaders must emphasize the importance of the release preparation portion of the mission, actively demonstrate their support in meeting this objective, and demand that staff perform in a manner consistent with this goal (e.g., role-modeling prosocial behaviors and appropriate interaction).

■ Federal Prison Industries (FPI)

Federal Prison Industries (FPI) is one of the agency's most important correctional work programs. This program is critical to the safety and security of agency institutions and helps it occupy about 18% of the work-eligible inmate population. Research has confirmed that inmates who work in FPI are 24% less likely to recidivate.[6]

Recent legislative changes significantly limited FPI's mandatory source status, making it necessary for FPI to compete for virtually all its sales. This adversely affected FPI's office furniture program, causing sales to drop and some factory closures. Congress continues to consider bills that would, if passed, significantly affect how FPI operates. Consequently, FPI is focusing its efforts on expanding the services, fleet management, and recycling business areas, which operate without any mandatory source preference and compete against private vendors (in some instances, even against low-cost providers from outside the United States). Again, by FPI leaders making a proactive decision to change based on their awareness of the political climate and public sentiment, FPI has been able to control its own future to the maximum extent possible.

■ Interagency Collaboration

Providing effective programming in prison is just one component of a successful reentry strategy. Corrections and treatment research demonstrate that treatment support to offenders entering the community under continued criminal justice supervision (i.e., transfer to a halfway house, probation, and parole) reduces recidivism. Thus, it is incumbent upon the agency to ensure continuity of appropriate programs, care, services, and support tailored to the specific needs of inmates, particularly for those with greater needs.

As partners in the criminal justice system consider the unique challenges related to community reentry, leaders must recognize some basic truths about what will be needed to succeed. No single agency or individual can do it alone; many agencies share some responsibility for ex-offenders. Leaders must ensure effective collaboration and communication during the entire incarceration process and well before release, involving the right people—in this case, involving all parties with a stake in the outcome. Agencies must make full use of available technology and automation to improve data flow within and across agencies and to reduce redundancies.

The National Offender Workforce Development Partnership (NOWDP) includes representatives from several different agencies and government departments. It emphasizes collaboration, information sharing, and resource development with the purpose of improving reentry success by increasing career-oriented employment opportunities for ex-offenders. The bureau's involvement in this partnership ties in perfectly to its Inmates Skills Development (ISD) initiative. BOP leaders understand that if ex-offenders have viable, reliable jobs that provide a reasonable living wage, they are more likely to stay crime-free. In fact, work programs have been a key component of the BOP since 1934 and have provided training to develop and enhance inmates' marketable skills since that time.

The BOP makes sure its employees understand that viable employment reduces the potential for rearrest and promotes a climate that encourages active support toward this objective. As change agents, leaders must share that awareness with staff, actively solicit and support innovation on their part that enhances collaborative efforts, and direct the implementation of those ideas that show promise or value. Various agency changes or activities have followed the decision to participate in the NOWDP, including:

- Guidance has been provided to all wardens on implementing partnerships at the institution level.
- The National Institute of Corrections (NIC) created and hosts a website that provides detailed information and points of contact for partner agencies.
- Joint Offender Workforce Development training is being provided by the NIC, the agency's ISD branch, and the Office of Probation and Pretrial Services for field staff and local community partners at targeted cost-effective geographic locations.

As one can see, a single decision (in this case, to be a member of the NOWDP) can easily trigger multiple consequences.

■ Forward Thinking

The seeds of the future are always planted in the present; the trick is to identify which will germinate. It is impossible to forecast some circumstances, such as what the consequences for the criminal justice system might be if there is another major successful terrorist attack, or a budget crisis, or a change in society's outlook about the criminal justice system's responsibilities regarding the drug trade and drug use. But it is a leader's responsibility to encourage innovative, future-oriented thinking and consider organizational enhancements to operational practices and culture.

The BOP strives to be its own best critic and to preserve a strong risk assessment capability. Critical self-examination readies the agency to meet future demands, as does the concept of forward thinking that was introduced in the agency by former Director Kathleen Hawk Sawyer in April 2001.

Many agencies have a forward-thinking process in place. In starting the agency down this path, Sawyer explained that the agency historically had done a great job strategically planning 3–5 years out. However, she recognized the need to plan strategically for the long term (e.g., 20–25 years into the future), a process that would involve framing what the future might look like and enhancing the agency's flexibility. To best position itself for the future, the BOP has focused on incorporating proactive thinking into its entire culture, still an ongoing process. Ultimately, this approach will spread across the agency and get everyone thinking of the big picture and future possibilities. The essence of this approach is creating a new way of thinking for the agency's future leaders.

In the years since Sawyer posed this challenge, BOP leaders have been immersed in the process of forward thinking, researching and analyzing trends that may affect it, scanning the environment, and creating scenarios that will help track and plan for the effects of various outside influences on the prison system—all to ensure the agency's continued success. To that end, a Forward-Thinking Review Team was established that oversees ongoing training to agency staff, dissemination of information related to this specific initiative, continued environmental scanning and trend identification and analysis, and the development of mechanisms to monitor scenarios. It also ensures the inclusion of a forward-thinking element in all new agency initiatives.

Research was conducted on a global scale in the categories of environment, justice, technology, and workforce to identify emerging trends. Commonalities in trends were evaluated to determine the likelihood of having an effect on the agency in 20–25 years. The Forward-Thinking Review Team further consolidated these trends and identified the top 30 trends potentially having an effect on the future of the agency. Information on these trends serves as a resource in the development of policy, recommendations for pilot programs, and preparation of executive staff papers. It provides a framework for discussing how the BOP is preparing to meet anticipated demands and changes, and provides some questions to challenge leaders or those aspiring to leadership positions.

Prevention, Rehabilitation, and Reentry

The review team found that partnerships with correctional facilities and their communities needed to focus on reentry programs for all offenders and that this should remain a primary goal of all correctional institutions in an effort to reduce recidivism. They issued a challenge to leadership: "What are correctional systems doing now, collectively or as individual agencies, that will effectively prepare the agencies for this future scenario?"

Inmate Work and Vocational Training Programs

The review team also recognized that inmate work and vocational training programs should be designed in partnership with community business leaders to support local economies and help ease the transition of inmates into the community's workforce. Toward this end, leaders must seek to design programming efforts both in partnership with and in support of the local economy and not in competition against it. Inmate labor is valuable to both correctional institutions and their communities, providing both valuable work experience and service while reducing the likelihood of inmate misconduct. As such, vocational training and educational programs are crucial to correctional facilities. The review team challenged leadership in this arena as well by asking, "How can wardens obtain buy-in from local community business leaders for such partnerships?"

Resource Allocation

A shift in national priorities means that resources are moving toward terrorism prevention and public education and away from corrections. As such, the review team challenged correctional leaders to "identify changes that may need to occur to enable corrections and supervision agencies to successfully accomplish their missions in the future if more resources are pushed to other areas."

Workforce Demographics

Trends in the workforce indicate that advancing technology creates the need for more educated and skilled workers. As such, the role of corrections professionals is expanding, and they will be required to perform more advanced skills. For example, the health services' electronic medical record (EMR) initiative aims to enable all agency healthcare practitioners to access the healthcare records of all inmates housed in its facilities. The challenge in this area is assessing how technology will affect the "nuts and bolts" of corrections.

■ Conclusion

Many opportunities and challenges exist for individuals seeking leadership roles in the field of corrections. Each individual is entirely responsible for his or her own future, both personally and professionally. To have an effect, particularly in leadership roles, individuals must strive for and demand personal excellence of themselves. The field of corrections absolutely demands it. Adopting this strategy while maintaining one's sense of humanity will yield success and, more importantly, the greatest sense of fulfillment.

Chapter Resources

DISCUSSION QUESTIONS

1. Why is strong leadership important in the field of corrections?
2. What are the fundamental principles of an effective organization?
3. What is forward thinking, and how is it relevant to the field of corrections?
4. What forward thinking trends have been identified by the Federal Bureau of Prisons?
5. In what ways can the leadership of the BOP to the challenges of forward thinking?

ADDITIONAL RESOURCES

Federal Bureau of Prisons, http://www.bop.gov

Keith, K. L. (2012). Organizational Culture and Legitimacy in Prison Leadership. Available online from http://www.academia.edu/3518706/Organizational_Culture_and_Legitimacy_in_Prison_Leadership

National Institute of Corrections, http://www.nicic.org

UNICOR, Federal Prison Industries, Inc., http://www.unicor.gov

NOTES

1. Carson, E. A., & Sabol, W. J. (2012). *Prisoners in 2011* (December 17, 2012, ed.). Washington, DC: U.S. Department of Justice, Office of Justice Programs. NCJ 239808.
2. Langan, P., & Levin, D. (2002). *Recidivism of prisoners released in 1994.* Bureau of Justice Statistics Special Report. Washington, DC: U.S. Department of Justice, Office of Justice Programs.
3. Bureau of Prisons. (n.d.). *Federal inmate population.* Retrieved from http://www.bop.gov
4. Josephson, M., the Josephson Institute of Ethics, and Government Ethics Center Commission. (2005). *Preserving the public trust: The five principles of public service ethics.* Los Angeles, CA: Josephson Institute of Ethics.
5. Federal Bureau of Prisons Office of Research and Evaluation, internal agency unpublished documents.
6. Saylor, W. G., & Gaes, G. G. (1997). PREP: Training inmates through industrial work participation and vocational and apprenticeship instruction. *Corrections Management Quarterly, 1*(2), 32–43.

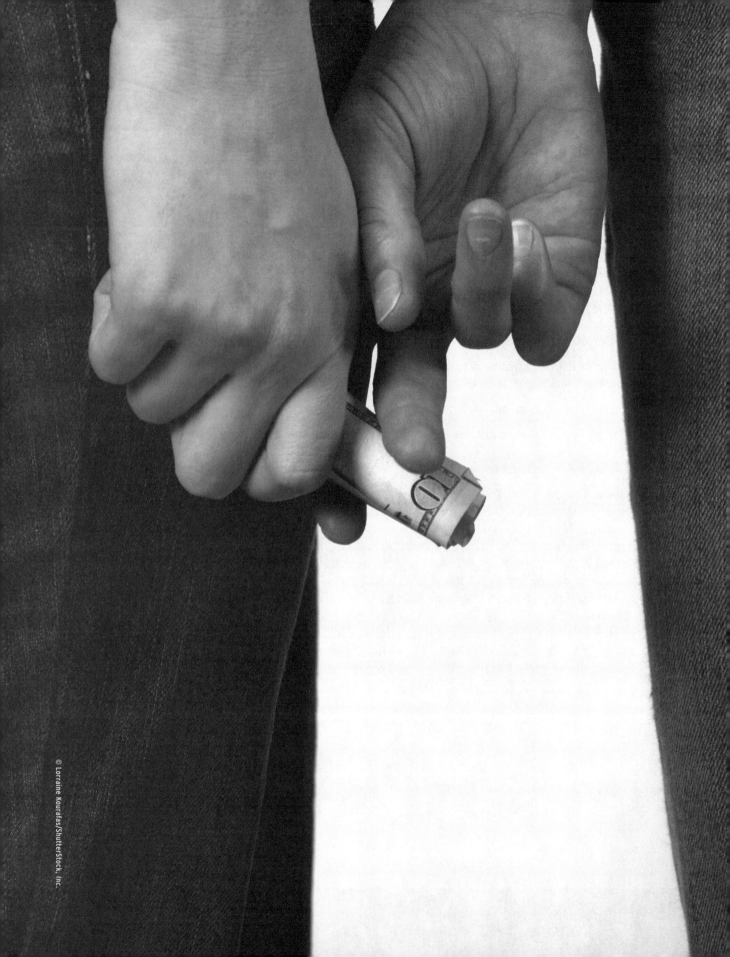

Deterring Corruption

Sam S. Souryal

CHAPTER OBJECTIVES

- Define public corruption.
- Discuss the main differences between public corruption and prison corruption.
- Describe the main characteristics of professionalism.
- Define acts of misfeasance.
- Explain how acts of malfeasance differ from acts of nonfeasance.

■ Overview

Corruption by prison personnel has traditionally been thought to be part of the broader spectrum of public corruption. However, prison corruption can be often much more harmful to society because prisons may *graduate* individuals who are more embittered and vengeful than common citizens. Such embittered and vengeful persons can be much more dangerous to society for a longer time. Furthermore, some aggravating factors can make prison corruption even more epidemic because (1) it is almost invisible because it is hidden behind high walls; (2) it is most often committed by individuals who were well immersed in corrupt acts before they were in prison; (3) public scrutiny of prison corruption is close to nonexistent because the public does not care, or want to care, about "sub-humans" who are locked up behind bars—where they belong; (4) prison corruption is almost undetectable in light of inmate culture that inflicts extreme punishment on inmates who cooperate with prison officials; and (5) there can be rather phantom supervision of inmates by correctional officers who may be ignorant or indifferent.

■ Public Service Corruption

When public officials display professionalism, they encourage trust. When they behave corruptly, they betray the public's trust. Corruption by public officials has been considered much more sinister than corruption by private sector employees, for several reasons:

First, citizens have no choice but to use the available public services (e.g., to drive a car, to run a business, to pay taxes, to petition for a license), whereas they can choose among the services offered by different organizations.

Second, public officials take an oath to faithfully execute the laws of the land and to serve society, making their failures, especially when unjustified, seem more "sinful."

Third, because of their sovereignty, public agencies can inflict greater damage on unsuspecting citizens than can officials in the private sector. When corruption is discovered, citizens can lose faith in their political system, their elected officials, and themselves.[1]

People, especially in a democracy, expect their public servants to be efficient and civil (hence the term "civil service") and to consider their duties sacred obligations. While people should expect public officials to demonstrate a higher level of integrity than the average person, private officials and contractors must adhere to the rules and practice good faith management.

Alert and conscientious managers can fairly estimate the extent of corruption by monitoring several indicators, including (1) formal and informal complaints filed against employees by dissatisfied customers, supervisors, or other employees; (2) disciplinary actions taken against employees for violating agency rules and regulations; (3) patterns of questionable behavior by workers such as involvement in alcoholism, drug use, or domestic violence, or patterns of depressive episodes; (4) erratic behaviors by workers such as more out-of-town trips than are customary, radical changes in their lifestyle that might indicate the sudden acquisition or loss of wealth, or unexpected requests for reassignment or resignation; and (5) graffiti on walls and inside bathrooms. Based on these indicators, management should be able to determine when to intervene.[2]

■ Definition of Prison Corruption

From a sociological standpoint, corruption in prisons and jails may be considered abuse of power because the term denotes the use of power to achieve a purpose other than that for which it is granted. An officer might hire or promote a less qualified worker because he or she is a relative of a superior or because that is the warden's desire, treat inmates preferentially because the inmates serve as house trustees, or deny civil rights privileges to a group of inmates because of their faith or religion.[3]

From a legal standpoint, corruption can involve the use of oppression or the use of extralegal methods to suppress the will of others. An officer might write up inmates for violations they did not commit because of their race or ethnicity, beef up charges against inmates (or other officers) because they are viewed as troublemakers, or permit physical abuses to be inflicted upon inmates (or other officers) because they are gay or lesbian.

From a moral standpoint, corruption may be the failure of staff to demonstrate compassion or to keep a promise; public officials are morally obligated to care for the needs of those in their custody or under their supervision. An officer might ignore an inmate's cries for medical attention believing that his or her shift is understaffed, trick an inmate into giving information regarding illicit or illegal activities of other inmates with the promise of better treatment that then is not rendered, or, in a parole hearing, withhold helpful testimony regarding the good behavior of an inmate because of his or her refusal to respond to the officer's sexual advances.

From an economic standpoint, corruption in the correctional environment could mean the abusing of authority for personal gain; public workers are forbidden to take bribes, kickbacks, or any unauthorized payments for discharging regular duties. An officer might write up a procurement contract that fits a specific vendor who had promised to pay a kickback if selected, exploit inmates by threatening to "make their lives miserable" unless their families pay a bribe, bring or sell contraband to inmates, or use prison equipment (e.g., a truck or a tractor) without authorization.[4]

Corruption among correctional workers occurs at all levels and in many different forms. In some cases, it is very limited in scope, such as a minor conflict with a staff member. In other cases, correctional officers have been terminated for smuggling contraband or for having inappropriate relations with an inmate. Other corruption cases involve more elaborate schemes and involve substantially more money. In 1998, the Kansas Court of Appeals overturned the conviction of a county jail administrator who took money from an inmate account (an account holding inmates' personal funds, abandoned inmate funds, and jail telephone commission profits) and put it into an interest-bearing bank account. The transferred money was used to buy equipment for the jail and pay jail commissary bills. Although the money was not used for the personal benefit of the administrator, the Court of Appeals ruled that the transfer was improper because it violated the terms of the trust, and the administrator, as custodian, was held responsible. However, because the money was neither county nor state property, the charge of "misuse of public funds" was inappropriate (see *Estate of McDonald v. Unified Government of Wyandotte County*).[5]

Also, in February 2006, the Secretary of the Florida Department of Corrections, James Crosby, was forced to resign following a large-scale state and federal investigation into the Florida Department of Corrections. The investigation uncovered widespread corruption including problems with contract vendor accounts and abuse of the department's athletic program. Allegedly, nonemployee "ringers" were furnished with department security identification cards to be able to participate in department softball games and were encouraged to use steroids. As a result, high-ranking officials in Florida's Department of Corrections were fired including two regional directors, four wardens, and three assistant wardens.[6]

Because of the enclosed environment of prisons, corruption can take the form of use-of-force violations, including punitive and excessive use of force. For example, in 1997, Wayne Garner, Georgia Commissioner of Corrections, was implicated in an alleged mass beating of inmates in Georgia's Hays State Prison. Garner allegedly watched while the inmates, some in restraints, were beaten until blood covered the walls.[7] It is noteworthy that the use of force in prisons and jails need not cause serious bodily harm to be excessive. In *Hudson v. McMillian*,[8] the Supreme Court held that inmates can maintain a claim of cruel and unusual punishment under the Constitution's Eighth Amendment even if a correctional officer's use of force did not result in serious bodily injury. In this case, Keith Hudson, a Louisiana inmate, was punched in the face and stomach while the correctional supervisor looked on and told the officers only not to "have too much fun." Hudson suffered minor bruises and swelling, and some loosened teeth in the beating. The Court determined that the malicious and sadistic nature of the use of force violated the inmate's rights.

As a result of these rulings, a new correctional law discipline was born. This new discipline articulated matters of civil liability, which will be discussed more in other chapters. Accordingly, inmates can now file lawsuits against prison officials seeking a change in prison conditions, policies, or procedures, as well as monetary damages. Federal civil rights lawsuits can now be filed by inmates under Title 42 U.S.C. §1983. The right of inmates to file such lawsuits (against correctional officials) was first endorsed by the Supreme Court in *Cooper v. Pate*.[9] Historically, under the doctrine of "sovereign immunity," governments could not be sued unless they consented to being sued. The Supreme Court later further clarified the application of §1983 lawsuits against government officials in *Monell v. Department of Social Services of the City of New York*.[10] The Supreme Court holds local governments, counties, and municipalities liable because they are considered "persons" and, as such, can be sued under §1983.

■ The Nature of Prison Corruption

Prison and jail corruption differs slightly from public corruption. These differences are uniqueness of the environment, function, occupational opportunities, and patterns of social relationships that develop inside the correctional institutions. Here are a few reasons:

First, not only do prison officials serve in environments that are relatively closed to public scrutiny (making it easier to carry out corrupt acts or to suppress evidence of such acts), but they are also engaged in unusually stressful jobs for much longer periods of time. In most instances, they are given the difficult task of controlling a reluctant, resistant, and sometimes hostile inmate population whose welfare may seem better served by corruption than by honest compliance with prison rules and regulations.

Second, because prisons and jails have played a major part in maintaining order in society, their operation has become a massive industry. More than 1.5 million Americans are now behind bars, and another 5 million are under some sort of correctional supervision. When huge numbers of inmates are confined to small spaces, prisonization increases. A culture of manipulation, violence, and—at times—barbarism may ensue. This can wear down the professional fiber of correctional officers, especially those assigned to highly stressful tasks. As a result, prison personnel may experience more resentment and cynicism than their counterparts in other public agencies.

Third, prison and jail operations have become too complicated and expensive. This can increase the opportunity for economic corruption, especially if the workers are not quite professional and supervision is lax. As the complexity of the operation and the amount of capital involved grow, corruption tends to increase. California, for example, spends $7.6 billion per year on prison operations, and five states have a corrections budget of more than $1.5 billion.[11]

Fourth, the demographics of confined inmates today may be more conducive to another kind of corruption: racial cruelty and racial oppression. Prison and jail populations do not proportionately represent the general population of Americans. This disparity has grown more pronounced in the last 30 years. Although African American males make up less than 12% of the U.S. population, they comprise almost half of prison and jail populations, while the majority of officers are Caucasian.

This composition of institution populations and the disparity between the racial distribution among inmates and staff may give rise to staff violence against minorities.

Fifth, correctional management has undergone a series of changes more radical than those confronted by any other public institution. In the last 20 years alone, an avalanche of new rules have emerged concerning overcrowding, judicial review, parole conditions, acquired immune deficiency syndrome, gang members, drug usage, the aging of inmates, and the use of tobacco products by inmates and correctional officers. These rapid changes can cause serious managerial problems, complicating the maintenance of discipline inside a correctional facility. As a result, officials— generally more attached to security issues than social issues—may feel hesitant to enforce the new rules, which they may consider vague, confusing, politically motivated, and possibly dangerous. The new rules, furthermore, have prompted the hiring of unprecedented numbers of correctional officers, creating yet another difficulty: inadequacies in screening and training. All in all, a state of institutional uncertainty seems to engulf prison operations, which, ironically, must be navigated every day by the least experienced personnel.[12]

Sixth, given the relatively low pay of correctional officers, especially of those at the lower levels, the potential gains from corrupt behavior may be too attractive to resist. Correctional officers may, over time, become dependent on inmates for the completion of some tasks or the smooth management of the tier. In return, they may overlook inmate infractions and supervise with some favoritism.[13] Also, young and inexperienced personnel especially can justify accepting graft as a lucrative albeit illicit way to supplement one's income—usually without significant risk.[14]

■ Categories of Prison Corruption

Prison corruption inevitably falls into one of the three following categories:

1. *Acts of misfeasance.* These are deviant acts that an official is supposed to know how to do legally (through education, expertise, and/or training) but are willingly committed illegally for personal gain. Misfeasance is most likely to be committed by high-ranking officials in the prison hierarchy or by others associated with the correctional facility through a political or a professional appointment. (One example would be a member of the oversight board who stretches the limits of his or her discretion, allowing for indiscretions by contractors that would undermine the public interest yet benefit the board member personally.)

2. *Acts of malfeasance.* These are basically criminal acts or acts of misconduct committed by institution officials in violation of the criminal laws of the state and/or agency regulations. Such violations are usually committed by officials at the lower or middle-management levels. (Examples include theft, embezzlement, trafficking in contraband, extortion, official oppression, or the exploitation of inmates or their families for money, goods, or services.)

3. *Acts of nonfeasance.* These acts constitute failures to act in accordance with one's administrative responsibilities. They are basically acts of omission or avoidance by an official. Acts of nonfeasance are committed across the board, regardless of people's positions in the agency's hierarchy. Because of their subtle nature, acts of nonfeasance may be more responsible for corrupting correctional officers than acts of misfeasance or malfeasance.[10] Two types of acts are common in this category: (1) selectively ignoring inmate violations of institutional rules, such as looking the other way when marijuana or other drugs are smuggled into the facility by inmates or visitors in return for payment; and (2) failing to report another employee involved in misconduct out of loyalty or as a repayment for a previous favor.

■ Prevention of Prison Misconduct

Official corruption cannot be prevented; it can only be minimized. Because workers are not born professional and cannot be counted on to police themselves—especially when faced with acute moral dilemmas—direction, guidance, and leadership must be provided. Ideally, a manager should serve as a role model, an arbitrator, a disciplinarian, and the conscience for all workers and inmates. However, this may be more easily said than done.[15]

To have any chance at success, management must first be credible. Senior staff must create a work environment that is conducive to honesty, fidelity, and obligation. Honesty is telling the truth at all times unless concealment is justified for a higher good. Fidelity is keeping all promises made to workers, inmates, and any other group associated with the prison enterprise. If management claims that it treats the officers fairly, fairness must be provided at each step of the officers' careers, including assignments, promotions, demotions, and discipline. Obligation is treating each rule, policy, or directive seriously, and not acting in bad faith. Therefore, if management declares that it will enforce a rule by which every officer is to be searched at a point of entry, everyone, including the warden, must be faithfully searched.

Ethical institution leaders must also be consistent, reasonable, and sympathetic to the needs of officers and inmates. Their behavior—in public as well as in private—must be above reproach and their managerial decisions borne by moral reasoning, regardless of who is to win or lose. The use of manipulation and hidden agendas must be shunned, because it can substantially add to the resentment and cynicism of prison personnel. The influence of management leadership should also be methodically exercised rather than casually discharged in occasional remarks at commencement ceremonies or staff meetings. If correctional officers note that their leaders do not truly care, they stop caring themselves, leading them to pursue personal interests that may be much more profitable.

To minimize prison corruption, management should articulate its position on corruption and corrupters, and develop and implement an anticorruption policy. Management should first and foremost prepare a policy statement outlining its position regarding corruption and corrupters and distribute it to every official. The message must be perfectly clear: professionalism counts, corruption will not be tolerated, and all employees will be held accountable for absolute integrity in everything they do. By publicizing such a policy statement, workers are put on notice that a concentrated effort is being aimed at raising the consciousness of workers about the depravity of corruption, that management supports high ethical conduct, that the agency will identify and deal with policy violators, and that no one is exempt from compliance with the agency's professional standards.

The Impact of Policy

An ideal policy statement should accomplish two basic activities[16]:

1. Articulate the activities generally accepted as being corrupt by prison or jail officials, including criminal acts such as theft, assault, forgery, bringing in contraband, maintaining an illegal sexual relationship with an inmate or another officer, and falsification of evidence (by a member of internal affairs).

2. Specify the investigatory procedures and penalties to be meted out in each of the previous categories. As a matter of policy, investigatory procedures should be conducted by the internal affairs division or an independent office and should not undermine the constitutional rights of the accused (e.g., the presumption of innocence, due process, and easy access to legal defense). Penalties should be fair and reasonable and may include suspension (with or without pay), termination, reassignment, payment of a fine, or, in more serious cases, a judicial sentence to be imposed during a court trial.

After identifying and categorizing the agency's anticorruption policy, management must establish an anticorruption action program. Wardens may be reluctant to pursue an overtly aggressive program because of concern about reactions from the correctional officers' union, concern for workers' morale, and an unfair or vindictive media response.

Anticorruption Programs

Prison administrators should design their anticorruption programs to fit their specific function, culture, and resources. Regardless of how such programs are designed, four strategies should be included. First, upgrade the quality of correctional personnel. A natural place to begin developing agency defenses against corruption is the recruitment office door. There are two significant obstacles to pursuing this endeavor: low entry-level pay for correctional officers, resulting in relaxed educational requirements, and a higher turnover rate than in other public agencies (the national turnover rate among correctional officers in 1995 was 22.6%, and in Texas, about 75% of these people quit prior to completing the probationary period).

Managers of correctional institutions who are intent on fighting corruption should[17]

First, make every effort to ensure that their hiring standards keep out high-risk applicants. Careful attention should be given to conducting background investigations and reference checks during the screening process. Advanced psychological testing should be utilized to check the character of those who make the final cut, and a mandatory interview by a hiring board should be a routine procedure prior to appointment.

Second, establish quality-based supervisory techniques. Traditional supervision in correctional facilities focused on quantitative standards, such as the classification of X inmates or the preparation of X meals, should be replaced with a quality-based supervisory system that focuses on how well the tasks are performed (and quantity). Supervisors should be trained that trivial policy violations can—and should—be overlooked, but serious transgressions must be reported and aggressively investigated—regardless of who the corrupters might be. In this respect, well-trained and quality-oriented supervisors are expected to possess the professional wisdom to know which is which—without being told. At the outset of the training initiative, management may have to face substantial employee resentment, and perhaps sabotage by some, but the eventual outcome should be worth the investment.

Third, strengthen fiscal controls. Most acts of official corruption involve the illegal acquisition of money. An effective tool to check corruption in correctional institutions is the proper design and administration of preaudit and postaudit controls within the agency. Internal auditors can determine whether bidding procedures have been followed, expenditure ceilings observed, and vouchers issued only for objects of expenditure. Toward that end, the American Institute of Certified Public Accountants has produced three volumes of comprehensive accounting and auditing standards, and the responsibility of internal auditors has been expanded to include the investigation of all aspects of fraud, waste, and abuse. But controls by internal auditors are obviously not foolproof. They may be deceived when superior officials collect checks for services that are not rendered, bribes are paid for negotiated contracts, overtime pay is collected by workers who are on vacation, travel expenses are absurdly padded, and institution equipment in good working condition is sold as scrap metal.

Furthermore, in corrupt agencies, it is possible that the auditors themselves are on the take. In such cases, the challenging question would be "Who then watches the watchdogs?" To establish accountability in correctional facilities, the prison director, the regional director, or the warden must ensure that internal auditors are honest, are experts in the latest advances in the accounting field, and are willing to check out every business transaction, regardless of how small or complex. Internal auditors must also be autonomous in their decisions, save only for scrutiny by state auditors and members of the General Accounting Office. Advanced methods of control now include the establishment of a telephone hotline where whistleblowers can pass on tips about misconduct they may observe. This brings about another important observation: The tendency of correctional agencies to accept and appreciate the practice of whistleblowing (rather than frantically fighting it) confirms their eagerness to cultivate a healthy ethical culture. In professional agencies, employees should be encouraged, rather than discouraged, to report misconduct, and managers should not be disturbed by such practices because they should have nothing to hide.

Fourth, emphasize true ethical training. Correctional institutions have been involved in serious training at all levels—basic, managerial, professional, executive, and so forth. The American Correctional Association has been responsible for determining the minimum amount of training for all prison and jail systems, and the Commission on Accreditation for Corrections has been offering far more for the accredited institutions. Some of the more popular courses offered have been in cultural diversity, sexual harassment, stress reduction, classification techniques, and job satisfaction. Ironically, one of the least popular courses has been about ethics in corrections. Although ethical training can make certain individuals feel guilty, it can make more people feel confident about themselves, their values, and the benevolence of their careers. Leaders of professional institutions should, therefore, make every effort to increase ethical training, both in-house and at national and regional conferences. They should be visible and active. They should subscribe to ethics journals and learn the arts of moral reasoning. They should participate in panel discussions debating what constitutes right and wrong behaviors, what distinguishes rational from irrational decisions, and how to promote a healthy ethical culture in their institutions. They should not shy away from facing their subordinates, engaging them in question-and-answer sessions, and guiding them in the pursuit of true professionalism. Anything short of this would defeat the purpose of establishing an anticorruption program.[12]

■ Conclusion

Professionalism and corruption are two most important concepts in institution management. Professionalism is an ideal toward which correctional personnel should strive, and corruption is a shameful reality from which they should distance themselves. As long as corrections is part of the mandate to "establish justice and ensure domestic tranquility," then correctional managers must by all the identified means redeem justice by stamping out corruption.

Chapter Resources

DISCUSSION QUESTIONS

1. What is public corruption?
2. What are the main differences between public corruption and prison corruption?
3. What are the main characteristics of professionalism?
4. What are acts of misfeasance?
5. How do acts of malfeasance differ from acts of nonfeasance?

ADDITIONAL RESOURCES

McCarthy, B. J. (1984). Keeping an eye on the keeper: Prison corruption and its control. *The Prison Journal*, *64*(2), 113–125.

Souryal, S. S. (2009). Deterring corruption by prison personnel: A principle-based perspective. *The Prison Journal*, *89*(1), 21–45.

Stewart, C. H. Jr. (1998). Management response to sexual misconduct between staff and inmates. *Corrections Management Quarterly*, 2(2), 81–88.

Sykes, G. M. (2007). *The society of captives: A study of maximum security prison*. Princeton, NJ: Princeton University Press.

NOTES

1. American Correctional Association. (1990). *The state of corrections*. Proceedings of Annual Conference. San Diego, CA.
2. Beaumont/Pt. Arthur Texas Channel 4 Homepage (msnbc.com-kjac tv). (1998, June 16). Panel reverses conviction of ex-Wyandotte county jail administrator. *The Kansas City Star*.
3. Braswell, M., McCarthy, B., & McCarthy, B. (1984). *Justice, crime, and ethics*. Cincinnati, OH: Anderson Publishing Company.
4. Donziger, S. R. (1994). *The real war on crime: The report of the National Criminal Justice Commission*. New York, NY: Harper Collins.
5. *Estate of McDonald v. Unified Government of Wyandotte County*, No. 92,699, 2006 WL 1170101 (Kan.App.).
6. Galnor, M. (2006). Prison system purge goes on, *Florida Times-Union*, Jacksonville, March 16, 2006, p. A1.
7. Cook, R. (1997). Guard recalls beatings as payback time, *Atlanta Constitution*, June 29, 1997, p. 01C.
8. *Hudson v. McMillian*, 503 U.S. (1992).
9. *Cooper v. Pate*, 378 U.S. 546 (1964).
10. *Monell v. Department of Social Services of the City of New York*, 436 U.S. 658 (1978).
11. Pollack, J. M. (1994). *Ethics in crime and justice: Dilemmas and decisions* (2d ed.). Belmont, CA: Wadsworth Publishing Company.
12. Souryal, S. (2003). *Ethics of criminal justice: In search of the truth*. Cincinnati, OH: Anderson Publishing.
13. Souryal, S. (1977). *Police organization and management*. Eagan, MN: West Publishing.
14. Gray, T. (2002). *Exploring corrections*. Boston, MA: Allyn and Bacon.

15. Farrington, D. P., & Nutall, C. P. (1980). Prison size, overcrowding, prison violence, and recidivism. *Journal of Criminal Justice*, 8(4), 221–231.

16. LA Times. (n.d.). *Overview on crowding in LA prisons*. Retrieved from http://realcostofprisons.org.2003/03/la_times_overi.html

17. Muraskin, R., & Muraskin, M. (2001). *Morality and the law*. Upper Saddle River, NJ: Prentice Hall.

Staff Sexual Abuse in Confinement Settings

Anadora Moss, Rachel Bosley, and Mara Dodson

CHAPTER OBJECTIVES

- Understand the historical context of addressing sexual abuse in confinement settings.

- Understand the definitions related to sexual abuse in confinement settings.

- Understand the evolution of data collection efforts in determining the prevalence of sexual abuse in confinement settings.

- Explore the importance of culture and leadership in creating safe environments.

- Understand the role of the National Standards to Prevent, Detect, and Respond to Prison Rape in addressing sexual abuse in confinement settings.

- Identify emerging issues and implications for further research.

Addressing sensitive issues in any profession can test the foundations of trust among members of the community, the corporate understanding of the "good" and the "bad" of its members, and the degree to which external opinions are received as credible. This is particularly true when competing perceptions of the identified problem vary widely among professionals, advocates, researchers, and legislative bodies, among others. Addressing staff sexual abuse in correctional settings, the subject of this chapter, is a sensitive issue with a fascinating journey of professional discourse, input from the advocacy community, and a broad range of influencing factors ultimately resulting in extensive changes in policy and practice now driven by national standards for the prevention of, detection of, and response to sexual abuse in confinement.

Since the first edition of this text, the body of knowledge in this area has grown considerably as the issues of sexual abuse in confinement continue to be understood and addressed by all levels of leadership within the corrections profession. Not only have corrections professionals gained greater understanding through increasing strategies to eliminate sexual abuse in confinement, but survivors, advocacy groups, researchers, and legislators also have contributed to the development of strategies both in corrections and in the larger community to better define staff sexual abuse in the context of an imbalance of power. In August 2012, after several periods of public comment on draft standards, the Department of Justice promulgated national standards designed to assist the field in addressing this issue. In the future, correctional textbooks may identify the Prison Rape Elimination Act (PREA) of 2003 and the resulting national standards as the "game changer" in addressing sexual abuse in confinement settings.

■ Historical Context and the Evolution of National Standards

On September 4, 2003, President George W. Bush signed PREA into law. Now, more than a decade since enactment, much of the intent of PREA is embodied in the promulgation of the National Standards to Prevent, Detect, and Respond to Prison Rape issued by the Honorable Eric Holder, 82nd Attorney General of the United States.

The PREA legislation addresses the rights and responsibilities of inmates in custodial confinement settings in the criminal justice system, including federal, state, and local prisons, jails, police lockups, juvenile justice facilities, private facilities, and community residential settings. The law speaks to the sexual abuse of inmates/youth by staff and additionally includes a major focus on sexual abuse occurring between inmates/youth. Although this chapter focuses primarily on the dynamics between staff and inmates resulting in staff sexual abuse—often referred to as staff sexual misconduct—the promulgation of the PREA standards clearly defines a larger discussion and requirement to address all sexual abuse in confinement settings. This chapter also limits the discussion to adult and prison settings with the full awareness that all settings under the law need careful study.

With the enactment of the law in 2003, federal resources were dedicated to engage the field in further research, technical assistance, information dissemination, and development of strategies in addressing sexual abuse. Many of these initiatives informed the development of the final standards.

Although PREA is considered by some to be one of the most significant reform initiatives in recent correctional history, the topic of sexual abuse in the profession was not new in 2003. In fact, prisoner sexual violence was documented in the United States as early as 1826, and research on the issue was published in the 1920s.[1] In the 1970s, there were credible reports of sexual abuse by staff against juveniles,[2,3] female offenders, and male inmates,[4-6] yet no substantive action to address these violations was adopted by the profession at large. Very little traction was developed to spur action in the field beyond individual system responses to local incidents until highly visible litigation in women's prisons "named" or acknowledged staff sexual abuse as an issue demanding a more in-depth discussion regarding correctional practice and response to survivors of abuse in confinement.

Influencing Factors 1990–2005

A number of factors contributed to an increased emphasis in the field of corrections on this important subject. By recognizing some of these key factors, students, practitioners, and policy makers can learn the ways in which the public, nongovernmental organizations, legislators, faith communities, litigators, and correctional leadership can become powerfully interrelated players in the development of public policy.

EARLY LAWSUITS IN WOMEN'S PRISONS. Just as cases in the media-highlighted issue of domestic violence came to national attention by the public and policy makers, highly visible cases in women's prisons raised awareness of the issue of staff sexual abuse in correctional settings. In 1992, allegations of widespread sexual abuse of women emerged from the Georgia Women's Institution in Milledgeville, Georgia. Corrections staff were found to have engaged in sexual assault, inappropriate viewing, and verbal degradation of female prisoners in their custody.[7] That same year, the Michigan Women's Commission identified the problem of staff sexual abuse in Michigan's prisons, which led to a U.S. Department of Justice investigation 2 years later in 1994. In 1994, a class-action suit, *Women Prisoners v. District of Columbia Department of Corrections* [877 F.Supp. 634 (D.D.C. 1994)], was brought in the U.S. District Court. The suit alleged discrimination and widespread abuse against female prisoners at three Washington, D.C., facilities (Washington, D.C., Jail; the Correctional Treatment Facility; and the Lorton Minimum Security Annex). The District Court in this case found that widespread abuses against women prisoners were occurring on a regular basis, including lack of privacy, vulgar sexual remarks, inappropriate touching, sex exchanged for food and goods, and sexual assault by correctional staff and male inmates. The Court further argued that this created a "sexualized environment" where the boundaries of expectations of behavior were not clear, and which were in violation of the Eighth Amendment's protection against cruel and unusual punishment.[8] Similarly, other state systems and the U.S. Federal Bureau of Prisons faced litigation that was documented in the 1996 Human Rights Watch publication *All Too Familiar: Sexual Abuse of Women in U.S. State Prisons*. The court orders and remedies in these cases provided models for policy and practice that served as the foundation of a correctional management framework for responding to an issue that affects all institutions. The monetary awards resulting from individual inmate cases also increased the concern of the public as well as correctional professionals, legislators, and advocates.

GROWTH OF CORRECTIONS. The prison population in this country grew from 1,078,542 in 1995 to more than 1,598,780 in 2011.[9] To the correctional practitioner, the reality of building new facilities, hiring large numbers of staff, and managing prisons during such extreme periods of growth had a tremendous impact on day-to-day institutional operations. With the growth of the offender population and prisons, more supervisors were needed to operate all aspects of prison and jail facilities. Promotions often occurred without personnel having the experience expected in earlier decades, and supervisors were often individuals who had worked as peers with the people they eventually supervised. This likely contributed to an environment in which many supervisors felt uncomfortable confronting sensitive issues at a time when correctional investigative practice did not include training on investigating allegations of sexual abuse in correctional settings.

ADVOCACY GROUPS AND GOVERNMENT ACCOUNTING OFFICE REPORT. The role that advocacy groups played during this period was significant to the passing of PREA and offers a student of social change a unique look into the effect that stakeholders external to the corrections field can have on policy and practice. During this period, several key human rights and advocacy groups documented the problem of sexual abuse in both male and female facilities and called for reform of these and all systems. Human Rights Watch, Amnesty International, Widney-Brown, and the United Nations High Commissioner noted serious concerns about female inmates' safety in America's correctional institutions.[10-15] Similarly, the Government Accounting Office (1999), through a mandate from the U.S. Congress, conducted its own study in a review of the same states addressed in the earlier report by the Human Rights Watch.[16] Although some of these reports were highly criticized by corrections officials, they served to further elevate the urgency of the national dialogue.

In addition to advocates for women in prison, advocates concerned with sexual abuse occurring in male facilities had long been championed primarily by survivors of custodial sexual abuse in male facilities and by a handful of researchers concerned with raising the visibility of such abuse. The nonprofit Stop Prisoner Rape, founded by male survivors, was established in 1980 and was renamed Just Detention International on September 4, 2008. Human Rights Watch also published a report in 2001 titled *No Escape: Male Rape in U.S. Prisons,* drawing further attention to the issue of prison rape in male facilities.

EVOLUTION OF STATE LAWS. The litigation that emerged from women's facilities in the 1990s identified the lack of state laws prohibiting staff sexual abuse. Further study by the National Institute of Corrections (NIC) and the National Women's Law Center indicated that even where laws existed, staff were often not aware of them or not trained on the substance of the law. In the 1990s, there were fewer than 10 state laws prohibiting staff sexual misconduct. As of 2013, every state has such a law, and the increase in state laws occurred as a result of several influencing factors. The NIC, through federally funded training programs, provided guidance in the development of state laws. In 2002, American University, Washington College of Law began hosting these training events for correctional administrators, emphasizing the importance of state laws and the key components of good law in this area. Technical assistance was also made available through NIC to support efforts in the field and the advocacy community, notably Amnesty International, continued to focus on the importance of this legislative effort.

Finally, as the issue of sexual safety in all confinement settings continued to emerge, there was recognition, particularly in the juvenile area, of the importance of additional laws addressing custodial staff sexual misconduct and related state laws. See **Figures 28-1** and **28-2** to see the evolution of state laws from 1990 through 2010.

EARLY WORK: THE NATIONAL INSTITUTE OF CORRECTIONS. Motivated to serve the corrections field through its mission of technical assistance to the profession, the NIC, under the U.S. Department of Justice, was a pioneer in developing a national strategy to address staff sexual abuse. Learning from the lawsuits in women's facilities in the early 1990s, the NIC developed a systemic model that provided the correctional field with an approach focused on effective correctional management practice, rather than an ad hoc response to a given crisis. It is not unusual for leaders in any field to be disappointed in colleagues abusing their power in a sexualized relationship, referring to the expression that all organizations have "a few bad apples." Although there may be some truth to this expression, the assumption behind it is that the management structure or leadership has little responsibility; these unfortunate issues just happen with those "few bad apples." The NIC was willing to support a different direction in addressing sexual abuse in corrections that assumed instead that although the majority of correctional staff conduct themselves professionally, there still is good reason to frame sexual abuse in corrections as a management issue worthy of a comprehensive management approach to prevention and response. Nearly two decades later, to the credit of the leadership at the NIC, thousands of correctional staff had been trained in a systemic model to address sexual abuse in corrections. Their work continues as they partner with other federal initiatives to broadly implement PREA. See **Figure 28-3** for a visual representation of the initial systemic model. The model continued to evolve over the years and ultimately provided a strong foundation for the implementation of PREA for those states and jurisdictions that received early NIC assistance.

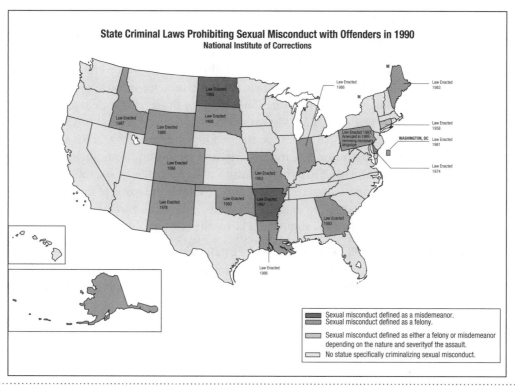

FIGURE 28-1 State laws in 1990

Source: 1997, *Fifty State Survey of Criminal Laws Prohibiting Sexual Abuse of Prisoners, Brenda V. Smith,* National Women's Law Center.

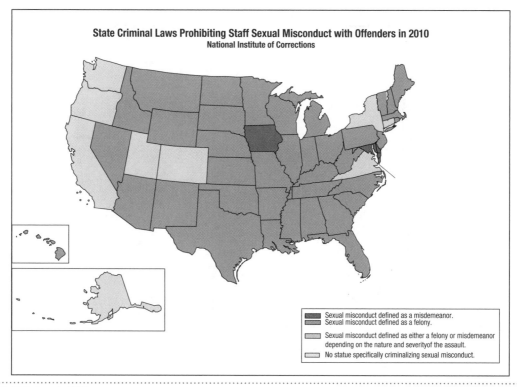

FIGURE 28-2 State laws in 2010

Source: September, 2001. Brenda V. Smith, The American University, Washington College of Law.

PASSAGE OF PREA. By the mid- and late 1990s, a diverse coalition of supporters addressing custodial sexual abuse began to form from advocacy groups such as Human Rights Watch, Stop Prisoner Rape (now known as Just Detention International), faith-based groups, and conservative and liberal policy makers, thereby elevating the discussion and demanding change. This ground swell of advocacy created a perfect storm of interest in Congress. Correctional leadership was able to advocate for a technical assistance approach to the implementation of the law through testimony before the passage of the legislation, ensuring federal funds to support the field through grants and other forms of assistance.

The result was the passage of PREA (Public Law 108-79) in September 2003. PREA demanded a "zero tolerance" standard, focused on prevention as a top priority, and established a number of important priorities for correctional agencies nationwide. Most importantly, Public Law 108-79 assembled the resources of a host of federal agencies to study, address, and respond to this problem. The name of the law over the next few years would create a good deal of discussion because the term "prison" doesn't represent the full spectrum of facilities covered under the law. The final standards clarify the scope of coverage.

PUBLIC INTEREST AND INCREASED AWARENESS OF ABUSE OF POWER. Costly lawsuits combined with the general public's frustration with crime contributed to an increased interest in corrections. Highly visible cases in the military, the academic community, churches, civic organizations, and the private and public sectors overall

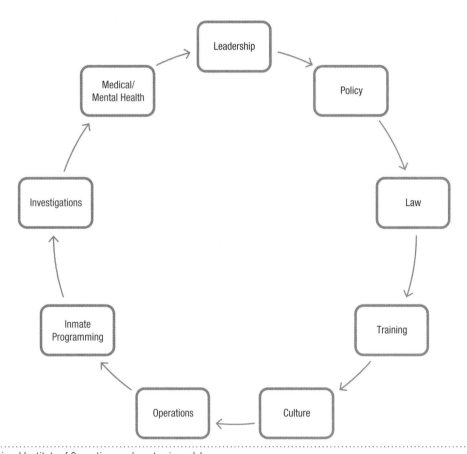

FIGURE 28-3 National Institute of Corrections early systemic model

raised the awareness of abuse of power in various settings. This increase of examples in other settings in which individuals hold authority over others affirmed the importance of addressing issues of sexual violence and abuse in correctional settings. Any social or cultural change begins by naming or acknowledging that the issue exists; by 2005, the correctional field was clearly moving into a new era of policy and practice addressing staff sexual misconduct by naming the need for a systemic management response.

Influencing Factors 2005 to Present

EMPIRICAL RESEARCH. The absence of systematic empirical research was of serious concern to members of Congress during the development of the PREA legislation. The limited data demonstrating the prevalence of sexual abuse in confinement settings made addressing the issue difficult. Anecdotal evidence and a limited but concerning scope of research was used to demonstrate both extremely high and extremely low rates of sexual abuse. In the last decade, research efforts have increased and practitioners have begun to develop more confidence in approaches to prevention, detection, and response to sexual abuse in their facilities. One of the key features of PREA was to have systematic, multimodal empirical studies conducted by the Bureau of Justice Statistics (BJS) to examine the prevalence of sexual assault in America's jails, prisons, and juvenile institutions. Although the methodology is complex and challenging because of the nature of the work, the multiyear trends and rich information have notably enhanced the field's knowledge of the prevalence of sexual abuse in confinement settings and the patterns that exist therein. The National Institute of Justice, consistent with PREA, conducted research through grant funding. This work further contributed to the body of knowledge.

ECONOMY. The final PREA standards arrived in an environment of cost containment where many states were cutting corrections budgets and reducing the inmate population. This challenging time in corrections affected agency responses to the PREA standards because of limited staffing and monetary resources. The significant controversy around the potential costs agencies might incur if mandated to comply with the standards spurred the Department of Justice to conduct a cost analysis of each standard. The final promulgated standards were designed to reflect findings in the cost analysis and included feedback from the field to alleviate some of the concerns.

ADVOCACY AND AGENCY COLLABORATION. The increased collaboration among advocacy groups, nonprofits, and corrections officials through the implementation phase of the PREA standards represents an encouraging approach to the prevention of sexual abuse in confinement. With the involvement of community partners, there is an increased focus on policy, practice, and a strong response to victims. Examples of these collaborative efforts are found in the development of facility–community partnerships with rape crises centers and local law enforcement.

THE NATIONAL PREA STANDARDS. The National Prison Rape Elimination Commission (NPREC), a nine-person committee, was appointed by Congress and the White House[17] and was tasked with the enormous responsibility of creating standards for the field, which would then be promulgated by the U.S. Attorney General. The NPREC released the draft standards in 2009 and subsequently disbanded as described in the law.

After what became a multiyear project, including several periods during which the corrections field and the public were asked to submit comments on the draft standards, the Attorney General released the National Standards to Prevent, Respond, and Detect Prison Rape[18] in May 2012 and promulgated the standards in August 2012. These standards include 12 domain areas, shown in **Figure 28-4**, and include requirements for both policy and practice across key operational areas affecting inmate sexual safety.

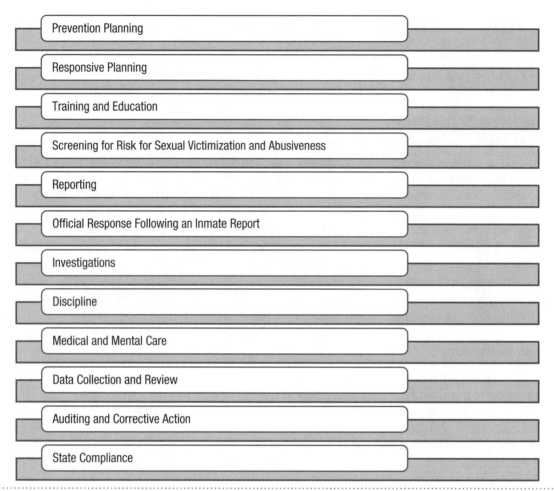

Prevention Planning

Responsive Planning

Training and Education

Screening for Risk for Sexual Victimization and Abusiveness

Reporting

Official Response Following an Inmate Report

Investigations

Discipline

Medical and Mental Care

Data Collection and Review

Auditing and Corrective Action

State Compliance

FIGURE 28-4 Domains of National Standards to Prevent, Detect, and Respond to Prison Rape
Source: Data from U.S. Department of Justice, 28 CFR Part 115, Docket No. OAG-131; AG Order No. RIN 1104-AB34, 2012.

■ Defining Sexual Abuse in Confinement Settings

To best guide the field and develop strategies that can be implemented with consistency and clarity, it is important to have consistent definitions. Defining behaviors or categories of behaviors that constitute the various forms of sexual abuse in confinement settings only began through the lawsuits of the 1990s in women's prisons, borrowing terms from state laws, domestic violence response, and nationally recognized organizations involved in addressing sexual violence. The definitions in these lawsuits were driven by the "naming" of staff sexual misconduct rather than the current expanded understanding of the range of behaviors identified with custodial sexual abuse. Without the development of consistent terms and the subsequent training of correctional staff, recognizing and effectively preventing subtle behaviors is difficult sometimes. Without consistent definitions, it has also been challenging to determine prevalence of sexual abuse and develop effective policy. The evolution of PREA required a thoughtful dialogue to continue clarifying definitions with legislation, state laws, and the BJS data collection efforts.

In the section "Data Collection, Reporting, and Determining the Prevalence of Sexual Abuse in Correctional Facilities," we discuss the role of the federal data collection process through the BJS (under the

Office of Justice Programs, U.S. Justice Department) as a component of Congress's mandates under PREA. To collect the most accurate data to determine prevalence of sexual abuse, the development of common definitions was a powerful and critical step. The definitions evolved over several years with input from experts and professional organizations around the country and have now resulted in a body of work that informs policy language and ongoing data collection efforts required by PREA. Specifically, the BJS definitions drive data collection and serve to create uniformity for greater fidelity in understanding prevalence and characteristics of sexually abusive behavior.

The national PREA standards include definitions for the field to use when working toward compliance with the standards. In addition to the term *sexual abuse*, the field often uses "staff sexual misconduct," which originated from litigation of women's prisons. This chapter uses the term *staff sexual abuse* rather than *misconduct* to be consistent with the PREA definitions. The Department of Justice defined staff sexual abuse as the following in the promulgated standards:

> ***Sexual abuse of an inmate, detainee, or resident by a staff member, contractor, or volunteer*** *includes any of the following acts, with or without consent of the inmate, detainee, or resident:*
>
> 1. *Contact between the penis and the vulva or the penis and the anus, including penetration, however slight;*
> 2. *Contact between the mouth and the penis, vulva, or anus;*
> 3. *Contact between the mouth and any body part where the staff member, contractor, or volunteer has the intent to abuse, arouse, or gratify sexual desire;*
> 4. *Penetration of the anal or genital opening, however slight, by a hand, finger, object, or other instrument, that is unrelated to official duties or where the staff member, contractor, or volunteer has the intent to abuse, arouse, or gratify sexual desire;*
> 5. *Any other intentional contact, either directly or through the clothing, of or with the genitalia, anus, groin, breast, inner thigh, or the buttocks, that is unrelated to official duties or where the staff member, contractor, or volunteer has the intent to abuse, arouse, or gratify sexual desire;*
> 6. *Any attempt, threat, or request by a staff member, contractor, or volunteer to engage in the activities described in paragraphs 1–5 of this section;*
> 7. *Any display by a staff member, contractor, or volunteer of his or her uncovered genitalia, buttocks, or breast in the presence of an inmate, detainee, or resident; and*
> 8. *Voyeurism by a staff member, contractor, or volunteer.*
>
> ***Voyeurism by a staff member, contractor, or volunteer*** *means an invasion of privacy of an inmate, detainee, or resident by staff for reasons unrelated to official duties, such as peering at an inmate who is using a toilet in his or her cell to perform bodily functions; requiring an inmate to expose his or her buttocks, genitals, or breasts; or taking images of all or part of an inmate's naked body or of an inmate performing bodily functions.*

The standards also address the issue of sexual harassment, which is defined as follows:

> ***Sexual harassment*** *includes—*
>
> 1. *Repeated and unwelcome sexual advances, requests for sexual favors, or verbal comments, gestures, or actions of a derogatory or offensive sexual nature by one inmate, detainee, or resident directed toward another; and*
> 2. *Repeated verbal comments or gestures of a sexual nature to an inmate, detainee, or resident by a staff member, contractor, or volunteer, including demeaning references to gender, sexually suggestive or derogatory comments about body or clothing, or obscene language or gestures.*

■ Data Collection, Reporting, and Determining the Prevalence of Sexual Abuse in Correctional Facilities

Reporting and the Effect on Data Collection

Historically, the occurrence of incidents of sexual abuse in correctional settings has been difficult to determine. Early work funded by the NIC resulted in gathering staff perspectives of the barriers to reporting that complicate the task of defining prevalence. Staff reported the barriers that hinder the collection of statistics on sexual abuse that they encounter as well as the barriers that inmates encounter in.

Staff Perspectives: Trends from Focus Group Interviews.[19] Some of the identified barriers include the following:

- Data on investigations have often been documented in more general categories not specific to sexual misconduct, such as assault or drug investigations.
- The degree to which sexual misconduct is reported may also parallel the historical underreporting of other forms of sexual assault in the world beyond corrections.
- Prisoners may not report sexual misconduct for fear of reprisal or fear that they will not be believed, or because the relationships meet their needs in some ways.
- Sexual misconduct is difficult to investigate, and investigative techniques that corroborate or add information beyond the word of the inmate are generally necessary to substantiate a claim.
- Staff may not recognize the signs indicating a potential problem.
- A "code of silence"[20] from either the inmate population or the staff may create a significant barrier embedded in the culture of a facility.
- Effective reporting mechanisms are not in place.
- Investigations are not perceived to be objective.

An historical perspective provides the following reasons why prevalence rates have been difficult to establish:

- *Detection.* Staff have not generally been trained in recognizing the signs that may indicate a potential problem. In addition, many staff have not been educated on the dangers of sexual abuse in confinement settings or the inevitable security risks that arise when staff are not where they are assigned or are otherwise not doing their jobs or following policy, which has meant that not all recognized signs of sexual abuse have been reported. Cultural codes of silence have also impeded reporting of detected abuse, particularly in cases of staff sexual abuse.
- *Reporting.* Of all crime categories, rape and sexual assault have traditionally been underreported because of fear, intimidation, and concern about safety,[21] which is even more challenging when reported in a correctional environment.[22] Prisoners may not report sexual abuse for fear of reprisal or fear that they will not be believed, or because the relationship meets their needs in some way. In addition, effective reporting mechanisms have not always been in place, which leads to inmates reporting without appropriate agency follow-up or documentation, or inmates refraining from reporting altogether. Inmates who do report may face retaliation, which may lead to noncooperation. When investigations are not perceived to be objective, this also leads to fewer reports.
- *Response.* Investigations of sexual abuse in corrections have often been categorized in more general categories, such as physical assault or drug investigations, and thus, there have not been clear data on the quantity of sexual abuse investigations. In addition, sexual abuse is difficult to investigate, and investigative techniques that corroborate or add information beyond the word of the inmate are generally necessary to substantiate a claim. Many corrections staff have not been trained in

trauma-informed interviewing techniques, which enhance cooperation from victims of sexual abuse. Agencies have often used outside investigators with limited or nonexistent correctional expertise who frequently find it difficult to substantiate a claim due to the unique challenges of a correctional setting, including difficulties in obtaining physical evidence, problems with maintaining confidentiality, and the complications inherent to navigating a facility culture.

Data Collection Mandate from Congress

Congress tasked the BJS with determining the actual prevalence of sexual abuse in corrections settings through a multiyear comprehensive data collection process. This task includes not only data collection concerning abuse between staff and inmates/youth but also required data regarding inmate-on-inmate or youth-on-youth abuse. Since 2003, the BJS has conducted administrative records collections in adult jails, prisons, and juvenile facilities to document the formal reports submitted by inmates, prisoners, detainees, and juveniles to correctional authorities, and has collected data on victimization reported by former and current state prisoners through BJS anonymous surveys. The reports resulting from the data collection are made available to the public the BJS website.

The data collected through this research were substantial, and although controversial in some aspects, clear patterns emerged with regard to inmate victimization and staff sexual abuse. The most recent National Inmate Survey[23] for inmates currently in custody in prison or jail found that 88,500 adult inmates self-reported being sexually victimized in the 12 months before the survey, which was 4.4% of the inmates in prisons and 3.1% of the inmates in jails. Percentages of inmates reporting sexual victimization by staff included 2.8% in prisons and 2.0% in jails. Of that number, 1.8% in prisons and 1.1% in jails indicated that they willingly (although note that *willing* does not reflect consent) participated in sex or sexual contact with staff.

Rates of self-reported victimization by staff were higher among black inmates (compared to white), inmates aged 20–24 (compared to ages 25 or older), inmates with a college degree (compared to those who had not completed high school), and inmates who had experienced sexual victimization before coming to the facility (compared to those who had not). Inmates with a sexual orientation other than heterosexual self-reported victimization by staff at a rate three times higher than heterosexual inmates.

Most perpetrators of staff sexual misconduct were females; among male victims of staff sexual abuse, 69% of those in prison and 64% of those in jails reported sexual activity with female staff. Of those male inmates reporting sexual activity with facility staff, 64% reported no force or pressure. In contrast, 70% of female inmates reporting sexual activity with facility staff reported that they were pressured by the staff to engage in the activity. Among the former prisoners interviewed in 2008, half of all those who self-reported victimization by staff stated that they had been offered favors or special privileges; a third said they had been persuaded or talked into it.[24]

These data points provide practitioners with important information. The characteristics reported by the inmate population indicate the need to explore prevention strategies that are targeted with sensitivity to gender, race, age, sexual victimization history, sexual orientation, and education level.

Role of the National Prison Rape Review Panel

The National Review Panel on Prison Rape was formed under PREA. The panel is responsible for conducting annual hearings to identify common characteristics of victims and perpetrators of prison rape, as well as to identify prisons and prison systems with high incidence and low incidence of prison rape.[25] The panel has helped to clarify general assumptions about sexual abuse through the hearing process. As a result, the corrections field is moving toward a greater understanding of the occurrence of sexual violence and abuse in our correctional systems. This increased understanding provides correctional administrators with refined and effective approaches in addressing sexual abuse.

■ The Importance of Culture and Leadership in Promoting Sexually Safe Environments

Long before the passage of PREA and the promulgation of the final standards, many correctional administrators have been developing ways to respond to this issue. What is important to note, and is acknowledged in the preamble of the national standards, is that the PREA standards alone are not enough to ensure sexually safe environments: Culture and leadership are key components that must be incorporated into an approach toward addressing sexual abuse. The final standards note:

> The success of the PREA standards in combating sexual abuse in confinement facilities will depend on effective agency and facility leadership, and the development of an agency culture that prioritizes efforts to combat sexual abuse. Effective leadership and culture cannot, of course, be directly mandated by rule. Yet implementation of the standards will help foster a change in culture by institutionalizing policies and practices that bring these concerns to the fore.[26]

The environment of a facility is complex because of the culture in which it exists. Although every organization has a culture founded on the attitudes, beliefs, values, norms, and prejudices of the individuals within the organization, a correctional facility culture is unique because of the purpose of the institution and the inescapable dynamics therein. The majority of the population within a correctional facility (the inmate population) is there involuntarily and depends almost entirely on the minority population (staff) to respond to their daily needs. Correctional staff spend many hours interacting with inmates, getting to know inmates through long-term supervision.

Most types of interactions that occur between individuals in a normal community also occur in corrections, but they are intensified by the correctional setting. Although transgender individuals in the community may find themselves avoiding certain areas or people to minimize unwanted stares and verbal or even physical harassment on the street, transgender inmates are unable to choose the individuals with whom they interact and instead must rely on correctional staff to help protect them. Although rival gang members may only interact occasionally in the free world, they may be living on the same unit in a correctional facility. Racism, sexism, and homophobia all exist in the free world, but the impact is more clearly felt in the artificial community of a correctional facility.

Cultural Collision

In addition to the staff–inmate dynamics caused by virtue of the individuals' positions as staff or inmates, correctional facility cultures often struggle with "cultural collisions"[27] as well. Cultural collisions can be characterized by competing priorities of various subgroups, policy directives, or leadership direction. For instance, prisons are often located in geographical locations far from an inmate's home area, and the life experiences of staff and inmates may be vastly different. If culture is defined by the behavioral norms of staff and offenders, then the behaviors that challenge these norms result in cultural collisions.

These cultural differences embedded in the day-to-day life of a prison can create challenges (collision) of perceptions, communication styles, life experiences, and values, creating difficulty in relationships among staff and offenders, both between and within groups. An increased loyalty among subcultures within the facility, both among staff and offenders, may contribute to a code of silence.

Paramilitary Structure and Effect on Culture

Staff and inmate interactions must be understood within the context of an environment that remains, in most settings, a paramilitary structure between inmates and staff. In such a culture, reporting infractions usually requires a prescribed reporting system within a chain of command. In a small community, reporting a colleague for any infraction, sexual or otherwise, can lead to alienation and isolation. An inmate reporting a staff person or another inmate for an infraction may face similar isolation or, in extreme cases, find himself or herself in physical danger.

In addition, as the cultural drivers mentioned above create divisions that become embedded in the day-to-day life of a facility, they can create a collision of perceptions, communication styles, life experiences, and values. The dynamics of a correctional facility lead to increased intergroup loyalty among subcultures within the facility, creating the potential for a code of silence.

False Allegations

Any discussion of staff–inmate dynamics and correctional culture would be incomplete without acknowledging staff concerns of false allegations from offenders. This difficult topic in correctional settings creates one of the major barriers to gaining staff confidence in addressing sexual abuse. Many staff still fear that inmates will manipulate the system through false reports. Although false allegations are a reality, if the investigative process is timely, efficient, and objective, inmates will soon learn that false allegations will not benefit them, and invisible retaliation from staff and inmates usually greets the false accuser. Both false allegations and invisible retaliation are addressed in the PREA standards with guidance to the field. If false allegations are a continuing problem in a facility, this may indicate other problems in the supervision of inmates. The concern about false allegations often seems to escalate into mythic proportions when compared to facility data. With the federal requirements for reporting all allegations, a much clearer picture of incidents of false allegations will continue to emerge. The encouraging news is that most practitioners understand that all allegations must be fully investigated whether they appear credible or not. Effective investigative practice results in staff recognizing that the investigative process serves to clear them from false allegations and protect them as well.

Reporting Culture

Although policies and the implementation of the national standards will move the field forward through strong guidance, the desired outcome of eliminating staff sexual abuse requires a willingness to promote a reporting and responsive culture. A reporting culture is characterized by staff and offenders knowing how to report abuse, being willing to report abuse, and having confidence that a response to reporting will be handled objectively. Reporting environments are characterized by an expectation that staff members will demonstrate professionalism every day in all aspects of daily operations. Appropriate language that demonstrates respect and encourages trust; objective investigations that are effective and timely; trained staff who understand their roles and responsibilities in preventing, detecting, and responding to sexual abuse; strong operational practices that enhance safety and minimize opportunities for sexual abuse; and appropriate inmate programming that minimizes inmate idleness and enhances reentry are all hallmarks of a reporting culture. These characteristics promote the culture as one that values prevention and increases physical and emotional safety as well as sexual safety.

Creating a culture that supports the reporting of sexual abuse is a dynamic process that must be valued by all levels of leadership. If the culture of the institution does not support objective reporting and response to nonsexual infractions, then the atmosphere for reporting staff sexual abuse is greatly hampered. A fear-based facility culture is one that characteristically is highly punitive and leaves little room for the consideration of complex human dynamics. Sometimes to "preserve the order," keeping things simple seems like an efficient management style of leadership. Addressing staff sexual misconduct in a correctional setting requires much more from leadership. Effective leaders in corrections allow for hope-based environments encouraging respectful and safe avenues for reporting any abusive behavior. The opportunity to report abusive behavior, as supported by the PREA standards, requires multiple ways in which staff or inmates can report safely.

■ Examples of Current and Emerging Issues

Employee Support and Training in Professional Boundaries

People may wonder why staff do not understand the simple directive not to have sex with inmates. However, most staff do understand this directive and would never intentionally violate their professional duties. Yet the boundaries between staff and inmates can become blurred, and not all staff sexual abuse involves overt coercion or force. Forms of staff sexual abuse range from force, coercion, and sex for favors to "willing" relationships in which the staff and inmate claim to be in love.[28] In addition, there are inmates who "groom" staff to develop affection for them for the purpose of accessing privileges and contraband, and warnings of the manipulative inmate are common in correctional officer trainings.

Although it is always the responsibility of the correctional staff to maintain professional boundaries to ensure that security is maintained in the facility and that all relationships are professional, staff members may feel isolated, depressed, or verbally abused themselves by peers or supervisors, which creates emotional vulnerability. Cases of staff sexual abuse have involved all levels of staff, and case examples demonstrate that even the staff members who might be thought least likely to become involved may sometimes cross the line. Staff feeling particularly stressed in their personal lives may have an increased vulnerability to "crossing the line" with inmates, especially if they have had minimum training and support in understanding the importance of professional boundaries. Research shows PTSD rates among correctional officers rivaling rates previously reported for emergency medical professionals, post-9/11 firefighters and police officers, and wartime military personnel.[29] The need to identify stress reduction strategies becomes even more apparent when we know that staff carrying high stress levels are vulnerable to diminished professional judgment.

Correctional staff are in close contact with those they supervise, but very few correctional training programs address the feelings and emotional dilemmas of officers or staff members when inmates become attached to or interested in them personally, or when the reverse is true. Although early training for clinical professionals such as psychologists, social workers, and clinical chaplains includes discussions of the critical boundaries between professionals and patients, training for correctional staff traditionally has not. Such training offers more understanding of the emotional challenges of the job and goes beyond a policy statement prohibiting inappropriate behavior. One might strongly argue that correctional staff simply need more "tools" for the emotional dynamics of the job. A low-cost tool might be a greater awareness among supervisors of the warning signs indicating staff isolation or high levels of stress exhibited by an individual staff member.

Women in Corrections

The BJS data reported in the section "Data Collection, Reporting, and Determining the Prevalence of Sexual Abuse in Correctional Facilities" brings forward challenges regarding violations of professional boundaries by some women staff in ways that threaten the public and the field's positive perceptions of the productive role women play throughout all areas of the profession. More importantly, some of the more egregious staff sexual misconduct violations have resulted in dangerous outcomes including loss of life during escapes that were orchestrated by female staff for their male inmate lovers. The data calls for corrections professionals, men and women, to share in a renewed awareness of the importance to develop an understanding of the environment in which they work. As discussed earlier in the chapter, staff sexual misconduct takes many forms. The data related to women in corrections indicate that 64% of inmates involved with female staff did not feel forced. This is notably different from and higher than the reporting of male staff involved with female inmates. Understandably, this is a complicated subject to address. The data do not ignore the fact that some males do feel forced to become involved in relationships with male and female staff. Seeing women staff as perpetrators is often more difficult for the corrections community, prosecutors, and the public. Emerging work in understanding the role of gender in staff sexual abuse is important in the strengthening of prevention strategies. This work is a priority of the Bureau of Justice Assistance (BJA)–funded National PREA Resource Center.

Inmate Orientation and Education

Prisoners do not leave their emotional needs or needs for the basic comforts of life in the courtroom. Just as the inmate population is keenly aware of vulnerable staff members, staff members recognize the vulnerability of inmates. Although effective staff training is critical, more recent understandings of the dynamics of staff–inmate sexual abuse have resulted in recognition of the importance of educating the inmate population about their rights to live in a correctional environment that is sexually safe. Although inmate orientation programs that address sexual abuse in custody have been implemented in some facilities for a number of years, the PREA standards require that programs provide information defining sexual abuse in custody and provide information on multiple ways to report sexual abuse in all facilities.

Understanding Pathways

The field's understanding of the dynamics of staff–inmate sexual abuse will be enhanced as we continue to learn more about the profile of prisoners in both men's and women's facilities, as well as the profiles of the staff supervising them. For instance, understanding more about the effects of childhood abuse and its impact on adult behavior patterns can be helpful in identifying ways to enhance day-to-day interactions between staff and inmates. Many inmates have histories of physical, sexual, and emotional abuse, and research shows that male and female inmates have experienced significant prior sexual victimization. Staff similarly bring the influences of their histories. The "journey" of both staff and offenders affects the corrections "mix."[30] The BJS data recognize past histories of sexual abuse as a factor in vulnerability to custodial sexual abuse. Training programs for staff need to be trauma informed so that the operations of a facility, investigative practice, and programming and work assignments are informed by pathways of offenders, many of which involve a trauma component. Not all pathways into crime are through childhood trauma; however, inmates often come from communities of families that have been marginalized because of poverty, lack of education, unemployment, and substance abuse.

Women Offenders

Meda Chesney-Lind suggests that there are gender differences in the dynamics that follow an abused child into adulthood, noting that girls are much more likely than boys to be victims of sexual abuse and that sexual abuse of girls often follows them into adulthood.[31] This may suggest that many women continue to be "frozen" in a victim role as they enter institutions. The studies report that between 40% and 88% of incarcerated women have been victims of domestic violence and sexual or physical abuse prior to incarceration.[32] These experiences with intimate violence create pathways to prison in two ways: First, trauma is typically untreated and is tied to initial entry into substance abuse, the primary reason for increasing female imprisonment. Second, repeated victimization in the lives of women can lead to defensive violence and other criminal behavior.[33] There is also a correlation between victimization and future offenses with the cycle of violence continuing through imprisonment and upon release. Professor Barbara Owen of Fresno State University is a national figure in the area of research on women offenders and emphasized in her testimony before the National PREA Review Panel that sexual violence should be understood in a gendered context. She and Dr. James Wells have developed a research-informed safety instrument funded by the National Institute of Justice (NIJ) and the NIC to assist practitioners in identifying women's perceptions of safety (including sexual safety) in women's facilities by housing unit.[34] The instrument's capacity to collect data on perceptions of sexual violence, among other types of violence, in women's facilities is promising and can enhance facility safety for staff and inmates.

Mentally Ill Offenders

The population of individuals with mental illness in the criminal justice system is growing, and the management of this population requires a unique skill set from officials and staff. A 2005 BJS report stated that more than half of all prison and jail inmates had a mental health problem. More than two-fifths of state prisoners and half of jail inmates reported symptoms that met the criteria for mania; almost one-quarter of state prisoners and one-third of jail inmates reported symptoms of major depression; and an estimated 15% of state prisoners and almost one-quarter of jail inmates met the criteria for a psychotic disorder.[35] This large population of mentally ill offenders has resulted in large part from the "deinstitutionalization" of persons with mental illness starting in the 1970s and has caused a crisis in corrections as staff struggle to manage complex populations with limited training, treatment, and staffing resources. Among several unique needs, this population is more likely to have experienced sexual and physical abuse prior to their incarceration,[36] which may increase their vulnerability to sexual abuse while in confinement. As the field of corrections moves forward, shifts in both training and culture will be necessary to keep this population physically and sexually safe. Providing administrators and staff with the tools to prevent, detect, and respond to sexual abuse and harassment in this unique population is a necessity in creating a culture of safety in a correctional setting.

Transgender Offenders

Transgender inmates, although a minority population, have featured in some of the most publicized lawsuits in corrections, including the 1994 Supreme Court case of *Farmer v. Brennan, Warden, et al.*, which determined that the deliberate indifference of a correctional officer to a substantial risk of serious harm to an inmate (physical, sexual, emotional) violates the cruel and unusual punishment clause of the Eighth Amendment. The population requires careful consideration as agencies attempt to determine appropriate placement, management, and treatment for their safety. Just as transgender individuals in the community face prejudice, confusion, and ignorance among their peers, transgender inmates face isolation, alienation, and, according to one research study done in California, a 59% chance of experiencing sexual assault.[37] Although more research is needed to determine the actual prevalence of sexual abuse among the transgender population in corrections, the field of corrections as a whole is working to address the needs of the population more generally and to establish best practices that will allow for the supervision of transgender inmates in a way that maintains their dignity, safety, and mental health.

Lesbian, Gay, Bisexual, Transgender, and Intersex Offenders

For many, the focus on transgender individuals in confinement is an opportunity to address the issues facing the lesbian, gay, bisexual, transgender, and intersex (LGBTI) population as a whole. BJS data demonstrate that inmates with nonheterosexual orientations are up to 10 times more likely to report abuse by other inmates and 3 times more likely to report abuse by staff.[38] The PREA standards require correctional staff to be trained in communicating effectively and professionally with all inmates, including LGBTI or gender-nonconforming individuals,[39] and require agencies to consider any gender-nonconforming appearance or manner or identification as LGBTI, and whether the inmate may therefore be vulnerable to sexual abuse, in intake screening processes and housing, bed, program, education, and work placements.[40] Many agencies are developing policies addressing the supervision and management of LGBTI populations in confinement that touch on all areas of operation, from professional boundaries and the role of personal values in managing and interacting with inmates to cross-gender supervision and distinguishing consensual sexual activity from sexual abuse. This is an arena where best practice is currently being developed.

Investigative Training

The skills needed to investigate sexual abuse in correctional settings were not well identified in the period prior to the evolution of state laws prohibiting staff sexual misconduct. The general thinking among many investigative units was that a good investigation is simply a good investigation. Just as the world outside corrections has learned that investigations of crimes of a sexual nature are a specialized area of professional expertise, the NIC identified the need for specialized training for investigators conducting sexual abuse investigations in a correctional environment and developed a national initiative to offer investigative training to correctional administrators through technical assistance and training.

The potential contamination of evidence through multiple interviews in a setting that is filled with institutional rumors and invisible retaliation; the high incidence of sexual abuse in the histories of the inmate population, particularly women; and the code of silence within a closed facility culture all affected a new paradigm for understanding investigating sexual abuse in confinement. Correctional investigative training is being conducted in many locations now and is often funded by the U.S. Department of Justice, BJA National PREA Resource Center because the PREA standards require specialized investigative training. For many years, the NIC funded programs through training at the American University, Washington College of Law and with technical assistance from the Center for Effective Public Policy. The evolution of this work from early lawsuits is one of the cornerstones of how the work has advanced in addressing staff sexual abuse. Experts now believe that correctional investigative training should be trauma informed, gender informed, and conducted to teach investigative skills that include an understanding of the corrections environment.

Audits

The PREA standards require compliance documented through an audit process. Audits will assess the degree to which an individual facility is in compliance with each PREA standard and will assist in establishing best practice in the field of corrections moving forward. This is a critical time in the evolution of national best practice, and the corrections field has the opportunity to accomplish measured results of the intent of the PREA legislation. As challenging as the journey has been for the development of standards and the audit process, few professions have accomplished a national initiative with such complexity and sensitivity.

■ Conclusion

Sexual abuse among staff and inmates is an issue that has come to the forefront in contemporary corrections because of factors inside and outside the correctional environment. Professional relationships between corrections personnel on the front lines and inmates often create challenges for staff and offenders alike. An understanding of the importance of professional boundaries and the role of correctional staff in an often emotional environment requires an understanding of inmate dynamics as well. An institutional culture is created and sustained through the example of leaders throughout the institution and the behaviors and values exhibited by all staff in adhering to policies and practices daily.

Meeting standards is not a new challenge for the correction's field; however, the PREA standards will only meet their intent by the day-to-day commitment of professionals to sexual safety. There are many examples of the seriousness with which correctional administrators, community partners, and stakeholders have taken their responsibilities to create a strong response to staff sexual abuse. Countless individuals have provided leadership in changing state laws, developing policy, conducting training, improving investigative practice, developing inmate orientation, and expanding reporting mechanisms. It is essential to the mission of corrections that the issue of staff sexual abuse is discussed openly with staff and inmates to promote understanding and support of the efforts to end staff sexual abuse.

Although PREA will likely define policy and practice for years to come, creating a sustainable culture of safety will always require diligence from correctional administrators, stakeholders, and the population we serve.

Chapter Resources

DISCUSSION QUESTIONS

1. Why is it important to consistently define sexual abuse for confinement settings?
2. How might facility–community partnerships assist the corrections facilities in assimilating PREA into their operations more effectively?
3. How has the passage of PREA and the development of the PREA standards affected corrections standards, and how will PREA affect future correctional practices?
4. What is necessary to integrate the mission of PREA into standard operations in corrections facilities as budgets and experience decrease?
5. Taking into account workload, experience, and culture, is it possible for corrections leaders and correctional officers to become proactive rather than reactive in prevention of sexual abuse in the confinement setting?

ADDITIONAL RESOURCES

American University, Washington College of Law an End to Silence, http://www.wcl.american.edu/endsilence/

BJS, PREA Data Collection Activities, 2012, http://bjs.gov/index.cfm?ty=pbdetail&iid=4373

Fleisher, M. S., & Krienert, J. L. (2009). *The myth of prison rape. Sexual culture in American prisons.* Lanham, MD: Rowman & Littlefield.

Implementing the Prison Rape Elimination Act: Toolkit for Jails, http://nicic.gov/Library/026880

The Moss Group, Inc., www.mossgroup.us

The National PREA Resource Center, www.prearesourcecenter.org

National Standards to Prevent, Detect, and Respond to Prison Rape, http://www.ojp.usdoj.gov/programs/pdfs/prea final rule.pdf

NOTES

1. Fleisher, M. S., & Krienert, J. L. (2006). *The culture of prison sexual violence.* Washington, DC: U.S. Department of Justice, National Institute of Justice.
2. Cole, L. (1972). Our children's keepers: Inside America's kids prisons. New York, NY: Grossman.
3. Wooden, K. (1976). *Weeping in the playtime of others: America's incarcerated children.* New York, NY: McGraw-Hill.
4. Bowker, L. H. (1980). *Prison victimization.* New York, NY: Elsevier.
5. Bowker, L. H. (1982). "Problems in Prison Life." In Bowker, L. (ed.), *Corrections: The Science and the Arts* (pp. 262-281). New York, NY: MacMillan Publishing.
6. Dumond, R. W. (1992). The sexual assault of male inmates in incarcerated settings. *International Journal of the Sociology of Law, 20*(2): 135-157.

7. *Cason v. Seckinger*, No. 99-11125., 11th Cir. (2000, October 24). *Women Prisoners of the District of Columbia Dep't of Corr. v. District of Columbia*, No. 93-2052 (JLG). United States Court of Appeals for the District of Columbia Circuit. December 13, 1994.

8. *Daskalea v. DC*, No. 98-7207. (2000, August 8). United States Court of Appeals for the District of Columbia Circuit (award of $350,000 for inmate forced to participate in cellblock striptease).

9. Carson, E. A., & Sabol, W. J. (2012). *Prisons in 2011*. (December 17, 2012 ed). Department of Justice, Office of Justice Programs. NCJ 239808.

10. Thomas, D. Q., et al. (1996). All too famliar: Sexual abuse of women in U.S. state prisons. Human Rights Watch. Available at http://www.hrm.org/legacy/reports/1996/Us1.html/. Accessed August 2, 2013.

11. Amnesty International. (1999). Not part of my sentence: Violation of the human rights of women in custody. Available at: http://www.amnesty org/en/library/asset/AMR51/019/1999/en.7599269ae33d-11dd-808b-bfd8d459a3de/amr510191999en.pdf. Accessed August 2, 2013.

12. Amnesty International. (2000). *Custodial sexual misconduct; Survey misconduct: Survey of all 50 states, DC, and the Federal Bureau of prisons*. New York, NY: Author.

13. Amnesty International. (2001). *Abuse of women in custody: Sexual misconduct and shackling of pregnant women*. Available at: http://www.amnestyusa.org/pdf/custodyissues.pdf. Accessed August 2, 2013.

14. Widney-Brown, A. (1998). Nowhere to hide: Retaliation against women in Michigan state prisons. *Human Rights Watch, 10*(2): 2-27.

15. Coomaraswamy, R. (1999). Report of the Mission to the United States of America on the Issue of Violence Against Women, Its Causes and Consequences, in Accordance with Commission on Human Rights Resolution 1997/44. United Nations Economic and Social Council: Commission on Human Rights. Available at: http://www.unhchr.ch/Huridocda/Huridoca.nsf/0/7560a6237c67bb118025674c004406e9. Accessed August 2, 2013.

16. General Accounting Office. (1999). Women in prison: Sexual misconduct by correctional staff. Washington, DC: United States General Accounting Office, GAO/GGD-99-104. Available at: http://www.gao.gov/archive/2000/gg00022/pdf. Accessed August 2, 2013.

17. Public Law 108-79 – September 4, 2003 Section 7 a and b.

18. U.S. Department of Justice, 28 CFR Part 115, Docket No. OAG-131; AG Order No. RIN 1104-AB34, 2012.

19. U.S. Department of Justice. (2012, August). *National standards to prevent, detect, and respond to prison rape*. Washington, DC: U.S. Department of Justice.

20. Code of silence refers to an unwritten code among groups that reporting infractions, abuse, or misconduct is not acceptable in the group. Breaking the code may have serious consequences for the member stepping out of line.

21. Bartol, C., & Bartol, A. M. (2004). Introduction to forensic psychology: Research and application. Thousand Oaks, CA: Sage Publications.

22. Dumond, R. W., & Dumond, D. A. (2002). Inmate sexual assault. In Hensley, C., (ed.), Prison Sex: Practice & Policy (pp. 89-100). Boulder, CO: Lynne Rienner Publishers.

23. Beck, A. J., Harrison, P. M., Berzokfsky, M., Caspar, R., & Krebs, C. (2010, August). *Sexual victimization in prisons and jails reported by inmates, 2008-09*. NCJ 231169. Washington, DC: United States Department of Justice, Office of Justice Program.

24. Beck, A. J., & Johnson, C. (2012, May). BJS Special Report: Prison Rape Elimination Act of 2003. *Sexual victimization reported by former state prisoners, 2008*. NCJ 237363. Washington, DC: United States Department of Justice, Office of Justice Program.

25. The official Review Panel website is http://www.ojp.usdoj.gov/reviewpanel/reviewpanel.htm

26. U.S. DOJ, 28 CFR Part 115, Page 3.

27. The term *cultural collision* in this context was coined by Andie Moss and was used in the earlier edition of this chapter. Cultural collisions within facilities often impact sexual safety as subgroups compete to achieve opposing goals.

28. Smith, B. V. (2006). Rethinking prison sex: Self-expression and safety. *Columbia Journal of Gender and Law, 15,* 185. American University, WCL Research Paper No. 2008-31.

29. PTSD in US correctional professionals: Prevalence and impact on health and functioning. Published by Desert Waters Correctional Outreach, 2012.

30. This language is pulled from Barbara Owen's work on the pathways of women offenders, mentioned later in this chapter. Though the theory is an application to understand primarily women offenders, this author believes that the research of correctional staff pathways could also be relevant.

31. Mauer, M., & Chesney-Lind, M. (2002). *Invisible punishment: The collateral consequences of mass imprisonment.* New York, NY: The New Press.

32. Owen, B., & Covington, S. (2003). *Gender-responsive strategies: Research, practice, and guiding principles for women offenders.* Washington DC: National Institute of Corrections.

33. Moss, A. (2007). PREA and implications for women and girls. *Corrections Today,* pp.44–47. Washington, DC: National Institute of Corrections.

34. Wells, J., Owen, B., Pollock, J., & Muscat, B. (2013). *Validation project for improving safety in women's facilities.* National Institute of Corrections. Washington, DC: Authors.

35. James, D., & Glaze, L. (2006, September). *Bureau of Justice Statistics Special Report: Mental health problems of prison and jail inmates.* NCJ 213600. Washington, DC: United States Department of Justice, Office of Justice Program.

36. Human Rights Watch. (2003). *Ill equipped: U.S. prisons and offenders with mental illness. Special report: Mental health and treatment of inmates and probationers.* Washington, DC: National Institute of Justice, Bureau of Justice Statistics.

37. Jenness, V., Maxson, C. L., Matsuda, K. N., & Sumner, J. M. (2009). *Violence in California correctional facilities: An empirical examination of sexual assault.* Irvine, CA: Center for Evidence-Based Corrections.

38. Beck, A. J., Harrison, P. M., Berzokfsky, M., Caspar, R., & Krebs, C. (2010, August). *Sexual victimization in prisons and jails reported by inmates, 2008-09.* NCJ 231169. Washington, DC: United States Department of Justice, Office of Justice Program.

39. U.S. Department of Justice. (2012, August). *National Standards to Prevent, Detect, and Respond to Prison Rape,* standard 115.33. Washington, DC: Author.

40. U.S. Department of Justice. (2012, August). *National Standards to Prevent, Detect, and Respond to Prison Rape,* standards 115.41 and 115.42. Washington, DC: Author.

Inmate Management

YOU ARE THE ADMINISTRATOR
■ Wet and Wild

There was no question that (fictional) Mid River Jail inmate Bosco Givens was difficult to have in custody. He was awaiting trial on a charge of rape and had been confined in the county jail for 85 days (though to staff and inmates, it seemed like 85 years). He had been difficult from the moment he arrived. During the admission processing, the admitting officer noted that Givens was acting spacey. He had pupils that were constricted to tiny specks, and he could not walk without support. Staff took him to the county hospital's emergency room where the ER physician determined that Givens was high on heroin.

Once he was back at the jail, Givens was constantly creating problems in the cell house. He had to be segregated after picking a fight with another inmate and often started arguments with staff members. He cursed at officers, threw food at them, and occasionally spit in their direction. The jail administration had a mental health professional evaluate Givens, but the psychologist reported that Givens was not mad... just bad.

Recently, Givens used his food tray to reach up and break the sprinkler head off the emergency fire suppression sprinkler in his cell. By the time the staff on duty managed to shut down the sprinkler system, Givens was soaked. The lieutenant on duty ordered that Givens be placed outside in the secure recreation cage while his cell and surrounding area were mopped up. This might have been a reasonable action, except that the temperature outdoors was 28°F, and Givens was left outside in cold, wet clothing for over an hour. Afterwards, Givens filed a complaint with the county jail authority through his attorney. The incident was reported in the local newspaper, and it seemed that everyone believed the jail staff had acted inappropriately. The local newspaper editor wrote an editorial condemning the jail personnel for their "Gestapo-like" punishment tactics.

- How should jail personnel have handled this incident?

- How would inmates that givens have been dealt with in the past?

- What aspects of prison architecture could offer potential solutions to dealing with difficult inmates?

- What technological developments could assist in similar situations in the future?

change the terms, conditions, and notices under
but not limited... by regularly reviewing these terms.
for regularly reviewing these terms... Web Sites are for your pers...
distribute, transmit, display, perform, rep...
transer, or sell any information, softw...

Rules

any expressly stated restrictions or
download and print hard copy portion
for your own noncommercial use
other use of materials on this
reproduction, republication, d...
of P&G is also...

Inmate Disciplinary Procedures

Clair A. Cripe

CHAPTER OBJECTIVES

- Describe the goals of an inmate discipline policy and outline the essential elements of a good disciplinary program.

- Explain the constitutional provision that governs inmate discipline procedures.

- Name major legal decisions governing prison discipline proceedings.

Social control of inmate behavior is critical to the successful governance of a correctional institution. To oversee inmates appropriately, positive discipline is necessary. An inmate discipline policy establishes the institution program that regulates inmate conduct, attempting to keep that conduct within the limits of acceptable standards of institutional behavior. Good inmate behavior helps ensure the orderly and safe running of any prison or jail. A functional and well-implemented inmate disciplinary policy will instill respect for authority. It is hoped that the good behavior and respect for authority will persist after the offender's release.

Importance of Inmate Discipline

Those who have worked in prisons or jails accept without question that an inmate disciplinary process is essential. Those who are new to corrections may wonder why it is necessary to have additional discipline when these persons are already locked away from society. What are correctional staff and administrators trying to achieve with their disciplinary procedures? Moreover, are those goals clear, and do their actions in disciplining inmates bring them closer to those goals?

Inmate discipline should achieve several agreed-upon goals:

1. Making inmate conduct conform to a standard of behavior that ensures a safe and orderly living environment
2. Instilling respect for authority
3. Teaching values and respectful behavior (in a group of people who, by definition, have not displayed good values and behavior) that inmates may continue to use once they reenter the community

Society has adopted rules of behavior for its own protection and well-being. These rules are called criminal laws. They are enforced by law enforcement officers. From the patrols and investigations of police officers, through prosecutions and criminal trials, into the correctional facilities that carry out the sentencing orders of the courts, the criminal justice system attempts to achieve the same kinds of goals that the inmate disciplinary system does within institutions: making behavior conform to accepted norms, protecting the safety and property of all, and instilling respect for authority.

When people visit a prison for the first time, most of them have the same reaction: "I am amazed at how much movement there is. At many times of the day, inmates appear to be moving in many directions. What is the purpose? How can all that activity be supervised and tolerated?" That reaction is nearly universal for two reasons. First, ideas about prisons and jails often have been formed by misleading sources such as movies, television shows, and media reports that portray correctional facilities as closely regimented, locked-down (i.e., with inmates in their cells all the time) facilities. Indeed, there are some locked-down, tightly regimented facilities, but there are only a few of them in the whole country. Second, most corrections facilities emphasize free movement of inmates during daytime hours and evening activities. This free movement allows for various programs such as work, education, and recreation. Inmate movement lessens tensions and normalizes day-to-day living, thus benefiting both inmates and staff.

However, the movement of inmates—and the large variety of workplaces, programs, and activities in which inmates are involved—also increase the need for discipline. Most inmates appreciate the opportunity to join a variety of activities, and they adjust to the requirements of living in a prison environment. To assist those inmates in their good adjustment to prison life and to help staff in their primary mission of maintaining a secure and safe institution, it is necessary to punish those who break the rules. For those reasons, inmate disciplinary procedures are necessary.

Essentials of Inmate Discipline

Keeping in mind the goals of disciplinary actions, there are three aspects of discipline essential to an effective inmate disciplinary program.

1. There should be a written set of rules defining expected inmate behavior and procedures for handling misconduct. Most institutions will have a misconduct code—a list of offenses that are subject to punishment in the prison or jail. An adjunct of that list of offenses should concern the types of sanctions that may be imposed if the rules are broken.

2. The rules for discipline must be communicated carefully and thoroughly. All staff members must be taught how the inmate disciplinary program works, in general and specific terms, because every employee may be involved (as a witness, or reporting official, or in some other capacity) in the disciplinary system. Inmates must also be given the details of the system. They must know the kind of responsible behavior that is expected of them, and they should learn the penalties for misbehavior. All staff and inmates should be given a written statement of the policy and hear an oral presentation explaining how the policy works, with the opportunity to have their questions answered.

3. The disciplinary policy must specify clearly how inmates will be notified of suspected misconduct, how sanctions will be imposed, and what their rights to be heard are (along with their rights to appeal, if any).

It is extremely important to have an inmate discipline program that is supported by written policies and specifies precise procedures. These procedures must be applied by staff who understand the importance of the disciplinary program and its procedural requirements. It is also important to apply the policy consistently to engender respect for the rules among staff and inmates.

■ Informal Resolution of Misconduct

It must be noted that informal handling of many kinds of misconduct occurs and is essential to the smooth running of any correctional system. Officers in correctional facilities are given authority to use their good judgment, and they will handle some misconduct informally. This does not mean that the inmate behavior is excused if it violates the rules. It means that there is official recognition that the goals of the disciplinary system (achieving a safer and more secure facility and instilling respect for authority) may be achieved in many cases without processing misconduct through the official system.

Informal handling is usually used for less serious misconduct. For example, an inmate, especially one who has just arrived, may violate a rule without knowing that the conduct is considered misbehavior. In these cases, the officer's reaction is more instructional than punitive: Taking the inmate aside and explaining the proper way to do things communicates the expected behavior for the institution, and it also may open the way for good relations between the officer and the inmate. When to handle such an incident in this way will obviously be a matter of judgment. The officer must assess the likelihood that the inmate did not understand what was expected. The officer's assessment should always take into account other factors, such as the seriousness of the behavior, the sophistication level of the inmate, and the effect this handling of the incident will have on other inmates. For example, being out of bounds, that is, in an unauthorized place at an unauthorized time, may be relatively innocent behavior for a naïve new inmate, but it could be extremely serious behavior for a sophisticated inmate.

As the behavior becomes more serious, or if an officer is not certain whether to have an informal discussion with the inmate or to write up charges, the matter can be referred to a supervisor who will make that decision. In addition to the officer on the scene, who may choose to refrain from filing certain charges, the correctional supervisor should be given authority to dispose of charges informally, rather than pursuing them in a formal disciplinary procedure. Again, these informal dispositions are to be used at the lower end of the spectrum (obviously, assaults, drug offenses, and escape attempts must be pursued with formal charges), but more than half of the offenses on the misconduct list can probably be handled informally in the right circumstances.

In a more sensitive type of informal disposition, the staff member is certain that the inmate has violated a rule, but a sanction is given without charges being filed. Sometimes, this is done by negotiating with the inmate ("I will drop the charges, if you agree to . . ."). More often, and preferably, staff may use certain minor and agreed-upon sanctions in these situations (e.g., extra work, restrictions in movement, or even changes in work assignments, recreation activities, or housing assignments). There need not be a written code for informal sanctioning, because these sanctions should consider an inmate's current and past behavior, though sanctions should be applied consistently. To that end, facility management and supervisory correctional staff must specify how informal sanctions may be used. Supervisors should check that the power given to staff to punish inmates informally is not abused. When power is abused, inmates lose respect for authority.

There are benefits of informal resolutions of inmate misconduct. The most obvious is that they help prioritize cases in the disciplinary process, reserving the procedural hearings for the more serious offenses. Inmates will have greater respect for staff who handle matters fairly but informally.

■ Due Process Requirements

The Fifth Amendment grants that no person may be "deprived of life, liberty, or property, without due process of law," and the Fourteenth Amendment says "nor shall any State deprive any person of life, liberty, or property, without due process of law; nor deny to any person within its jurisdiction the equal protection of the laws." Whenever a claim is made (e.g., by inmates claiming violation of their rights because of disciplinary action), there is first the question of whether there has been any deprivation of life, liberty, or property. Not every type of government action that a person dislikes raises a due process question. Generally, due process is considered a set of procedures that ensure that the action taken is fair, given the circumstances. Again, as a general rule, the more serious the action taken by the government, the more procedural protections (due process) will be required. The U.S. Supreme Court has looked at disciplinary actions in prisons and established some relevant constitutional standards based on a variety of cases.

Sandin v. Conner (1995)

The Supreme Court gave new guidance as to the circumstances under which due process is required in prison actions in the case of *Sandin v. Conner*.[1] The Court greatly simplified the constitutional standard to be used to decide when prison action amounts to a deprivation of liberty that requires due process. The Court recognized in *Sandin v. Conner* that the purpose of prison disciplinary action is to achieve good prison management and prisoner rehabilitative goals. As long as disciplinary action is in pursuit of those goals and does not add to the sentence already being served or go beyond the conditions contemplated in the sentence being served, the disciplinary action does not create a liberty interest. The Court held that Conner's discipline in segregated confinement did not present the type of atypical, significant deprivation in which a state might conceivably create a liberty interest. The regime to which he was subjected as a result of the misconduct hearing was within the range of confinement to be normally expected for one serving an indeterminate sentence of 30 years to life.

Thus, the question is not whether the inmate is punished or even punished severely. The question is whether the punishment is within the range of conditions, restrictions, and sanctions that are contemplated for the type and length of sentence that the particular inmate is serving. This substantially reduces the number of cases where due process protections are constitutionally required because the action taken by prison officials deprives inmates of liberty. Lower courts have been busy interpreting the scope of the *Sandin v. Conner* ruling. From the facts of the case and the Court's language, segregated confinement (or other housing restrictions or the withdrawal of privileges) would not trigger due process requirements, but actions that might extend the time to be served (such as good time awards being taken away or parole release being affected) would require a due process hearing. Some correctional agencies, as a matter of caution as well as fairness, continue to require certain procedural protections for any serious act of inmate misconduct.

Wolff v. McDonnell (1974)

Wolff v. McDonnell is the leading case in the Supreme Court on inmate discipline.[2] The Supreme Court recognized the special nature of prison disciplinary proceedings and specifically rejected claims for procedures (such as representation of inmate by lawyers) that would "encase the disciplinary procedures in an inflexible constitutional straitjacket that would necessarily call for adversary proceedings typical of the criminal trial." In other words, prison hearings are "administrative" and call for much less procedural protection than court proceedings.

There are five minimum due process standards for a prison disciplinary hearing:

1. There must be advance written notice to the inmate of the claimed violation.

2. The hearing should be held at least 24 hours after the notice, so that the inmate has time to prepare for his or her appearance.

3. The inmate should be allowed to call witnesses and to present documentary evidence, unless permitting him or her to do so would be unduly hazardous.

4. A representative (who may be an inmate or a staff member) should be allowed to assist the inmate if the inmate is illiterate or if there are complex issues involved.

5. There should be a statement by an impartial disciplinary committee of the evidence relied on to support the fact findings and the reasons for the disciplinary action taken.

Two requirements that had been strenuously sought for inmate hearings were specifically denied in *Wolff v. McDonald*: There was no requirement for the inmate to be permitted to confront and cross-examine adverse witnesses (because of the special hazards, those actions could present in a prison setting), and there was no requirement for allowing inmates to have legal counsel.

Other Relevant Cases

Other Supreme Court cases added more guidelines for prison disciplinary hearings.

In *Baxter v. Palmigiano* (1976), the Court reiterated its ruling that inmates are not entitled to either retained or appointed counsel in disciplinary hearings.[3] A new issue was the inmate's right to remain silent in the disciplinary proceeding. The Court said that it was permissible for officials to tell inmates that they could remain silent, but that their silence could be used against them (to draw an adverse inference) at their hearing. However, the inmate's silence by itself would be insufficient to support a decision of guilt by the disciplinary committee. In addition, if the inmates were compelled (i.e., ordered) to furnish testimony that might incriminate them later in a criminal proceeding, that testimony could not be used against them in the criminal trial.

But can the inmate be punished twice—once inside the prison and again in criminal court? This raises the issue of another constitutional protection: the double jeopardy clause. The Fifth Amendment to the Constitution provides that no one shall be "twice put in jeopardy of life or limb" for the same offense. Inmates have protested that it is a violation of this provision if they are punished in prison for an offense and then are prosecuted for the same offense in a criminal trial. The Supreme Court has not ruled on this precise issue. However, lower courts have considered it and have consistently ruled that it is not a constitutional violation for an inmate to be proceeded against in both places—in a prison disciplinary action and criminal prosecution.

Courts have said that the double jeopardy clause protects only against multiple *criminal* punishments for the same offense. Prison disciplinary action is not considered a criminal punishment. As one court ruled, "The Double Jeopardy Clause was not intended to inhibit prison discipline, and disciplinary changes in prison conditions do not preclude subsequent criminal punishment for the same misconduct."[4]

In the case of *Superintendent v. Hill* (1985), the Court ruled on the amount of evidence that was required, constitutionally, to support a prison board's findings.[5] The Court said that due process required only that there be "some evidence" to support the findings of the disciplinary board—about the lowest standard of proof that could be devised.

■ Use of Informants

There are some issues of inmate disciplinary proceedings that have not been addressed by the Supreme Court. One of the most troublesome is the use of evidence that comes from confidential informants or develops as a result of the information given by such informants. Much information for the safer control of correctional facilities is supplied by inmate informants. Many correctional supervisors and officers rely on this information to keep track of sensitive inmate misconduct. In fact, officers often develop regular sources of such confidential information and even provide rewards to the informants. (Again, this practice has its counterparts in the outside community's law enforcement activities.) Because a central goal of prison management is the maintenance of security and safety, there is a need to have such suppliers of information. However, to ensure the fairness of the disciplinary process (to have some due process in prison hearings), there must be protection against inmates fabricating information or providing false accusations, which they may do for a variety of reasons.

Although the U.S. Supreme Court has not addressed this issue, lower courts (and correctional officials and lawyers) have considered it and have concluded that there must be some way to ascertain the reliability of informants' stories. Informants, to protect their safety, cannot be called as witnesses at hearings. By the same token, their identities cannot be revealed to the accused inmates. In the policy of most agencies, the disciplinary committee makes inquiry, apart from the accused, as to the reliability of informant information that is present in the case. A conclusion that the informant is reliable is entered into the record. That conclusion may be based on the circumstances of the case, in which the informant's assertions have been corroborated by other facts; on a report from an investigating officer who gives reasons for believing the informant; on other situations where the informant gave reliable information; or on detailed information that could be known only by someone who was present to observe the facts that otherwise proved true.

Until the Supreme Court provides firm guidance in this area, correctional staff will have to look to any rulings that have been made by courts in their jurisdiction and follow those rulings. Staff responsible for drafting policy must make certain that the inmate disciplinary policy reflects any court rulings on use of informant information (and any other area where local courts may have special requirements, outside of or beyond those given by the Supreme Court). Line staff implementing the disciplinary policy must be able to rely on its accordance with any court rulings that apply in the local jurisdiction. With the Supreme Court's ruling in *Sandin v. Conner*, the exposure of staff to individual liability for constitutional violations in disciplinary proceedings has been greatly reduced but not eliminated.

■ Inmate Appeals and Grievances

Appeals from disciplinary decisions have not been required by the courts as a necessary component of inmate discipline procedures. For the more serious levels of misconduct, an appeal system is common under administrative policy. There may be one or two levels of appeal of disciplinary action. In some systems, appeals would be made to the disciplinary hearing officer or committee, or to the warden. In agencies with regional organization, there may be a level of appeal to the regional office, and many agencies do allow appeal to the headquarters level.

Because inmates are often unhappy with the results of the disciplinary proceedings, it is no surprise that disciplinary matters are appealed frequently. In some agencies, inmate disciplinary actions may be appealed through the inmate grievance system, in the same way other prison actions or conditions may be grieved. Many agencies do not allow disciplinary matters to be taken into the regular grievance system; in these agencies, there will be a separate procedure for review or appeal of inmate disciplinary actions. In those agencies where discipline actions are grievable, it is common for appeals concerning discipline to account for the greatest number of inmate complaints. Similarly, when inmates go to court, disciplinary actions are, in most jurisdictions, the most frequent category of matters taken into court.

Review of disciplinary actions on appeal is typically limited to procedural review. The records (the discipline offense report, the investigation report, and the written report of the hearing officer or hearing committee) are examined to ensure that the procedures required by the agency's disciplinary policy have been followed. The facts of the case and the sanction imposed are summarily reviewed. Some evidence must exist to support the findings of the disciplinary authority. The reviewer ensures that the sanction imposed is within the range of punishments authorized for that offense. There is a legal requirement that the hearing officer or committee record the evidence relied on to support the conclusion reached and that the reasons for the sanction(s) imposed be given.

There are other significant legal requirements for inmate disciplinary proceedings, and corrections staff should be aware of them. As noted previously, the inmate disciplinary program attempts to establish respect for authority. For the inmate disciplinary program to receive respect, it must be administered fairly and according to rules of due process. Apart from being the law, these rules are important for maintaining a fair and humane living environment in correctional facilities.

■ Personal Liability

Legally, it is also essential that staff follow rules to avoid exposure to personal liability. In litigating inmate complaints over the last 40 years, the most frequently used legal action has been under the Civil Rights Act of 1871, particularly what is usually called a Section 1983 lawsuit.[6] That federal statute provides that:

> Every person who, under color of any statute, ordinance, regulation, custom, or usage, of any State or Territory, subjects, or causes to be subject, any citizen of the United States or other person within the jurisdiction thereof to the deprivation of any rights, privileges, or immunities secured by the Constitution and laws, shall be liable to the party injured in an action at law, suit in equity, or other proper proceeding for redress.

This law allows people who claim that their constitutional rights have been abridged to go into federal court for legal relief. (While Section 1983 only applies to state actions and state employees, its standards have been applied equally to federal actions and employees by the Supreme Court.[7]) Section 1983 has been popular for inmates to use for several reasons. In most states, federal courts were seen as being more liberal and more receptive to inmate complaints than state courts. Legal rulings were obtained in one part of the country, which could then be used as leverage to get favorable rulings in federal courts in another part of the country.

Section 1983 could be used to obtain two kinds of relief. If constitutional violations were proved, the federal courts could give injunctive relief and also monetary damages against the offending officials. Injunctive relief could require an agency to stop doing something it had been doing, to change its procedures, or to start doing something that was constitutionally required. Many changes were required by courts in injunctive orders under Section 1983. More threatening to the individual official is the risk of being ordered to pay monetary damages because of constitutional violations.

A corrections worker may be held personally liable if he or she does not follow constitutional requirements that have been established by court rulings at various levels. A ruling by the U.S. Supreme Court is the most authoritative and must be followed throughout the country. There may also be rulings in lower federal courts or in state courts that govern a particular type of activity covered by the Constitution or state statutes. It is the responsibility of lawyers for each correctional agency to make sure that employees are aware of any such local rulings and that agency policy reflects the current constitutional requirements that have been given in court rulings.

Correctional staff can protect themselves by receiving staff training, which points out legal standards and constitutional requirements, and following agency policy, which must be most carefully done in those areas of possible constitutional liability where the courts have ruled. All staff must be careful to follow those rules established by the courts with regard to disciplinary actions.

■ Conclusion

Disciplinary policy must be written carefully to ensure fairness and to guarantee basic due process standards. Staff must follow that policy carefully to protect themselves from liability and maintain the integrity of the correctional environment.

Chapter Resources

DISCUSSION QUESTIONS

1. Why is it necessary to have a prison's discipline policy spelled out in writing?
2. What are the benefits and risks of handling inmate misconduct informally?
3. Would having an attorney present at a prison discipline hearing to represent the inmate be a good or a bad thing?
4. What are the benefits and risks of using inmate informants to take disciplinary actions against other inmates?
5. To what extent is an inmate discipline process similar to the criminal law process, and how is it different?

ADDITIONAL RESOURCES

Cripe, C., Pearlman, M., & Kosiak, D. (2012). *Legal aspects of corrections management* (3rd ed.). Burlington, MA: Jones & Bartlett Learning.

NOTES

1. *Sandin v. Conner*, 585 U.S. 472 (1995).
2. *Wolff v. McDonnell*, 418 U.S. 539 (1974).
3. *Baxter v. Palmigiano*, 425 U.S. 308 (1976).
4. *United States v. Simpson*, 546 F.3d 394 (6th Cir. 2008).
5. *Superintendent v. Hill*, 472 U.S. 445 (1985).
6. Civil Rights Act of 1871, U.S. Code vol. 42, sec. 1983 (1871).
7. *Bivens v. Six Unknown Federal Narcotics Agents*, 403 U.S. 388 (1971).

Grievance Procedures in Correctional Facilities

Kevin I. Minor and Stephen Parson

CHAPTER 30

CHAPTER OBJECTIVES

- Explore the interrelated trends and convergence of interests that gave rise to the rapid adoption of prisoner grievance procedures in the 1970s.

- Compare and contrast the influence of CRIPA and PLRA on modern grievance procedures.

- Compare and contrast the principles of model grievance procedures, commonly adopted grievance elements, and actual practice.

- Explore the effects of prison culture and bureaucratic co-optation on the implementation and operation of prisoner grievance procedures.

Three official avenues for addressing disputed issues in correctional facilities include (1) passage of statutes by legislative bodies; (2) case law rulings by state and federal courts; and (3) promulgation of administrative regulations and policies by executive branch agencies. This chapter examines the latter. Of various administrative dispute resolution mechanisms that have been used, this chapter focuses specifically on prisoner grievance procedures.

With a movement in corrections away from concerns like prisoner rights and rehabilitation, the topic of grievance procedures has received little attention in the literature during the past few decades. Numerous observers have described this period as involving heightened public fear, massive increases in use of incarceration, emphases on custody and punishment, and expanded deference to prison officials.[1] Although grievance procedures have not been a priority in the literature, we will see that implementation of the Prison Litigation Reform Act (PLRA) dramatically increased the significance of these procedures in actual prison operations.

Grievance procedures exist in some form in virtually all prisons and are fairly common in local jails and other correctional facilities (e.g., halfway houses). If properly designed and operated, these procedures can have important benefits for both staff and prisoners.[2] A not necessarily fundamental goal of these procedures is to permit expression of individual prisoners' grievances and encourage resolution through a standardized process. These procedures set out written steps and channels to follow when investigating and attempting to resolve issues. Procedures typically define (a) the types of issues that can be grieved such as a policy, condition, action, or incident applicable to a facility; (b) the time frames associated with the process, including provisions for dealing with emergencies; (c) specific actions to be performed whether filing or responding to a grievance; (d) channels for appeal, normally one or two levels above the level of the initial filing; and (e) the possible remedies available.[3] Restrictions are commonly placed on what issues can be grieved and on the remedies possible. Procedures exist on a vertical continuum of formality, ranging from initial efforts at relatively informal discussion and resolution at the bottom to progressively higher levels of formalized review and decision.[4]

Written policies set out the professed intent and design of grievance mechanisms but do not necessarily portray the reality of how mechanisms are implemented and operated. This is because of differentials in power between prisoners and correctional officials, as well as between the correctional administration and line staff subordinates.[5] Correctional grievance procedures are a microcosm of the complex and hierarchical bureaucracies in which they are implemented, shaping and being shaped by the needs and dynamics of those bureaucracies. It is here that one begins to see potential for tension between what Rothman terms "conscience," reflected in genuine efforts to handle prisoners' issues in a fair and responsive way, and "convenience," reflected in practical efforts to run the organization and further its interests as efficiently as possible.[6] To the extent that conscience and convenience collide, power differentials become more evident, and potential grows for displacing or co-opting the fundamental goal of grievance procedures, which is to fairly and efficiently resolve institutional problems, thereby promoting order and justice.[7]

Appreciating that grievance procedures are affected by bureaucratic dynamics provides only partial understanding. This is because grievance procedures also exist in relationship to the culture of correctional facilities, including both the staff and prisoner subcultures. These subcultures exist in all facilities but are usually most pronounced in prisons. Like other dispute resolution mechanisms, correctional grievance procedures are situated at the nexus of conflict between opposing parties. Thus, a complete discussion of grievance procedures must reckon with their wedging between organizational bureaucracy on the one hand and staff and prisoner subcultures on the other.

■ Origin and Evolution of Grievance Procedures

Systematic, multilevel procedures allowing prisoners to grieve disputes not resolved less formally were rare in American corrections before 1970. By 1980, however, most facilities had such procedures in place.[8] The rapid adoption of formalized grievance procedures can be traced to three interrelated trends that led the interests of judges, prisoners, and prison officials to converge in favor of such procedures.[9] These trends included (a) rising politicization, militancy, and unrest among prisoners sparked by poor conditions and unfair practices in many facilities; (b) growing recognition of the legitimacy and utility of the right of prisoners to complain; and (c) increasing intervention of the courts in correctional matters (i.e., partial and temporary relaxation of the "hands-off doctrine," under which the courts had traditionally avoided responsibility for prison operations). Importantly, these mutually reinforcing trends played out in the context of, and drew strength from, the broader civil rights movement of the 1960s and early 1970s.

Politicization, Militancy, and Unrest

The ethos of the wider civil rights movement helped to politicize prisoners and render them increasingly militant. As early as the 1950s, prisoners began using riots as a means of airing complaints.[10] Before that, riots were relatively rare, spontaneous, opportunistic events not intentionally launched to air collective complaints.[11] Beginning in the 1950s, however, riots occurred with greater frequency and began to display political and activist overtones. Spurred on by poor conditions, combined with inadequate or nonexistent grievance procedures and very limited access of prisoners to the courts, a growing portion of riots occurred for the purpose of collectively expressing grievances. Oftentimes, prisoners protested deplorable conditions and practices. In many prison systems before 1970, when officials responded at all to prisoner complaints, they did so informally, without structured guidelines or checks on discretion provided through review of decisions. The result was inconsistency, perceptions of unfairness, and heightened contentiousness. Thus, throughout the 1950s and 1960s, institutions not only saw more riots but also other indicators of increased frustration and collective protest (i.e., work stoppages, hunger strikes, and sit downs).[12] In trying to understand the reasons for this unrest, it is essential to realize that to prisoners, the lack of a fair complaint procedure (whether perceived or genuine) was equal in importance to the substantive issues generating the complaints.[13]

Growing Recognition of the Right to Complain

Along with the prison unrest just described, there was also growing recognition from respected governmental, professional, and public interest organizations of the legitimacy and utility of the right of prisoners to complain.[14] This recognition occurred in three temporal stages. First, some organizations began to call for fair and effective grievance procedures. For example, in 1955, the First United Nations Congress on Prevention of Crime and Treatment of Offenders adopted a rule entitling every prisoner to make complaints with prison authorities and requiring authorities to promptly reply to nonfrivolous or grounded complaints.[15] However, it was not until the President's Commission on Law Enforcement and the Administration of Justice echoed this call in its 1967 Task Force Report on Corrections, followed by endorsements from the National Council on Crime and Delinquency and the National Advisory Commission on Criminal Justice Standards and Goals, that corrections began to take notice. Second, certain organizations, mobilized by these calls, conducted research and developed model grievance procedures. Most notable was the Center for Community Justice, which in 1975 articulated nine model "essential" principles of effective grievance mechanisms.[16] Third, other organizations including the American Correctional Association and the American Bar Association subsequently adopted and disseminated those model procedures. All these efforts are important because they established the foundation from which modern grievance processes were constructed.

Increased Intervention of the Courts

By the mid-1960s, amid the civil rights movement, it was becoming evident to the judiciary that left to their own devices, some prison systems could not be relied upon to operate institutions according to constitutional standards. Building on earlier case law that helped prisoners gain access to the courts, in 1964 the U.S. Supreme

Court allowed prisoners to bypass state courts and bring constitutional claims directly to the federal courts under section 1983 of the Civil Rights Act of 1871.[17] This development began to ease the hands-off doctrine. The number of suits filed by prisoners increased considerably, prisoners won a series of important rights, and in some cases, courts mandated that certain correctional facilities, or entire correctional systems, improve practices and conditions. Court intervention, punctuated by such prison disturbances as the highly publicized 1971 riot at New York's Attica Prison that claimed 43 lives, helped to raise both public awareness of prison issues and receptivity of criminal justice officials to formal grievance procedures.[18]

Convergence of Interests

It was in this context that the interests of various groups converged around having grievance mechanisms for prisoners. Grievance procedures found favor with many prisoners who were seeking greater power in prison decision making, less arbitrariness from officials, and less delay in having complaints addressed than characteristic of court filings. Prison officials recognized the need for ways to ameliorate prisoner unrest, reduce negative publicity, and avoid relinquishing authority to the judiciary; and some had a genuine interest in opening lines of communication with prisoners and promoting greater fairness.[19] The courts began favoring these mechanisms as concern grew about the increased volume of prisoner cases. Some cases were perceived as frivolous, and others were seen as potentially meritorious but better resolved without court intervention.[20] Also, some courts saw grievance procedures as a means of monitoring prison official compliance with judicial rulings. By the close of the 1970s, grievance procedures had become commonplace in correctional facilities.[21]

Grievance Mechanisms and Legislation

In addition to the judicial and executive branches, the legislative branch has shaped the evolution of correctional grievance procedures. Drawing in part on the model grievance principles developed by the Center for Community Justice, Congress passed the Civil Rights of Institutionalized Persons Act (CRIPA) of 1980 in response to reports of constitutional rights violations.[22] CRIPA authorized the U.S. Department of Justice to directly oversee state and local institutions housing various populations (e.g., prisoners, the elderly, and mental patients).[23] The act required the U.S. Attorney General to establish minimum standards for institutional grievance procedures and set up a process whereby state and local authorities could voluntarily submit procedures for federal certification. Adult state and local convicted prisoners filing federal lawsuits under section 1983 were required to run through, or exhaust, administrative remedies available through certified grievance procedures if the court in question deemed exhaustion appropriate. However, failure to exhaust a grievance process was not necessarily grounds for dismissal of the lawsuit, and grievance procedures had to satisfy certain criteria for certification. The criteria included provisions for input from staff and prisoners, expedited processing, preventing retaliation for filing a grievance, time limits for decisions, and independent external review.[24] However, use of the certification process was sporadic and rather short-lived. Relatively few states had grievance procedures certified under CRIPA before mid-1996, and no state or local grievance procedure has been certified since.[25]

Then in 1995, Congress passed PLRA, which from a practical point of view rendered the CRIPA certification provision defunct.[26] PLRA took effect in 1996 and modified a key portion[27] of CRIPA to read: "No action shall be brought with respect to prison conditions under section 1983 of [the Civil Rights Act of 1871] or any other Federal law, by a prisoner confined in any jail, prison, or other correctional facility until such administrative remedies as are available are exhausted." The significance of this modification is threefold. First, it expands the scope of the requirement to exhaust administrative remedies from covering *only* section 1983 lawsuits to include *all* federal lawsuits except habeas corpus actions that challenge the fact or duration of confinement. Second, it makes exhaustion of administrative remedies *mandatory*, rather than *contingent* upon court discretion or federal certification of the grievance system. Finally, it potentially undermines the quality of grievance procedures by eliminating from CRIPA several pages outlining minimum standards and certification requirements and replacing them with the single phrase, ". . . such administrative remedies as are available...." Furthermore, CRIPA, as modified by PLRA, states: "the failure of a State to adopt or adhere to an administrative grievance procedure shall not constitute the basis for an action under [this law]." Thus, although CRIPA had not required establishment, certification, or exhaustion of state and local grievance processes, PLRA mandated that prisoners exhaust such processes, regardless of their quality or extent, before bringing actions under any federal law.[28] Additionally, PLRA applies to prisoners at all levels of government and those of all ages, permits dismissal of lawsuits where administrative remedies are not deemed exhausted, and eliminates CRIPA's time period of 180 days for processing a grievance.[29]

PLRA is the most important component of the shift toward a "due" or "substantial" deference philosophy under which courts and lawmakers generally defer wide authority to the discretion of correctional administrators.[30] PLRA has sharply curtailed prisoner access to courts and diminished judicial oversight of prisons.[31]

Concurrently, we find an increase in both the bureaucratic co-optation of grievance procedures and in negative influences from prison culture (see later sections of this chapter). When the hands-off doctrine was relaxed in the 1960s, the result was a flood of litigation prompting court officials, correctional officials, and others to seek such alternatives as grievance procedures. Just as these procedures were becoming institutionalized by the end of the 1970s, the courts began adopting the due deference posture, later culminating with PLRA. The typical product was a diluted version of the model grievance procedures developed during the 1970s, lodged between the prison's administrative bureaucracy and the prison culture. With PLRA in place, correctional facilities have less motivation to operate high-quality grievance procedures and more latitude to adulterate these procedures and/or co-opt them to serve bureaucratic ends. This is evidenced by the fact that modern grievance procedures rarely incorporate the two most important elements contained in the model principles—*meaningful participation* by prisoners and line staff and *external review* of grievances or grievance procedures. Paradoxically, then, at the same time that PLRA made grievance procedures more important by mandating exhaustion, it undermined their quality by removing minimum standards and certification requirements. Nevertheless, the U.S. Supreme Court has refused to recognize exceptions to the exhaustion requirement and required strict compliance with all institutional rules for filing grievances.[32]

■ Model Principles, Common Elements, and Actual Practice

As presented in the second column of **Table 30-1**, the Center for Community Justice developed model principles for effective correctional grievance procedures. These principles were cast by the Center as "essential" elements and originally received widespread support from such diverse stakeholders as court officials, prisoners, government agencies, public interest organizations, researchers, and correctional officials; indeed, the principles were a foundation for CRIPA. Nevertheless, the principles have rarely been incorporated intact into a correctional grievance mechanism. The third column of Table 30-1 displays the elements that do commonly comprise the grievance procedures in use today. The fourth column contrasts both the model/essential principles (column 2) and common elements (column 3) with the actual or everyday practice of grievance processes in most institutions.[33]

It can be seen that the model principles differ appreciably from commonly adopted grievance elements. Most importantly, commonly adopted elements usually do not include (a) independent, external review of grievances or (b) line staff and prisoner participation in design and operation of the process. Even when a policy does contain these key elements, the elements are often among the first targets of co-optation and dilution efforts or outright removal. Other differences between model principles and common elements are readily apparent in the table. Moreover, the table reveals that the reality of actual practice is usually even further detached from the model principles.

TABLE 30-1 Comparison of Model Grievance Principles, Commonly Found Elements, and Actual Practice

Principle	Model/Essential Principles for an Effective Grievance Procedure	Common Elements of Grievance Procedure Policy	Actual/Everyday Practice of Grievance Procedures
1. Review (Note: Although periodic independent review of the grievance system as a whole is important, this principle refers primarily to the ongoing potential for independent review of individual grievances.)	The mechanism must include some form of *independent review*, that is, review by people outside the correctional structure. The more totally independent of official governmental control such review is, the more likely it will be to promote inmates' belief in the mechanism's fairness and their willingness to use it.	In most cases, the initial version of a grievance system policy (a) did not contain an independent review provision; (b) provided for independent review that is advisory only (i.e., had no authority); or (c) considered the potential of an appeal beyond the local institution (e.g., to DOC headquarters) to be independent.	In practice, most facilities with grievance systems that provided for independent review based on actual authority, later attempted, and in most cases succeeded in (a) removing the independent review provision; (b) converting it to an advisory role; or (c) converting it to an "appeal to headquarters" provision, thereby co-opting it to serve as a tool of the central administration to monitor and control the local facility, rather than as a safeguard of the fairness of the grievance system.[a]
2. Participation	Line staff and inmates must *participate* in the design and operation of a grievance mechanism. Only participation can give these critically important constituencies a vested interest in the success of the mechanism. In addition, participation seems to be the only possible way to overcome initial apprehension on the part of line staff and distrust on the part of inmates.	Relatively few modern grievance systems provide for meaningful participation of line staff or prisoners. Although some grievance procedures provide for limited advisory roles for these important groups, most provide for very little or no participation.	Actual line staff and prisoner participation in the formulation and operation of grievance procedures was fairly common in the 1970s when most formalized procedures emerged. In the years since, with the decline of the civil rights movement and court intervention in corrections, increasingly punitive sentiments, and bureaucratization and co-optation, such participation has been sharply curtailed or eliminated from most systems.
3. Time limits	The mechanism must have relatively *short, enforceable time limits.* These limits must apply to both the making and implementation of decisions. Every mechanism should also provide for the handling of emergency grievances.	Grievance policies typically permit prison officials relatively lengthy, flexible time frames—usually 20–30 days to respond at each level. Failure to adhere to these guidelines typically results in no penalty, a mandatory extension, or automatic appeal to the next level. In some cases, prison officials' failure to respond to an appeal within the time frame constitutes a denial of the appeal. Prisoners, on the contrary, are usually held to short, firm deadlines—typically 5–10 days for an initial grievance and 2–5 days for an appeal. Failure to meet these deadlines results in grievance dismissal except in rare cases.	The short time limits normally imposed on prisoners are at odds with the practical realities of incarceration, and with the grievance policy itself. Most grievance procedures encourage or require attempts to resolve problems informally. In some facilities, several stages of informal attempts are required. Yet incarceration entails numerous, often extended delays in movement and access to resources, such as grievance forms, staff pertinent to informal resolution attempts, and administrative staff. Time limits frequently expire while attempting such informal resolutions.

4. Responses	There must be *guaranteed written responses* for every complaint submitted to the mechanism. Written answers must give reasons for adverse decisions.	Although written responses are a requirement for nearly all modern multilevel grievance procedures, many do not include the "reasons" provision of the model principles. Some policies allow an appeal to be denied simply by not responding to it, effectively eliminating not only the written response requirement but also the time frames and evidence of exhaustion.	There is a tendency in corrections to view prisoners' allegations with extreme suspicion. At the same time, perhaps based in part on a sense of moral superiority and staff subcultural solidarity, there is a tendency to uncritically accept staff responses to prisoner allegations. It is fairly common for grievance coordinators and other officials responding to grievances to identify and respond to an error, weakness, or peripheral remark in grievance, while ignoring or marginalizing substantive comments. This often produces contrived responses based on flimsy reasoning.
5. Planning and leadership	The implementation of a successful grievance mechanism requires *effective administrative planning and leadership.* Correctional administrators must take the lead in assessing needs, determining resource requirements, and allocating sufficient resources in order to create successful mechanisms. In addition, they must participate actively in an effort to win the commitment of subordinate administrators to establishing effective mechanisms.	Most existing grievance procedures were initially drafted (in the 1970s) at the headquarters level and were subsequently imposed on local institutions with (a) little or no input or notice; (b) scant consideration for variation between institutions; and (c) little effort to win the buy-in of local administrators or staff. However, more recently, there have been increasing efforts toward better planning, orientation, and training. Some jurisdictions have localized their policies (e.g., issued field instructions to each local institution).	The lack of effective administrative planning and leadership had, and continues to have, significant effect on the day-to-day reality of interfacing with grievance procedures. For example, local administrators, staff, and prisoners all struggle with grievance polices that were adopted en masse from other states, with little or no modification. Likewise, procedures implemented without adequate training, orientation, and resource allocation are more often viewed by staff as threatening or burdensome, and by prisoners as insincere, ineffective, or futile, or simply as distractions or barriers.
6. Training	Administrative, line staff, and inmate personnel, key to the operations of a mechanism, must be *trained* thoroughly in the skills and techniques requisite for the effective investigation, hearing, and disposition of inmates' grievances.	Although correctional policies and budgets often provide some training for administrative personnel, such as grievance coordinators, they often have to rely on self-study and on-the-job training. In contrast, line staff and prisoners, where they are involved in the grievance procedure at all, are seldom provided formal training.	In practice, the essential principle of quality training, at least as it relates to line staff and prisoners, is related to the principle of participation. For line staff and prisoners, both training and participation in grievance system formulation and operation are often curtailed in the course of bureaucratic co-optation and centralization of control.

(continues)

TABLE 30-1 Comparison of Model Grievance Principles, Commonly Found Elements, and Actual Practice (cont.)

Principle	Model/Essential Principles for an Effective Grievance Procedure	Common Elements of Grievance Procedure Policy	Actual/Everyday Practice of Grievance Procedures
7. Orientation program	Every institution with a grievance mechanism must develop an effective, persuasive, continuing program for the *orientation* of staff and inmates to the nature, purpose, and functions of the grievance mechanism.	Most correctional facilities distribute literature describing the grievance procedure to newly arriving prisoners and make policy manuals available in the law library or elsewhere. Some facilities discuss grievance procedures during an orientation or indoctrination phase and/or post flyers/memos on bulletin boards in breezeways or living units.	Often these efforts give little concern to issues of literacy or intellectual functioning, mental health status, housing or segregation status, or other impediments to accessing, understanding, or acting on grievance procedure literature.
8. Monitoring and evaluation	There must be a continuing system to *monitor and evaluate* the effectiveness of each operating grievance mechanism. At a minimum, the monitoring and evaluation system should operate at the institutional and departmental levels; it is preferable that some outside monitoring take place at least periodically.	Although considerable variation exists, most grievance procedures are monitored and evaluated to some moderate extent. An example is the Ohio Correctional Institution Inspection Committee, a group of state legislators with a full-time staff of inspectors who, among other things, inspect grievance procedures and issue biennial reports.	Much of the monitoring and evaluation of grievance systems is superficial and self-justifying (e.g., a low number of grievances or a low percentage of appeals is often taken as evidence of a successfully functioning system, rather than as an indication that most prisoners have dismissed the system as unfair or ineffectual).
9. Codification	Once a department has tested and evaluated its mechanism thoroughly, it should move to make it a permanent part of its program by having it statutorily enacted in appropriate *legislation*. (Notice that this recommendation would offer some stability for a grievance procedure by partially insulating it against changing political winds, changing administrations, and bureaucratic co-optation.)	Although many grievance procedures currently rest on statutory or administrative law, this primarily stemmed from a "top-down" central office bureaucratization of corrections, rather than from "bottom-up" local facility efforts to stabilize programs. Contrary to the spirit of the essential principle, the legal authority for most existing grievance procedures grants broad authority to the central office to promulgate policy.	As a practical matter, this "top-down" centralization of authority often results in overly standardized grievance procedures and other policies that fit poorly at some institutions. One method many corrections departments have employed to address this issue is the use of localized "field instructions" to supplement the broad, standardized policy manuals.

10. Reprisals	N/A	Most modern grievance system policies explicitly forbid reprisals against grievants.	In practice, such protections are nearly nonexistent. The prisoner subculture prompts harsh and violent responses against prisoners who grieve other prisoners or, in some cases, certain staff or situations. Forbidding such reprisals is akin to, and about as successful as, forbidding violence or rule infractions. Likewise, line staff misuse of disciplinary procedures; manipulation of housing, job, education, or other assignments; and countless other means of reprisal are nearly impossible to prevent or prove.
11. Applicability of procedure	N/A	Grievance procedures commonly apply to issues that (a) personally affect the grievant; (b) are within the authority of the institution or system in which s(he) is housed; and (c) are not subject to a separate appeal process.	Owing to practical (social and structural) impediments stemming from the nature of grievance procedures, indeed prisoners themselves being wedged between prisoner and officer subcultures and the prison bureaucracy/power structure, large segments of the correctional landscape are essentially off limits and are not subject to grievance.
12. Appeal	N/A	Modern, multilevel grievance systems usually provide for three or four levels of grievances, with two or three potential appeals (one between each level).	The reality of the appeal process is intertwined with the principles of participation, review, and time frames (see principles 1, 2, and 3 above). Almost since the inception of formalized grievance procedures, the trend has been for prison officials to sharply limit or eliminate

TABLE 30-1 Comparison of Model Grievance Principles, Commonly Found Elements, and Actual Practice (cont.)

Principle	Model/Essential Principles for an Effective Grievance Procedure	Common Elements of Grievance Procedure Policy	Actual/Everyday Practice of Grievance Procedures
			participation by line staff and prisoners in, and external review of, grievance procedures. With limited participation and review, time frames have grown more lax for officials. The suppression and co-optation of these three essential principles have in turn undermined and co-opted the appeal process. Although initially intended to serve as a safeguard on fairness and equity, the appeal process, indeed grievance procedures in general, has grown increasingly biased and ineffective.
Sources	The information in this column is quoted from Keating et al. (1975, p. 33).[b] Emphases are added.	The information in this column is derived from a review of a sample of grievance policies from 10 state departments of corrections. The policies reviewed are indicative of policies generally.	The information in this column is based on one of the author's field experience working with correctional grievance procedures.

[a]See, for example, Bordt, R. L., & Musheno, M. C. (1988). Bureaucratic co-optation of informal dispute processing: Social control as an effect of inmate grievance policy. *Journal of Research in Crime and Delinquency, 25,* p. 19; and *Inmate Grievance Procedure Review.* (2006, May 23). http://www.ciic.state.oh.us/reports/igp.pdf, a biennial report of the Ohio Correctional Institution Inspection Committee, p. 10.

[b]Keating, J. M. Jr., McArthur, V. A., Lewis, M. K., Sebelius, K. G., & Singer, L. R. (1975). *Grievance mechanisms in correctional institutions.* Washington, DC: U.S. Government Printing Office.

Source: Data from Keating, J. M. Jr., McArthur, V. A., Lewis, M. K., Sebelius, K. G., & Singer, L. R. (1975). *Grievance Mechanisms in Correctional Institutions.* National Institute of Law Enforcement and Criminal Justice, Law Enforcement Assistance Administration. Washington, DC: U.S. Government Printing Office.

■ Bureaucratic Co-Optation

Bureaucratic co-optation occurs when a given bureaucracy takes over or neutralizes a policy or procedure for the bureaucracy's own purposes, particularly through absorption or assimilation into established, long-standing bureaucratic structures and practices. As applied to correctional grievance procedures, co-optation has proceeded subtly and, in most instances, without any grand design or overarching intent. Nonetheless, the structures and practices into which grievance procedures have been absorbed were often contributing to the very issues being grieved. The "solution" became part of the "problem." As such, some correctional agencies have inadvertently undermined the prospects for grievance mechanisms to encourage longer term resolution of disputes by improving conditions and practices.

It is instructive to examine the roots of this. The introduction of grievance procedures is but a small component of an historical trend toward the professionalization and bureaucratization of corrections.[34] A vast punishment infrastructure has emerged over the past two centuries, with extensive chains of authority and divisions of specialization and expertise. Increasingly, social control is achieved in subtle, less overtly repressive ways through objective-looking, managerial policies and procedures, the very delineation of which is self-legitimating.[35] Introduction of grievance procedures into the prison stemmed from and contributed to this bureaucratization. Bearing in mind Rothman's concept of convenience, it is not hard to see why these procedures are responsive to the needs, and shaped by the dynamics, of the bureaucracies of which they are part.

The limited research available demonstrates that grievance procedures are shaped by bureaucratic prerogatives. For example, Bordt and Musheno studied a pre-PLRA state grievance policy and concluded that "the implementation process, when dominated by bureaucratic interests, can transform a procedure intended to resolve disputes into a means of increasing social control. . . ."[36] These researchers found that correctional personnel manipulated implementation of the grievance procedure, redefining its goals to make their work easier and redirecting actions to fit the interests of the organization in exercising control. Findings like this assume added significance in the post-PLRA era given that prison officials, now motivated by the exhaustion requirement, typically implement grievance procedures that are demanding and cumbersome for prisoners to navigate.[37] Based on a study of California's post-PLRA grievance procedures, Swearingen concluded that the "procedures dramatically alter the focus of the complaint process from one concerned primarily with the declaration of rights and wrongdoings to one focused on a prison's organizational goal of resolving disputes quickly and to its own advantage."[38] Swearingen conceptualized these procedures as an internal mechanism of legal compliance that allows prisons to regulate themselves, except that the compliance is typically more cosmetic than real. And although Hepburn and Laue generally reported positive findings about the grievance procedure they studied, the researchers also discovered "many instances in which clearly indicated and important policy changes were aborted by the tendency to view grievances independently and resolve them case by case," as opposed to the alternative of promoting systematic changes aimed at the source of problems.[39] As a concrete illustration, consider a successful grievance that: (a) results in a refund of $25 that was accidentally deducted from a prisoner's account but (b) fails to address the inadequate technology and/ or staffing pattern that routinely leads to such errors. (See column 4 of Table 30-1 as well as the next section for other concrete illustrations of co-optation.)

The most fundamental question is not whether a grievance procedure can allow the communication of complaints, conciliate disgruntled prisoners, avert lawsuits, or even resolve individual disputes. If grievance procedures are to accomplish any of these things effectively over the long term, the more fundamental issue, as Hepburn and Laue suggest, is the extent to which these procedures have potential to advance resolution of conditions, policies, or practices that are demonstratively problematic and at the root of commonly grieved issues. Ultimately, neither prisoners nor correctional line staff, the parties usually affected most directly in grievances, will accord much legitimacy to a procedure lacking the capacity for advancing such resolution. This is why Branham's analysis concludes that it is essential to link prison grievance processes to problem-solving mechanisms and services.[40]

It is not necessary that all, or even most, grievances produce final systematic resolutions; such an expectation is unrealistic. Some grievances will be frivolous, and others will be totally or partially unsuccessful though having some merit. Even among successful grievances that are granted in full, many address isolated or individual issues. It is important that these be resolved. But for those grievances that address systemic problems such as inadequate policy, unfair practices, or dangerous conditions, a finding of merit must lead to systemic action/resolution, rather than mere individual resolution. In any grievance situation, there is need to fairly balance the concerns of prisoners with the needs of the facility to expend limited resources efficiently and manage masses of people in a way that preserves order and safety. Nevertheless, the potential has to exist for any given nonfrivolous grievance to bring the resolution of problematic issues closer; otherwise, the process risks being perceived as a farce. In terms of co-optation, then, the major question is whether the values and motives underpinning the operation of a grievance procedure will (a) prioritize the control interests of the correctional bureaucracy, more or less irrespective of the merits of a given grievance or (b) strive toward fairly balancing the interests of all parties involved, thus moving closer to resolution of key issues.

■ Grievance Processes and Prison Culture

In addition to the correctional bureaucracy, grievance procedures are also wedged between the cultural dynamics of correctional facilities, including both staff and prisoner subcultures. This has significance for any complete understanding of grievance processes.

Staff Subcultural Dynamics

In most facilities, especially larger ones, a staff member(s) is assigned to coordinate grievances, and by definition, such staff members face role conflict. On the one hand, prisoners expect a grievance officer to handle complaints fairly and expeditiously. Among other things, this means recognizing that grievances have potential for legitimacy and maintaining a balanced, neutral posture when conducting investigations and carrying out the process; simply, this means to avoid siding with "the man" in an *a priori* way. Behavior short of this on the coordinator's part is likely to arouse cynicism about the grievance process among prisoners and engender a search for alternative, possibly illegitimate, means to address issues.

On the other hand, a grievance coordinator often faces expectations from his or her coworkers to defer to prison officials—to err on their side—and this can permeate the process with bias, especially in the eyes of prisoners. A central feature of staff subculture in some facilities is a disparaging perception of prisoners as morally inferior.[41] Furthermore, some staff are suspicious of any prisoner grievance from the outset and are reluctant to grant credence.[42] Even a hint of appearing to take the prisoner's side can be equated with disloyally undermining security or other institutional objectives and falling prey to convict manipulation, both of which can produce disrespect and ostracism in the staff subculture. In addition, institutional administrators may occasionally pressure grievance coordinators to curtail the sheer number of grievances, or at least the number consuming larger amounts of time and moving to higher levels of formality and appeal. Administrators may also censor the written responses of coordinators. Analogous to the situation with prisoners, then, behavior on the part of the grievance coordinator that falls short of these expectations can promote staff cynicism about the grievance process.

Grievance coordinators respond to these competing pressures in various ways. Although the factual circumstances surrounding a grievance are certainly important, a simplistic strategy of letting the facts "speak for themselves" is unlikely to prove viable, at least not on a consistent basis. Facts must be interpreted, and almost invariably, the interests of the interpreter will skew interpretation, particularly when (as is typical of grievances) the contested issues are emotionally charged. No doubt a good number of coordinators see their ultimate allegiance as resting with coworkers and administrators, and they behave accordingly using any of a number of subtle strategies. For example, a coordinator may identify a relatively insignificant or weakly supported component of a grievance and respond to this in isolation of the substance of the complaint as a whole. Depending on the situation, this may preoccupy, distract, discourage, placate, or confuse the grievant, but the effect is to complicate an appeal because the grievant must address the tangential response in addition to the underlying substance. (This is why some jailhouse lawyers advise grievants to state complaints in a single, carefully worded sentence.) By contrast, a coordinator might respond by trying to see that each party to a grievance gets some of what they are seeking (i.e., by trying to please everyone to some degree). Of course, the risk here is that, in the absence of exceptional tact and skilled communication, there is a good chance that all parties to the grievance will feel slighted and grow cynical.

Prisoner Subculture

The prisoner subculture is also a potent force affecting the grievance process. Substantial barriers exist to a prisoner choosing to initiate a formal grievance or follow through on one that has been initiated. Some barriers stem from prisoner characteristics, such as high rates of illiteracy, or from institutional practices, such as high levels of segregation that physically restrict the capacity to pursue a grievance. But some of the most important barriers emanate from the dynamics of the prisoner subculture.

As mentioned earlier, prisoners may share cynicism about the fairness and efficacy of the process. The reasons are not difficult to appreciate. Prisoners tend to play even less of a role than line staff in formulating, operating, and reviewing grievance procedures. Participation is often sharply curtailed. Furthermore, accountability of the process may be lacking. Although typically there is some form of oversight from internal sources (e.g., a warden or state director), there is rarely oversight from objective external sources (e.g., a neutral citizen review board) and attempts to achieve oversight commonly meet resistance from institutional officials. With the PLRA exhaustion requirement, the sentiment has become widespread among many prisoners that the grievance system is simply a roadblock to the courts—a stall or deflection device that, although superficial and pointless, casts a guise of bureaucratic legitimacy and fairness.

Another subcultural barrier is fear of retaliation from staff and other prisoners.[43] Grievants or prospective ones may be concerned about staff retaliation, which can assume such forms as transfers to a less desirable facility or living unit; disciplinary action for filing a grievance judged to be groundless; extra cell shakedowns; being set up for problems with staff or other prisoners; reassignment to a less desired job; and encroachment on visitation, phone, commissary, or other privileges. In the world of the prison, staff retaliation can take very subtle and covert forms as it plays out in the context of interaction between the staff and prisoner subcultures. Robertson argues that in making prison grievance procedures prominent, the PLRA exhaustion requirement gives correctional staff greater incentive to retaliate against grievants. Grievances are typically filed by persons seeking redress (potentially judicial relief) for misconduct by prison officials, and retaliation (or the threat thereof) may help dissuade prisoners from the formal grievance path. Robertson contends that retaliation is integral to the staff subculture in many institutions and can be a normative reaction to a grievance.[44]

A significant portion of grievable issues in any correctional facility stem not from the actions of staff, but from the actions of other prisoners. Yet filing a formal grievance (or even informing a staff member) can land the aggrieved party a "snitch" label. Such a label invites all sorts of victimization (e.g., harassment, antagonism, extortion, robbery, and assaults ranging from minor through deadly). Negative treatment can come from the prisoner who was the target of the grievance, from the general population, or from a subgroup thereof (e.g., a clique). A written grievance regulation prohibiting retaliation, even one vigorously enforced and with harsh penalties (though this is seldom the case), carries little practical weight in the face of the daily realities of the prison culture. Prison culture largely dictates the levels of violence in prisons.[45] The prisoner subculture has its own norms and informal mechanisms of social control for addressing interpersonal conflict among prisoners, and given the stigma of the snitch label, these mechanisms are usually preferred over the formal procedures of the institution.

Large areas of disputed terrain are off limits to the grievance process in the prisoner subculture. Even targeting a staff member with a grievance can be considered "dry" or indirect snitching, if doing so could have adverse consequences for other convicts or their close associates. And if such a grievance is filed, the grievant might word it so that a collective issue is individualized, in the hope of not negatively affecting other prisoners. However, staff members could respond by finding in favor of the grievant and then take actions that adversely affect other prisoners, thereby prompting retaliation intended to teach the grievant a "lesson" in doing time.

Thus, all grievances, whether pondered or actually filed by prisoners, play out against the interaction of the staff and prisoner subcultures and the organizational bureaucracy. As Douglas concluded based on comparison of various prison grievance mechanisms in England/Wales, Sweden, and Denmark:

> In all three countries . . . existing mechanisms . . . seem unsatisfactory. Internal mechanisms are not independent and so may not be regarded as fair by the aggrieved prisoner. They may be dealt with more from the standpoint of upholding authority than from achieving a fair result. Bureaucratic or peer-group concerns may take priority over the merits of the case.[46]

Or as Cohen articulates in more rhetorical terms: "When you take a group already cynical about legal process and run them through . . . grievance procedures that are cumbersome and irrational, the cynicism is simply hardened. Does that matter? Only if one strives to change attitudes and behavior."[47]

■ Conclusion

Although literature on correctional grievance procedures has been sparse in recent decades, previous writers have identified several potential benefits, some quite general and others more specific, of having an effective procedure.[48] Without an attempt at prioritization, potential benefits include

- Promotion of justice and fairness
- Promotion of order, security, and stability in correctional facilities
- Alleviation of tension, frustration, and hostility
- Contribution to a more civilized, more humanized, and less totalitarian environment
- Reduced individual and group violence
- Improved communication between prisoners and staff
- Reduced opposition between the prisoner and staff subcultures
- Enhanced monitoring of conditions, practices, and policies so as to better identify problems that need attention from authorities and to prompt improvements
- Timely resolution of disputes and conflict between individuals and groups
- Systematic and long-term improvements in conditions, practices, and policies
- Reduced litigation
- Provision of documentation of issues surrounding disputes and problems
- Gaining of experience/skills in constructive resolution of conflict for prisoners and staff
- Promotion of consistency in the approach to resolving conflict

Although there is obviously some overlap here, it is clear that there are significant advantages to prisoners, line staff, middle and upper management, and the public if effective mechanisms are in place. The fundamental and ultimate goal is to advance resolution of problems that give rise to grievances.[49] All parties benefit to the extent that this goal is achieved. Although thousands of grievances are filed each year in the nation's correctional facilities, unfortunately the goal of resolving underlying problems remains unattained by most grievance systems.

This chapter implies two directions for improving grievance procedures and their capacity to remedy underlying problems. First, the trend toward bureaucratic co-optation should be recognized and reversed because it has compromised the potential of grievance procedures to resolve problems. The task is formidable but can be approached by revisiting and fully, rather than selectively, implementing the model essential principles as originally suggested in 1975 (see column 1 of Table 30-1). Most important in this respect are (a) opportunities for meaningful participation by line staff and prisoners in the development, implementation, and operation of procedures in order to promote buy-in from both groups and (b) provisions for objective independent review of grievances by parties external to the correctional system, what Swearingen calls a neutral arbiter (e.g., courts or citizen review boards) to promote accountability.[50] Concomitantly, there must be short, enforceable time limits for correctional officials so as to circumvent problems associated with undue delays. Such time limits have obvious advantages for prisoners but can also benefit staff. For example, Collins points to potential for staff liability under the Eighth Amendment if lengthy grievance processes are judged to constitute deliberate indifference to prisoner health care.[51] Also, rather than having overly restrictive limitations on the types of issues than can be grieved, if the procedure is to be meaningful, it must apply to a broad range of issues.[52] Likewise, if the types of remedies the procedure can provide are too restricted, systematic improvements of conditions, practices, and policies will be precluded.

The second direction is more encompassing. The capacity of the staff and prisoner subcultures to subvert the efficacy of grievance procedures must be recognized and diminished. Concrete steps must be taken to overcome the various disincentives presently found in these subcultures to participate in fair grievance processes. Accomplishing the first direction outlined above would certainly help accomplish this one too, but ultimately, norms pertaining to violence and other kinds of victimization in the prison culture must be changed. Although both directions are formidable, unless they are pursued, the potential benefits of grievance procedures will remain unrealized.

Chapter Resources

DISCUSSION QUESTIONS

1. What three interrelated trends gave rise to the rapid adoption of prisoner grievance procedures in the 1970s, and why?
2. How did the passage of the Prison Litigation Reform Act increase the significance of grievance procedures?
3. What are the two most important principles of model grievance procedures, and why are they rarely incorporated intact in actual grievance procedures?
4. How does bureaucratic co-optation influence the functioning of grievance procedures?
5. How is prison culture related to the functioning of grievance procedures?

ADDITIONAL RESOURCES

Alderstein, D. M. (2001). In need of correction: The iron triangle of the Prison Litigation Reform Act. *Columbia Law Review, 101*, 16–81.

Fathi, D. (2009). *No Equal Justice: The Prison Litigation Reform Act in the United States.* Retrieved from http://www.hrw.org/reports/2009/06/16/no-equal-justice-0

Slutsky, A. (2004). Totally exhausted: Why a strict interpretation of 42 USC 1997e(a) unduly burdens courts and prisoners. *Fordham Law Review, 73*, 22–89.

NOTES

1. Austin, J., Bruce, M., Carroll, L., McCall, P., & Richards, S. (2001). The use of incarceration in the United States. *Critical Criminology, 10*(1), 17–41; Clear, T. R. (1994). *Harm in American penology: Offenders, victims, and their communities.* Albany, NY: State University of New York Press; Clear, T. R. (1997). Ten unintended consequences of the growth in imprisonment. In E. J. Latessa, A. Holisinger, J. W. Marquart, & J. R. Sorensen (Eds.), *Correctional contexts: Contemporary and classical readings* (2nd ed., pp. 71–82). Los Angeles, CA: Roxbury; Garland, D. (2001). *The culture of control: Crime and social order in contemporary society.* Chicago, IL: University of Chicago Press; Irwin, J. (2005). *The warehouse prison: Disposal of the new dangerous class.* Los Angeles, CA: Roxbury; Irwin, J., & Austin, J. (1997). *It's about time: America's imprisonment binge* (2nd ed.). Belmont, CA: Wadsworth; Robertson, J. A. (2006). The Rehnquist court and the "turnerization" of prisoners' rights. *New York City Law Review, 10*, 97; Simon, J. (2007). *Governing through crime: How the war on crime transformed American democracy and created a culture of fear.* New York, NY: Oxford University Press; Simon, J. (2000). The "society of captives" in the era of hyper-incarceration. *Theoretical Criminology, 4*(3), 285–308.
2. Cripe, C. A., & Pearlman, M. G. (2005). *Legal aspects of corrections management* (2nd ed.). Boston, MA: Jones & Bartlett; Cole, G. F., & Silbert, J. E. (1984). Alternative dispute-resolution mechanisms for prisoner grievances. *The Justice System Journal, 9*, 306–324; Ducker, W. M. (1983/1984). Dispute resolution in prisons: An overview and assessment. *Rutgers Law Review, 36*, 145–178; Hepburn, J. R., & Laue, J. H. (1980). Prisoner redress: Analysis of an inmate grievance procedure. *Crime & Delinquency, 26*, 162–179; Keating, J. M. Jr., McArthur, V. A., Lewis, M. K., Sebelius, K. G., & Singer, L. R. (1975). *Grievance*

mechanisms in correctional institutions. Washington, DC: U.S. Government Printing Office; Wall II, A. T. (1999). Inmate grievance procedures. In P. M. Carlson & J. S. Garrett (Eds.), *Prison and jail administration: Practice and theory* (pp. 268–274). Gaithersburg, MD: Aspen.

3. American Correctional Association. (2003). *Standards for adult correctional institutions* (4th ed.). Lanham, MD: Author; Baker, J. E. (1985). *Prisoner participation in prison power*. Metuchen, NJ: Scarecrow Press; Cripe and Pearlman (2005); Wall (1999).

4. Bordt, R. L., & Musheno, M. C. (1988). Bureaucratic co-optation of informal dispute processing: Social control as an effect of inmate grievance policy. *Journal of Research in Crime and Delinquency, 25*, 7–26.

5. Bordt and Musheno (1988).

6. Rothman, D. J. (1980). *Conscience and convenience: The asylum and its alternatives in progressive America*. Boston, MA: Little, Brown.

7. Ducker (1983/1984).

8. Baker (1985); Ducker (1983/1984).

9. Baker (1985); Bordt and Musheno (1988). Also see Bernstein, B. (1976). The Federal Bureau of Prisons administrative grievance procedure: An effective alternative to prisoner litigation? *American Criminal Law Review, 143*, 779–799.

10. Ducker (1983/1984).

11. Keating et al. (1975).

12. Baker (1985).

13. Baker (1985); Hepburn and Laue (1980); Keating et al. (1975).

14. Baker (1985); Ducker (1983/1984); Hepburn and Laue (1980).

15. Baker (1985). Baker errs in listing this in the Fourth United Nations Congress; it was actually the First. The Fourth was held in 1970.

16. Keating et al. (1975, p. 33). The Center for Community Justice was known as the Center for Correctional Justice from its inception in 1971 until the late 1970s.

17. *Civil Rights Act of 1871*, U.S. Code, vol. 42, sec. 1983. (1871); *Ex parte Hull*, 312 U.S. 546 (1941); *Cooper v. Pate*, 378 U.S. 546 (1964). Also see *Monroe v. Pape*, 365 U.S. 167 (1961).

18. Swearingen, V. (2008). Imprisoning rights: The failure of negotiated governance in the prison inmate grievance process. *California Law Review, 96*, 1353–1382.

19. Wall (1999); Bernstein (1976).

20. See The Harvard Law Review Association. (1991). Resolving prisoners' grievances out of court. *Harvard Law Review, 104*, 1309–1329; Goldfarb, R. L., & Singer, L. R. (1973). *After conviction*. New York, NY: Simon and Schuster.

21. It is worth noting that formal grievance procedures were only one administrative mechanism introduced during the 1970s for addressing prisoners' complaints. The ombudsman system was another. Typically, this system involved bringing in an official (or panel) from outside the institution to investigate and review complaints. The individual overseeing the hearing was able to make recommendations for corrective action but was prohibited from recommending any other form of relief. Another mechanism involved the use of a prisoner advisory group or council to review grievances. A group comprised solely of prisoners reviewed all complaints and made recommendations regarding appropriate actions. As with the ombudsman system, recommendations were limited to those entailing corrective action. One of the most commonly utilized mechanisms during this time period was hearing panels. A committee of staff members reviewed complaints. Although these committees were also limited to remedying the situation through corrective action, committees were often empowered to order, rather than simply recommend, such action. Although

the stated purpose of these various mechanisms was to provide a forum for complaint resolution, many of them employed disorganized, informal processes that produced inconsistent and contentious results. Most fell short of achieving their stated aims. See Cole and Silbert (1984). Also see Ducker (1983/1984).

22. Baker (1985); *Civil Rights of Institutionalized Persons Act*, U.S. Code, vol. 42, sec. 1997 (1980).
23. Branham, L. S. (2001). The Prison Litigation Reform Act's enigmatic exhaustion requirement. What it means and what congress, courts, and correctional officials can learn from it. *Cornell Law Review, 86*, 483–545.
24. Branham (2001).
25. J. Fuller (personal communication, August 30, 2011).
26. *Prison Litigation Reform Act of 1995*, U.S. Code, vol. 42, sec. 803 (a) (1996).
27. 42 U.S.C. § 1997e(a).
28. The U.S. Supreme Court has upheld the PLRA exhaustion requirement, even if the remedies available under the grievance system do not allow for the specific remedy being sought by the prisoner filing the grievance. *Booth v. Churner*, 532 U.S. 731 (2001).
29. Branham (2001).
30. McShane, M. D. (2008). *Prisons in America*. New York, NY: LFB Scholarly Publishing; Minor, K. I., Wells, J. B., & Soderstrom, I. R. (2003). Corrections and the courts. In J. Whitehead, J. Pollock, & M. C. Braswell. (Eds.), *Exploring corrections in America* (pp. 61–107). Cincinnati, OH: Anderson.
31. Human Rights Watch. (2009). *No Equal justice: The Prison Litigation Reform Act in the United States*. New York, NY: Author.
32. *Booth v. Churner*, 532 U.S. 731 (2001); *Woodford v. Ngo*, 548 U.S. 81 (2006).
33. Contemporary professional standards for grievance procedures, such as those of the American Correctional Association (ACA), are also dilutions of the model principles. By and large, such standards align more closely with commonly adopted elements (column 3 of Table 30-1) than with model principles (column 2 of Table 30-1). For instance, ACA recommends supervisory review over independent/external review, thereby giving the institution total control over the procedure.
34. Garland, D. (1990). *Punishment and modern society: A study in social theory*. Chicago, IL: University of Chicago Press.
35. Foucault, M. (1979). *Discipline and punish: The birth of the prison*. New York, NY: Vintage.
36. Bordt and Musheno (1988, p. 22). See also Hepburn and Laue (1980).
37. Human Rights Watch (2009).
38. Swearingen (2008, p. 1378).
39. Hepburn and Laue (1980, p. 177).
40. Branham (2001).
41. Irwin (2005).
42. Hepburn, J. R. (1984). The erosion of authority and the perceived legitimacy of inmate social protest: A study of prison guards. *Journal of Criminal Justice, 12*, 579–590.
43. The Commission on Safety and Abuse in America's Prisons. (2006). *Confronting confinement*. New York, NY: Vera Institute of Justice.
44. Robertson, J. E. (2009). One of the dirty secrets of American corrections: Retaliation, surplus power and whistleblowing inmates. *University of Michigan Journal of Law Reform, 42*, 611.
45. The Commission on Safety and Abuse in America's Prisons. (2006).

46. Douglas, G. (1992). Dealing with prisoners' grievances. In M. K. Carlie & K. I. Minor (Eds.), *Prisons around the world: Studies in international penology* (pp. 279–295). Dubuque, IA: Wm C. Brown (quote from p. 293).

47. Cohen, F. (2010). Grievance procedures and futility. *Correctional Law Reporter, 22*(1), 11 (quote from p. 11).

48. Cripe and Pearlman (2005); Cole and Sibert (1984); Ducker (1983/1984); Hepburn and Laue (1980); Keating et al. (1975); Wall (1999).

49. Branham (2001).

50. Swearingen (2008).

51. Collins, B. (2010). Can a grievance system be deliberately indifferent to inmate medical needs? *Correctional Law Reporter, 22*(3), 33.

52. Wall (1999).

Protective Custody

Kevin I. Minor and
Stephen Parson

CHAPTER OBJECTIVES

- Define protective custody and its forms, including differentiation of protective custody from other types of segregation.
- Explain the stigma of protective custody.
- Understand protective custody as a component of the wider prison subculture.
- Discuss the legal considerations pertinent to protective custody.
- Identify the policy implications that emerge from this chapter.

T his chapter addresses several considerations related to protective custody (PC). It defines the term, estimates the number of PC prisoners, and addresses procedural and operational considerations, including entry to, life in, and transition out of PC. It also discusses the effects of segregation and the major legal considerations involved with its use. Finally, this chapter explores PC as a component of the wider prison subculture, acknowledging the need for greater attention to clarifying legal issues and safely transitioning prisoners out of protective status.

■ Defining Protective Custody

First introduced in the 1960s, official PC is defined by the American Correctional Association (ACA) as "a form of separation from the general population for inmates requesting or requiring protection from other prisoners for reasons of health or safety."[1] Officially speaking, PC is a formal custody status assigned to prisoners by staff during classification procedures. Many jurisdictions include an official definition of PC in their statutes or policy documents. Formal PC typically involves specialized, segregated housing for several different types of prisoners. Informally, however, PC can involve prisoners disengaging themselves from threats in the prison environment or staff disengaging certain prisoners through such routine management practices as housing assignments. Informal PC activities do not necessitate a formal PC designation.

Table 31-1 outlines elements of PC as well as similar types of segregation including disciplinary segregation (whereby those prisoners believed to have violated rules are isolated from the general population as discipline or punishment) and administrative segregation (whereby continued presence of the prisoner in the general population might pose a serious threat to security). Although terminology varies across jurisdictions, this threefold distinction is representative of most prison systems. PC is sometimes treated as a subset of administrative segregation, but the two are actually quite distinct. Administrative segregation is a generalized tool of management and control that many prison officials readily embrace and many prisoners perceive as enhancing their status. PC is a strategy targeted specifically around protection that officials and prisoners perceive in more distasteful terms.

Application

Prison staff determine who is placed in formal PC. At the same time, the prison subculture exerts considerable influence over PC assignments by fomenting aggressive and other negative behaviors toward certain types of prisoners that can culminate in PC placement. The subculture negatively skews the official definition of PC by attaching stigma to the status itself and to those prisoners (and even staff) assigned to PC.

PC is much more than official transfers to a PC unit. Informal PC status is more subjective, and less readily defined and identified, than formal PC. The key distinction between informal PC and other protective activities undertaken by prisoners and staff is that informal PC involves stigmatizing change in custody or prisoner activities. Unofficial PC status is achieved through some stigmatizing modification in the custody or activities of an individual prisoner other than placement in a formal PC unit or program. Although it may or may not be regarded as a formal custody change by staff, the change is no less real in effects because the lifestyle and movement patterns of the prisoner are altered significantly.

Self- or Staff-Imposed Protective Custody

Not every action taken by staff or prisoners to promote protection qualifies as PC. Dick Franklin argues that many prisoners, instead of seeking official PC status, take alternative protective actions within the prison subculture—a "self-imposed protective custody."[2] This includes

- Intentionally breaking institutional rules to receive administrative or disciplinary segregation (commonly known as "taking a fall")

TABLE 31-1 Types of Segregation

Question	Disciplinary Segregation	Administrative Segregation	Protective Custody
Who typically assigns the prisoner to segregation?	A standing disciplinary committee or hearing officer	An ad hoc committee or single official with the authority to do so	A standing classification committee
What is the process?	Relatively open, formal hearing with rules of evidence, witnesses, and so on, and the prisoner present; focus on specific action or occurrence alleged to have taken place; result is a finding of fact or determination of guilt; availability of a standard appeals process	Relatively closed informal hearing or discussion often without the prisoner present; focus on ongoing or emerging general circumstances; result is a finding of likelihood or probability of what might take place if segregation is not imposed; appeals process is nonstandard or nonexistent	Prisoners may request PC placement and have the request reviewed by prison officials; alternatively officials may recommend PC status, but prisoners often have an option to sign a waiver and opt for non-PC status
What is the length of segregation?	Definite or set period	Indefinite period	Indefinite period
Where is the prisoner segregated?	The disciplinary segregation unit, or in prison argot, "the hole"	Any of several secure units or facilities (e.g., separate administrative segregation unit, disciplinary segregation unit, protective custody unit, county jail, out-of-jurisdiction unit)	A separate protective custody unit or within a larger segregation unit housing non-PC segregated prisoners
Why is the prisoner segregated?	As punishment for a specific rule infraction to which the prisoner has admitted or for which he or she has been convicted; actual outcome is specific (i.e., intended deprivations and punishment)	To disrupt or prevent an ongoing or potential security threat; actual outcomes are variable and general (e.g., prevention of security threats, unintended or intended punishment of select prisoners)	For protection against victimization; actual outcomes include possible temporary protection, unintended deprivation, short- and long-term stigmatization in the eyes of both staff and other prisoners, as well as a potentially higher likelihood of future victimization

- Organizing activities to avoid interaction with the person or group believed to be a threat (commonly known as "PC-ing up")
- Establishing patterns of close affiliation with staff, as in the case of certain trustees (commonly known as "hangin' on the man's leg")
- Establishing affiliation with other individual prisoners or groups of prisoners, such as a gang (commonly known as "cliquing up")
- Seeking protection themselves through aggression directed at the perceived threat (commonly known as "spinning out")

Only the first three of these constitute informal PC in that each is a disengaging custodial modification carrying stigma in the prison subculture. Stigma attaches from the fact that each entails retreat from the general population and the perceived threats therein (despised signs of weakness in a hyper-macho prison subculture), as opposed to confronting threats directly. By contrast, "cliquing up" and "spinning out" are engaging or confrontational adaptations to perceived threat that signify strength and, as such, do not carry stigma in the subculture.

Similarly, staff frequently take initiatives to promote protection of prisoners that do not entail official PC designations. Some of these (e.g., increased surveillance of a particular area, altering population movement patterns) involve management of the aggregate population and, as such, are not viewed as informal PC in the subculture. But other initiatives disengage or remove individual prisoners from "the mix" in the general population (e.g., transfer of an assault victim to another facility, altered housing arrangements for a prisoner deemed vulnerable to victimization) and, therefore, are viewed as informal PC and stigmatized as such. Staff-initiated informal PC takes place when an individual prisoner is managed in a way that gives other prisoners the impression of special handling for purposes of protection. These points are summarized in **Table 31-2**.

Stigma

Prison subculture applies a kind of normative, universal stigmatization to PC status, which includes a lack of social acceptance and diminished respect from others. Prisoners who formally or informally adopt the PC role are perceived as subhuman and treated accordingly in the subculture. The "PC punk" label, as it is commonly perceived, can set the stage for the PC prisoner to be the target of extreme degradation and violence.

Although the stigma initially derives from the reason the prisoner acquired PC status (e.g., having entered prison upon conviction of child molestation), an added stigma results from the sheer act of opting for the PC

TABLE 31-2 Illustrative Typology of Protective Activities

Initiating Party	Formal PC	Informal PC	Non-PC Protective Activities
Prisoner	Seeking out PC status on one's own accord	Disengaging adaptations to threats (e.g., avoiding certain areas and/or people, skipping meals or recreation)	Engaging adaptations to perceived threats (e.g., physically attacking the source of the threat)
Staff	Recommending PC during classification activities	Managing individual prisoners to promote protection through disengagement (e.g., individual housing reassignments or transfers for vulnerable prisoners)	Managing prisoners in the aggregate to promote protection (e.g., increased surveillance of particular areas)

label, rendering PC prisoners vulnerable to numerous forms of victimization at the hands of other prisoners and staff.[3] Again, it is important to remember that many protective acts do not entail disengagement of prisoners from the general population and carry no stigma in the prison subculture.

■ Estimating the Number of PC Prisoners

Estimating the prevalence of PC is difficult because it is impossible to know the number of informal PC cases, and terminology differs across jurisdictions. However, estimates range from 6,000 to 8,000 persons in PC nationwide, or approximately 1% of the total prison population.[4] Although data are lacking on unofficial PC and non-PC protective activities, it is safe to conclude that both are far more common in the prison environment than official PC designations and operations.[5]

■ Formal PC Procedures and Operations

At the most basic level, prisoners acquire formal PC status through one of two procedures.

1. Inmates may request the status and then have it granted at the discretion of institutional staff, frequently after having served the staff in the capacity of informant or "snitch" to justify PC placement.
2. Staff members working in the area of classification may decide that a particular prisoner should be housed in PC and classify the prisoner accordingly, although prisoners can typically waive PC status.

Issues surround both of these procedures. PC consumes money and staff time because of the special provisions it entails. Even when a separate PC housing unit is not made available, special arrangements have to be made within whatever segregated housing unit does exist, and many PC prisoners require single cells. Although PC prisoners often live under restrictive and deprived conditions, the same services and programs provided for the general population should be accessible to them, because in theory they are being segregated for protection rather than punishment.

As such, depending on a jurisdiction's laws and policies, as well as space availability, officials often screen requests, under the assumption that a substantiated rationale for PC should exist. It is clear that some prisoners who might benefit from PC are reluctant to seek it. They may see the designation of PC status as incapable of guaranteeing protection—as actually increasing the risk of harm through the stigma of the label—or they may see it as incompatible with their sense of who they are and the norms of the prison subculture.[6]

What may be more difficult is to determine whether all prisoners who request PC belong there. For example, there may not be a genuine and serious threat against the person making the request, the requestor may be attempting to achieve some outcome besides safety (e.g., a one-person cell and greater solitude or a transfer to another facility), or the requestor may even pose a threat to prisoners in the PC population. On the contrary, prison officials traditionally have been concerned that denial of requests for protection may increase their legal liability.

The challenge for staff is to balance liability concerns against the need to weed out illegitimate requests. But genuine threats can be difficult to discern. In some situations, certain prisoners are identified as "marks" by other prisoners who wager bets on who can drive their mark to check in to PC first, making it difficult to distinguish genuine and serious threats from manipulations posing little real or long-term threat to safety. In addition, staff can actually heighten a prisoner's vulnerability to victimization, and potentially their own legal liability, by insisting that prisoners who ask to enter PC first act as informants about certain illicit activities of other prisoners or even divulge (snitch) everything they know about illicit activities in the subculture as a means of establishing the threat. In such instances, some prisoners will exaggerate, embellish, or outright fabricate information to make their case for a threat and to be taken seriously, especially when staff press to know more and more.

Equally important issues are associated with a decision by staff to classify a prisoner as PC. This decision can produce enormous stress and anxiety for prisoners who view the status of PC as stigmatizing them and rendering them more vulnerable to harm over the long term. These prisoners may take the fact that staff have recommended them for PC as proof of their vulnerability.[7] Prisoners who object strongly to a PC housing assignment can become difficult to manage, so in most places, they can waive PC status. Even if a prisoner has no angst or objection to a PC assignment, there is still the difficulty of accurately determining whether he or she should be classified as PC, as there are few objective, empirically established guidelines to follow. As Austin observes, external classification systems are much more advanced than internal ones, and PC is an internal classification matter (i.e., it involves deciding where a prisoner will be housed *within* a specific institution rather than deciding to which institution *across* the jurisdiction the person will be sent).[8] Finally, there is the possibility of staff abusing the PC status. For example, in an effort to gain some kind of needed cooperation from a prisoner in the general population, staff may threaten the prisoner with a transfer to PC (and its associated stigma) in hopes of coercing cooperation.

Given the difficulties of internal classification and the issues discussed above, most institutions with PC units end up with a diverse population in those units. A given unit may contain persons vulnerable to various victimizations (e.g., psychological abuse and manipulation, economic exploitation, sexual assault, physical assault) as a result of their

- Physical attributes (e.g., perceived to be weak, frail, or otherwise incapable of defending themselves)
- Mental attributes (e.g., mentally ill/unstable, low functioning)[9]
- Behaviors, especially those that violate subcultural norms (e.g., snitching, failure to pay debts, getting in someone else's business)
- Crime categories (e.g., crimes against children, sex crimes, anything perceived to be "freakish" or "unnatural")

PC units can also contain various other individuals, such as those seeking to manipulate special privileges (e.g., a single cell or transfer to a more desirable facility) or those seeking to gain access to someone in PC for purposes of retaliation.

Such diversity can present serious management challenges within the PC unit itself. The problem may be compounded when PC prisoners are housed in or close to a larger administrative or disciplinary segregation unit that houses predatory prisoners.

Limited research has been conducted on the distinguishing characteristics of those entering PC.[10] A Missouri study compared PC and non-PC prisoners and demonstrated that PC prisoners exhibited greater deficiencies on measures of physical, psychological, and social functioning. PC prisoners were found to be serving longer sentences, and a disproportionately high number had been convicted of sex crimes and homicide.[11] However, a Canadian study by Wormith et al. uncovered more similarities than differences between these groups.[12] Wormith et al. did find more evidence of substance abuse and mental disorder among those in PC, and sex offenses were also more common. Furthermore, PC prisoners had been exposed to more aggression in the general population, were significantly more fearful, and held more negative perceptions of treatment received from staff. Another Canadian study by Zinger et al. also uncovered greater psychological problems among segregated prisoners.[13]

Living in PC

The conditions under which PC prisoners live vary widely across jurisdictions (and even within them). An institution may have a separate PC unit or may house PC prisoners as part of a larger segregation unit that contains administrative and/or disciplinary cases. Where separate PC units exist, they are typically small, averaging fewer than 50 persons. Either dormitory or cellblock living space may be provided.[14]

PC prisoners need maximum-security protection irrespective of their own individual custody levels assigned at classification.[15] For this reason, a low-custody PC prisoner who presents little threat to anyone, but is nonetheless at high risk of being victimized, may live under conditions similar to those for a high-custody segregation prisoner who poses significant threats to other prisoners or staff. As a general principle, ACA standards (which many institutions attempt to follow for accreditation purposes) hold that "inmates in PC should be allowed to participate in as many as possible of the programs afforded the general population, providing such participation does not threaten institutional security."[16] In addition to having access to programs like mental health, religion, and education, PC prisoners should generally receive services and privileges (e.g., food, hygiene, medical, phone, mail, recreation) that, although not necessarily identical to those provided the general population, are as comparable as possible, absent a compelling security rationale.

The reality is that enormous variations in conditions exist across institutions. Like other policies and procedures, the ACA standards leave much leeway for staff to justify PC conditions that differ appreciably from conditions found in the general population. Moreover, despite some exceptions, the standards tend to treat all segregated populations as a single category for purposes of specifying conditions, meaning that there is minimal room for distinguishing PC prisoners from those in disciplinary segregation. This contributes to the fact that PC prisoners have been reported to live under conditions that are often far more restrictive and depriving than those found in the general population.[17]

On a related note, some researchers have reported that PC populations experience negative stereotyping and treatment, not only at the hands of other prisoners, but also staff.[18] Where negative attitudes and treatment are found on the part of staff, these may arise from various issues.

- Stigmas attached to the types of crimes for which many PC prisoners have been incarcerated
- The problem behaviors of these prisoners in the general population that culminated in their seeking or being assigned to PC
- A perception that some prisoners are in PC in order to manipulate special privileges
- A general demeanor toward PC prisoners as weak and inferior
- The ongoing challenges posed by daily interactions and work with PC populations

In summary, PC prisoners may experience a double dose of negative bias—one from fellow prisoners and the other from staff—with each one compounding and reinforcing the other.

This is not to say that life in PC is entirely or universally negative. Some prisoners derive genuine protection from such a placement, and evidence has been reported that many individuals feel safer and experience less stress in PC.[19] In addition, some prefer the relative solitude and tranquility.[20] At the same time, however, it is clear that some (but certainly not all) PC units experience a disproportionately high number of problems. These can include psychological breakdown among prisoners (resulting in such things as suicide attempts, self-mutilations, and psychotic symptoms), physical and verbal attacks directed toward other prisoners and staff, group disturbances, fire setting, and property destruction, as well as sexual assaults and pressure for sexual favors.[21] Although such problems derive in part from the peculiar mix of prisoners found in PC, they can also derive from excessive idleness and a paucity of services and programming.[22]

Transition from PC

Stays in PC range from very brief to permanent. Prison classification and casework officials make decisions about the length of stay. Prisoners may transition from PC to the outside world, to another institution or community-based facility, or to the general population in the same prison.

Although prison officials normally hope to transition as many prisoners as possible out of PC because of the drain on resources, such transitions are sometimes inadvisable. Regardless of the setting to which the person is transitioning, an important consideration is the extent to which threats to the person's safety exist or persist in that setting. These may be threats that have carried over from the time preceding PC placement or new ones that have emerged for reasons at least partly related to the PC stay. The fact is that many PC prisoners have exhibited specific behaviors deemed highly offensive in the prison subculture (e.g., sex crimes on the outside, failing to pay debts, snitching), and the mere act of entering PC is regarded as offensive as well.

Contempt for persons in PC can be so intense that members of the general population who do not capitalize on an opportunity to victimize a PC inmate may end up endangering themselves. Despite the potential gravity of this issue, few jurisdictions have been found to have systematic programs for transitioning PC prisoners.[23] Instead, transition efforts seem to be unsystematic and grafted onto such extant practices as counseling, classification reviews, security investigations, and prisoner transfers.[24] Far more attention appears to have been directed to deciding who belongs in PC than to deciding how to transition prisoners to a safe environment following PC.

Yet if the goal is really to provide protection, neglecting transition is a serious mistake, especially given the rather elaborate informal systems of prisoner communication that exist, not just within and across institutions, but also with the outside world. It is obvious enough how prisoners doing time in the same institution could easily learn of a prisoner's impending return from PC to the general population. But prisoners hoping to victimize those coming out of PC (or hoping to have them victimized by others) can communicate with friends and associates housed in facilities to which former PC inmates will be transitioning. They can also communicate with potential victimizers on the streets. Elaborate gang networks are hardly a prerequisite for all this to take place. Underestimation of the prisoner subculture in this respect can result in death or serious injury to a person transitioning from PC to another environment.

■ Effects of PC

In principle, it is difficult to disagree with the assertion that a properly administered protection unit can contribute to a more orderly, stable, and humane institutional environment. Positive effects of PC include protection from victimization, feeling safer, and experiencing less stress. However, this section focuses on some of the negative, often unintended, consequences of PC, especially with regard to its associated stigma, because stigmatization lies at the crux of many of the negative outcomes associated with PC.

The negative effects of PC range from the most infamous and extreme to the subtle and sometimes unrecognized. At the infamous end are events that transpired in February 1980 at the Penitentiary of New Mexico (La Pinta) at Santa Fe, when an enraged mob of drugged prisoners forced their way into the protection unit and executed a "hit list" of segregated inmates with such objects as metal rods and acetylene torches.[25] At the more subtle, far less publicized end are prisoners who jeopardize parole release by entering PC, in part because their PC status is interpreted as evidence by officials that they are incapable of adjusting to prison.[26] In short, although protective segregation can help shield a prisoner from physical, psychological, economic, and social forms of victimization, it can also contribute to such victimization and, indeed, can lead these forms of victimization to interact with and feed off one another.

Some research has addressed the sociopsychological effects of PC. For example, Brodsky and Scogin uncovered various "psychopathological consequences" (e.g., extreme anxiety, sleep dysfunctions, psychosomatic symptoms, delusional thoughts, depression) among two-thirds of the PC prisoners at two of the institutions studied; PC prisoners in these institutions had little, if any, access to programs and spent most of their time in their cells. However, the researchers found no comparable consequences in a prison that permitted PC prisoners more mobility and access to programs. This suggests that the negative psychological effects of PC are situational and contingent on the particular segregation environment.[27] Zinger et al. found that although those entering segregation displayed more psychological problems than nonsegregated prisoners, there was no evidence of deteriorated psychological functioning after 2 months in segregation.[28] So although certainly a possibility, measurable negative psychological effects are by no means an inevitable outcome of PC.

Owing to their disrespected status, PC prisoners become tagged as easy and deserving marks for general population prisoners seeking to enhance their own status as convicts or unleash pent-up hostilities. Additionally, in many institutions, a general population prisoner who passes an opportunity to intimidate or otherwise victimize a PC prisoner can face serious repercussions from other members of the general population.

On the basis of Erving Goffman's classic study of stigma, PC prisoners may respond to disqualification and stigmatization in several, sometimes overlapping, ways. They may

- Try to correct the source of the stigma, such as by arranging to pay off a gambling debt
- Adopt the unconventional identity implied by the stigma (e.g., admitting that one is weak)
- Use the stigma as an excuse for shortcomings or to gain favors
- Come to view the stigma in beneficial terms and, correspondingly, direct focus to the negative characteristics of those not possessing or approving of it
- Come to avoid contact with peers who lack the stigma
- Approach interaction with nonstigmatized persons with much uncertainty, apprehension, and anticipation of how to act, constantly looking for signs and making adjustments during the course of daily interaction
- Feel that "minor failings or incidental impropriety" are being interpreted by others as further evidence of the stigma; in other words, the stigma can begin to overshadow normal ways of relating to others, resulting in exaggerated acts of "cowering" or "bravado"[29]

Goffman's insights provide a sense of how everyday social interaction patterns and individual identities are shaped around the stigma associated with the PC status. In addition to adversely affecting the way the PC prisoner is perceived by others, PC status can have deleterious effects on the perception of self and accompanying behaviors. Lemert described how initial acts of deviation from a particular set of norms (what he called primary deviance) can, when followed by stigmatizing reactions from others, result in the person gradually slipping into secondary deviance. A person who has undergone such slippage begins to regard him- or herself as deviant and reorganizes life activities accordingly, including the possible commission of further deviance.[30] The process of mortification of self that Goffman sees as typically transpiring in closed institutional settings is likely to be exacerbated for PC prisoners, because they confront double stigmatization—stigmatization from the prison society as well as from the outside society because of their criminal status.[31] The effect can be a radical and long-term alteration of self-perception.

It is worth noting that efforts to undo the stigma of PC status will ordinarily have little, if any, success in prison. To understand why, it is useful to extend Lemert to differentiate between primary and secondary stigmatization. Applied to PC, primary stigmatization attaches to whatever reason(s) a prisoner incurred PC status. But in the prison subculture, PC status in and of itself (whether formal or informal) carries a secondary stigma above and beyond any "transgression" that initially gave rise to it. In short, stigma can act as both cause and effect of the PC status.

■ Legal Considerations

Existing legal precedent is most applicable to formal assignment to PC and conditions/practices therein. Potential legal issues arise when a prisoner is assigned to PC against his or her desire or when a prisoner seeks but is denied protection. As mentioned earlier, often prisoners can waive a PC classification decision if they see PC as less desirable than staying in the general population. However, in some instances, prison officials may be concerned enough about a prisoner's safety and/or their own liability that PC placement is involuntarily imposed. In these situations, the question is whether a prisoner is entitled to due process under the Fourteenth Amendment.

The U.S. Supreme Court has not addressed involuntary PC placement but has set due process precedent on related classification and transfer matters. Prisoners are not constitutionally entitled to due process when facing transfer to another prison in the same jurisdiction or to a prison in a different jurisdiction.[32] Likewise, in the key disciplinary segregation ruling of *Sandin v. Conner*, the Court held that a liberty interest is created (and due process thus required) only when segregation "imposes atypical, significant hardship . . . in relation to the ordinary incidents of prison life" and is outside "the range of confinement to be normally expected." The majority further stated that in the *Sandin* case "disciplinary segregation mirrored those conditions imposed upon inmates in administrative segregation and protective custody."[33] Applying this precedent subsequently, the Court deemed transfer to supermaximum confinement sufficiently atypical to necessitate due process but also held a multilevel review of the classification decision to be adequate.[34] The Court has required significantly greater due process for involuntary transfer from a prison to a mental hospital, owing partly to the stigma such hospitalization carries.[35] Given the above precedent and especially the subjective criteria propagated in *Sandin*, it is difficult to envision constitutional due process being mandated for involuntary PC classifications; this is notwithstanding the stigma of the status and the risk for serious danger during transition out of PC. Exceptions could arise in unlikely situations where authorities are convinced that PC imposes hardships or deprivations significantly greater than "normal" confinement or that it extends sentence length.

Refusing PC to a prisoner who seeks it can open legal risks. There is no right to PC upon request, and some prisoners who request it have illegitimate rationales for doing so. Refusal has constitutional ramification when the requestor confronts a "pervasive risk" of assault, and failure to segregate would deny the prisoner a reasonable measure of safety.[36] This combination represents deliberate indifference by prison officials, the standard for Eighth Amendment cruel and unusual punishment violations.[37] To establish deliberate indifference, prisoners must show that corrections officials did not take reasonable actions "despite . . . knowledge of a substantial risk of serious harm."[38]

Transferring a prisoner facing pervasive risk to the PC unit is a reasonable action to avert risk, but this alone will not guarantee safety. Whether safety ensues depends largely on conditions and practices in PC. For example, Robertson argues that a PC unit does not provide reasonable safety unless there is control of access to the unit, partitioning of the unit population into subgroups as necessary to promote safety (e.g., separation of PC and disciplinary segregation prisoners), sufficient numbers of trained correctional officers, and a physical layout conducive to proactive staff responses to security threats.[39]

As with assignment decision making, questions of Eighth Amendment liability within PC turn on deliberate indifference. The Supreme Court has held that mere staff negligence that results in injury to a prisoner is not actionable under the Fourteenth Amendment's equal protection clause;[40] of course, depending on the laws and policies of a particular jurisdiction, tort liability may attach. Moreover, the deliberate indifference standard is used not only to evaluate claims about safety but for claims about all conditions of confinement in PC (e.g., medical care, programming, sanitation).

As mentioned earlier, compared to general population standards, life in PC is often more restrictive. For example, PC prisoners have challenged restrictions on religious practices, legal services, programming, and exercise.[41] In recent years, the Supreme Court has required that such claims (indeed, all constitutional claims except those involving cruel and unusual punishment and racial segregation) be evaluated using the so-called *Turner* test.[42] Under *Turner*, prisoners who challenge PC restrictions are unlikely to prevail on constitutional grounds where prison officials can demonstrate that the restrictions are reasonably related to legitimate penological interests, paramount of which are institutional order and security. Under *Turner*, courts consider (a) whether there is a valid, rational connection between the disputed practice and a legitimate penological interest; (b) whether there are alternative means available for the prisoner to exercise freedoms; (c) how accommodation of the prisoner might affect staff, other prisoners, and resources; and (d) whether the penological interest could be furthered in a manner less encroaching on prisoner freedoms.[43] It is generally not very challenging for officials to justify restrictions on these grounds, particularly when (as with PC) issues of personal safety are involved.

Correctional staff enjoy qualified immunity, meaning that they cannot be held civilly liable unless they are shown to violate a "clearly established statutory or constitutional right of which a reasonable person would have known."[44] Therefore, it is important for staff to be trained in any statute or regulation concerning PC in the particular jurisdiction and also in the deliberate indifference and *Turner* standards.

■ Conclusion

Three main directions for future policy emerge from this material. First, PC status is a unique one in the prison and jail environment, and the courts need to clarify the major issues surrounding it. At minimum, attention should be directed to clarifying the rights of PC prisoners vis-à-vis those living in the general population, administrative segregation, or disciplinary segregation. Administrators must also consider liability if prisoners who requested and were denied PC status are subsequently harmed. Furthermore, although there is minimal legal guidance concerning formal PC, there is less guidance still regarding staff liability and informal PC.

Second, far greater attention should be given to systematically and safely transitioning prisoners from official PC status to other settings. The ethical obligation to provide protection does not end when a person leaves the protective unit. Indeed, based on what is known about prisoner communication and networking systems, the obligation may only be beginning. Disproportionate attention has been given to the issue of screening people entering PC, to the neglect of those leaving it. Far more is needed in this area by way of research, development of effective procedures, dissemination of information about effective practices through training and publications, and clarification of legal guidelines.

Third, prison subculture must be considered when exploring PC. Treating PC as detached from subcultural norms, values, and practices can promote a false sense of security or protection, both within facilities and across them. The mere fact that a protective unit is needed at all in an institution is symptomatic of problems endemic to the prison environment, especially as regards violent, intimidation, and predatory behavior. When persons are sentenced to institutional environments where safety is so lacking in the general population that they must live in constant fear, it is unreasonable to suppose that a safe haven can exist in those environments, effectively protecting those who need it indefinitely.

Humane imprisonment involves undertaking long-range, and at times expensive or politically unpopular, efforts to change the underlying sources and correlates of prison victimization, to the point that formalized PC becomes largely superfluous.[45] This means finding ways to address issues that are deeply embedded in the prison and its social organization—crowding and the associated competition over resources; problematic race relations; gang formations; illicit sub rosa activities and the control thereof through institutionalized snitch systems; and norms and traditions condoning intimidation, retaliation, and predation, to cite some interrelated examples.

Although there is certainly a place for PC in contemporary prison management, ultimately PC is a band-aid approach to symptoms that reflect the prison subculture and, indeed, the totality of prison environments in the United States. Penologists should avoid becoming so focused on the technical aspects of PC management that they lose sight of the conditions needed to curtail or eliminate its use.

Chapter Resources

DISCUSSION QUESTIONS

1. Why do confined offenders need PC?
2. Should correctional personnel encourage PC status or encourage inmates to try to survive in general population?
3. How would you suggest that correctional officials head off the negative effects of PC or disciplinary status housing?
4. What distinguishes formal PC from informal PC?
5. What steps should be taken to assist inmates transitioning out of PC?

ADDITIONAL RESOURCE

Henderson, J., & Phillips, R. L. (1990). *Protective custody management in adult correctional facilities: A discussion of causes, conditions, attitudes, and alternatives.* Washington, DC: National Institute of Corrections.

NOTES

1. American Correctional Association. (2004). *2004 standards supplement* (p. 318). Lanham, MD: Author.
2. Franklin, D. Protective custody: A window to institution culture. In *Contemporary issues in prison management: Additional readings.* Retrieved September 10, 2007, from http://www.nicic.org/Library/015778.
3. Bowker, L. H. (1980). *Prison victimization.* New York, NY: Elsevier.
4. Austin, J., & McGinnis, K. (2004). *Classification of high-risk and special management prisoners: A national assessment of current practices.* Washington, DC: National Institute of Corrections.
5. Carriere, K. (1989). Protective custody in Canada: A review of research and policy responses. *Canadian Criminology Forum, 10,* 17–25.
6. Toch, H. (1977). *Living in prison: The ecology of survival.* New York, NY: Free Press.
7. Toch, H. (1975). *Men in crisis: Human breakdown in prison.* Chicago, IL: Aldine.
8. Austin, J. (2003). *Findings in prison classification and risk assessment: Prison division—issues in brief.* Washington, DC: National Institute of Corrections.
9. Angelone, R. (1999). Protective custody inmates. In P. Carlson & J. Garrett (Eds.), *Prison and jail administration: Practice and theory* (pp. 226–231). Sudbury, MA: Jones & Bartlett Publishers.
10. Perez, A., & Hageman, M. (1982). Dilemma in protective custody: Some notes. *Journal of Offender Counseling, Services, and Rehabilitation, 7,* 69–78.
11. Pierson, T. (1989). Social and psychological correlates of protective custody (PC) status: A comparison of PCs and Non-PCs. *Journal of Offender Counseling, Services, and Rehabilitation, 14,* 97–120.
12. Wormith, J., Tellier, M., & Gendreau, P. (1988). Characteristics of protective custody offenders in a provincial correctional centre. *Canadian Journal of Criminology, 30,* 39–58.

13. Zinger, I., Wichmann, C., & Andrews, D. (2001). The psychological effects of 60 days in administrative segregation. *Canadian Journal of Criminology, 43*, 47–83.

14. Henderson, J. (1991). *Protective custody management in adult correctional facilities*. Washington, DC: National Institute of Corrections.

15. Gendreau, P., Tellier, M. C., & Wormith, J. S. (1985). Protective custody: The emerging crisis within our prisons? *Federal Probation, 49*, 55–63.

16. American Correctional Association. (1990). *Standards for adult correctional institutions* (3rd ed.). Laurel, MD: Author.

17. Brodsky, S., & Scogin, F. (1988). Inmates in protective custody: First data on emotional effects. *Forensic Reports, 1*, 267–280.

18. Priestley, P. (1980). *Community of scapegoats: The segregation of sex offenders and informers in prisons*. New York, NY: Pergamon.

19. Alarid, L. (2000). Sexual orientation perspectives of incarcerated bisexual and gay men: The county jail protective custody experience. *The Prison Journal, 80*, 80–95.

20. Toch, H. (1977). *Living in prison: The ecology of survival*. New York, NY: Free Press; Wormith, J., Tellier, M., & Gendreau, P. (1988). Characteristics of protective custody offenders in a provincial correctional centre. *Canadian Journal of Criminology, 30*, 39–58.

21. Alarid, L. (2000). Sexual orientation perspectives of incarcerated bisexual and gay men: The county jail protective custody experience. *The Prison Journal, 80*, 80–95; Perez, A., & Hageman, M. (1982). Dilemma in protective custody: Some notes. *Journal of Offender Counseling, Services, and Rehabilitation, 7*, 69–78; Toch, H. (1977). *Living in prison: The ecology of survival*. New York, NY.

22. Brodsky, S., & Scogin, F. (1988). Inmates in protective custody: First data on emotional effects. *Forensic Reports, 1*, 267–280.

23. Austin, J., & McGinnis, K. (2004). *Classification of high-risk and special management prisoners: A national assessment of current practices*. Washington, DC: National Institute of Corrections.

24. Henderson, J. (1991). *Protective custody management in adult correctional facilities*. Washington, DC: National Institute of Corrections.

25. Hirliman, I. (1982). *The hate factory: The story of the new Mexico penitentiary riot*. Agoura, CA: Paisano Publications.

26. Perez, A., & Hageman, M. (1982). Dilemma in protective custody: Some notes. *Journal of Offender Counseling, Services, and Rehabilitation, 7*, 69–78.

27. Brodsky, S., & Scogin, F. (1988). Inmates in protective custody: First data on emotional effects. *Forensic Reports, 1*, 267–280.

28. Zinger, I., Wichmann, C., & Andrews, D. (2001). The psychological effects of 60 days in administrative segregation. *Canadian Journal of Criminology, 43*, 47–83.

29. Goffman, E. (1963). *Stigma: Notes on the management of spoiled identity*. New York, NY: Simon and Schuster, Inc.

30. Lemert, E. (1967). *Human deviance, social problems, and social control*. Englewood Cliffs, NJ: Prentice Hall.

31. Goffman, E. (1961). *Asylums: Essays on the social situation of mental patients and other inmates*. New York, NY: Doubleday.

32. *Meachum v. Fano*, 427 U.S. 215 (1976); *Montanye v. Haymes*, 427 U.S. 236 (1976); *Olim v. Wakinekona*, 461 U.S. 238 (1983).

33. *Sandin v. Conner*, 515 U.S. 472 (1995).

34. *Wilkinson v. Austin*, 545 US. 209 (2005).
35. *Vitek v. Jones*, 445 U.S. 480 (1980).
36. Robertson, J. E. (1987). The Constitution in protective custody: An analysis of the rights of protective custody inmates. *University of Cincinnati Law Review, 56*, 91.
37. *Wilson v. Seiter*, 501 U.S. 294 (1991).
38. *Farmer v. Brennan*, 511 U.S. 825 (1994).
39. Robertson, J. E. (1987). The Constitution in protective custody: An analysis of the rights of protective custody inmates. *University of Cincinnati Law Review, 56*, 91.
40. *Daniels v. Williams*, 474 U.S. 327 (1986).
41. Robertson, J. E. (1987). The Constitution in protective custody: An analysis of the rights of protective custody inmates. *University of Cincinnati Law Review, 56*, 91.
42. *Johnson v. California*, 543 U.S. 400 (2005). Also see Robertson, J. E. (2006). The Rehnquist court and the "turnerization" of prisoners' rights. *New York City Law Review, 10*, 97.
43. *Turner v. Safley*, 482 U.S. 78 (1987).
44. *Harlow v. Fitzgerald*, 457 U.S. 800 (1982).
45. Silberman, M. (1995). *A world of violence: Corrections in America*. Belmont, CA: Wadsworth.

Help me

Preventing Suicide

Daniel W. Phillips III

CHAPTER 32

CHAPTER OBJECTIVES

- Outline the prevalence of suicide in the United States and in its prison populations.
- Explain the correlation between social and individual characteristics and suicide.
- Describe the steps needed to construct a proper correctional suicide prevention and treatment program.

Suicide is a major problem in the United States, claiming more than 38,000 lives per year.[1] Prison suicide rates are only slightly higher, but jails have a suicide rate more than four times that of the U.S. population. Fortunately, jail and prison suicide rates have been dropping significantly for the past 20 years.[2] The U.S. suicide rate for those not incarcerated dropped from the early 1990s to 2000 but then by 2009 rebounded to its previous early 1990s rates.[1]

■ Social and Individual Considerations

Research indicates that the suicide rate is correlated with certain social factors (e.g., race, gender, and age) and individual factors (e.g., mental illness and substance abuse).[3] Sociologists believe that certain demographic factors, such as gender, cause people to experience life differently, to encounter a different number of stressors, and to develop different coping skills. For example, boys may be encouraged more to use guns than girls are, and a boy is therefore more likely to use a gun to end his life than his female counterparts. Girls may invest in interpersonal relationships more than boys do and may therefore have bigger networks of relationships to fall back on when they experience stress, thus decreasing the likelihood that they will commit suicide.[4]

In the United States, males constitute 80% of all completed suicides.[5] In fact, suicide is the eighth leading cause of death for males.[6] Although men are four times more likely than women to complete suicides, women self-report that they attempt suicide three times more often than men.[7] One reason for this great differential may be the specific methods preferred by each gender. Men are more likely to use a firearm, a method of suicide that is more than 90% successful, when they commit suicide.[8]

Race and age are also strongly correlated with completed suicides. Caucasians are twice as likely as African Americans to complete a suicide. Young people (those aged 15–24) have very low rates of death, but suicide is the third leading killer in people of this age group.

In addition, there are many individual suicide risk factors, including:

- History of mental illness
- Substance abuse
- Previous suicide attempts
- Isolation
- Relationship loss
- Feelings of hopelessness
- Physical illness

Individuals may benefit from several protective factors, including:

- Family and community support
- Interpersonal coping skills
- Cultural or religious beliefs that suicide is wrong[9]

Jails and prisons often use suicide checklists to screen inmates when they first arrive, although the checklists can be used at other times as well. The checklists produce a score; if the score breaks a certain threshold, the person is considered to be a suicide risk. A specific correctional suicide checklist called the *Suicide Assessment Manual for Inmates* (SAMI), created by Dr. Patricia A. Zapf, is found in **Exhibit 32-1**. The SAMI checklist asks inmates about their psychiatric and criminal justice involvement backgrounds as well as their current mental health, substance abuse, and suicidal symptoms.[10]

■ Stigma

Religious organizations have differing attitudes toward suicide. Some religions state that suicide leads to eternal damnation, whereas others are careful to treat the deceased and his or her family with the utmost respect.

EXHIBIT 32-1 SUICIDE ASSESSMENT MANUAL FOR INMATES RATING FORM

Name of Inmate: _____

CSC Number: _____

Date of Birth: _____

Name of Assessor: _____

Date: _____

Risk Factors   Rating (0, 1, 2)

1. Marital Status _____
2. History of Drug/Alcohol Abuse _____
3. Psychiatric History _____
4. History of Suicide Attempts _____
5. History of Institutional Suicide Attempts _____
6. Family History of Suicide _____
7. Arrest History _____
8. History of Impulsive Behavior _____
9. High-Profile Crime/Position of Respect _____
10. Current Intoxication _____
11. Other Major Life Problems _____
12. Hopelessness/Excessive Guilt _____
13. Psychotic Symptoms/Thought Disorder _____
14. Depressive Symptomatology _____
15. Stress and Coping _____
16. Social Support _____
17. Recent Significant Loss _____
18. Suicidal Ideation _____
19. Suicidal Intent _____
20. Suicide Plan _____

GRAND TOTAL _____

Notes/Other Concerns:

Imminent Risk of Suicide   H   M   L

Actions to Be Taken

Monitoring Recommended: Y   N

Frequency: 24 hr   15 min

Refer to Mental Health: Y   N

Comments/Other Recommendations:

Time: _____   Date: _____

Assessor's Signature: _____

Source: Zapf, P. A. (2006). *Suicide Assessment Manual for Inmates.* Burnaby, BC. Courtesy of Mental Health, Law, & Policy Institute, Simon Fraser University.

Socially, Americans are still likely to punish the family of a suicide victim. People sometimes shun the victim's family or imply that the family is at fault for the suicide. Sometimes people do not attend the victim's funeral or grieve with the family. Research indicates that some families carry around the grief and guilt of a suicide for generations.[11]

Those who attempt suicide may also be stigmatized. Because the public already has negative ideas about inmates in general, they may look at suicidal inmates as a group not worth saving. Pubic perceptions are important because even a well-designed suicide prevention program will not work if the corrections officers who are supposed to implement it devalue the suicidal person. Suicide prevention programs must focus on suicide stigma reduction and a revaluation of suicidal inmates.

The stigma of suicide combined with the stigma of being incarcerated leaves the suicidal inmate as one highly stigmatized individual. This may explain why saving suicidal inmates' lives has not been a priority in the past. Correctional staff must learn to value inmates' lives so that they can save those who are suicidal.

■ Correlates of Suicide

Past research by the Department of Justice has revealed many correlates of jail and prison suicide. Studies have indicated that small jails (those with fewer than 50 detainees) have a suicide rate five times that of the largest U.S. jails. Males and white people were most likely to kill themselves, as is true in the general U.S. population. Jail suicide rates increased significantly with age, although 18-year-olds also had a high rate of suicide in correctional settings. Although male and female prisoners had similar suicide rates, male jail inmates had a suicide rate 50% greater than female inmates. Jail suicide was concentrated in the first week, but two-thirds of prison suicides took place after the first year.[12] Hanging was the most common suicide method used in jail and prison.[13]

■ Legal Considerations

The legal responsibility of jail and prison staff with respect to inmate suicide depends on the concept of *deliberate indifference*. This concept comes from U.S.C. Title 42, Section 1983, which allows incarcerated people to sue jail and prison workers and officials for deliberately not providing medical treatment such as the kind needed to prevent a suicide. Lawsuits filed under Section 1983 have to meet the deliberate indifference standard, which means that corrections workers must have known that a person was suicidal (possibly from a record of previous suicide attempts or knowledge of a person's serious mental health problems) and did nothing about it. This failure to act or provide treatment must then result in real damage such as a death by suicide or serious impairment from a suicide attempt. Deliberate indifference is a higher standard to meet than mere negligence or even gross negligence. Simply making a mistake is not enough to be sued successfully under Section 1983.[14]

■ Attitudes and Training

In the past, people have viewed suicides as inevitable and therefore unpreventable. However, most people who attempt suicide will never complete it. Sometimes a prisoner attempts suicide in an effort to gain attention but ends up killing himself or herself.

Since the early 1980s, jails and prisons have invested money and time to reduce the number of suicides. Staff members have been trained, and procedures have changed. Staff members ask incoming inmates about suicidal risk factors such as previous suicide attempts and mental health or substance abuse problems. Staff may prevent at-risk inmates from being alone (because more than 80% of all jail and prison inmates who kill themselves do so in their cells) and may refer such inmates to a mental health or substance abuse professional.[15] Smaller jails have partnered with community mental health facilities to provide mental health care, whereas prisons and large jails have hired full-time mental health staff.

Lindsay Hayes of the National Center on Institutions and Alternatives (NCIA) developed a six-point framework for developing a written suicide prevention policy in institutions.[16]

1. *Training*—Jail and prison staff members need to receive training on suicide prevention (as well as CPR and first aid) as they are being trained to become correctional officers. Officers need to understand why it is important to save the life of a person who is suicidal. This needs to be followed up by regular in-service training. Training should include information about suicide and its underlying causes, how to best prevent suicide, and how to intervene should the occasion present itself.

2. *Identification and assessment*—There must be a way of identifying and assessing people who may be suicidal. Corrections officers interview inmates with these surveys and score them based on the number of suicide risk factors. Suicidal persons may be evaluated by someone with clinical training such as a psychiatric nurse or licensed clinical social worker.

3. *Housing*—Solitary confinement, segregation from the general population, and placement in mental health or medical units should be seriously considered for suicidal inmates.

4. *Levels of supervision*—The more suicidal an inmate, the more often he or she should be observed. Some must be observed constantly and others once every few minutes, while others are observed once every 15 minutes. Still controversial is the use of fellow inmates to watch those who may be suicidal in the general population. Suicidal inmates do not do best by themselves. If the inmate has to be removed from the general population, it is still best if he or she is not alone.

5. *Intervention*—Each facility should have a plan to deal with a suicide attempt before an incident occurs. Officers have found themselves in the unenviable situation of watching from outside a cell as an inmate inside a cell dies from self-inflicted wounds. The officer was following rules that stated that no officer should enter a cell alone. Although technically the officer would have been abiding by institution rules, this sort of scenario would be very uncomfortable for jail or prison management to recount during a civil trial.

6. *Follow-up/administrative review*—Every aspect of the suicide incident should be reviewed. All involved personnel, such as the medical staff, mental health staff, corrections officers, and management, should be queried about the incident. Policy should be reevaluated, and the training of those involved in the incident should be examined. Changes should be made based on the results of the review.

■ Program Example: Jail Mental Health Crisis Network

The high rate of suicide in Kentucky jails prompted an investigation in 2002. This crisis was the impetus for needed change. Mental health training is now required for all jail personnel, and legislation funds an innovative program offering a system of care to the state jails. The Jail Mental Health Crisis Network, developed and operated by the Bluegrass Regional MH-MR Board, provides jails the following services:

1. Training for jail personnel on the signs and symptoms of suicide and mental illness.

2. Screening instruments to identify the risk and needs of people who have a current or past history of mental illness or suicide risk.

3. Assessment by a licensed mental health professional in a toll-free telephonic triage system to identify four risk levels for suicide or mental illness.

4. Management protocols for each risk level, including protocols for housing, supervision, and management.

5. Mental health follow-up for face-to-face crisis counseling, consultation, and diversion by a local mental health professional.

Since its inception, the Kentucky Jail Mental Health Crisis Network has reduced the rate of suicide in participating jails by 84%. This program saves lives and provides an unprecedented handshake between jails and mental health service providers.[17]

■ Community Health Workers

A study of Kentucky jails revealed that in rural states, many mental health services are not provided by in-house mental health staff but rather by private psychiatrists, psychologists, and social workers. Other jail systems contract for mental health services with their local community mental health centers.[18]

Community mental health centers employ several different types of workers, including psychiatrists, psychologists, or social workers. Their services can be paid for by the jail or prison. Often, correctional facilities have standing contracts with community mental health centers to provide services. There is, however, concern that with two agencies coordinating activities, a mental health worker might not be located quickly in an emergency.

■ Conclusion

Since the 1980s, suicide in correctional settings has decreased significantly more than in the general U.S. population. Yet suicide still happens in correctional settings and much more so in jails than in prisons. Research has uncovered correlates of suicide so that correctional management can better prevent suicide in jails and prisons. Suicide prevention programs have been advanced by knowing that half of all jail suicides occur during the first week of incarceration and that those with mental health and substance abuse problems are more likely to kill themselves. Correctional management must take suicide seriously, and correctional staff should be well trained to detect and deal with suicide. Additionally, jails and prisons should employ mental health professionals to treat suicidal inmates.

Chapter Resources

DISCUSSION QUESTIONS

1. What is the best allocation of resources to help prevent inmate suicide?
2. Should jails be expected to have full-time mental health staff to deal with persons with mental illness, or should they contract with local community mental health centers or doctors in private practice in the community?
3. Why are the rates of suicide in jails higher than the rates in prisons and society at large?
4. What is the correlation between race and gender and suicide?
5. Why is this correlation so strong?

ADDITIONAL RESOURCES

Criminal Justice/Mental Health Consensus Project, http://consensusproject.org

Jail Suicide/Mental Health Update, http://66.165.94.98/cjjsl.cfm

National Center for Injury Prevention and Control, http://www.cdc.gov/ncipc/factsheets/suifacts.htm

National Commission on Correctional Health Care, http://www.ncchc.org

NOTES

1. Center for Disease Control and Prevention. (2012). *Trends in suicide rates among persons ages 10 years and older, by sex, United States, 1991–2009*. Atlanta: Author.
2. Hanson, A. (2010). Correctional suicide: Has progress ended? *Journal of the American Academy of Psychiatry and the Law Online, 38*(1), 6–10.
3. Centers for Disease Control and Prevention, National Center for Injury Prevention and Control. (2006). *Suicide: Fact sheet*. Retrieved March 6, 2007, from http://www.cdc.gov/ncipc/factsheets/suifacts.htm
4. Butler, L., & Nolen-Hoeksema, S. (1994). Gender differences in responses to a depressed mood in a college sample. *Sex Roles, 30*, 331–346.
5. Centers for Disease Control and Prevention, National Center for Injury Prevention and Control. (2012). *Web-based injury statistics query and reporting system*. Retrieved March 7, 2007, from http://www.cdc.gov/ncipc/wisqars/default.htm
6. Anderson, R., & Smith, B. (2003). Deaths: Leading causes for 2001. *National Vital Statistics Report, 52*(9), 1–86.
7. Krug, E. G., Mercy, J. A., Dahlberg, L. L., Zwi, A. B., Lozano, R. (2002). *World report on violence and health: Summary*. Geneva, Switzerland: World Health Organization.
8. Physicians for Social Responsibility. (2003). *Firearms and suicide*. Washington, DC: Physicians for Social Responsibility.
9. Health and Human Services. (1999). *The surgeon general's call to action to prevent suicide*. Washington, DC: Author.

10. Zapf, Z. A. (2006). *Suicide assessment manual for inmates*. Burnaby, British Columbia, Canada: Simon Fraser University.

11. Dunne, E. J., McIntosh, J. L., & Dunne-Maxim, K. (Eds.). (1987). *Suicide and its aftermath: Understanding and counseling the survivors*. New York, NY: W.W. Norton and Company.

12. Mumola, C. (2005). *Suicide and homicide in state prisons and local jails*. Washington, DC: Bureau of Justice Statistics.

13. Goss, J. R., Peterson, K., Smith, L. W., Kalb, K., & Brodey, B. B. (2002). Characteristics of suicide attempts in a large urban jail system with an established suicide prevention program. *Psychiatric Services, 53*, 574–579.

14. Middleton, M. (2013). *Typical section 1983 claims, find law for legal professionals*. Retrieved March 7, 2007, from http://library.findlaw.com/1999/Jan/1/126485.html

15. Mumola, C. (2005). *Suicide and homicide in state prisons and local jails*. Washington, DC: Bureau of Justice Statistics.

16. Hayes, L. (1995). *Prison suicide: An overview and guide to prevention*. Washington, DC: National Institute of Corrections.

17. Adams, J., & Shipley, S. (2002). Locked in suffering: Kentucky jails and the mentally ill. *Louisville Courier Journal, Four-Part Series*. February 24–March 3, 2002.

18. Phillips, D., & Mercke, C. (2003). Mental health services in Kentucky jails: A self-report by jail administrators. *Journal of Correctional Health Care, 10*(1), 59–74.

Programs and Operations Unique to Institutions

YOU ARE THE ADMINISTRATOR

■ Is There a Problem with Requiring Work from Prisoners?

Convict labor in prisons has been expected since the early days of American institutions in New York. The Auburn model of prison facilities in the early 1800s developed congregate work, the silent system, and extremely physical punishment for those who violated the rules of silence. Prison labor and industry operations developed from the desire to have convicted offenders "earn their keep" by making products that could be sold in the free community—with the money made used to offset the cost of confinement to the taxpayer. Prison labor was also seen as a reasonable way to keep inmates busy rather than giving them time to relax and concoct more negative uses of their time. Prisons in the south used inmates in agricultural fields, again to make money. Other prisons were authorized to accept contracts where officials leased or rented inmates to private businesses and farmers. Additionally, many prison systems made prisoners produce goods for use within the state's correctional system: clothing, shoes, mattresses, and food. All these programs were intended to give convicted offenders a productive task, save the government money, and further the concept of "just desserts."

Concerned citizens have often expressed displeasure at the harsh use of inmate labor, the perception of the state taking advantage of the confined population as cheap labor, and the idea that prison-made goods present an unfair advantage over the less competitive and more costly to operate factories outside prisons. Reformers and trade unions tend to complain bitterly during economic downtowns in our country. Federal legislation restricting the use of prison-made products was conceived in the 1930s during the Great Depression; many feared that jobs in the free world would be lost to cheap convict labor. The Hawes-Cooper Act of 1935 and the Ashurst–Sumners Act of 1940 made interstate trade in prison-made goods illegal. An exception to these restrictions was later created with the Prison Industry Enhancement (PIE) program. This legislation was created by Congress in 1979 to encourage states to create institutional work opportunities for prisoners that approximate work opportunities in the community; products of these joint ventures are allowed to be sold in the free market. In order to qualify for such a program, state and federal prisons would have to develop partnerships with private companies; the companies are required to pay inmates the prevailing wage for the industry. In return, inmates would be required to pay for their room and board in the correctional facility. One important benefit for inmates is that they learn marketable skills that are viable in today's employment marketplace.

Prison and jail authorities have, for the most part, welcomed the relaxation of laws that allow employment opportunities for prisoners. Labor organizations and private companies still resent the competition from convicted offenders.

- Should correctional leaders be allowed to use inmate labor to offset the costs of confinement?
- Do you think prison-made goods should be allowed to compete with outside industry?
- What do you think our society should expect for a daily routine for prisoners?
- Do you believe inmates should be required to work?

Prison Work and Industry

Robert C. Grieser, Steve Schwalb, and J. C. Keeney

CHAPTER OBJECTIVES

- Describe the importance of written work policies and the benefits of inmate work assignments.

- Explain the role of administrators in work supervision and the benefits of prison industry programs.

- Outline issues associated with prison industry programs and the laws that have been enacted to address these concerns.

rison administrators have long known the benefits of having inmates involved in meaningful work or program assignments, such as academic or vocational education. Institutions operate much better when most inmates have a detailed work assignment or a scheduled program to which they must report each day. There is contentious debate in some sectors about prison industry programs, yet such programs continue to thrive because everyone agrees that offenders should work while incarcerated. The benefits of prison industry programs include

- Reducing the debilitating effects of idleness and boredom
- Improving the safe management of prisons
- Teaching inmates valuable work skills
- Improving inmates' chances of success upon release

This chapter examines work policy and philosophy as well as the types of work inmates perform and potential concerns around work assignments. It also discusses the prison industry in general, dating back to the early history of corrections, and its benefits and drawbacks, as well as the legal framework surrounding it and the public policy questions it raises.

Work Policies

All prison and jail facilities with work programs must have a written philosophy in place clearly defining the departmental policies concerning inmate employment. Correctional agencies should also have a written departmental policy that delegates to various facilities and the authority to develop institutional policies and procedures covering the areas of inmate maintenance assignments. The commissioner or director of the agency must clearly define the agency's philosophical position relating to inmate labor. It is also his or her responsibility to put this position in the form of a departmental policy or directive. These policies must concur with those of the legislative body to whom he or she reports.

In turn, the chief administrative officer of each facility must develop written institutional policies and procedures and make them available to all staff and to the incarcerated population. Such policies help establish the staff principles of inmate management, promote consistency of action by staff, and ensure that staff are operating within the scope of their responsibilities and the law. This written document must be based on the departmental principles statement and must be understood by all staff and inmates.[1]

A policy document that establishes an inmate work program should include

- The types of maintenance jobs available
- The skill levels required for each position
- The pay ranges of the individual positions (if there is an applicable inmate pay system)
- Nonmonetary benefits associated with working, such as extra "good time"
- Any other items that merit defining

Privately owned and operated facilities must have a written corporate policy concerning inmate work assignments that allows the individual facilities to develop policies and procedures. When private facilities contract with public entities for inmates, the contract must spell out the expectations of both parties concerning inmate work assignments. Because privately operated facilities are usually contracted on a daily bed cost rate per inmate, it makes economic sense and is good correctional practice to use inmates in as many maintenance assignments as is feasible from a security standpoint.

Staff and inmates must be aware of the procedure by which inmates will be assigned to work details. In some jurisdictions, inmate assignments are under the purview of classification. In some facilities, there are assignment officers who take inmate applications and assign inmates to the various job openings. The system must be consistent, and both staff and inmates must understand how it works.

Inmate talents and skills should be utilized as much as possible. Presentence investigations and inmate history sections may give some indication of work experience and employment history in and outside institutions. In addition, there are a variety of vocational interest and ability tests given during the reception process at the beginning of the incarceration period. It is normally the case worker's or counselor's responsibility to assess an inmate's skill level, vocational training accomplishments, educational level, and work history and make a recommendation as to the type of institutional assignment that would be most appropriate.

■ Types of Work

The types of jobs available at a given facility will vary depending on the facility's security level. Obviously, it is easier to employ more inmates in lower-custody-level institutions than in maximum security facilities; maintenance assignments in higher-security-level facilities must be evaluated carefully.

Maintenance work assignments are among the most common jobs inmates perform. They not only help create a healthy atmosphere in the institutional setting but reduce operating costs. Common maintenance assignments include assistance with food service, cleaning, and custodial tasks.

One of the largest users of inmate labor in a facility is the food service department. In this department there are various positions, including porters, bakers, meat cutters, diet cooks, fry cooks, general cooks, servers, and janitors. There are many opportunities for inmates to start in food service in an entry-level, low-skill position and later advance to a more skilled position.

Inmates should be responsible for cleaning their own living areas. Staff should not have to clean up after inmates. Staff should clean areas such as control rooms that are restricted from inmate access. Common use areas such as bathrooms, day rooms, and dining rooms should also be cleaned by inmates.

Supervisory staff must be alert and observe these activities because, on occasion, staff will allow overly ambitious inmates into restricted areas to clean, thus relieving employees of this responsibility. This activity can seriously jeopardize the security of the facility. Supervisors need to be observant and tour the facility on all shifts so that they are aware of staff activity. Detailed assignments must be given to inmate janitors so that they clearly understand their areas of responsibility. Staff must supervise housing unit janitors, and precautions need to be taken so that janitors are not able to access other inmates' personal property. In the event that there is a problem of theft in the housing units, inmate janitors are instantly suspected. If the problem persists, inmate janitors may be the victims of violence.

Skilled inmates may practice their trades assisting electricians, painters, welders, and heating and air-conditioning specialists. Plumbing services may also be provided by inmate maintenance plumbers working under the supervision of security staff. Inmates may also help paint to cover any graffiti or worn paint areas or maintain lawns, shrubs, and the grounds in general.

There are various other areas that can benefit from inmate maintenance workers. The medical department and the administrative area of the facility will need inmate janitors. The motor pool can have inmates wash and service vehicles. The education department may use inmate clerks, library aides, teacher aides, janitors, and tutors.

■ History

The idea of having prisoners work dates back to the early history of corrections.[2] To reduce the debilitative effects of incarceration and better prepare the inmate for employment upon release, inmates were allowed to work by themselves in their cells on shoemaking, tailoring, and other tasks. Thus administrators began to focus on the economics of prison industry—the goal being to generate revenue in excess of the cost of maintaining the prisoner. In the early 19th century, the state of New York, an early leader in many corrections reforms, developed the congregate system, whereby inmates worked together in prison factories under very rigid discipline. This group production technique allowed the manufacture of items that could not be made efficiently by an inmate in a cell. Items produced included carpets, clothing, barrels, and furniture. Products were sold on the open market to American customers or exported, and the proceeds were used to reduce prison operation costs.

As the 1800s progressed, some other states (particularly those in the Midwest and South, where agricultural production was prominent) developed prison labor programs in which inmates were leased to private businesses. The prisons benefited because the lease payments were used to reduce the cost of prison operations. The private businesses gained many long hours of virtually free labor. There were complaints, however, that inmates were abused by contractors. Despite these complaints, the prevalence of convict lease programs increased after the Civil War, as the southern states scrambled to partially replace slavery.

■ The Legal Framework

The open market sale of prisoner-made goods incited free labor and private business to unite to bring about legal restrictions on the sale of inmate products. They managed to eliminate certain prison industry operations. Several states enacted laws that restricted inmate work and training programs. At the federal level, several statutes were passed, including the Sumners-Ashurst Act. Passed in 1940, this law made it a federal crime to knowingly transport convict-made goods in interstate commerce for private use, regardless of what state law allowed.

In 1979, Congress passed the Justice Systems Improvement Act (commonly called the Percy Amendment after its leading proponent), which permits waivers of the Sumners–Ashurst restrictions on the interstate sale of prison-made goods with several stipulations.

1. Inmates should be paid the prevailing wage with appropriate deductions for taxes, room and board, and court-ordered commitments such as restitution, child support, and alimony.
2. Local labor union officials should be consulted and must approve assignments.
3. Free labor must be determined to be unaffected by such programs.
4. Consultation with private industry must occur before establishing a program.

This amendment also created the PIE certification program wherein the U.S. Justice Department certifies applicant programs for an exception from the Sumners–Ashurst restrictions.

Perhaps the most noteworthy development from the struggles among government and prison industry officials, private businesses, and labor leaders was the state use system. Initiated in New York, this system precludes the sale of prison-made products to the public but promotes their purchase by the state (that unit of government of which the prison industry is an integral part). Today, state use sales are by far the most common market for prison industry products across the country.

■ Benefits

There are many benefits to prison industry programs. First, they save taxpayers money. Most prison industry programs are at least partially self-sustaining, generating their income from the sale of goods and services. To the extent that these programs can be self-sustaining, a work program can be provided to the inmates without appropriated funds. Thus, the cost to the taxpayers of operating prisons is reduced. Furthermore, some of the wages paid to inmate workers are applied to restitution, fines, child support, and alimony. Inmates also send some of their earnings home to their families. These revenues can reduce outlays for public assistance of various types. In this era of fiscal conservatism, reducing the taxpayer burden is an important attribute of prison industries.

Second, prison industries contribute to the safe management of prisons. By providing productive work and reducing inmate idleness, the presence of prison industry programs reduces the likelihood of disruptions and other violent inmate behavior, so prisons become safer places for staff and inmates. A well-managed prison is also a better neighbor to the host community than a poorly managed prison.

Third, prison industry experience improves inmate success upon release. Several research projects have tracked inmates after release. One of the more comprehensive was conducted by the Federal Bureau of Prisons; more than 7,000 inmates with comparable characteristics were evaluated for as long as 12 years following release. The results indicated that inmates who worked in Federal Prison Industries (FPI) while in custody were 24% less likely to recidivate and, thus, more likely to successfully reintegrate into society as a law-abiding, tax-paying citizen upon release.[3]

When former inmates are employed and not engaged in criminal behavior, the obvious additional benefits include

- A reduction in crime
- Improved public safety
- Greater contributions to the gross domestic product
- Increased tax revenues

In addition, prison industries may create jobs for law-abiding citizens, because they require raw materials, supplies, services, and equipment purchased from the private sector, thus creating jobs for various businesses. For example, supervision of inmate workers is provided by staff, whose salaries are normally paid from industrial revenues. Some of the monies paid to inmates are spent in prison commissaries, which stock items procured from local private sector vendors.

In summary, the number of civilian jobs created by prison industry revenues is substantial. This is an important consideration in evaluating the effect of prison industries on the private sector.

■ Concerns

A well-rounded work and program environment can assist greatly in maintaining a safe, secure, and healthy institution, but there are several areas of potential concern.

Diversity. It is important that the chief executive officer of the facility have a written policy stating that all work assignments should be filled by inmates of all races or ethnicities, in proportion to the makeup of the inmate population. Traditionally, there have been certain work assignments that inmates of certain races or ethnicities prefer; this should not be allowed. Inmate gangs also attempt to control some work areas of an institution, so the intelligence staff must ensure that gang-affiliated prisoners are tracked closely.

Access to information. Caution should be exercised to ensure that inmate clerks do not have unmonitored access to computers. Inmates may create all sorts of mischief on a computer system, including illegally accessing staff databases. If inmates are given access to computers, the machines should not be networked, offer access to sensitive information, or have a modem or another way to contact other networks.

Dependence. Inmates should not be assigned to the same job for an extended period of time. They may become possessive, and there is danger of staff becoming overly friendly or dependent on an inmate who has been on the same assignment for years. Rotating job assignments helps to avoid these problems.

Authority. An inmate should never be put in a position of authority over other inmates. Staff should handle all direction, instruction, and supervision. If "lead" inmate mentors are not well controlled, prisoners may become abusive in the use of their power.

Manipulation. Putting policies in writing is critical in all aspects of prison and jail administration. Not having written policy and procedures covering work assignments can give the inmate population the perception that the system can be manipulated and that favoritism is the norm. All aspects of the process (e.g., work applications, waiting lists for specific assignments) need to be spelled out in detail.

Quality. The quality of an inmate work program is sometimes neglected or given insufficient attention by managers. This can be a fatal mistake due to the sensitive nature of many of the inmate work assignments. Food service, in particular, needs to be monitored on a daily basis. In the history of corrections in this country, there probably have been more incidents and disturbances relating to inconsistent or poor quality of food preparation or serving than any other single issue. The food service department should never be the dumping ground for malcontents or problematic inmates.

Overload. Most correctional facilities require all able-bodied inmates to have a work assignment. This requirement can easily overload inmate crews. If it only takes five inmates to do a job and ten are assigned, the extra inmates on the crew may make trouble. The facility would be better served working two five-person crews for 4 hours each rather than having 10 inmates on a job doing little or nothing for 8 hours.

Supervision. It is important that supervisors and senior managers of an institution remain sensitive to all aspects of the work assignment and selection process as well as the quality of work accomplished on a daily basis. Supervisors should tour the facility each shift to observe and assist staff in this endeavor. Effective chief executive officers are inside the facility regularly to observe and talk to staff and inmates.[4]

There are often arguments against prison industries that center on their adverse effect on the private sector. There are several concerns in this arena. First, antagonists of prison industry programs argue that a provision commonly referred to as the mandatory source provides prison industries an unfair advantage. Because many prison industry programs are confined to state use sales, there are often statutes or regulations requiring that the government agencies buy first from the prison industry program. The private sector companies feel that this essentially locks them out of a percentage of the government market, which is unfair and has an adverse effect on their businesses. They advocate competition between prison industries and the private sector for all government business. Noteworthy is the fact that these mandatory source rules are rarely enforced and—in recent times—have been eroded by new laws that have further limited or weakened their original intent.

Second, critics argue that low inmate wages provide an unfair advantage to prison industries. These critics do not consider the assertion by prison industry officials that the constraints of prison work programs such as increased civilian supervision, tool control, pat searches, and unskilled workers substantially increase the total overhead costs. With the exception of the aforementioned PIE programs, inmates are paid only a small amount for their labor. Low inmate wages, however, do not equate to low inmate labor costs when operating prison industries.

A third argument—that prison industries take too much work away from the community—points to a crucial debate, namely how to determine fairly the share of the market that prison industries should have. There is no magic formula, and the current practice varies widely. On the one hand, for instance, there is essentially no commercial production of license plates in the country. Virtually all are made in prison industries. On the other hand, there are numerous products purchased by the government that prison industries will never make, including computers, aircraft, ships, and weapons systems. However, on more common items such as office furniture, there needs to be a balance between the percentage of government contracts awarded to prison industries and to the private sector. Typically, correctional industries' share of the overall domestic U.S. market is less than 1% or 2% for most items made and supplied by inmates. Increasingly, many of these commercial-type items made by prison industries would otherwise be manufactured in whole or in part by nondomestic U.S. labor off-shore.

As the prison inmate populations rises, so will the need for more inmate labor, increasing the probability of elevated market share for prison industries. This elevation will come at a time when many private sector firms are facing increased competition, both domestically and from imports, and when many of them will rely more heavily on sales to the government.

■ Conflicting Mandates

Prison industries have a checkered history, and a wide spectrum of opposition still exists. Therefore, it is no surprise that prison industries are deemed a success based on the extent to which they can demonstrate the most benefit to the greatest number of constituents. The FPI statute, for example, requires that FPI diversify production as much as possible to

- Minimize the effect on any one industry
- Employ as many inmates as practicable
- Perform work in a deliberately labor-intensive manner
- Be financially self-sustaining
- Sell products only to the federal government
- Produce products that are comparable to those of the private sector in features, quality, and delivery and that do not exceed current market prices
- Produce no more than a reasonable share of the federal government purchases, so as to avoid an undue burden on private sector business and labor
- Teach inmates a marketable skill

Taken individually, almost everyone would agree with these mandates. Putting them together, however, creates what Warren Cikins, a criminal justice consultant and former senior staff member at the Brookings Institution, calls a "convergence of righteousness," describing the tension associated with simultaneously pursuing these competing demands in a balanced way.[5] Ultimately, the debate is not about whether prison industries should exist; rather, it is about the manner in which prisoners should work.

■ Public Policy Questions

There are many public policy questions associated with prison industries, and none of them have clear answers.

Should Prison Industry Programs Be Required to Be Self-Sustaining?

Those who answer "yes" would argue that this requirement encourages prison industries to be more efficient and businesslike. It also reduces the burden on taxpayers, because if the prison industry program were not self-sustaining, more appropriated funds would be required for an alternative program.

Those who answer "no" would suggest that the private sector businesses that compete with prison industries are bearing an unfair share of the burden. They would also suggest that if the manufacturing done by prison industries were turned over to the private sector, the additional taxes collected from the increased sales would offset much if not all of the increased appropriated funds required to fund replacement programs.

Should Prison Industries Be Labor-Intensive?

Idleness reduction is a critical contribution of prison industry programs. The less labor-intensive programs are, the more idleness there will be. On the contrary, as the economy becomes less and less labor-intensive, the extent to which inmates are being provided market-based skills becomes questionable, yet this also argues that the effects of prison labor on private sector jobs wanes with each passing year. Those who support labor intensity in prison industries argue that inmates are being taught a work ethic, which is one of the most important skills that employers desire in new hires.

Should Prison Industries Have a Mandatory Source?

Those in favor of retaining this preference suggest that when it was agreed to limit prison industry sales only to the government, there was consent between private industry and labor that a certain amount of the government's business would be reserved for prison industries. Opponents argue that having a mandatory source keeps the government from getting the most "bang for its buck" through full and open competition.

Should Inmates Be Paid Minimum Wage?

There is no support for inmates being paid minimum or higher wages without deductions for room and board, taxes, and so on. If an employer had to pay minimum wage, the number of inmate jobs would reduce dramatically, because the labor costs would be far too high to be competitive. This could affect the total number of inmates employed and increase idleness. An argument can also be made that when the government provides room and board, education, and medical care at no cost to the inmate, lower tax-free inmate wages can be paid and the net income for the inmate is virtually the same as minimum wage with deductions. With the exception of the PIE programs, inmate wages were intended to serve as gratuities, to support inmate skills development as part of their participation in the prison industries training program.

Should Prison Industries Be Permitted to Sell Their Products to the Private Sector?

Advocates of this approach (which would essentially constitute a repeal of the Sumners–Ashurst Act) argue that the United States imports products from foreign countries that pay their workers wages comparable to prison industry wages in this country. Some economists would argue that any value added in the economy, regardless of the source, is advantageous. Opponents, however, envision a return to the abuses of the past. Trade experts also question whether statutes and foreign trade treaties should disallow the sale of prison-made goods in the domestic economy. Should inmates be granted the ability to produce items and repatriate work that is otherwise performed outside the United States, the net overall effect on jobs in the U.S. economy could be positive.

To What Extent Should the Private Sector Be Allowed to Operate Prison Industries?

Some advocate granting greater access to inmate labor by private industry. Others suggest that private companies should operate the current industrial programs run by the government, injecting the business principles at which the private sector is arguably more adept.

■ Conclusion

The provision and maintenance of a sense of order in the correctional environment are critical to institution management. Staff must provide daily routines for prisoners that facilitate a normal, calm, and stable atmosphere. Work assignments contribute a great deal to this quality of life. Inmates should be assigned to meaningful work assignments to enhance the operations of a correctional institution. Maintenance work assignments for inmates make an institution more cost-effective and contribute to other important aspects of corrections including assisting inmates in the process of reentry and teaching a positive work ethic.

The Reentry Policy Council has recommended that training and job assignments in correctional facilities provide meaningful work experience that will assist offenders in preparing for employment opportunities in the free community. Training and work should be conceived and developed while keeping in mind the job opportunities that will be available for inmates in their home communities. All institutional programs and activities should help inmates prepare for success in the future as they return home.[6]

Prison administrators should understand the critical contributions that prison industry programs make to the safe operation of correctional facilities. Legislators should appreciate that prison industries may reduce costs and make prisons more manageable. The private sector is legitimately concerned that prison industry growth will come at an expense, and there are sometimes difficult choices among the various options and competing interests. Successful industrial programs are the by-product of good communication, quality production programs, and skill in juggling these competing interests.

Chapter Resources

DISCUSSION QUESTIONS

1. What act allows for the interstate sale of prison-made goods? What are the major provisions of this act?
2. What arguments are presented against prison industry programs?
3. Should legal restrictions exist for the sale of prison-made goods?
4. Should prison-made goods be sold in the open market?
5. What role does the private sector played in prison industries?

ADDITIONAL RESOURCES

DiIulio, J. (1991). *No escape: The future of American corrections*. New York, NY: Basic Books.

Federal Prison Industries, http://www.unicor.gov

National Correctional Industries Association, http://www.nationalcia.org

Reynolds, M. (1996). *Factories behind bars*. Dallas, TX: National Center for Policy Analysis.

NOTES

1. Fleisher, M. (1989). *Warehousing violence* (p. 85). Newbury Park, CA: Sage Publications.
2. Roberts, J. (1996). *Work, education and public safety: A brief history of federal prison industries*. Washington, DC: Federal Prison Industries.
3. Saylor, W., & Gaes, G. (1996). *PREP: Training inmates through industrial work participation, and vocational apprenticeship instruction* (pp. 21–23). Washington, DC: Federal Bureau of Prisons.
4. Cikins, W. (1994, May 19). Remarks before the Subcommittee on Crime, House Judiciary Committee.
5. Cikins, W. (1994, May 19). Remarks before the Subcommittee on Crime, House Judiciary Committee.
6. Re-Entry Policy Council. (2005, January). *Charting the safe and successful return of prisoners to the community*. New York, NY: Council of State Governments. Retrieved from http://www.reentrypolicy.org/reentry/THE_REPORT.aspx

Prison Visitation

Reginald A. Wilkinson and
Tessa Unwin

CHAPTER OBJECTIVES

- Explain the benefits and drawbacks of visitation in a prison setting.
- Identify the challenges presented to institution security by the inmate visiting program.
- Outline the role that visitation plays in successful prison and jail administration.

T he operation of a visitation program is integral to any correctional system. Hundreds of thousands of relatives and friends visit the confined each year. Experienced correctional managers know that visitation improves the prison environment. Thus, all institutions should encourage visits from family and friends. Visits give inmates something to look forward to, an incentive to participate in rehabilitative programs, and a mechanism to help them cope with life behind bars. Although visitations present challenges to security, an elaborate system of rules and regulations governs the process, and overall, the benefits of visitations greatly outweigh the potential risks.

■ Benefits

Correctional institutions encourage visiting with family and friends for several reasons. The most important becomes evident after release. The prisoner who has maintained contact with supportive individuals has a safety net when he or she returns to the community. And to the community they will return; it is estimated that 97% of those who are incarcerated will ultimately be released. Family and friends provide a feeling of belonging to a group. They often help released offenders seek and find employment and conduct themselves in a positive, constructive manner after release. Newly released prisoners are more likely to see themselves (and be seen by others) with the stigma ascribed to former convicts if they do not maintain desirable social roles while incarcerated. These ex-convict roles are more likely to lead inmates back to criminal behavior.[1]

Prison visitation research has consistently found a positive effect on recidivism[2] for those offenders who have the benefit of visits from family, friends, and other supportive individuals. The Minnesota Department of Corrections examined the effects of prison visitation for more than 16,000 inmates released from their custody between 2003 and 2007 and found a significant positive outcome in terms of a successful transition from prison to the home community.[3]

Visitation is also an incentive for good behavior, providing management with a powerful tool. Prisoners are fully aware that the visiting environment for general population inmates is significantly freer than for those in disciplinary status.

Offender reentry can only be enhanced by positive, nurturing experiences in the visiting room. The idea of family involvement is critical to successful community reintegration. Important, continuous relationships with friends and family can play a positive role in inmates' rehabilitation. Many benefits can result if visitors maintain relationships following the release of the offender. If the inmate has children, the bonding experience can be continued in a healthy way, serving to lessen the shock and stigma of incarceration. It should be the duty of correctional administrators to help facilitate these visiting opportunities, even if special arrangements must be made.

■ Potential Risks

There are also drawbacks to allowing visits for a confined population, including contraband, illegal activities, and inmate tension. But risks are also a part of the everyday operation of a correctional facility.

Visitors can be a pipeline for the smuggling of drugs and other contraband into a facility. Contraband is defined as anything not allowed into a particular facility and varies depending on the type and security level of that facility. Most systems divide contraband into two categories: major and minor. Major contraband consists of drugs and alcohol, tools, weapons, explosive ordnance, ammunition, currency, cellular devices, and the like, whereas minor contraband often consists of nuisance items such as excessive food. Most prison systems today disallow bringing or sending food items to prisoners. Nevertheless, inmates and their visitors have devised many ingenious ways to attempt to smuggle items into detention facilities.

Drugs seem to be the contraband of choice. Inmates, and their trafficking conspirators, deploy many creative methods to traffic drugs into prison. They have been found in diaper linings, shoe heels, tubes of shampoo and toothpaste, felt-tip markers, stamps, greeting cards, and books. Illegal substances have been thrown over institution fences, taped to trash cans and toilets in the visiting room, sent in with packages of clothing, and left outside crew worksites. As such, significant numbers of alert staff are required, not only to supervise visits carefully but also to conduct background checks on visitors and to search packages or any items given to inmates. They must also search recreation yards, packages, and so on.

Some prisoners use the visiting process to make contact with potential crime partners or gullible new friends whom they may later use to convey contraband into the prison or conduct illegal activities. In many instances, prisoners first make contact with outsiders through pen pal organizations and then quickly exploit the friendship. Inmates also abuse the visiting privilege by convincing sympathetic visitors to bring them money or even participate in criminal activity requiring outside assistance. Certain visitors may be partners in crime who help the inmate to continue running illegal street enterprises during incarceration.

Some inmates schedule their visiting to get out of job assignments, while others become depressed because they have no visitors at all. A wise correctional manager knows that prison visiting is a sensitive and emotionally charged subject. Just as visiting provides a powerful incentive for good behavior, unfair treatment regarding visits, whether real or perceived, can create undesirable tensions. If a prisoner feels that his or her mother, spouse, or other family member has been unnecessarily hassled or in some way insulted, an outburst may result. Sensitivity training and professionalism are essential for staff involved in the visiting process.

It is incumbent on prison managers to be aware of the climate for visitors, both during the entry procedure and in the visiting room. A correctional officer who abuses his or her position by bullying and humiliating visitors creates a domino effect negatively affecting the visit, the inmates, staff, and prison security. Just as some employees excel in managing inmates or finding contraband, others have the skills and personality to work best with visitors. Corrections officers who know how to balance security and safety with dignity and empathy should be recognized as positive models for other officers.

■ Rules and Regulations

Prison systems have a myriad of rules, regulations, and procedures regarding visits. Rules vary widely according to tradition, security needs, and the availability of staff and visiting space. Informing staff, visitors, and inmates of the rules and regulations ensures a smooth operation; perceived or actual inconsistency and arbitrariness add unnecessary tension to the process. Many agencies include detailed visiting information in early correspondence mailed home by the inmate during the reception process. A courteous, informed, and professional staff can make the visiting experience positive for everyone. In addition, every effort should be made to inform visitors of restrictions or delays caused by special circumstances (such as fog alerts, extra or extended counts, lockdowns, or disturbances) as soon as possible.

Searches

Searches are imposed to provide adequate safeguards against the introduction of contraband into correctional facilities. All searches should be conducted in a professional manner, without violating the legal rights of visitors and with respect for human dignity. Searches may include a body cavity search, strip search, pat-downs or pat-frisks, metal detector, or X-ray. Entering a prison, for a visitor as well as for staff, is not unlike what one would undergo at an airport. In most correctional jurisdictions, strip and body cavity searches must be approved by the warden or designee and are performed only when there is a specific reason to suspect that the visitor has contraband. In most states, only a medical professional is permitted to conduct an intrusive body cavity search. Most corrections departments partner with local law enforcement in the interdiction of drugs or weapons into a prison and the arrest of people known to be carrying drugs. Some systems also utilize drug-detecting canines. High-tech drug detection devices such as ionizer systems have also been deployed to detect drugs and explosives. As we have seen in airports, more sophisticated technology is constantly being introduced.

Visit Terminations

Violation of prison rules may result in the termination of a visit. The visitor may also be suspended or removed from the approved visitation list. Violations include refusing to be searched, possessing contraband, attempting to convey contraband to an inmate, attempting to visit while intoxicated, presenting falsified identification, loaning identification to others, wearing inappropriate clothing, or engaging in prohibited physical contact, sex, or other behavior. If caught bringing illegal contraband into a prison, a visitor may be detained, arrested, and possibly prosecuted. Visitation obviously may be curtailed or terminated during prison emergencies.

■ Visitation List

Most prisoners develop their visiting list while still in the reception process. Lists generally include family, friends, attorneys, and clergy members. The list names the visitors, their address, phone number, and relationship to the inmate. After the individuals listed are screened and a background check is completed, some correctional systems actually interview visitors to determine their suitability for the prison setting. To avoid problems and conflict, prohibitions to visiting lists usually include known felons, former inmates, parolees and probationers, vendors, and prison volunteers; there are exceptions, of course. Some inmates are granted visits with individuals who are not on a visiting list for unusual situations such as to accommodate someone traveling a long distance or to address a family crisis.

Courtesy of the Ohio Department of Rehabilitation and Correction.

General Population Visits

The number, frequency, and duration of visits are limited by space, personnel constraints, scheduling, and security considerations. Upon arriving at the prison, visitors are required to present photo identification and may need to be searched. Visitors are also informed of what constitutes contraband and the sanctions in place to punish those who attempt to convey contraband into the facility.

Conjugal Visits

The argument may be made that allowing conjugal visits between husbands and wives further strengthens family bonds, helping to minimize the deleterious effects on the family of separation caused by incarceration. A stronger home and family relationship may also smooth the reentry of the offender into the community upon his or her release.

About half of America's prison inmates claim to be married, and six states (California, Connecticut, Mississippi, New Mexico, New York, and Washington) allow conjugal visitation.[4] In some jurisdictions, conjugal visits may be viewed as an unnecessary prisoner privilege and frowned upon by the general public and other stakeholders. Jules Burstein compares this American conservatism with the more liberal attitudes in other countries and asserts that the acceptance of conjugal visits in other countries is generally attributable to two factors: a less puritanical and hypocritical attitude toward sex and a greater emphasis on the family as a primary and vital social unit. Many foreign cultures view conjugal visits, along with home furloughs, as an individual's right.[5]

Visits with Children

Bringing families together is a laudable endeavor, yet one must wonder about the lasting effects on children of seeing a parent in prison. Robert R. Ross and Elizabeth A. Fabiano have argued that the variety of prison visiting arrangements is a reflection of the complex social and moral issues involved in the question of whether children should be separated from their incarcerated mothers or exposed to prisons, including:

- Effects of such visits on the mother and child when the visit ends
- Feelings of other inmate mothers who do not have contact with their children
- Effects on the child of seeing the often-frightening physical structure of prisons
- Possible long-term effects on children who may live in a prison for short or long periods of time
- Effects of separating children, particularly infants, from their mothers while they are in prison[6]

Most correctional agencies, recognizing the value of keeping families together, try to make the visiting area conducive to child visitations by providing children's reading areas, toys, games, or outdoor picnic or playground areas. Partnerships with area churches, schools, and charitable organizations can help maximize the resources available to enhance the visiting experience for children. A positive visit can help children see their incarcerated parent in a more normalized environment, allowing bonding and parenting to continue throughout the period of incarceration and beyond. A strong relationship with their children is a major incentive for many inmates to work toward a positive reentry to the community.

Innovative programs have sprung up nationwide to counter the deleterious effects of prison visits on children. For example, the Girl Scouts of America has formed partnerships with some women's prisons to pilot scout troops behind bars. Incarcerated women and their daughters work together on projects, earning merit badges and learning how to be successful teammates. In some women's prisons, overnight and weekend visits are granted as rewards for successful completion of parenting programs. Other states—such as Ohio and Nebraska—include unique incentive programs designed to increase an offender's awareness of responsibilities to the family with positive nurturing and interaction.

Televisiting

The advent of technology is always something to keep in a correctional administrator's visiting tool chest. While slow to catch on in a widespread way, creative persons are exploring the idea of televisiting. Televideo conferencing and telemedicine are common usages of this technology. This is how it could work. At a remote location, approved visitors would be connected to the inmate, who would be escorted to a prison location equipped with the electronic equipment to facilitate the connection. Many potential visitors such as the elderly and the infirmed may not be able to travel to an institution. Some inmates are housed in prisons that are not easily accessible; therefore, the cost of traveling is a concern. On the other hand, there is a cost attached to administering this technology. Cash-strapped correctional systems, consequently, are not quick to purchase the necessary equipment.

Legal Representation

The American Correctional Association's Commission on Accreditation for Corrections requires that provisions be made to ensure attorney–client confidentiality, including special arrangements for such communications. These provisions include telephone communications, uncensored correspondence, and visits.[7]

Whenever possible, separate visiting rooms are provided for inmates and their attorneys. This courtesy may also be extended to public officials and members of the media.

Types of Visiting

Institutional visiting is generally divided into two categories: contact and noncontact. Contact visiting is when visitors can actually "touch" the visitor. Touching, however, is very carefully defined and monitored. Anything excessive, or that might compromise security, will be curtailed. Nonetheless, holding hands or an occasional hug is permitted. The notion is that this is more humane and facilitates normal human interactions. But contact visiting is a privilege, not an entitlement. Contact visiting can easily be denied for violating visiting or prison rules. Some contact visits can be denied permanently. Contact visits may be restored after a suspension period in other cases.

Noncontact visiting typically is reserved for high-risk prisoners, that is, those who are continually in trouble and those who are housed in high-security confinement. This type of visiting is typical of what one would see in movies. The visitor and inmate are in two separate rooms. Visiting is conducted on either side of a secure, unbreakable, Plexiglas-type barrier. Discussions are conducted either via telephones on either side of the barrier or through a grid with holes in the barrier sufficient to facilitate communication.

Concerns with High-Risk Inmates

In the case of death row, administrative segregation, disciplinary detention, and protective custody inmates, security concerns outweigh concerns about family closeness. Thirty-four states plus the federal government and the U.S. military have the death penalty. High-risk prisoners or those in disciplinary housing are often restricted to noncontact visits using screens, handcuffs, and leg irons at the discretion of the facility.

■ Role of the Community

Community agencies and businesses may be involved in the visiting process in various ways. Specialized bus companies offer regular charters to prisons from large cities, helping to alleviate the problems caused by long distances. Local businesses such as motels, restaurants, and gas stations benefit from visitors who patronize these establishments. In many communities, volunteer visitors offer friendship to prisoners providing guidance and support while the individual is incarcerated and assistance with finding employment and a place to live after release.[5]

■ Facility Design

The design of visiting areas should allow for adequate supervision and control. Visiting rooms should provide a comfortable visiting environment that is neat and clean, has adequate light and ventilation, and includes separate lavatory facilities for visitors and inmates. Today's visiting rooms must also be fully accessible for those with disabilities.

■ Conclusion

Correctional agencies, prisoners, visitors, and society in general can all benefit from an efficient, humane, and secure visiting program. Regular contact with visitors significantly enhances an inmate's quality of life and establishes a lifeline with the free community. Ties with family members, friends, and other loved ones are critical to inmates' successful return to the community, and visitations help inmates maintain these important relationships. Today's forward-thinking correctional agencies recognize that returning an offender to the community prepared to begin a productive new life is a hallmark of successful corrections. The seamless support of family and friends is crucial to that success, especially considering the difficulties a formerly incarcerated person can experience once released.

Chapter Resources

DISCUSSION QUESTIONS

1. Why do prison administrators encourage visits to inmates by friends and family?
2. What are some of the drawbacks to allowing inmate visitation?
3. What controls can prison administrators put in place to minimize concerns around visitation?
4. In what ways can communities be involved in visitation?
5. Should young children be permitted in institutional visiting rooms? Why or why not?

ADDITIONAL RESOURCE

Tewksbury, R., & DeMichele, M. (2005). Going to prison: A prison visitation program. *The Prison Journal*, *85*, 292–310.

NOTES

1. Dickinson, G., & Seaman, T. (1994). Communication policy changes from 1971–1991 in state correctional facilities for adult males in the United States. *Prison Journal*, *74*(3), 371–382.
2. Clark, T. A. (2001). The relationship between inmate visitation and behavior: Implications for African-American families. *Journal of African American Men*, *6*(1), 43–58; Casey-Acevedo, K., & Bakken, T. (2001). Effects of visitation on women in prison. *International Journal of Comparative and Applied Criminal Justice*, *25*(1), 31–48; Bales, W. D., & Mears, B. M. (2008). Inmate social ties and the transition to society: Does visitation reduce recidivism? *Journal of Research in Crime and Delinquency*, *45*, 287–321.
3. Duwe, G., & Clark, V. (2013). Blessed be the social tie that binds: The effects of prison visitation on offender recidivism. *Criminal Justice Policy Review*, *24*(3), 271–296.
4. Camp, C., & Camp, G. (2003). *The corrections yearbook 2002* (p. 149). Middletown, CT: Criminal Justice Institute.
5. Burstein, J. (1977). *Conjugal visits in prison* (p. 24). New York, NY: Lexington Books.
6. Ross, R., & Fabiano, E. (1986). *Female offenders: Correctional afterthoughts* (p. 58). New York, NY: McFarland and Company.
7. American Correctional Association. (1990). Standard 3-4263. *Standards for adult correctional institutions* (3rd ed.). Lanham, MD: Author.

Gang Management

Mark S. Fleisher

CHAPTER OBJECTIVES

- Recognize how the U.S. Constitution influences American state and federal prisons.

- Identify the reasons that minor misconduct and serious infractions committed by members of prisoner groups are particularly difficult to prevent and disrupt.

- Identify the reasons why prison quality of life can positively or adversely influence prisoner's behavior.

- Identify the influence of security threat groups on their members' behavior.

- Identify the function of prisoner classification systems.

- Identify the influence of computer technology on prison management.

S ince 1990, the U.S. prison population had increased to nearly 1 million prisoners. In 2009, more than 3,000 jails and nearly 2,000 state and federal prisons housed approximately 1.7 million prisoners, a majority of whom were convicted of murder, nonnegligent homicide, rape, and other sexual offenses.[1] California and Texas confined the highest number with roughly 170,000 prisoners each. Florida held just over 100,000. Georgia, New York, Ohio, and Pennsylvania confined between 50,000 and 60,000 prisoners each, and 19 states incarcerated fewer than 10,000 prisoners each. Other states confined 60,000–100,000 prisoners each. The Federal Bureau of Prisons (BOP), an agency within the U.S. Department of Justice, imprisoned nearly 210,000 prisoners. The mid-2008 per capita cost of state corrections exceeded police protection by about 10% in eight states.[2] Jails abided the criminal justice system's heaviest burden: at year-end 2009, when nearly 250,000,000 people were arrested and processed by jails.

The U.S. Constitution outlines the rights of all U.S. residents, both citizens and noncitizens. The complexity of prisoners' constitutional rights requires that prison authorities acknowledge prisoners' rights and protections and their responsibility to maintain safe and secure prisons and protect prisoners' right to confinement in healthy prison communities. Reliable oversight of prison operations and programs test the patience and skills of even the most accomplished administrators. The responsibilities of prison authorities are continuously tested by highly disruptive prisoners and also by prisoner social groups who deliberately engage in violence and misconduct that, if left unchecked, create social disorder.

Correctional systems are service organizations that ensure public safety and protect prisoners' well-being. The absence of prison security and prisoner well-being has effects similar to those in disorderly communities where crime and violence go hand in hand with a disregard for the rights of fellow citizens. Prisons that are well managed are best suited to offer a quality of life that endorses prisoners' positive behavior. Prison disorder studies show that prisons well balanced with rewards and sanctions create a prison climate that strongly supports a healthy quality of life and allows an ease of positive behavioral expression through education, recreation, employment, and leisure time activities.

■ Creating a Healthy Prison Environment

American prisons are places of numerous human service industries. Like the Joint Commission on Accreditation of Healthcare Organizations that assesses and accredits hospitals, the American Correctional Association establishes prisoner quality-of-life standards of care and health and offers a complete assessment of physical facilities and operations and programs in state and federal prisons.

Over recent decades, well-managed, healthy state and federal prison communities are evident in relatively low rates of severe violence. That fact indicates that prisons facilitate and enable social order; that as a consequence of a healthy prison environment, prisoners choose to engage in and encourage and endorse prison regulations; and that prisoners actively promote social order. Opposition to social order comes from state and federal prisoners who actively disregard and disdain prison regulations and endorse violations of fellow prisoners' right to confinement in a safe prison.

■ Threats to a Healthy Prison Community

In the 1980s, the War on Drugs cracked down on drug importation and distribution. While law enforcement agencies arrested and courts convicted local and international purveyors of illegal drugs, law enforcement also targeted international and domestic terrorists, hate-group members, and cartels that operated through urban street gangs. Aggressive law enforcement and prosecution swelled state and federal prison populations. As the prison incarceration rate increased, the relative percentage of violent prisoners increased as well. However, imprisonment did not end their violent behavior nor prevent an appearance of prison-based gangs that carried on crime and violence and threatened prisoner and prison personnel safety and prison security.

The imprisonment of violent criminals in the late 1980s and 1990s added to the already dangerous roster of prisoners who belonged to *prison gangs* that are crime-oriented prisoner groups with an origin inside prison, an origination history that distinguishes them from street gangs. Prison gangs slowly emerged in the 1950s and 1960s and continued to expand criminal activities as more violent street criminals were confined under deplorable prison conditions. A documented history of the origin of prison gangs remains elusive, but stories abound among prison personnel and prisoners that describe most assuredly an origin that with close examination appears more apocryphal than an accurate historic account.

First to appear were notoriously violent prison gangs such as the Mexican Mafia (*La Eme*), Black Guerilla Family, Aryan Brotherhood, *La Nuestra Familia*, and Texas Syndicate.[3] When the scope and severity of prison gangs' criminality accelerated and the prisoner populations expanded and included terrorists, hate groups, and international gangs, prison authorities were compelled to rethink the designation *prison gang*. In its place was coined the term *security threat group* (STG) that identifies prisoner social groups that have an internal hierarchy of leaders (order givers) and rank-and-file members (order takers) and systematically pursue criminal activity within prisons.

STGs represent a relatively low percentage of state and federal prisoners but are particularly and continuously troublesome and posed an even more daunting management challenge as the number of street gang members increased and their members comingled with prison gangs. The crime and disorder caused by prison and street gangs did not end when gang members were released. Social ties between prison and street gangs inside prison opened opportunities for criminal activities outside and also for a formation of criminal conspiracies between prisons and communities.

■ Curbing a Threat of Violence

STGs rely on leaders' power and influence to compel the behavior of rank-and-file members to act out violently and further STG criminal ventures. A 1991 study of STG-related violence and other prison misconduct was conducted in nearly 300 prisons in 45 states and surveyed nearly 14,000 state inmates and 8,500 federal inmates. This study learned that approximately 6% of all surveyed prisoners engaged in criminal activities while STG members.[4] A 2002 study of the effect of STGs on their members' behavior in federal prisons learned that STG members, and non-STG members influenced by STGs, engaged more often in violent acts than prisoners who had no social ties to STGs.[5] All STG members did not engage in misconduct, nor did all non-STG prisoners refrain from misconduct. But these studies illustrated STG members' propensity toward violent behavior, a propensity that led to acts of violence, or endorsed violent acts, or encouraged non-STG prisoners to commit violence.

■ STG Crime

STGs' scope of criminal activity increased and complicated prison authorities' responsibilities. STGs' internal structure and cohesion that attaches members to one another create a social group more resilient to prison authorities' intervention than a loosely organized street gang and activity-based prisoner groups such as weightlifters and softball players. Internal group structure and cohesion facilitate STGs' capacity to plan and enact criminal activities and even advance STG's criminal agenda by coercing street gang members' and non–gang members' participation. STG-instigated crime worsened still when released prison gang members plotted with their cronies inside prison to smuggle contraband into prisons through visiting room interactions. From time to time, prison personnel hopeful of a quick and profitable payday accepted payoffs from prison gangs to smuggle contraband such as cell phones, concealing them in clothing or lunch sacks. When apprehended, prison personnel stand trial and, if convicted, are sentenced to prison and face stiff financial fines.

■ STG Management Strategies

If left unimpeded, STGs spawn social discord and violence. A diffusion of minor-to-serious misconduct provokes social disorder and an erosion of cautious respect among prisoners and between prisoners and staff personnel, a respect for peaceful interactions, and a sense of civility among thousands of prisoners and between them and hundreds of staff personnel. If civility continuously erodes, its consequences are social hostility and tension and a permeating sense of fear of the inevitability of aggression and violence. Once embedded in a network of social interactions, fear and tension are difficult to alleviate, and a restoration of civility and social order may be unreachable.

■ Prisoner Classification, a First Approach to Prison Safety

A rational approach to prison population management does more than focus on disruptive groups but rather creates an inclusive framework, a prison *inmate classification system*. Predicated on the tenets of social science, inmate classification systems abstract and summarize an array of complex variables that described the nature of prisoners' behavioral, cognitive, emotional, social, and criminal history and severity of conviction offense. That analysis yields the concept of *security level*, a measure of prisoners' dangerousness.

The BOP uses an array of prison facility designations, each of which implicitly conveys prisoners' dangerousness.[6] Security level creates a ranked order of federal prison facilities from minimum to high security, meaning that prisoners assigned to minimum-security prisons are far less dangerous than those in high-security prisons. State correctional systems' prison designations vary widely across the country but recognize elements similar to those in federal designations.

Official designations of federal prisons are federal prison camp, federal correctional institution, and United States penitentiary. Each designation signifies a security level denoted by characteristics of prisons' physical features such as towers and fences; security equipment like fence-line detection devices; and multiple types of prisoner housing including dormitories and cell blocks. Federal prison designations inherently signify prisoners' dangerousness but also extend to prisoners' need for substance abuse management, medical and mental health treatment, and educational and vocational training, as well as complementary types of program services.

Inmate classification provides a standardized set of measures and compiles it into a formal procedure that matches prisoner dangerousness and needs and then places prisoners in security-level prisons that match both dangerousness and needs. Prisoners who pose a low degree of danger as based on statistical predictions are least likely to act out violently and endanger other prisoners and staff personnel and might be assigned to a federal prison camp. Prisoners whose background provides evidence of flagrantly dangerous and violent behavior and a disregard of and disdain for the well-being of others might be assigned to a United States penitentiary.

Inmate classification extends beyond security level. Additional assessment criteria are necessary as well. The federal inmate classification system refers to these additional criteria as public safety factors (PSFs), a set of criteria that further elaborate prisoners' dangerousness and adjust security-level assessment. PSFs are assigned to prisoners whose criminal history precludes a designation that might otherwise threaten prison and community security and safety. PSFs are issued to prisoners who are, for instance, sex offenders, or escape risks, or STG members.

The federal prison system's prisoner classification serves as a shorthand, or a summary of key facts, about prisoners' criminal history and a complex assessment and a prediction of the likelihood of prisoners' future behavior. A comprehensive prisoner classification provides a critical first step in the management of all prisoners and particularly STG members who pose a continuous risk to their own safety and others and threaten prison security.

■ STG Disorder, Modes of Intervention

That prisons achieve a zero rate of violence and disruptive behavior rests well outside realistic expectations, but prison policies and regulations aim to establish procedures of formal social control that apply to an entire prison population. Formal social control procedures refer to specific rules and regulations that prescribe prisoners' proper behavior and, by doing that, proscribe specific types of inappropriate, offensive, and criminal behavior. Specific acts of nonviolent and violent misconduct are defined along a continuum that engenders disciplinary behavior from minor sanctions to filing new criminal charges.

Discipline systems and schemes of sanctions that increase with misconduct severity or repeated rule violations are predicated on an assumption that even minor prisoner rule violations levy an implicit threat to the safety of prisoners and security of a prison. A conundrum of prisoner misconduct occurs when nonviolent behavior that might be interpreted as inconsequential outside prison, like gambling and tattooing, has repeatedly created violence inside, like an unpaid gambling debt that leads to an assault, or a new tattoo that indicates STG affiliation that eventually causes victimization.

Prisons establish STG management policies and procedures that specifically state a prison's STG management guidelines and create a set of rules that prison personnel abide by subsequent to an infraction. But STG criminality extends beyond prison boundaries. STGs' linkage to community criminal groups led to policies and procedures that take into account procedures necessary to prevent and investigate STG criminality that extends beyond the confines of a prison. STGs' in-prison criminality may involve paroled prisoners, or family members, or romantic partners, or even prison personnel. Those circumstances require joint investigations with local, state, or federal law enforcement. Federal prisons' STG investigations of serious infractions like escape, killing, and staff personnel involvement in crime involve the FBI.

STGs' members are carefully monitored but without reasonable cause cannot be confined in administrative detention, a type of confinement required during an investigation, nor can STG members be punished more harshly than non-STG members for the same infraction. Nevertheless, STG members' behavior comes under more intense supervision, their behavior is monitored more carefully, and investigations of serious infractions, like aggravated assault and killing or smuggling contraband like cell phones, weapons, and illegal drugs, involve diverse investigative procedures and might include local, state, and federal law enforcement agencies. Regardless of STG affiliation, disciplinary procedures apply to all prisoners and require that behavior infractions be met by graduated sanctions, a set of rank-ordered institutional responses that account for infraction severity and prisoners' frequency of infractions. Behavior control sanctions are scaled from minor disciplinary action that imposes limits on access to recreation, to more serious sanctions that necessitate disciplinary segregation, and to severe sanctions that require transfer to another prison of the same or higher security level.

Egregious infractions like violent assault on staff personnel, killing, attempted escape, and possession of lethal weapons require sanctions that prescribe a period of time in a supermaximum security prison, a "supermax" or "lockdown" prison, where prisoners are confined most hours of the day. STG members, like non-STG members, may be charged in state and federal court on new criminal charges and, if convicted, receive an additional prison sentence.

Conventional wisdom errs in its assumption that prisoners have *nothing to lose*. The overwhelming population of state and federal prisoners serves time in *mainline* prisons that allow a relatively open social life and permit prisoners more than a modicum of free access to prison services like employment and hobby shops and a library. Sentence length notwithstanding, more freedom affords greater benefits than less freedom. An additional term of imprisonment, even one added to prison sentence of life plus 150 years, has grim consequences if a prisoner moves from a mainline prison to a supermax, where years of confinement are spent locked down 23 hours a day.

■ Prison Management, Technology

The late 20th century saw rapid maturation of the information age that appeared just in time to aide prison managers. The sophistication of Internet hardware and software technology and its worldwide expansion from the late 1980s into the 2000s allowed creation of law enforcement agencies' and state and federal correctional systems' networks of information management systems that monitored international and domestic threats of violence and international criminal conspiracies.

Paper-and-pencil record keeping and phone communication of the 1960s and 1970s would not have been able to sustain security and crime intelligence requirements that an international cross-section of dangerous prisoners posed to state and federal prisons. Before the Internet became as common as steel gates, prison security and investigation personnel were limited both in their breadth of knowledge on prisoners' criminal histories and in knowledge derived from the integration of local, regional, and national sources. The Internet opened speed-of-light information transmission between state and federal prisons and local, state, and federal law enforcement agencies.

The conversion from paper to electronic files and implementation of management information systems not only improved prison personnel's management ability but also enhanced prisoner classification systems and sped analysis of violence and nonviolent misconduct. Modern computer technology and information management systems revolutionized correctional administration and management and had dramatic effects on types and quality of prisoner supervision and management and enhanced prison security. Prison technology today has improved surveillance, improved architectural design, and sharpened and polished crime analysis and intelligence-gathering strategies.

Modern technological advances improve prisons' access to police gang units and multiagency crime intelligence centers that integrate multiple sources of crime data and track movements of and crime committed by paroled STG members. State prisons customarily notify local law enforcement agencies when STG prisoners are paroled. Those data and parolee photographs enter into police databases and enable patrol officers to recognize parolees and pay particular attention to STG members.

Advancements in forensic and information science improve in-prison criminal investigation, but while technology has become a critical necessity and vital to prison security, it cannot fill the social space between prisoners and prison staff. That social space has to be filled with continuous and positive interaction between prison staff and prisoners. Modern technology aside, state and federal prisons are places of intensive interpersonal interaction, and that interaction, along with modern technology, creates safe and secure prisons.

■ Conclusion

A common cliché declares that prisons are not for punishment, but that a convicted felon goes to prison as punishment, meaning that a prison sentence removes a person from daily life and that removal constitutes punishment. The cliché's wisdom raises doubts. Anyone who has worked in or served a term of confinement knows that prison life, in and of itself, constitutes punishment. The challenge for prison authorities is to create a balance between imprisonment as punishment and the benefits derived from it.

Experience has taught parents and teachers that deliberate punishment and deliberate indifference to the needs of youth and adolescents do not encourage their cooperation and inspire them to obey school and community rules and respect their peers, family, and teachers. Prison authorities have learned that lesson as well. Deliberate punishment and indifference to prison conditions and arbitrary restrictions and sanctions do not engender prisoners' prosocial behavior and promote a sense of civility within a prison community. Correctional experts know well that confinement designed to be punitive has effects opposite to those expected—that prisoners abide by prison rules and regulations if they are treated well and humanly and, within limits imposed by security and safety concerns, are afforded privileges that people outside prison enjoy, like recreation, education, employment, and sanitary living conditions.

Public outpourings to remove prison privileges and impose more punitive and restrictive conditions are irrational and have never had the desired outcome, to punish prisoners so strongly, "to teach them a lesson," that they transform themselves into law-abiding citizens. Prison authorities and prisoners alike agree that time served in prison does not, in the long run, serve the best interests of communities.

Chapter Resources

DISCUSSION QUESTIONS

1. If you were the director of a state correctional system, would you advise wardens to restrict prisoners' activities or encourage more activities and programs?
2. Do you accept the idea that prisons should be "healthy communities?"
3. Prisons confine nonviolent and extremely violent felons. Would you endorse the release of nonviolent felons? Should nonviolent felons even go to prison?

ADDITIONAL RESOURCES

Carlson, P. M. (2001). Prison interventions: Evolving strategies to control security threat groups. *Corrections Management Quarterly, 5,* 10–22.

Fleisher, M. S. (1989). *Warehousing violence.* Newbury Park, CA: Sage Publications.

Fleisher, M. S., & Decker, S. H. (2007). Gangs behind bars: Prevalence, conduct, and response. In R. Tewksbury & D. Dabney (Eds.), *Prisons and jails: A reader* (pp. 1–28). New York, NY: McGraw-Hill.

Fleisher, M. S., & Krienert, J. L. (2009). *The myth of prison rape: Sexual culture in American prisons.* New York, NY: Rowman & Littlefield.

Pyrooz, D., Decker, S. H., & Fleisher, M. S. (2011). From the street to the prison, from the prison to the street: Understanding and responding to prison gangs. *Journal of Aggression, Conflict and Peace Research, 3*(1), 12–24.

NOTES

1. U.S. Census Bureau. (2011). *Statistical abstract of the United States: 2012* (131st ed.). Washington, DC: Author. Retrieved from http://www.census.gov/compendia/statab/
2. Retrieved from http://www.census.gov/compendia/statab/2012/tables/12s0345.pdf
3. Carlie, M. (2002). *Into the abyss: A personal journey into the world of street gangs.* Retrieved from http://people.missouristate.edu/MichaelCarlie/
4. Gaes, G. G., Wallace, S., Gilman, E., Klein-Saffran, J., & Suppa, S. (2002). The influence of prison gang affiliation on violence and other prison misconduct. *The Prison Journal, 82*(3), 359–385.
5. Gaes, G. G., Wallace, S., Gilman, E., Klein-Saffran, J., & Suppa, S. (2002). The influence of prison gang affiliation on violence and other prison misconduct. *The Prison Journal, 82*(3), 359–385.
6. Federal Bureau of Prisons. (2006, September 12). *Program statement: Inmate security designation and custody classification.* Washington, DC: U.S. Department of Justice. Retrieved from http://www.bop.gov/policy/progstat/5100_008.pdf

The Death Penalty

Julie C. Eng

CHAPTER OBJECTIVES

- Describe the role of religious and activist groups in the capital punishment debate.

- Explain why the death penalty has become such an emotional topic in the administration of justice in the United States.

- Examine how states differ in their capital punishment laws.

apital punishment is a highly controversial topic that raises many important questions: Is the death penalty morally wrong? Is it an effective punishment? Is it cruel and unusual? Is it consistently used across the country? For prison and jail administrators, capital punishment raises many other questions about the details of housing and caring for inmates sentenced to death.

■ A Brief History

The history of capital punishment goes back to the earliest human cultures, when methods of execution were extremely cruel. The goal of the punishment was to create a painful experience; stoning, whipping, and boiling were common. With the passage of time and the evolution of ideas, punishments have changed. Early in the 20th century, death-sentenced inmates in the United States were executed by hanging, electrocution, or firing squad. Now, these practices are more limited (see **Table 36-1**). There are five methods used in the United States: lethal injection, electrocution, lethal gas, firing squad, and hanging.[1] New execution methods allow the government to execute criminals in the most civilized and humane manner, with the least amount of suffering, which means, in most states, lethal injection. States that use more than one method of execution allow sentenced inmates to choose their method of death.[2] Nebraska is the sole state that uses electrocution as the only method of execution.

Between 1976 and 2011, the number of executions in the United States was 1,265 (see **Figure 36-1**). Currently, executions seem to be declining somewhat because of questions arising about the effectiveness and accuracy of the death penalty.

TABLE 36-1 Methods of Execution

Method	Number of States Permitting
Lethal injection	37
Electrocution	9
Lethal gas	4
Hanging	3
Firing squad	3
Death penalty is legal in a total of 37 states and the federal government. Most states have multiple methods of execution.	

Source: Snell, T. (2006). *Capital punishment, 2005.* Washington, DC: U.S. Department of Justice, Bureau of Justice Statistics.

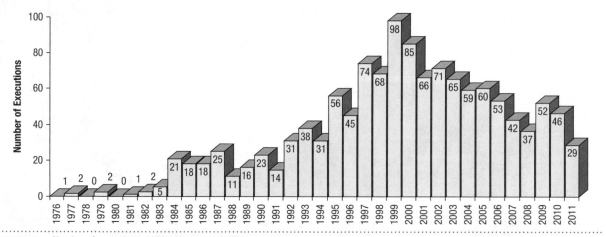

FIGURE 36-1 Number of executions, 1976 to 2011; total: 1,263 (as of December 31, 2011)
Source: Courtesy of Death Penalty Information Center.

Particular problems noted with the electric chair have encouraged the development of new methods of executions. Several executions have been documented where the electricity administered was not enough to kill the condemned person. Some executions have resulted in which the condemned person was burned in various parts of the body but did not die. The most infamous example of this occurred in Alabama in 1983, during the execution of John Louis Evans. Three separate attempts of 1,900 volts of electricity were required to complete Evans' punishment. In Florida, during an electrocution on March 25, 1997, the electricity created flames that erupted from convicted murderer Pedro Medina's masked head during the execution. An international outcry resulted, causing many states to review of this method of execution.

Although some states (such as Michigan, Rhode Island, Wisconsin, Minnesota, and Maine) abolished the death penalty in the early 1900s, other states abolished the death penalty only to reinstate it later.[3] Most states have maintained their capital punishment laws with little change, except for court-required restrictions. However, there are states reconsidering the use of the death penalty. New Jersey abolished the death penalty in 2007, New Mexico abolished it in 2009, and Illinois abolished it in 2011. In addition to 37 states using the death penalty the federal government and the U.S. military use the death penalty as well.[4]

After the Supreme Court articulated a new standard in the 1970s for the use of the death penalty, states returned to a greater use of the death penalty as their ultimate sanction. From 1930 through the 1950s, those who were sentenced to death were generally executed promptly. Nearly 4,000 men and women were executed in the United States during this time. In the 1960s, executions slowed dramatically as courts became more involved in this arena, and death row inmates often exercised lengthy appeals. This trend culminated in the U.S. Supreme Court's ruling in *Furman v. Georgia* (1972) that capital punishment was cruel and unusual.[3]

In *Furman*, the Court held that the decision to execute as a punishment was not applied fairly to all defendants. As a result of this ruling, the death penalty was annulled in 39 states. Many jurisdictions then embarked on an effort to rewrite their sentencing laws to deal with the issue of arbitrariness. To combat the Supreme Court's charges, state legislators mandated capital punishment for certain offenses and created specific guidelines for the judicial system to follow when deciding whether to implement the death penalty. In 1976, the first test of the new laws came before the Court in *Gregg v. Georgia*.[4] Although the Supreme Court ruled against mandating the death penalty for certain crimes, the guidelines for juries to follow were approved. Accordingly, the Georgia version of the guidelines became the model for many other states.

■ Arguments Against the Death Penalty

As the death penalty became more common in the United States, so did the controversy surrounding it. Critics have raised several complaints, which are as follows.

Long Waits on Death Row

The greatest argument against capital punishment seems to be that few individuals are actually executed. On January 1, 2007, about 3,350 inmates were awaiting execution. The state with the highest number of total executions—Texas—has a current backlog exceeding 390 people. In California, 660 inmates are currently on death row. Between 1973 and 1995, only 5% of inmates on death row nationwide were executed.[5] Despite these statistics, judges and juries continue to hand out an average of 2,300 death sentences each year.[6]

Unclear Qualifications

The lack of clarity around who qualifies for the death penalty has contributed to the debate over its use. Federal and state prisons have an immense backlog of death row inmates simply because the laws addressing this controversial issue are nebulous. Although the goal of the moratorium imposed by the *Furman* decision was to reduce capricious sentencing, inmates today are able to find myriad loopholes in the laws to prolong their time on death row.

Determined lawyers manage to contest capital punishment rulings in creative ways, often because of the lack of consistent sentencing guidelines across state and federal jurisdictions. This inconsistency stems from ambiguous standards in the law. Most death penalty sentencing guidelines are based on seven criteria:

1. Murder committed in the commission of a felony (e.g., robbery, rape, or kidnapping)
2. Multiple murders
3. Murder of a police or correctional officer acting in the line of duty
4. Especially cruel or heinous murder
5. Murder for financial gain
6. Murder by an offender having a prior conviction for a violent crime
7. Causing or directing another to commit murder

Because these guidelines are defined loosely, interpretations may differ radically among judges and juries in various state and federal jurisdictions. "Multiple murders" could refer to hundreds of deaths resulting from a bomb exploding in a large office building or the shooting of two individuals during a robbery. Another judge could believe that a single murder is particularly cruel. Thus, when the courtroom deliberation finally results in a decision on how to apply the law—a process that can be extremely lengthy—this decision can become the basis of many appeals.

Complexity of Appeals

All three branches of government are concerned about the time delays and complexity of death penalty appeals. The Anti-Terrorism Effective Death Penalty Act (1996) was intended to shorten the lengthy and cumbersome state and federal appeal process. It limits the appellate process for those under sentence of death to one federal appeal; if the individual seeks additional appeals, he or she must first receive approval from a three-judge panel.

With the current death penalty laws, an estimated 40% of capital punishment decisions are reversed.[7] The inmate is then resentenced, which starts a new cycle of retrying cases and appealing decisions. Taxpayers are left paying for keeping men and women on death row in prison for years while their cases await judicial review. Even if the current rate of execution were to double, it would take nearly half a century for the backlog of sentenced inmates to be executed.

High Financial Cost

Another major shortcoming of capital punishment is the immense cost. Many Americans support capital punishment because they believe it to be less expensive than a life sentence in prison without parole. Contrary to this conventional wisdom, capital punishment is actually the more costly option. Considering the average age of incarceration and typical life expectancy, the estimated cost ranges from $750,000 to $1 million per execution.[8] Some states even estimate the cost to be much higher. These costs are not affected by the method of execution but by the cost of extended legal review. Retaining attorneys and expert witnesses and conducting the investigation create significant expenses. In Florida, the average cost of trying and executing one person is $3.2 million. This is almost three times the cost of a single Florida inmate's imprisonment for 40 years.[9]

Racial Discrimination

When debating the death penalty, one cannot avoid the argument that the process discriminates against some races and ethnicities. Dr. David Baldus, professor of law at the University of Iowa, points out that "About half of all the people who are murdered each year in the United States are black. Yet since 1977, the overwhelming majority of people who have been executed—more than 80 percent—had killed a white person. Only 11 percent had killed a black person."[10] These statistics suggest that the judicial system appears to value the lives of Caucasian citizens more than the lives of individuals of other races or ethnicities. Baldus also completed a study in Georgia that revealed that convicted offenders with Caucasian victims received the death penalty 4.3 times more often than those with African American victims.

Other studies also reveal bias with respect to the death sentence. In 2006, 53 inmates in 14 states were executed. All were men; 61% were Caucasian, and 39% were African American. If the statistics mirrored the U.S. population, only about 22% of the death row population would be African American, although in 2005, 42% of inmates on death row were African American.[11] Sociologist Michael Radelet has concluded from his studies that those of lower social class and poor economic status are also disproportionately given death sentences.[12]

Limited Effect on Deterrence

Many argue that the infrequency with which capital punishment is imposed can hardly be expected to deter others from crime. In the study of capital punishment in Georgia, Baldus determined that a mere 23% of death penalty–eligible criminals received that punishment.[13] The irregularity and inconsistency of dispensing the death penalty may be its greatest weakness.

Failure of Legal Representation

The American Bar Association (ABA) voted in February 1997 to seek a halt to the death penalty. Its primary concern stemmed from the inconsistent quality of legal representation provided to criminal defendants facing the ultimate sanction. Some ABA attorneys argued that these critical judicial decisions turn not on the nature of the crime but on the quality of representation for the accused, citing examples of lawyers who were inadequately paid or incompetent.

Unfair Application Based on Location of the Crime

Locations of crimes also have a large effect on whether a criminal is assigned the death penalty. The University of Maryland and the Nebraska Crime Commission have each released studies that show prosecutors in urban areas seek the death penalty as much as five times more frequently than those in rural areas.[14]

Wrongful Execution

Opponents of the death penalty also argue that the possibility of killing an innocent human being is a weakness of capital punishment. They believe the chance that an innocent person may be wrongly killed is enough of a reason to ban the death penalty altogether. Since 1973, 138 people have been found to be innocent and released from death row; more than a dozen of these were exonerated due to DNA testing.[15]

In fact, most states have exonerated at least one inmate, with Florida absolving the greatest number (see **Figure 36-2**). This raises questions about the extent to which the legal system is accurately able to investigate and try suspects of crimes.

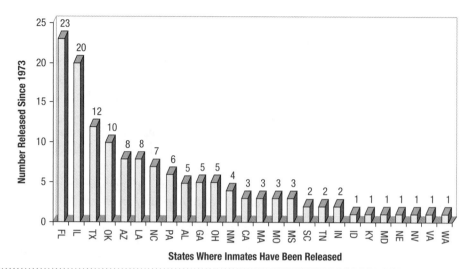

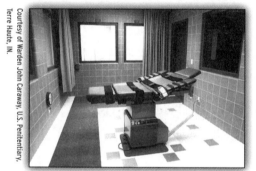

FIGURE 36-2 Death row exonerations by state; total: 138
Source: Courtesy of Death Penalty Information Center.

Methods of Execution

In 2008, the U.S. Supreme Court approved the "three-drug cocktail" as not comprising "cruel and unusual punishment."[5] This cocktail is actually three different injections: first, sodium thiopental, which is an anesthetic; second, Pavulon or pancuronium bromide, which paralyzes the muscle system and stops the breath; third, potassium chloride, which stops the heart. With this method generally being used (the exception is Ohio, which uses a one-drug method), there are still concerns that this is not the most humane method. Doctors are not allowed to administer the injections for reasons of medical ethics. Thus, injections are frequently performed by medical technicians, nurses, or prison staff. This may lead to injections into the muscle, rather than the vein, causing pain. In addition, the anesthetic may wear off before the lethal dose is administered.

■ Support for Capital Punishment

Even with the negative publicity concerning its costs and delays, many people still favor the death penalty, based on some of the following arguments. First, death penalty advocates argue that although every life should be valued and every American is guaranteed due process of law by the Fourteenth Amendment, this right does not confer the power to enjoy, as Raymond Paternoster calls it, "super due process."[16] While the Supreme Court has repeatedly claimed that the death sentence requires a more in-depth case study, the time-consuming appeals process has become extreme. If capital trials are not extensively prolonged and the appeals process is simplified, costs would be significantly lower in capital punishment cases than life imprisonment ones. Only when the judicial aspect of the death penalty is accelerated does capital punishment become substantially more economical than life imprisonment.

Others contend that the death penalty is valid because it deters would-be criminals from committing violations. Because death is the ultimate sanction a court can deliver, some believe that those criminals who consider the consequences of committing certain acts will certainly refrain rather than become a member of the death row population. Paul Rubin coauthored a 2001 study that found that the death penalty deterred 18 crimes per execution, and polls find that 40% of people believe that capital punishment deters crime.[17]

Perhaps the greatest reason that people support the death penalty is that it offers merited punishment, known as "just desserts." According to this argument, a person who takes the life of another has forfeited the right to his or her own existence, and the moral fiber of a community is strengthened when it takes the life of a murderer because it can express its outrage. Even if little crime reduction or deterrence results from the death penalty, the public continues to embrace the deserved punishment theory.

Walter Berns readily explains this argument:

> We surely don't expect to rehabilitate [murderers], and it would be foolish to think that by punishing them we might thereby deter others. The answer is clear: We want to punish them in order to pay them back. We think that they must be made to pay for their crimes with their lives, and we think that we, the survivors of the world they violated, may legitimately exact that payment because we, too, are their victims.[18]

Berns' argument allows the public the right to be angry with criminals and to act on that anger.

The overwhelming amount of support for the death penalty shows how deeply the concept of retribution is rooted in the United States. A belief in justice—the creed of "an eye for an eye" (in this case, a life for a life)—holds that retribution is the justification for capital punishment. People need absolute assurance that a convicted murderer will never again have the opportunity to become a repeat offender, and only the death penalty can offer this comfort.

Finally, some people contend that the death penalty comforts the families of victims, giving them a sense of relief and greater peace of mind. On the other hand, the long appeals process can be particularly frustrating to families of victims as they spend hours inside courtrooms during repeated testimonies during the inmate's appeal process. Finally, some victims' families oppose the death penalty.

■ Death Row Operations

Condemned inmates in U.S. penal facilities spend many years on death row. The average inmate spends 147 months (12.25 years) on death row before being executed.[19] Operating institutions that house those sentenced to death is a unique challenge. Each correctional system must consider how to house and treat these inmates. Prison administrators must decide if they will place these individuals with the general population or operate a separate death row housing area.

Several states have elected to mainstream their death-sentenced inmates and allow them to participate fully in general population work, education, recreation, and other program opportunities. These jurisdictions do not separate the inmate from others until the individual's date of execution is imminent. However, most state correctional agencies have developed separate death row operations. Generally, prison administrators have chosen to run these cellblocks as segregation units, highly controlled custodial environments that offers a high degree of accountability for these inmates who are deemed to present the most extreme threat to society. These individuals spend the majority of their time in secure cells and are out solely for minimal periods for recreation and showers. Other death row operations keep this group apart from the general population but permit relatively free interaction among the individuals under sentence of death. These units generally offer communal dining, recreation, and work experiences. Inmate programming (such as religious or educational programming) is often offered to these inmates within the boundaries of the unit.

■ The Emotional Ordeal of an Execution

Correctional administrators have expressed concern about the emotional toll that carrying out the death penalty takes on the staff.[20] Despite the harsh rhetoric engaged in by proponents of capital punishment, even by correctional staff, it is extremely difficult to participate in an execution without experiencing personal trauma. Participating staff should be selected carefully.

Many wardens responsible for an execution personally pick the staff who will participate in the death watch during the 2 or 3 days prior to an execution and use only the most mature and experienced staff for the actual execution. This selection process often involves staff who volunteer for the task, with final selection made based on their experience and ability. Some agencies will not utilize staff who volunteer; instead, they ask certain individuals if they would be willing to participate. Many institutions carefully protect the identities of staff who are involved.

The use of medical staff in an execution is another very sensitive matter. Many physicians will not participate in the actual execution and limit their involvement to the pronouncement of death. The American Medical Association sternly speaks out against physicians' participation and has stated that it is a violation of their professional ethics and the Hippocratic oath. This can present a dilemma for those states that use lethal injection as the method of execution, because it is a medical procedure. Accordingly, most executioners are nurses or emergency medical technicians who are skilled at inserting a needle into an individual's arm. All jurisdictions offer complete anonymity for these individuals.

After an execution, it is important to debrief all those who participated. This emotional time is the most difficult for the execution team, and senior staff work very hard at providing necessary social services support.

■ Special Exemptions: Juveniles and People with Mental Retardation

Two groups of people are now exempt from capital punishment: juveniles and people with retardation.

Juveniles are defined differently according to particular states. Most states have designated 17 or 18 minimum years of age, with a few states making this designation at 16 years of age. Arguments in favor of juvenile capital punishment tend to focus on this issue of crime prevention, citing statistics that homicide committed by juveniles is worse in the United States than in most other countries. Public fear of juvenile homicide is extremely high, and some argue that juvenile offenders seem to be nonresponsive to other, nonviolent types of crime prevention efforts.[21]

The argument against the death penalty for juveniles contends that youth offenders do not have fully matured brain impulse control, which usually develops in the late teens or early twenties. Juvenile offenders may have endured terrible childhoods, and they may lack a realistic understanding of death, thus strongly diminishing the deterrence factor associated with the death penalty.

While scholars may continue to debate the merits of and objections to juvenile executions, *Roper v. Simmons* (2005) effectively has ended the legal discussion. In this case, the U.S. Supreme Court ruled that offenders under the age of 18 when they committed their crimes may not be put to death, because this violates the Eighth Amendment ban on cruel and unusual punishment. The Supreme Court also decided in *Atkins v. Virginia* (2002) that it is considered cruel and unusual punishment to execute mentally handicapped persons (see **Table 36-2**).[22]

TABLE 36-2 Relevant Supreme Court Cases

Furman v. Georgia (1972)—The death penalty does not violate the Constitution, but the way that states assign it is considered cruel and unusual based on the prevalence of racial discrimination in sentencing.
Gregg v. Georgia (1976)—The sentencing phase of capital trials must be separate from the case trial.
McClesky v. Kemp (1987)—Georgia state death penalty is constitutional even though there is racial bias in the application of sentencing and executions.
Thompson v. Oklahoma (1988)—The Court ruled that offenders under the age of 16 at the time they committed the crime cannot be executed.
Stanford v. Kentucky (1989)—Executions for offenders who were 16 or 17 when they committed their crimes are constitutional.
Atkins v. Virginia (2002)—Executing mentally retarded criminals violates the Constitution's ban on cruel and unusual punishment.
Roper v. Simmons (2005)—Offenders who were younger than 18 when they committed their crimes may not be executed.

■ **Conclusion**

The government-sanctioned taking of a life is a contentious and emotionally charged issue. Nearly every argument for or against capital punishment can be refuted by opponents. Whether one invokes economic, moral, social, or legal reasoning, it is not enough to convince the other side of the rightfulness or wrongfulness of the law. The debate over the death penalty has not been resolved by logic. Clearly, emotional arguments are more significant and influential than arguments of reason. As long as most Americans believe in the concept of just desserts, it seems clear that the death penalty will remain a viable force in criminal justice for years to come. With convicted inmates such as Oklahoma City bomber Timothy McVeigh requesting his execution to be publicly broadcast, there will continue to be death penalty concerns, debates, and legal reviews. This topic is far from being concluded in the United States.

Chapter Resources

DISCUSSION QUESTIONS

1. Do you support or oppose the idea of capital punishment?
2. Why does the American public consider some offenders to be worthy of capital punishment and not others?
3. Do you feel that the execution of juvenile or mentally handicapped offenders constitutes cruel and unusual punishment?
4. How can the disparity of capital punishment based on location and age be resolved?
5. How should death penalty laws be framed to consider these concerns?

ADDITIONAL RESOURCES

Death Penalty Information Center, http://www.deathpenaltyinfo.org

Mandery, E. (2005). *Capital punishment: A balanced examination*. Sudbury, MA: Jones & Bartlett Publishers.

National Center for Policy Analysis, www.napa.com

Zimring, F. (2003). *The contradictions of American capital punishment*. Oxford, UK: University Press.

NOTES

1. *Clark County Prosecuting Attorney. Methods of execution.* Retrieved from www.clarkprosecutor.org/html/death/methods.htm
2. Snell, T. (2006). *Capital punishment, 2005*. Washington, DC: U.S. Department of Justice, Bureau of Justice Statistics.
3. Keve, P. (1981). *Corrections* (p. 468). New York, NY: John Wiley & Sons, Inc.
4. *Gregg v. Georgia*, 428 U.S. 153 (1976).
5. Death Penalty Information Center. *Death row inmates by state and size of death row by year.* Retrieved from http://www.deathpenaltyinfo.org/article.php?scid=9&did=188#year; Leibman, J. (2000, June). *A broken system: Error rates in capital cases, 1973–1995.* Retrieved from http://www2.law.columbia.edu/instructionalservices/liebman
6. NAACP Legal Defense Fund and Educational Fund. *Death row USA.* Retrieved from http://www.naacpldf.org/content.aspx?article=297
7. Bartle, L. (1996). *Current death penalty statistics*. Washington, DC: Death Penalty Information Center.
8. Costanzo, M., & White, L. (1994). An overview of the death penalty and capital trials: History, current status, legal procedures, and cost. *Journal of Social Issues*, 50, 1–18.
9. Costanzo, M., & White, L. (1994). An overview of the death penalty and capital trials: History, current status, legal procedures, and cost. *Journal of Social Issues*, 50, 10.
10. Eckholm, E. (1995, February 23). Studies find the death penalty tied to race of victim. *New York Times*, p. 1.

11. Death Penalty Information Center. Retrieved from http://www.deathpenaltyinfo.org; Bureau of Justice Statistics. *Correctional trends*. Retrieved from http://ojp.usdoj.gov/bjs/glance.htm#cptrends

12. Radelet, M. (1989). *Facing the death penalty* (p. 10). Philadelphia, PA: Temple University Press.

13. Eckholm, E. (1995, February 23). Studies find the death penalty tied to race of victim. *New York Times*, p. 1.

14. American Civil Liberties Union (ACLU). (2004, March 5). *Scattered justice: Geographic disparities of the death penalty*. Retrieved from http://www.aclu.org/capital/unequal/10532pub20040305.html

15. The Justice Project. Retrieved from http://www.thejusticeproject.org/

16. Paternoster, R. (1991). *Capital punishment in America*. New York, NY: Lexington Books.

17. Rubin, P. (2003). *Does capital punishment have a deterrent effect? New evidence from post-moratorium panel data*. Emory University Economics Working Paper No. 01-01. Retrieved from http://ssrn.com/abstract=259538

18. Berns, W. (1979). *For capital punishment: Crime and the morality of the death penalty* (p. 152). New York, NY: Basic Books.

19. Death Penalty Information Center. *Time on death row*. Retrieved from http://www.deathpenaltyinfo.org/article.php?&did=1397

20. Watson, R., personal interview, Smyrna, Delaware, October 13, 1994.

21. Streib, V. (1973, January 1 – 2004, April 30, May 4). *The juvenile death penalty today: Death sentences and executions for juvenile crimes*. Retrieved from www.internationaljusticeproject.org/pdfs/JuvDeathApril2004.pdf

22. *Roper v. Simmons*, 543 US 551 (2005); *Atkins v. Virginia*, 536 U.S. 304 (2002).

COOK COUNTY
DEPARTMENT OF CORRECTIONS
DIVISION XI FACILITY

Volunteering Inside

Richard L. Stalder

CHAPTER OBJECTIVES

- Explain the role of volunteer work in a correctional environment.
- Outline the best mechanism to recruit and secure volunteers.
- Determine the methods to ensure long-term success of volunteer programs.

Administrators of correctional programs must meet expanding service requirements with a resource base that is shrinking on a real-dollar-per-capita basis, yet long-term solutions to crime require meaningful programs that provide an opportunity for change—an opportunity that helps inmates develop basic skills and new ways of thinking. The only solution is to marshal the help of volunteers to compensate for inadequate financial resources. In the future, volunteers will be the cornerstone of correctional programs that fully meet the demands of society and the needs of the offender. Volunteers will no longer be peripheral; they will be essential to fulfilling the mission of correctional facilities.

■ Types of Volunteers

There are two primary classifications of volunteers in a correctional program: direct service and indirect service volunteers.

Direct Service Volunteers

Direct service volunteers generally provide onsite service to the program, its staff, or offenders. The scope of services may range from infrequent brief participation with a large group of volunteers to daily or weekly involvement as individuals. This category of participation typically demands the greatest sacrifice of time from a participant and may involve additional risk, depending on the area in which an individual is serving. Direct service volunteers are the core of most successful programs. They interact with staff and offenders and, in a properly administered volunteer initiative, can be very effective in contributing to the success of agency goals.

Indirect Service Volunteers

Indirect service volunteers are typically not involved onsite and generally do not have contact with the primary receivers of service. However, they can offer valuable assistance. Indirect service volunteers participate in a variety of tasks. Tasks may include fundraising; developing policy, procedure, and training manuals; offering technical assistance in the review of budgeting, accounting, and financial audit issues; and donating materials and supplies, among others.

Many programs have come to rely on the fundraising assistance of outside organizations to enable them to provide services that are not included in their core budgets. Indirect service volunteers often provide or coordinate access to facility beautification funds that are not otherwise available. Individuals who sacrifice their time to raise money are real volunteers who have a real impact.

Volunteers may be professionals in administrative and training areas and offer advice and assistance in their areas of expertise. Volunteers can contribute by developing or reviewing core policy documents and training curricula or manuals. Many professionals will donate time to assist correctional institutions in areas for which budgeted funds are not available.

Often overlooked are volunteers who solicit or donate materials or supplies for various projects. Important elements of community restoration are often not possible without this type of involvement. In Louisiana, for example, appropriated money was not available to provide supplies to an inmate artist who wanted to paint pictures for patient rooms in a local hospital; volunteers convinced individuals and organizations to donate the materials. Other inmates were interested in making toys for needy families at Christmas. Again, budgeted funds were not available for wood, glue, tools, and the other supplies needed to make the project a success. Volunteers came to the rescue and provided everything necessary to build thousands of toys.

■ Sources of Volunteers

Sources of both direct and indirect volunteer services include:

- Individuals with particular skills known by key agency or facility staff
- Civic clubs

- Religious organizations and churches
- Fraternal organizations
- Crime victims
- Special-purpose organizations

Perhaps the best mechanism to meet a defined volunteer need is to identify and solicit, through key staff, individuals who can provide the specific service. All staff must help develop a resource bank of individuals who can be called upon and who will provide assistance. In an ideal world, citizenship through service would be a part of everyone's agenda, and prison, jail, and field service staff would simply call on individuals when they were needed. Regrettably, this ideal is rarely met. Therefore, the likelihood of securing individual participation may improve if potential volunteers are contacted by someone they know who is familiar with the program.

The support of civic, religious, fraternal, and special-purpose organizations is critical to any volunteer initiative. Civic clubs (such as Lions, Rotary, Optimist, Toastmasters, and Jaycees clubs) consider service to their communities one of their primary functions. They do not discriminate against corrections and are underutilized only when they are not called upon. Their service can be both direct and indirect. Many individuals from these organizations are community leaders. Their volunteer service helps them become better informed, more effective advocates for corrections.

Religious and fraternal organizations generally have outreach programs that are related to corrections initiatives. Although the scope or type of service may be defined by the organization and not the agency, the ultimate goals typically coincide. Many mainstream religious denominations, as well as the Volunteers of America and the Salvation Army, have core service commitments to criminal justice. They provide strategic assistance to offenders and their families in areas where there would otherwise be a void.

Crime victims have been used effectively in some correctional jurisdictions. This group offers a unique perspective in terms of their ability to reflect and focus inmates on how crime has affected their lives in significant ways. Such programs have been developed and utilized in community-based correctional organizations.[1]

Special-purpose organizations also enable and enrich the delivery of critical services. Alcoholics Anonymous and Narcotics Anonymous best typify this category of organization. Broad-based programs of substance abuse education and counseling simply would not be available in many correctional institutions and work release centers or to probationers and parolees without these groups. There is little question of their importance because the majority of the individuals under correctional supervision have substance abuse experiences that relate to their criminality. Without Alcoholics Anonymous and Narcotics Anonymous, many inmates would not change their substance abuse behaviors and, therefore, would be less likely to succeed after release.

■ Components of an Effective Volunteer Program

The components of an effective volunteer program include initial development and organization, recruitment, selection, orientation, training, and recognition.

Development and Organization

The initial development and organization of the volunteer program in a correctional institution will help ensure its ultimate effectiveness. Initially, policies and procedures must be drafted and incorporated into the formal structure of the departmental program that utilizes the volunteers. This will minimize the possibility of disruption and provide consistency and direction to volunteers and staff alike. Inherent in this effort should be the establishment of clear lines of authority and the appointment of a volunteer coordinator. Whether full-time or part-time, this important position will improve communication among volunteers and staff and allow for the clear definition of expectations.

Recruitment

Recruitment strategies must be well defined. Failure to enlist the support of enough volunteers will endanger the program's success. Too many people can be overwhelming and can result in chaos with reduced productivity. Recruitment strategies must aim for the right number of the right kind of volunteers. The volunteer coordinator must use the personal contacts of staff and the reputation of established organizations to ensure that recruitment is successful. If well-known organizations have integrated their volunteers in the institution successfully, others will be encouraged to do so.

Selection

Selection follows recruitment. Improper volunteer selection will weaken a program. Neither the agency nor the volunteer nor the community benefits from informal selection practices. Unfortunately, in volunteering, one size does not fit all. Senior citizens who were very successful in hospital programs may find that the stress of a foster grandparent assignment in a secure juvenile correctional facility renders them ineffective. Interviews, education about agency expectations, and discussion of what the potential volunteer wants to accomplish are essential elements of proper selection practices. Because there are so many areas in which volunteers participate, a motivated individual can almost always be utilized in some capacity.

Background checks are important, especially in direct service. Current or recent clients of the criminal justice system are generally not the best candidates for facility volunteer assignments. Anyone who visits an inmate in a secure facility must be restricted from participating as a volunteer. Relationships with offenders in direct volunteer service must be limited to the boundaries of the volunteer duties. Formal recruitment and selection procedures are the best first line of defense to ensure that a volunteer program does not jeopardize the security of the facility. Programs involving juveniles must use extra scrutiny in volunteer selection.

Orientation

Prior to beginning their duties, volunteers should participate in a structured orientation program that covers at least the following topics:

- The basic mission and goals of the criminal justice system and the agency in which services will be provided
- The facility or field service area and the specific division in which services will be provided
- The basic security procedures appropriate to the program security level (including definitions and control of contraband and the importance of maintaining professional relationships with offenders)
- Safety and emergency procedures
- Cultural diversity awareness

Training

It is often feasible to use existing staff to train volunteers. The curricula and the length of training will vary in accordance with the scope and frequency of services provided. Initial orientation training—including a system of registration and identification that will track the volunteer throughout the period of active service—should be completed before any volunteer activity begins. Short in-service training segments often can be combined with appreciation banquets or similar functions.

Recognition

Perhaps one of the most important elements of ensuring the long-term success of a volunteer program is the formal recognition of volunteers' contributions. Plaques and letters of commendation become important mementos of service rendered. The simple act of saying "thank you" can help foster goodwill and commitment.

■ Volunteer Programming Ideas

The effect of a comprehensive program of volunteer services can be very positive. The result of volunteers' efforts may be seen in many areas, including religious services, recreation, staff training, social services, substance abuse treatment, and pre- or postrelease programs. These are only examples of areas in which volunteers can assist. Each institution will have unique needs and opportunities. For example, volunteers may also be used in institutional library settings, administrative support roles, legal service programs for staff and offenders, and health care.

Religious Services

Perhaps the most traditional and largest area of volunteer service in a jail or prison is religious programming. In fact, this is one of the oldest types of volunteer programs in American corrections; members of the clergy first became involved in prison programs in the 1700s and 1800s. Their primary purpose was to "help offenders repent."[2] The staff chaplain often handles the overall coordination of volunteers. Facilities typically are unable to provide assistance to all faith groups without the help of volunteers. Under federal law, institutions must ensure access to (often obscure) religious faiths and practices. Volunteers may make the difference in whether compliance can be achieved and maintained.

Recreation

Another important area of service is recreation. The community is an important ingredient in sports programming in a facility. Leadership and sportsmanship can be taught very effectively by volunteers who compete as individuals or teams, participate in training officials, or serve as coaches or fans. This organizational component of most institutions is often unsupported by appropriation and therefore depends on volunteer involvement.

Staff Training

Staff training represents an often overlooked area where volunteers can make a contribution. Many institutions do not have sufficient staff or funds for outside contractors to provide training in areas such as cultural diversity, employment law, management and supervision practices, and technical medical and mental health issues. The professional development of staff is a good way to involve the community in the institution.

Social Services

Offender education programs require volunteer support to provide service to any significant number of inmates who need to develop academic and vocational skills. Volunteers can work in literacy, adult basic education, and job skills development programs. Education is a cornerstone of any program to reduce recidivism by improving opportunities for legitimate employment after release. Education is also traditionally underfunded. Therefore, it should be a primary focus of the volunteer initiative.

Substance Abuse

As previously mentioned, without volunteers, the ability of facilities to provide broad-based programs of substance abuse education would be severely diminished. Alcoholics Anonymous and Narcotics Anonymous have a long, widely heralded record of accomplishment in correctional institutions. The commitment of individual volunteers, many of whom have previously conquered substance abuse problems, is a significant factor in this success.

Pre- and Postrelease

Pre- and postrelease programs are other examples of critical areas that receive too little budgetary support given their importance in meeting correctional goals. Volunteers fill this gap (see **Table 37-1**). They provide

TABLE 37-1 Suggestions for Starting and Maintaining a Volunteer Program

Evaluate the need: After determining what tasks are not getting done or are overextending staff, decide whether these tasks could be handled effectively by volunteers.

Develop goals and job descriptions: Write up the goals of the volunteer program, as well as job descriptions for volunteers, so that administrators, staff, and the volunteers themselves know what volunteer positions entail.

Involve staff: Be sure to include staff (especially staff who will work directly with volunteers) in all planning and implementation of volunteer programs. If their input is included, staff will have a greater desire for the program to succeed because they will share a sense of program ownership.

Actively recruit volunteers: There are many organizations one can contact to find volunteers. Churches, civic groups, retirement organizations, and colleges and universities are all good choices for volunteer recruitment.

Explain security needs to volunteers: Instruct volunteers on the institution's security policies and procedures, and explain why they are needed. Otherwise, volunteers may resist institution security precautions simply because they do not understand their purpose.

Give volunteers the big picture: Teach volunteers about the institution's mission and services so they have a sense of how their contributions are a part of the facility's overall operations.

Evaluate program effectiveness: Once a volunteer program is in place, it is crucial to know how well it works. All volunteer activities must be carefully documented so program and volunteer effectiveness can be evaluated. Once the program has been established, it also should be formally evaluated by staff, inmates, and volunteers. With this information, one can make sure the program's purpose is being served.

Recognize the volunteer's contribution: Volunteers, like all of us, need to be recognized for their work and accomplishments. A pat on the back can go a long way, particularly in a demanding field like corrections. Recognizing volunteers for their contributions can help keep them motivated and involved.

Educate volunteers about inmates: Before inmate contact begins, caution volunteers on the pitfalls that await those who are not familiar with the inmate culture and who may be easy prey for manipulative inmates. This is necessary to protect volunteers from being used and to maintain the institution's security.

Source: Reprinted with permission from Ogburn, K. R. (1993). Volunteer program guide. *Corrections Today, 55,* 66; American Correctional Association, Alexandria, VA.

service—not just enrich what is already provided. Community support to the released offender is frequently the only support available. Involvement begins at the institution with education in a prerelease setting about how to access services. The involvement continues after release, with volunteers serving as mentors and providing guidance and support.

■ Conclusion

Everyone is a winner in a properly organized and administered volunteer program. Inmates receive services they would otherwise not receive; this can only improve the odds for successful adjustment in and out of the institution. Staff receive the benefit of community expertise, allowing them to sharpen their professional skills and be more effective in their jobs. The agency and facility are opened to the community, helping erase traditional misconceptions about jails and prisons as external support increases. The most important player, the volunteer, is also a winner; citizenship through service is its own reward.

Chapter Resources

DISCUSSION QUESTIONS

1. How do direct and indirect volunteer service providers differ?

2. Why should volunteers be required to undergo an orientation process before working with offenders in an institutional setting?

3. What types of information about inmates should volunteers be exposed to and why?

4. What are the advantages of a properly organized and administered volunteer program?

5. What types of pre- and postrelease programs can help an offender make a successful reentry into his or her home community?

ADDITIONAL RESOURCES

American Correctional Association. (1993). *Helping hands: A handbook for volunteers*. Laurel, MD: Author.

Love, B. (1993). Volunteers make a big difference inside a maximum security prison. *Corrections Today*, *55*, 76–79.

Prison Literacy Project. (1993). *Prison literacy project handbook*. Philadelphia, PA: Author.

Sigler, R., & Leenhouts, K. (1985). *Management of volunteer programs in criminal justice*. Denver, CO: Yellowfire Press.

Weston, P. (1977). *Volunteers in justice*. Washington, DC: National Association of Volunteers in Criminal Justice.

NOTES

1. Costa, J., & Seymour, A. (1993, August). Crime victims, former offenders contribute a unique perspective. *Corrections Today*, *55*(5), 114–117. Laurel, MD: American Correctional Association.

2. Coleman, J. (2003, December). Chaplains: God's partners in prison. *Corrections Today*. Retrieved from http://www.correctionalchaplains.org/gods%20partners/gods%20partners.html

Emergency Preparedness

YOU ARE THE ADMINISTRATOR
■ Rioting in New Castle

Riots broke out in Indiana's privately run New Castle Correctional Facility on April 24, 2007. For two hours, about 500 inmates ran wild, burning mattresses, smashing windows, and throwing furniture. Before response teams arrived on the scene, several guards and maintenance workers barricaded themselves in a room to avoid dozens of raging inmates wrapped in masks and wielding sticks and knives. Two staff and seven inmates suffered minor injuries, including cuts, scrapes, and tear gas exposure.

According to Indiana Department of Correctional Commissioner J. David Donahue, the rioting began after several newly transferred inmates took of their shirts in the prison's recreation area in protest. Later, a spokeswoman for the prison management company said that inmates had been complaining about the lack of recreation and other inmate programming.

After the incident, the state analyzed the events and recommended pressing charges against 26 inmates, most of whom were recently transferred from another facility in Arizona. Their report concluded that the transfer happened too quickly as an effort to combat overcrowding in the privately managed Arizona prison. The Department of Corrections insisted that in the future more time be allowed to hire and train staff to prepare for large transfers.

- What does this event show about causes of institutional unrest?

- What steps could have been taken to prevent this riot?

- What use of force is appropriate in circumstances like this?

Source: Charles Wilson, "Prison Riot Charges May Come in July" Associated Press, June 26, 2007, available at http://www.indystar.com/apps/pbcs.dll/article?AID=/20070626/LOCAL/706260430& template, accessed July 26, 2007; "Indiana Halts Transfer of more Ariz. Inmates," Associated Press, April 25, 2007, available at http://www.msnbc.msn.com/id/18294136/, accessed July 26, 2007.

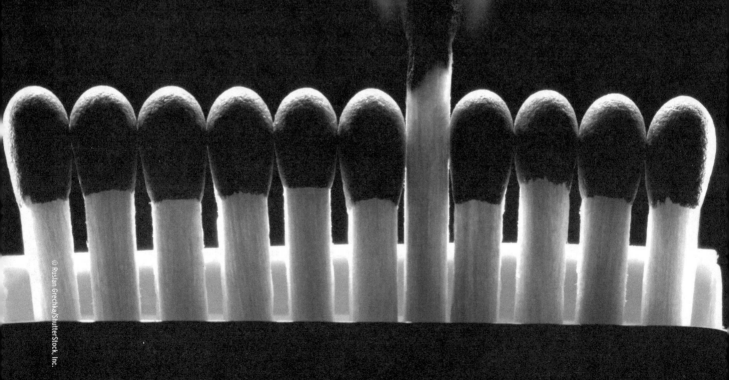

Causes of Institutional Unrest

John J. Armstrong

CHAPTER 38

CHAPTER OBJECTIVES

- Describe the basic mission of a prison under a confinement model.
- Give examples of the varied sources of unrest in correctional facilities.
- Explain the relationship of prison management practices to prison unrest.

P rison riots resulting from unrest have occurred in the United States since before the Revolutionary War. If correctional professionals fail to recognize, understand, and control the causes of unrest, unrest will remain an unfortunate hallmark of correctional administration.

■ Causes of Unrest

The sources of unrest are as varied as the correctional facilities that have experienced violence. Researchers suggest several causes, including:

- Crowding
- Insufficient funding
- Gang activity
- Racial and cultural conflict
- Changes in policy
- Poor management practices
- Insufficient staff training
- Inadequate facility security
- Poor living conditions
- External events

Despite the complexity and diversity of disturbances, the American Correctional Association has narrowed the causes of prison unrest to three general categories: inmates, conditions of confinement, and correctional management. Unrest often involves a failure in more than one category.

Inmates

Felons incarcerated as a consequence of a lack of self-control present special challenges. These inmates are often angry and antisocial and seek immediate gratification when faced with a problem. Inmate-created unrest does not always spring from a sudden or specific cause. An unhealthy facility climate frequently sparks unrest. Effective staff can recognize subtle verbal and nonverbal changes in inmate behavior. If they do not, investigation and control measures may be limited to reactive, after-disturbance efforts, rather than proactive ones.

The presence and influence of gangs also contribute to inmate-created unrest. Gang activity in a prison focuses on dominance and turf control, often along racial or geographic lines. Gang rivalries spawn a climate of tension, violence, and coercion. New gang members are recruited by force. Nonaligned inmates often arm themselves for protection against gang activities. Staff can control this threat to the well-being of a facility by installing mechanisms to gather intelligence and to identify gang members and leaders. These mechanisms are reviewed regularly to check that they are performing well and incorporate due process protections. Staff recognize gang-affiliated inmates by their tattoos, association with other known gang members, personal property, involvement in group activity of a negative nature (assaults, etc.), and by their own admission.

Unrest also results when predators are not separated from particularly vulnerable inmates, such as those who are very young or very old, are weak, are retarded, or have disabilities. An effective inmate classification system, in addition to staff that promptly recognize such problems and responds appropriately, undermines this type of threat.

Conditions of Confinement

Some unrest may appear inmate created but instead is rooted in the conditions of confinement and is related to communication, sanitation, food, idleness, inadequate facility maintenance, cell space, access to medical or mental health care, work, school or addiction programs, or innumerable other service delivery areas.

The conditions of confinement leading to unrest generally develop gradually over time and are typically multifaceted. It is important that the correctional team recognize changes that are occurring within a facility environment that would evidence a growing instability. A declining quality of the staff–offender relationship is a key factor, as are increases in the number and severity of disciplinary reports, inmate grievances, and incidents, particularly those involving dangerous contraband, interpersonal violence, and staff use of force. The aforementioned factors are often occurring concurrently with waning facility sanitation, and offender compliance with dress and grooming standards.

Frequently, these indicators are initially met with a stiffening of custodial approaches and a further hardening of the conditions of confinement. Although understandable as an interim measure, in the long term, this response would promote rather than address developing unrest.

An area of particular concern toward the conditions of confinement is inmate grievances concerning inmate access to programs and services. Although the quality and quantity of medical and mental health services may be the most urgent and compelling, this source of tension affects most of the population as it also relates to meaningful work, education, training, visitation, chaplaincy, and counseling programs.

A significant factor of unrest may appear, over time, in the style of correctional management embraced by the agency in pursuit of the complex goals of the correctional mission. Specifically, the manner and approach of setting activities in motion toward the achievement of the multiple goals of incarceration is vital to the level of unrest that may manifest at a particular facility. This is especially important when considering the custody–treatment relationship as it pertains to the mutual support of a full range of meaningful and accessible inmate programs.

Crowding has been the most explosive condition in recent correctional history. Unprecedented prison population growth has plagued jurisdictions throughout the country at a time when public sector funding has continued to decline as a social priority. Population growth affects everyone—staff, inmates, and the public. Overcrowding reduces the quality of life in a facility, burdens its physical plant, and increases staff stress. These environmental, physical, and social pressures serve as a seedbed for destructive perceptions that lead to a sense of hopelessness in inmates and staff alike.

Correctional Management

Correctional managers promulgate policies and procedures based on established correctional standards and continually review them against set performance measures. Effective management practices lead to staff success, high employee retention rates, and little or no unrest.

Facility and departmental policy and procedure manuals and post orders supply staff with the organization's mission, values, and expectations; the basis of authority; and an outline of each position's responsibilities. Consistent policies that govern inmate conduct and accountability are the foundation of facility security, order, and safety. In a secure facility, staff and inmates perceive consistency, fairness, and justice as uniform standards applied in the absence of discrimination.

In recognizing correctional management's role in directing staff toward the accomplishment of the organization's mission, values, and expectations through policy development, it is important to stress that the leadership team must constantly strive to achieve balance among the complex goals involved. Punishment, incapacitation, rehabilitation, and deterrence are the predominate goals, but can create an exceptional challenge to meet together within the intrinsically punitive environment of the prison.

Above all other goals, a common propensity of a correctional agency is to view its primary mission as custodial. Although this tendency may be easily understood in terms of public and political pressures to maintain custody and control over their wards, other equally important goals may be reduced in value and significance by day-to-day security interests.

For example, the goal of providing secure correctional facilities to ensure the safety of the public, the staff, and offenders tends to collide with and often diminish the value of promoting sound correctional programs that reduce tension and foster opportunities for offenders to improve their skills, behaviors, and lifestyles.

Those agencies that view prison order shortsightedly tend to focus on a high degree of regimentation, close custody monitoring, and overly restrictive movement within facilities. These highly structured environments can decrease opportunities for inmates to engage in programs that reduce aggression, boredom, and idleness; improve facility climate; build self-esteem; and lower inmate misconduct.

Corrections professionals recognize that prisoner misconduct disrupts order, endangers lives, and results in considerable costs.[1] In one study, it was determined that inmates completing substance abuse programs were 74% less likely to engage in misconduct.[2] Other studies have indicated that prisoners who participate in programs have broader perspectives, recognize the consequences of their actions, and are less likely to be involved in violence in prison.[3]

Prisons with a full range of viable programs including recreation, counseling, religion, education, vocational education, visitation, and substance abuse treatment are seldom the sites of major incidents or serious disorder. Programs are an effective management tool that provides positive outlets and sets the tone for an environment built on cooperation and is conducive to safety, security, and order.

A final deliberation of a narrow custodial mission is the potential of creating a detrimental and enduring contention among the custody and treatment ranks. In leading a correctional mission, communal and undivided support for the collective mission and goals is essential to fully understand, sustain, and nurture the complex interrelationships that reduce unrest and support healthy facility outcomes.

To be effective, disciplinary, grievance, and classification appeal processes must be easily understood by inmates and supported by staff. Fair and uniform appeal process outcomes are important to avoid unrest. By investigating and reviewing incidents, an administrator can evaluate circumstances leading to unrest. In addition, institutions should have a clear mission statement, the foundation for all policy development and decision making. It serves as the benchmark for all operations, as the prime reference and resource for agency and facility administrative directives. When staff apply policies, procedures, and support structures to climate-related problems, they balance their actions against the agency standards and values established in the mission statement.

■ Prison Management

Almost every major prison riot in recent history has involved a security breach. To maintain facility security, staff must be able to rigidly control all operational elements. A comprehensive program of security audits ensures compliance with established standards and the requirements stated in the operations manual. Security auditing often will reveal vulnerabilities and offer correctional management an ongoing method by which to document, correct, and consistently improve operations and security. The consistent application of the principles of auditing—specifically, evaluation, correction, and follow-up—reduce the potential of the security breach as a precursor to a critical incident.

A unit's operations manual is the blueprint that outlines several key areas of management:

- Essential plans, systems, and post orders
- Proper reporting procedures
- Practices for issuing and controlling keys, tools, and weapons
- Techniques for conducting routine and random searches for contraband
- Methods for conducting urinalyses, inspections, tours, and visiting
- Systems for maintaining inmate documentation

Managers also carefully establish the framework in which they communicate with each other, their subordinates, and the news media. A clear chain of command with clean lines of authority reduces inmate unrest resulting from mismanaged information or indecisiveness. Established channels of communication to staff and inmates eliminate confusion, misinformation, and destructive rumors.

For example, changes in operating policies disrupt highly structured prison routines and the expectations of inmates and staff. The prudent distribution of information, accompanied by explanation when necessary, lightens the impact of the message. Nevertheless, change—whether in policy, privileges, or living conditions—always heightens tension in a prison. Consequently, timing becomes a paramount concern when implementing change.

Accessible and responsive administrators and staff lead inmates to feel free to communicate and to know that they will receive appropriate and timely feedback. Reasonable questions and concerns are met with reasonable responses. Staff effectively counter externally driven causes of inmate unrest (such as issues reported in the media) with open and honest communication. Managers also counter externally driven causes by explaining to reporters, legislators, and governmental officials the effect of their messages on corrections. For example, reports of "get tough on crime" proposals are often interpreted by staff and inmates as fact, even before legislation has been introduced.

Effective managers also recognize that agency and facility stability results from recruiting quality applicants and maintaining high-quality preservice and in-service training programs. The challenges facing modern corrections also require training in cultural sensitivity. For example, a common problematic social dynamic found in many American prisons is that staff from predominantly suburban or rural areas supervises urban inmates. (Inevitably, most inmates are from major metropolitan areas, and most prisons are located in isolated areas.) It is difficult to develop open communication between staff and inmates from such diverse backgrounds. Staff must be taught to view all offenders the same way; fairness is the key. Instances of perceived disrespect or injustice involving staff-driven or inmate-driven cultural or racial stereotypes create conditions resembling a tinderbox waiting for a spark.

■ Actively Gauging the Climate

Staff in direct contact with offenders are a facility's eyes and ears, its primary resource for identifying unrest indicators. Their evaluation of the inmate population is dynamic and continual. Facility security depends on how effectively these professionals deal with offenders and how the professionals use their training and interpersonal skills to evaluate the institution's climate.

Among all correctional professionals, correctional officers have the most daily interaction with the largest number of inmates. When the health, safety, and welfare of inmates are preserved, when their lifestyles of criminality are altered, chances are responsibility lies not with the psychiatrists or social workers, but with skilled and concerned correctional officers. Dedicated and vigilant correctional professionals are the linchpin in the effort to achieve institutional safety and security.

Facility tours can act as another barometer of facility climate. All employees—including medical and program staff and administrators—should conduct area inspections and evaluate trends in incident and disciplinary reports, offender grievances, confiscated contraband, recreational grouping, and commissary activity.

Effective management depends on rumor control, and rumor control depends on rumor identification. Responsive line staff monitor rumors. Disregarding rumors places a prison climate at risk. Most rumors start with a grain of truth; otherwise, they would not be transmitted. Some, however, are propelled by personal issues. After filtering the information they gather informally, staff must be empowered to investigate and defuse a rumor or a consequent condition. Such empowerment should be tempered by the observance of communication priorities and the chain of command.

■ Management by Walking Around

Managers frequently walk through a facility, not just to be seen, but also to observe, listen, respond, and evaluate. Meeting the correctional mission requires management by walking around: paying attention, interacting with staff and inmates, and identifying and addressing problems.

An unannounced or random walk often helps an administrator check on the eight dimensions of criminal justice performance measures for prisons: security, order, activity, conditions, safety, care, justice, and management.[4] All management staff are encouraged to do this. If prison wardens want staff to be their eyes and ears, they must set the example by daily visits throughout the facility. Staff tend to emulate the leadership style and organizational values and expectations that are demonstrated regularly by senior management officials.

The agency commissioner and the facility warden hold the most visible positions in corrections and determine whether a department is successful. They ensure public protection, staff safety, and the maintenance of a secure, safe, and humane facility in a climate promoting high standards of professionalism, respect, integrity, dignity, and excellence.

■ Interpreting the Indicators and Achieving Performance

Indicators of unrest and prison performance measures appear dissimilar (see **Table 38-1**), yet one set of indicators cannot be assessed without considering the others. Assessment is crucial to the effective and active management of a prison climate; all such data are linked and, together, provide a valid overview of the institutional environment.

TABLE 38-1 Predictors of Riots and Disturbances

Separation of inmates by racial or ethnic groups
Increase in purchases of food items at inmate canteens
Transfer requests
Staff requests for sick leave
Inmates gathering with point people facing away from the group
Increase in disciplinary cases
Increase in voluntarily lockups
Inmate–employee confrontations
Direct and indirect inmate intimidation of officers
Threats against officers
Inmate sick calls
Inmate violence against other inmates
Increase in number of weapons found in shakedowns
Harsh stares from inmates
Drop in attendance at movies or other popular functions
Unusual and/or subdued actions by inmate groups
Appearance of inflammatory and rebellious materials
Warnings to "friendly" officers to take sick leave or vacation
Employee demands for safety
Staff resignations
Letters and/or phone calls from concerned inmate families demanding protection for inmates
Unusual number of telephone inquiries about facility conditions
Outside agitation by lawyers or activists
Increase in complaints and grievances

Source: Reprinted with permission from *Preventing and Managing Riots and Disturbances* (p. 131), American Correctional Association, Alexandria, VA.

■ Conclusion

Prevention is an everyday event in a prison—on every shift for every employee. An agency attuned to detecting problems can identify a problem in its early stages and resolve it before it becomes a crisis. Forestalling unrest requires active monitoring of the prison environment, detection of unrest predictors, investigation of problems, and quick and appropriate resolution.

Chapter Resources

DISCUSSION QUESTIONS

1. Are riots an inevitable consequence of the prison environment?
2. What are the most effective strategies to reduce prison unrest and the violent disturbances that may result from such unrest?
3. How should a prison administrator develop an awareness of inmate tension?
4. Why is prevention of institutional unrest considered a key component of good correctional leadership?
5. Are public expenditures better focused on crisis response planning, disturbance suppression training and riot equipment, or prevention-centered activities?

ADDITIONAL RESOURCE

Wright, K. (1994). *Effective prison leadership*. Birmingham, NY: William Neil Publishing.

NOTES

1. Lovell, D., & Jemelka, R. (1996). When inmates misbehave: The costs of discipline. *Prison Journal, 76,* 165–179.
2. Langan, P., & Pelissier, B. (2002). The effect of drug treatment on inmate misconduct in prisons. *Journal of Offender Rehabilitation, 34,* 21–30.
3. Edgar, K., & Martin, C. (2001). Conflicts and violence in prisons. *Journal of the Economic Research Council, 42,* 1–3.
4. Logan, C. (1993). Criminal justice performance measures for prisons. In J. DiIulio (Ed.), *Performance measures for the criminal justice system*. Washington, DC: U.S. Bureau of Justice Statistics.

Emergency Management

E.A. Stepp

CHAPTER OBJECTIVES

- Describe the role a prison administrator plays in emergency preparedness.
- Explain the stages of response: planning, active management, and aftermath.
- Differentiate between emergency response and emergency preparedness.

Prison and jail riots or disturbances continue to be the nightmare of institution administrators. Although events necessitating full-scale emergency response are rare, they are ever-present in prison managers' minds. Any number of small, isolated, and seemingly unimportant events that occur frequently can mushroom into full-blown emergencies. Emergencies can occur in isolated portions of a facility or, when not immediately contained, engulf the entire prison.

Disturbances range from passive demonstrations by inmates (i.e., food or work strikes) to violent acts against property, staff, or other inmates. Whether an event is planned by a few individuals or orchestrated by a large group, it can escalate quickly into a worst-case scenario, such as a riot, hostage situation, or escape.

How, then, do prison administrators operate safe and secure institutions? How can staff move from routine daily operations to the highest level of emergency response? After the events of September 11, 2001, how can prison administrators prepare for traditional responses to prison emergencies and ensure that emergency plans incorporate new response standards established by the federal government? To answer these questions, one must take a look at the entire process of prison emergency preparedness and the new coordinated, all-hazards approach to emergency management.

■ Planning

The planning stage of emergency response includes development of established, specific emergency response plans, training, and assignment of resources. Before anything happens, management must ensure that staff are prepared to recognize and respond to a multitude of different emergencies. Each type of situation may require an individualized, specific response plan. If the first stage of emergency response is emphasized, a system of emergency preparedness can be established. There is a huge difference between emergency preparedness (preparation, planning, training, and budgeting) and emergency response (active management, intervention, containment, and resolution). The goal of any administrator must be to establish an emergency preparedness program to ensure that actual emergency response is effective.

The first step in preparing a response to emergency situations is to develop site-specific plans for each type of emergency. An overall emergency plan for an institution contains several contingency plans for specific emergencies. These include plans to resolve riots, escapes, hostage situations, weather emergencies, food or work strikes, fires, and situations that could necessitate evacuation of inmates and staff from the institution. Planning for these and other types of emergencies will require establishing a contingency-planning team consisting of different staff experts from various departments in the institution.

Internal Cooperative Contingency Planning

Planning for emergency response requires a "big picture" approach that examines all available resources. All contingency plans must define the responsibilities of staff from various departments. This is true when planning for even small situations. Plans must be developed through cooperative means, using the collective experience of staff from all departments in the institution. In cases where emergency plans are written by security staff, with little or no input from other departments, unrealistic or dangerous assumptions may be made.

All emergency plans should cover certain general elements clearly:

- *Communication of the initial alarm.* Once an emergency situation is identified, all staff must know how to alert management and others of the situation.
- *Securing the scene and initial containment of incident.* Most emergencies begin small and spread quickly if initial containment actions are not effective. It is critical to the final resolution of any incident to contain the incident to the smallest area possible by locking the affected area or building.

- *Command structure.* All plans should specify responsibilities for immediate emergency response command. Everyone must know who the initial on-scene commander is before the arrival of senior management staff.
- *Notification and callback procedures.* Emergency situations must be communicated swiftly and clearly to the facility chief executive officer. A standard process of timely and urgent recall of staff to the institution should be in place.
- *Command center location and operation.* The location of the command center must be established clearly. Appropriate equipment and instructions for activating a command center must be in place in a secure location. Because predicting the location of an incident is impossible, the command center should be located in an area inaccessible to inmates. In most cases, this requires establishing a command center outside the secure portion of the institution. Emergency plans, communication equipment, and enough space for several staff to work are essential when planning for a command center.
- *Preparation of emergency response teams.* Before correctional administrators can begin to develop strategies to resolve emergencies in their facilities, it is critical that decisions be made regarding resources that will be not only needed but also dedicated to the emergency response.

Emergency Response Teams

Different levels of response are required, contingent on the type of emergency faced. For each level of response, different teams with incident-specific training are required. Regardless of team membership and levels of specialty expertise, common qualities apply to all. All teams must be composed of volunteers, receive specialized training in specific skills, and be highly trained in agency policy regarding use of force. All staff selected for membership on any team should be required to pass physical, academic, and psychological screening.

TRADITIONAL DISTURBANCE CONTROL TEAMS. The first level of response to disturbances is the traditional disturbance control team (DCT). DCTs are trained in riot control formation and the use of defensive equipment such as batons, stun guns, and chemical agents. DCTs are trained to control and contain both large and small groups of inmates involved in disturbances. Application of "less lethal" technologies usually falls to DCTs. Extensive training is necessary and should include minimum proficiency standards. A certification process must be included that requires a knowledge of agency policy and emergency plans as well as proficiency in the use of related equipment.

ARMED DCTs. While traditional DCTs should be viewed as the primary emergency response team for incidents requiring containment and control, a higher level of response may be necessary to deal with a difficult scenario that has escalated to one that requires the use of deadly force. This type of incident requires managers to respond with a specially trained team; the use of an armed DCT should be limited to situations where staff or inmate lives are in imminent danger. Training and certification standards increase as the manager of the incident follows an escalating use-of-force continuum. Use of armed DCTs implies that management has accepted that lethal force may be used.

TACTICAL RESPONSE TEAMS. Tactical response teams are the most highly trained and skilled emergency response staff. These teams, known as correctional emergency response teams or special operations response teams, are similar to traditional special weapons and tactics teams found in most police departments. Tactical teams required advanced levels of training in barricade breaching, hostage rescue tactics, and precision marksmanship with pistols, rifles, and assault weapons.

External Cooperative Contingency Planning

Most emergency situations in correctional institutions require assistance from outside law enforcement sources. Since 9/11, there has been a renewed emphasis on cooperative contingency planning. This requires effective cooperation with entities outside of correctional agencies or departments. Historically, correctional facilities have developed emergency plans with an emphasis on self-directed, self-sustained response. Agreements with local, state, and federal agencies were often ill-defined or nonexistent. Failure to establish relationships with outside agencies will contribute to an already chaotic situation and prolong incident resolution.

Managers must ensure that institution emergency plans include mutually agreed-upon cooperative contingency plans with outside agencies. Plans may be as simple as assistance with site access and traffic control or as complicated as meshing institution tactical teams with outside tactical resources and hostage rescue attempts. Regardless of the level of assistance, preexisting memoranda of understanding establishing limits of assistance and command and control will reduce confusion and delay. Managers must be able to implement plans and take actions to resolve the situation and not debate questions of philosophy regarding expertise, resources, or how to accomplish a given goal.

Cooperative contingency plans should be signed by the outside agency representative and the institution warden. Once this is accomplished, role definition is achieved. Institution managers must also realize that coordination with local or state emergency action centers is important. Intelligence briefings regarding both domestic and international terrorism threats can be provided so long as mutual assistance agreements exist. Outside groups such as terrorist organizations may believe it newsworthy to target government facilities, including prisons. Prison administrators can no longer take an "inside out" approach to emergency planning. Planning must also include an "outside in" review and plan.

Training and Mock Exercises

A realistic training program must include all key staff. Because not all staff will be available to respond during an emergency, managers must ensure that cross training of staff occurs. Staff will be much more prepared and effective when they can perform multiple tasks and assume a variety of roles during an emergency.

For any emergency plan to succeed, all staff must be familiar with their responsibilities and management expectations. The only way to determine whether a plan is effective is to conduct regular tests and analyze results. Management must evaluate emergency plans, devise training scenarios, and analyze staff performance. Major exercises involving all staff and outside agencies should be conducted at least annually. This type of mock exercise requires planning, use of resources, and coordination with each cooperative contingency plan outside the agency. In most cases, however, emergency plans can be tested with little or no disruption of normal institution operations.

Small, internal training exercises that test specific parts of plans should also occur regularly. These tests include communication devices, staff recalls, command center setup, and area containment. Having staff who are trained properly in their roles and in the requirements to implement emergency plans is the goal, as it limits the amount of time required to contain and ultimately resolve a crisis. The beginning of any emergency is the most critical time. There is often an early window of opportunity to resolve or, at a minimum, contain the incident. Managers should demand effective, well-rehearsed emergency plans to ensure that confusion and delay do not become the reality of the response.

One of the most important aspects of emergency preparedness is knowing the capabilities and limitations of various emergency response teams. Practicing scenarios where each team participates with other groups, including outside agencies, will provide this critical information to crisis managers.

Testing emergencies plans should include the following steps:

1. Identify those staff who are to respond and those to be used as role players.
2. Ensure that staff are cross-trained.

3. Ensure that staff know how to assume their various roles.

4. Assign monitors to evaluate and criticize the exercise.

5. Provide a method of terminating the exercise should a real incident occur.

6. Establish a code word or signal to alert staff should an actual emergency occur.

7. Conduct a debriefing with all staff participants.

The debriefing is a critical component. This evaluation of the exercise should provide useful feedback from participants. Gathering information from training participants allows management to assess the organization of emergency teams, the adequacy of communication, and the overall use of resources. On the basis of this feedback, administration can revise plans to achieve better results in actual emergencies.

Meeting Legal Requirements

A final step in the training portion of preparation is ensuring that all prearranged agreements with other agencies have been reviewed by the respective legal representatives. Short-notice implementation of these agreements will be required. Before implementation, everyone in the institution should know what staff from other agencies legitimately can and cannot do during a crisis.

Tactical Options

Tactical planning and preparation for crisis resolution is an important element of overall emergency response training. Standard tactical plans will not be incident specific but will be based on certain known factors. These include agency philosophy and goals and tactical capabilities of teams. Flexibility of response is necessary. Standard, preexisting tactical plans based on agency management philosophy can then be tailored to specific situations as intelligence and information from the crisis develop.

A crisis manager can use any of the following three options to resolve major incidents in a correctional setting:

1. Negotiation—involves the least amount of force

2. DCTs—involves nonlethal technologies and options such as chemical agents and distraction devices

3. Use of deadly force—involves intervention by an armed team

An effective emergency management structure relies on the use of all resolution options because options only work properly when used together. Negotiations cannot succeed without tactical options. Tactical options cannot succeed without information and intelligence obtained by negotiators. All components of the emergency management structure must cooperate and train together to ensure success. Success for one is success for the entire emergency management structure.

It is nearly impossible to plan a specific response to all the different crisis situations that could arise in a correctional setting. However, an effective emergency preparation program should include plans for accessing all areas of the institution during an emergency. Preplanned breach points and means of entry provide the needed flexibility to develop an incident-specific tactical plan during active management of the emergency situation. Preestablished breaching plans should include the following:

- *Identification of a staging area.* There should be primary and secondary staging areas for teams that are not visible to inmates, media, or the public.
- *Plan of approach.* Primary and secondary approaches should exist to areas that provide concealment.
- *Preparation for entry.* Again, primary and secondary points of entry into all buildings should be established in advance of a crisis.

- *Required physical hardware and equipment necessary to effect entry*. Every building inside the secure perimeter of the institution should have blueprints that identify doors, windows, hatches, tunnels, and all locking devices. The type of construction and strength of walls, doors, and so on must be known in advance.
- *Identification of the method-of-entry options for opening or removing by force*. Each entry point must be planned in advance. All possible entry methods should be documented, including keys, cutting tools, torches, saws, and explosives.
- *Assignment of primary entry teams*. Tactical teams must work together and practice the techniques before attempting forced entry in an actual situation. Incident-specific plans can then be developed based on known variables in the preexisting breach and forced entry plans.

All staff members must understand the institution's policy on use of force. Managers plan the resolution phase during active management of a crisis in accordance with a use-of-force continuum. A use-of-force (particularly deadly force) policy is based on the reasonable response from staff to actions by the inmate. A sequence of escalating steps lead to the top of a continuum. At each level, the policy should define clearly what response from staff is acceptable in response to actions initiated by an inmate or group. Response by staff must meet the threat level presented. The response and the policy are governed by law. Active management of a crisis in a correctional setting does not include rules of engagement—a military term that permits a more flexible strategy of response. The response to each emergency is always governed by preexisting use-of-force policy that remains consistent and legally and morally acceptable, regardless of the nature of the crisis or incident.

■ Prediction

Prediction is the phase of emergency preparedness that precedes the implementation of a well-planned emergency response. This phase will develop the methods to identify the possibility of an emergency, the probable type of incident, and the best response. The prediction phase requires daily communication of risk factors identified in the prison population. Emergencies can often be predicted if disturbance factors can be identified and evaluated properly.

Prison administrators should develop a risk analysis mechanism designed to predict the degree of possibility for an emergency. This risk analysis should include intelligence information, an assessment of inmate grievances and complaints, and a review of any possible common ground issues (factors that affect the entire inmate population) discovered. These issues may include

- Medical care
- Food service and preparation
- Disciplinary programs
- Inmate work assignments
- Safety
- Sanitation
- Grievance procedures

■ Prevention

Prevention is the phase of emergency preparedness that enables the prison administrator and the staff to maintain or restore safe, humane, and professional conditions of confinement of the inmate population. This phase, like prediction, requires constant monitoring and communication among staff. Prevention includes appropriate programs for inmates and effective safety, security, and sanitation programs. The most important factor in prevention is consistent enforcement of rules, policies, and directives. In almost every prison in the United States, establishing a daily routine and communicating expectations must be a priority. Communication of any changes to the inmate routine reduces the risk factors and serves as a means of prevention. The bottom line is that prevention requires complete reporting of disturbance risk factors and responding with actions that mitigate these factors.

New and Additional Emergency Preparedness Elements

With the likelihood of intense scrutiny both during and after any prison disturbance, utilization of all available outside resources will be required. Additionally, managing a disturbance or emergency in a prison requires planning and execution of strategies that are familiar to other law enforcement and emergency response agencies.

Continuity of Operations Plan

A continuity of operations plan (COOP) is designed to ensure continuing facility operations of personnel and technical infrastructure. Terms of the plan should be tailored to meet the requirements of the National Incident Management System (NIMS) (discussed in the next section). The COOP is a concept that requires evolution of traditional response into protection of electronic and communication, water, power, and sewer systems, along with designations of key personnel who would assume direction of various operations in worst-case scenarios. COOP plans are broken down into three main topical sections. Each section may contain as many as 12 subsections of specific required activities and coordination. These plans are designed to cover a wide range of potential incidents.

An example taken from the Florida Division of Emergency Management includes the following areas:

1. Contact information (state, county, and agency and facility name)—All primary response personnel and alternates should be listed with primary and secondary contact information.

2. Policy and administration—Objectives, responsibilities, planning assumptions, plan execution, and postincident review and remedial actions should be documented.

3. Essential elements criteria—This includes procedures; clearly defined mission; essential functions; delegations of authority; orders of succession; alternate facilities; interoperable communications; vital records and databases; logistics and administration; security, physical, and operational coordination of personnel; and testing, training, and implementation of emergency plans.[1]

National Incident Management System

NIMS was established by the Secretary of Homeland Security to standardize emergency responses from differing jurisdictions and disciplines. The theory behind NIMS is to enable responders to work together more quickly and effectively when responding to natural disasters and other large-scale emergencies. NIMS focuses on a unified approach to incident management and command structures and emphasizes mutual aid agreements among agencies.

Although it may be difficult to view a local prison disturbance in the same light as a disturbance that occurs on a national scale, the concept of NIMS does translate to local jurisdictional mutual aid agreements as detailed earlier. The national plan incorporates best practices (lessons learned) from incident managers at the federal, state, and local levels as well as in the private sector. All emergency preparedness planning and training should incorporate the elements of NIMS into local plans. Just as the prison administrator wants to eliminate common ground issues from the inmate population, law enforcement, through NIMS, attempts to lay a common ground framework for all potential emergency responders.

National Response Framework

A National Response Plan, developed by the Department of Homeland Security and superceded in 2008 by the National Response Framework (NRF), is a comprehensive approach to emergency management that goes hand in hand with NIMS and the Incident Command System (ICS). It establishes protocols for national, state, and local jurisdictions as well as the private sector to coordinate responses to a crisis. The principles of the NRF are

1. *Engaged partnership.* Leaders from all levels of government will be partners and contributors. This collective response to emergencies will help ensure that no one agency or level of government is overwhelmed by a crisis.
2. *Tiered response.* This idea is to ensure that all incidents are managed efficiently and effectively at the lowest level of government and are augmented by additional support only when necessary.
3. *Scalable, flexible, and adaptable operational capabilities.* This principle references the concept that all incidents are unique and can escalate or diminish over time. Partnership assets can be requested through ICS and NIMS and activated/deactivated as necessary.
4. *Unity of effort through unified command.* The ICS/NIMS activity will work closely with each agency's chain of command structure with a goal of seamless coordination and use of resources.
5. *Readiness to act.* This highlights the principle of preparation in advance of an incident so all involved agencies are ready for any emergency.

The NRF establishes goals from an emergency response point of view and provides insight to prison administrators in preparing local plans.[2]

Dealing with the Aftermath

After a crisis situation is contained and resolved, the prison administrator's toughest challenge may just be beginning. In all major crises in a correctional setting, returning the institution to a normal, pre-event status is a unique challenge for administrators. Administrators must have a plan to deal with inmates and their needs. Just as important, they will need a plan to deal with staff and their needs. Feelings of guilt, disbelief, and failure are common among staff following a major prison incident. Support functions for both staff and the inmate population will be critical in returning the facility to normal operations. Staff from both the chaplain's department and the psychology department should play an important role in dealing with and resolving deep-seated feelings among staff and inmates. Support and counseling for everyone involved must be available and be a part of the institution's emergency preparedness planning and response.

Conclusion

Emergency preparedness plans require utilization of all available resources to ensure an effective and practical system of response that can also be implemented in concert with outside resources. The use of NIMS and ICS and a review of the NRF will result in a better and more realistic emergency plan. However, planning for emergencies in a prison setting still requires the use of traditional first responders.

Chapter Resources

DISCUSSION QUESTIONS

1. Do you support the use of deadly force for resolution of disturbances?
2. Does the cost of preparation and training affect active emergency management and crisis resolution?
3. Have prisons and jails been affected by domestic and international terrorism?
4. What are the differences in emergency planning in today's world compared to the planning done before September 11, 2001?
5. What role do Homeland Security and the NRF play in local planning?

NOTES

1. County Coordination Checklist—Continuity of Operations, Division of Emergency Management, Department of Community Affairs. (2004). "County coordination checklist for agency COOP plans in accordance with chapter no. 2002-43: Relating to disaster preparedness—Amends 252.365," Florida Division of Emergency Management. Retrieved September 23, 2007, from http://www.floridadisaster.org/documents/COOP/CountyCoordination Checklist.pdf
2. Department of Homeland Security. *National response framework*. Retrieved June 2, 2013, from http://www.fema.gov/national-response-framework

SECURITY

Crisis Negotiation in Correctional Settings

Thomas J. Fagan and Dyona Augustin

CHAPTER OBJECTIVES

- Describe three types of critical incidents encountered in correctional settings.

- Discuss advantages and disadvantages that correctional administrators have in responding to critical incidents compared to community law enforcement officers.

- Describe the typical negotiation team structure and discuss the roles of each team member.

- Explain the major steps or tasks needed to successfully resolve a hostage incident.

- Discuss proactive steps that a correctional administrator can take to prepare for correctional critical incidents.

■ Introduction

Law enforcement officials, including correctional administrators, are tasked with resolving various types of critical incidents such as riots, victim-focused events, and hostage incidents every year.[1] Each type of incident has its own set of presenting characteristics and requires a response strategy that addresses these unique characteristics.[2] Common response strategies employed by law enforcement include such tactics as contain and wait, snipers, chemical agents, tactical assault, and/or negotiation.[3] Although the presenting characteristics of critical incidents may vary across community and correctional settings and among different perpetrators, negotiation has become the preferred response strategy for a number of critical incidents in law enforcement since its inception in the early 1970s.[4,5] Specifically because it is relatively easy to implement in the early stages of an incident, it has the potential to de-escalate the emotional tenor of the situation, it allows other incident responders the time they need to gain intelligence, and it allows tactical teams the time they need to develop and practice tactical solutions should they be needed.[6,7] In short, seeing as how talking is never lethal, law enforcement officials continue to use negotiation to defuse critical incidents because it has a long track record of saving lives.[8]

■ Types of Critical Incidents

As noted above, there are three types of critical incidents commonly faced by law enforcement personnel: riots, victim-focused events, and hostage incidents. A riot is defined as an uncontained situation (i.e., no clearly defined perimeter) characterized by individuals in a highly emotional state with limited direction and leadership and few well-defined demands.[9] In correctional riots, prisoners may roam the prison wreaking havoc wherever they go, cause physical and/or psychological injury to staff and other inmates, destroy prison property, and even take hostages. Clearly in cases such as this, the primary focus for correctional administrators is to contain the situation as quickly as possible to minimize damage, prison escape, and potential loss of life. Thus, tactical options may be more effective in achieving this objective than negotiation because the latter strategy may be more difficult to impose in an uncontained situation without clearly defined demands or leadership.

Victim-focused incidents occur when an individual takes a specific person captive with the intention of expressing emotions (e.g., anger, rage, lust, frustration) he has toward the victim.[10] For example, a man may take his ex-wife captive as a result of his jealousy over her moving on to another man. Similarly, an inmate may take a correctional officer captive if he believes that the officer has treated him unfairly. In victim-focused events, the incident is typically well contained from the onset; however, the captor is typically in a highly emotional state, is acting impulsively, and has no clearly defined objective other than directing his emotional turmoil at a specific individual who he believes is responsible for his emotional distress.[11,12] Typical victim-focused events include barricaded subject incidents and domestic violence events.[13] In cases such as this, the captor does not need law enforcement officials, including negotiators, to assist them with anything. Everything they need is contained within their environment, and their only request to law enforcement officials may be to leave.[14] In victim-focused incidents, the initial goal of law enforcement officials is to try to stop violence aimed at the victim before actively trying to resolve the incident.

A hostage incident occurs when an individual takes another individual captive and uses the captive as leverage in order to get demands met by law enforcement officials. Hostage incidents are goal directed in the sense that the hostage taker uses a hostage as a bargaining chip in order to meet his *instrumental* (or tangible) needs; that is, in order to gain access to things to which he would not otherwise have access (e.g., drugs, escape, political/social change, money).[15] Hostage situations tend to be contained events with defined goals—goals that can only be met with the assistance of law enforcement personnel. Although hostage incidents tend to be rare in correctional facilities, they can be incredibly costly when they do occur in terms of their short- and long-term consequences (e.g., physical injury, property damage, psychological trauma, and even death).[16] The correctional administrator's goal during a hostage incident is to gain the safe return of the hostage(s) while also minimizing property damage, loss of life, and major concessions to hostage takers.

■ Correctional Versus Community Incidents

Although all three types of incidents occur in both community and correctional settings, the frequency of occurrence differs across settings. In particular, community law enforcement officials are more likely to face victim-focused events, whereas correctional administrators are more likely to encounter riot and/or hostage incidents, albeit at relatively low frequencies.[17]

In comparison with community law enforcement administrators, Fagan notes that correctional administrators may have several advantages (and relatively minor disadvantages) in managing incidents in correctional facilities.[18] For example, prison walls or fences provide correctional administrators with some degree of initial containment; in contrast, community law enforcement officers must first establish a perimeter before working toward problem resolution. Also, though correctional administrators have quick access to previously gathered psychological, criminal, and medical data (that can be helpful in terms of profiling the perpetrator and his motives), community law enforcement officials must gather and then sort through this information—a process that can be time-consuming. Moreover, community law enforcement officials may be called to sites with which they have limited or no familiarity, whereas correctional officials are often familiar with the layout of their facilities.

Another issue that may affect the management of an incident is the amount of disruption that may be caused by an event. In the course of establishing a secure perimeter, community law enforcement personnel often cause considerable disruption to the general public by detouring traffic, establishing roadblocks, or evacuating buildings or entire neighborhoods. In contrast, though containing a correctional event may cause some disruption to basic prison or jail operations, such activities as periodic lockdowns, restricted movement, and use of boxed meals (i.e., the kinds of actions that may result from a critical event in a prison or jail) occur periodically in correctional settings in response to various activities. Although no one likes their routine to be disrupted, correctional populations may tolerate these disruptions for longer periods of time compared to the general public allowing correctional managers more time to resolve the situation. Finally, correctional personnel are at an advantage in that they are constantly searching the facility for weapons and confiscating them when they are discovered. Although certainly not guaranteeing the absence of all weapons, it does reduce the number and types of weapons available to inmates. Community law enforcement personnel may face greater personal risk in terms of the weapons available to perpetrators in the community.

Although correctional administrators may have several small advantages in managing correctional incidents, they also have two potential disadvantages. First, community incidents most typically involve a single perpetrator, whereas correctional incidents have greater potential to involve multiple perpetrators with competing issues and demands. Second, when a community event ends, the instigators of the event will likely end up in a correctional setting. Although they may be unhappy with the outcome of the incident or blame community law enforcement for unmet promises, their dissatisfactions are directed at community law enforcement, not correctional personnel. Conversely, when a correctional event ends, the perpetrator remains in the correctional setting. Thus, any animosities resulting from the incident remain and may reappear in subsequent incidents if left unresolved.

■ Examples of Correctional Hostage Incidents

Correctional hostage incidents may be sparked by any number of precipitants. Some of the most common causes of correctional incidents include inmates who get caught in the middle of a crime (e.g., stealing drugs, escaping) and then seize the person(s) who discovered them; inmates dissatisfied with prison conditions (e.g., health care or food choice or quality); and inmates who are frustrated and angered by abusive, disrespectful correctional staff members.[19,20] Accordingly, hostage incidents may be planned as a means of bringing public attention to prison conditions or may evolve spontaneously as a result of some minor precipitating event. Even though an event may begin as one type of incident (e.g., a prison riot), it can eventually evolve into a hostage incident as the situation unfolds. The examples that follow are used to illustrate the causes and outcomes of three well-documented correctional incidents.

Attica Penitentiary—September 1971

The Attica penitentiary is a large correctional facility located in upstate New York. At the time of the event, the institution was populated predominantly with African American and Puerto Rican inmates from New York City but staffed primarily with white correctional officers from the surrounding rural communities. Additionally, the situation was further exacerbated in at least a couple of ways.[21] First, racial tensions were high and further fueled by the black power movement of the 1970s. Second, in addition to correctional administrators being "old school" (i.e., firm believers in infrequent talk with inmates and frequent use of segregated housing for discipline), prison conditions were described by inmates as being harsh (e.g., crowded living conditions, lack of adequate medical treatment, a dearth of programming opportunities, and rough treatment from staff). Although the prisoners had protested these harsh conditions through brief prison protests as well as letters to the warden and governor, their concerns seemingly fell on deaf ears.

Consequently, on September 9, 1971, following an incident in the prison's dining room, inmates began to riot. Correctional officers were quickly overpowered by inmates, and these inmates eventually broke into the institution's control room, freeing inmates in other cellblocks. As these inmates moved through the prison, acts of brutality and violence were directed toward both staff and other inmates; eventually, one officer and three inmates were killed, and additional staff members were taken hostage. Given the mistrust engendered by the warden and his staff, attempts to negotiate with the prisoners proved futile, as did negotiation attempts made by the New York State Corrections Commissioner. Eventually, on September 13, 1971, the New York governor ordered the state police to retake the prison. Although it only took state police 6 minutes to rescue the captured staff and about an hour to secure the facility, 39 people (including 10 hostages) were killed, and an additional 80 individuals were wounded in the process.[22,23] Although the results of this incident were tragic, they did highlight the need for more effective communication among responders, the need for emergency planning, and the need for better emergency preparedness training.[24] The lessons learned from this single event served as an impetus for other correctional institutions throughout the country to develop, implement, and practice emergency management procedures.

Federal Correctional Institution, Oakdale, Louisiana, and U.S. Penitentiary, Atlanta, Georgia—November 1987

These lessons were put to the test in November 1987 when the Federal Bureau of Prisons lost two facilities to inmate rioters in the span of 2 days.[25] Both the Oakdale and Atlanta prison disturbances, which began 2 days apart, were precipitated by an agreement between the U.S. State Department and the Cuban government calling for the return of 2,700 Cuban detainees who were in federal custody pending deportation to Cuba. Many of these Cubans had fled Cuba and the Castro regime several years earlier and had no desire to return to Cuba. When detainees from both prisons (which housed primarily Cuban inmates) heard about this agreement, tensions rose quickly, riots broke out in both facilities, government property was destroyed, buildings were set on fire, and staff members were taken hostage—28 in Oakdale and 110 in Atlanta.[26] Almost immediately, negotiators began to work around the clock in order to secure the release of hostages. After 9 and 11 days, respectively, the negotiators were able to successfully address inmate concerns by securing an additional layer of review by immigration officials prior to any deportation. Despite the magnitude and duration of these incidents and the extensive resulting property damage, loss of life was minimal and negotiation proved its effectiveness.

Southern Ohio Correctional Institution, Lucasville, Ohio—April 1993

Following a series of incidents in 1990 that resulted in the murder of a staff member and several inmates, prison officials at the Southern Ohio Correctional Institution developed a plan to tighten prison security.[27] Included in this plan were such steps as introducing controlled movement to the institution, restricting programming time and opportunity, implementing more frequent shakedowns of inmate housing units, and removing inmates from jobs where they might have access to sensitive information. Consequently, in April 1993, hundreds of prison inmates began to riot in response to these initiatives, and eventually 12 staff members were taken hostage. During the initial inmate takeover, four staff hostages were seriously injured, and on the fifth day of the incident, one staff hostage was murdered. In addition to requesting amnesty for participating in the riot, inmates demanded the replacement of the current warden, improved medical care, reviews of the current mail and visitation policies, and freedom of religious speech for Muslims.[28] Ultimately, negotiators were able to secure the release of some hostages during the incident in exchange for such concessions as allowing a radio broadcast of inmate demands, and the remaining hostages were released on the 11th day, when a negotiated settlement was reached. During this event, nine inmates were murdered by their peers—two of them after the negotiated settlement had been reached.[29]

■ Negotiating Correctional Incidents

Before and at the time of the Attica disturbance, most correctional critical incidents were managed using tactical solutions with negotiators serving in a supportive role. However, as negotiation has proven its effectiveness repeatedly since the Attica disturbance, it has evolved into the preferred response option in most situations.[30] Nonetheless, research suggests that the success of negotiation is based in large part on how well it is integrated into the larger institutional response protocol.[31] **Figure 40-1** presents a sample organizational chart to illustrate the many components needed to successfully respond to a critical incident while also simultaneously managing those remaining portions of the prison that are not actually involved in the incident.

This chart should trigger a few observations. First, there are many response components needed to successfully resolve a critical incident. Second, during a critical incident, it might be relatively easy for any one responder to get bogged down in whatever role he or she is assigned, thus losing sight of the big picture. From a correctional administrator's perspective, all response components are important, and their individual issues need to be addressed in order to bring an event to a successful conclusion. However, decision making may be delayed, and this can be frustrating for individual response components. Third, with so many response components working on different aspects of the event, it is vital that a clearly defined response plan be developed and articulated to all responders so that individual response components are working in conjunction with and not against one another. In other words, a unified response strategy that is clearly communicated to all operational components is essential to a successful outcome of the incident. Having highlighted the "big picture," the remainder of this section will focus on the negotiation response component.

The Negotiation Team

The negotiation team utilizes verbal strategies to engage the hostage taker, de-escalate the emotional intensity of the situation, and resolve the incident with minimal injury or property damage.[32] Additionally, the negotiation team also serves as a vital source of information for correctional administrators and tactical teams. At a minimum, an effective negotiation team will be composed of at least three members—a team leader, a negotiator, and a recorder.[33-36] However, a typical team will consist of a team leader, an assistant team leader, a primary negotiator,

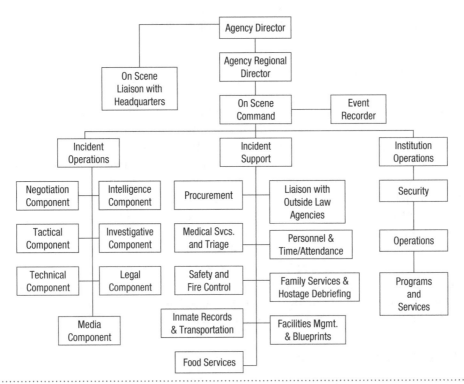

FIGURE 40-1 Critical incident management: An organizational chart

Source: Reprinted with permission of the American Correctional Association, Alexandria, VA.

a secondary negotiator (coach), a recorder, and a mental health consultant.[37,38] The size, scope, and duration of an incident may necessitate a much larger team or the formation of multiple teams.[39] Descriptions of the negotiation team members, as delineated by both Fagan and Noesner, will be described later in text.[40,41]

Negotiation Team Membership

As the name suggests, the team leader directs the entire negotiation team. The team leader coordinates all team activities, represents the negotiation team in the command center, provides feedback to the on-scene commander about the status of the negotiation process, and relays information and command center decisions back to the negotiation team (usually through the assistant team leader). The assistant team leader is responsible for organizing and managing the operations of the negotiation team in the negotiation operations center (i.e., where the actual negotiation occurs); for relaying negotiation information, reports, and proposed strategies to the team leader; and for settling disputes between team members as they arise.

The primary negotiator is the only person who maintains actual verbal contact with the hostage taker. It is, therefore, important that he possess certain qualities/characteristics (e.g., good verbal and interpersonal skills, flexibility, objectiveness, maturity) that will enable him to develop rapport with the perpetrator as well as determine which strategies would work best in terms of bringing about a successful resolution to the crisis incident. The secondary negotiator is the primary negotiator's helper. His role is to coach the primary negotiator when the need arises (e.g., when the primary negotiator drifts into an unproductive area), to serve as a second set of ears for the primary negotiator, listening

Delaware Department of Corrections crisis negotiation team.

for what the negotiator is missing or not hearing from the hostage taker, and to filter information from the team members to the primary negotiator so as not to distract the primary negotiator from his duties.

The recorder keeps a detailed, chronological record of the negotiation process as it is unfolding, maintains situation boards (i.e., lists of important items like demands, names of hostage takers and hostages, important medical issues, deadlines) for the team that serve to facilitate their memory and focus, and may prepare periodic situation reports that summarize key developments in the negotiation process for other response components. Lastly, the mental health consultant is usually a mental health professional who joins the team either as a full member or as a consultant brought into situations as needed. The mental health consultant brings a unique knowledge base to a critical incident and may aid the negotiation team by developing psychological profiles of the hostage takers, helping to craft negotiation strategies/tactics, proposing activities that can help foster cohesiveness among negotiation team members, and crafting training scenarios that assist team members in proactively improving their skills.

In addition to these basic team members, some agencies also include a tactical liaison and an intelligence liaison in their basic team configuration. These additional positions on the negotiation team highlight the importance of maintaining constant communication between negotiation and tactical team members and sharing information among all response components.

The Process of Negotiation

Similar to critical incidents that occur in the community, correctional incidents share the same ultimate goals, that is, to save lives, to minimize property damage, and to restore order.[42] However, reaching these goals can follow an uneven, frustrating path filled with emotional highs and lows. Thinking of negotiation as a process with specific steps, phases, or tasks can make a challenging task more manageable. Additionally, it can also assist both negotiators and correctional administrators in more accurately measuring the progress of negotiation. Although different researchers conceptualize the negotiation process in different ways, the current authors propose negotiation as a six-step process or as a series of six tasks that need to be accomplished generally in a sequential fashion with each step or task making the next step easier to accomplish.[43] These tasks include

1. Establishing contact with the hostage taker and opening a line of communication
2. Restoring calm to the situation
3. Gathering information
4. Developing a plan or negotiation strategy
5. Selling the plan first to on-scene commanders and then to the hostage taker
6. Preparing for the release of hostages and the surrender of hostage takers

The first step that the negotiator must take is to establish contact with the hostage taker(s) by opening a reliable line of communication (e.g., via a hostage "throw" phone, cellular telephone, conventional telephone, bullhorn). During this stage, the negotiator must speak to the identified hostage taker(s), establish rapport with the hostage taker, and eventually establish personal authority as the hostage taker's only communicative link to the outside world. Although this step sounds easy, it can easily become complicated by the availability of appropriate communication equipment, the availability of tactical resources to safely deliver the equipment to the hostage taker, the willingness of the hostage taker to speak to the negotiator, the presence of multiple hostage takers, and the elimination of other individuals who may also be speaking to the hostage taker. The successful completion of this task makes all subsequent tasks easier to accomplish.

Once a communication link is established, the negotiator must assess the emotional tenor of the situation and attempt to restore calm to the situation. Frequently, the early stages of a hostage incident are extremely stressful—emotions are in overdrive and behavior can be erratic and impulsive. Until these emotions are brought under control, hostage takers will not be able to effectively participate in the rational give-and-take that is essential to the negotiation process. During this stage, the negotiator will typically use various active listening skills (e.g., sharing observations, mirroring, open-ended questions, minimal encouragers, labeling emotions) to calm the hostage taker, and in doing so, the negotiator gives the hostage taker the opportunity to express his feelings and emotions. By taking the time to actively listen to the hostage taker, the negotiator may build some rapport with the hostage taker;[44] this may increase the likelihood that the hostage taker will comply with the negotiator's later requests. Although the duration of this stage may vary from incident to incident, this stage tends to take longer to accomplish in victim-focused incidents where expressive needs represent the primary motivation for the event.

Once the hostage taker has calmed down, the negotiator can move on to the task of gathering relevant information in a more systematic way. Questions about the hostage taker's motivations, demands, issues, external support systems, and problem-solving resources are much easier to assess once the hostage taker is calmer and thinking more rationally. In this stage, the negotiator may use techniques such as probing questions (e.g., "Could you tell me more about . . . ?"), clarifying questions (e.g., "Could you clear this up for me?"), and summarizing statements (e.g., statements that capture the main elements of what has been said). These techniques can help the negotiator understand what is significant to the hostage taker, how the hostage taker perceives the incident (as well as its antecedents), and what the hostage taker believes is needed in order to end the event positively. Information gathered during this stage may also benefit other response components (e.g., the tactical team or command center) in their emergency response planning and decision making.

During the fourth and fifth stages, the negotiator uses all the information obtained during the previous stages to develop a negotiation plan that addresses the hostage taker's issues and demands and that can lead to a successful outcome. Brainstorming techniques and role-playing various strategies may help negotiation teams arrive at the best strategy. Once a strategy has been crafted, it must be approved by the on-scene commander and reviewed by other response components before being introduced to the hostage taker(s). In introducing the plan to the hostage taker(s), the negotiator must determine the best way to present the plan. Essentially, the negotiator must create an environment in which the hostage taker feels that (a) his complaints are being heard, (b) the negotiator is reasonable and willing to make compromises, and (c) complying with the negotiator's requests represents a win-win situation for both the hostage taker and the negotiator. This stage ends when the hostage taker has agreed to release the hostages and surrender.

In the sixth and final step, the negotiator determines all the details of the hostage taker's surrender and puts them into effect in order to successfully resolve the situation. Issues such as how and to whom hostages are to be released or who will surrender first—hostages or hostage takers—must be worked out with tactical teams and on-scene commanders to avoid confusion during the actual release and surrender.

Understanding the Hostage Taker

The six steps outlined earlier can be helpful in guiding the negotiation team through the negotiation process and can be useful indicators of progress. Knowledge about three other factors—the motivation of the hostage taker for precipitating the incident, the basic personality structure of the hostage taker, and the hostage taker's propensity for violence—can also assist the negotiation team in their strategizing and planning.[45-47] For example, as mentioned earlier, some hostage takers are very goal-directed and view hostage taking as a means to achieve a desired end (i.e., instrumental motivation). Others view hostage taking as a way of seeking revenge or retaliation for real or perceived wrongs (i.e., expressive motivation). Assuming that the negotiator has taken the time to assess the hostage taker's motivation, then the negotiator can usually make some predictions about how the negotiation process will progress and which techniques will be warranted. For example, perpetrators with primarily instrumental needs will likely spend more time in the latter stages of the negotiation process (i.e., because they already know what they want and know that they will need the authorities to assist them in achieving their goals). However, perpetrators with primarily expressive needs will tend to spend more time in the earlier stages because emotional expression is their primary motivation. Once expressed, these hostage takers may become more realistic, realize the seriousness of their predicament, and seek a quick, safe exit from the situation.

Similarly, knowledge about the personality structure of the hostage taker may help inform negotiators about possible strategies. For example, a psychopathic individual characterized by aggressiveness, impulsivity, egocentrism, manipulative behavior, disregard for the law and the rights of others, and an absence of empathy, remorse, and/or guilt may warrant more straightforward negotiation strategies that appeal to the hostage taker's ego, keep the hostage taker focused on personal survival, and give the hostage taker the illusion of personal control. In contrast, seriously mentally disturbed individuals such as those suffering from various forms of psychosis may present negotiators with psychological symptoms like delusions, hallucinations, tangential speech, bizarre behaviors, and confused thinking. Negotiators may have a more difficult time with these types of individuals because they tend to be unclear in their thinking patterns, reasoning, and speech. In these cases, the negotiator may need to spend considerable time keeping the hostage taker focused on reality-based issues that can be managed successfully. By tailoring the negotiation strategy to the hostage taker's unique personality dimensions, negotiators enhance the probability of a successful outcome.

Perhaps the single most important question for both the negotiator and other responders to address in the early stages of the negotiation process is the hostage taker's propensity for violence. The mental health consultant can be especially helpful in evaluating the many factors that contribute to a careful risk assessment for both violence and/or suicide.[48] However, even without the guidance of a mental health consultant, the negotiator can gather information about the hostage taker's past history of violent behavior; past history is often the best predictor of current behavior.[49] Factors such as the presence and types of weapons available to the hostage taker along with their lethality must also be considered. Similarly, any previous relationship between the hostage and hostage taker may shed some light on the violence potential inherent in the situation.

Other Factors to Consider

There are a few other factors that can have an effect on the negotiation process and will be briefly mentioned here. There has been much written about Stockholm syndrome—a psychological process where the hostage may begin to identify with the captor and may eventually see law enforcement officials as the "enemy."[50] Researchers have debated whether this syndrome routinely forms in all hostage events and have identified the passage of shared time and space as primary contributors to the syndrome's development.[51] To the extent that correctional incidents can sometimes span several days with hostages and hostage takers in proximity, the possibility that hostages may develop positive feelings toward their captors and may become more sympathetic to the hostage taker's cause cannot be ignored. This identification with their captor might become an important issue for correctional administrators to consider when evaluating information provided by these hostages who are released before the incident's conclusion.

Although individual inmates may take hostages for their own personal reasons, so too might groups or gangs of inmates take hostages to address the instrumental and/or expressive needs of the group. For example, a street gang might feel singled out and discriminated against by correctional staff. Hostage taking may be their way of expressing their frustration or their way of obtaining a wider audience toward which to express their concerns. Individual gang members may have different or competing issues that can complicate the negotiation process. In other words, the negotiator may be negotiating with several inmates simultaneously until the group can articulate a single set of demands.

Offenders housed in America's prisons and jails (especially those located in urban areas) come from all parts of the globe—each offender bringing his or her own customs and beliefs. Knowledge of the ethnic, cultural, and racial composition of an institution as well as the unique beliefs and values of these different groups is important if these individuals become involved in a hostage incident.[52]

During hostage events, it is not uncommon for individuals (e.g., family members of hostage takers, community leaders) to offer their assistance to negotiators. Additionally, hostage takers will sometimes ask to negotiate directly with community representatives (e.g., local reporter or newscaster). These people are sometimes called "third-party intermediaries" and are defined as individuals who are allowed to converse with the hostage taker even though they are not a member of the law enforcement response team.[53] Although the use of third-party intermediaries may seem appealing, especially when the negotiation process has stalled, these individuals are not trained in law enforcement emergency response procedures and can sometimes make promises that are difficult for law enforcement to accomplish and equally difficult to undo once made. Current conventional wisdom is to either avoid the use of third-party intermediaries or to carefully script and rehearse them before allowing them to speak to the hostage taker.

■ Emergency Preparedness

As is evident from the above discussion, hostage incidents begin for various reasons, are motivated by different factors, and involve individuals with different personality, racial, ethnic, and cultural characteristics. Managing these events can be time-consuming, labor-intensive, stressful, and disruptive to the orderly running of a correctional institution. Although correctional administrators can do much to avoid these incidents through proven correctional management principles, history indicates that these events will nonetheless occur occasionally. History also suggests that thinking about and preparing for the possibility of such events is a sound proactive strategy. Preparation may take the form of developing specific policies and procedures for managing various types of correctional critical incidents (e.g., fires, hurricanes, riots, hostage incidents), or it may take the form of staff training.

Policy and Procedure Development in Emergency Preparedness

Correctional institutions have many general policies in place to facilitate the smooth, routine running of the institution. Developing policies and procedures to address the management of critical incidents in advance of their occurrence has several advantages.[54] First, it allows staff to discuss response options in a calm, thoughtful manner rather than in a rushed, reactive manner during an actual incident. Second, it allows staff to collect and place material and equipment that may be needed in emergency situations in locations where it can be easily accessed during an emergency. Third, it affords correctional administrators the opportunity to contact other law enforcement agencies and work out agreements regarding how each agency will respond to a correctional incident. Fourth, policy can define chain-of-command structure both within individual response components and across response components. Fifth, it can define certification or qualification standards for team membership within specific response components that require specialized knowledge or skill. Sixth, it can define specific training timetables for each response component. And seventh, policy may provide the content around which staff training can occur regarding emergency response procedures. At a minimum, staff training focused on correctional hostage incidents should concentrate on at least four key areas—first responder training, hostage survival skills training, specific team training (e.g., negotiation team training), and joint training exercises for all response components.[55]

First Responder Training

Critical incidents may occur at any time, and any institutional staff member may be first person on the scene of a critical incident. Accordingly, all institutional staff should receive basic training on what to do if they are the first person to arrive on the scene. This training should discuss the importance of containing and stabilizing the situation before making contact with the individual. It should also define steps that should be taken to establish contact with hostage taker(s) and, more importantly, behaviors that should be avoided in order to minimize harm to hostages and optimize the chances for a successful resolution to the incident.

Hostage Survival Skills Training

All correctional workers are aware of the fact that they can potentially be taken hostage at any time. Thus, correctional facilities must also make sure that all correctional workers are taught basic hostage survival skills. As the name suggests, hostage survival skills training involves a set of skills or techniques that, if implemented, can help the correctional worker reduce the likelihood of being victimized while being held captive and help maximize his chances of surviving a hostage incident. Essentially, staff members learn to remain calm during a hostage incident, refrain from engaging in actions/behaviors that will increase the hostage taker's stress level, and exhibit human qualities (which can potentially endear the hostage taker to the hostage, making it less likely that he will hurt the hostage). Most institutions offer this type of training on at least an annual basic to ensure that all correctional staff remain mindful of these techniques.

Negotiation Team Training

Being selected as a negotiation team member should mark the beginning of a training regimen that provides team members with the knowledge and skills they need to carry out their specific team assignments. Negotiation team training often focuses on (a) learning to avoid errors that have been made in the past in other critical incidents and by other teams; (b) developing specific techniques, strategies, and skills that can be useful in defusing volatile situations and bargaining with hostage takers; (c) identifying specific roles and job functions within the negotiation team; (d) understanding how personality and motivational factors can affect a hostage taker's behavior and requests; (e) discussing the ways in which critical incidents can affect those directly and indirectly involved (i.e., the

Delaware Department of Corrections crisis negotiation team during routine training exercise.

responders); (f) becoming familiar with different equipment used during the negotiation process; (g) engaging in role-playing activities that help negotiation team members practice the skills they have acquired; and (h) learning more about other factors (e.g., Stockholm syndrome, the effect of culture/race) that may affect the negotiation process. In order for negotiation team training to be effective, it must occur regularly, be progressive and extensive, and address team deficiencies as they are identified.

Delaware Department of Corrections crisis negotiation team. Recorder passing information to the primary negotiator during a training exercise.

Joint Training Exercises

If individual team training (e.g., negotiation, tactical, intelligence gathering, public information officers) is effective, then individual teams will develop considerable proficiency in their specific areas of expertise. However, unless teams learn how to integrate their skills into the institution's larger response strategy, the success of the overall institution response may be jeopardized. Joint training exercises or maneuvers provide one way for different teams to practice coordinating their activities with other response components in order to achieve a single, unified response during an actual critical incident.

◼ Conclusion

Hostage incidents are one of several types of critical incidents that can occur in correctional settings. Although they tend to occur infrequently, their effect can be significant in terms of the short-term (e.g., property damage) and long-term (e.g., psychological trauma, physical trauma) consequences on staff and inmates alike. Although the tactical option used to be the primary strategy used by law enforcement officials to deal with critical incidents, past history suggests that negotiation may be the safest and easiest first step to employ in successfully resolving a hostage incident. Successful resolution of hostage events can be facilitated in a number of ways. Specifically, correctional facilities can increase the likelihood that their efforts will be successful by making sure that their negotiation teams are well trained; ensuring that team members are well integrated into the overall response strategy of the institution; and certifying that all staff members are proactively made aware of the institution's policies and procedures regarding hostage events, among other things. Although following all these steps cannot ensure that an institution's negotiation efforts will be completely successful, it can help to decrease the occurrence of preventable errors that might adversely affect the negotiation process.

Chapter Resources

DISCUSSION QUESTIONS

1. It is often said that negotiation is the easiest thing to do in a hostage incident. Do you agree with this statement? Explain your position.
2. In this chapter, several sequential steps or tasks were detailed regarding the negotiation process. Why is it important to complete each step or task before moving on to the next step?
3. What is the value of training all correctional workers in hostage survival skills?
4. Explain how expressive versus instrumental needs can influence the course and outcome of a correctional incident.
5. Why is it essential that correctional administrators adopt a unified response strategy when responding to a critical incident in a correctional setting?

ADDITIONAL RESOURCES

International Association of Hostage Negotiators (IAHN), www.hostagenegotiation.com

National Council of Negotiation Associations, www.ncna.us

The Negotiator Magazine, www.negotiatormagazine.com

NOTES

1. Fagan, T. J. (2003). *Negotiating correctional incidents: A practical guide*. Lanham, MD: American Correctional Association.
2. Stepp, E. A. (2007). Emergency management. In P. M. Carlson & J. S. Garrett (Eds.), *Prison and jail administration: Practice and theory* (pp. 469–478). Sudbury, MA: Jones & Bartlett Publishers.
3. Strentz, T. (2006). *Psychological aspects of crisis negotiation.* Boca Raton, FL: CRC Press.
4. Strentz, T. (2006). *Psychological aspects of crisis negotiation.* Boca Raton, FL: CRC Press.
5. Vecchi, G. M., Van Hasselt, V., & Romano, S. J. (2005). Crisis (hostage) negotiation: Current strategies and issues in high-risk conflict resolution. *Aggression and Violent Behavior, 10,* 533–551.
6. Browning, S. L., Brockman, A. M., Van Hasselt, V. B., & Vecchi, G. M. (2011). Crisis situations: Communications, goals and techniques. In C. A. Ireland, M. J. Fisher, & G. M. Vecchi (Eds.), *Conflict and crisis communication: Principles and practice* (pp. 53–73). New York, NY: Routledge.
7. Lanceley, F. J. (2003). *On-scene guide for crisis negotiators* (2nd ed.). Boca Raton, FL: CRC Press.
8. Regini, C. (2002). Crisis negotiation teams: Selection and training. *FBI Law Enforcement Bulletin, 71,* 1–5.
9. Fagan, T. J. (2003). *Negotiating correctional incidents: A practical guide*. Lanham, MD: American Correctional Association.
10. Fagan, T. J. (2003). *Negotiating correctional incidents: A practical guide*. Lanham, MD: American Correctional Association.
11. Vecchi, G. M., Van Hasselt, V., & Romano, S. J. (2005). Crisis (hostage) negotiation: Current strategies and issues in high-risk conflict resolution. *Aggression and Violent Behavior, 10,* 533–551.
12. Noesner, G. W. (1999). Negotiation concepts for commanders. *FBI Law Enforcement Bulletin, 68,* 6–14.

13. McMains, M. J., & Mullins, W. C. (2010). *Crisis negotiations: Managing critical incidents and hostage situations in law enforcement and corrections* (4th ed.). New Providence, NJ: Anderson Publishing.

14. Noesner, G. W. (1999). Negotiation concepts for commanders. *FBI Law Enforcement Bulletin, 68*, 6–14.

15. Vecchi, G. M., Van Hasselt, V., & Romano, S. J. (2005). Crisis (hostage) negotiation: Current strategies and issues in high-risk conflict resolution. *Aggression and Violent Behavior, 10*, 533–551.

16. Fagan, T. J. (2003). *Negotiating correctional incidents: A practical guide.* Lanham, MD: American Correctional Association.

17. Fagan, T. J. (2003). *Negotiating correctional incidents: A practical guide.* Lanham, MD: American Correctional Association.

18. Fagan, T. J. (2003). *Negotiating correctional incidents: A practical guide.* Lanham, MD: American Correctional Association.

19. Schmalleger, F., & Smykla, J. (2009). *Corrections in the 21st century.* New York, NY: McGraw-Hill Education.

20. Fagan, T. J. (2003). *Negotiating correctional incidents: A practical guide.* Lanham, MD: American Correctional Association.

21. Fagan, T. J. (2003). *Negotiating correctional incidents: A practical guide.* Lanham, MD: American Correctional Association.

22. McMains, M. J., & Mullins, W. C. (2010). *Crisis negotiations: Managing critical incidents and hostage situations in law enforcement and corrections* (4th ed.). New Providence, NJ: Anderson Publishing.

23. Hatcher, C., Mohandie, K., Turner, J., & Gelles, M. G. (1998). The role of the psychologist in crisis/hostage negotiations. *Behavioral Sciences and the Law, 16*, 455–472.

24. Fagan, T. J. (2003). *Negotiating correctional incidents: A practical guide.* Lanham, MD: American Correctional Association.

25. Useem, B., Camp, C. G., & Camp, G. M. (1996). *Resolution of prison riots: Strategies and policies.* New York, NY: Oxford University Press, Inc.

26. Fagan, T. J. (2003). *Negotiating correctional incidents: A practical guide.* Lanham, MD: American Correctional Association.

27. Fagan, T. J. (2003). *Negotiating correctional incidents: A practical guide.* Lanham, MD: American Correctional Association.

28. McMains, M. J., & Mullins, W. C. (2010). *Crisis negotiations: Managing critical incidents and hostage situations in law enforcement and corrections* (4th ed.). New Providence, NJ: Anderson Publishing.

29. Fagan, T. J. (2003). *Negotiating correctional incidents: A practical guide.* Lanham, MD: American Correctional Association.

30. Strentz, T. (2006). *Psychological aspects of crisis negotiation.* Boca Raton, FL: CRC Press.

31. Birge, R. (2002). Conducting successful hostage negotiations: Balance is the key. *Law & Order, 50*, 102–106.

32. Hatcher, C., Mohandie, K., Turner, J., & Gelles, M. G. (1998). The role of the psychologist in crisis/hostage negotiations. *Behavioral Sciences and the Law, 16*, 455–472.

33. Call, J. A. (2008). Psychological consultation in hostage/barricade crisis negotiation. In H. V. Hall (Ed.), *Forensic psychology and neuropsychology for criminal and civil cases* (pp. 263–288). Boca Raton, FL: CRC Press.

34. Noesner, G. W. (1999). Negotiation concepts for commanders. *FBI Law Enforcement Bulletin, 68*, 6–14.

35. Regini, C. (2002). Crisis negotiation teams: Selection and training. *FBI Law Enforcement Bulletin, 71*, 1–5.

36. Wind, B. A. (1995). A guide to crisis negotiations. *FBI Law Enforcement Bulletin, 64*, 7–11.

37. Fagan, T. J. (2003). *Negotiating correctional incidents: A practical guide.* Lanham, MD: American Correctional Association.

38. McMains, M. J., & Mullins, W. C. (2010). *Crisis negotiations: Managing critical incidents and hostage situations in law enforcement and corrections* (4th ed.). New Providence, NJ: Anderson Publishing.

39. Birge, R. (2002). Conducting successful hostage negotiations: Balance is the key. *Law & Order, 50,* 102–106.

40. Fagan, T. J. (2003). *Negotiating correctional incidents: A practical guide.* Lanham, MD: American Correctional Association.

41. Noesner, G. W. (1999). Negotiation concepts for commanders. *FBI Law Enforcement Bulletin, 68,* 6–14.

42. McMains, M. J., & Mullins, W. C. (2010). *Crisis negotiations: Managing critical incidents and hostage situations in law enforcement and corrections* (4th ed.). New Providence, NJ: Anderson Publishing.

43. Fagan, T. J. (2003). *Negotiating correctional incidents: A practical guide.* Lanham, MD: American Correctional Association.

44. Noesner, G. W., & Webster, M. (1997). Crisis intervention: Using active listening skills in negotiation. *FBI Law Enforcement Bulletin, 66,* 13–19.

45. Fagan, T. J. (2003). *Negotiating correctional incidents: A practical guide.* Lanham, MD: American Correctional Association.

46. McMains, M. J., & Mullins, W. C. (2010). *Crisis negotiations: Managing critical incidents and hostage situations in law enforcement and corrections* (4th ed.). New Providence, NJ: Anderson Publishing.

47. Van Hasselt, V. B., Baker, M. T., Romano, S. J., Schlessinger, K. M., Zucker, M., Dragone, R., & Perera, A. L. (2006). Crisis (hostage) negotiation training: A preliminary evaluation of program efficacy. *Criminal Justice and Behavior, 33*(1), 56–69.

48. Fagan, T. J. (2003). *Negotiating correctional incidents: A practical guide.* Lanham, MD: American Correctional Association.

49. McMains, M. J., & Mullins, W. C. (2010). *Crisis negotiations: Managing critical incidents and hostage situations in law enforcement and corrections* (4th ed.). New Providence, NJ: Anderson Publishing.

50. McMains, M. J., & Mullins, W. C. (2010). *Crisis negotiations: Managing critical incidents and hostage situations in law enforcement and corrections* (4th ed.). New Providence, NJ: Anderson Publishing

51. Fagan, T. J. (2003). *Negotiating correctional incidents: A practical guide.* Lanham, MD: American Correctional Association.

52. Fagan, T. J. (2003). *Negotiating correctional incidents: A practical guide.* Lanham, MD: American Correctional Association.

53. Lanceley, F. J. (2003). *On-scene guide for crisis negotiators* (2nd ed.). Boca Raton, FL: CRC Press.

54. Fagan, T. J. (2003). *Negotiating correctional incidents: A practical guide.* Lanham, MD: American Correctional Association.

55. Fagan, T. J. (2003). *Negotiating correctional incidents: A practical guide.* Lanham, MD: American Correctional Association.

Use of Force

Marie L. Griffin and John R. Hepburn

CHAPTER OBJECTIVES

- Describe circumstances in which an officer may use force in a correctional setting.
- Discuss critical elements of an agency's use-of-force policy.
- Identify relevant constitutional amendments and how they have been applied to cases involving the use-of-force.

Correctional institutions are extremely coercive organizations in which all activities are carried out in an environment of uncertainty. In both jails and prisons, where staff are usually unarmed and always outnumbered by the population of resistant prisoners, the ability of staff to control the prisoners is a matter of major importance.

For the most part, staff rely on their legitimate power; that is, prisoners accept that staff have the authority to give reasonable instructions related to inmates' daily activities.[1] Of all the types of power, legitimate power ensures compliance by the largest number of prisoners, over the widest scope of prisoner activities, and over the greatest amount of time and effort involved in those activities. In contrast, coercive power is most effective when it is always available but seldom used. In prisons and jails, coercive power is an ever-present resource that can be mobilized to provide the force necessary to support legitimate power.

Lethal force is a rarely used type of coercive power that represents the extreme end of the continuum of force. Lethal weapons are issued routinely only to those who guard the perimeter of an institution. Few, if any, officers working within the population are armed with lethal weapons unless they are responding to an internal disturbance. Nonlethal force is used much more often than lethal force; officers routinely rely on direct physical contact with prisoners to maintain control and security. For the most part, this use of force involves only some form of hands-on contact with the prisoners. However, such nonlethal weapons as stun devices and chemical sprays are becoming more prevalent in jails and prisons.[2]

■ Incidence of the Use of Force

It is generally agreed that deadly force is rarely used and that nonlethal force is frequently used, but there are few studies that provide data about how often the different types of force are used. Each institution keeps its own records of the use-of-force incidents that occur, but totaling these incidents across institutions or making comparisons between institutions is difficult, if not impossible. Institution policies have different definitions of force, different requirements about when incidents involving force should be reported, and different specifications about the type and completeness of such reports.

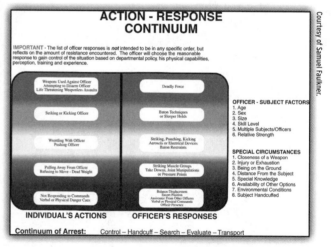

In 1993, the American Correctional Association (ACA) conducted a national survey of the use of force in 325 prison facilities, representing 49 state correctional systems and the Federal Bureau of Prisons (BOP). This survey showed that in the 12 preceding months, the number of incidents ranged from 0 (in 17 facilities) to more than 200 (in 8 facilities, with 1 facility with 652 incidents). Most facilities fell between these extremes, however, reporting between 7 and 90 incidents. Overall, facilities reported a mean of 70 and median of 34 incidents.[3]

In prisons, the incidence of the use of force is greater in larger facilities and in maximum security facilities. In contrast, force may be used more frequently in jails, especially in the intake units that receive arrestees who are intoxicated, angry, or frightened. A study of use-of-force incidents in the Maricopa County, Arizona, jail system found 2,995 reported use-of-force incidents (used or threatened) over a 2-year period.[4] More than half of these incidents (1,808) occurred in the intake facility, whereas the other 1,187 incidents occurred in the remaining six jail facilities.

Lethal force is most likely to be used against escaping inmates and to control group disturbances, whereas nonlethal force is most likely to be used when officers become involved in inmate-on-inmate fights or when an inmate refuses to comply with lawful orders.[5] Most incidents of nonlethal force are spontaneous, use only hands-on force, occur in housing units, and involve only one inmate. Although lethal force is designed to have deadly consequences, nonlethal force rarely results in injuries to either officer or inmate. Most inmate injuries and nearly all officer injuries from nonlethal force are minor abrasions or scrapes.

■ Use and Effectiveness of Nonlethal Weapons

Studies by the ACA and the Institute for Law and Justice reach similar findings with regard to the availability of nonlethal weapons in correctional facilities. These reports indicate that

- Nonlethal weapons are present in most facilities, although prisons are more likely than jails to have such weapons.
- Chemical irritants and batons (or some type of impact weapon) were available for use in nearly all the prisons studied, but in only about half of the jails.
- Less-than-lethal projectile guns were available in nearly half the prisons and less than 20% of the jails, and a stun device was available in approximately one-third of both the prisons and the jails.[6]

Not all officers are routinely equipped with these weapons, however. Instead, these weapons are more likely to be stored in a central arsenal or distributed only to certain, perhaps supervisory, staff. As a result, many jails and prisons report that the weapons were not used during the preceding year. Even in those facilities in which these weapons had been used at least once during the past year, only the chemical irritants were used an average of 10 or more times.

When surveyed about the effectiveness of nonlethal weapons, prison and jail administrators considered all the following nonlethal options to be effective, rated in order of effectiveness: less-than-lethal projectile gun, chemical irritants (such as oleoresin capsicum—pepper spray), stun devices, batons, and other nonlethal weapons.[7] After overcoming initial resistance by jail personnel, stun devices and pepper spray quickly became integral tools for officers' responses to altercations with inmates. One study noted that the mere display or threat of a nonlethal weapon often was enough to control inmates and terminate an altercation. As such, pepper spray use was found to be infrequent and more likely to be used when only one officer was involved with more than one inmate, especially when controlling inmate-to-inmate altercations. Stun devices and pepper spray were likely to totally incapacitate noncompliant inmates, and their level of effectiveness was consistently high regardless of gender or size of inmate or the degree of resistance encountered.[8] Research has demonstrated that nonlethal weapons are effective in gaining control over noncompliant inmates except when used against inmates with a mental or substance impairment.

■ Officer Attitudes Toward the Use of Force

Unlike the policing literature, few studies examine correctional officers' attitudes toward the use of force.[9] Studies have found that detention officers with increased levels of punitive and custodial orientation, greater satisfaction with the quality of supervision, or more concerns about role conflict, fear of victimization, and personal authority reported an increased readiness to use force.[10] It is important to note, however, that readiness to use force on the part of correctional officers is neither necessarily punitive nor indicative of the potential for misuse of force. A competent corrections officer is required to maintain a certain level of readiness to use force. Both correctional training and policy emphasize that officers should be prepared to use legitimate force to gain the compliance of or maintain control over inmates.

■ Civil Liability of Lethal Force

Different standards are used to judge the civil liability of the use of lethal force by police and correctional officers. For police, the appropriate use of lethal force is judged in terms of the Fourth Amendment's prohibitions against unreasonable seizure. The standard is defined by the Supreme Court's decision in *Tennessee v. Garner* (1985), which specifies that deadly force is only appropriate to seize a fleeing suspect when, under the wtotality of the circumstances, "the officer has probable cause to believe that the suspect poses a significant threat of death or serious physical injury to the officer or others."[11]

In contrast, civil liability for correctional officers is defined in terms of the Eighth Amendment, which provides that "Excessive bail shall not be required, nor excessive fines imposed nor cruel and unusual punishments inflicted." Although the cruel and unusual punishment clause is an explicit "intention to limit the power of those entrusted with the criminal law function of government," it protects against only those actions that are "repugnant to the conscience of mankind."[12]

As a result, correctional officers have more latitude than police officers in the use of force. First, the courts begin with the (often false) assumption that all escaping prisoners are dangerous, so evidence of a threat is not required to justify the use of lethal force. Second, warning shots and shooting to maim cannot be justified by current standards that govern police, but can be justified, and may even be preferred by the courts, in correctional settings. Warning shots may be more safely used when prisons are separated from the neighboring populace by open fields. If the situation permits less-than-deadly force, then deadly force should not be used—disabling force is always preferred to deadly force.[13]

Finally, the courts have established that only the unnecessary and wanton infliction of pain constitutes cruel and unusual punishment as forbidden by the Eighth Amendment.[14] In *Whitley v. Albers*, a case involving an officer who shot an inmate during a disturbance, the Supreme Court concluded that "whether the particular measure undertaken inflicted unnecessary and wanton pain and suffering ultimately turns on whether force was applied in a good faith effort to maintain or restore discipline or maliciously and sadistically for the very purpose of causing harm."[15]

Civil Liability of Nonlethal Force

Correctional officers may use force lawfully in a correctional institution in defense of self or others or to enforce prisoner rules and regulations, prevent a crime from occurring, or prevent escape. In all cases, the degree of force used must be shown to have been reasonable under the totality of the circumstances known at that time.[16] A successful claim of excessive force must demonstrate that, either intentionally or through gross negligence or recklessness, officers used excessive force that inflicted bodily harm under circumstances when officers knew (or should have known) that it was an unnecessary and wanton infliction of pain.[17] Force applied in a good faith effort to maintain discipline is not excessive; a successful plaintiff must prove that the force was applied maliciously and sadistically to cause harm. In a recent case, *Wilkins v. Gaddy*, the Supreme Court clarified for lower courts the need to measure the validity of an excessive-use-of-force claim not by the severity of the alleged bodily harm, but the more critical issue of whether the force was applied in good faith. The Court found that as long as the alleged harm "rises above the level of trivial," then inquiry as to whether the use of force was in good faith should proceed.[18]

Litigation typically occurs under one of four conditions:[19]

1. Those cases that assert that an officer reacted improperly to an inmate, either by overreacting to a resistant inmate or by using or threatening to use force against a nonresistant inmate; the use, or continued use, of a nonlethal weapon is examined in terms of the officer's reasonable belief that such force was necessary.

2. Negligent use of nonlethal weapons contrary to the manufacturer's recommendations; this implies carelessness, not wanton harm, and is judged against the standards of use expected of any trained officer.

3. Failure to provide timely medical aid to an inmate who has been injured. In *Estelle v. Gamble*, the Court ruled that there must be a deliberate indifference to the inmate's medical needs and not simply an inadvertent failure to provide medical care.[20] Indifference implies culpability whenever a reasonable person would have known that medical aid was needed. Furthermore, the deliberate indifference must result in substantial harm to the inmate.[21]

4. Legal liability for any misuse of a nonlethal weapon may extend to supervisors or administrators. Supervisors may be liable whenever it can be established that they (1) failed to intervene at the scene to prevent an officer's excessive use of force, (2) assigned an officer to a duty or issued to the officer a weapon that he or she was not trained to use, or (3) failed to investigate or discipline an officer who was known to have misused nonlethal weapons. Administrators who fail to provide training or establish clear policies regarding the proper and appropriate uses of lethal and nonlethal weapons may also be liable.[22]

■ Policies and Training

The National Sheriffs' Association, the National Association of Chiefs of Police, the Commission on Accreditation of Law Enforcement Agencies, the ACA, and other national organizations have provided guidelines and model use-of-force policies. In general, these associations recommend that agencies should have a written use-of-force policy, use-of-force training, systematic institutional review of all incidents in which force is used, and clearly articulated and appropriate institutional responses to the misuse of force. Following such policies should reduce an agency's legal liability for excessive force claims.

Use-of-Force Policy

The ACA recently reviewed and approved a *Public Correctional Policy on Use of Force*.[23] According to its policy statement,

> use of force includes the use of restraints (other than for routine transportation and movement), chemical agents, electronic devices and weapons. Force is justified only in instances of self-defense, protection of others, protection of property, prevention of escapes, and maintaining or regaining control, and then only as a last resort and in accordance with appropriate statutory authority.

In an effort to ensure that the use of force by officers is legal (i.e., justifiable and appropriate), the ACA suggests that agencies establish a set of policies that include such measures as prohibiting the use of force as a means of retaliation or punishment, designing strategies to minimize the need to use force, and, when used, calling for the minimum amount of force necessary to control the situation.

The ACA and other associations suggest that policies should also include reporting requirements, review procedures, and a statement of disciplinary actions that may result from the excessive use of force. The policy must include a clear statement regarding the need to consider factors such as age, gender, health, and mental health status before any use of force by officers, as well as the need to provide medical aid and medical review following the use of force.

If nonlethal weapons are available, the policy should indicate which weapons are authorized for use, which officers are authorized to carry or use such weapons, and when and how officers will be trained to use such weapons. The policy should also

- Include a statement that locates the weapons on the continuum of force (e.g., is a chemical spray less severe than, more severe than, or the same severity as the use of hands-on contact with an inmate?)
- Give specific directions or limitations for their use (e.g., stun devices may not be applied to the head or the genitals, and batons are not to be applied to the head or the neck)

- Define any situations in which, or persons (e.g., pregnant women, older persons, or persons who are mentally ill) against whom, nonlethal weapons are not to be used
- Prohibit restraint techniques (e.g., hogtie) that could cause positional asphyxia.

The use of lethal weapons must also be included in any use-of-force policy. These policies are likely to be tailored to the individual needs of each correctional facility. The BOP, for instance, stipulates that deadly force may be used to prevent escapes from secure facilities or to stop an inmate whose actions present imminent danger to others. Moreover, firearms are generally not to be used in a minimum security institution; they may be used to prevent an escape from a minimum security institution only when specifically authorized by a warden.[24] In addition, deadly force policies should clarify expectations with regard to such related matters as the use of warning shots and shooting to maim, as both practices are preferred by some jurisdictions and prohibited by others. Indeed, Nebraska, Texas, and some other states have policies that explicitly state that disciplinary actions may be taken against officers who fail to use deadly force to prevent an escape.

Use-of-Force Training

As a result of the often spontaneous and unplanned nature of inmate violence, correctional officers rarely have the time to plan or prepare a use-of-force response. As such, officers must rely on training and experience. It is critical, then, that agencies provide all officers with entry-level and in-service training in the use of force. Training should include a review of all institutional policies pertaining to the use of force as well as some general guidelines about the officer's civil liability when using force. Training should incorporate a review of technical information and physical training regarding the proper use for each authorized force technique or weapon, whether handholds, physical restraints, or such nonlethal weapons as stun devices and chemical irritants. Trainees should also receive basic information about rendering temporary medical assistance to those who may be harmed by the use of force, especially by chemical irritants. Finally, the training should acquaint officers with a large number and variety of situations through role-playing activities that require them to exercise discretion along the entire use-of-force continuum. It is important to train for de-escalation of force and to emphasize that verbal communication skills are the preferred means of inmate control.[25]

Systematic Institutional Review

Agencies should develop and maintain a process by which all instances of the use of force are systematically recorded and reviewed.[26] All incidents of any physical contact with an inmate, regardless of whether they result in an injury, should be recorded and reviewed, as should all incidents in which an inmate is threatened with a lethal or nonlethal weapon. Systematic and formal review will help to identify problem areas and problem inmates within the institution and officers who may need further training or formal sanction. Unacceptable behaviors by officers or supervisors must be addressed and, if appropriate, sanctioned according to a set of written disciplinary guidelines. The Ohio Department of Rehabilitation and Corrections requires greater review of incidents wherein more than minimal use of force is used.[27] Use-of-force incident reports must be completed by those officers involved or witnesses to the incident, and supervisors must obtain a voluntary written statement from the inmate against whom force was used describing the inmate's version of the event. Discrepancies in these reports often lead to a more detailed investigation and, some suggest, a more accurate description of the circumstances surrounding the use-of-force incident.[28]

■ Utility and Costs

Use-of-force policies, practices, and training vary widely across correctional institutions.[29] There is no single standard or model that fits all institutions. For that matter, there is no consensus about what is defined as use of force or what is an appropriate response to a given situation. Systematic data on use-of-force incidents are almost nonexistent. The state of current knowledge about the use of force in corrections is best illustrated by the fact that these simple questions remain unanswered.

1. How often, and in what contexts, is lethal (or nonlethal) force used annually?
2. What types of inmates and officers are involved, and what situational factors are present, in use-of-force incidents?
3. How many inmates and staff are injured annually as a result of lethal and nonlethal force incidents, and what is the extent of their injuries?

Although the use of force is a common and expected occurrence in correctional settings, little is known about its utility and its costs.

The question of utility revolves around the issue of what type or level of force is most useful in maintaining safety and control. Today, the focus is on the utility of nonlethal weapons in corrections. The Science and Technology Division of the National Institute of Justice supports many efforts to examine the usefulness of chemical irritants, electronic stun devices, intense pulsating lights, sticky foam, capture nets, projectile launchers, stun grenades, and other less-than-lethal weapons in prisons and jails. The limited data available suggest that nonlethal weapons can be used effectively in corrections, but more research is needed to discern which weapons are effective and which weapons are ineffective (or worse, counterproductive) for specific situations or settings.[30] The following questions still need to be addressed:

1. Should such nonlethal weapons as chemical irritants and handheld stun devices be issued to all officers?
2. Will the presence or threat of a nonlethal weapon calm or exacerbate the situation?
3. Will the use of a nonlethal weapon be more effective than conventional hands-on force in gaining control over the inmate and in reducing injuries to the inmate and officer involved in the incident?

The use of force involves many potential costs. One is the direct financial cost associated with injuries that occur to inmates or officers in the application of force. For inmates, these direct costs comprise the medical treatment received; for officers, these costs include medical treatment, workers' compensation claims, and lost work days. Indirect financial costs to the institution accrue in the form of the time and dollars spent to process inmate grievances, to respond to civil lawsuits alleging excessive force, and to address governmental (e.g., U.S. Department of Justice) and nongovernmental (e.g., Amnesty International) investigations into the misuse of force.

The use of force also has emotional costs for those who use force, especially deadly force. Law enforcement agencies routinely require some level of counseling following shooting incidents. How (if at all) does the use of force, especially deadly force, by correctional officers lead to feelings of guilt, remorse, or despair that affect an officer's quality of work and interpersonal relationships with family and friends? Unfortunately, these questions remain largely unanswered.

■ Conclusion

Available data on the incidence of the use of lethal and nonlethal force in correctional institutions suggest a wide disparity within and among federal, state, and local jurisdictions. It is generally agreed, however, that lethal force is restricted to use against escaping inmates and in response to group disturbances, whereas nonlethal force is generally applied to individual inmates as a means of control. Nonlethal weapons most commonly used in prisons and jails are chemical irritants and batons. Less-than-lethal projectile guns and stun devices are available in about one-third of all correctional institutions and, together with chemical irritants, are generally considered to be most effective in controlling inmate behavior.

Issues of civil liability revolve around both lethal and nonlethal force. Although given more latitude than the police in resorting to lethal force, correctional officers are held to the cruel and unusual punishment prohibition contained in the Eighth Amendment to the U.S. Constitution as interpreted by several federal courts. Appropriate nonlethal force must generally meet the tests of reasonableness, nonnegligence, timely medical aid for injuries resulting from the use-of-force, provisions for adequate training, and the existence of clear policies regarding the use of force.

To avoid liability for claims of excessive force, agencies should have a written policy on the use of lethal and nonlethal force. Such a policy should establish a continuum of force available to correctional officers and associate the levels of force with the levels of inmate resistance or threat. An effective use-of-force policy that provides line staff with specific and practical information is less likely to be viewed as adversarial or antistaff by officers and thus is more likely to be followed.[31] Training in the use of hands-on techniques for control of inmates, as well as lethal and nonlethal weapons, should be mandatory and updated regularly. A process of supervisory review is also critical.

Issues surrounding the utility and costs of the use of force by correctional officers remain largely unresolved. The level of force and type of weapon best suited to a particular incident remain the subject of continuing debate. Injuries to both inmates and correctional officers and the economic effects of medical treatment, processing inmate grievances, and civil lawsuits should be seen as real costs likely to be incurred when even reasonable, nonexcessive force is used.

Chapter Resources

DISCUSSION QUESTIONS

1. What costs are associated with the misuse of force by correctional officers?
2. How does the court assess allegations of misuse of force by a correctional officer?
3. What are the relative advantages and disadvantages of alternative, nonlethal weapons in a correctional setting?
4. In what instances may correctional officers use force lawfully in a correctional institution?
5. How might officer attitudes toward the work environment influence their readiness to use force against an inmate?

ADDITIONAL RESOURCES

Johnson, R. (2002). *Hard time: Understanding and reforming the prison* (3rd ed.). Belmont, CA: Wadsworth.

Marquart, J. (1986). Prison guards and the use of physical coercion as a mechanism of prisoner control. *Criminology, 24,* 174–188.

Zimbardo, P. (2013). *The Stanford prison experiment: A simulation study of the psychology of imprisonment.* Conducted at Stanford University. Retrieved from http://www.prisonexp.org

NOTES

1. Hepburn, J. (1985). The exercise of power in coercive organizations: A study of prison guards. *Criminology, 23*(1), 145–164.
2. Hemmens, C., Maahs, J.,& Pratt, T. (2000, January/February). Use of force in American jails: A survey of current policies. *American Jails,* 47–52; Henry, P., Senese, J., & Ingley, G. (1994). Use of force in America's prisons: An overview of current research. *Corrections Today, 56,* 108–114.
3. Henry, P., Sense, J., & Ingley, G. (1994). Use of force in America's prisons: An overview of current research. *Corrections Today, 56*(4), 108–114.
4. Hepburn, J., Griffin, M., & Petrocelli, M. (1997, September). *Safety and control in a county jail: Nonlethal weapons and the use of force.* A report submitted to Maricopa County Sheriff's Office, National Sheriffs' Association, and the National Institute of Justice.
5. Senese, J. (1994). *Summary report: Institutional use of force reports.* A paper presented at the American Correctional Association Open Symposium on Use of Force, Orlando, FL, pp. 6–7.
6. Institute for Law and Justice. (1993). *Less than lethal force technologies in law enforcement and correctional agencies* (pp. 3–12). Alexandria, VA: National Institute of Justice.
7. Onnen, J. (1993). *Oleoresin capsicum: Executive brief.* Alexandria, VA: International Association of Police Chiefs.
8. Hepburn, J., Griffin, M., & Petrocelli, M. (1997, September). *Safety and control in a county jail: Nonlethal weapons and the use of force.* A report submitted to Maricopa County Sheriff's Office, National Sheriffs' Association, and the National Institute of Justice.

9. Griffin, M. (2001). *The use of force by detention officers*. New York, NY: LFB Scholarly Publishing.

10. Griffin, M. (1999). The influence of organizational climate on detention officers' readiness to use force in a county jail. *Criminal Justice Review, 24*(1), 1–26; Griffin, M. (2002). The influence of professional orientation on detention officers' attitudes toward the use of force. *Criminal Justice and Behavior, 29*(3), 250–277.

11. *Tennessee v. Garner*, 471 U.S. 1 (1985).

12. *Estelle v. Gamble*, 429 U.S. 97, 98 (1976).

13. Walker, J. (1996). Police and correctional use of force: Legal and policy standards and implications. *Crime and Delinquency, 42*, 144–156.

14. *Wilson v. Seiter*, 501 U.S. 294 (1991).

15. *Whitley v. Albers*, 475 U.S. 312 (1986).

16. Deland, G., & R. Billings, R. (2010). *The use of force in corrections facilities*. Corrections Managers' Report, no. 3. pp. 33–48.

17. *McRorie v. Shimoda*, 795 F.2d 780, 9th Cir. (1986).

18. Adelman, S. (2010, June). Court reaffirms rules governing excessive-use-of-force lawsuits. *Corrections Today, 72*, 73–75.

19. Institute for Law and Justice. (1993). *Less than lethal force technologies in law enforcement and correctional agencies* (pp. 3–12). Alexandria, VA: National Institute of Justice.

20. *Estelle v. Gamble*, 429 U.S. 97, 98 (1976).

21. *May v. Enomoto*, 633 F.2d 164 (CA9 1980).

22. Daane, D., & Hendricks, J. (1991). Liability for failure to adequately train. *Police Chief, 58*(11), 26–29.

23. American Correctional Association. (2010, April). 2009 Winter Conference Jan. 9–14, 2009. *Corrections Today*, 87–92.

24. Federal Bureau of Prisons. (1996). *Program statement 558.12 firearms and badges* (p. 6.). Washington, DC: Author.

25. Nicoletti, J. (1990). Training for de-escalation of force. *Police Chief, 57*(7), 37–39.

26. Lyons, D. (1990). Preventive measures cut physical force suits. *Corrections Today, 52*, 216–224.

27. Ohio Administrative Code 5120-9-02; Ohio Administrative Code. Retrieved August 14, 2011, from http://codes.ohio.gov/oac

28. Collins, W. (2010, April/May). Will inmate reports enhance the quality of use of force reviews? *Correctional Law Reporter, 22*, 93.

29. Hemmens, C., Maahs, J., & Pratt, T. (2000, January/February). Use of force in American jails: A survey of current policies. *American Jails*, 47–52.

30. Institute for Law and Justice. (1993). *Less than lethal force technologies in law enforcement and correctional agencies* (pp. 3–12). Alexandria, VA: National Institute of Justice; Hepburn, J., Griffin, M., & Petrocelli, M. (1997, September). *Safety and control in a county jail: Nonlethal weapons and the use of force*. A report submitted to Maricopa County Sheriff's Office, National Sheriffs' Association, and the National Institute of Justice.

31. Schwartz, J. (2010, January/February). Fixing use-of-force problems. *American Jails, 23*, 37–47.

Legal Issues

YOU ARE THE ADMINISTRATOR

■ Is a "Shy Bladder" an Excuse to Avoid Urine Surveillance?

Drug testing in correctional facilities is routine in most correctional jurisdictions as a means of deterring the use of illegal substances. Prison and jail administrators regularly test randomly selected inmates of an institution, and if their findings are positive, the inmate is subject to disciplinary action and will be placed on a repeat testing protocol.

Correctional authorities who utilize drug testing programs require inmates to provide a urine sample for testing in the presence of institutional staff. A small sample of a correctional population is chosen randomly, or an individual could be selected for testing if the prisoner's behavior is suspected of drug use.

Policies are typically developed to require an inmate to void in a sample bottle under direct staff supervision within a reasonable time frame after he or she is requested. Protocols often allow an individual extra time if he or she is unable to urinate at the time requested, and many jurisdictions will allow an offender to drink limited additional amounts of water to facilitate the process.

But what if an inmate is unable to "produce"? A state prisoner in Alaskan custody has recently brought suit against the state and alleges that he suffers from paruresis, a medical condition that creates an inability for an individual to urinate in front of others—a shy bladder. Loren Larson claims that he was required to provide a sample for random testing every 3–4 months, and his contention is that his medical issue renders him unable to void urine under supervision. He is then forced to drink additional water until he absolutely must release his bladder involuntarily, and this process creates pain and suffering (*Larson v. State of Alaska DOC*, 284 P.3d 1 (Alaska 2012)).

- Do you believe a random drug testing protocol is necessary for all inmates? Do you believe this to be an important drug control program? Why do some institutions not require this?
- Should correctional authorities make special provisions for inmates with such medical issues? What accommodations might be made?
- Is it reasonable for inmates to be able to seek court intervention for such institutional concerns? Why? Defend your answer.

Prisoner Access to the Courts

William C. Collins

CHAPTER OBJECTIVES

- Describe the history and development of the constitutional right of access to the courts as it pertains to prisoners, and discuss the role of the U.S. Supreme Court in prison law and in right-of-access law.

- Describe the major provisions of the Prison Litigation Reform Act and the effects it has had on inmate litigation. Outline the pivotal role that the lower federal and state courts play in interpreting and applying the decisions of the Supreme Court.

- Describe other issues related to the implementation of the right of access to the courts based on both Supreme Court and lower court decisions.

H ow could a nation like America that puts great value on the civil and other legally protected rights of persons not have a right of access to the courts, that is, access to the forum empowered to enforce those rights? Deny access to the courts and "rights" become meaningless, particularly individual rights that define the limits of governmental powers. But what "access to the courts" means in the context of prisons and jails has been the source of much litigation and several Supreme Court decisions.

Despite the apparent obviousness of a right of access to the courts, it is still not even clear where the right finds its constitutional roots. In *Christopher v. Harbury*, the Court noted that over the years, it has "grounded the right of access to the courts" in five different places in the Constitution, including the Article IV privileges and immunities clause, the First Amendment petition for redress of grievances clause, the Fifth Amendment due process clause, and the Fourteenth Amendment equal protection and due process clauses.[1] Arguments about what portion or portions of the Constitution provide the foundation of the right of access to the courts can be left to legal scholars. This chapter is more concerned with the contours of the right as it affects both inmates and correctional agencies and administrators.

Inmates typically file two types of lawsuits: habeas corpus petitions and civil rights claims.

- A habeas corpus petition asks for the inmate's release from custody because of constitutionally significant flaws in the legal proceedings that led to the inmate being in custody. A federal habeas corpus proceeding cannot be filed until the petitioner has exhausted available state remedies.
- Civil rights claims are most commonly filed under a federal statute passed in the post–Civil War reconstruction era, 42 U.S.C. §1983. The statute gives all persons in the country the right to sue persons acting "under color of state law" in federal court for violations of rights protected by federal statutory or constitutional law. The statute creates no substantive rights, but only a vehicle for someone to get into federal court. Federal inmates are not protected by §1983, but can bring an equivalent action in federal court as a result of a Supreme Court decision, *Bivens v. Six Unknown Named Agents of the FBI*.[2]

■ Access to the Courts and the Supreme Court

Supreme Court decisions addressing access to the courts can be divided into three eras. The first dealt with prison rules that had the effect of preventing inmates from getting cases to court. The second era, which emerged in the mid-1970s, dealt with the principle that prison officials[3] had an affirmative duty to provide some form of assistance to inmates seeking to file and prosecute civil lawsuits. This era lasted for two decades and spawned a great deal of lower court litigation over the adequacy of resources that facilities were providing, particularly the facility law library. Finally, the third era, which continues as this book is published, began in 1996 when the Supreme Court almost reversed the affirmative duty principle. The duty still exists, but as a mere shadow of its former self.

The Barrier Era

Years before the "inmate rights" began, prison staff in Michigan intercepted an inmate's mail to a court because the inmate had not submitted it first for review by a lawyer who represented the state parole board. Michigan policy required a lawyer to review all inmate legal pleadings to determine whether they were "properly drawn." With his father's cooperation, the inmate later managed to smuggle a letter to the clerk of the Supreme Court, explaining that prison officials were confiscating his letters to the Court. This smuggled letter became the basis of *Ex Parte Hull*.[4]

Hull presented two issues. The first issue was whether the pleading approval rule was illegal and the second whether the inmate's conviction was valid.

On the first issue, the Supreme Court's response was terse:

> The regulation is invalid. The considerations that prompted its formulation are not without merit, but the state and its officers may not abridge or impair petitioner's right to apply to a federal court for a writ of habeas corpus. Whether a petition for writ of habeas corpus addressed to a federal court is properly drawn and what allegations it must contain are questions for that court alone to determine.[5]

That short paragraph is the sum total of the Court's analysis of the Michigan practice of reviewing legal pleadings. Why was the Michigan rule invalid? Did it violate an unidentified provision of the Constitution or a congressionally created statutory right allowing inmates to file habeas corpus petitions in federal court? The opinion in *Hull* left those questions unanswered.

Having summarily disposed of the Michigan rule, the Court went on to decide that the inmate's attack on his conviction had no merit. So although the inmate won a procedural victory that enshrined his name in the annals of access-to-courts litigation, he didn't get out of prison.

Fast forward to 1969 and *Johnson v. Avery*.[6] The inmate rights movement in federal courts was still in its infancy.[7] Tennessee prison officials disciplined Billy Joe Johnson, an inmate jailhouse lawyer, for helping another inmate to prepare a legal pleading. The district court overturned the disciplinary result, saying that the rule prohibiting one inmate from assisting another to prepare habeas corpus pleadings effectively prohibited illiterate inmates from access to federal habeas corpus relief and therefore conflicted with a right created by federal habeas statute.[8] On appeal, the Sixth Circuit reversed, saying that state interests in prison discipline and limiting the practice of law to licensed attorneys justified the restriction.

The Supreme Court acknowledged the legitimacy of the Sixth Circuit's concerns but felt that they were not strong enough to justify the rule because it effectively barred illiterate inmates from filing habeas petitions because they had no other means of obtaining assistance. Justice Fortas, writing for a 7–2 majority, twice said that such a rule would be unconstitutional without specifying what constitutional provision would be violated.

Justices White and Black dissented, challenging the majority's assumption that help from other prisoners would necessarily be of any benefit and questioned why the petitioner should be entitled to any relief, because he was the offeror of legal assistance, not the illiterate inmate who might have been denied access to the courts by Tennessee's "no assistance" rule.

The Affirmative Duty Era

The second era began with what could be described as a "stealth opinion" from the Supreme Court, a 1971 *per curiam* decision in the case *Younger v. Gilmore* that had far more impact than appeared from this terse decision:

> On this appeal, we postponed the question of jurisdiction pending the hearing of the case on the merits. Having heard the case on its merits, we find that this Court does have jurisdiction and affirm the judgment of the District Court for the Northern District of California.[9]

This short decision does not even state the issue of the case. A "per curiam" opinion is one issued in the name of the court, rather than identified by its author. *Younger* fits this definition. Usually, such opinions deal with routine or noncontroversial issues. *Younger* does not fit this definition.

What one does not know from reading the Supreme Court's *Younger* decision is that it affirmed a district court decision that found that legal materials the California Department of Corrections provided inmates were inadequate and ordered the state to develop a more comprehensive process by which inmates could exercise their right of access to the courts.[10] *Younger* embraced the principle that the right of access to the courts created an affirmative duty for the institution to provide some level of legal resources for inmates but did so in a way that required an eagle-eyed observer to notice the decision, let alone appreciate its implications.

Three years later, the Supreme Court touched on access to the courts again in a case better known for its holding regarding inmate disciplinary proceedings, *Wolff v. McDonnell.*[11] *Wolff* found that the constitutional source for the right of access to the courts was the due process clause of the Fourteenth Amendment.[12]

The main holding in *Wolff* was that the right of access to the courts extended to §1983 cases that challenged prison conditions or practices as well as habeas corpus petitions, which were the focus in *Hull* and *Avery*. It also approved the court of appeals decision requiring the district court to review the "adequacy of legal assistance" that the state of Nebraska was providing its inmates,[13] thus reaffirming the affirmative duty aspects of *Avery* and *Younger*. But at this point, it was not clear what a state's affirmative duty might be.

That uncertainty was largely resolved in 1977 in what was to be the landmark access-to-courts decision for the next 20 years, *Bounds v. Smith.*[14] At issue was the validity of a remedy ordered by the district court that required the North Carolina Department of Corrections to provide law libraries for inmates.

Bounds is the Court's first exhaustive examination of the right of access to the courts. The district court held that the department's law library system was "severely inadequate" and that there was no other form of legal assistance available to inmates.[15] The Court ordered the department to develop a remedy and eventually accepted the department's proposal of two systems of seven regional libraries serving its 77 prison units holding 13,000 inmates in 66 of the state's 100 counties.

North Carolina's proposal called for temporarily moving inmates to the library prisons on an appointment basis for up to one full day of legal work. The state's plan included a list of the materials that would be provided in each of the main libraries that complied with recommendations of various national organizations, including the American Bar Association. The substantial collection included various state and federal statutes, court rules, texts, and state and federal reporters (large sets of books containing the reported decisions of various levels of state or federal courts).

The Supreme Court agreed with the lower courts that the plan was acceptable and implicitly approved the law library collection that the lower court had approved. For years, the library collection approved in *Bounds* became the benchmark for prison law libraries.

In *Bounds*, the Court was faced directly with the question of what "access to the courts" meant.

> We hold, therefore, that the fundamental constitutional right of access to the courts requires prison authorities to assist inmates in the preparation and filing of meaningful legal papers by providing prisoners with adequate law libraries or adequate assistance from persons trained in the law.[16]

Note the use of the disjunctive "or." Prison authorities *did not* have to provide a law library—they could instead provide assistance from persons "trained in the law" who did not even have to be lawyers. But whichever side of the "or" a correctional agency might choose, *Bounds* made clear that the agency had an affirmative duty to provide some form of assistance regarding the preparation of legal pleadings.

When *Bounds* was written, there was federal funding available to support some form of professional or quasi-professional legal assistance to inmates. Some states took the advantage of this funding to meet the *Bounds* obligations, but law libraries were the preferred option for most prisons systems and virtually all jails.

Many administrators and staff felt uncomfortable with a lawyer representing inmates constantly peering over their shoulders. Many inside and outside the institution opposed giving state dollars to lawyers to represent inmates suing the state and state officials. As inmate populations soared in the 1980s and 1990s and federal support for lawyer programs dried up, budget pressures grew and state funding for inmate lawyers was an easy item to cut.

But for various reasons, lawyer-centric access-to-courts programs failed to flourish, and *Bounds* became the "law library" case. The library book list from *Bounds* became, at a minimum, the starting point for any discussion of what must be included in an inmate law library.

BOUNDS **AND NORTH CAROLINA: AN IRONY**

The logistics of moving inmates back and forth between their assigned prisons and the law library prisons would prove too much for North Carolina to meet, and a decade after the *Bounds* decision, the Fourth Circuit court of appeals heard a new appeal in the case[17] and affirmed the district court's decision that the department had failed to implement the program in various ways, including denying a large number of law library requests "without explanation."[18] The appellate court approved the district court's order that the department begin a program of providing assistance from lawyers. The "law library" case had morphed into a lawyers-for-inmates case.

In that appeal, the department offered a surprising defense, claiming that it had documented its compliance but the lawyer who had represented it through the entirety of the litigation had somehow failed to present that material in court. Whether the lawyer accidentally left his client's defense in a file drawer is not known. What is known is that the state's claim came too late in the day to save it.

The Aftermath of Bounds

Before *Bounds*, many prisons and at least some jails had what purported to be a "law library." However, the collections in such libraries were typically haphazard and often out of date.

For nearly two decades after *Bounds*, litigation over the adequacy of an institution's law library collection and library access was common. Many such cases dealt with issues involving the general population[19] but others dealt with narrower issues, such as access to legal materials for inmates in segregated confinement units who could not get physical access to the main library[20] or rights of illiterate inmates.[21]

It was often easy to find fault with a law library—the collection was deficient in some way, the library was too small or not open enough, and small prisons did not have adequate libraries even though the demand was apt to be small.

When *Bounds* was decided, legal research depended on books, mostly very large sets of "reporters," which would include virtually all of the decisions of a given level of court. An "adequate" law library for a prison in a given state would include the reporters from the state's appellate courts and reporters from the federal district courts, circuit courts of appeal, and the Supreme Court. All these comprised hundreds of books and were constantly expanding. Occasionally, questions would arise about inmates transferred from one state to another and how that inmate might access legal materials from his home state, which would not be provided in the receiving state that might be a thousand miles or more away from the inmate's home state.

A properly researched case could require reviewing statutes, court rules, and many cases and require many trips to the law library both to prepare the case originally and to pursue through to final decision.

Today, researching a legal issue by pulling individual reporter volumes off library shelves is a throwback to a bygone era. Those books are still available, and are now accessible through comprehensive computerized legal research systems such as LEXIS™ or WESTLAW™ or other services. These systems, which allow faster and more in-depth research than "book-based" techniques, developed as the *Bounds* law library era was ending. Some jurisdictions provide access to computerized research systems, but courts have not reached the question of whether such systems might be required instead of the traditional law library.

The Actual Injury Era

The *Bounds* era ended with a bang. Two themes had been slowly developing in lower court access-to-the-courts decisions after *Bounds*. The first related to the specific requirements of the right, as lower courts interpreted *Bounds* and tried to fill in blanks in the decision. The second was more subtle and dealt with the remedial powers of a federal court. What sort of remedy could a federal district court judge order, having found a violation of a constitutional right? Could the judge order the institution to do or provide things that, taken in isolation, were not required by the Constitution? This question was not limited to access-to-the-courts issues, but arose with regard to other large prison "system" issues such as medical care, systemic misuse of force, and so on.

These two developing themes reached their climax in a case from Arizona, *Lewis v. Casey*,[22] an action that attacked the Arizona Department of Corrections' entire access-to-the-courts system. *Lewis* followed close on the heels of a similar case that dealt only with the Arizona state prison, *Gluth v. Kangas*.[23] The case resulted in a very broad order in favor of the inmates. *Lewis* resulted in an order that was, if anything, even broader in scope. Although *Gluth* went no farther than the Ninth Circuit, *Lewis* reached the Supreme Court and is, as this is written, the Court's last decision on access.

Lewis was controversial and hotly contested, with the district court judge being on the receiving end of harsh public criticism from department officials and the media. *Lewis* followed much the same pattern as had *Gluth*. The district court judge found the department's access-to-the-courts system unconstitutional and appointed a special master to develop a proposed remedy, the same person who had performed this function in *Gluth*. The judge adopted the master's very detailed recommendations almost without change. The Ninth Circuit affirmed the lower court decision in all major respects.[24]

Two parts of the Ninth Circuit's opinion demonstrate the aftermath of *Bounds*. At one point, the Ninth Circuit discussed the importance of direct inmate access to the law library, almost espousing a "right to browse:"

> . . . legal research often requires browsing through various materials in search of inspiration; tentative theories may have to be abandoned in the course of research in the face of unfamiliar adverse precedent. New theories may occur as a result of a chance discovery of an obscure or forgotten case.[25]

Elsewhere, the circuit affirmed its prior position that *Bounds* allows a state to provide either a law library or assistance from persons trained in the law but went on to approve the lower court's order requiring the state to provide both libraries *and* trained inmate law clerks. Why? Because a library alone could not meet *Bounds'* requirement that the state provide "meaningful" access to the courts for inmates unable to read English. Nearly 15% of Arizona's prison population could not even speak, let alone read, English.[26] Such a result was a logical extension of *Bounds'* demand that officials provide meaningful assistance in some form to inmates.

The Supreme Court Decision

Two issues reached the Supreme Court. First, the prison officials argued that there could not be a violation of the right of access to the courts unless inmates could show they had suffered an "action injury" of some sort. Second, they argued that the remedy went too far. The Supreme Court agreed with both arguments

While paying homage to *Bounds'* holding that prison officials have a constitutional duty "to assist inmates in the preparation and filing of meaningful legal papers by providing adequate law libraries or adequate assistance from persons trained in the law,"[27] Justice Scalia's majority opinion drains almost all content out of *Bounds* in various ways.

Most notably, *Lewis* adds a requirement that to have standing to sue over an alleged access-to-the-courts violation, the plaintiff/inmate must show that he suffered an "actual injury" as a result of the actions or inactions of the defendants. Justice Scalia's majority opinion gives two examples of what could constitute "actual injury:"

> [The inmate] might show, for example, that a complaint he prepared was dismissed for failure to satisfy some technical requirement which, because of deficiencies in the prison's legal assistance facilities, he could not have known. Or that he had suffered arguably actionable harm that he wished to bring before the courts, but was so stymied by inadequacies of the law library that he was unable even to file a complaint.[28]

To support this standing requirement, Justice Scalia cites the Court's major inmate medical case, *Estelle v. Gamble*,[29] a decision based on the Eighth Amendment's cruel and unusual punishment clause. Justice Scalia wrote that while *Estelle* established that prison officials' "deliberate indifference to serious medical needs"[30] violates the Eighth Amendment, a healthy inmate could assert an Eighth Amendment violation by arguing that the prison infirmary was a deficient argument. The inmate must have suffered some sort of injury because of the inadequacies. To Justice Scalia, *Bounds* did not create "an abstract, free-standing right to a law library" but needed to be read as including an actual injury requirement.[31]

But in reading an injury requirement into *Estelle*, the majority ignored its own precedent, *Helling v McKinney*.[32] In *Helling*, the Court said an inmate could state an Eighth Amendment claim if the inmate could show that a prison condition put him at "substantial risk of serious harm."[33] The potential harm in *Helling* was exposure to secondhand cigarette smoke. The Court did not say that exposure violated the Eighth Amendment, but did say that the inmate was entitled to try to prove that his exposure had created a substantial risk of serious harm.

Under Justice Scalia's written logic in *Lewis*, the same inmate or inmates cannot successfully argue that a prison's access-to-the-courts system is so abysmal that it presents a substantial risk that inmates will not be able to present claims to a court. So, for example, a class of illiterate inmates would not have standing to claim that a court access system that relied exclusively on written materials was unconstitutional unless at least some members of the class could show that they had been unable to bring a nonfrivolous lawsuit about some issues other than the court access system because they could not read.

In addition to the new "actual injury" standing requirement and emphasizing that there is no right to a law library per se, *Lewis* narrowed the right of access to the courts in other ways. It indicated that "some minimal access to legal advice and a system of court-provided forms"[34] might suffice. Agencies should be encouraged to experiment with access-to-the-court programs, which would be presumptively valid until an inmate could "demonstrate that a nonfrivolous legal claim had been frustrated or was being impeded."[35] The effect of this statement was to allow agencies to defend access-to-the-courts claims by attacking the validity of the legal claim the inmate wanted to bring.

Later, Justice Scalia wrote that in various ways, "*Bounds* went beyond the right of access recognized in earlier cases. . . ."[36] For example, the majority "disclaimed" any statement from *Bounds* that might appear "to propose that the State must enable the prisoner to *discover* grievances and to *litigate effectively* once in court."[37] Taken literally, this says that the institution could deny inmates access to legal materials from which they might learn of a potential violation of their rights and deny access to legal materials once a case was filed. At least one court has interpreted this to mean that "*Lewis* does not require that [an inmate] ever be permitted access to the law library, only that he be permitted to file a complaint or appeal."[38] Other courts say this is too narrow a reading of *Lewis*. In *Marshall v. Knight*,[39] the district court ruled that *Lewis* only protected the ability to file the complaint, but the Seventh Circuit court of appeals disagreed:

> A prisoner states an access-to-courts claim when he alleges that even though he successfully got into court by filing a complaint . . . his denial of access to legal materials caused a potentially meritorious claim to fail.[40]

The *Marshall* approach is more in tune with reality than a "right stops when the complaint is filed" rule. How can access be "meaningful" if an inmate cannot access legal materials to research whether he might have a claim and then again after a complaint has been filed to develop and demonstrate his case? Without access to court rules, the inmate litigant will inevitably violate various procedural rules that will result in a lawsuit being dismissed. He will have no knowledge of how to conduct discovery. Without access to legal research materials, he will be unable to either present his case or reply to pleadings filed by the defendants intelligently.

Despite the *Marshall* decision in 2006, the question of whether the right of access to the courts extends past the filing of the initial complaint remains unresolved.

THE IMPACT OF *LEWIS*. The effect of *Lewis* cannot be understated. It is this author's sense that *Lewis* has virtually eliminated successful access-to-courts class actions dealing with the question of what sort of assistance agencies must furnish. Case after access-to-the-courts case now founders on the actual injury requirement.

Lewis raised, but did not answer, new questions about the scope of the right of access to the courts, which makes it much harder for the correctional administrator who wants to create a defensible access-to-the-courts system in a time of constant budget crisis. The old "*Bounds* library" is not required. But what can adequately replace it? Some authorities have hired contract lawyers or paralegals given very limited powers to assist inmates. Sufficient? Hard to tell, because there have been no broad challenges to their adequacy.

Written materials cannot provide "meaningful access" for an illiterate inmate. Some sort of assistance is required, but what? A reader? A person "trained in the law"?

Lewis ends any debate about the scope of the right of access to the court, holding that the right only protects direct or collateral attacks on the inmate's sentence (criminal appeals and habeas corpus petitions) and §1983 actions. In other words, *Bounds* does not guarantee inmates the wherewithal to transform themselves into litigating engines capable of filing everything from shareholder derivative actions to slip-and-fall claims.[41]

Few inmates file shareholder derivative actions; some may have legitimate slip-and-fall or other tort claims against an agency or its employees. Others may have valid concerns about parenting or other family law issues. But at any rate, according to *Lewis*, the state has no obligation to offer assistance in any form regarding such issues.

After more than 15 years of life with *Lewis*, the scarcity of successful inmate access-to-courts cases suggests that the "do little or nothing" approach creates little real legal jeopardy for the agency. There is a temptation for the agency to do virtually nothing on the assumption that it may be a long time before an inmate who is unable to bring a nonfrivolous legal claim will find a way to get to court to complain about the lack of assistance that cost him that claim.

LEWIS AND THE RELIEF POWER QUESTION. The court's relief power in *Lewis* also warrants brief mention. The lower court's very comprehensive relief order ran headlong into a trend that had been building up in the Supreme Court decisions for several years that said federal courts should generally defer to the judgment calls of correctional administrators.

When appellate courts criticize lower court judges for one reason or another, they generally put their criticism in gentle terms such as "the learned judge. . . ." No such niceties in *Lewis*. Justice Scalia took off the gloves and waded into the district court judge: "His order was inordinately—indeed, wildly—intrusive . . . representing the *ne plus ultra* of what our opinions have lamented as a court's 'in the name of the Constitution, becom[ing] . . . enmeshed in the minutiae of prison operations.'"[42]

Justice Thomas's dissent went on for pages criticizing the relief order, concluding that "It is a stark example of what a district court should not do when it finds a state institution has violated the Constitution."[43]

Lewis delivers a very strong statement about lower courts deferring to prison administrators, the need for courts to give administrators prominent roles in developing proposed relief orders, and keeping relief orders minimally intrusive. In this respect, *Lewis* mirrors portions of the Prison Litigation Reform Act (PLRA) intended to curb what Congress felt were overbroad relief powers of federal courts. (A detailed discussion of the PLRA appears below.) *Lewis* was decided about 6 months after the PLRA was passed, but none of the four majority concurring and dissenting opinions in *Lewis* mention the PLRA.

INTERFERENCE WITH ACCESS. In addition to the "affirmative duty" decisions such as *Bounds* and *Lewis*, there is a second largely separate prong of the access-to-the-courts right that warrants mention—the right of inmates to access courts without what the Ninth Circuit refers to as "active interference" from prison officials.[44] In *Silva*, the inmate alleged that California prison officials had seized all his legal files and had transferred him between prisons frequently to frustrate his litigation efforts. The court stated that these allegations, if proven, could show a violation of the right of access to the courts.

Actions by officials such as limiting the amount of legal materials the inmate may possess in his cell, which could be viewed as interfering with the inmate's access to the court, or at least making it more cumbersome, will not only face the *Lewis* "actual injury" hurdle[45] but also can be justified if officials can show that the restriction is reasonably related to a legitimate penological interest (most commonly security).[46]

■ Congress and Inmate Access to the Courts

Congress rarely dips its toe into the ocean of "inmate rights," but it waded into the waves with passage of the PLRA of 1995.[47] The PLRA has two major purposes: (1) to make it more burdensome for inmates to file civil rights complaints in federal court and (2) to limit the relief powers of federal courts after a constitutional violation is found. The PLRA does not alter any substantive inmate rights.

■ Increasing the Burden: Inmates Filing §1983 Lawsuits

There are several components to this portion of the PLRA.

- *Exhaustion*. Inmates must completely exhaust any "available" administrative remedy such as a grievance process before filing a complaint in federal court.
- *Filing fee payments*. Courts can no longer routinely waive the $350 fee to file a new case in federal district court or the $450 fee to file an appeal in a federal court of appeals for indigent inmate litigants. Payment can only be deferred and spread out over time.
- *Case screening*. Federal district court judges have long had the discretionary power to screen and dismiss an inmate complaint deemed to be "frivolous" or "malicious," both legal terms of art. The PLRA makes screening a mandatory duty and expands it to include a determination of whether the complaint "fails to state a claim upon which relief can be granted" or seeks damages from an official who is immune from damages. Such dismissals take place without the defendants even knowing the suit has been filed.
- *Three strikes*. An inmate who has had three cases dismissed as frivolous or malicious or for failing to state a claim must pay the full filing fee when filing any new suit and is not eligible for the "deferred" payment mentioned earlier, except in extraordinary situations.
- *Attorney's fees*. Limitations are placed on the amount of attorney's fees that can be awarded to the successful inmate plaintiff's lawyer.
- *Damages*. No damages may be awarded to a winning plaintiff for mental or emotional injury unless the inmate can show an actual physical injury.

The Exhaustion Requirement

If prison officials named as defendants in a §1983 suit can show that the inmate–plaintiff failed to exhaust administrative remedies, the court must dismiss the inmate's claim.[48] "Failure to exhaust" typically means the inmate either did not file a grievance or did not pursue the process completely. The dismissal will be "without prejudice," meaning that the inmate could file the suit again if he could exhaust his administrative remedies. Nevertheless, most grievance systems or administrative appeal remedies have time limits that would have long since expired in almost all situations, so a dismissal for failure to exhaust is the effective death knell for the inmate's claim, regardless of its merits.

The Supreme Court has looked at the exhaustion rule several times and found no major faults.

- Exhaustion is required even if the grievance process cannot award the relief the inmate seeks, such as money damages.[49] If the process is "available," it must be exhausted, even if all it might do is apologize to the inmate for a mistake.

- The rule applies to all civil rights claims.[50] The Second Circuit court of appeals had tried to exempt suits brought by a single inmate about a single incident by a strained reading of the statute,[51] but a unanimous Supreme Court rejected that reading.

- The entire grievance process must be exhausted, from start to finish. If the inmate is barred from completing the process by, for example, missing a mandatory time deadline, the inmate has failed to exhaust and his case will be dismissed.[52]

Not surprisingly, the Supreme Court saw things differently, declaring that "exhaustion" means *complete* exhaustion of the *entire* process. This would further the goal of allowing prison officials to correct their own mistakes short of litigation. Less than complete exhaustion would "turn [the PLRA exhaustion requirement] into a largely useless appendage."[53] Inmates wanting to avoid the grievance process for some reason, such as the inmate in *Booth,*[49] who saw the grievance process as futile because it could not give him monetary damages, could simply miss the first filing deadline and be off to federal court.

Consider the effect of *Ngo v. Woodford* (see side bar). The inmate who fails to meet a mandatory procedural requirement in the grievance process and therefore cannot access the entire process is barred from having his complaint heard in federal court, regardless of its merits, at least as long as he remains in custody. If a grievance process contains a mandatory time for filing a grievance, the effective statute of limitations for filing a §1983 action becomes measured not in years but in the days in which the inmate must file a grievance.

Note the different perspectives of the Ninth Circuit and the Supreme Court. The former worried that a complete exhaustion rule would lead to grievance systems loaded with mandatory procedural requirements designed to trip up inmates, make complete exhaustion difficult, and bar a number of inmates from raising claims in federal court. The latter worried that without a strict exhaustion requirement, inmates would effectively boycott the process and subvert the remedial, early problem-solving goal of grievance processes. The PLRA exhaustion requirement thereby becomes a significant legal procedural tail that threatens to wag the entire grievance procedure dog.

CASE IN POINT: COMPLETE EXHAUSTION

Viet Mike Ngo was a California inmate. A disciplinary infraction involving something he did in the prison chapel resulted in his being barred from participating in various religious programs. Six months after the restrictions were imposed, Ngo filed a grievance that was promptly denied because it was not filed within 15 days of the ban being imposed. His appeal of that decision was denied.

The Ninth Circuit, a court that has historically favored inmate cases, went through a lengthy and complicated analysis of legal concepts of exhaustion of remedies and "procedural defaults" that need not be analyzed here. Suffice it to say the circuit decided that if an inmate took a grievance as far as he could, he will have "exhausted" the process, even if he was not able to move through every step of the process. Therefore, Ngo had exhausted his remedies. If the court ruled the other way, it said:

prisoners' access to courts would be based on their ability to navigate procedural minefields, not on whether their claims had any merit. Moreover, prison administrators should not be given an incentive to fashion grievance procedures which prevent or even defeat prisoners' meritorious claims.[54]

Inmate grievance systems originally were created in the hope that they would provide inmates with elementary ways of raising complaints with correctional officials about conditions and practices in the institution. If legitimate inmate complaints could be resolved in a matter of days or weeks, some inmate frustrations and tensions might be mitigated, inmate–staff relationships improved, and lawsuits avoided. The PLRA may be doing little to further those aspirations.

Although it is beyond the scope of this chapter, a question worth discussing is what message the operational quality of a grievance process sends to inmates. Does the process operate to give inmates the belief that it at least fairly evaluates their complaints, or does it tell them that the system will bend over backward to avoid admitting mistakes or attempting to remedy them?

Filing Fee

As of this writing, the fee to file a lawsuit in federal court is $350. Filing an appeal costs $450. However, if a litigant is indigent, the court may waive the filing fee and allow the person to proceed "IFP" or, in legal Latin, "in forma pauperis." However, the PLRA altered the fee waiver rules as applied to inmates.

Historically, most inmate suits are filed "pro se," that is, without the assistance of an attorney, and courts routinely waive the filing fees for inmates.

Federal courts opened their doors to inmate complaints around 1970. Between that year and 1995, the number of civil rights claims from local, state, and federal inmates grew from less than 2,300 to more than 39,000. See **Table 42-1**. Although most of these cases went nowhere, they still took a toll on agency time and resources to defend.

In fiscal 1995, federal district courts terminated just over 39,000 inmate civil rights cases. One study concluded that more than four of five resulted in a pretrial dismissal in favor of defendants.[55]

The PLRA changed the IFP rules, replacing the complete waiver with a rule that said the indigent inmate would have to pay the full filing fee but because of his indigence, the payment could be spread over time. The court now sets the payment schedule based on the amount of money passing through the inmate's institution account. What amounts to a down payment and periodic payments thereafter are made by the institution to the court clerk.[56] Congress reasoned that if an inmate had to pay several hundred dollars to get to court, he would think twice about filing a frivolous case, let alone make a hobby of filing lawsuits. Although there was undoubtedly some truth to this reasoning, it neglected to consider that the same financial burden would also deter inmates with meritorious claims.

The change in the IFP requirements is probably the single most important factor for an immediate and startling dropoff in the number of suits inmates have filed since passage of the PLRA. Inmate civil rights filings plummeted from an all-time high of 39,008 in 1995 to 24,245 in 1998. The drop is even more dramatic when measured by the number of inmate civil rights claims filed per 1,000 inmates, dropping from 24.6/1,000 inmates in 1995 to just over 11.1/1,000 in 2010. See Table 42-1.

■ Attorney's Fees

Federal law allows a court to award attorney's fees to the prevailing party in a §1983 case, including inmate cases.[57] Case law makes it difficult for the prevailing defendant to be awarded such fees. In general, these fees are computed by multiplying the number of hours the lawyer spent working on the case times the hourly billing rate for lawyers of similar skill in the federal district where the case was heard. In a large class action, the lawyer or lawyers representing the inmate class could devote thousands of hours to the case. When the PLRA was passed in 1996, it was not difficult to find such lawyers billing at $200/hour or more, meaning the attorney's fee in a major lawsuit could run well into the millions of dollars. Even small cases could result in an attorney's fees award far in excess of what the inmate won, because there was no link between the size of the inmate's award and the hours-times-rate computation of the attorney's fees.

TABLE 42-1[58] Inmate Civil Rights Claims Filed per 1,000 Inmates

Year	Total Number Incarcerated (Federal, State, Local Jails)	Inmate Civil Rights Claims Filed in Federal Court	Filings per 1,000 Inmates (Estimates)
1970	357,292	2,267	6.3
1980	503,586	13,047	25.9
1990	1,148,702	24,004	20.9
1995	1,585,586	39,008	24.6
1998	1,816,931	24,245	13.4
2001	1,995,705	22,206	11.4
2010	2,266,832	25,057	11.1

Source: Inmate Litigation, Schlanger, Margo, 116 Harvard Law Review 1555,1583.; Sourcebook of Criminal Justice Statistics, http://www.albany.edu/sourcebook/pdf/t5652010.pdf

The PLRA tries to limit attorney's fee awards in two ways. It limits the hourly rate to 150% of the hourly rate paid to court-appointed counsel in criminal cases in the federal district where the case was filed, which is $125/hour as of this writing. Although $187.50/hour may sound substantial, it is still considerably lower than the hourly rates could receive under the old hours-times-rate approach.

The PLRA requires that the fee be proportionate to the relief ordered. Thus, nominal damages award of $10 will no longer support an attorney's fee award of several thousand dollars computed using the traditional hours-time-rate method. The effect of this may be to deter attorneys from representing inmates in damages cases where the potential damage award will be relatively small.

Limitations on Damages

The PLRA says "no federal civil action may be brought by a prisoner ... for mental or emotional injury suffered while in custody without a prior showing of physical injury."[59] This inartfully worded provision is subject to a variety of interpretations, but courts generally say that it applies to suits brought by prisoners while prisoners, not suits brought after their release. It prevents the award of compensatory damages for mental or emotional injury, but not nominal or punitive damages. It does not limit actions for injunctive relief. Its biggest effect may be in barring compensatory damage awards in cases involving religious or other First Amendment rights where there will not be any physical damages.

The Three-Strike Rule

Anyone who has worked around inmate litigation knows about "frequent filers," the very small group of inmates who file a disproportionately large number of lawsuits. A Washington state inmate attempted to file more than 200 proceedings in federal court between 1979 and 2004. All were filed IFP. In 1984, the federal district court revoked the inmate's IFP privileges, invoking a seldom-used judicial power that was a precursor of the three-strikes portion of the PLRA.[60]

The PLRA provides that if an inmate has had three cases dismissed as frivolous or malicious, or as failing to state a claim upon which relief can be granted, the inmate must pay the full filing fee at the time the complaint was filed with the court unless the inmate can show he is in "imminent danger of serious physical injury."[61] Appeals dismissed on any of the three grounds also count as strikes.

Dismissals for frivolity or maliciousness are relatively rare, but dismissals for failure to state a claim are relatively common in inmate litigation, so the three-strike rule directly affects the great majority of would-be frequent filers.

"FRIVOLOUS CASES"

The poster-child example of a frivolous inmate lawsuit is the legendary crunchy peanut butter case. Although a citation to this case cannot be found in LEXIS, its facts have been thrown out in almost every discussion about inmate litigation abuses since the 1970s. The allegations go something like this: Inmate X orders crunchy peanut butter from the prison commissary. He gets smooth (or perhaps vice versa). He files a federal lawsuit.

But there is an inconvenient and overlooked aspect to this tale. It is incorrect. According to Judge Jon O. Newman, a retired judge from the Second Circuit, the case was really about money. The commissary delivered the wrong peanut butter to the inmate, who gave it to an officer, who in turn promised to return the next day with the correct peanut butter. But during the night, the inmate was transferred to another prison. The $2.50 he paid for the peanut butter remained deducted from his account. The unrefunded money was what the inmate sued about.

Was $2.50 worth filing a federal lawsuit? Realistically, probably not. But had the prison officials properly acknowledged their mistake and either refunded the money or given the inmate the right kind of peanut butter, the brouhaha would never have happened. By wronging the inmate, the officials should not have been surprised if the inmate tried to raise his complaint in another forum.[62]

Some number of legally meritless suits fall into this category: The institution makes a mistake but refuses to correct it, antagonizing the inmate and unnecessarily provoking a lawsuit.

■ Restrictions on Judicial Power

The PLRA imposes various restrictions on the power of federal judges that are beyond the scope of this chapter. These restrictions include limitations on injunctions and consent decrees ("prospective relief" in PLRA terms) that are similar to the admonitions about the scope of such orders that appeared in *Lewis*. The law also makes it more difficult for a court to impose a prisoner release order and makes it considerably easier for a defendant to have a prospective relief order terminated.

■ Other Issues

Legal Mail

Mail to and from inmates is generally protected by the First Amendment, but the limitations still leave considerable room for officials to control both the flow and content of mail.[63] But are there categories of mail, led by correspondence between and inmate and lawyer, that enjoy enhanced, "privileged" protection?

In 1974, the Supreme Court in *Wolff v. McDonnell* addressed inmate rights associated with mail from attorneys, that is, "legal mail;" "assumed" inspection of legal mail was protected by the Constitution; and approved Nebraska's practices of practices requiring mail to be clearly marked by the sender as privileged and opening, but not reading, such mail in the presence of the inmate-recipient.[64]

Despite the Court's equivocation about whether legal mail received any special constitutional protection, lower courts after *Wolff* have generally held that mail from attorneys and paralegals is privileged and generally confidential. Officials should not read such mail short of some sort of emergency, and privileged mail should be opened only in the presence of the recipient and outgoing privileged mail should generally be not opened.[65] To enjoy special protection, agencies may require the mail to be specially marked by the sender in some way as "privileged." Thus, a return address from an attorney alone will not establish a letter as privileged.

There is some question as to what mail, beyond that from attorneys and paralegals, qualifies as privileged. Mail from legal organizations such as the ACLU qualifies, at least when it deals with a legal matter. However, cases such as *Sallier v. Brooks*[66] indicate that questions remain as to whether mail from other government officials is privileged, especially when such correspondence is part of the public record. In *Sallier*, the court addressed with several types of mail, saying that because the American Bar Association does not protect legal advice or direct legal services, its mail was not privileged, nor was mail from a county clerk. There is disagreement among courts about whether mail to an inmate from a court is privileged.[67]

Retaliation

Regardless of the vitues of a lawsuit an inmate may file, prison officials may not retaliate against the inmate for filing it. To do so exposes the officials to liability for the retaliation, even though the inmate's original claim was meritless.

Retaliation claims can arise when officials take some sort of negative action against an inmate who is in temporal proximity to the inmate filing or winning a lawsuit. However, a time link between the inmate's legal activity and the activities of officials alone does not prove an improper retaliatory motive. For the retaliation claim to succeed, a court must find that (1) the inmate engaged in constitutionally protected content, for example, he filed a lawsuit; (2) some adverse action was taken by officials against the inmate that would "deter a person of ordinary firmness from continuing to pursue the protected conduct;" and (3) there is a causal connection between the first two elements "motivated at least in part by the plaintiff's protected conduct."[68]

In general, the key element in a retaliation claim is the motive behind the officials' actions: Would the action have been taken regardless of the inmate's legal activity?

Basic Supplies

In *Bounds*, the Supreme Court said, "It is indisputable that indigent inmates must be provided at state expense with paper and pen to draft legal documents, with notarial services to authenticate them, and with stamps to mail them."[69] From this general statement of principle come various questions, including what qualifies an inmate as "indigent" and whether indigent inmates are entitled to free copying and to typewriters.[70] All questions about lack of access to basic supplies are now subject to the "actual injury" requirement from *Lewis v. Casey*.

■ Conclusion

The feast or famine history of the right of access to the courts over the last 40 years provides a clear example of the conservative shift in the Supreme Court during those decades. In *Wolff* and *Bounds*, the Court barely took the time to establish the right somewhere in the Constitution and described the officials' affirmative duties in terms—providing "meaningful" access—that invited expansion of those duties.

Twenty years after *Bounds*, a different Supreme Court decided *Lewis* and gave a new sort of "less is more" meaning to "meaningful." One wonders whether the 1996 Supreme Court (and certainly the 2013 Court) would reduce the scope of the right of access to the courts even more were it not stuck with the precedent of *Bounds*. But old cases can be overruled, and it would not be surprising if at some point the Court decides that the right of access to the courts does not create any affirmative duties for prison officials, but only prevents them from actively impeding inmate attempts to access the courts.

Chapter Resources

DISCUSSION QUESTIONS

1. Discuss the possible effect on the inmate rights movement and corrections in general had the Supreme Court said, in *Younger v. Gilmore* (1971), that prison officials did *not* have an affirmative duty to provide any resources that inmates could use in challenging prison conditions or practices.

2. Assume that a federal appeals court released a decision in a habeas corpus proceeding filed by an inmate in State A that called into question a substantial number of criminal convictions or sentences of inmates in other states in the circuit. Officials in State B in the same circuit, relying on a decision saying that the right of access to the courts required only that an inmate "be permitted to file a complaint or appeal," provided inmates with no resources or assistance that addressed substantive inmate rights issues, leaving no way for the inmates to find out about the decision. Should officials in State B have any obligation to make inmates aware of the decision?

3. Two prisons are essentially identical with regard to such things as physical plant, inmate population characteristics, staffing, and resources, but inmates in one file less than half the civil rights cases as inmates in the other. What might explain this disparity?

4. You are counsel to a corrections agency. The agency asks you to review a draft of a proposed new grievance system that contains a large number of mandatory requirements (time deadlines, content requirements, etc.). In response to your query about the new procedural requirements, an official confides in you, "I wouldn't say this publicly, but we want to make it hard for inmates to exhaust their administrative remedies so we can get more inmate civil rights cases dismissed quickly." Is this permissible under the PLRA? Does it raise possible constitutional access-to-the-courts issues?

5. If the unstated intent of the proposed rule to make it harder for inmates to present claims in court became known, there could be an access-to-the-courts issue raised, but how courts would resolve the issue is unknown. Could the proposed grievance system be seen as an unconstitutional barrier to court access, comparable to the situations in the *Hull* and *Avery* Supreme Court cases?

6. Should the right of access to the courts include an affirmative obligation for prison officials to provide some resources by which inmates could learn about their substantive legal rights with regard to their criminal convictions and sentences and about issues of prison conditions and practices? Why or why not?

ADDITIONAL RESOURCES

Boston, J., & Manville, D. E. (2010). *Prisoners' self-help litigation manual* (4th ed.). New York, NY: Oceana.

Civil Rights Litigation Clearinghouse, http://www.clearinghouse.net/

Collins, W. C. (2010). *Correctional law for correctional officers* (5th ed.). Alexandria, VA: American Correctional Association.

Mushlin, M. B. (2009). *Rights of prisoners* (4th ed., 4 volumes with supplements). Eagan, MN: West Publishing.

NOTES

1. 536 U.S. 403, 415, fn. 12 (2002).
2. 403 U.S. 388 (1971).
3. In general, references to "prison" in this chapter include jails.
4. 312 U.S. 546 (1941).
5. 312 U.S. at 549.
6. 393 U.S. 483 (1969).
7. In 1961, the Court breathed life back into §1983 by holding that it gave federal courts jurisdiction over claims that state or local officials had violated federal statutory or constitutional rights, *Monroe v. Pape*, 365 U.S. 167 (1961). Three years later, the Court held that state or local inmates could sue prison officials directly in federal court over prison-related issues, without taking their cases through state court first, *Cooper v. Pate*, 378 U.S. 546 (1964). These cases opened the federal courthouse door for inmate suits, but it took a while for the message to sink in. As Table 42-1 shows, inmates filed fewer than 2,300 §1983 claims in 1970.
8. 28 U.S.C. §2242.
9. *Younger v. Gilmore*, 404 U.S. 15 (1971).
10. *Gilmore v. Lynch*, 319 F. Supp. 105, 110 (N.D. Cal., 1970).
11. 418 U.S. 539 (1974).
12. 418 U.S. at 570.
13. 418 U.S. at 580.
14. 430 U.S. 817 (1977).
15. 430 U.S. at 818.
16. 430 U.S. at 828.
17. *Bounds v. Smith*, 813 F.2d 1299 (4th Cir., 1987).
18. 813 F.2d at 1303.
19. *U.S. v. Janis*, 829 F. Supp. 512 (S.D. Cal., 1992), inmate has right of access to courts for general civil matters, a right of 2 hours of law library time 5 days a week.
20. *Abdul-Akbar v. Watson*, 4 F.3d 195 (3rd Cir., 1993).
21. See Boston, J., & Manville, D. E. (2010). *Prisoners' self-help litigation manual* (4th ed., p. 239). New York, NY: Oceana. There were fewer cases addressing the issue of illiterate inmates than one might have expected, because by definition, a person who cannot read is not going to be able to use the best law library.
22. 581 U.S. 343 (1996).
23. 951 F.2d 1504 (9th Cir. Ariz., 1991).
24. *Casey v. Lewis*, 43 F. 3d 1261 (9th Cir., 1994).
25. Id., at 1267.
26. Id., at 1261.
27. 518 U.S. at 346, quoting *Bounds*.
28. 518 U.S. at 351.
29. 429 U.S. 97 (1976).
30. 429 U.S. at 104.
31. 581 U.S. at 351.
32. 509 U.S. 25 (1993).
33. 509 U.S. 25 (1993), *Farmer v. Brennan*, 511 U.S. 825 (1994).
34. 518 U.S. at 352.

35. 518 U.S. at 353.

36. 518 U.S. at 354.

37. Id. Emphasis in original. Does this implicitly reject the Ninth Circuit's comments about the importance of browsing through a law library?

38. *Shidler v. Moore*, 409 F.Supp.2d 1060 (N.D. Ind., 2006).

39. 445 F.3d 965 (7th Cir., 2006).

40. 445 F.3d at 969.

41. 518 U.S. at 355.

42. 518 U.S. at 362, citing *Bell v. Wolfish*, 441 U.S. 520 (1979).

43. 518 U.S. at 392.

44. *Silva v. Vittorio*, 658 F.3d 1090 (9th Cir., 2011).

45. *Monroe v. Beard*, 536 F.3d 198 (3rd Cir., 2008).

46. *Nevada Department of Corrections v. Cohen*, 582 F.Supp.2d 1085 (D. Nev. 2008), citing *Turner v. Safley*, 482 U.S. 78 (1987). *Turner* defined the legal test for determining the validity of prison regulations or practices that infringe on inmates' constitutional rights. The test generally favors the interests of the officials.

47. §§801-810, 110 Stat. 1321-66 to 1321-77. Public Law 106-274.

48. *Jones v. Bock*, 549 U.S. 199 (2006).

49. *Booth v. Churner*, 121 S.Ct. 1819 (2001).

50. 534 U.S. 516 (2002).

51. 534 U.S. at 522.

52. *Woodford v. Ngo*, 548 U.S. 81 (2006).

53. 548 U.S. at 93.

54. *Ngo v. Woodford*, 403 F.3d 620, 631 (2005).

55. Schlanger, p. 1598. An earlier pre-PLRA study of a nine-state sample of cases found that 94% resulted in "court dismissal" or "dismissal on defendant's motion." Hanson, R., & Daley, H. W. K. (1995). *Challenging the conditions of prisons and jails*. Washington, DC: Bureau of Justice Statistics. Retrieved from, http://bjs.ojp. usdoj.gov/index.cfm?ty=pbdetail&iid=544. The Hanson study contains an intriguing table that shows a huge disparity between the rate at which inmates file §1983 claims from one state to another. In 1991, 129 of every 1,000 inmates in Iowa filed a §1983 claims. In Rhode Island, the rate was 2.7 lawsuits per 1,000 inmates. The median was approximately 30. Why are inmates in some states so much more litigious than in other states? Are the rates tied primarily to actual poor conditions and practices? Could overall relations between staff and inmates be a driving factor also?

56. 28 U.S.C. §1915.

57. 42 U.S.C. §1988.

58. Schlanger, M. (2003). Inmate Litigation. *Harvard Law Review, 116*, pp. 1555, 1583. The data in the last line of the table come from the *Sourcebook of Criminal Justice Statistics*, http://www.albany.edu/sourcebook/ pdf/t5652010.pdf. I computed the filings per 1,000 inmates figure.

59. 42 U.S.C. §1997e(e).

60. *Demos v. Kincheloe*, #C-80-152 (and 28 additional cases), June 27, 1984, unpublished.

61. 28 U.S.C. §1915(g).

62. http://www.uscourts.gov/News/TheThirdBranch/00-02-11/Judiciary_apos_s_Goal_Outstanding_ Service_at_Reasonable_Cost.aspx

63. *Procunier v. Martinez*, 416 U.S. 396 (1974), *Turner v. Safely*, 4821 U.S. 78 (1987).

64. *Wolff v. McDonnell*, 418 U.S. 539, 577 (1974).

65. See *Prisoners' self-help litigation manual* (p. 193).

66. *Sallier v. Brooks*, 343 F.3d 868 (6th Cir., 2003).

67. *Sallier*, supra (privileged) *Keenan v. Hall*, 83 F.3d 1083 (9th Cir., 1996) (not privileged except in rare circumstances.

68. *Thaddeus-X v. Blatter*, 175 F.3d 378 (6th Cir., 1999).

69. 430 U.S. at 824–825.

70. Id.

IN CONGRESS, JULY 4, 1776.

The unanimous Declaration of the thirteen united States of America

When in the Course of human events, it becomes necessary for one people to dissolve the political bands which have connected them with another, and to assume among the powers of the earth, the separate and equal station to which the Laws of Nature and of Nature's God entitle them, a decent respect to the opinions of mankind requires that they should declare the causes which impel them to the separation. ———— We hold these truths to be self-evident, that all men are created equal, that they are endowed by their Creator with certain unalienable Rights, that among these are Life, Liberty and the pursuit of Happiness. —— That to secure these rights, Governments are instituted among Men, deriving their just powers from the consent of the governed, —— That whenever any Form of Government becomes destructive of these ends, it is the Right of the People to alter or to abolish it, and to institute new Government, laying its foundation on such principles and organizing its powers in such form, as to them shall seem most likely to effect their Safety and Happiness. Prudence, indeed, will dictate that Governments long established should not be changed for light and transient causes; and accordingly all experience hath shewn, that mankind are more disposed to suffer, while evils are sufferable, than to right themselves by abolishing the forms to which they are accustomed. But when a long train of abuses and usurpations, pursuing invariably the same Object evinces a design to reduce them under absolute Despotism, it is their right, it is their duty, to throw off such Government, and to provide new Guards for their future security. —— Such has been the patient sufferance of these Colonies; and such is now the necessity which constrains them to alter their former Systems of Government. The history of the present King of Great Britain is a history of repeated injuries and usurpations, all having in direct object the establishment of an absolute Tyranny over these States. To prove this, let Facts be submitted to a candid world. ————

He has refused his Assent to Laws, the most wholesome and necessary for the public good.
—— He has forbidden his Governors to pass Laws of immediate and pressing importance, unless suspended in their operation till his Assent should be obtained; and when so suspended, he has utterly neglected to attend to them.
—— He has refused to pass other Laws for the accommodation of large districts of people, unless those people would relinquish the right of Representation in the Legislature, a right inestimable to them and formidable to tyrants only.
—— He has called together legislative bodies at places unusual, uncomfortable, and distant from the depository of their public Records, for the sole purpose of fatiguing them into compliance with his measures.
—— He has dissolved Representative Houses repeatedly, for opposing with manly firmness his invasions on the rights of the people.
—— He has refused for a long time, after such dissolutions, to cause others to be elected; whereby the Legislative powers, incapable of Annihilation, have returned to the People at large for their exercise; the State remaining in the mean time exposed to all the dangers of invasion from without, and convulsions within.
—— He has endeavoured to prevent the population of these States; for that purpose obstructing the Laws for Naturalization of Foreigners; refusing to pass others to encourage their migrations hither, and raising the conditions of new Appropriations of Lands.
—— He has obstructed the Administration of Justice, by refusing his Assent to Laws for establishing Judiciary powers.
—— He has made Judges dependent on his Will alone, for the tenure of their offices, and the amount and payment of their salaries.
—— He has erected a multitude of New Offices, and sent hither swarms of Officers to harrass our people, and eat out their substance.
—— He has kept among us, in times of peace, Standing Armies without the Consent of our legislatures.
—— He has affected to render the Military independent of and superior to the Civil power.
—— He has combined with others to subject us to a jurisdiction foreign to our constitution, and unacknowledged by our laws; giving his Assent to their Acts of pretended Legislation:
—— For Quartering large bodies of armed troops among us:
—— For protecting them, by a mock Trial, from punishment for any Murders which they should commit on the Inhabitants of these States:
—— For cutting off our Trade with all parts of the world:
—— For imposing Taxes on us without our Consent:
—— For depriving us in many cases, of the benefits of Trial by Jury:
—— For transporting us beyond Seas to be tried for pretended offences:
—— For abolishing the free System of English Laws in a neighbouring Province, establishing therein an Arbitrary government, and enlarging its Boundaries so as to render it at once an example and fit instrument for introducing the same absolute rule into these Colonies:
—— For taking away our Charters, abolishing our most valuable Laws, and altering fundamentally the Forms of our Governments:
—— For suspending our own Legislatures, and declaring themselves invested with power to legislate for us in all cases whatsoever.
—— He has abdicated Government here, by declaring us out of his Protection and waging War against us.
—— He has plundered our seas, ravaged our Coasts, burnt our towns, and destroyed the lives of our people.
—— He is at this time transporting large Armies of foreign Mercenaries to compleat the works of death, desolation and tyranny, already begun with circumstances of Cruelty & perfidy scarcely paralleled in the most barbarous ages, and totally unworthy the Head of a civilized nation.
—— He has constrained our fellow Citizens taken Captive on the high Seas to bear Arms against their Country, to become the executioners of their friends and Brethren, or to fall themselves by their Hands.
—— He has excited domestic insurrections amongst us, and has endeavoured to bring on the inhabitants of our frontiers, the merciless Indian Savages, whose known rule of warfare, is an undistinguished destruction of all ages, sexes and conditions.

In every stage of these Oppressions We have Petitioned for Redress in the most humble terms: Our repeated Petitions have been answered only by repeated injury. A Prince whose character is thus marked by every act which may define a Tyrant, is unfit to be the ruler of a free people. Nor have We been wanting in attentions to our British brethren. We have warned them from time to time of attempts by their legislature to extend an unwarrantable jurisdiction over us. We have reminded them of the circumstances of our emigration and settlement here. We have appealed to their native justice and magnanimity, and we have conjured them by the ties of our common kindred to disavow these usurpations, which, would inevitably interrupt our connections and correspondence. They too have been deaf to the voice of justice and of consanguinity. We must, therefore, acquiesce in the necessity, which denounces our Separation, and hold them, as we hold the rest of mankind, Enemies in War, in Peace Friends.

We, therefore, the Representatives of the united States of America, in General Congress, Assembled, appealing to the Supreme Judge of the world for the rectitude of our intentions, do, in the Name, and by Authority of the good People of these Colonies, solemnly publish and declare, That these United Colonies are, and of Right ought to be Free and Independent States; that they are Absolved from all Allegiance to the British Crown, and that all political connection between them and the State of Great Britain, is and ought to be totally dissolved; and that as Free and Independent States, they have full Power to levy War, conclude Peace, contract Alliances, establish Commerce, and to do all other Acts and Things which Independent States may of right do. —— And for the support of this Declaration, with a firm reliance on the Protection of divine Providence, we mutually pledge to each other our Lives, our Fortunes and our sacred Honor.

John Hancock

Button Gwinnett
Lyman Hall
Geo Walton.

Wm Hooper
Joseph Hewes
John Penn

Samuel Chase
Wm Paca
Thos. Stone
Charles Carroll of Carrollton

Robt Morris
Benjamin Rush
Benj. Franklin
John Morton
Geo Clymer

Josiah Bartlett
Wm Whipple
Saml Adams
John Adams
Robt Treat Paine
Elbridge Gerry

Th Jefferson
Chs. Livingston
Fras. Lewis
Lewis Morris

Edward Rutledge

Compliance with the Constitution

John R. Shaw

CHAPTER
43

CHAPTER OBJECTIVES

- Discuss why and when the U.S. Supreme Court shifted away from the "hands-off doctrine" and began to ensure many constitutional rights to convicted offenders.

- Explain how the right of habeas corpus led to prisoners generally having access to the courts, and describe how the right of access to the courts affects the operation of correctional facilities.

- Identify common legal issues that arise in correctional institution settings and discuss how the courts have responded to these issues.

t is clear that all prison and jail administrations, as well as their employees, must comply with the provisions of the U.S. Constitution. Failure to do so can result in disruptive lawsuits, imposition of severe judicial remedies, monetary awards, and even personal employee liability. What is not so clear is exactly which provisions of the Constitution actually apply to the many challenges posed by operating this country's vast variety of federal, state, local, and privately run prisons and jails. This area of the law is extensive and complex, requiring courts to review and decide prisoner lawsuits challenging almost every aspect of corrections operations filed every year. Each of these cases turn on constitutional or statutory rights that will dictate the outcome. In this chapter, we will concentrate on the U.S. Constitution and examine whether, and how, its provisions apply behind the prison and jail walls. With this knowledge, we will be able to see how correctional administrators and their employees can ensure that they comply with the Constitution.

The Constitution, the Supreme Court, and Corrections

The U.S. Constitution is the supreme law of the land. All laws, regulations, rules, and other types of legislative provisos and governmental actions that affect the affairs of citizens (and for that matter noncitizens, or even to some degree persons in the country illegally) are subject to constitutional scrutiny to determine whether they fall under the umbrella of constitutional requirements. The arbiter of what is and what is not constitutional falls to the judiciary. The ultimate judicial authority is the U.S. Supreme Court ("the Supreme Court" or "the Court"). A ruling of the Supreme Court regarding an interpretation of the Constitution as it relates to a federal, state, or local governing body statute, regulation, or rule dictates whether such provision may permissibly continue in force.

Over the last 50 years, the Supreme Court decided many dozens of cases concerning management of U.S. prisons and jails, determining how far the U.S. Constitution reaches inside these facilities to provide prisoners constitutional protections and limit the unfettered discretion of prison administrators. As will be seen, the Court has struggled with balancing the constitutional rights of prisoners with the discretion that must be accorded prison administrators charged with the extremely difficult task of safely and efficiently operating correctional institutions.

It would be impossible in one chapter to even begin to touch on the many issues that can arise under the Constitution relating to operating U.S. corrections facilities. Instead, this chapter will present a brief overview of the more important constitutional issues and concepts as decided by the Supreme Court that affect the operations of U.S. prisons and jails, as well as the rights prisoners retain when detained and incarcerated.[1] We will also look at legislative initiatives that have affected these issues.

The Shifting Supreme Court View of Prisoner Rights and the Constitution

For almost 200 years after the signing of the Constitution and the Bill of Rights, courts left all authority over prison issues to those who ran the prisons. This total deference by the courts to prison administrators is often referred to as the "hands-off" doctrine. Indeed, the prevailing view was that a prisoner was a mere "slave of the state" who "not only forfeited his liberty, but all his personal rights except those which the law in its humanity accords him."[2] However, even in the 1800s, there were a few Supreme Court decisions that acknowledged a prisoner's right to petition the courts for habeas corpus relief. For instance, in 1894, the Supreme Court accepted and considered that a federal prisoner's habeas corpus petition alleging his incarceration in a state penitentiary was in violation of the federal statute for which he was convicted.[3] Over the decades, these cases eventually led to a broadening of the Court's view as to not only what types of prisoner petitions and lawsuits the federal courts should accept but also what constitutional rights prisoners retained while incarcerated.

Whether one believes the Constitution is a "living, breathing" document or an "original intent" legal contract, there is no question the Court's view of prisoner rights and limitations on prison administrative independence has shifted to the left and to the right, depending to a large degree on the philosophical makeup of the nine Supreme Court justices and the president who nominated them, along with the Senate who approved the nominations. So, as we will see, the Court's view of constitutional requirements sway back and forth, just as society changes its positions as to the important issues of the day.

If this chapter had been written in 1960 instead of today, it would have taken perhaps one paragraph to provide a complete analysis of the Constitution as it applies to prisons and prisoner rights. However, during the late 1960s up until the time of this writing, the U.S. Supreme Court has repeatedly analyzed the constitutionality of laws, regulations, and rules governing the operation of U.S. prisons and jails. It can be stated with some certainty that every chapter of this textbook has constitutional implications. For those of us who follow closely this area of the law and advise prison administrators of constitutional standards, it is difficult to say with assurance that advice given today will still be the case in future. Matters that seemed settled can be reopened by the Court, leading to dramatic changes in constitutional interpretation of issues. Adding to this mix, the U.S. Congress has on occasion enacted legislative provisions that limit or expand the rights of prisoners, even setting standards that affect constitutional requirements with regard to certain aspects of prison life and the authority of the courts to intervene. Thus, whatever conclusions we state today regarding the rights of those incarcerated in our prisons and jails, and the authority to restrict those rights by prison administrators, will almost surely be subject to revisions and amendments over the coming years.

In the remaining portions of this chapter, we will touch briefly on the constitutional and legislative provisions that affect the operation of U.S. prisons and the rights of their prisoners.

■ Habeas Corpus, the End of the "Hands-Off" Doctrine, and Access to the Courts

Habeas Corpus

The one provision in the U.S. Constitution that specifically provides any right to prisoners is contained in Article I, §9, of the Constitution, which states: "The Privilege of the Writ of Habeas Corpus shall not be suspended, unless when in Cases of Rebellion or Invasion the public Safety may require it."[4] As noted above, historically there had been a trickle of cases decided by the Supreme Court that considered prisoner habeas corpus petitions. However, these cases dealt with traditional attacks on the legality of the sentence being served by the petitioner, and not with the conditions of the confinement. Thus, for many years, the "hands-off" doctrine was uncontested. One of the first cases to expand the traditional scope of habeas corpus petitions was the Supreme Court decision of *Ex Parte Hull* (1941).[5] In that case, the Court found that a Michigan prisoner who had been required to submit his habeas corpus petition for approval to the institution welfare office prior to submission to the Court had the right to contest his conviction, and that "[t]he state and its officers may not abridge or impair the petitioner's right to apply to a federal court for a writ of habeas corpus."[6] Even though the Court did not provide any guidance as to why it found that the prison administration could not hamper a prisoner's right to petition the courts for habeas corpus relief, it presumably believed that the Constitution's protection of the right of habeas corpus was meaningless unless the right was unhampered by prison authorities. Other cases followed in *Hull's* footsteps over the next 30 years, expanding the protection to file habeas petitions such as prohibiting the state from limiting the right to file habeas corpus petitions to those inmates who could afford the filing fee,[7] or finding unconstitutional a prison rule prohibiting inmates from assisting other prisoners in filing habeas corpus petitions (unless the state provided other reasonable alternatives).[8] So, although the Court slowly moved away from the "hands-off" doctrine as to the right to habeas corpus protections, other protections found in the Constitution, in particular the liberty interests in the first 10 amendments, or Bill of Rights, remained largely on the sidelines.[9]

The End of the "Hands-Off" Doctrine

By the late 1960s and into the 1970s, the Supreme Court had clearly moved away from limiting its review of prison matters to habeas matters and was actively deciding a variety of prisoner rights issues. In a landmark case that you will see cited in this text regarding several constitutional issues, the Court stated that "[t]here is no iron curtain drawn between the Constitution and the prisons of this country" (*Wolff v. McDonnell* (1974)).[10] *Wolff* went on to acknowledge that

> [t]he demarcation line between civil rights actions and habeas petitions is not always clear. The Court has already recognized instances where *the same constitutional rights might be redressed under either form of relief.* (Emphasis added).

Thus, if it were not clear before, the Court now had shed notion of courts limiting prisoner complaints to narrow habeas issues, and the era of "hands off" had ended.

Access to the Courts and Law Libraries

In 1977, the Supreme Court tackled another important issue regarding access to the courts. While the Court had found for the fundamental rights of prisoners to present their legal claims to the courts, and that inmates could assist one another in filing such claims unless the state provided other alternatives, the Court had not addressed whether the states must provide further access to the courts. In the case of *Bounds v. Smith* (1977),[11] the Court held that

> The fundamental constitutional right of access to the courts requires prison authorities to assist inmates in the preparation and filing of meaningful legal papers by providing prisoners with adequate law libraries or adequate assistance from persons trained in the law.

Because most, if not all, state systems chose not to attempt to travel down the "adequate assistance" alternative path, prison law libraries are now found in most federal, state, and local corrections facilities. This case is mentioned not only to discuss access to the courts but also to highlight a point made earlier: Matters that seem settled can and are revisited by succeeding Supreme Courts, made up of different justices in a different era. *Bounds* was decided when the Supreme Court was actively examining many prisoner rights issues; the Court's decision in *Bounds* was written by Justice Marshall, who had championed many prisoner rights issues during his tenure.

Highlighting the concept of evolving views of the Constitution and prisoner rights, the Supreme Court again took up the issue of prison law libraries 19 years after *Bounds* was decided. In *Lewis v. Casey* (1996),[12] the Court, through Justice Scalia, reiterated that there is a constitutional right of access to the courts "that the States must affirmatively protect." However, the Court went on to say that "[i]t must be acknowledged that several statements in *Bounds* went beyond the right of access recognized in the earlier cases on which it relied. . ." Furthermore, the Court emphasized that State prisons should be run by state officials with the expertise for running such institutions and that "absent the most 'extraordinary circumstances,' federal courts should refrain from meddling in such affairs." With a poke at the lower court's far-reaching findings, the Court lectured that "[a]n overbroad remedial decree can make an already daunting task virtually impossible." The Court then went on to limit the scope of *Bounds*, requiring prisons to provide only those tools necessary for inmates to "attack their sentences, directly or collaterally, and in order to challenge conditions of their confinement." *Lewis* holds that there is no guarantee in the Constitution that inmates must be provided "the wherewithal to transform themselves into litigating engines capable of filing everything from shareholder derivative actions to slip-and-fall claims." Thus, prison law libraries today can be much more limited than was first thought under *Bounds*.

Prison Litigation Reform Act

One final word about access to the courts: Although it is up to the judiciary to define constitutional provisions, the legislature has the authority to enforce its provisions. Thus, through legislative actions, Congress can affect and enforce various parts of the Constitution, and how they apply to the government and its citizens.

For example, in response to crowded court dockets, perceived abuses by prisoners of the legal system, and over-reaching by federal courts in prison matters, the U.S. Congress enacted the Prison Litigation Reform Act (PLRA) in 1996.[13] This legislation sets forth procedural requirements that prisoners must meet when filing lawsuits and limits the power of federal courts in ordering relief in prison condition matters.

One important provision in PLRA requires that a prisoner must exhaust all available prison administrative remedies prior to instituting a suit involving prison conditions, including civil rights actions under §1983. Thus, an effective administrative remedy program not only is important in addressing legitimate inmate grievances and remedying those issues but also serves to protect the prison administration and its employees against premature and frivolous lawsuits. In addition to the exhaustion provision of PLRA, other portions of the statute further limit inmate lawsuits, including:

- An inmate-plaintiff must pay the applicable court filing fee in full. If the prisoner is indigent, there are still requirements to pay a deposit, based on the prisoner's average trust fund account balance, and monthly installments thereafter until the full filing fee is paid.

- If a prisoner's lawsuit or appeal is dismissed because it is found to be frivolous or malicious, or does not state a proper claim, it is considered a "strike." If a prisoner accumulates "three strikes," the prisoner is barred from filing any further lawsuits as an indigent (*in forma pauperis*) unless the full filing fee is paid (unless there is a threat of suffering immediate serious physical injury).

- A prisoner must show a physical injury when claiming money damages for mental or emotional injury.

PLRA also limits federal courts in fashioning relief involving prison conditions. Among other things, federal courts are limited in ordering prospective relief unless "the relief is narrowly drawn, extends no further than necessary to correct the violation of the Federal right, and is the least intrusive means necessary to correct the violation of the Federal right." Also, PLRA limits preliminary injunctive relief to 90 days, and any prospective relief ordered is limited to 2 years.

The net result of PLRA has been a reduction of inmate civil rights violations lawsuits. No doubt, it is more difficult for prisoners to file §1983 actions, and the courts are limited as to the relief they can fashion even if there is a finding of constitutional violations.

During the 1970s and 1980s, the pace of Supreme Court cases analyzing prisoner rights picked up steam, resulting in at least one or two decisions a year. Thus, today, we have many Supreme Court cases analyzing almost every aspect of prison administration and the constitutional protections afforded to those who are incarcerated. Although it is well beyond the scope of this chapter to detail with any specificity the courts findings in these many and problematic cases, some general conclusions can be drawn about some of the more important aspects of prison administration and prisoner rights. Because the Supreme Court is the final authority in interpreting the Constitution and, as we have noted, it has issued numerous rulings on almost all of the important constitutional rights and limitations issues arising out of incarceration, we will rely on those rulings in this chapter.

Besides the right of access to the courts that we have discussed previously, what other constitutional rights survive incarceration? Over the past 50 years, the Supreme Court has found that certain of the protections found in Bill of Rights, plus the Fourteenth Amendment, are applicable to prison operations and the rights of prisoners. Although the Court has consistently found that these constitutional rights are severely constrained because of the necessities attendant with incarceration, they do protect in limited form the rights of U.S. prisoners and detainees. We will turn to each of the constitutional amendments that are applicable in the prison setting—the first, fourth, fifth, and eighth—to see generally what areas of prison life they protect, and how these protections are interpreted by the courts. The Fourteenth Amendment is also relevant because it confers to state citizens the rights found under the Fifth Amendment due process clause and also requires the states to provide equal protection of the laws. Thus, the constitutional amendments we will review apply to actions of the federal government and the states in equal force. The portions of these amendments relevant to our discussion are:

- *Amendment 1*

    Congress shall make no law respecting an establishment of religion, or prohibiting the free exercise thereof; or abridging the freedom of speech, or of the press; or the right of people peaceably to assemble, and to petition the Government for a redress of grievances.

- *Amendment 4*

    The right of the people to be secure in their person, houses, papers, and effects, against unreasonable searches and seizures, shall not be violated. . . .

- *Amendment 5*

    No person shall . . . be deprived of life, liberty, or property, without due process of law. . . .

- *Amendment 8*

    . . . nor cruel and unusual punishments inflicted.

- *Amendment 14*

    . . . No State shall make or enforce any law which shall abridge the privileges or immunities of citizens of the United States; nor shall any State deprive any person of life, liberty, or property, without due process of law; nor deny to any person within its jurisdiction the equal protection of the laws.

■ The First Amendment

The First Amendment has always been cherished as perhaps the most important of our constitutional freedoms. However, in the prison environment, the Court has found that the constitutional rights of prisoners, including the First Amendment, are more limited in scope than the constitutional rights held by individuals in society at large. Although the Court has made it clear that it will protect the fundamental constitutional rights of prisoners, it also will defer in great measure to the judgment of prison authorities because "courts are ill-equipped to deal with the increasingly urgent problems of prison administration and reform."[14] Furthermore, the courts should exercise judicial restraint because "the problems of prisons in the US are complex and intractable, and, more to the point, they are not readily susceptible to resolution by decree."[15] With these principles in mind, the Court has determined a wide array of prison First Amendment issues.

Freedom of Speech and Right of Association

Freedom of speech encompasses not only "speech" in the traditional sense, but important in prison matters are other issues that fall under the freedom of speech umbrella such as whether prison authorities can place restrictions on incoming and outgoing mail, impose limitations and rejections of incoming books and publications, limit and/or prohibit media visits and interviews, prohibit prisoners' unions, reject incoming letters in foreign languages, or reject enclosures in correspondence. The list could go on, and there are hundreds of lower federal court decisions and more than a dozen Supreme Court decisions that have considered the broad array of prison freedom of speech issues. By way of example, Supreme Court decisions in this area include:

- Rejecting California prison regulations that prohibited inmates from mailing out letters that "unduly complain" or "magnify grievances." The Court found that when limiting prisoner First Amendment speech rights that involved also the rights of the members of the general public, prison officials must show the regulation related to a substantial governmental interest of security, order, or rehabilitation, and that the regulation was no greater than necessary.[16] The Court found that the regulation was unduly broad and failed to show how it furthered a legitimate governmental interest.[17]

- Upholding a prison regulation that prohibited face-to-face media interviews with individual inmates. The Court found that prison officials had presented legitimate reasons for the regulation, and their response was not "exaggerated."[18]

- Agreeing with the state that it could prohibit prisoners conducting prisoner union activities such as conducting meetings and soliciting other inmates to join the union. The Court found that speech rights "were barely implicated" in this case, and association rights could be curtailed by prison officials if they reasonably conclude that such associations possess the likelihood of disruption.[19]

- Upholding a Federal Bureau of Prisons' (BOP) regulation that inmates could only receive hardbound books directly from the publishers, book clubs, or bookstores. The Court found that the prison regulation was a "rational response" to a clear security problem.[20]

- Concurring with the state that it could restrict noncontact visitation based on legitimate penological concerns.[21]

Finally, in the pivotal case of *Turner v. Safely* (1987), the Supreme Court undertook to promulgate an encompassing "standard of review for prisoners' constitutional claims that is responsive both to the 'policy of judicial restraint regarding prisoner complaints and [to] the need to protect constitutional rights.'"[22] This case involved two First Amendment issues: inmate marriages and inmate-to-inmate correspondence. In considering the competing interests of the inmates and the prison administration, the Court stated that "when a prison regulation impinges on inmates' constitutional rights, the regulation is valid if it is reasonably related to legitimate penological interests." The Court provided four factors that are relevant when determining the reasonableness of a prison regulation that affects prisoner rights:

- "[T]here must be a 'valid, rational connection' between the regulation and the legitimate governmental interest put forth to justify it."

- "[W]hether there are alternative means of exercising the right that remain open to prison inmates."

- "[T]he impact the accommodation of the asserted right will have on guards and other inmates, and on the allocation of prison resources generally."

- "[T]he absence of ready alternatives is evidence of the reasonableness of a prison regulation."

Using these factors, the Court overturned the prohibition of inmate marriages because the regulation was not related to legitimate penological interests. However, the Court agreed with the state that the prohibition of inmate-to-inmate correspondence was related to valid corrections goals.

While *Turner* is a First Amendment freedom of speech case, the Court has since used the standard and rationale put forth to consider a wide array of prisoner constitutional rights cases. It remains the linchpin when testing the constitutionality of a prison regulation, except in matters of First Amendment religion issues. This exception is discussed later in this chapter.

Freedom of Religion and Establishment of Religion

Apart from the *Cutter* case, which is addressed below, Supreme Court decisions relating to prisons and religion have centered on the free exercise clause of the First Amendment, and not the establishment clause. In *Cruz v. Beto* (1972), the Court reversed the dismissal by the district court and court of appeals of an inmate's complaint that he could not practice his Buddhist religion in the same manner as was accorded to inmates of other religions. Without a lot of analysis, the Court returned the case to the lower court, finding that if Cruz was a Buddhist, and if he was denied reasonable accommodation to pursue his religion comparable to the opportunity afforded to other prisoners of conventional religions, then there was "palpable discrimination."[23] Some 15 years later, the Court considered the case of *O'Lone v. Shabazz* (1987).[24] In that case, plaintiff Muslim inmates claimed a violation of the free exercise clause when they were not permitted to leave their work details, outside the prison, to return to the prison during the day to attend Friday Jumu'ah prayers. Citing its recently decided standard in *Turner*, the Court found that even though the weekly prayer was of "central importance" to the prisoners' religious practices and beliefs, the regulation and rationale prohibiting them from reentering the main prison during the day "were reasonably related to legitimate penological objectives." Therefore, the regulation was upheld. However, a few years later, the *Turner* standard used by the Court in First Amendment cases would be challenged by the U.S. Congress.

RELIGIOUS FREEDOM RESTORATION ACT. Under the *O'Lone* decision, it seemed well settled that the *Turner* approach to determining the standard for review of prison regulations implicating the First Amendment was the law of the land. However, in a nonprison case, *Employment Division v. Smith* (1990), the Court upheld an Oregon statute criminalizing the use of peyote in Native American religious rituals.[25] This triggered concerns that the Court had abandoned its earlier decisions of compelling interest before finding that a religious activity could be restricted by the government. Therefore, in 1993, Congress enacted the Religious Freedom Restoration Act (RFRA), mandating a strict scrutiny, compelling interest standard before the government could substantially burden the free exercise of religion.[26] There is no exception for prison regulations in the legislation.

Within a few years, the Court was presented with a case contesting the constitutionality of RFRA. In the *City of Boerne v. Flores* (1997), the Court ruled RFRA to be unconstitutional, finding that Congress had overstepped its power.[27] The Court stated that it held the sole power to define the substantive rights guaranteed by the Fourteenth Amendment and that Congress did not have "the power to determine what constitutes a constitutional violation." Because this was a Fourteenth Amendment case, it has been interpreted as applying to the states, but activities of the federal government are bound by RFRA. However, even this Supreme Court decision was not the end of the matter.

RELIGIOUS LAND USE AND INSTITUTIONALIZED PERSONS ACT OF 2000. In 2000, Congress again entered the fray of First Amendment freedoms by passing the Religious Land Use and Institutionalized Persons Act (RLUIPA).[28] The act applies specifically to prisoners, mandating that no state government "shall impose a substantial burden on the religious exercise of a person residing in or confined to an institution," unless the burden furthers a compelling state interest and uses the "least restrictive means" test. The other portion of the act relates to protection of land use by religious organizations and will not be addressed in this chapter. RLUIPA worked its way around the Court's ruling in *Boerne* by applying its provisions only to state programs that use federal funding.

The Supreme Court took up the constitutionality of RLUIPA in *Cutter v. Wilkinson* (2005).[29] The Court reviewed only that portion of the act that dealt with prisoners. This time, a unanimous Court found that the "compelling interest" standard required of the states was within the purview of Congress. The state had argued that by advancing religion over other constitutionally protected rights, Congress had violated the establishment clause of the First Amendment. In perhaps the only Supreme Court case dealing with the establishment clause and prisons, the *Cutter* Court found that "institutionalized persons are unable to attend to their religious needs freely and are therefore dependent on the government's permission and accommodation for exercise for their religion." Thus, accommodation of religious practices in the prison context does not violate the establishment clause. Further, the Court found that "the Act does not elevate accommodation of religious observances over an institution's need to maintain order and safety," nor does it "differentiate among bona fide faiths." The courts will be busy over the coming years deciding the exact parameters of RLUIPA as it applies to prisoner religious practices and institutions' interests in discipline, order, and security.

■ The Fourth Amendment

As you will recall, the Fourth Amendment protects the right of the people to be secure in their person, houses, papers, and effects, against unreasonable searches and seizures. What, if any, part of the Fourth Amendment survives incarceration? The Court has considered a string of Fourth Amendment prison cases over the years and has consistently found that the amendment has little applicability given the necessities of running safe and secure prisons and jails. These cases generally deal with searches of prison cells and searches of inmates, including strip searches. Some of the leading Supreme Court cases addressing the Fourth Amendment include

- *Bell v. Wolfish* (1979).[30] This case involved a wide range of alleged constitutional violations at the BOP's New York City jail, the Metropolitan Correctional Center (MCC). The facility housed both pretrial detainees and sentenced offenders. We have previously discussed one of the issues decided in this case relating to the First Amendment and the MCC requirement that inmates could only receive hardbound books directly from the publishers, book clubs, or bookstores. As to the Fourth Amendment claims raised in this case, there were two issues. First, could the facility conduct searches of inmate living quarters outside the presence of the inmate? The other was whether the institution could permissibly strip-search, including a visual body cavity inspection, after every contact visit with a person from outside the institution. Acknowledging that pretrial detainees did retain some Fourth Amendment rights upon commitment to a corrections facility, the Court held both the room searches and the strip searches were justified responses to legitimate, nonpunitive security concerns, and were therefore constitutional. The Court noted that "[t]he Fourth Amendment prohibits only unreasonable searches."

- *Block v. Rutherford* (1984).[31] In *Block*, the Court outlined the risks presented when jail visitors have contact visits with detainees. The Court held that the Los Angeles County Jail could ban all contact visits because of the threat they posed and that there was a "valid, rational connection" between the ban and internal security of a detention facility. There was not a violation of the Fourth or Fifth Amendments triggered by the ban.

- *Hudson v. Palmer* (1984).[32] This case involved a state prisoner alleging constitutional violations in the manner his cell was searched and claimed a Fourth Amendment right to be free of unreasonable searches of his cell and seizures of his property. The Court strongly disagreed with the prisoner, and while it was cautious in finding that the Fourth Amendment could be inapplicable in the given contexts,

  > We hold that society is not prepared to recognize as legitimate any subjective expectation of privacy that a prisoner might have in his prison cell and that, accordingly, the Fourth Amendment proscription against unreasonable searches does not apply within the confines of the prison cell.

  Privacy rights for prisoners in their cells "simply cannot be reconciled with the concept of incarceration and the needs and objective of penal institutions." The Court went on to say that because the respondent did not have a reasonable expectation of privacy under the Fourth Amendment, he still had a remedy for alleged calculated harassment or willful destruction of his property under the Eighth Amendment, along with state court and common law remedies.

- *Florence v. Chosen Freeholders* (2012).[33] This Supreme Court case addressed the question of whether a detainee charged with a minor offense, and who was assigned to the general jail population, may be required to undergo a close visual inspection while undressed. The Court reviewed its previous rulings concerning the Fourth Amendment limitations in prisons and jails (see above) and concluded that "courts must defer to the judgment of correctional officials unless the record contains substantial evidence showing their policies are unnecessary or unjustified response to problems of jail security." In this case, the Court noted the many risks associated with the introduction of contraband when being admitted to the facility. The Court also observed that "people detained for minor offenses can turn out to be the most devious and dangerous criminals." Therefore, the Court upheld the practice of subjecting all detainees being placed in the jail's general population to a visual search while the detainee was undressed. (I am careful here not to use the term "strip search" because the Court found it to be imprecise, noting that strip searches could include touching or not touching body parts. In the *Florence* facts, there was no actual touching.)

These cases make it clear: The Supreme Court finds little room for Fourth Amendment prisoner privacy protections of their persons, houses, or papers. Other types of "searches" also fall under the Fourth's reach in the nonprison world, such as monitoring conversations and phone calls. However, the courts have generally found that in the prison context, no such protection can be asserted. The exception is the privacy of attorney–client communications, which would be protected under the Sixth Amendment, and possibly the Fourth, if both parties thought their communication was confidential.

■ The Fifth Amendment and Fourteenth Amendment

The Fifth Amendment applies to the actions of the federal government and protects its citizens from deprivation of ". . . life, liberty, or property, without due process of law." The Fourteenth Amendment extends due process to the states and their citizens. The Fourteenth Amendment also prohibits states from denying ". . . to any person within its jurisdiction the equal protections of the laws." In prison matters, these due process clauses protect prisoners by requiring some procedural "process" before a protected interest in life, liberty, or property may be taken. So there is a two-step inquiry: First, is there an interest that is to be protected? Second, if there is a protected interest, what process is due? Generally speaking, the higher the interest, the more due process is required to ensure fairness.

No doubt, the most due process accorded under the Constitution is before the government can deprive one of "life" in capital punishment matters. Also, depriving a defendant of his liberty in a criminal case requires much due process. As the deprivation becomes less important, such as the taking of private property or revocation of a license, the process due is less than in criminal matters but is not eliminated.

In the prison setting, most of the cases have dealt with what Fifth Amendment and Fourteenth Amendment protections survive incarceration. For example, the Court has found that the equal protection clause protects prisoners from invidious discrimination based on race (*Lee v. Washington* (1968)).[34] The due process clause, and how it applies in the prison setting, has been the subject of many Supreme Court decisions. One of the most important, and still relevant today, is the case of *Wolff v. McDonnell* (1974).[35] This case set forth the due process requirements that must be accorded to an inmate in certain disciplinary matters. *Wolff* concerned an inmate who had been found to have committed a serious rule violation and as part of his punishment forfeited good time credit. The Court found that the Constitution itself does not guarantee good time credit, but here the state had provided a statutory right to good time and specified that it was to be forfeited only for serious misbehavior. Therefore, the Court concluded that the state, by the mandatory nature of its statute and the fact that deprivation of good time affected the inmate's sentence length, had created a liberty interest that entitled the prisoner to some minimum due process procedures to ensure that his state-created right was not "arbitrarily abrogated."

In addition, *Wolff* contained a footnote that indicated that the due process requirements it articulated when good time credits were forfeited would also apply when solitary confinement was at issue because that was also a punishment the state had reserved for "instances where serious misbehavior has occurred."

The footnote stated that solitary confinement represents "a major change in the conditions of confinement" requiring minimum procedural safeguards as a "hedge" against arbitrary determinations by corrections officials. This opened the door to many inmate due process lawsuits claiming that some state regulation had created a liberty interest or that a change in conditions could trigger due process protections. Over the next 15 years, the Supreme Court issued more than a half dozen decisions dealing with various aspects of the due process clause and whether liberty interests could be found in the Constitution or state regulations requiring some procedural protections.

Finally, the Court decided that many of its decisions since *Wolff* had gotten off base with regard to finding liberty interests solely in the language of state regulations. In *Sandin v. Conner* (1995),[36] the Court said that as this judicial methodology took hold, "no longer did inmates need to rely on a showing that they had suffered a 'grievous loss' of liberty retained even after sentenced to terms of imprisonment." Instead, by relying on the state-created right standard, the Court had produced several undesirable effects. First, it had created "disincentives for States to codify prison management procedures" for fear of creating "liberty" interests, thus causing "standardless discretion on correctional personnel." Second, it had "led to the involvement of federal courts in the day-to-day management of prisons," which was contrary to the often-stated view of the Court that the federal courts should afford "deference and flexibility to state officials trying to manage a volatile environment." Also, the Court noted that by focusing its liberty interest inquiry "to one based on the language of a regulation, the Court encouraged prisoners to comb regulations in search of mandatory language on which to base entitlements to various state-conferred privileges."

Sandin, while stating that it was not "technically" overruling its previous prisoner due process cases, abandoned its earlier approach because "in practice [it] is difficult to administer and . . . produces anomalous results." Instead the Court said that unless the interest can be found in the due process clause "of its own force" (such as transfer to a mental hospital or involuntary administration of psychotropic drugs), the clause would be limited to those cases where the state has imposed "atypical and significant hardship on the inmate in relation to the ordinary incidents of prison life," regardless of what is stated in a statute or regulation. In the particular matter presented to the Court in *Sandin*, Conner argued that the hearing he was accorded was prior to his placement in disciplinary segregation. The court found that the hearing was irrelevant because "discipline in segregated confinement did not present the type of atypical, significant deprivation in which a State might conceivably create a liberty interest." Thus, while the states may continue to provide disciplinary hearings as a matter of statute or regulation, the due process constitutional requirement to do so is limited to cases where the length of the sentence is implicated or where the condition of confinement causes an "atypical and significant hardship" and is not "within the range to be normally expected."

■ The Eighth Amendment

The Eighth Amendment prohibits the government from inflicting "cruel and unusual punishments." This amendment has been the basis of many issues decided by the Supreme Court. For purposes of this section, we will examine what direction the Court has given as to the standards required by the Eighth Amendment when considering prison conditions of confinement. In particular, the Court has reviewed issues such as whether crowding, or "overcrowding," is so serious that if affects basic requirements of providing humane living quarters, adequate food, medical and mental health treatment, and other necessities of life. The Court has also used the cruel and unusual clause when considering whether alleged excessive use of force violates the Constitution. This area of law is broad and beyond a detailed review in this chapter, but we will consider some of the leading cases and general principles articulated by the Court that guide prison administrators today.

- *Estelle v. Gamble* (1976)[37] was the first case in which the Supreme Court addressed medical care in prisons and the requirements of the Eighth Amendment. The Court stated that the government did have an obligation to provide medical care for prisoners and concluded that "deliberate indifference to serious medical needs of prisoners constituted the 'unnecessary and wanton infliction of pain' proscribed by the Eighth Amendment." However, the Court warned that "this conclusion did not mean that every claim by a prisoner that he had not received adequate medical care states a violation of the Eighth Amendment." The Court found that mere negligence or inadvertent failure to provide medical care did not state a constitutional claim. "In order to state a cognizable claim, a prisoner must allege acts or omissions sufficiently harmful to evidence deliberate indifference to serious medical needs." This "deliberate indifference" rule remains the standard in Eighth Amendment considerations.

- In *Rhodes v. Chapman* (1981),[38] the Court found that "double celling" did not constitute cruel and unusual punishment. The Constitution "does not mandate comfortable prisons," and only those deprivations so serious that they deny "the minimal civilized measure of life's necessities" form the basis of an Eighth Amendment violation.

- During a riot at the Oregon State Penitentiary, an inmate was shot as officers regained control of a cell block. As it had in *Estelle*, the Court found that "inadvertence or error in good faith" is not sufficient to prove an Eighth Amendment violation, but "[i]t is obduracy and wantonness . . . that characterize the conduct prohibited by the Cruel and Unusual Punishments Clause" (*Whitley v. Albers* (1986)).[39]

- In *Wilson v. Seiter* (1991),[40] the Court considered a claim by an Ohio prisoner that a number of conditions of his confinement, such as overcrowding, excessive noise, inadequate heating and cooling, and so on, constituted cruel and unusual punishment. The Court issued several important limitations and requirements when considering prisoner Eighth Amendment claims. First, "overall conditions" do not rise to the level of cruel and unusual punishment "when no specific deprivation of a human need exists." This portion of the decision has come to be interpreted that each challenged condition must be examined by the court individually, and unless conditions are "mutually enforcing," such as low temperatures at night combined with a failure to issue blankets, will not be consolidated into an "overall conditions" case resulting in sweeping judicial remedies. *Wilson* is also important in that in addition to determining whether a particular condition violates the Eighth Amendment, it requires a subjective inquiry into the defendant prison official's state of mind. The Court emphasized what it had stated in *Whitley*, that "only the unnecessary and wonton infliction of pain . . . constitutes cruel and unusual punishment forbidden by the Eighth Amendment." To make such a finding, the court must look at the subjective intent of the official as to whether he or she intended to cause "wanton" punishment.

- Thus far, we may conclude that given the Supreme Court standards as to what constitutes cruel and unusual punishment, the bar is quite high before a court will find a violation of the Eighth Amendment. However, in 2011, the Supreme Court showed that it will not turn a blind eye to prison Eighth Amendment claims. In *Brown v. Plata* (2011),[41] the Court issued a startling decision in ordering the State of California to cap its prison population at 137% of design capacity—resulting in the potential release of up to 46,000 prisoners—because of inadequate medical and mental health care caused by overcrowding. The Court found that this and a consolidated case had been ongoing for more than 15 years. The lower courts had found "overwhelming" evidence of serious constitutional violations regarding the state's delivery of medical and mental health care. The Court found that in spite of these findings and the remedies fashioned by the lower courts, the state still had not corrected the violations. Over the strenuous objections of the dissent, the Court concurred with the three-judge panel—which had been appointed pursuant to PLRA requirements—that the only possible remedy was to order California to either increase its prison capacity or to reduce its population to an acceptable level. The Court found that even though various stringent provisions of the PLRA limit such a drastic remedy, here there was no acceptable alternative. Thus, *Brown* demonstrates that even with the limitations posed by Supreme Court precedent and the provisions of PLRA, the Court will still recognize and protect the basic constitutional rights of prisoners.

■ Conclusion

It is incumbent on those responsible for writing and implementing the rules that regulate the institutions under their control to be mindful of various limitations that may affect their decisions. Along with budgetary, legislative, political, and operational issues, important legal and constitutional issues must be considered. Every corrections agency or entity has subject matter experts to assist decision makers. As far as legal issues are concerned, administrators have the assistance of agency legal counsel or attorneys who can provide guidance as to constitutional aspects of proposed rules and regulations. It is imperative that this advice is followed if the agency is to avoid legal problems down the road.

Although it is unrealistic to expect employees of corrections facilities to be specifically knowledgeable about a wide-ranging area of the law that has been in a state of flux for many decades, it is important that every corrections worker realize that prisoners do retain some protections under the Constitution. It is the responsibility of those who write and promulgate agency rules, regulations, and policies to conform them to constitutional standards. It is the responsibility of corrections employees to be aware of those provisions that apply to their particular jobs, and to follow those rules precisely. In doing so, these employees may safely rely on these provisions as meeting constitutional requirements.

Chapter Resources

DISCUSSION QUESTIONS

1. What are the protected interests found in the Fifth Amendment? What initial inquiries should be made when considering whether a prisoner has due process protections in a particular matter?
2. Why did the Supreme Court decide to revise its standard when examining due process claims by prisoners?
3. Give some examples of where the Supreme Court altered its view of constitutional rights in the prison setting.
4. What are some of the provisions in RFRA that limit prisoner lawsuits?
5. What is the subjective intent standard required when a court is determining whether an Eighth Amendment violation has occurred?

ADDITIONAL RESOURCES

Collins, W. C., & Collins, A. W. (1996). *Women in jail: Legal issues.* Washington, DC: National Institute of Corrections. Available online and accessed June 2, 2013, at http://www.wcl.american.edu/endsilence/documents/Women_in_Jail_Legal_Issues.pdf

Cripe, C. A., Pearlman, M. G., & Kosiak, D. (2013). *Legal aspects of corrections management.* Sudbury, MA: Jones & Bartlett Learning.

Ross, D. (2013). *Legal issues and concepts.* An online forum sponsored by Corrections One. Accessed June 2, 2013, at http://www.correctionsone.com/writers/columnists/Darrell-Ross/

Smith, C. E. (2000). *Law and contemporary corrections.* Belmont, CA: West/Wadsworth Publishing Company.

NOTES

1. There have been literally thousands of prisoner cases decided by federal district and appellate courts since the 1960s. However, as we have discussed, the Supreme Court is the ultimate arbiter of the Constitution, and its rulings control constitutional rights and limitations in federal, state, and local corrections systems.
2. *Jones v. North Carolina Prisoners' Labor Union, Inc.*, 433 U.S. 119, 139 (1977) (Marshall, J., dissenting) (quoting *Ruffin v. Commonwealth*, 62 Va. 790, 796 (1871)). There may have been some support for the "slave of the state" concept in the Thirteenth Amendment, which was passed after the Civil War, prohibiting slavery "except as punishment for crime whereof the party shall have been duly convicted. . . ." U.S. Constitution, Amendment 14.
3. *In re Bonner*, 151 U.S. 242 (1894).
4. U.S. Constitution, Article I, §9.
5. *Ex Parte Hull*, 312 U.S. 546 (1941).
6. Unfortunately for *Hull*, while acknowledging that he had the right to apply for the writ of habeas corpus, the Court denied the petition on its merits.
7. *Smith v. Bennett*, 365 U.S. 708 (1961).
8. *Johnson v. Avery*, 393 U.S. 483 (1969).

9. However, as early as 1964, the Court granted a review (or writ of certiorari) as to a §1983 suit brought by an Illinois inmate alleging that he was denied the right to purchase certain religious publications and denied other religious privileges. The Court reversed the Court of Appeals and found that the complaint did state a cause of action. *Cooper v. Pate*, 378 U.S. 546 (1964).

10. *Wolff v. McDonnell*, 418 U.S. 539 (1974).

11. *Bounds v. Smith*, 430 U.S. 539 (1977).

12. *Casey v. Lewis*, 518 U.S. 343 (1996).

13. Title 42, U.S. Code, §1997(e).

14. *Procunier v. Martinez*, 416 U.S. 396 (1974).

15. Id. at 416 U.S. 404–405.

16. Id. at 416 U.S. 413–414.

17. *Martinez* used a "strict scrutiny" test when it considered censorship of outgoing inmate mail, but the Court in *Turner* limited *Martinez's* applicability to matters that involved First Amendment rights of the nonprisoner mail recipients.

18. *Pell v. Procunier*, 417 U.S. 817 (1974).

19. *Jones v. North Carolina Prisoners' Union*, 433 U.S. 119 (1977).

20. *Bell v. Wolfish*, 441 U.S. 520 (1979).

21. *Overton v. Bassetta*, 539 U.S. 126 (2003).

22. *Turner v. Safely*, 482 U.S. 78 (1987), citing *Martinez* at 416 U.S. 406.

23. *Cruz v. Beto*, 405 U.S. 319 (1972).

24. *O'Lone v. Shabazz*, 482 U.S. 342 (1987).

25. *Employment Division v. Smith*, 494 U.S. 872 (1990).

26. Title 42, U.S. Code, §2000bb.

27. *City of Boerne v. Flores*, 521 U.S. 507 (1997).

28. Title 42, U.S. Code, §2000cc.

29. *Cutter v. Wilkinson*, 544 U.S. 709 (2005).

30. *Bell v. Wolfish*, 441 U.S. 520 (1979).

31. *Block v. Rutherford*, 468 U.S. 576 (1984).

32. *Hudson v. Palmer*, 468 U.S. 517 (1984).

33. *Florence v. Board of Chosen Freeholders*, 566 U.S. (2012).

34. *Lee v. Washington*, 390 U.S. 333 (1968).

35. *Wolff v. McDonnell*, 418 U.S. 539 (1974).

36. *Sandin v. Conner*, 515 U.S. 472 (1995).

37. *Estelle v. Gamble*, 429 U.S. 97 (1976).

38. *Rhodes v. Chapman*, 452 U.S. 337 (1981).

39. *Whitley v. Albers*, 475 U.S. 312 (1986).

40. *Wilson v. Seiter*, 501 U.S. 294 (1991).

41. *Brown v. Plata*, 563 U.S. (2011).

External Constituencies

YOU ARE THE ADMINISTRATOR
▪ How Much Media Access Is Good?

Lieutenant Kidd was feeling the stress of the busy institution. The county jail had experienced a serious inmate-on-inmate assault at 3 P.M. in the long-term jail wing, and now the local media was pressing for more information on the incident. The lieutenant had followed jail policy and refused to release the specifics of the incident until it had been appropriately investigated, but the media had heard from some unknown source—probably an inmate phoning his family—that the victim was a high-profile offender recently sentenced in local court for embezzlement to an 8-year prison term. The local newspaper was demanding confirmation of the identity and condition of the injured prisoner and where he was being treated. The local television station requested to interview the victim; another reporter went so far as to threaten Lt. Kidd with a law suit. The veteran lieutenant responded to the reporter that he was sorry he could not be of more help.

Press organizations nationwide have been protesting what some indicate has been an attempt to hide from public scrutiny of jail and prison operations. Citing their concerns for institutional safety and increasing numbers of requests for interviews with well-known inmates, institution officials in some states have been taking firmer stances in dealing with representatives of the media. Florida and Michigan have proposed policy modifications that would reduce media access to inmates in state prisons. In Texas, officials are considering restricting access to prisoners to what the its Department of Corrections defines as legitimate news media representatives.

Historically, the U.S. Supreme Court has limited journalists' access to America's prisons and jails. In the 1974 cases *Saxbe v. Washington Post* and *Pell v. Procunier*, the Court ruled that media representatives should have no more access to correctional facilities than the general public. The Court specified that institutions could curtail interviews with prisoners based on inmate privacy and institutional security needs. In other words, the Court gave great latitude to correctional administrators. Despite these Supreme Court rulings, many prison and jail administrators have been very open with the media and have allowed journalism representatives to meet with and interview inmates under prearranged rules and conditions. But the trend in recent years has been to tighten institution policies and further restrict media contact. This trend is not being well received by journalists who claim the correctional authorities are trampling on the First Amendment.

- Do you think the media should have the right to unimpeded access to a detention, jail, or prison operation? What should a reasonable policy specify?
- Place yourself in the shift supervisor's role. Should Lt. Kidd be legitimately concerned about a future lawsuit? Why?
- What is the "watchdog" value to our communities of allowing the media greater freedom of access?
- Would inmates take advantage of less restriction on the press? How?

Working with the Media

Judith Simon Garrett

CHAPTER OBJECTIVES

- Explain the positive and negative aspects of media access to prisons from the perspectives of the public and of prison administrators.

- Identify the key elements of an effective media strategy.

- Outline aspects of good media training.

The public is fascinated with crime and criminals, and such fascination does not stop when an offender is hauled off to jail or prison. The interest simply shifts from the crime itself and the workings of the criminal justice system to the prison system and life behind bars. Accordingly, reporters frequently produce stories about inmates and the prisons in which they are housed. Unfortunately for prison and jail administrators, the stories usually center on the plight of the inmates. Some stories focus on the harsh conditions that offenders face, the violence reputed to pervade prison life, or misconduct by staff (ranging from physical abuse of inmates to mismanagement of government funds).

Most stories portray prisons negatively and rarely provide an accurate description of what goes on behind institutional walls and fences. Media stories often fail to mention the many positive things that transpire in institutions and instead distort the motives and actions of staff. Prison and jail administrators should work with media representatives to provide the public a more accurate, positive picture of what goes on inside correctional institutions.

Most prison administrators will have to respond to a news media request to interview an inmate or do a story about some aspect of his or her institution's operations. Such a request may involve making an inmate available in the visiting room for 30 minutes, allowing a reporter to shadow a staff member for a week, or anything in between. Therefore, a written policy regarding the handling of media requests is very helpful. Media policies should strike a balance between the burden on prison staff associated with accommodating a media request (including any potential risks to the safety of inmates, staff, and the community) and the need for the media to inform the public about prison operations (including prisoners' rights to express themselves through the media). The media does not have the right to enter a correctional institution to complete a story, and inmates do not have the right to unlimited or unrestricted access to media representatives. But appropriate media coverage can help keep the public informed about prison operations and the expenditure of tax dollars.

■ Media Access: Legal Considerations

How much access should the media have to prison and jail operations? Some correctional agencies permit representatives of print and electronic media into their facilities upon request. Other agencies believe such contact with inmates can be disruptive and a threat to the orderly running of the institution. In 1974, in *Pell v. Procunier*, the Supreme Court upheld the California Department of Corrections' prohibition on face-to-face interviews between individual inmates and representatives of the news media.[1] The Court concluded that this restriction was permissible because inmates had other avenues of communicating: They could correspond with the media and receive visits from family and friends. Thus, prisoners had adequate means of expressing their concerns about their conditions of confinement. Furthermore, journalists were permitted tours of the prisons and could ask inmates questions while visiting.

At the same time the Court decided *Procunier*, it decided another media access case involving the Federal Bureau of Prisons (BOP). In *Saxbe v. Washington Post*, the Court ruled that the First Amendment does not provide the press a constitutional right of access to information that is not generally available to the public.[2] The Court upheld the BOP's rationale that giving individual inmates access to the media would create undue attention for specific inmates who may already be notorious (the "big wheel" theory), potentially causing tension among inmates or between inmates and prison personnel. Even though the BOP won this legal battle, the agency does permit media representatives to interview individual inmates under clearly identified policy parameters and on terms set by the agency.

On occasion, state legislatures have stepped in to try to require departments of corrections to alter their policies to ensure that the media are granted appropriate access to prison facilities. In one state, the legislature passed a bill that reversed an agency policy that prohibited members of news agencies from securing interviews with particular inmates.

◼ Interview Considerations

Many correctional jurisdictions believe it is important to permit representatives of the media into institutions to interview specific prisoners. In these situations, there are significant questions that should be asked and evaluated before granting approval.

Who Is Making the Request?

- Does this person have press credentials, such as an affiliation with a newspaper, television station, radio station, magazine, or book publisher?
- Does this person have a relationship with the inmate, a victim of the inmate's crime(s), or a member of the staff?
- Does this person have a known agenda that is likely to substantially bias the reporting?

What Is the Purpose of the Intended Story?

- Is the inmate who is the focus of the story particularly well known (or notorious)? Did his or her case generate substantial media interest before and during the trial phase?
- Is the author hoping to garner sympathy or support for a particular inmate's case?
- Is the author hoping to encourage a public outcry against the treatment of one or many prisoners held at the facility?
- Are prison operations being targeted as being corrupt or excessively harsh?

What Will Be the Demands on Staff?

- How many people will be interviewed and for how long?
- How many people will be entering the prison in order to complete the story?
- For how long will the media representative be in the institution?

What Will Be the Effect on Prison Operations, Including Security?

- To what extent will the media representative disrupt daily operations? Will the visit prevent scheduled activities from taking place?
- How are the inmates likely to react to the presence of the media representative and to the completed story?
- How are people (including other members of the media) likely to react to the completed story? Are they likely to demand changes to prison operations or make additional media requests?
- To what extent will any pictures that are taken provide members of the public or inmates with information that could be used to fashion an escape or plan other disruptive activities?

There are no right or wrong answers to these questions, nor should the answer to any one question necessarily mandate a particular conclusion, but consideration of these questions will help make the administrator aware of the many possible ramifications of granting or denying media requests.

Administrative Concerns

The administrator's foremost responsibility is to maintain the safe and orderly operation of the prison facility. At times, fulfilling this responsibility will conflict with granting a media request, in which case the media representative must accept, if not understand, the reason that the request has been denied. For example, permitting extensive filming of staff training, prison perimeter fencing, and control room operations could create security concerns. Allowing substantial or sustained media coverage of a particular inmate has the potential to create difficulties for that inmate (who may become the target of jealousy and anger from other inmates) and for prison administrators (if the inmate decides he or she has special status and wants special treatment).

In cases where the media request can be accommodated with minimal disruption and little chance of a threat to the safe and secure operation of the prison, it may make sense to grant the request. It should always be assumed that denying a media request will give rise to accusations that the institution is attempting to hide something or that the prison administration is silencing an inmate in order to protect itself, an elected official, or some other government representative.

Media Access Policies

In general, the more restrictive the access policy is, the more a correctional agency stands at risk of angering the public, representatives of the media, and elected representatives. Severe restrictions on access prevent correctional staff from gaining the public's confidence and support. In the face of the public pressure to rehabilitate criminals and use tax funds wisely, it is important that prison and jail administrators be held accountable for their stewardship of public funds. The best means of disseminating information is welcoming outsiders into the closed environment of the prison or jail. Finally, administrators should be cautious not to routinely grant media requests made by one source and deny requests from another. Doing this would create a perception of favoritism that could result in various problems.

The accreditation process of the American Correctional Association requires a prison or jail to have a written policy that provides for reasonable access between inmates and media representatives, subject only to limitations necessary to maintain good order and security, and to protect an inmate's privacy.[3]

An institution's written policy regarding access by the media should include various key provisions, including the following:

- All media requests should be in written form and should include an acknowledgment by the requestor stating that he or she is familiar with institution's rules and regulations and agrees to comply with such rules.
- The representative must make reasonable attempts to verify all allegations leveled against inmates, staff, or the institution and provide the institution with an opportunity to respond to allegations before publishing the story.
- The media representative must make an appointment to visit the institution.
- Inmates may not receive compensation for interviews with the media.
- The request for an interview with news media representatives may originate with the representatives or with an inmate; an inmate's request or consent to be interviewed must be in writing.
- The administrator should approve or disapprove media requests in a timely fashion, and all denials shall be provided in writing. Reasons for denial may be based on various factors, including the inmate's medical or mental condition, a threat to the health or safety of the interviewer, a threat to the safety and good order of the institution, a threat to the safety of the inmate, or a court order forbidding news interviews.

■ Media Representatives

When the prison or jail accommodates a media request, it is the responsibility of the institution's liaison or spokesperson to work with the author or producer to learn as much as possible about what the story will say and to try to minimize distortions of prison operations. The public information officer (PIO) is responsible for managing media requests and all communications with the media. This person should be screened appropriately and given extensive training in how to work effectively with the media. The training can be provided in-house by staff with experience in media relations, or the PIO can attend one of the many commercially available classes. This training will help the PIO develop strategies and techniques for communicating effectively with the media.

An effective PIO will shape a response to the media request by providing effective "sound bites" to ensure the most positive portrayal of the institution and its staff. Additionally, an effective PIO makes clear the parameters governing the media's access to inmates, staff, and the institution at the outset. Finally, an effective PIO will ensure that media representatives respect the right to privacy that all inmates and staff enjoy and acknowledge the institution's responsibility to protect this right.

There are occasions when newsworthy events occur at an institution and the administrator or PIO should contact the news media. Examples of such events include escapes, disturbances, and deaths of inmates. When such events occur, administrators should provide information to the media that is considered public, such as an inmate's name, register number, and sentencing data. Similarly, information about staff that is generally considered public includes position title, job assignment, years of service, and previous duty stations. Any incident that has the potential to give rise to criminal prosecutions should be discussed only in the most general terms and, to the extent possible, with the advice of legal counsel. As a general rule, it is wise to provide few details at the outset, at least until all relevant facts have been established to a substantial degree of certainty.

■ Community Coverage

Sometimes media representatives will request access to write or produce a story about a positive aspect of prison operations. On a rare occasion, the media will become interested in a particular program or aspect of prison operations, such as a program to permit women inmates to care for their young children inside prison. It is more likely to be the case that the prison or jail administrator will have to actively solicit media support for worthy programs. The chief executive officer or administrator might occasionally invite representatives of the news media to visit the institution and observe particular programs or operations. It would be inappropriate to extend such invitations on a regular basis because it might give the impression that administrators were more concerned with attracting media attention than with operating the facility.

Another means of obtaining positive media coverage is through members of the community. Garnering support in the community for prison programs and operations is generally an effective strategy to gain positive media coverage. Many prison administrators create a community relations board (CRB) comprising senior prison staff and members of the community, including representatives from local businesses, elected officials, and others. Through this board, potential conflicts between the prison and the community, such as expansion of the prison or a change in the security level, can be often avoided by facilitating factual discussions rather than emotionally charged debates. Such debates are often played out in the media, and thus it is important to expend considerable resources to avoid conflict at the outset. Additionally, CRBs often give rise to partnerships between the community and the prison that effectively serve the interests of all participants. For example, prison inmates can assist the community by building homes for underprivileged families or building toys for needy children from scrap materials. The community benefits through free labor, the inmates benefit from the satisfaction gained from helping others, and the prison staff benefit because inmate idleness tends to breed unrest.

■ Conclusion

Granting media representatives access to correctional institutions, staff, and inmates is a sensitive matter that must be considered carefully and managed by experienced personnel. The focus of media coverage undoubtedly will vary; there will be opportunities for positive exposure for the institution and the community, and thus it is essential to maintain positive relationships with representatives of the media.

Clearly, the media play a significant role in shaping public opinion. Correctional administrators must think of communication specialists as information messengers. Through media representatives, administrators can convey a sense of the challenges and complexities of working in and managing correctional institutions.

Chapter Resources

DISCUSSION QUESTIONS

1. How much access should the media have to prisons and prisoners?
2. What are some key strategies to ensure accurate media coverage from the perspective of prison administrators?
3. What role does the media play in shaping public perception about prison life?
4. What aspects of media relations pose challenges to prison and jail administrators?
5. What are the crucial elements of an effective media strategy?

ADDITIONAL RESOURCES

Hickman, R. Q. (2007). Politics, power, the press and prisons. *Corrections Today, 69*(1), 46-48.

Levenson, J. (2001). Inside information: Prisons and the media. *Criminal Justice Matters, 43*(1), 14-15.

Mason, P. (2006). *Captured by the media: Prison discourse in popular culture*. Cullompton, UK: Willan Publishing.

Muraskin, R., & Domash, S. F. (2006). *Crime and the media*. Upper Saddle River, NJ: Prentice Hall.

Yousman, W. (2004). *The prisons outside and the prisons in our heads: Televison and the representation of incarceration*. Electronic Doctoral Dissertations for UMass Amhurst AAI3136799. http://scholarworks .umass.edu/dissertations/AAI3136799

NOTES

1. *Pell v. Procunier*, 417 U.S. 817 (1974).
2. *Saxbe v. Washington Post*, 417 U.S. 843 (1974); Cripe, C., & Pearlman, M. (2005). *Legal aspects of corrections management*. Sudbury, MA: Jones & Bartlett Publishers.
3. American Correctional Association. (1989). *Foundation/core standards for adult correctional institutions*. Washington, DC: St. Mary's Press.

Community Relations Boards

Paul McAlister

CHAPTER OBJECTIVES

- Describe the primary purpose of a community relations board (CRB).
- Outline the goals of successful CRBs.
- Explain the logistics involved with setting up and running CRBs.

S ociety has become dependent on correctional institutions. The incredible growth of the number of prisons has made their presence undeniable, yet few people want a correctional facility nearby. A community relations board (CRB) can help a community and a correctional institution live together as neighbors and partners in the effort to deal with the reality of criminal behavior. Institutional personnel can become aware of community concerns. The community can learn that institution staff are members of the community too and share community concerns. Through ongoing dialogue, communities can learn ways to help strengthen the effectiveness of neighboring institutions, not just endure their presence.

■ Composition of CRBs

There is no prescribed number of CRB members; the number should be determined by each facility. Nominations may be sought from appropriate agencies or individuals. Those individuals may be approved by the board, but final selection should be made by the warden. Each local facility will need to tailor a CRB to fit its specific situation and circumstances; CRB models are highly adaptive. However, there are several groups of community members who should be represented on a CRB, including:

- People most directly affected by the physical presence of the facility (i.e., immediate neighbors and realtors)
- Local officials with whom the institution will want to build relationships (e.g., police, city council, and county commissioners)
- Outreach members who provide a link to the rest of the community (e.g., educational representatives, clergy, civic groups, charitable organizations, multiethnic organizations, and others)

■ Objectives of CRBs

There are many objectives commonly associated with an institution's CRB, including improved communication, easing reentry, and community involvement.

Improved Communication

First and foremost, a prison or jail administrator should use the CRB to improve communication with the local community. This requires CRB members to become educated in all aspects of institution operations so that they can serve as effective information conduits to other citizens. In turn, CRB members can provide honest and worthwhile feedback to senior correctional managers from the community.

Since the early 1980s when CRBs began to develop, their central goal has been to enable the exchange of accurate information between the institution and the community. Honesty is critical to effective institution–community communication. CRB members need to be given accurate information about facility functions and policies and encouraged to ask honest questions. If the institution does not provide honest information, the effectiveness of the CRB will be undermined. Board members must be encouraged to express the concerns of the community openly to the institution.

Through effective and open communication, the CRB can also help to build goodwill and trust between the institution and the community. It can help remind community representatives that staff members live in the same neighborhoods that they do, and like them, they want these neighborhoods to be pleasant and safe places to work and live. CRBs can enhance the facility's existing programs by promoting and supporting community volunteer efforts. The board can also suggest ways that the institution can contribute to the community.

Although most communities recognize the need for prisons and jails, they typically do not want one nearby. CRBs can help diminish a community's fears by sharing their insight and experience with communities where institutions may be built.

On occasion, incidents occur at correctional facilities that are of heightened interest and concern to the community. Board members should be knowledgeable about institution incidents that would be of public concern. The CRB members can be contacted with accurate information regarding events and can then provide a measure of reassurance and calm to the community. If incidents occur that will be covered by the news media, the CRB should be informed promptly. If it takes days or weeks for an incident to be resolved, reassurance may be an ongoing need.

Ease of Reentry

Currently, some legislative bodies, and many communities, are debating the issue of the reentry of inmates. With the ever-growing prison population comes the recognition that most of those currently incarcerated will be released. Faced with this reality, citizens demand good information and reassurance. The issue of reentry is vital to end the cycle of recidivism (often referred to as the revolving door of corrections). Accountability and support for inmates returning to public life is a vital task. CRBs can serve as important bridges to the community to provide for effective reentry. Community input is indispensable to the development of meaningful reentry programs. If the institution elicits community support for reentry, it should anticipate that the community may ask for additional information, and the institution must respond honestly and appropriately to these requests. Discussion motivated by budgetary consideration concerning possible early release dates should heighten the importance of reentry programs.

Community Involvement in Intuitional Programming

CRBs also may help enhance community involvement and volunteer participation in institution programs. Inmates will realize that there are people other than correctional staff who honestly care about them. CRBs may also provide options for the inmates to be involved, as appropriate, in community service. CRBs also help the community recognize staff as community members and contributors.

Institutions should provide CRB members with information about trends, programs of the institution, and the difference between facility policy and government-mandated programs or policies. This education can be provided at regularly scheduled CRB meetings or on specific training days. Because policies change regularly, education must be ongoing.

Each board meeting can include a different aspect of the program and introduce staff members involved with that program area. Possible agenda items include emergency preparedness planning, medical and drug programs, reaction to national trends, changes in the institution's mission, and construction or expansion plans. Placing the institution's issues in the context of national trends, legal concerns, and expansion pressures helps enhance CRB members' understanding of their local facility's program needs and mandates.

Educating the community also includes working with educational institutions, civic groups, religious groups, and media representatives. With appropriate concern for safety and inmate privacy, tours also may be an effective aspect of community education. Each institution should provide staff with an internal list of areas that tours would cover so that tours are consistent and key community concerns are always addressed.

The CRB can look for opportunities to suggest that community members become involved with the institution through volunteer programs. Positive changes in inmate behavior are often inspired by dedicated volunteer efforts. The community has a vested interest in inmates' rehabilitation.

The CRB also may help develop programs in which inmates provide the community with needed services. This may be some inmates' first positive experience of giving to someone else. Such opportunities can boost an inmate's self-image and awaken a desire to contribute more to society. Worthwhile projects might involve helping warn at-risk young people about the costs of criminal behavior, providing assistance during emergencies, and supporting charitable activities, such as home repair projects for low-income community members.

It must be said that the CRB is not a policy-making entity but a vehicle for the exchange of information between the institution and the community. The CRB may be called on to make recommendations to prison or jail administrators. If the administration has good information to work with concerning community perceptions and concerns, decision makers can anticipate community reactions and help community members accept institutional decisions.

It is important for prison staff to be respected by the community and for community members to feel gratitude toward them. Activities that increase public contact with staff should be encouraged. When staff are seen as having a vested interest in maintaining a pleasant and safe community for themselves and their families, it builds trust between the community and the institution.

■ Logistics

CRB members should help decide on meeting times. It is not always easy to find a meeting time that works for everyone. Institution staff should inform prospective members of scheduled times before they are asked to participate. Noon meetings often are preferred, but certain members of the community may have difficulty attending during the day because of employment obligations. Early evening or early morning meetings may also work well. Meetings may be monthly, bimonthly, or quarterly. Special meetings can be called if there is a crisis or some decision about which the CRB may be asked to make recommendations. Because a truly representative CRB is the goal, every effort should be made to make full participation as likely as possible.

CRB members may be involved in events outside regular meetings. To enhance the CRB's understanding of the institution and its staff, CRB members may be encouraged to attend certain social events. During these events, CRB members can learn from staff about what institution programs need enhancement. Board members also may be invited to certain staff meetings such as a staff recall. At such meetings, CRB members will learn more about institutional goals and needs and report what they learned to the community. Although confidentiality is necessary in some aspects of institutional operations, CRB members should not feel that the institution is hiding things that the community should know.

Board members' terms will be established by each institution in conjunction with actual community members. There is an advantage to allowing some members to serve for a specified period of time: People can participate and yet not commit themselves too far into the future. A 2- or 3-year term may be appropriate. It is difficult to provide the education necessary to contribute to the function of the CRB if the term is any shorter. In some cases, members may be willing to commit to an extended period of service. They can provide expertise that is beneficial to all. By allowing automatic reappointments after a term ends, a board can reduce the need for renominating and/or approving existing members who wish to continue serving. The downside of the extended term is that others who wish to serve are not able to fill a vacated position.

The CRB chair facilitates meetings through handling introductions and working through the meeting agenda. He or she can also contribute to the development of meeting agendas by making suggestions. Each agenda should be sensitive to developing issues and address ongoing information and education issues. The chair should be nominated by the board members, who also will decide the chair's term. A term of 1 year with the possibility of reappointment is common.

Each facility and CRB may draft its own bylaws. The bylaws normally will be structured by the warden or superintendent with input from members and should spell out details concerning membership, terms of service, and functions. Bylaws may also cover issues of security and confidentiality.

There needs to be a public awareness of the CRB and its members. If the community members do not know who the CRB members are, they cannot learn about the institution or give their opinions about the institution to CRB members. An article in the local paper can help community members learn about the CRB, its role, and its members.

■ Conclusion

Community relations have become a very important aspect of institutional planning. A CRB can contribute greatly to an institution and its surrounding community.

Boards are only as effective as their ability to establish open and honest lines of communication. Perfunctory CRBs are doomed to failure. Institutions need to provide honest answers to questions generated by CRB members or communicated by the CRB on behalf of the community. The capacity of the CRB to react to incidents or to prevent confusion in the community can be a great service to all. Wardens can use CRB members as sounding boards. CRBs must carry information and understanding from the facility to the community and from the community to the facility. Both directions of this information channel must remain open for CRBs to be effective. The growing number of people incarcerated and the ongoing need for new institutions mean that the issue of community relations will remain very important for many years to come.

Serving on a CRB is a privilege. CRB members often feel a sense of meaningful investment in developing a partnership between the community and the facility and in helping to ensure a safe and effective approach to criminal justice. Members of a CRB have a significant opportunity to contribute to this vital partnership and make a difference in a local community.

Chapter Resources

DISCUSSION QUESTIONS

1. How can citizens provide useful insights to institutional administration?
2. What difficulties are there in the use of CRBs?
3. What opportunities do CRBs offer?
4. How can a CRB assist with media coverage?
5. Who should serve on a CRB?

ADDITIONAL RESOURCES

American Correctional Association. (1993). *Helping hands: A handbook for volunteers.* Laurel, MD: ACA Press.

Jones, J. (1991). Community relations boards. *Federal Prisons Journal, 2*(2), 19–22.

Political Involvement

Judith Simon Garrett

CHAPTER OBJECTIVES

- Distinguish between a spoils system and career service.
- Outline the importance of correctional administrators working with legislators.
- Identify the types of issues posed by implementing legislation in the correctional environment.

n the 1990s, while the Uniform Crime Reports data indicated that crime rates were declining, the fear of crime remained a primary concern for most Americans.[1] Legislators, eager to be responsive to their constituents, remained steadfast in their "tough on crime" and "war on drugs" approaches that began in the 1980s. While this trend has slowed in the last two years, today, there are more than 1.6 million adults in prisons in the United States.[2] State and local governments spent nearly $60 billion on corrections in 2001, an increase of 529% since 1982. During the same period, spending for police and the judiciary increased only 281%.[3]

Following the terrorist attacks of September 11, 2001, the country's priorities concerning justice administration shifted dramatically, focusing almost exclusively on preventing acts of terrorism on American soil and eradicating the forces that allowed them to occur in the first place. Accordingly, the federal budget available for issues other than homeland security and war-related functions became very limited. The public's tolerance for continuing to spend billions of dollars on imprisonment seems to be waning for the first time in many years.

Although crime and criminal justice remain largely state and local issues, the legislative and executive branches of the federal government attempt to influence state and local laws and policies through grants and other means. Congress and the president more directly influence federal law through statutes, regulation, and executive orders. Elected representatives and also those seeking election do not hesitate to use public forums and the media to express their increasingly conservative views about crime and criminal justice administration.

■ Political Interest in Prison Operations

As a result of their desire to influence criminal justice policy and demonstrate their commitment to being tough on crime, federal and state legislators attempt to substantially affect correctional operations. The combination of enacting longer sentences and placing new restrictions on early release mechanisms (such as limiting or abolishing parole and good time) has been directly responsible for the tremendous increase in prison and jail populations across the country since the 1980s. At around that same time, legislators forced correctional officials to reduce or eliminate many programs and recreation opportunities in an attempt to create "no frills" correctional institutions with the belief that a harsher environment will increase the deterrent effect of prisons. For example, the Federal Bureau of Prisons (BOP) is prohibited from repairing, replacing, or purchasing new weightlifting equipment and musical instruments. Other legislation is introduced regularly that requires inmates to work 50 hours per week or be confined to their cells (for 23 hours per day) if they are not medically able to work.

It is unfortunate that most lawmakers have little or no direct knowledge of prison operations. Many would benefit substantially from an educational tour of a correctional institution. Most corrections managers would disagree with legislators' views that prison programs (including recreation opportunities) and modest amenities such as television rooms are frills that make prisons less of a deterrent. According to most correctional managers, these programs and amenities can be instrumental in ensuring an inmate's successful reintegration into the community following release from prison.

Institution recreational opportunities allow inmates the opportunity to release some of the anxiety and stress that are inherent in prison life and help create an environment with less tension for the staff and inmates. Research has found that prison programs help offenders reintegrate successfully into the community through lower rates of recidivism and higher rates of employment. This supports correctional professionals' belief that institutional programs (e.g., education, vocational training, prison industries, substance abuse treatment) are essential to effective correctional settings. Nearly all prison administrators agree that making prisoners' lives needlessly uncomfortable and unpleasant does little more than make the jobs of staff, particularly correctional officers, more difficult.

Some correctional managers are proponents of the spartan prison existence and help foster the misconception described above; they invite legislators to mandate that all prisons be operated in a no-frills, severe manner. Sheriff Joe Arpaio from Maricopa County, Arizona, was a classic example of this philosophy. He required some inmates to sleep in tents and required sex offenders to wear pink underwear.[4] In contrast, most correctional administrators believe that prisons should be decent places in which to live and should offer reasonable program and recreation opportunities that provide self-improvement activities, offer a safe and healthy environment, and properly control inmate behavior. Institution operations should not seek to embarrass prisoners or create unnecessary resentment.

■ Implementation of Laws

The degree to which politics influence the administration of government agencies has evolved with time. Woodrow Wilson, former U.S. president, is largely responsible for abolishing the spoils system in the federal government. His 1887 essay, "The Study of Administration," presented the philosophy of the Progressive Movement, created by reformers unhappy with the spoils system.[5] Under the spoils system, employees of government agencies were fired each time a new political party was elected. Political patrons of the party in office were brought in, and the entire direction of the government entity was subject to major change. Federal patronage had a particularly large influence on government operations. The Progressive Movement lobbied to establish a professional civil service that would be neutral on political issues. Over time, the system of political spoils was abolished at the federal level, except for a limited number of high-level positions such as cabinet heads and select senior members of their staff.

For government administrators to run their institutions effectively, they must avoid the strife of politics. As Wilson stated many years ago, the administration of an agency is a function of business and must be removed from the arena of political rhetoric. Professional administrators in all areas of government must focus on the impartial governance of their agencies. Public administration is the systematic and detailed execution of public law; legislators establish policy, and administrators implement their decisions.

In the federal prison system, leaders at all levels have always been career civil servants—individuals who worked their way up the organization. However, in many states, the directors of the departments of corrections are political appointees who serve at the pleasure of the governor. Turnover in these states is generally quite high, posing challenges for the professional correctional administrator. In many states, it has been common for prison wardens to also be political appointees—an individual who had assisted the governor with the election was rewarded with the warden's job in return. These wardens rarely had any relevant experience prior to arriving at the prison. Their ability to effectively manage a prison and lead a staff varied greatly. In many instances, they merely served as figureheads, and the associate warden or other career staff directed prison operations.

Regardless of whether the wardens are political appointees or career civil servants, it is essential that corrections administrators implement laws in a timely and effective manner, with the least possible disruption to institution operations. The personal views of the administrators regarding the wisdom of the laws are irrelevant.

Institution administrators should not become involved in the political process. Institution chief executive officers should be seen as impartial, professional administrators who have a responsibility to implement legislation and executive orders fairly.

As experts in corrections, professional administrators sometimes are called upon to share their expertise and facilitate the consideration of proposed changes in the law. Although senior institution staff should always welcome the opportunity to educate lawmakers, they must be cautious not to give the appearance that they are trying to influence the legislative process. One approach to educating legislators is to provide educational tours to members of Congress and their staff. The BOP demonstrates the realities of institutional management by opening its prison doors to elected officials and the public. Many legislators and, more frequently, their staff take advantage of such opportunities and find the experience interesting and enlightening.

■ Political and Societal Changes Affect Penal Facilities

Political winds shift with the times, sometimes quite rapidly, causing dramatic shifts in prison operations. During the 1970s, prison wardens would proudly show their college campus prisons and well-funded vocational training programs. Today, the public expects prison and jail environments to be more severe and punishing, with special attention paid to preventing radicalization of inmates and the recruitment of terrorists.

It is difficult and dangerous to withdraw privileges or programs from prisoners once these privileges and programs have been given to them; such withdrawals must be planned and implemented carefully. Therefore, when implementing laws that impose new restrictions on prisoners, administrators must communicate with inmates (through staff–inmate interaction, posted memos, and other means) and emphasize that the change in practice must be accepted by everyone—prisoners and staff alike. They must make prisoners understand that misbehaving in response to the planned change will result in swift and certain punishment and will not forestall the intended implementation.

At different times, all aspects of the reasons for confinement (punishment, rehabilitation, general deterrence, and specific deterrence) will be emphasized. Prison administrators must accept these changes and not become publicly or emotionally invested in any particular political approach. Administrators are not precluded from holding their own personal and professional views regarding the most appropriate manner in which to operate a prison, but as civil servants, all staff are expected to fulfill the requirements of the law as set forth by their legislative bodies. The public is best served by prison and jail leaders who implement policy established by elected officials effectively. The legislators' newfound interest in the administration of justice is significant and should be considered a positive development.

In a text on prison management, Richard McGee, California's venerable correctional administrator from 1944 to 1967, postulated that officials should fight political pressure.[6] He strongly advised penal leaders to avoid outside turmoil and maintain a tightly organized and operated environment inside the institution. Rather than joining in on the political dialogue external to the agency, his advice was to focus on making prisons and jails as safe, manageable, and humane as possible. He affirmed, however, the need to make institution operations accessible to external players who have great influence in political dialogue so that they can understand the facts of life behind bars.

■ Conclusion

Correctional systems demand a substantial portion of state and federal criminal justice budgets. As a result, politicians and the public are increasingly interested in prison operations, and they demand results, such as reduced recidivism. In addition, the public wants to know that terrorists are not taking advantage of the captive prison audience to recruit warriors to their cause. Correctional administrators often resist the interest of outsiders, viewing it as undue interference with daily operations by those who know very little about the difficult tasks faced by prison and jail staff on a daily basis.

Senior staff of U.S. prisons and jails must exert leadership behind the fences and in the world beyond. It is not appropriate for civil servants to lobby or otherwise directly seek to influence elected representatives of the people. However, it is acceptable and desirable for those who are experts in managing prisons and jails to educate the judicial and legislative branches of government. Correctional systems will not adapt well to today's turbulent external pressures unless they manage these sources of influence successfully. Leaders must comprehend the political context and appropriately position their agencies to withstand the political winds of change.

Successful leaders of correctional agencies are those who can cultivate the outside support necessary to counter individuals who are intent on wholesale change of the institution's regimen. Outside support is necessary in the local, state, and national communities and is generally composed of the media, the judiciary, and the popularly elected legislative bodies. The image of corrections is very much in the hands of chief executive officers of facilities and heads of correctional agencies. Effective leaders in these roles will gather support for their work by being responsive to their constituencies and bringing them inside to show them the realities of institutional management.

As public administrators, the leaders of institutional operations must be responsive to those who pay the bills and operate according to one of the important principles on which the United States was established—the rule of law.

Chapter Resources

DISCUSSION QUESTIONS

1. What are the pros and cons of a spoils system compared with career civil service?
2. Why should the public and legislators be interested in prison operations?
3. In what ways can corrections administrators develop a positive relationship with legislators?
4. How have expectations of the public and legislators changed regarding prison operations?
5. Why should correctional administrators be concerned about the political process?

ADDITIONAL RESOURCES

Ismaili, K. (2006). Contextualizing the criminal justice policy-making process. *Criminal Justice Policy Review, 17*(3), 255–269.

Lapi-Seppala, T. (2008). Trust, welfare, and political culture: Explaining differences in national penal policies. *Crime and Justice, 37*(1), 313–387.

Stolz, B. (2002). The roles of interest groups in US criminal justice policy making—Who, when, and how. *Criminology and Criminal Justice, 2*(1), 51–69.

Zimring, F. E., & Johnson, D. T. (2006). Public opinion and the governance of punishment in democratic political systems. *The Annals of the American Academy of Political and Social Science, 605*(1), 265–280.

NOTES

1. National Crime Prevention Council. (2000). *Are we safe? The 2000 national crime prevention survey.* Washington, DC: U.S. Department of Justice.
2. Bureau of Justice Statistics. (2011). *Correctional populations in the United States.* Washington, DC: U.S. Department of Justice. Accessed June 3, 2013, at http://www.bjs.gov/content/pub/press/p10cpus10pr.cfm
3. Bureau of Justice Statistics. (2004). *Justice expenditures and employment extracts.* Washington, DC: U.S. Department of Justice.
4. Hill, J. (1999, July 27). Arizona criminals find jail too in-'tents'. Retrieved from http://www.cnn.com/US/9907/27/tough.sheriff/
5. Mosher, F. (Ed.). (1981). *Basic literature of American public administration, 1787–1950.* New York, NY: Holmes and Meier.
6. McGee, R. (1981). *Prisons and politics.* Lexington, MA: Lexington Books.

YOU ARE THE ADMINISTRATOR
■ Making it on the Streets

Duvantre Cantrell had been back on the streets of Newport News for almost 2 weeks and was no closer to landing a job today than he had been 13 days ago. The Downton Street Halfway House had been trying to help him, but not one employer with a position could ever get past the question "Have you ever been convicted of a crime?" Duvantre was getting frustrated as he returned to the halfway house empty-handed again and again. Today, he voiced his anger to the counselor on duty: "What are my *^#! chances of getting hired when the question on the first page of the job application asks about a criminal record? This stops the hiring process before it gets started! Should I start lying about this?"

Duvantre had been worried about this for most of his 4-year sentence in the Virginia State Prison at Sussex. He had been locked up for dealing heroin and had never learned a job skill in his 24 years of life; he only knew how to make money selling drugs. His friends were all druggies, and he had always found it easy to make money illegally, but he knew in his soul that this would send him back to prison.

It's not that he minded selling the liquid gold; a quick drug deal would bring a profit of $400. He was good at it, really. But the downside—prison—had become overwhelming. So he really wanted to find a real job, despite the fact that he would only make minimum wage. He knew this would be hard, but he was convinced that he wanted to try. But today he felt like he was running out of steam.

He just didn't want to be sent back to the joint. But his determination was wearing thin. What should he do next?

- What should correctional facilities do to prepare inmates for their return to the community?
- How do we overcome an employer's reluctance to hire an ex-felon? Would you hire someone with this background?
- Can a halfway house or transitional program offer real help to inmates trying to make it in the free community? How?

Institution Prerelease Programs

Stefan Lobuglio

CHAPTER OBJECTIVES

- Discuss the range of prerelease services offered in secure and community-based correctional settings.

- Demonstrate the application of evidence-based rehabilitative principles in the prerelease services offered by community-based correctional facility.

- Describe the detailed integration of services, programs, and accountability measures in the operations of the Montgomery County Pre-Release Center.

The phrase "prerelease services" refers to rehabilitative programming and reentry strategies designed for incarcerated individuals during a period just before release. Although all services offered before release are by definition "prerelease services," the term generally applies to specific short-term programs and interventions that provide practical and logistical support to assist the incarcerated individual to manage their transition from confinement in jail or prison to liberty in the community.

The types, quality, duration, and providers of these prerelease services can vary significantly from one institution, department, and state to another. The services might constitute the entirety of institutional efforts to provide transitional support in a single jail or prison or serve as the final phase of a well-developed and choreographed reentry plan involving many different types of rehabilitative programming and spanning multiple institutions. Similarly, the specific services can range from the simple and inexpensive act—albeit largely ineffective—of providing a handout of community program provider contact information to incarcerated individuals at the time of release to the placement of an incarcerated individual in a community correctional facility with extensive treatment programming several months before release. Some of these programs might be offered by correctional officers, institutional case management staff, or representatives of community organizations as part of an in-reach effort to encourage individuals to enroll in their programs after release.

As local, state, and federal prisons systems rapidly expanded during the latter part of the 20th century and moved away from rehabilitative ideals, the composition of the prison systems changed by classification levels. Newer facilities were more often classified as medium- or higher security facilities, and the proportion of low- and minimum-security facilities including correctional camps and halfway houses where prerelease services were most often provided declined. As such, prerelease services are also not facility dependent today. A maximum-security prison could offer prerelease services to an individual scheduled for release and who, for whatever reasons, was not stepped down to a lower security setting. Similarly, individuals classified to medical units or medical correctional facilities or placed in categories such as protective custody may receive specialized prerelease services.

Since 1999, many systems have begun to reevaluate their efforts to prepare incarcerated individuals for release, and to begin designing new prerelease services as part of a larger reentry effort. As described in earlier chapters of this book, some of this rethinking was do the reality that so many more individuals were leaving jails and prisons, and so many were returning and overcrowding these facilities and bursting local and state budgets. Coupled with new evidence-based research about effective reentry strategies, many correctional systems have begun prerelease services in their correctional systems. In recent years, the Federal Bureau of Prisons (BOP) has committed itself to placing all incarcerated individuals in halfway houses when they are within 6 months of release and in home detention programs when they have completed 90% of their executed sentence. Although this represents an example of a significant commitment to institutionalizing prerelease services, recent articles in the *New York Times*[1] have exposed the severe variances of the services offered by different halfway houses. In New Jersey and in Brooklyn, New York, the *Times* revealed great irregularities in the quality and scope of services provided by the halfway houses and drew attention to unsavory political connections between the operators of these halfway houses and local and state political actors.

At the state level, Washington and other state prison systems have attempted to design prerelease services into a set of newly designated regional correctional facilities to which incarcerated individuals from these regions are sent within a year or two of release. Other states are exploring models where they transition state inmates to local county correctional facilities where they would receive prerelease services.[2] The Massachusetts Department of Correction has long utilized the excellent prerelease services of the Hampden County Sheriff's Department to place individuals returning to the Western part of Massachusetts in the Hampden House of Correction when they are within 1 year of release. Finally, there has been considerable increase in the number of local correctional agencies offering prerelease services to the jail population. For several years, the National

Institute of Corrections (NIC) has developed a transition model called Transition from Jails to Communities (TJC),[3] which it has promulgated through technical assistance grants to many jurisdictions. Because the stay of incarcerated individuals in jails typically is brief, this model helps local correctional agencies design a number of different strategies to quickly identify and place individuals into programs that can be offered in short periods of time. Historically, many local jails have used work release programs to allow individuals with jobs and transportation to begin working before release. These individuals are typically low-risk incarcerated individuals and will leave the jail during the day to work and return to custody afterward.

To illustrate the design and operation of fully developed prerelease services, the remaining section of this chapter focuses on one nationally regarded program that actually operates at the local, state, and federal levels. For 40 years, the Prerelease and Reentry Services (PRRS) Division of the Montgomery County Department of Correction and Rehabilitation has provided transitional services for more than 17,000 incarcerated individuals returning to the Washington metropolitan area. Although the program is operated by the county's correctional department, the program has been contracted by the Maryland State Division of Correction and the BOP to serve their incarcerated populations who are returning to this area as well.

PRRS operates a 171-bed residential community correctional center called the Montgomery County Pre-Release Center (PRC). Additionally, PRRS manages a home confinement program that allows individuals the opportunity to live in their homes but report regularly to the PRC for case management services and drug testing. Those on home confinement are also under electronic monitoring.

■ Target Population

The PRRS's target population is all convicted and sentenced inmates in the jail who meet the eligibility criteria (explained in the next section) and incarcerated individuals leaving state and federal correctional facilities and returning to the county. The target population includes individuals who have been convicted of a wide range of crimes from misdemeanor offenses to murder. It serves both men and women and individuals of both low and high rates of assessed risk-to-recidivate levels. The only individuals barred from the PRC are those who have been convicted of a prior escape charge. The inclusive criteria stem from the original charter for the county correctional department. In 1972, the newly created Montgomery County Department of Correction and Rehabilitation was mandated to apply the best concepts of community corrections toward two goals: first, to manage the jail population and, second, to materially assist those released from incarceration to the county and its environs. As such, PRRS operates with the premise that its services will benefit all transitioning incarcerated individuals and their families. Importantly, the program also recognizes the benefits to the larger community by having these individuals contribute to the local labor market and have reduced rates of recidivism.

Secure detention facilities and prisons may limit prerelease services to those incarcerated individuals who are assessed as the highest risk to recidivate. Although all soon-to-be-released individuals could benefit from prerelease services, program resources are finite, and priority should be given to those for whom the value of the intervention is greatest. Unfortunately, many facilities do not assess risk either with a standardized and normalized risk assessment instrument or through a basic interviewing process. Often, enrollment in these programs is voluntary and, as a consequence, may attract those individuals who have the greatest motivation but also the lowest risk to recidivate. Determining positive outcomes in these programs proves difficult given the self-selection bias and the fact that most low-risk individuals do not need the benefit of the services in order to successfully transition back to the community.

Secure correctional facilities can also make the mistake of excluding from prerelease services high-risk individuals who may fall into a certain offense category. Sex offenders and violent offenders are the groups most often barred from these programs, and these exclusionary criteria may be imposed from the funding source, such as a grant program or legislative action, or by a political decision made by the correctional agency. Unfortunately, high-risk individuals in these categories are actually those who would stand to gain the most from prerelease services, and in a secure facility where the possibility of escape is miniscule, there is very little justification to adopt these policies. By contrast, prerelease services offered in community correction settings such as halfway houses do incur greater risk by serving high-risk individuals, and many do have a long list of exclusionary criteria for program enrollment. Although this is more understandable than in a secure correctional facility, the exclusionary criteria that may screen out high-risk incarcerated individuals may limit the effectiveness of the program for the same reasons described above.

■ Selection Process

PRRS employs a multifaceted selection process for two overriding reasons. First, clients need to be legally eligible for enrollment in the program as defined by the county and state statute that governs the program's operation. As a work release program, clients must be eligible to live and work legally in the United States and cannot have any outstanding serious charges. For instance, an individual serving a sentence for a drug possession charge would not be eligible for enrollment if they were still facing charges for first-degree assault. The rationale for this policy is that such an individual would have an incentive to escape if moved to the community-based program given that he might face an additional sentence for the assault that would significantly increase his total time of incarceration. Once the assault case is adjudicated, he then could be considered for the program. These stipulations were put in the originating legislative requirements at the county and state levels governing the creation of PRRS in the late 1960s and early 1970s.[4] Second, clients need to volunteer for the program. This not only is a statutory requirement but also serves to put the onus on the client to declare their interest in this reentry program. In practice, more than 95% of potential clients volunteer to be screened for the program given the enormous advantages to them of being in a community correctional setting.[5] The incentives of being allowed to work, earn money, have contact visits more freely with family, dress in civilian clothes, and have access to the community and their homes are strong. However, a few individuals who would otherwise be eligible do make a calculated decision to stay in the detention center in the belief that they will be able to earn greater diminution credits and complete their sentences quicker. Many of them also make a realistic assessment that they are not ready to assume the responsibilities of increased freedom and liberty, and might wind up violating the strict rules of the community correction program and being revoked. Individuals revoked can actually lose diminution credits—often referred to as good time—and serve longer sentences. Those who commit crimes while on community correctional status also stand to receive stricter and longer sentences for these charges given that they were incurred during an opportunity for them to prepare themselves for release. Third, statutorily, the program can serve incarcerated individuals who are within 1 year of release—either time served or parole. Typically, clients on the program serve between 30 days and 9 months; also, the program can serve individuals with as short as 5 days remaining and up to 1 year remaining.

PRRS uses a structured questionnaire that is administered during a 1- to 2-hour interview. Reentry assessment specialists conduct these interviews in the local detention facility, and the questionnaire incorporates the questions of a standardized risk needs assessment instrument that is scored afterward. In addition to collecting information during the interview, PRRS runs a complete criminal background check on all clients and gathers information from prior institutions and community supervision programs about their conduct, their compliance with rules, and their reentry efforts and progress. All of this information is gathered in a 3-day process: on Monday, the individuals to be assessed for eligibility are determined from lists of individuals recently sentenced to the jail; on Tuesday, the interviews are conducted in the jails. For individuals from the state and federal prison systems, a "paper" review is conducted, and if and when the individuals are approved for placement at the PRC, they are interviewed when they arrive. If the information gathered by the paper review process fails to uncover some serious concerns discovered during the interview, PRRS retains the right to reverse its decision to accept the individual into the program and can arrange for his or her return to the sending institution.

On Wednesday afternoon, the reentry assessment specialists present each case to the deputy chief of programs and services for final review. Ultimately, the review process aims to answer two questions, which, if answered affirmatively, will lead to a decision to accept the individuals into the program: first, can the individual be managed safely in a community correction program, and second, will the individual benefit from the reentry services and opportunities provided by the program. In practice, nearly 95% of all individuals screened are accepted into the program. For the remaining 5%, most either voluntarily withdraw from consideration or a last-minute warrant or medical issue arises. In the latter cases, these individuals may still be considered for the program at a later date.

Once PRRS approves the eligibility of incarcerated individuals for placement in the program, it must then seek approval from the sentencing judge. Many of the judges have given PRRS a "blanket" authorization that allows the program to move individuals the following Monday. Other judges will be sent an authorization for transfer form requesting their consent to place this individual in the program. Note that although PRRS requires the consent of the sentencing judge in order to bring an individual into the program, judges cannot sentence individuals directly to the program. PRRS retains the right to determine eligibility. This is an important distinction and one that is not commonly practiced. In many other jurisdictions with community-based prerelease programs, judges have the authority to sentence individuals directly into these programs. The disadvantage of having direct sentencing is that prerelease programs can then become part of a plea negotiation, and factors that should be taken into consideration before a placement decision is made can be ignored. For instance, a defense attorney may argue that his client is working and is the sole breadwinner for his family. Perhaps he will layer on a compelling fact that the family's home is near foreclosure and without the defendant's ability to work and earn money, the home will be lost. Statements made in court are hard to fact-check, and PRRS has demonstrated in a number of cases where the factual basis for the defense attorney's argument for placement of an individual in the prerelease program was faulty. The defense attorney was not lying but merely repeating claims made by the defendant that could have only shades of the truth.

The ability to identify, interview, review criminal offense history and institutional and supervisor conduct, approve, and actually move individuals from the detention center to the prerelease program in 1 week is a great strength of the program. Because jail sentences are typically shorter term, agencies must develop a methodical and nimble decision-making process in order to determine eligibility for prerelease services. Too much time spent in assessment and review may prevent the program from actually serving the client. Although there is always additional information that might prove helpful, PRRS has developed the confidence to identify the key factors in determining eligibility and placement decisions. If a key piece of information is missing, the incarcerated individual's screening may be delayed a week, but this rarely occurs. Again, the longevity of the program has given the program the ability to quickly and accurately make these placement decisions. For prerelease services in detention facilities where the risk of escape is miniscule, the facility should be in a position to determine eligibility quickly if the leadership and resources are present to do so.

◼ Orientation

Individuals from the local jail placed at the PRC arrive by noon on Monday mornings. Individuals from the state and federal systems actually arrive the Thursday before. As soon as they come in the door, they are taken to one of the four assigned housing units where they meet with the supervising correctional officer, who is called a residential supervisor (RS). On the housing units, the RS explains to the new program participants (hereafter also referred to as residents) the program's escape policy first and foremost before they are given room assignments, linens, and towels. The RS explains in detail that individuals who are found accountable will face first- or second-degree escape charges and will be prosecuted to the full extent of the law. The new residents are then required to sign an acknowledgment form indicating that they understand the policy and also agree to give up extradition rights should they be charged with escape.

PRRS goes to extraordinary lengths to hammer home the escape policy to new residents, and by signing acknowledgment and consent forms during initial admission, they will hear about the consequences of escape from multiple individuals during their first 2 days. In the afternoon orientation, the division chief speaks to the new resident and explains the escape policy in further detail. He tells them that escapes jeopardize the community, political, and criminal justice stakeholder support of the program. Often, he will cite the case of Willie Horton, whose escape from a furlough program in Massachusetts in 1988 and subsequent criminal act while on fugitive status halted the use of all prerelease beds in the state for 21 years. It also played a role in the presidential election that year, and many cite the effective use of this case by the opponent of the Massachusetts governor, who was the Democratic candidate for president, as a reason for the governor's landslide loss in the general election.

At PRRS, individuals who leave the building without authorization are immediately charged with first-degree escape. Those who fail to return to the facility from an approved community pass are charged with second-degree escape. First-degree escape is a felony, and the sentencing guidelines are 5–10 years in state prison. Furthermore, Maryland law mandates that no part of an escape sentence can be suspended, nor can it run concurrently with any other sentence. In all cases, before the criminal charge is filed, every attempt is made to contact family members, visitors, workplace, and other individuals listed in the case file to ensure that the individual's failure to return is not the result of confusion or an error. Often, family members will play a significant role in encouraging their loved ones to return to the facility. However, once the charges are filed before a Maryland Commissioner, the warrant seeking the arrest of the individual is hand delivered to the sheriff's department, and they take over the apprehension effort. They have a unit that tracks down individuals with outstanding warrants and prioritize escapees from the prerelease program. As a result, almost all individuals return voluntarily or are found within 72 hours.[6]

Escapes are rare in the prerelease program. In 2012, the program experienced eight escapes and served more than 500 individuals.[7] At the writing of this chapter, all individuals who escaped from the PRC are in custody. For every escape, the PRRS division chief works closely with the Maryland State Attorney's Office for Montgomery County to vigorously prosecute the cases. At sentencing, the division chief will actually address the court and describe the harm that the escape has done to the program and will indicate his support of a strict sentence to the Maryland Division of Corrections. Because sentences greater than 18 months are sent to the state, he will typically request a sentence of between 3 and 5 years.

On Monday afternoon, new arrivals attend a 90-minute orientation session during which the facilitator, who is a case manager, reviews the rules and structure of the program. It closely follows a resident guidebook that is available to all residents. The 65-page guidebook is accessible on the PRRS website, and an electronic copy is also available on computers located on each of the housing units. Besides providing important information on the key policies of the program such as visiting, accounting, contraband, search, and discipline, the orientation is aimed to encourage residents to fully utilize the services and opportunities of the program. It identifies the case manager and work release positions who most closely work with clients on issues related to programs, treatment, family engagement, and employment. During the orientation, the new arrivals are told that they will participate in in-depth intake meetings during which they will be asked to explain their goals for the program. This occurs on Tuesday afternoon and typically is the time where the individual residents meet their case managers and work release coordinators. Other case managers on the housing units will also attend these "team meethings" along with other staff members in order to contribute to the conversation and to familiarize themselves with all the new clients on the unit.

On Tuesday and Friday mornings, residents receive several hours of job-readiness training and are informed fully of the program's expectations that they need to find work within 28 days of their arrival. They are told that they can access a career resource center that is composed of 23 computers with Internet access between 8:30 A.M. and 11:30 A.M. and between 1:30 P.M. and 4:30 P.M. In fact, during these "business hours," unemployed residents are expected to be looking for work and going out on interviews. The TVs in the housing units are off and recreation in the courtyard is limited to those individuals who are working. For the rest of that first week, residents meet with the community health nurse to review any issues related to their health and medication. The nurse also coordinates meetings with the department's psychiatrist. Finally, the new residents attend an 8-hour class on workplace digital literacy skills, which teaches them how to use the Internet and other resources effectively for job searches. This program was developed by the Second Chance Act provided by the U.S. Department of Justice, and the curriculum was developed by Montgomery College. The grant also provides opportunities for residents with the necessary aptitude, interest, and motivation to pursue industry-accepted certificate classes such as for Microsoft help desk support technician. By the Monday following their arrival, residents are fully expected to meet all rules and expectations of the program.

◼ Case Management and Work Release Services

The core rehabilitative and programmatic services are coordinated by case managers and work release coordinators. As described earlier, each resident of the program is assigned a case manager who maintains a caseload of between 20 and 30 residents. By contrast, each work release coordinator is assigned to a housing unit, and the three male housing units have between 46 and 50 beds plus those individuals assigned to home confinement.

Case Management Services

The case managers work with each resident to develop a reentry plan that is individualized to their needs. The risk/needs assessment instrument used by the reentry assessment specialist actually provides the case managers with a horizontal bar chart that characterizes the level of need for the clients in each of 10 "criminogenic" domains from low to high. These include criminal history, education/employment, family, financial, housing, leisure/recreation, companions, alcohol/drug abuse problems, emotional/personal, and attitudes and orientation. Each of these factors has been found to have "statistical power" to influence recidivism, and the goal of the reentry plan is to develop strategies in those areas that indicate high need and risk. For instance, an individual assessed as high risk/need in recreation/leisure would be encouraged to develop activities and interests that were healthy and prosocial outside of work and family. Likewise, case managers would assign individuals needing educational services to the appropriate programs whether they need literacy instruction, want help preparing for an alternative high school diploma, or want to pursue a college degree.

The individualized reentry plan combined with the strong involvement of family members is one of the great strengths of program. Family members are invited to participate in "contracting" sessions with the case manager and the program participant and are seen as allies in the reentry process. PRRS actually offers a separate evening program only for family members that educates them about the program and describes how they can assist the program to ensure that their loved ones accomplish the mutually shared goals of success. The evening "sponsor" program also serves as a support group for family members, and the facilitator spends time discussing how they can most effectively assist their husbands, daughters, sons, and so on in the reentry process. The importance of families in the reentry process is demonstrated by the liberal visiting policy at the facility that offers visiting hours 5 hours a day, 7 days a week. Also, program participants are incentivized to reach out to family members and have them agree to participate in the sponsor group meetings. If the family member participates in six classes, the participant may be eligible for an extended pass to the home of the family member ranging from 8 to 40 hours.

Prerelease services that do not differentiate between offender's assessed risks or needs and do not seek family member involvement ignore much of the recent evidence-based literature on offender rehabilitation. Although one-size-fits-all services to offenders are advantageous to the institution in terms of achieving economy of scale in services, these perfunctory services have no basis in research for effectiveness. Furthermore, families are an underappreciated resource that programs often ignore. Worse, through the inconvenient visiting and security policies, correctional institutions can send a disrespectful message to families that they are complicit with their loved ones' offenses and have no value to the institution. By contrast, the partnership formed by family members and PRRS significantly improves services. During case management meetings, family members are often the first to point out to their loved ones their need to seek treatment and comply with the reentry plans. The relationship between the case manager and the family member also establishes a greater intimacy in the relationship with them and leads to reentry plans that are more relevant and challenging to the specific situation of the client.

The reentry plan will refer clients to many programs offered in the community. Substance abuse and mental health counseling, AA/NA meetings, sex offender treatment, college classes, and day programs for individuals with cognitive impairments are a few of the many programs offered by government and nonprofit providers. As a community-based program, PRRS actually seeks to have its residents engage in these services rather than offer programs at the PRC and operate with the rationale that residents are more likely to continue to attend to these resources postrelease if they are not held on-site. Correctional agencies with community correctional centers can make the mistake of centralizing all services in the center and thereby re-create a jail and miss out on the comparative advantage of their ability to send clients into community programs. In essence, these agencies attempt to mitigate the risk of their community correctional centers by placing individuals in these centers, but then restrict their access to the community, which can be self-defeating to the purpose of classifying individuals to this lowered security level. At PRRS, individuals are allowed in the community only on an approved pass, and accountability is maintained by verifying their whereabouts using various methods including mobile teams in the community, electronic monitoring, and requiring participants to bring back verification materials.

Nevertheless, there are a number of programs offered at the PRC that the program has determined are important and not fully accessible in the community. These include GED preparation, parenting classes, child support counseling, and workplace digital skill training. PRRS introduced a cognitive behavior treatment program called Thinking for a Change, which was developed by the NIC. Five of the 24 sessions are provided to all of the program participants, and those assessed as needing the full program continue on in the following weeks. In addition, volunteers offer programs in meditation, mediation, relapse prevention, and literacy tutoring. The Archdiocese of Washington also receives some county funding to offer a mentoring program called Welcome Home. The program recruits and trains volunteers from the community who will commit to spending at least 1 year assisting program participants with their transitions. The program maintains a cadre of more than 40 mentors, and many of the mentor/mentee relationships continue after the release of the resident. The success of the program is due to the excellent training provided to mentors on boundary setting, the process of matching appropriate clients and mentors, and the continued level of support provided to mentors and mentees through periodic group meetings and individual contacts provided by the Welcome Home coordinator.

Case managers also work with residents to develop a budget and help them manage their funds. All monies earned by residents are deposited to a trustee account held by PRRS. Twenty percent of gross income, to a cap of $460/month, is taken for program fees that revert to the county fund—not PRRS or the Department of Correction and Rehabilitation. After restitution, family support, and other required costs are met, residents submit check requests to their case managers for their other financial needs ranging from transportation funds to mortgage payments. Each request is carefully scrutinized, and case managers use these requests as an opportunity to help residents prioritize their needs and plans for the future. On numerous occasions, case managers have challenged residents on their purported need for expensive clothing or haircuts, and helped them find cheaper alternatives.

Work Release Services

All PRRS residents must seek and secure full-time work. After 1 week of orientation, which includes 6 hours of job readiness, they are expected to find their own jobs—or return to preexisting ones—within 28 days of arrival. After this point, they are subject to disciplinary action that can result in the removal of good time. As such, PRRS subscribes to the "work first" methodology that pressures residents to rapidly attach themselves to the labor market and then circles back to work with them to develop longer-term career goals.

Work release coordinators (WRCs) in each of the four housing units oversee employment services and decisions. They ensure that individuals are actively seeking jobs and also ensure that jobs are appropriate for individuals given their experience and offense background. It is no surprise that sex offenders and drug offenders cannot work in K–12 school setting, nor can residents convicted of retail theft work in jobs in malls. However, in special circumstances, WRCs have authority to override certain agreed-upon conventions that they follow. Several years ago, an individual serving time for his repeated driving while intoxicated conviction was allowed to return to his job as a salesman for alcohol spirits and was allowed to drive a vehicle in which he had open samples in the trunk. In this case, the WRC made an exception given that the client had worked in this position for decades and was close to retirement from a well-paying job. Also, his DUIs in the past had always occurred at night, off the clock. Through an interlock device connected to his car and a GPS tracker, PRRS mitigated risk and allowed him to work and retain this job while ensuring that he remained alcohol free while in the program.

At intake, each resident meets with his or her WRC and discusses their employment goals and concerns. For those individuals with preexisting jobs—about 25% of the population—the WRC facilitates their return. In all cases where a job is tendered, the WRC will contact the employer to confirm their understanding of the incarcerated individual's offense and the prerelease program and will also seek to execute an employer contract. This contract essentially asks the employer to confirm that they have been informed about PRRS and understand their obligation to report to PRRS any problems with punctuality, absences, or behavior.

Often residents will complain that the WRC jeopardizes jobs by requiring that the resident disclose immediately to a prospective employer that they are participating in the prerelease program. Some employers do in fact lose interest in prerelease residents, but the purpose of the policy is twofold. First, PRRS wants to ensure that employers are not surprised by individuals' custodial status and are comfortable hiring these individuals for their businesses. In this way, PRRS seeks to be an honest broker with employers. Second and more importantly, the program is training residents to be forthcoming about their background up front given the widespread use of criminal background checks by employers. In the 1990s, the Department of Justice estimated that just over half of employers conducted background checks; by 2005, the percentage was over 95%.[8] This change in practice was driven both by the greater availability of criminal history and greater concern about tort liability and has increased the penalty of having a criminal history. Often called the collateral costs of criminal offending, PRRS's policy trains the residents to develop a "script" that they can deliver to allay concerns to a prospective employer about their backgrounds and that speaks to their ability to contribute to the employer's bottom line. Although forcing them to disclose this information is uncomfortable and does lead to the closing of some job opportunities, it is a lifelong skill that these individuals will need to use repeatedly in their work lives. There are many cases where employed individuals who were not forthcoming with their criminal background are fired abruptly when it does surface, and they then lose the ability to reference this work in future employment.

The only exceptions to PRRS's work requirement for residents are individuals attending high school full-time, disabled, and retired residents and individuals who are assigned to work details in the institution. These individuals must be workforce "engaged" but do so through education, community services, and institutional jobs. Work details are used at PRRS to assist the highest risk individuals first become acclimated to the community correction setting before requiring them to venture out and work. Typically, they are sentenced to the kitchen or maintenance details for 60–90 days during which they are held accountable to 40 hours of work a week at $2 per day. Although they are working the institutional details, they also pursue their reentry plan developed with their case managers.

As described before, in June 2006, PRRS introduced a new Internet-based career resource center to serve soon-to-be-released inmates participating in its work release program. The career resource center assists them in preparing resumes and cover letters, searching and applying for jobs, and identifying community resources that will assist in their transitions. In June 2011, the career resource center was expanded to 23 computers, and the center is kept open 25–35 hours a week with no additional permanent staff. Carefully trained volunteers work with RSs to provide most of the supervision in the center with assistance from WRCs. The design and operation of the center has incorporated important safeguards that have resulted in few and minor instances of inappropriate use, which is particularly remarkable given the clientele.

Having Internet-accessible computers in corrections is rare. However, given that PRRS places enormous pressure on residents to find jobs within 1 month, the program was able to argue the necessity of these tools. Historically, residents have used classified ads in newspapers, listings of businesses in telephone books, and networking with each other and staff to identify promising employment opportunities to pursue. However, over the past decade, the Internet has become an indispensable tool for job searches, and in fact, many companies now require applicants to apply and submit resumes online.

On a typical day during the week, unemployed residents are required to attend a meeting at 8:00 A.M. that serves to ensure that they are up and dressed and participate in an encouraging and interesting 15-minute conversation about employment-related issues. They spend from 8:30 A.M. to 11:30 A.M. and 1:30 P.M. to 4:30 P.M. in the career resource center filling out applications online and preparing resumes. They also utilize a phone bank to follow up on employment opportunities and immediately inform their WRC when they been able to obtain an interview and also confirm that they have disclosed their offense and the fact that they live at the PRC. Before allowing the resident to leave, the WRC and other staff confirm with the employers that they are hiring and that they are aware that the individual is a participant in the prerelease program.

Level System

PRRS incentivizes residents to obtain work and follow their reentry plan through a level system that offers graduated privileges as they increase from level 1 to 6. Individuals arrive in the program and, after the first week of orientation, are assigned to level 1, where they can receive three visits per week, participate in group recreational trips, and have a curfew at 10:00 P.M. To get to level 2, residents must obtain critical identification documents, finalize their reentry plan, and obtain employment. At this level, curfew moves to 11:00 P.M., and they can receive an unlimited number of visits. They can also take an 8-hour home pass once a month if they have involved a family member in the sponsor program. At level 6, there is no curfew, and they can earn up to four home passes per month, each lasting 40 hours (7:00 A.M. Saturday to 11:00 P.M. Sunday). In addition to these extended privileges, residents can earn diminution credits off their sentences in the amount of 10 days per month (in addition to 5 days per month earned through statutory good time). Several years ago, Rutgers economist Anne Piehl interviewed 22 residents and reported in her paper for the Manhattan Institute that most could articulate the level system chart by memory, indicating to her that the incentives were clearly understood by the population. In her report for the Manhattan Institute, "The Power of Small Rewards," she also reported how seemingly small incentives—such as an increase in curfew for 1 hour—could significantly motivate residents to make full use of the program.[9]

■ Security/Accountability

PRRS ensures the safety, cleanliness, and good order of the Montgomery County PRC. Every day, RSs conduct room and personal searches, and individuals caught with contraband are disciplined. Residents in possession of drugs or weapons are subject to immediate removal, and less serious items mean discipline through due process hearings.

Drug testing is conducted randomly on all residents on a host of illicit drugs, and they are subject to alcohol breath analysis every time they leave or return to the facility and while they remain in the facility. Positive findings result in immediate suspensions and disciplinary write-ups. First-time offenders are typically suspended in the jail for a number of days, and lose good conduct time, but are allowed to return.

Also, accountability of residents in the community is assisted with electronic monitoring equipment. All sex offenders wear GPS tracking devices, and other residents whose criminal offense or work situation raise an issue of unaccountability may also be required to use this equipment as well. Those living on home confinement are also subject to regular breath alcohol tests administered remotely, and they are monitored either by GPS or by home curfew electronic equipment.

There are many rules to the program, and the disciplinary process is codified in the guidebook and categorizes offenses by four levels: 400-level offenses are minor, not subject to appeal, and administered directly by staff; 300-level offenses are also minor but have greater sanctions; 200-level offenses are serious offenses and sanctions include suspension, revocation, and loss of statutory good conduct time; and 100-level offenses are the most serious and require immediate removal from the facility.

RSs staff the center 24/7/365 and carry out many security protocols, similar to a correctional officer. However, RSs, who are all required to have bachelor's degrees, play an important role in the rehabilitative mission of PRRS and deliver programs and mentor and counsel residents. While maintaining clear boundaries, they have excellent interpersonal skills and develop encouraging and constructive rapport with clients.

The PRC is accredited by the Maryland Commission on Correctional Standards and the American Correctional Association.

■ Performance Statistics

PRRS reports its data using different metrics including jail bed days saved, percentage of released residents with jobs and housing, and the total amount of monies earned and distributed in taxes and family support. On any given day, approximately 25% of all sentenced incarcerated individuals in Montgomery County are managed in the prerelease program, and thus, the program plays a critical role in ensuring that the detention centers are not overcrowded. In terms of programmatic indicators, for 2011, the data are as follows:

- 607 residents served (468 transfers + 139 average daily population 1/1/11)
- 81% program completion rate
- 87% released with employment (2007 statistic)
- 95% released with housing
- $1.25 million in gross income (down $2 million in 2007)
- $204.6K taxes
- $230.6K program fees collected
- $122.8K family support
- $4K fines/restitution
- 6 escapes (all apprehended, charged, prosecuted, and convicted)[10]

In terms of recidivism, the prerelease program does not track this metric at the time of this writing but is looking to institute a methodology to do so in the future. Recidivism rates prove to be difficult to measure and interpret based on study methodologies and the "risk" set of the targeted population. Differing definitions of recidivism and the use of selective data sources can significantly skew recidivism rates. Furthermore, programs, like PRRS, that house individuals of comparably high risk (60% are assessed at the medium- to high risk level) will have a higher recidivism rate than prerelease programs that target lower-risk individuals, and the different rates do not provide useful comparative information regarding program quality.[11]

■ Conclusion

Prerelease services have become a staple of quality correctional operations whether practiced in state and federal prisons or in city and county detention centers. As the rehabilitative goal of corrections has resurfaced, more departments and agencies are making use of the vast materials and technical assistance available to them to design prerelease services appropriate for specific institutions. The NIC has funded a number of research publications and technical assistance grants that provide tool kits and guides to develop quality prerelease services. Also, programs like the Montgomery County PRRS division are often visited by jurisdictions to learn about the specific practices in well-developed and established programs.

Chapter Resources

DISCUSSION QUESTIONS

1. What are the goals of prerelease services?
2. How are prerelease services differentiated from drug treatment, education, and other programs offered in a correctional setting?
3. What are the economic and political factors that a correctional administrator or policy maker would consider in advocating for prerelease services? In a jail or prison? In a community-based program?
4. What performance metrics are appropriate for measuring the effectiveness of prerelease services?
5. What are the strengths and weaknesses of the Montgomery County Pre-Release Center model of prerelease services?

ADDITIONAL RESOURCES

National Institute of Corrections, http://nicic.gov

National Reentry Resource Center, http://nationalreentryresourcecenter.org/

Urban Institute Reentry Roundtables, http://www.urban.org/projects/reentry-roundtable/

NOTES

1. Dolnick, S. (2012, December 12). A halfway house built on exaggerated claims. *New York Times,* p. A1.
2. Solomon, A. L., Osborne, J. W. L., LoBuglio, S. F., Mellow, J., & Mukamal, D. A. (2008, May). *Life after lockup: improving reentry from jail to the community,* p. 5. (BJA 2005-RE-CX-K148). Washington, DC: Urban Institute.
3. Transition from Jail to Community (TJC). Retrieved May 8, 2013, from http://nicic.gov/jailtransition
4. Rosenblum, R., & Whitcomb, D. (1978). Montgomery County work release/pre-release program: An exemplary project, p. 12–13. (Stock No. 027-000-00673-6). Washington, DC: Office of Development, Testing, and Dissemination, U.S. Department of Justice.
5. PRRS Overview Presentation. (2013). Retrieved May 8, 2012, from http://www6.montgomerycountymd.gov/content/docr/pdfs/prrs_presentation_1_9_13.pdf
6. LoBuglio, S. F. (2013). Personal interview.
7. PRRS Quarterly Chief's Report – DRAFT. (2012, September 13–December 6). Retrieved May 8, 2013 from http://www6.montgomerycountymd.gov/content/docr/NewsAdvisoryCommitte/PRRS/chiefs_report_12_06_12_draft.pdf
8. Rodriguez, M. N., & Emsellem, M. (2011, March). *65 million need not apply: The case for reforming criminal background checks for employment.* The National Employment Law Project. Retrieved from http://www.nelp.org/page/-/65_Million_Need_Not_Apply.pdf?nocdn=1
9. Piehl, A (2009, May). *Preparing prisoners for employment: The power of small rewards.* Civic Report No. 57, p. 5.
10. PRRS Overview Presentation. (2013). Retrieved May 8, 2012, from http://www6.montgomerycountymd.gov/content/docr/pdfs/prrs_presentation_1_9_13.pdf
11. PRRS Overview Presentation. (2013). Retrieved May 8, 2012, from http://www6.montgomerycountymd.gov/content/docr/pdfs/prrs_presentation_1_9_13.pdf

Reentry and Reintegration

Peter M. Carlson and Lior Gideon

CHAPTER 48

CHAPTER OBJECTIVES

- Understand the concept of reentry and its goals.
- Explore the paradox of corrections as an agent of change.
- Outline possible impediments to reentry and treatment programs.

The Bureau of Justice Statistics (BJS) indicated that at year-end 2011, federal and state prisons and local jails housed approximately 2.5 million prisoners.[1] Taking into consideration that 93% of all inmates will eventually return home, it was estimated that approximately 700,000 inmates will be released back to their home communities in each of the following years. In fact, Travis calculated that 1,700 inmates are released each day.[2] Unfortunately, soon after these offenders are released, many of them are rearrested and reincarcerated. According to BJS, approximately 80% of those released from incarceration will be released to parole supervision. Therefore, it is not surprising that studies show that nearly 80% of released prisoners are back behind bars within 10 years of release, as most of them are returning because of technical violations and other noncriminal-related activities that result from such requirement. As such, reentry has become the new buzzword in correctional reform and an important concern (along with rehabilitation and reintegration) for policy makers, criminologists, and the entire field of corrections,[3] thus diverting the attention to practices that promote successful reintegration while lowering recidivism rates.

The offender's future, the effect on his or her family, the cost of returning the individual to prison, and the effect on already overcrowded penal facilities are serious outcomes in which all parties have a stake. The success or failure of an inmate's transition back to his or her home community has many significant effects on public safety and health as well. Reentry is obviously one of the most crucial points in the offender's journey from prison back to society, as reentry not only symbolizes the end of incarceration but is also the starting point of a long and challenging process of reintegration, which is highly critical to the offender.[4]

■ Responsibility

Whose responsibility is it when a released offender returns to jail or prison? In many cases, it is very easy to place the blame for failure directly on the offender. After all, according to the classical school of criminology, each individual makes choices in life, and the violator of society's laws has chosen this course of behavior. Many will agree that it is not possible to change another person's attitude or moral standards; an individual chooses to either follow the law or violate it. The principle of free will asserts that an individual contemplates various actions and then selects the most desirable one by weighing the benefits of committing a criminal act against the negative outcomes of getting caught.

However, according to the positivist school of criminology, other circumstances may interfere with an individual's ability to choose the right course in life. Genetic mental deficiencies, social or economic circumstances, drug or alcohol addiction, or one's choice of associates may cause an individual to override his or her good judgment and create a pathway to crime.

Research shows that many offenders were unemployed before arrest, are functionally illiterate, or have some form of mental health problems. Similarly, studies have demonstrated that most inmates are poorly educated, lack vocational skills, struggle with drugs and alcohol abuse, and suffer from some form of mental illness.[5] Despite these issues, offenders are still released back into society, trying to succeed without a system to assist them in dealing with the problems that are often associated with future criminality.

Consequently, one cannot ignore the need for correctional institutions to have a stake in the rehabilitation, reentry, and reintegration of the offenders released from its jurisdictions. Correctional systems must make every effort to prepare a convicted offender for a successful return to the community. In truth, the process of helping to prepare an inmate for his or her eventual release is a key element in the criminal justice system in the United States. The National Commission on Safety and Abuse in America's Prisons conducted a comprehensive review of correctional facilities and concluded that reinvestment in programming for prisoners to reduce recidivism is an essential reform for correctional programs and operations nationwide.[6]

In their current state, many prisons and jails are not adequate places for rehabilitation. The current model of prison operations is based solely on incapacitation and not on inmate rehabilitation or preparation for successful release.[7] However, scholars have argued that even with rehabilitation goals in mind, prisons still fail to effectively deter offenders. In fact, the corrections system resembles a "revolving door of justice."[8] Similarly, as prisons become overcrowded, many correctional officials are forced to release offenders early, thus creating a backfire effect.[9] Policy in the United States that commits billions of dollars to lock up offenders for increasingly longer periods of time has proven to be ineffective. Some critics propose that these dollars would be better spent on programs designed to improve the success rate of prisoner reentry. Furthermore, the high recidivism rates should suggest that the existing model for corrections is not solving the crime problem, and if anything, it is only perpetuating the crime crisis. This paradox should be acknowledged, as it lies at the heart of any reintegration and reentry discussion.

■ Inmate Reentry Programs

Reentry is not a single event but is part of a process—a series of interrelated events that culminates in the physical release of the individual to the community. Joan Petersilia defines reentry as the collective effect of all institutional programs and activities that work together to help prepare offenders for a successful return to their home communities where they can live within the law. Petersilia believes that an effective reentry process relies on inmate participation in a continuum of activities during confinement, an effective release process, and the accountability/supervision of the offender once he or she is back in the free community.[10] Other scholars identify reentry as a specific point in time, an event that indicates transition from prison back to community.[11] While acknowledging the fact that reentry is indeed a crucial point of a continuum, a process, reentry by itself is a significant event, the point of transition, and symbolizes the beginning of a long reintegration process on the outside.[11]

The reentry process should begin at the presentence report stage and during initial intake stages at the facility, when the newly convicted offender walks his or her first steps as an inmate. Such assessment should be done in stages, beginning with inmate classification or assessment. This stage includes classification of the inmate and staff determination, in partnership with the inmate, of the risk and needs of each individual inmate. It determines what programs may help prepare that inmate for his or her return to the community and outlines the inmate's participation in all planned activities. Essentially, one can argue that an inmate reentry program consists of every program offered in the correctional system in which the inmate participates. Programs such as teaching an individual to read and write, drug abuse treatment, counseling, work assignments, life skills, and anger management groups are all good examples of institutional activities and can all be classified as helping prepare for reentry. In fact, the time spent behind bars should be devoted to prepare the inmate for the time of reentry by providing the skills needed for successful reintegration that is expected to follow the point of reentry.

Inmate Programming

Several aspects of inmate programming can assist in preparing incarcerated offenders for the ultimate point of reentry:

- Educational and vocational training
- Life skills programs
- Individual counseling
- Medical and psychiatric care
- Drug treatment programs
- Therapeutic communities
- Faith-based/religious programs

Studies have concluded that participants who had correction-based education, vocation, and work programs recidivate at a lower rate than nonparticipants and that such programs may help provide opportunities for a successful path after release.[12] Recent research also suggests that prisoners are more likely to reoffend if they are unemployed, use drugs or abuse alcohol, or have extensive criminal histories.[13] Other studies suggest that untreated mentally ill inmates pose a danger to themselves as well as to public safety if not treated during incarceration and if not guided and followed upon release.[14] Therapeutic communities have proven to be especially effective in a correctional institution setting because of their characteristic as a total treatment environment that isolates participants from the rest of the prison population, segregating them from drugs, violence, and other aspects of prison life commonly associated with ineffective rehabilitation efforts.[15] Alternatively, faith-based programming may offer inmates a way to cope with the harsh prison environment and ward off negative emotions, although studies examining the effect of religious programming are just developing.

Prerelease Activities

Prerelease programs should focus on the issues the individual will have to deal with in the future, such as finding a residence, looking for employment, dealing with expectations of parole officers, reuniting with family, avoiding stressful situations, and learning how to improve, build, and foster positive social capital.[16] These programs are generally conducted in the last 180 days before an inmate's release and should involve, when appropriate, community agencies and family members with whom the inmate will reunite. Effective programs often use practitioners who will work with inmates upon their release, including parole officers, halfway house supervisors, and employers.

Transition

There are many facets in a good transitional program. Inmates being released should have a prearranged residence and community assistance in terms of seeking employment. Mental health inmates should be released with a 30-day supply of any medication that has been part of their treatment regimen and should have prearranged appointments with a community mental health program. Similar arrangements are needed for offenders who are chronically ill and pose a danger to public safety because of their medical condition. Such transition requires carefully thought-out discharge planning that involves correctional case managers, inmates, their families, and relevant agencies in the community.[17]

■ Motivation

Motivation is an essential part of successful reintegration and as such is also essential to the process of reentry. No matter what programs are offered by and available from correctional staff, lack of inmate's motivation can be a crucial factor in such program success,[18] so the challenge for correctional staff is to motivate the inmate to prepare for his or her future, even when reentry is years away. At least 95% of all state prisoners are released from prison at some point, and this fact alone should be enough to justify the development and continuation of rehabilitative programs in the correctional environment.[19]

One might think that inmates generally have poor attitudes and are not motivated to prepare for or make a successful reentry to their home areas. However, research by the Urban Institute found that before release, most offenders expressed a strong desire to change and held positive attitudes, especially feelings of high self-esteem and control over life.[20] This evaluation confirms what correctional practitioners already know—that the vast majority of incarcerated inmates, if given the opportunity, will engage in self-help programs and work hard at improving their personal situations. Even the most difficult and challenging offenders are often interested in making productive use of their time while confined and find hope and excitement in solid institutional self-help programs.

Researchers have concluded that excellence in institutional leadership results in high-quality correctional operations; the quality of inmate care and security are in direct proportion to the quality of a facility's organizational and management practices.[21] These same factors have a huge influence on the ability of staff to positively influence inmates. Quality inmate program opportunities create a better institutional environment and lead to inmates who are statistically more likely to succeed when they return to their homes.[22] Inmate attitudes are improved by participation in programming, and the outcomes upon reentry are significant.

Methods of Release

Parole

The concept of parole began in the 1700s as a means of releasing military prisoners of war and first appeared in the United States in the 1800s. New York first authorized this reduction in time based on meritorious conduct and hard work. Over time, other states adopted this practice of releasing inmates back to the community under the threat that these same inmates would be returned to confinement if again caught in criminal acts.

As the correctional model shifted toward an emphasis on rehabilitation, indeterminate sentencing increased. According to this model, offenders were sentenced to a term of unspecified length, such as 4–8 years, with parole release after 4 years if the individual demonstrated good behavior, completed institution programs, and demonstrated a sincere desire to conduct himself or herself according to the law. However, as society lost faith in the capacity of rehabilitation and the effectiveness of subsequent parole release, state and federal laws shifted toward greater determinacy in sentencing. As such, parole has been discontinued in federal jurisdictions for all offenses that have occurred since November 1984.

Expiration of Sentence

Offenders who complete their entire term of confinement must, by law, be released to their home community or to the jurisdiction of the local area where they were originally sentenced. Inmates who have completed their entire term of confinement are typically released without the requirement of community supervision.

Halfway House

Regardless of whether an inmate is released by parole or by completion of his or her sentence, most correctional jurisdictions will attempt to place the offender in a halfway house for the last 3–6 months of the term of confinement. These supervised residential institutions allow the offender to decompress from the routine of a prison in a more gradual manner and give the inmate a place to reside as he or she transitions to freedom. Community halfway houses also assist inmates in finding employment and help them with other mundane but necessary tasks such as getting a driver's license. Some offer special assistance to deal with special situations such as drug problems or mental illness.

Aggravating Factors

Many inmates leaving correctional facilities have complex social and medical problems. Some have lengthy histories of mental illness, and many have serious and potentially debilitating medical concerns. Others report histories of drug and/or alcohol abuse, whereas many are functionally illiterate or have learning disabilities and have no plans or capability for meaningful employment. These factors are ample evidence that correctional personnel have a major responsibility to offer rehabilitative and retraining programs to inmates in their care. These programs must be made available to inmates early in their confinement and must be of sufficient number and quality to offer all inmates the opportunity to improve their futures.

It is important that correctional authorities target all offenders with program options, especially the more difficult and high-risk group of inmates. Research has demonstrated the efficacy of intervening with the neediest offenders early in their incarceration.[23] Policies and programs are necessary to ensure that the future of our public's safety is served by intervening with these offenders as early as possible.

■ Conclusion

Former U.S. Supreme Court Chief Justice Warren Burger once said, "We must accept the reality that to confine offenders behind walls without trying to change them is an expensive folly with short-term benefits—winning the battles while losing the war. It is wrong. It is expensive. It is stupid."[24]

Society has yet to realize that merely locking up offenders is a partial solution to the problem of crime. Serving time in prison is not adequate to rehabilitate offenders and may even interfere with reintegration and successful reentry. According to Ortmann, the prisonization process experienced by inmates during their incarceration prevents them from being rehabilitated while incarcerated.[25] Incapacitation is limited, and the results of it have a strong effect on both individual offenders and society. In fact, Elliot Currie argues that the tendency for incarceration to make some criminals worse is one of the best-established findings in criminology.[26] Yet there is strong evidence in support of prison-based treatment and rehabilitation.[27] Prison-based drug treatment programs, therapeutic communities, educational and vocational training, and faith-based programs all show promising results in terms of their effect on rehabilitation, reentry, and successful reintegration.

As such, policy makers should invest more resources in treating and rehabilitating offenders while they are incarcerated. This investment will help ease the process of reentry and provide released offenders with true opportunities to rehabilitate and reintegrate back into the normative noncriminal community as functioning members. Inside correctional facilities, reentry planning must commence early, at the intake stage, and be a guiding principle during confinement.

Today's challenging inmate has a very high chance of becoming tomorrow's failure as offenders legally exit the secure perimeters of correctional institutions. The task of correctional professionals is to use every possible means to turn the statistics in favor of each individual inmate's success and end the revolving door phenomenon. The safety and well-being of all our communities depend on it.

Chapter Resources

DISCUSSION QUESTIONS

1. How would you respond to a citizen who believes rehabilitative programs are a total waste of tax dollars?
2. What should serve as the primary goal of confinement: punishment or rehabilitation? Why?
3. When should planning for an inmate's release begin?
4. What impediments may be faced by released offenders in their effort to reintegrate back into society?
5. Former Supreme Court Chief Justice Warren Burger said, "We must accept the reality that to confine offenders behind walls without trying to change them is an expensive folly with short-term benefits—winning the battles while losing the war." Do you agree with this statement? Why or why not?
6. Discuss the difference between reentry and reintegration.

ADDITIONAL RESOURCES

American Correctional Association. (2006). *Reentry today: Programs, problems, and solutions*. Alexandria, VA: Author.

Prisoner Reentry Institute at John Jay College of Criminal Justice, http://www.jjay.cuny.edu/centersinstitutes/pri/pri.asp

Rehabilitation and Reentry, The National Institute of Justice, http://www.ojp.usdoj.gov/reentry/publications/inmate.html

Seiter, R. (2004, January/February). Inmate reentry: What works and what to do about it. *Corrections Compendium*, *29*(1), 33–35.

NOTES

1. Bureau of Justice Statistics. (2012). *Prisoners in 2011*. Washington, DC: U.S. Department of Justice. NCJ239808.
2. Petersilia, J. (2003). *When prisoners come home: Parole and prisoner reentry*. New York, NY: Oxford University Press; Krisberg, B., & Marchionna, S. (2006). *Attitudes of U.S. voters toward prisoner rehabilitation and reentry policies*. Retrieved May 9, 2007, from http://www.nccd-crc.org/nccd/pubs/2006april_focus_zogby.pdf; Travis, J. (2005). *But they all come back: Facing the challenges of prisoner reentry*. Washington, DC: The Urban Institute Press.
3. Austin, J. (2001). Prisoner reentry: Current trends, practices, and issues. *Crime and Delinquency*, *47*(3), 314–334.
4. Gideon, L., & Sung, H. E. (2011). Conclusion: Integrative triple R theory: Rehabilitation, reentry, and reintegration. In Gideon, L., & Sung, H. E. (Eds.), *Rethinking corrections: Rehabilitation, reentry, and reintegration* (pp. 399–407). Thousand Oaks, CA: Sage Publishing.
5. Petersilia, J. (2003). *When prisoners come home: Parole and prisoner reentry*. New York, NY: Oxford University Press; Travis, J. (2005). *But they all come back: Facing the challenges of prisoner reentry*. Washington, DC: The Urban Institute Press.

6. Commission on Safety and Abuse in America's Prisons. (2006). *Confronting confinement*. Washington, DC: Vera Institute of Justice.

7. Seiter, R. (2006). Inmates reentry: What works and what to do about it. In Clayton, S. L. (Ed.). *Reentry today: Programs, problems, and solutions* (pp. 77–90). Alexandria, VA: American Correctional Association.

8. Petersilia, J. (2003). *When prisoners come home: Parole and prisoner reentry*. New York, NY: Oxford University Press; Freeman, R. (2003, May). *Can we close the revolving door? Recidivism vs. employment of ex-offenders in the United States*. Urban Institute Reentry Roundtable; Travis, J. (2005). *But they all come back: Facing the challenges of prisoner reentry*. Washington, DC: The Urban Institute Press.

9. Walker, S. (2006). *Sense and non-sense about crime and drugs: A policy guide*. Washington, DC: The Urban Institute Press.

10. Petersilia, J. (2003). *When prisoners come home: Parole and prisoner reentry*. New York, NY: Oxford University Press.

11. Gideon, L., & Sung, H. E. (2011). Conclusion: Integrative triple R theory: Rehabilitation, reentry, and reintegration. In Gideon, L., & Sung, H. E. (Eds.), *Rethinking corrections: Rehabilitation, reentry, and reintegration* (pp. 399–407). Thousand Oaks, CA: Sage Publishing.

12. Tischler, E. Making a place of change. *Corrections Today*, 61(4), 74; Davis, C. (2000, December). *Education: A beacon of hope for the incarcerated. Enhancing public safety*. Washington, DC: U.S. Department of Justice Office of Community Oriented Policing Services. Retrieved May 9, 2007, from http://www.urban.org/UploadedPDF/411061_COPS_reentry_monograph.pdf

13. La Vigne, N., Solomon, A., & Beckman, K. (2006). *Prisoner reentry and community policing: Strategies for enhancing public safety*. Washington, DC: U.S. Department of Justice, Office of Community Oriented Policing Services. Retrieved May 9, 2007, from http://www.urban.org/UploadedPDF/411061_COPS_reentry_monograph.pdf; Petersilia, J. (2001). *Prisoner reentry: Public safety and reintegration*. New York, NY: Oxford University Press; Petersilia, J. (2003). *When prisoners come home: Parole and prisoner reentry*. New York, NY: Oxford University Press; Travis, J. (2005). *But they all come back: Facing the challenges of prisoner reentry*. Washington, DC: The Urban Institute Press.

14. McMullen, E. C. (2011). Seeking medical and psychiatric attention. In Gideon, L., & Sung, H. E. (Eds.), *Rethinking corrections: Rehabilitation, reentry, and reintegration* (pp. 399–407). Thousand Oaks, CA: Sage Publishing.

15. Prendergast, M., & Wexler, H. (2004). Correctional substance abuse treatment programs in California: A historical perspective. *The Prison Journal*, 84(1), 8–35.

16. Gideon, L. (2010). *Substance abusing inmates: Experiences of recovering drug addicts on their way back home*. New York, NY: Springer.

17. Cruz, R. (2008). *Discharge planning for incarcerated inmates*. Thesis submitted as part of the requirements for Masters of Art, New York, NY: John Jay College of Criminal Justice; also see Mellow, J., Mukamal, D. A., LoBuglio, S. F., Solomon, A. L., & Osborne, J. W. L. (2008). *The jail administrator's toolkit for reentry*. Joint report by the Urban Institute, Washington, DC; John Jay College of Criminal Justice, New York, NY; Bureau of Justice Assistance, Washington, DC.

18. Gideon, L. (2010). Drug offender's perceptions of motivation: The role of motivation in rehabilitation and reintegration. *International Journal of Offender Therapy and Comparative Criminology*, 54(4), 597–610.

19. Hughes, T., & Wilson, D. J. *Reentry trends in the United States: Inmates returning to the community after serving time in prison*. Washington, DC: U.S. Department of Justice, Bureau of Justice Statistics. Retrieved June 3, 2006, from http://www.ojp.usdoj.gov/bjs/reentry/reentry.htm

20. Visher, C., LaVigne, N., & Travis, J. (2004). *Returning home: Understanding the challenges of prisoner reentry. Maryland pilot study: Findings from Baltimore.* Washington, DC: The Urban Institute Press.

21. Carlson, P. (2004). Something to lose: A balanced and reality-based rationale for institutional programming. In Krienert, J., & Fleisher, M. (Eds.), *Crime and employment: Critical issues in crime reduction for corrections.* Walnut Creek, CA: Altamira Press; also see Gideon, L., Shoam, E., & Weisburd, D. L. (2010). Changing prison to therapeutic milieu: Evidence from the Sharon prison. *The Prison Journal, 90*(2), 179–202.

22. Gideon, L., Shoam, E., & Weisburd, D. L. (2010). Changing prison to therapeutic milieu: Evidence from the Sharon prison. *The Prison Journal, 90*(2), 179–202.

23. Lowencamp, C., & Latessa, E. (2004). Understanding the risk principle. In *Topics in community corrections.* Washington, DC: U.S. Department of Justice, National Institute of Justice.

24. Quoted in Petersilia, J. (2003). *When prisoners come home: Parole and prisoner reentry* (p. 93). New York, NY: Oxford University Press.

25. Ortmann, R. (2000). The effectiveness of social therapy in prison: A randomized experiment. *Crime and Delinquency, 23,* 591–601.

26. Currie, E. (2002). Rehabilitation can work. In Gray, T. (Ed.), *Exploring corrections: A book of readings.* Boston, MA: Allyn & Bacon.

27. Andrews, D. (1990). Does correctional treatment work? A clinically relevant and psychologically informed meta-analysis. *Criminology, 28*(3), 369–404; Cullen, F. (1985). Attribution, salience, and attitudes toward criminal sanctioning. *Criminal Justice and Behavior, 12*(3), 305–331; Gendreau, P., & Ross, B. (1987). Revivification of rehabilitation: Evidence from the 80s. *Justice Quarterly, 4*(3), 349–408; Greenwood, P., & Zimring, F. (1985). *One more chance: The pursuit of promising intervention strategies for chronic juvenile offenders.* Santa Monica, CA: U.S. Office of Juvenile Justice and Delinquency Prevention; Hamm, M., & Schrink, J. (1989). The conditions of effective implementation: A guide to accomplishing rehabilitative objectives in corrections. *Criminal Justice and Behavior, 16*(2), 166–182; Inciardi, J., Martin, S., & Butzin, C. (1997). An effective model of prison-based treatment for drug-involved offenders. *Journal of Drug Issues, 27*(2), 261–278; Lipton, D., Franklin, G., & Wexler, H. (1992). Correctional drug abuse treatment in the United States: An overview. In Tims, F., & Leukefeld, C. (Eds.), *Drug abuse treatment in prison and jails* (pp. 8–29). Rockville, MD: National Institute on Drug Abuse.

Creating the Future

YOU ARE THE ADMINISTRATOR
■ Change Ahead?

Correctional leaders and their employees face many challenges on a daily basis: personnel matters, inmate management issues, operational and support glitches, funding shortages, and changes in the local, state, national, and international environment. All successful practitioners in the field will have to consider every opportunity to do their jobs with open minds to new ways of taking care of business.

Put yourself in the shoes of Julie Albright, the warden of the high-security prison at Big Meadow. Would Warden Albright consider approving a procedure in which a prison computer is permitted to clear an evening count at her institution without staff reviewing the process? How about approving a camera as a stand-alone security system on the institution's fence line with no officers assigned to immediately respond to an alarm? Would the warden permit a software program to compute an inmate's sentence—and release date—without staff oversight?

Warden Albright could probably more easily envision flying a personal jet bike home than she could consider turning over such significant institution operations to a machine with artificial logic and intelligence. Is the warden an albatross or a throwback to the age of dinosaurs? No, probably not, but experience has taught her that important custodial processes require the expertise and knowledge of well-trained staff members.

Yet most correctional leaders have come to depend on technology to help us work more efficiently and more cost effectively. All correctional facilities are using computers to enhance staff members' work; few in today's workforce can remember the days before word processing replaced typewriters in the 1980s. Nearly all institutions use computers to track housing and work assignment changes today, and security devices help protect institutional personnel with their surveillance and tracking devices. New geographic information systems (GIS) let us visualize, analyze, interpret, and understand data to reveal relationships, patterns, and trends. These systems are very helpful in revealing weaknesses and highlighting areas of our institutions that may require more staff or electronic supervision.

Change, change, change! Institutional accountability and basic management principles must be the standard, but correctional personnel also must change with the times. If Warden Albright is unable to mesh new process with the tried-and-true methods of the past, she will not be demonstrating forward-thinking leadership. What will be your contributions to the field of corrections?

- How can Warden Albright—and each of us—know when new technology or any change will be safe and a positive move rather than a security or safety liability?
- How does a correctional leader establish an institutional environment that is receptive to new ways of operating a safe and secure facility?
- What are the obstacles to implementing a new approach to an important institutional procedure or process?
- Should a senior staff member involve line staff in the planning for the future? Why?

Restorative Justice

Dominick P. Ignaffo and
Lior Gideon

CHAPTER OBJECTIVES

- Understand the concept of restorative justice and its goals.
- Recognize the benefits of restorative justice as an alternative to revenge and retribution.
- Identify the benefits of restorative justice as part of the rehabilitation, reentry, and reintegration efforts.
- Outline possible impediments to reentry and treatment programs.

■ Introduction

The mission of corrections is to "carry out the sentence of the court" (p. 5–6).[1] However, many correctional administrators see a much broader mission of corrections, one that balances the needs of security and public safety with the desire to rehabilitate and reintegrate offenders back to society. Consequently, corrections is not just to administer court-ordered sentences and to punish offenders but also to correct offenders' behavior and by that repair the harm caused to society by his or her behavior, and thus allowing a returning prisoner the chance to reintegrate or earn back the responsibilities and privileges of citizenship.[2-5]

It is in this context that restorative justice gained renewed attention during the 1980s and 1990s, addressing the disappointment of many criminal justice scholars and policy makers from the way in which the criminal justice system deals with its offenders, victims, and the community. Under this approach, the equilibrium in society must be restored in order for the victim, his surrounding community, and the offender to get on with their lives. Using such a holistic approach, the *restorative justice movement* brought forth a philosophy of justice that focused more on the interrelationship among the offender, government, victim, and the community in cases involving delinquency and crime.[6] Restorative justice is a future-oriented approach[1] that focuses on preventive measures based on the assumption that the crime's origins are rooted in social conditions, and therefore, the response to criminality must take into account the social context of crime.[7] Consequently, there is a need to increase the role of the community in promoting changes that will monitor and prevent the conditions that lead to criminal behavior and the need for criminal justice intervention.

The principle components of restorative justice have traditionally been incorporated in the context of informal processing of first-time, nonviolent offenders; however, this traditional approach is shifting to include violent and high-risk offenders as well. The successful application of restorative justice practices has been the subject of criminological research for the past several years, with programs throughout the United States embracing the opportunity to provide state legislatures with the assurance that their funding resources are being used effectively to serve victims, offenders, and the community.

The promising outcome of restorative justice practices has been the subject of recent literature on its possible application during the process of prisoner reentry.[4,8,9]

■ The History of Restorative Justice

Most of the research indicates that restorative justice is a movement occurring worldwide in the past 30–35 years. In fact, the ideology of restorative justice has biblical roots. The Bible offers a different view of justice and love. Both are integral parts of God's character. God is a righteous judge (Psalm 7:7; 2 Timothy 4:8). At the same time, God is love (1 John 4:8). Followers of Jesus are asked to "act justly and to love mercy and to walk humbly with . . . God" (Micah 6:8) and to "love your neighbor as yourself" (Leviticus 19; Matthew 22:39).

Although not referred to as restorative justice, its principles were the dominant theme/model of criminal justice in Western countries before the 11th century and embedded in numerous indigenous cultures throughout the world. **Table 49-1** summarizes a list of countries and cultures that are known to use restorative justice principles as guidelines to their justice systems. For example, it is the dominant theme of African customary law, of the indigenous Maori culture of New Zealand, and of the aboriginal people of North America to use restorative justice ideology to solve disputes and to restore peace to their communities. Specifically, the countries and cultures given in Table 49-1 are built on the deep understanding that all things are connected and interconnected through relationships. Our current interpretations of justice, the rule of order, take priority over harm done. The state, rather than the victim, is the primary stakeholder, and the focus on guilt and punishment is rather recent.

It was after the Norman invasion of Britain that a major paradigm shift occurred, in which there was a turning away from the established understanding of crime as a victim–offender conflict in the context of

TABLE 49-1 **Indigenous Justice in Different Countries and Cultures: Practices That Express Restorative Values**

Afikop dispute resolution in Nigeria
Celtic Brehan Laws
Gacaca village courts in Rwanda
Hoho pono among Native Hawaiians
Lok Adalet mediation by village elders in India
Maori justice in New Zealand
Navajo peacemaker courts
Peacemaking circles among Native Americans and First Nations people of Canada
Sulha process among Arabs and Palestinians

community. William the Conqueror's son, Henry the first, issued a decree securing royal jurisdiction over certain offenses (robbery, arson, murder, theft, and other violent crimes) against the king's peace. This decree established that the fines that had been paid by offenders to their victims would now be paid to the state in the person of the king.[10]

To better understand restorative justice in its historical context, one must consider the alternatives, revenge and retribution, as these are the most natural reactions to crime. The most basic reaction to harm by another was to *retaliate* against the wrongdoer. This is the primitive and most pure reaction to crime. When society cannot protect its members from offenders, *revenge* becomes the most prominent type of behavior. However, society cannot function by letting its members react to crime on individual bases, as revenge can lead to a dreadful deadly spiral. As an alternative, *retribution*, or *lex talionas*, as stated in the ancient code of Hammurabi, became a more systematic approach to dealing with offenders, by declaring the price of the crime for everyone to see and know. Such an approach encourages rule of law and human rights. There exists a primal sense of pleasure or, in other words, provides people with the sense that justice is served. It also has weaknesses; this type of justice tends to be punitive, impersonal, focused on guilt and blame, and it discourages responsibility on the part of the perpetrators. While being heavy on punishment, it becomes mired in process (see **Figure 49-1**). This figure describes the current criminal justice system and the way

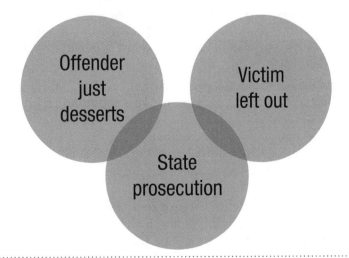

FIGURE 49-1 Traditional systems in criminal justice: Retribution model

in which it deals with offenders and criminals. As can be seen in the figure, there is no interaction between offender and victim, and the criminal justice system processes the information of both victim and offender to decide the punishment, which is, most times, retributive in nature. The state plays a major role and by that neutralizes the victim from the important equation; as a result, the offender does not face the consequences of his or her wrongful acts.

To overcome the barrier of both revenge and retributive models, an attempt was made to bridge offender and victim, whereas the criminal justice system provides the much-needed platform. Thus, restorative justice gained favor worldwide. Restoration is "essentially harm-focused, meaning that victims' needs and rights are central, not peripheral. People—not the state—are seen as the victims of the crime, and offenders are encouraged to understand the harm they have caused and to take responsibility for it".[11]

> *"Resentment is like drinking poison and expecting someone else to die."*
>
> Malachy McCourt

In other words, the focus on the individual and fostering communication among the victim, the offender, and the community become more visible. Variations on restorative justice show promise in navigating the differences between the therapeutic and retributive models of justice. See **Table 49-2**. Its advocates laud restorative justice's community-centered and cite statistics that demonstrate high victim satisfaction, reduced recidivism, and safer streets (http://www.sas.upenn.edu/jerrylee/RJ_full_report.pdf). In addition to statistical efficacy, advocates also claim that restorative justice approaches lead to an increased emphasis on personal accountability and thus empower individuals and communities to invest and identify solutions to community problems, while creating, affirming, and reaffirming community standards.

■ Different Definitions and Interpretations of Restorative Justice

Howard Zehr, one of the dominant figures in the restorative justice movement, offers the most succinct and accepted definition. According to him, "[r]estorative justice is a process to involve, to the extent possible, those who have a stake in a specific offense and to collectively identify and address harms, needs, and obligations, in order to heal and put things as right as possible" (p. 37).[12] Zehr further describes restorative justice as an "obligation to make things right. Justice involves the victim, the offender and the community in a search for solutions which promote repair, reconciliation, and reassurance" (p. 181).[11] Differently, Wolterstorff offers another insight into this model by defining it as "liberating justice; that is to say, one can seek to bring it about that the victim is freed from the injustice being perpetrated on him" (p. 175).[13]

Both definitions by Zehr and Wolterstorff place the victim at the heart of the process. This means that the harm done to the victim takes precedence and therefore guides the interaction between all key players. This does not mean that the victim controls the process but rather takes an active part in it. As per Umbreit and Armour,[14] restorative justice views accountability as central to the rehabilitation of offenders, while drawing upon the strengths of the offender and victim, and their ability to address the need to repair the harm caused.

As the scenario in **Box 49-1** and its corresponding link describe, first attention is given to the victim, second to the surrounding community, and then to the offender. **Figure 49-2** illustrates the restorative justice model, which focuses primarily on the victim. This is new thinking that shifts the attention from the offender to the victim and the community by emphasizing the damage done, and the need to address both the victim's and the community's needs.

TABLE 49-2 **Restorative Versus Retributive Justice: Summary**

	Retributive	Restorative
Crime	A violation of the law and the state	Violation of people and relationships
Violations	Create guilt	Create obligations
Justice	State determines blame community members in an effort to *punishment*	Involves victims, offenders, and *guilt*; imposes pain; identifies responsibilities; and promotes healing
Focus	Just desserts	Victim reparation, offender responsibility
Outcomes	Pain, suffering, harm by offender and victim, problem solving, harm to offender	Needs, obligations identified for both offender and victim, balanced by healing
	Offender and sometimes victim ostracized from community	Reentry for offender, victim made whole, both embraced and reunited by community restoration

BOX 49-1 WHO SHOULD BE THE FOCUS OF ATTENTION?

Dennis Maloney, former director of the Deschutes County Department of Community Justice of Oregon, confronted students of restorative justice with this scenario: A woman is assaulted and lying in the street. Her children and closest friends surround her. Observing this scenario, who should be the main focus? Who should be the focus next? Check the following link: http://www.youtube.com/watch?v=Y7MhQG5BiYQ to listen to the full scenario and explanation of the principle of restorative justice and the sense of justice.

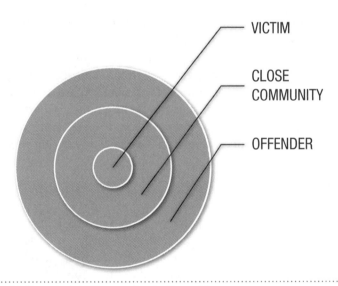

VICTIM

CLOSE COMMUNITY

OFFENDER

FIGURE 49-2 Restorative justice model: Conceptual shift from previous justice models

■ The Importance of Restorative Justice to Correctional Practice

As an approach, restorative justice can be applied to prevent crime by using mediation to resolve conflicts before they reach the threshold of criminal behavior. However, as discussed earlier, it is more often effective as an approach to repairing harm caused by crime while holding the offender responsible for his or her actions, and by providing an opportunity for the victim(s), offender, and community to identify and address their needs while seeking a resolution that affords healing, reparation, and reintegration, thus preventing future crime.

An example is the experience of the South African Truth and Reconciliation Commission (TRC), which was established to repair the pains of apartheid, which was characterized by violence and human rights abuses from all sides. The TRC was a court-like body assembled to address the needs of anyone who felt victimized. Perpetrators of violence could also give testimony and request amnesty from prosecution.

■ Recidivism

Overall studies have shown that introduction of restorative justice to the process of rehabilitation and reintegration results in reduction of recidivism. For example, Latimer, Dowden, and Muise[14] conducted a thorough meta-analysis of more than 25 years of literature on restorative justice and analyzed 22 studies to find that restorative programs were significantly more effective in reducing recidivism. Their findings are consistent with earlier analysis done by Bonta, Wallace-Capretta, and Rooney.[15]

In a study conducted in Belgium from 2001 to 2003, using a New Zealand model of conferencing for juvenile offenders, 58% of the juveniles in the stated time period who did not participate in conferencing were rearrested, whereas 22% of the juveniles who participated in the conferencing were rearrested. In other words, 78% of the juveniles who participated in conferencing did not recidivate.[16] These results are consistent with the findings of a more extensive research project by Maxwell and Morris conducted in New Zealand. Maxwell and Morris found a low recidivism rate (25%) for juveniles who completed conferencing. Further research by Hokwerda in the Netherlands found that restorative justice tends to have a strong positive effect on more serious crime—that is, the more serious the crime is, the more effective was restorative justice in reducing recidivism.

Four meta-analyses have addressed recidivism issues. Nugent, Umbreit, Winamaki, and Paddock in 2001 conducted a rigorous meta analysis of recidivism data reported in four previous studies involving a total sample of 1,298 juvenile offenders: 619 who participated in victim–offender mediation (VOM) and 679 who did not. The authors determined that VOM youth recidivated at a statistically significant 32% lower rate than non-VOM youth. Those who did reoffend committed less serious offenses than non-VOM youth.[14]

From the above, it is clear why restorative justice should be an integral part of any correctional practice aiming at reducing recidivism while promoting public safety. Consequently, restorative justice should be embraced by prison and jail administration as an essential strategy for treating offenders and preparing them for reentry and reintegration.

■ Forms of Restorative Justice

Restorative justice is a concept that takes many shapes. In its most basic form, restorative justice utilizes VOM. VOM is the oldest, most widely developed and empirically grounded expression of restorative justice dialogue. It provides interested victims the opportunity to meet the offender directly, in a safe and structured environment. The goal is to hold the offender directly accountable for his or her behavior while providing important assistance and compensation to the victim. These meetings occur with one or more mediators facilitating them. Eventually many of these programs morphed into victim–offender reconciliation programs.

Family group conferencing is another format widely used in juvenile restorative justice. In 1989, the New Zealand legislature passed a landmark act of Parliament. The Children, Young Persons, and Their Families Act made family group conferences (FGCs), not the courtroom, the hub of the youth justice system. Possible participants in FGCs include offenders, family members of the offender, police representatives, victims, victim representatives and supporters (including family members of their choice), and other advocates including nonadversarial lawyers. These groups have also been successful on the adult level.

Peacemaking circles are yet another variation of restorative justice derived from native traditions, and in particular those of native tribes in Canada. Circles can deal with various conflicts, including sentencing.*

Community reparative boards/victim impact panels are similar in nature and makeup. The main goal of these panels is for the offender to learn about the impact of crime on the community, make amends to the community, and learn ways to avoid reoffending. Panels are effective in communities that are experimenting or orienting themselves to the whole restorative justice process. They are usually made up of key individuals in the community, particularly people who have been victimized in the past. The current victim of the crime being addressed is often not a member of this panel, by choice. Otherwise members are similar to those on peacemaking conferences. Community reparation boards are particularly popular in Vermont.

■ Surrogate Dialogue Programs in Prisons

There is an emerging victim–offender dialogue occurring across American prisons regarding crimes involving severe violence. This proves to be quite effective and is victim initiated. Most restorative justice in-prison programs rely on prison-based ministries that aim to facilitate the offender's character transformation through the development of religious practice and/or moral orientation.[17]

In-prison programs are generally not used as tools to reduce recidivism. They are a means to empower offenders to take responsibility for their actions and make amends to victims and their communities. Because more than two-thirds of released prisoners reoffend within 3 years, these innovative programs promote successful transition and reintegration of offenders into the community.[14] One excellent example of such a program is Bridges to Life (BTL) in Houston, Texas. It operates in more than 20 prisons in Texas and has expanded to other states including Colorado, Mississippi, and Florida. BTL uses restorative justice models; basically, the goal is for victims to tell "their story" and explain how these crimes affected their lives.†

BOX 49-2 EXPERIENCE FROM THE FIELD

Teaching a class at a local inpatient drug treatment center in the northeast, one of the students approached me with a problem that was haunting him. He explained he was involved in a fight between two gangs, and he pushed from behind a member of the other gang onto the street and into a car. This occurred in such a way that the victim was severely injured and is now a paraplegic. The student wanted forgiveness; he wanted to tell the victim, who actually was a friend of his, how remorseful he was. The victim never knew who pushed him. My brain was flooded with suggestions. I wanted to tell the student all he could do to make reparations, but then I thought it is easy to give advice, to tell someone to do the right thing, but meaningless if it does not come from within. I ended up suggesting that he find a way to forgive himself, and he could start by figuring out what the victim needs. The student looked at me quizzically with pain in his eyes. It was the end of the semester, and I do not know what he did with the ideas I tried to plant; I am sure he would never stop using drugs, however, unless he pursued the path of forgiveness. Programs like BLT would have certainly led him and the victim on paths of restoration.

---

* For an excellent expose on peacemaking circles, see Mikaelsen, B. (2001). *Touching spirit bear.* New York, NY: HarperCollins; and Umbreit, M., & Armour, M. P. (2011). *Restorative justice dialogue.* New York, NY: Springer.

† Also see Blackard, K. (2005). *Restorative peace: Using lessons from prison to mend broken relationships.* Houston, TX: Bridge to Life Publishing.

■ Current Restorative Justice Practices in Prisons

Daniel W. Van Ness,[‡] executive director of the Centre for Justice and Reconciliation at Prison Fellowship International, has written about ways in which restorative justice might fit into the context of a prison.

One is when prisoners have decided that they want to find ways to make amends and to meet with their victims. A second is when leaders in correctional circles become champions of restorative justice (two good examples can be found in Canada and Minnesota). "Corrections" is a broader term than prison; it can include community-based sanctions such as probation and parole. A third is when those responsible for prisoner rehabilitation have discovered that it is necessary to deal with prisoners' responsibilities to those they have harmed as part of a process of reentry. The last is when victims of serious crime decide that they would like to meet with their offender.

> "*I have always found that mercy bears richer fruits than strict justice.*"
>
> Abraham Lincoln

Furthermore, Van Ness argues that restorative programs in prison may be categorized by their objectives[18]:

1. Some programs seek to help prisoners develop awareness and empathy for victims.
   a. The Focus on Victims program in Hamburg, Germany, helps prisoners think generally about victimization, consider people they know who have been victimized, reflect on their own experience of being victimized, and then look at the consequences and aftermath of victimization. It concludes with an introduction to VOM.[19]
   b. The Victim Offender Reconciliation Group, initiated by prisoners at the California Medical Facility, operates weekly meetings in which they invite various victim groups to make presentations and participate in dialogue.[20]
   c. There are other programs that organize conversations between prisoners and surrogate victims. The victim experience becomes real for prisoners who develop a relationship with victims, hear their stories, and reflect together on how crime affects their lives. The Sycamore Tree Project, run by Prison Fellowship in a number of countries, is an example of this.[18]

2. A second objective is to make it possible for prisoners to make amends to their victims.
   a. Belgium gives prisoners access to a fund that allows them to earn money by doing community work. The money is applied to restitution to their victim.[21]
   b. In other places, there is an emphasis on the community as an indirect victim. In New York, inmates have painted churches and constructed parks, particularly the foundation for the "fun forest," in Hyde Park, NY.

3. A third group of restorative programs is aimed at facilitating mediation between prisoners and their victims, their families, and their communities (Van Ness RJ in Prisons).
   a. The State of Texas, at the request of victims, facilitates meetings between victims or survivors and their offenders. There is a lengthy preparation process to ensure that the meeting will not result in secondary victimization.
   b. Communities can be fearful and angry at the prospect of prisoner reentry. In Zimbabwe, the Prison Fellowship affiliate acts as a facilitator in conversations between the leader of the prisoner's village and the prisoner related to the prisoner's return to the village.[18]

[‡] A paper presented at Symposium on Restorative Justice and Peace in Colombia, California (Colombia, February 9–12, 2005).

4. A fourth objective was set by the Restorative Prison Project in the United Kingdom to strengthen ties between prisons and the communities in which they are situated.[18] Strategies included public awareness activities, recruitment of volunteers to help in the prison, and negotiation of community service projects.[22]

5. The fifth objective is to create a culture in the prison in which conflict is resolved peacefully.

6. Lastly, the sixth and most ambitious objective is to create an environment in which the prisoner's entire self may be transformed (Van Ness). Cullen refers to this as a Virtuous Prison, where restorative justice and rehabilitation are combined in an effort "to foster 'virtue' in inmates, which is usually defined as 'moral goodness.' . . . There are standards of right and wrong and offenders must conform to them inside and outside of prisons. The notion of a virtuous prison, however, also suggests that the correctional regime should be organized to fulfill the reciprocal obligation of providing offenders with the means to become virtuous" (p. 268).[23]

■ Potential Obstacles to the Implementation of Restorative Justice

Implementing restorative justice inside correctional facilities is not an easy task. Introducing such methods requires a thorough understanding of the ideology behind restorative justice and the potential impediments that may accompany it in a restrictive environment, where the culture of both inmates and staff may impede proper dialogue. It cannot be said enough that before any correctional institution proceeds down the path of utilizing restorative justice programs, it needs to prepare the foundation, set meaningful goals, and prepare all participants as to what the goals are and what to expect. If a participant's personal agenda is at odds with the goals of the restoration, it is likely to backfire. For example, consider the following unusual example: A violent crime victim was invited to speak to the person who had shot and killed her fiancé with a stray bullet. Reluctantly, she attended the meeting and came away angrier than ever. She had no doubt the offender was disingenuous and was using the meeting in the hope of attaining early release. The victim's anger and revulsion for the system was revitalized and resulted in advocacy for the death penalty. But not many cases are offender initiated, and it is the victim's initiative to take part in such VOM sessions.

The office of probation and community corrections in Dutchess County, New York, successfully interacted with victims. The officers sought out their input on sentencing and were very aggressive and successful in the collection of restitution. They often required juveniles to write empathy letters to their victims in the hopes that this would cause them to seriously contemplate the harm they caused. Victims were welcome to read these, and many did. The Dutchess County probation officers also utilized VOM whenever it was possible and available through the local mediation center. Such practice had favorable results in terms of the victims expressing their hurt and emotional pain suffered by the criminal act. In addition, offenders acknowledged the harm caused to their victims and were able to develop a sense of accountability. Unfortunately, they failed in their efforts to organize a community board or victim panel.

■ Evaluation

No matter what a corrections agency decides to do, it should employ a victim survey, sent out to all victims, to measure the service provided. The agency or institution should be prepared to receive a heaping amount of criticism, especially at first, but this is beneficial because it can help the provider of victim services design a program around victims' needs in their respective communities.

> *"Without forgiveness there is no future."*
>
> Bishop Desmond Tutu

■ Conclusion

In conclusion, as can be seen, there are many opportunities and perils in introducing restorative justice to corrections and correctional settings. History and experience are proof that restorative programs can be of significant value to victims, their closest communities, and the offenders.

Nothing is more synonymous with justice than the pair of scales sign: a symbol of equilibrium and harmony, what should be the true aim of the criminal justice system—to restore peace and balance in society, while providing people with security. This is the true ideal of restorative justice, an ideal that regained momentum in recent years, and in the face of booming incarceration in the United States.

As mentioned in earlier chapters, incarceration rates in the United States had boomed over the past two and a half decades; such reliance on incarceration as the leading response to crime has proven to be of very little benefit to society because the costs of incarceration—both monetarily and socially—are tremendous and contribute very little to victims, offenders, and society as a whole. In fact, incarcerating first-time offenders may even increase their odds of becoming career criminals because very little is done to address their needs and the needs of victims and society. It is in this context that restorative justice models can benefit sentencing and correctional practices while promoting safer communities. Inviting victims to take an active part of the criminal justice process not only promotes the sense of justice but also enables the offender to face the true cost of his or her actions, which in turn is assumed to promote more accountability and social responsibility toward the victim and society by making amends. This method is also beneficial in terms of taxpayer money, because nonviolent low-risk offenders are expected to "make right" and restore the peace and harmony violated by their criminal act. Restorative justice thus becomes relevant in parole hearings, where the incarcerated offender faces his or her victim and pleads for forgiveness while presenting the victim with the progress he or she made during incarceration. It is also a place where the victim can rely his or her expectations from the correctional agency on how to deal with the offender in such a way that will better serve the goal of punishment while also bring the restoration of community peace one step forward. Restorative justice programs in jails and prisons are not tools to reduce recidivism; they are geared toward empowering offenders—an important step toward inmates taking responsibility for their actions and making amends to victims and their communities. Such responsibility and accountability are important parts of the rehabilitation process and of successful reintegration because they develop a sense of responsibility and accountability in people who may not have had them before.

Chapter Resources

DISCUSSION QUESTIONS

1. Discuss the differences between restorative justice, revenge, and retribution.

2. What form of restorative justice, as discussed in this chapter, is more adequate for adoption in prisons and jails? Why?

3. Consider the following scenario: A young child of about 10 years old shoplifts can of soda from a small neighborhood store. When his mother finds out about this, she drags her son to the store and makes him apologize and pay for the soda out of his allowance. The store owner accepts the apology. The child promises this would never happen again. What happened here? A crime occurred, but 911 was not called. Discuss the ramifications of the mother's course of action. In your opinion, was the mother's response adequate to the child's delinquent behavior? Who took responsibility for the wrongdoing?

4. In your opinion, should parole boards incorporate victims' input in their decision? Why or why not? Explain by using proper concepts discussed in this chapter.

ADDITIONAL RESOURCE

Restorative Justice Evaluation—Dennis Maloney, http://www.youtube.com/watch?v=el1OMxeSKU4

NOTES

1. Seiter, R. P. (2011). *Correction: An introduction* (3rd ed.). Upper Saddle River, NJ: Prentice Hall.
2. Maruna, S. (2006). Who owns resettlement? Towards restorative reintegration. *British Journal of Community Justice, 4*(2), 23–33.
3. Burnett, R., & Maruna, S. (2006). The kindness of prisoners: Strengths-based resettlement in theory and in action. *Criminology and Criminal Justice, 6*(1), 83–106.
4. Bazemore, G., & Maruna, S. (2009). Restorative justice in the reentry context: Building new theory and expanding the evidence base. *Victims and Offenders, 4*, 375–384.
5. Wilkinson, R. A., Bucholtz, G. A., & Siegfried, G. M. (2004). Prison reform through offender reentry: A partnership between courts and corrections. *Pace Law Review*, 609–629.
6. Dorne, C. K. (2008). *Restorative justice in the United States.* Upper Saddle River, NJ: Pearson/Prentice Hall.
7. Maiese, M. (2003). *The aims of restorative justice.* Retrieved August 9, 2011, from www.beyondintractability .org/essay/restorative_justice
8. Bazemore, G., & Boba, R. (2007). "Doing good" to "make good": Community theory for practice in a restorative justice civic engagement reentry model. *Journal of Offender Rehabilitation, 46*(1–2), 25–56.
9. Bazemore, G., & Erbe, C. (2004). Reintegration and restorative justice: Towards a theory and practice of informal social control and support. In S. Maruna & R. Immarigeon (Eds.), *After crime and punishment: Pathways to offender reintegration* (pp. 27–56). Portland, OR: Willan Publishing.
10. Johnstone, G. (2002). Restorative justice: Ideas, values, debates. New York, NY: Routledge.
11. Zehr, H. (1990). *Changing lenses: A new focus of crime and justice.* Scottsdale, PA: Herald Press.
12. Zehr, H. (2002). *The little book of restorative justice.* Beaverton, OR: Good Books Publishing.
13. Wolterstorff, N. (2011). *Hearing the call.* Devon, UK: William Publishing Co.
14. Umbreit, M., & Armour, M. P. (2011). *Restorative justice dialogue.* New York, NY: Springer Publishing Co.

15. Bonta, J., Roonery, J, & Wallace-Capretta, S. (1998). Restorative justice: An evaluation of the restorative resolutions. Retrieved August 6, 2013 from http://www.cehd.umn.edu

16. Vanfraechem, I. (2005). Evaluating conferencing for serious juvenile offenders. In E. Elliott & R. M. Gordon (Eds.), *New directions in restorative justice: Issues, practices, and evaluation.* Devon, UK: Willan Publishing.

17. Armour, M. P., Windsor, L. C., Aguilar, J., & Taub, C. (2008). A pilot study of a faith-based restorative justice intervention for Christian and non-Christian offenders. *Journal of Psychology and Christianity, 27(2),* 159-167.

18. Van Ness, D. (2005, February 9–12). *The practice of restorative justice in prison reform.* Presentation given at Columbia CA.

19. Hagemann, O. (2003). Restorative justice in prison? In L. Walgrave (Ed.), *Repositioning restorative justice* (pp. 221–236). Devon, UK: Willan Publishing.

20. Braithwaite, S., & Liebmann, M. (1999). *Restorative justice in custodial settings: Report for the restorative justice working group in Northern Ireland* (pp. 17–18). Restorative justice Ireland network. Retrieved August 9, 2011, from http://www.restorativejustice.org.uk/About_RJ/pdf/Restorative%20justice%20in%20custodial%20settings_Marian%20Liebmann%20and%20Stephanie%20Braithwaite.pdf

21. Newell, T. (2001). Responding to the crisis—Belgium establishes restorative prisons restorative justice in prison project. The International Centre for Prison Studies (p. 4). Retrieved August 9, 2011, from www.kcl.ac.uk/depsta/rel/icps/restorative_prison_paper4.doc

22. Coyle, A. (2001, May). *Restorative justice in the prison setting* (p. 10). Paper presented at the International Prison Chaplains' Association conference. Driebergen, Holland. Retrieved August 9, 2011, from www.kcl.ac.uk/depsta/rel/icps/restorative_justice.doc

23. Cullen, F. T., Sundt, J. L., & Wozniak, J. F. (2001). Virtuous prison: Toward a restorative rehabilitation. In H. N. Pontell & D. Shichor (Eds.), *Contemporary issues in crime and criminal justice: Essays in honor of Gilbert Geis* (pp. 265–286). Upper Saddle River, NJ: Prentice Hall.

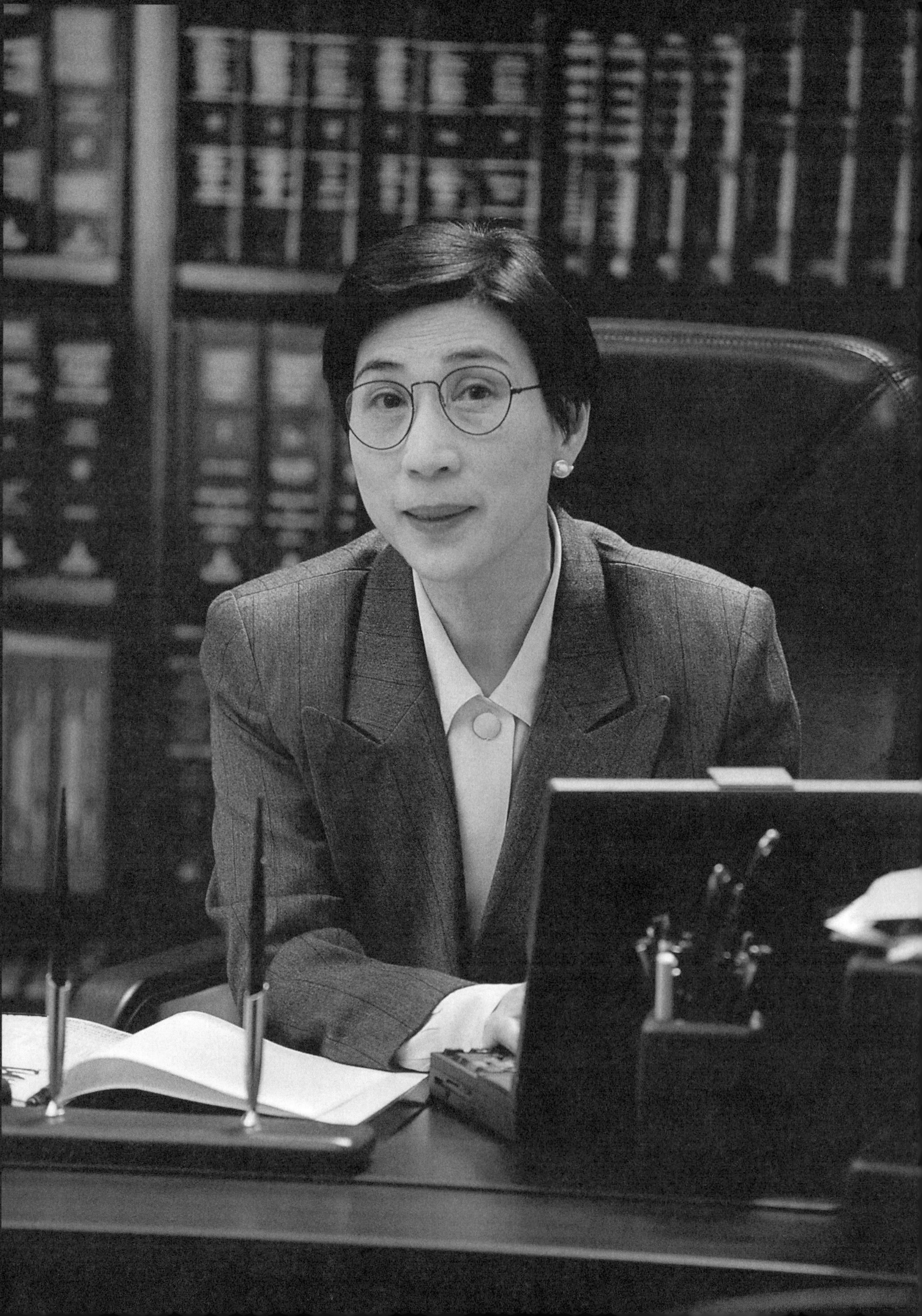

Sentencing and the Future

Phyllis J. Newton, Julius Debro, and Peter M. Carlson

CHAPTER OBJECTIVES

- Explain how sentencing in criminal cases has changed in recent decades.
- Differentiate between determinate and indeterminate sentencing and identify the benefits and drawbacks of each.
- Discuss the purposes of sentencing guidelines and the current legal status of guidelines.

Think about the criminal justice system. What role does sentencing play in that system? What impact does sentencing have on the system? Is the sentence reasonable or fair? Can the system be seen as impartial if the sentence is unfair? Does the judge (or court) determine what the sentence will be? What part does the public play in determining the sentence? What about the prosecution and lawmakers? Do they play a role in sentencing? In thinking about sentencing as part of the criminal justice system, then, the role it plays is neither simple nor straightforward. American society, legislatures, and the courts have struggled with determining the appropriate sentence or sanction since the early colonial period, and that struggle continues today.

The most public face of sentencing is the judge, who frequently laments, "Sentencing is the hardest job I have. I better be pretty sure I'm right." Historically, it has not always been the judge who determines the sentence or sanction for someone who has violated the law. In fact, the determining entity has varied depending on the period in history and the philosophy of punishment of the day. In the early years of American history, magistrates generally imposed sentences that included some form of public punishment often consisting of public humiliation, as with stockades. The young American legal system used the laws with which it was familiar—those they brought with them from England and Europe. As the United States became more urban and industrial, the theory of law and punishment adapted to societal demands and exigencies of the times. This adaptive practice in developing laws and meting out punishment consistent with societal desires and sensibilities has continued to the present day. See chapter 1 for a discussion of these historical practices.

Many factors play a role in the practice of sanctioning a person who has broken the laws of the state. The judge may impose the sentence, but the importance of the role of societal beliefs, legislative bodies, and happenstance cannot be overstated. Society and legislators are deeply affected by the shocking crimes committed around them and by those who commit those crimes and have definite opinions about the punishment those "criminals" deserve. When we think of a nefarious, harmful criminal act, such as a terrorist bombing of innocent people, a serial murderer preying on a city, or a rapist or child molester, we tend to want extreme punishments. On the other hand, we tend to be more lenient when we consider an appropriate punishment for white-collar offenders in which no one was "hurt."

■ Recognized Purposes of Sentencing

Throughout history, four purposes of sentencing have dictated the severity of punishment offenders receive: just punishment (retribution), deterrence, incapacitation, and rehabilitation. When imposing a sentence, judges generally adhere to one overriding purpose for the sanction; however, a judge may use multiple purposes of sentencing to underscore the seriousness he or she equates with both the offender and the criminal offense. In general, judges do not pronounce sentence based, consciously, on one of these principles but will recognize, in retrospect, that the sentence he or she imposed falls within one or more of these categories.

Just punishment or retribution looks back at the offense committed and the guilt or culpability of the offender. It addresses the need to reflect the seriousness of the offense and to promote respect for the law. As a purpose of sentencing, just punishment argues that the convicted offender should be punished for his or her criminal behavior commensurate with the seriousness of that behavior. The sanction, here, emphasizes the wrongful behavior, and the sentence is intended to overcome the bad effects or harm caused by the crime.

On the other hand, *deterrence* aims to keep the offender from committing future crimes (specific deterrence) and to discourage others from committing crime (general deterrence). Utilitarian theorists argue that people are intelligent and rational beings capable of comparing the relative costs and benefits of criminal behavior. In other words, people are able to weigh the utility of breaking the law. Deterrence in many ways defines classical criminology, and for sentencing purposes, the rational person can weigh the benefits anticipated from the criminal activity against the severity of the sanction should he or she be caught and determine whether he or she should commit the crime. Deterrence theory argues that if the sanction is sufficiently harsh, the rational person will not commit the crime.

Incapacitation addresses the need to protect the public from future crimes committed by the offender. The incapacitation purpose of sentencing calls for the removal of the convicted offender from the community and, thus, protecting society from his or her future criminality. If the offender is incapacitated behind prison walls, he or she is not able to commit crimes against the law-abiding public, resulting in enhanced public safety.

Rehabilitation came to the forefront of sentencing in the United States in the late 1800s and remained in vogue until the early 1970s, when questions began to arise about whether rehabilitative or reform programs had any positive effect on the convicted offender. In the United States, rehabilitation took the form of offering corrective programs to those convicted of harming others with the goal of returning improved individuals to the community following their terms of imprisonment. The rehabilitative programs came in many forms, including improving one's academic and/or vocational education, providing cognitive awareness by way of drug programs, improving one's English proficiency, counseling, anger management courses, or other means of assisting offenders to prepare for a successful and law-abiding transition back to their home communities.

■ Indeterminate Versus Determinate Sentencing

Hand in hand with the rise of the rehabilitative purpose of sentencing came indeterminate sentencing, that is, sentencing to imprisonment with no fixed term of years. Consistent with rehabilitation, the indeterminate sentence called for a sanction that allowed sufficient time for the convicted offender to be transformed (or according to the medical model, cured). Unable to know how long the cure would take, judges sentenced convicted offenders to an indeterminate sentence of incarceration that consisted of a range of years. The range could be from 1 year to life, meaning the offender had to serve a minimum of 1 year but could serve his or her entire life in prison. As long as a judge sentenced within a range consistent with criminal law, there were no rules to govern the amount of time a judge could impose. This structure allowed a person to serve, often, many years in prison without any knowledge of when he or she would be released.

Under indeterminate sentencing, an administrative parole board generally determined the amount of time a person served in prison. Theoretically, an offender would remain in prison until he or she was rehabilitated, and it was the parole board that determined whether rehabilitation occurred. In the early 1970s, academic research findings began calling into question the fairness of indeterminate sentencing and the appropriateness of continued sentencing under this imprecise system of sanctions. Serious questions were raised about disparity[1] in sentencing under an indeterminate sentencing system in which the judge imposed a sentence without stating his or her reasons for the sentence on the record. Other research findings raised serious doubts about the rehabilitative model and questioned its ability to rehabilitate offenders.[2] Sentencing reform advocates called for the abolishment of indeterminate sentencing, calling it ineffective, capricious, and discriminatory.[3]

Ultimately, the complaints about indeterminate sentencing led to an investigation by the U.S. Senate Judiciary Committee. The Judiciary Committee noted that indeterminate sentencing resulted in an outdated and unworkable model of rehabilitation, stating that

> *Recent studies suggest that this approach has failed . . . the rehabilitation model is not an appropriate basis for sentencing decisions. We know too little about human behavior to be able to rehabilitate individuals on a routine basis or even to determine accurately whether or when a particular person has been rehabilitated.*[4]

The results of this investigation served as a major setback for indeterminate sentencing and rehabilitation. And, in 1974, Robert Martinson and his colleagues dealt rehabilitation a severe blow from which it never recovered.[5] In response to the near-universal dissatisfaction with indeterminate sentencing, federal and state legislators turned to determinate sentencing, the polar opposite of indeterminate sentencing, as the answer to fairness in sentencing. Under determinate sentencing, the sentence a judge imposed was the time in prison an offender actually served. The days of uncertainty and waiting for an offender to be cured were over.

■ Sentencing Disparity

Sentence disparity can be warranted or unwarranted and can take various forms, for example, too harsh or too lenient. Warranted sentence disparity results, for example, when offenders convicted of the same offense receive disparate sentences because one offender played a more prominent role in the offense than the other. Similarly, offenders convicted of the same offense receive different sentences (warranted) because one offender had a vast criminal record, whereas this was the other offender's first offense. On the other hand, unwarranted sentence disparity occurs when similarly situated defendants convicted of similar offenses receive very different sentences. Under indeterminate sentencing, the reason for these very different sentences could not be determined, and research suggested that factors such as race, sex, and social class played a role in reaching these disparate sentencing decisions.[6]

After listening to a heated debate about the disparity in sentencing under an indeterminate sentencing structure, a federal judge suggested, only partially in jest, "If all judges would sentence the way I do, there would be no sentencing disparity." Under indeterminate sentencing, judges' sentencing decisions were made in a black box in which they were not required to state their reasons for imposing a sentence. Often in the mid-to-late 1970s and early 1980s, prosecutors and defense attorneys alike went in search of judges on whom they could count to impose a sentence to their liking. Commonly referred to as "shopping for judges," attorneys sought judges who imposed lighter or more severe sentences depending on the sentencing outcome desired.

Quite often, sentences imposed by judges were harsh and inconsistent.[7] Persons committing the same offense but appearing before a different judge could, and often did, receive vastly different sentences. Judge Marvin E. Frankel, often referred to as the father of sentencing reform, produced a series of journal articles published in the *University of Cincinnati Law Review* that deliberated the need for sentencing reform. In one such article, Judge Frankel concluded:

> *The evidence is conclusive that judges of widely varying attitudes on sentencing, administering statutes that confer huge measures of discretion, mete out widely divergent sentences where the differences are explainable only by the variations among the judges, not by material differences in the defendants or their crimes.*[8]

■ Sentencing Guidelines

The hue and cry over the unfairness and unwarranted disparity of indeterminate sentencing ultimately led to determinate sentencing and, in many jurisdictions, the establishment of sentencing guidelines. According to most legislators and sentence reformers, the major purpose of sentencing guidelines was to eliminate disparity and move away from rehabilitation as the goal for punishment. In some jurisdictions, the guidelines had also been used to limit prison population growth by tailoring sentences to prison capacity.

In the federal system, Congress sought to achieve three primary objectives in its efforts to establish a fair and just sentencing system.[9] First, Congress wanted to establish an effective and fair sentencing system—one that would avoid the confusion and uncertainty that arose under indeterminate sentencing. Second, Congress wanted a system that provided reasonable uniformity among sentences imposed for similar offenses committed by similar offenders. And, finally, Congress wanted proportionality in sentences whereby offenders would receive different sentences for criminal conduct of differing severity.[10]

In general, sentencing guidelines establish sentences based mainly on the severity of the offense and the defendant's prior criminal record. Many guideline systems across the country rely on a sentencing grid to determine a sentence that takes into account severity and prior record (see **Table 50-1**). In some states and in the federal system, judges can depart from the guidelines, but they must state their reasons for the departures on the record.

TABLE 50-1 Sentencing Table (in Months of Imprisonment)

Offense Level	Criminal History Category (Criminal History Points)					
	I (0 or 1)	II (2 or 3)	III (4, 5, 6)	IV (7, 8, 9)	V (10, 11, 12)	VI (13 or more)
Zone A 1	0–6	0–6	0–6	0–6	0–6	0–6
2	0–6	0–6	0–6	0–6	0–6	1–7
3	0–6	0–6	0–6	0–6	2–8	3–9
4	0–6	0–6	0–6	2–8	4–10	6–12
5	0–6	0–6	1–7	4–10	6–12	9–15
6	0–6	1–7	2–8	6–12	9–15	12–18
7	0–6	2–8	4–10	8–14	12–18	15–21
8	0–6	4–10	6–12	10–16	15–21	18–24
Zone B 9	4–10	6–12	8–14	12–18	18–24	21–27
10	6–12	8–14	10–16	15–21	21–27	24–30
11	8–14	10–16	12–18	18–24	24–30	27–33
Zone C 12	10–16	12–18	15–21	21–27	27–33	30–37
13	12–18	15–21	18–24	24–30	30–37	33–41
Zone D 14	15–21	18–24	21–27	27–33	33–41	37–46
15	18–24	21–27	24–30	30–37	37–46	41–51
16	21–27	24–30	27–33	33–41	41–51	46–57
17	24–30	27–33	30–37	37–46	46–57	51–63
18	27–33	30–37	33–41	41–51	51–63	57–71
19	30–37	33–41	37–46	46–57	57–71	63–78
20	33–41	37–46	41–51	51–63	63–78	70–87
21	37–46	41–51	46–57	57–71	70–87	77–96
22	41–51	46–57	51–63	63–78	77–96	84–105
23	46–57	51–63	57–71	70–87	84–105	92–115
24	51–63	57–71	63–78	77–96	92–115	100–125
25	57–71	63–78	70–87	84–105	100–125	110–137
26	63–78	70–87	78–97	92–115	110–137	120–150
27	70–87	78–97	87–108	100–125	120–150	130–162
28	78–97	87–108	97–121	110–137	130–162	140–175
29	87–108	97–121	108–135	121–151	140–175	151–188
30	97–121	108–135	121–151	135–168	151–188	168–210
31	108–135	121–151	135–168	151–188	168–210	188–235
32	121–151	135–168	151–188	168–210	188–235	210–262
33	135–168	151–188	168–210	188–235	210–262	235–293
34	151–188	168–210	188–235	210–262	235–293	262–327
35	168–210	188–235	210–262	235–293	262–327	292–365
36	188–235	210–262	235–293	262–327	292–365	324–405
37	210–262	235–293	262–327	292–365	324–405	360 to life
38	235–293	262–327	292–365	324–405	360 to life	360 to life
39	262–327	292–365	324–405	360 to life	360 to life	360 to life
40	292–365	324–405	360 to life	360 to life	360 to life	360 to life
41	324–405	360 to life	360 to life	360 to life	360 to life	360 to life
42	360 to life	360 to life	360 to life	360 to life	360 to life	360 to life
43	Life	Life	Life	Life	Life	Life

Source: United States Sentencing Commission, Guidelines Manual, Chapter Five, Part A (Nov. 2012).

Sentencing reform through determinate sentences and sentencing guidelines have taken many forms in different parts of the United States. Some states and the federal government have established sentencing commissions to develop and adapt sentencing guidelines as appropriate and consistent with state and federal law. Other states have established temporary committees to study the states' sentencing systems and write sentencing guidelines. Some guidelines are advisory, whereas others are compulsory. Some states have moved to descriptive guidelines designed to help judges follow more consistently existing sentencing norms.[11] Despite the variation, the goal for reform was the same: eliminate sentencing disparity and uncertainty by turning to determinate sentencing.

■ Mandatory Minimum Sentences

Registering similar dissatisfaction with indeterminate sentencing at about the same time as the proliferation of sentencing guidelines, legislatures across the country began enacting mandatory minimum sentences for offenses they deemed deserving of at least a minimal sentence of incarceration. While drastically expanding the breadth of offenses covered, mandatory minimum sentences enacted in the 1980s were not new to sentencing philosophy or practice in the United States. Throughout its history, Congress periodically enacted mandatory terms of incarceration for certain offenses, for example, introducing quite severe penalties in the Narcotics Control Act of 1956. In fact, as early as 1790, Congress began establishing mandatory sentences for capital offenses.[12]

Although the breadth and severity of mandatory minimum penalties in the federal system have garnered the vast majority of publicity and criticism, states began enacting mandatory minimum laws even before the U.S. Congress made its concerted effort to introduce mandatory minimum sentences on a broad scale in 1984 and 1986. In fact, by 1983, 49 of the 50 states had passed at least some mandatory minimum laws.[13]

Mandatory minimum penalties and sentencing guidelines had not been in effect long before conflicts between the two began to arise. This was true particularly in the federal system in which mandatory minimum sentences for drug trafficking offenses were based on the amount of drugs involved in the offense. Sentencing judges were offended by the harsh sentences they were required to impose under the mandatory minimum statutes, and some elected to retire rather than impose those lengthy sentences. Others sentenced according to the mandatory minimum requirements but voiced their displeasure on the record.

In its report to Congress,[14] the U.S. Sentencing Commission identified three principal ways in which the mandatory minimum sentences crossed purposes with the sentencing guidelines' ability to build and sustain a system designed to impose equitable sentences based on the totality of an offender's criminal conduct: (1) The guidelines were designed to provide proportional increases in sentence length based on additional acts committed in the course of the convicted offense. On the contrary, mandatory minimum sentences frequently called for very different sentences for criminal conduct in cases in which the conduct varied minimally one from the other. (2) By providing a single mandatory minimum sentence, the potential for individualizing a sentence based on characteristics of the offense and/or the offender was lost. (3) Perhaps most importantly, a mandatory sentence became available only when the prosecutor elected to charge and the defendant was convicted of a specific offense that carried the mandatory sentence penalty, shifting considerable discretion from the judge to the prosecutor.

In addition to the problems between the sentencing guidelines and mandatory minimum sentences, the U.S. Sentencing Commission's mandatory minimum report to Congress described disturbing results of its study on mandatory minimum sentences and sentencing disparity:

The disparate application of mandatory minimum sentences in cases in which available data strongly suggest that a mandatory minimum is applicable appears to be related to the race of the defendant, where whites are more likely than non-whites to be sentenced below the applicable mandatory minimum; and to the circuit in which the defendant happens to be sentenced, where defendants sentenced in some circuits are more likely to be sentenced below the applicable mandatory minimums than defendants sentenced in other circuits. This differential application on the basis of race and circuit reflects the very kind of disparity and discrimination the Sentencing Reform Act, through a system of guidelines, was designed to reduce.

Source: United States Sentencing Commission, Report to Congress: Mandatory Minimum Penalties in the Federal Criminal Justice System, Washington, DC: U.S. Sentencing Commission, 1991.

■ Role of the Prosecutor

One inadvertent outcome in the advent of sentencing guidelines and mandatory minimum sentences shifted sentencing authority from the judge to the prosecutor. In the American system of justice, the prosecutor has always enjoyed significant power in determining the ultimate outcome (sentence) that results from a defendant's conviction. Historically, the prosecutor has exercised almost unlimited discretion in deciding whether criminal charges should be brought against a defendant and what those charges should be, whether certain evidence should be introduced in court or not, and whether the defendant would be charged with an offense that carries a mandatory minimum sentence penalty or not. Under a guideline system, particularly the federal guideline system in which the judge is constrained by the guideline's sentencing recommendation, the shift in discretion from the sentencing judge to the prosecutor is even more pronounced.

Criticism raised against the freewheeling discretion of judges and their willingness to impose sentences within a black box has similarly shifted to the prosecutor. Prosecutor decisions as to charge and the nature of the charge are decisions made at the sole discretion of the prosecutor, without knowledge or recourse from anyone else. The result has been that critics of judicial discretion now have shifted and heightened their criticism of the prosecutor's discretion.

■ Courts and Sentencing Guidelines

The U.S. Supreme Court has made several rulings that have influenced significantly the use of federal and state sentencing guidelines in sentencing decisions. These decisions, generally, reduced the judge's sentencing discretion even under sentencing guidelines. In one case, *U.S. v. Booker*, in fact, the Court went further, requiring that the federal sentencing guidelines become voluntary.

The *Booker* decision has had mixed results on federal sentencing practices according to a study by the U.S. Sentencing Commission. The Commission found that "the sentencing guidelines have remained the essential starting point in all federal sentences and have continued to exert significant influence on federal sentencing trends over time."[15] Somewhat disturbing, however, the Commission found that regional disparities have increased and that "demographic characteristics are now more strongly correlated with sentencing outcomes than during previous periods," although the Commission is quick to note that it "does not suggest that this correlation indicates race or gender discrimination on the part of judges."[16]

The first influential U.S. Supreme Court decision with respect to sentencing involved a case in which the sentencing judge used facts that went beyond the scope of the plea bargain to sentence the defendant to a longer period of incarceration (see *Apprendi v. New Jersey*).[17] In this case, the defendant, Charles Apprendi, entered into a plea agreement with the state prosecutor, pleading guilty to unlawful possession of a firearm—an offense that carried a prison term of 5–10 years in New Jersey. However, the sentencing judge noted that as part of the offense, Apprendi had fired several shots into the home of an African-American family in an effort to convince them to move from his neighborhood. The sentencing judge deemed this action a hate crime and used sentencing enhancement procedures to add to Apprendi's sentence of confinement.

The U.S. Supreme Court overturned the judge's decision, ruling that a judge may not impose an enhanced sentence based on facts that were not included in the plea bargain. The Court determined that the lower court had erred in applying sentencing enhancements based on aggravating factors that were not findings of fact from a jury or admitted by the defendant and that this violated the due process requirements of the Fifth Amendment and the jury guarantees of the Sixth Amendment.

In a second notable case, *Blakely v. Washington*,[18] the U.S. Supreme Court again ruled against a sentencing enhancement called for by the sentencing judge. In this case, Ralph Howard Blakely, an estranged husband, kidnapped his wife and transported her in a wooden box in the back of his pickup truck from her home in the state of Washington to Montana. Blakely ordered their teenage son to follow in a separate car, threatening to shoot his mother if he did not comply. While traveling, the teenager managed to notify the police, and Blakely was arrested. He subsequently pleaded guilty to kidnapping, which carried a maximum sentence of 53 months under Washington state sentencing guidelines.

However, the judge departed from these guidelines and sentenced Blakely to 90 months, based on a belief that Blakely's offense was deliberately cruel. Upon appeal, the U.S. Supreme Court found that the facts in support of Blakely's enhanced sentence were neither admitted by the defendant nor found by a jury and, therefore, violated the defendant's right to a jury as guaranteed under the Sixth Amendment of the Constitution.

Finally, the U.S. Supreme Court ruled in *U.S. v. Booker* and *U.S. v. Fanfan*[19] (2005) that the U.S. sentencing guidelines were unconstitutional as applied and that the problem could be remedied only by making the guidelines voluntary for federal judges.[20,21] In *U.S. v. Booker*, a federal judge added time to the offender's sentence based on "additional facts by a preponderance of the evidence." The U.S. Supreme Court ordered the judge to either sentence within the guidelines or hold a separate sentencing hearing before a jury. In *Fanfan*, the federal sentencing judge, mindful of the *Blakely* decision, concluded that he could not impose an enhanced sentence. The government appealed this decision, but the Court sided with the judge, concluding that the Sixth Amendment, as construed in *Blakely*, applies equally to federal sentencing guidelines.

■ Current Issues in Sentencing

Today, we have come full circle in terms of sentencing philosophy; that is, legislatures now are seeking sanction methods that do not involve long prison sentences. Many proponents of the "tough on crime" era of the past 30 years have come to realize that offenders sentenced to very long imprisonment terms eventually leave prison and return to society. After so many years in prison, the transition back to society can be difficult (e.g., family changes, lack of jobs, and housing problems). Another important realization for these advocates has been the effect of mandatory minimum and long determinate sentences on prisons that were not built to house the burgeoning inmate population.

America's rate of incarceration is the highest in the world. The "get tough on crime," determinate sentencing, and sentencing guidelines of the past three decades have led to a massive increase in U.S. jail and prison populations. By 2011, the number of prisoners under the jurisdiction of state and federal correctional authorities was 1,598,780.[22] However, there is some indication that the upward trend in prison populations has begun to reverse. The Bureau of Justice Statistics reports that 26 state departments of corrections reported decreases in their prison populations in the past 3 years. As witness to the shifting sentencing philosophy, state prison populations have begun to decline; however, the Federal Bureau of Prisons continues to report federal population increases.

One of the promising developments that has accompanied the nascent shift in sentencing philosophy is the use of research to identify evidence-based practices/programs to which the criminal justice system can turn for guidance as it addresses the issues that arise as a result of this shifting philosophy. The influence public sentiment, particularly outrage, has on sentencing practices will not end, but the turn to evidence offers hope that new solutions will be scientifically based and rationally implemented.

■ Conclusion

In our ever-changing society, sentencing reform often appears to be a permanent fixture associated with the criminal justice system. From the colonial period to the present, America has been in the business of trying to figure out how best to sanction individuals who commit crimes against society (and individuals). Although the public generally focuses its ire on judges who are "soft on crime" or want "to lock everyone up," the underlying crux of its concern is sentencing.

Sentencing practices mirror societal beliefs, and as society's views change, so do the rules that apply to sentencing. Sentencing reform, then, becomes chronic, with ebbs and flows in purpose and severity that correspond with societal norms of the day. In addition, as economic conditions in this country remain uncertain, state legislatures and the federal government are forced to consider adopting sentences that do not involve incarceration. States, primarily, do not have the funds required to imprison the number of offenders sentenced to incarceration. Budgetary cuts have forced some states to close some of their prisons because they cannot afford to run them anymore. Other states have come under federal consent decree because of the severe overcrowding in their prison facilities.

As mentioned earlier, 26 state departments of corrections reported decreases in their prison populations in the past 3 years. Although there are undoubtedly many causes for this decline, much results from states' reconsideration of the mandatory minimum penalties and the severity of their sentencing laws. For example, California voters have defeated the state's "three strikes" law, arguing that this sentencing rule was indiscriminately adding extremely lengthy prison sentences and flooding an already overcrowded prison system. In addition, the mandatory sentences associated with the war on drugs have lost some momentum as voters in Washington and Colorado voted to legalize marijuana in 2012. And finally, the cost of confining offenders—many offenders—has begun to hit home as states have struggled to pay for prisons and jails.

Sentencing rests at the heart of the criminal justice system but often is overlooked for the important role it plays. The general public, policy makers, and scholars often think of the criminal justice system as police, courts, and corrections. In this era of American concerns about criminal behavior and public safety, sentencing influences the police as they make arrests, prosecutors as they determine whether and what to charge, courts as judges deliberate and impose appropriate penalties, and corrections as it faces increasing and decreasing numbers of inmates entering and exiting correctional facilities.

Chapter Resources

DISCUSSION QUESTIONS

1. What are the primary differences between determinate and indeterminate sentencing?
2. What are sentencing guidelines, and why were they created?
3. How can the problems with sentencing guidelines be resolved?
4. Why were determinant sentencing structures enacted?
5. What are some of the problems attributed to determinate sentencing?

ADDITIONAL RESOURCES

Families Against Mandatory Minimums, http://www.famm.org

The Sentencing Project, http://www.sentencingproject.org

United States Sentencing Commission, http://www.ussc.gov

NOTES

1. See, for example, Clancy, K., Bartolomeo, J., Richardson, D., & Wellford, C. (1981). Sentence decision-making: The logic of sentence decisions and the extent and sources of sentence disparity. *The Journal of Criminal Law & Criminology, 72*(2), 524–554; Wheeler, S., Weisburd, D., & Bode, N. (1982). Sentencing the white-collar offender: Rhetoric and reality. *American Sociological Review, 47*(5), 641–659; Diamond, S., & Ziesel, H. (1975). Sentencing councils: A study of sentence disparity and its reduction. *University of Chicago Law Review, 43*(1), 109–149; Chiricos, T. G., & Waldo, G. P. (1975). Socioeconomic status and criminal sentencing: An empirical assessment of a conflict proposition. *American Sociological Review, 40*, 753–722; Clarke, S. H., & Koch, G. G. (1976). The influence of income and other factors on whether criminal defendants go to prison. *Law and Society Review, 11*(1), 59–92; Gibson, J. L. (1978). Race as a determinant of criminal sentences: A methodological critique and a case study. *Law and Society Review, 12*, 455–478; and Lizotte, A. J. (1977). Extra-legal factors in Chicago's criminal courts: Testing the conflict model of criminal justice. *Social Problems, 25*(5), 564–580.
2. Martinson, R. (1974). What works? Questions and answers about prison reform. *The Public Interest, 35*, 22–54.
3. Chambliss, W. J., & Seidman, R. B. (1971). *Law, order, and power*. Reading, MA: Addison-Wesley Publishing Company.
4. Reform of the Federal Criminal Laws: Hearing Before the Subcommittee on Criminal Laws and Procedures of the Senate Judiciary Committee, 92d Congress, 1st Session, 1971.
5. Martinson (1974) concluded that very few rehabilitative programs operating in this country, in fact, work, and existing methods of rehabilitation offer little support of our ability to positively change offenders.
6. See footnote 1 above.
7. Katz, L. (1980). *The justice imperative: An introduction to criminal justice* (p. 32). Cincinnati, OH: Anderson Publishing Company.
8. Frankel, M. (1972). Lawlessness in sentencing. *University of Cincinnati Law Review, 41*(1), 1–54.

9. Many of the state legislatures used the same objectives in developing their sentencing schemes, although often stated somewhat differently.

10. United States Sentencing Commission. (1991). *The federal sentencing guidelines: A report on the operation of the guidelines system and short-term impacts on disparity in sentencing, use of incarceration, and prosecutorial discretion and plea bargaining.* Washington, DC: Author.

11. Fraser, R. (1993). Prison population growing under Minnesota guidelines. *Overcrowded Times, 4*(1), 10–12.

12. United States Sentencing Commission. (1991). *Report to Congress: Mandatory minimum penalties in the federal criminal justice system.* Washington, DC: Author.

13. United States Sentencing Commission. (1991). *Report to Congress: Mandatory minimum penalties in the federal criminal justice system.* Washington, DC: Author.

14. United States Sentencing Commission. (1991). *Report to Congress: Mandatory minimum penalties in the federal criminal justice system.* Washington, DC: Author.

15. U.S. Sentencing Commission. (2012). *Report on the continuing impact of United States v. Booker on federal sentencing.* Washington, DC: Author.

16. U.S. Sentencing Commission. (2012). *Report on the continuing impact of United States v. Booker on federal sentencing.* Washington, DC: Author.

17. *Apprendi v. New Jersey,* 530 U.S. 466 (2000).

18. *Blakely v. Washington,* 542 U.S. 296 (2004).

19. *U.S. v. Fanfan,* 25 S.Ct. 738 (2005).

20. United States Sentencing Commission. (1991). *Report to Congress: Mandatory minimum penalties in the federal criminal justice system.* Washington, DC: Author.

21. *Blakely v. Washington,* 542 U.S. 296 (2004).

22. Carson, E. A., & Sabol, W. J. (2012, December). *Prisoners in 2011.* Washington, DC: U.S. Department of Justice, Bureau of Justice Statistics, NCJ 239808.

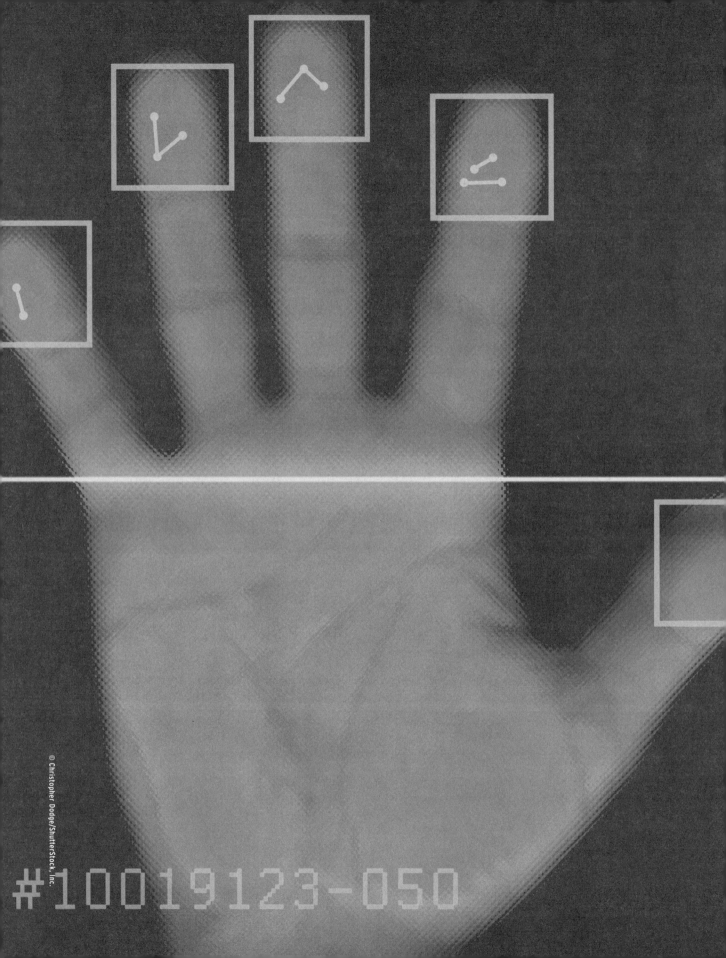

#10019123-050

Developing Technology

CHAPTER 51

Peter M. Carlson and
Sonya Thompson

CHAPTER OBJECTIVES

- Examine technological developments in the field of corrections.
- Outline concerns about new technology and institutional security.
- Grasp implementation techniques to increase the acceptance of new technology.

Just as technology can be used to enhance people's daily lives, it can be used in correctional settings to aid staff in performing their jobs, rehabilitate inmates, and protect society. Yet, in the past, prisons and jails have not demonstrated an affinity for change because of increasing concerns about security. Prison and jail administrators must learn to appreciate the benefits of new technology in the correctional setting and find ways of developing and implementing this technology that further the overall goals of their institutions.

■ Development of New Technology

Most criminal justice agencies are struggling to do their work in the face of burgeoning inmate populations and increasingly stark budgets in support of the daily institution operations. Correctional practitioners are striving to do more with less, and new technology and automated processes can allow staff to cover more ground in an age of dwindling resources. Like it or not, today's leaders in prisons and jails must leverage technology to enhance productivity.

Despite the reticence about new concepts, the corrections field has undergone as much technological change as any other business or industry in the United States and the world. Daily prison and jail routines are very different today than they were just a few years ago.

Many new technologies used in corrections have been adapted from applications developed by the National Aeronautics and Space Administration (NASA) and the Department of Defense.[1] Agencies like the National Institute of Justice (NIJ) have been working at this adaptation since 1989. NIJ's National Law Enforcement and Corrections Technology Center has been a major force in bringing the research community together to offer affordable, market-driven technologies to work in state and federal prison systems.[2] Many military innovations have proven to be very adaptable to the prison and jail setting, including less lethal chemical weapons, contraband detection, and identification verification equipment.

Information Management Systems

Information management systems and computers have transformed many aspects of correctional facilities. Computers monitor many aspects of institutional life, ranging from tracking actual inmate counts to status reports on open security doors. They can alert staff to problems, help track and order supplies, and manage documentation. With computers, correctional institution staff can monitor inmates throughout their confinement and easily access information on an individual prisoner, a specific institution, or the entire correctional system. The advent of new technologies has increased availability of systemic information and efficiency in many aspects of prison and jail administration.

One of the best uses of technology in a correctional environment is the electronic management of inmate data. Depending on the size and complexity of the system, almost all aspects of an inmate's confinement can be managed, modified, and controlled through an information system. For example, an inmate's housing assignments can be tracked and monitored to ensure that he or she is not confined with persons who are potential victims or potential threats. Similarly, inmates' disciplinary records, program and work assignments, educational needs, and medical needs can be managed through an information management system. Using such a system yields many benefits, because staff can access updated information and make real-time operational decisions. Additionally, in this centralized system, information travels with inmates as they move throughout the correctional system, and multiple members of inmate management teams can share and coordinate activities more easily. This information can also be shared with other law enforcement agencies to conduct criminal investigations or monitor intelligence.

After the terrorist attacks of September 11, information-sharing initiatives have become a necessity. Many individual states have coordinated data sharing among their own state agencies with the support of the Justice Technology Information Network (JUSTNET); in other instances, states are developing and using federal or regional information-sharing initiatives to share data among regional, state, and federal law enforcement entities.[3] Although these systems may be more difficult to develop and manage (because each participating agency wants a specific configuration and list of access and distribution), benefits are numerous:

- More data available that are shared across agencies;
- Encourages sharing of other types of communications;
- Shared costs, which helps smaller agencies gain access to information they would otherwise not be able to see.

Information systems may also interface with outside civilian agencies such as medical contractors and court systems. To ease information exchange, information systems should be built using commonly accepted protocols and standards so that systems owned by different organizations can exchange data using standardized specifications and interoperate. For example, the National Information Exchange Model (NIEM)—developed by the U.S. Department of Justice, Department of Homeland Security, and Department of Health and Human Services—is a set of standards and processes designed to facilitate information exchanges across disparate agencies, particularly in the event of an emergency.[4]

The availability of information to the public sector has also been enhanced by the proliferation of computers and the expansion of Internet resources. For example, the public can view the names of violent inmates soon to be eligible for release and contact the state division of parole to comment on an inmate's bid for parole. Victims may use computerized services such as the Victim Information and Notification Everyday (VINE) network to get up-to-date information about custody status, bond status, and court dates of convicted offenders. Geographic information systems (GIS), regularly used in community settings, are also making their way into correctional settings to chart locations of assaults, review offender demographics, and track offender movement.[5]

Prisoner Identification

Prisoner identification has also been enhanced greatly by the development of new technology, which in turn increases institutional security and efficiency. From facial, iris, and voice recognition equipment to the expedited capture and verification of finger and palm prints, technology is helping update prisoner identification, processing, and tracking throughout correctional facilities. Additionally, mobile barcode scanning and radio frequency identification (RFID) tagging equipment allows staff to inventory, record, and track facility and inmate personal property.

As mentioned earlier in the chapter, real-time tracking of inmates is also now available to monitor the physical location of inmates within a correctional facility. Such tracking is available through a radio-signaled wristbands or barcoded armbands so that reporting is made to receptors located throughout the prison. Using such a system, inmates and staff members can be recognized and tracked individually. In the event of an emergency, this type of system allows personnel to retrieve and identify all offenders who were in the area at the time of the incident. If an inmate attempts to tamper with the tracking device, the system notifies staff.[6]

Perimeter Security

Technology has improved perimeter security systems to lessen the likelihood of escapes; such technology includes the use of motion detectors, less lethal electric fences, visual surveillance, and entrance and exit monitoring systems. This technology enhances staff ability to monitor fence lines, institution boundaries, and other secure areas.

MOTION DETECTORS. Motion detectors can monitor an institution's perimeter for unauthorized movement. Historically, the probability of detection (increased sensitivity of the sensor) led to false alarms, but through advanced digital signal processing, today's adaptive sensors can detect moving targets based on size or mass and movement to minimize false alerts. Intelligent video motion systems can be configured to alert if inmates stray into prohibited areas or zones or focus the image on a specific field of view to minimize alerts about minor activity. Additionally, these systems can be integrated with electronically measured perimeter lighting such that lights come on or brighten when an intrusion is detected.

ELECTRIC FENCES.   Electric fences are exceptionally effective means of deterring escape attempts. These fences offer the opportunity to cut back on staffing in towers and external mobile patrols. They function by sending a nonlethal shock to anyone attempting to cut, climb, or tamper with the fence. Attempts to tamper or short-circuit the fence also generate an alarm. Fencing can be partitioned by zones to indicate the attempted breach point. Because some of these fences may inadvertently injure or kill birds and other wild animals, special netting can be installed, which allows the lethal fences to protect the perimeters and keep wildlife off the electrical grids.

VISUAL SURVEILLANCE.   Closed-circuit television (CCTV) has been a great technological addition to staff supervision in correctional environments. Most secure facilities have used camera supervision to monitor and record inmate visiting rooms to help supervise the areas and help prevent drugs or other contraband from entering the institution. Intelligent CCTV can also be used to determine whether suspicious objects are being placed at or over fence lines for retrieval by inmates. Monitoring can be accomplished from remote stations, giving management the ability to add to the duties of some posts. High-security penitentiaries have found that cameras in cell houses, dining rooms, recreation areas, and work production zones have a positive effect on the level of violence. Video recordings have also been very effective in subsequent prosecutions of those inmates who choose to assault others under the eye of the camera. Formerly stored as analog recordings, video surveillance can now be transmitted through a network and stored digitally on network digital video recording units. This process allows for greater amounts of data to be stored in less space. It also provides additional features such as remote management of cameras, email notification of system events and alerts, and remote, offsite viewing of high-resolution video. Staff members also appreciate the additional sense of security provided by the presence of the cameras.

ENTRANCE AND EXIT PROCEDURES.   New technologies also focus on perimeter security by monitoring points of ingress and egress by the use of

- Identification cards with magnetic barcodes or smart chips
- Voice, facial, iris, and fingerprint scanners and readers
- Heartbeat detectors in vehicle sallyports (detects the heartbeat of an intruder or escaped inmate who may be hiding in the vehicle)
- X-ray screening (newer models create a profile of metal content per inmate [surgical pins, unremoved bullets, etc.] so as to alert if the content changes [e.g., because of the introduction of a smuggled knife or shank])
- Drug-detection screening systems (screens for the scent or trace of up to 40 different explosives or narcotic substances on visitors' clothing or bodies)

More recent technologies such as whole-body imaging scanners, which use ionizing radiation, have made their way from private sector space, such as airports, to corrections.[7] These technologies are used to detect concealed objects on or inside an inmate's person and are helpful for detecting nonmetallic objects that X-ray machines cannot.

Inmate Programming

Because many inmates often come to prison with little education, minimal exposure to computers, and few job skills, inmate programming that teaches about technology and computer skills can greatly ease reintegration. Proficiency in basic computer skills such as word processing and data entry can make inmates more marketable for entry-level jobs. Some corrections systems partner with private companies and employ inmates in computer-based jobs, including responding to customer assistance calls, data quality assurance, and directory assistance. Apprenticeships and vocational training programs may provide an opportunity for inmates to use sophisticated information systems, including computer-assisted drafting and desktop publishing. Training opportunities can be made available to inmates at minimal cost thanks to computer labs outfitted with donated or recycled computers. In almost all instances, computer-based training for inmates is offered with tight security controls (e.g., no Internet or cross-network access, no access to sensitive or personal information, no administrative rights to install software) to prevent illegal or inappropriate behavior. Studies have shown that inmates who participate in educational and vocational training programs or prison industry jobs have a lower recidivism rate than inmates who do not.[8]

Medical Services

Management of inmate medical records is a substantial challenge for many corrections departments, particularly large systems where inmates transfer to many different institutions during their terms of incarceration. The use of electronic medical records in prisons allows healthcare providers to concentrate their limited resources on treating inmates rather than locating files, taking down histories, and requesting redundant lab tests. Many available electronic medical record systems allow providers to input information about the patient during the visit, thereby increasing the likelihood that the information is accurate and complete. This information can then be made available to all subsequent treating practitioners, even if the inmate transfers institutions, thus minimizing mistakes and opportunities for inmates to manipulate the system. Adding a pharmacy component to such a system that tracks prescribed and dispensed medications can also be a very useful enhancement.

Advancements in digital imaging and data transmission have enhanced the provision of medical care in prisons by allowing for remote diagnosis and treatment of various conditions in specialties ranging from radiology to psychiatry to orthopedics. Specifically, this technology allows medical staff, or even the patient, to view records that may be located thousands of miles away, thereby avoiding the costs and security concerns associated with transporting inmates to community hospitals or prison medical facilities for care.

Crisis Management

Emergency response equipment has improved significantly in recent years. Nonlethal—or more appropriately, less lethal—weapons are now the first level of response in crisis situations thanks to advances in technology. These include stun guns, chemicals (pepper spray, tear gas, and stink bombs), distraction devices (flash bangs, laser dazzlers, and bright lights), and blunt force projectiles, instead of firearms. Additionally, directed energy devices—used by the U.S. military—are being evaluated for use in corrections. Such devices can emit a focused beam of millimeter wave technology to repel individuals without injuring them.[9] Overall, less lethal technology reduces risk of harm to staff and inmates during crisis management.

Cell Phone Detection and Management

An increased focus of technology in prison is related to the prevention of contraband cell phones in prison. Inmates have used smuggled cell phones to plan escapes, continue criminal enterprises, or threaten witnesses. Such phones are often introduced into the facility by visitors, contractors, or corrupt

Courtesy of the Metropolitan Detention Center, Guaynabo, Puerto Rico.

Metal detectors are routinely used in prison and jail facilities to prevent the movement of serious contraband, such as a knife, from being transported into or within the institution. This photo depicts a scanner at the front entrance sallyport of the Federal Bureau of Prison's Metropolitan Detention Center, Guaynabo, Puerto Rico.

staff. Several jurisdictions, including the federal government, have either passed or are considering legislation making it a specific crime for an inmate to possess a cell phone in prison.[10] In light of this increased focus, three types of technology are emerging as preferred methods to combat contraband cell phones:[11]

- *Managed access systems:* These systems intercept communication between the cell phone and the cell tower and reroute it to a managed access base station for potential retransmission to the commercial outside network. Because such systems can be used with "whitelists," they can permit 911 and known authorized calls. Such systems require authorization from the Federal Communications Commission and the applicable telecommunication carriers in the vicinity.
- *Jamming devices:* These devices disrupt communications between the cell phone and cell tower by emitting the same radio frequency as the phone. Because these devices are prohibited by the Communications Act of 1934 and may cause interference with 911 and authorized calls from the public, they have not been authorized in the United States at the time of this writing.
- *Detection systems:* These systems attempt to track and identify the source of radio transmissions, including those generated by cell phones. Detection systems do not disrupt or interfere with communications, and so they are legal, but they may become confused by the large number of metal doors and the amount of rebar used in prison construction so as to be less effective.

Regardless of any technology being used, prison officials know it must not take the place of sound correctional principles that include visual monitoring and inspection of inmates and analysis of inmate movement and behavior.

■ Protecting Information

Prison officials have access to a great deal of personal information, either collected as part of the criminal justice proceeding or collected during the inmate's custodial stay. In providing staff with access to new technology, it is critical that they be trained in protecting access to systems and technology, as well as protecting information from being disclosed to unauthorized persons. Security breaches may result in inmate fraud, abuse, escapes, and potentially the loss of innocent lives. Careful measures need to be taken to ensure that information security is not compromised.

The easiest control to put in place is developing procedures to secure technology when not in use by authorized persons. Computers, laptops, and mobile computing devices such as smartphones should be issued only to approved persons, and data on the devices should be encrypted to prevent disclosure if lost or stolen. Additionally, only specific persons should be authorized to approve the purchase of IT equipment to ensure that unapproved technology is not in use in the facility. Finally, staff should be trained thoroughly in security best practices to ensure that they understand when and how information can be disclosed.

Access

The National Security Administration and National Institute of Standards and Technology advise that employees should only be given access to information that is required to perform their jobs. Human resources staff should not have access to financial systems, and correctional services line staff should not be able to view sensitive medical data and systems. Strictly controlling who has access to each system ensures that the risks of unauthorized disclosures, particularly to inmates, are minimized.

Software systems or applications that store private or sensitive staff or inmate data should employ user access controls and hard-to-guess passwords.[12] Other simple measures that can be deployed include

- Password-protected screensavers
- Privacy screens on monitors

- Well-enforced IT security policies
- Staff training about how to protect data and report security breaches

Additional measures can be taken to ensure that the above-described practices are actually being carried out. One valuable tool is the use of audit trails; by incorporating audit capabilities into applications and systems, investigations can be supplemented to review when or if users viewed, edited, or deleted relevant data from a system. Property audits should be performed on a routine basis to ensure that equipment has not been stolen or lost.

■ Implementation of Technological Change

Despite all the ways in which new technology can enhance the correctional environment, correctional workers often express ambivalence toward new technology and change. On the one hand, they may be interested in high-tech equipment that makes their jobs easier or more efficient, but new technology is expensive and often represents a departure from the traditional direct supervision of offenders. These competing interests tend to slow the adoption of new technology in the correctional world.

Because some ill-conceived technologies have resulted in security concerns that threatened the well-being of staff and inmates, this hesitation may not be unfounded. Additionally, new technology may be expensive and can be seen as a replacement for direct inmate care and surveillance. Lastly, new equipment and facility enhancements are often hyped solely as a means of improving efficiencies rather than as ways to help staff work more effectively.

For new technology to be accepted fully, it must be seen as a helpful tool that facilitates staff responsibilities, not as an additional burden or a threat to institutional personnel. Rather than replace personal interaction, high-tech products must make tasks easier and more efficient.

Staff reluctance to adapt to new procedures creates a significant management issue as institution administrators try to modernize their operations. Careful planning is necessary to effect development and integration of new technology to ensure that it is designed properly and is helpful to staff, tailored to local operations, and user-friendly. Additionally, teamwork—including involvement of correctional staff in the process of developing and implementing technology—is a key to success.

■ Conclusion

As correctional systems have expanded, so have the interest and scrutiny of external constituencies. Corrections-related expenditures have grown exponentially and are often one of the largest expenses in local, state, and federal budgets. Elected representatives in state legislatures, government budget personnel, and representatives of the media all have become extremely interested in prison and jail operations. Specifically, they want to know the logic behind institutional management decisions. The implication for the world of prisons and jails is significant. New technology is not just important—it is critical for survival. If used wisely, it can promote efficiency and improve staff's ability to perform operational tasks. But to be effective, today's correctional leaders must overcome the inertia that slows the acceptance of change.

Changes in the administration of confinement facilities have come slowly over the years, but the last decade has brought extraordinary and astonishing new concepts to a very old business. To meet the demands of the future, correctional leaders will need to seek out new ways of doing this business without losing sight of the most basic goal—to operate safe, secure, and humane correctional programs for those who live and work inside.

Chapter Resources

DISCUSSION QUESTIONS

1. Are lethal weapons an ethical means of maintaining institutional and perimeter security?
2. How can information systems be used to enhance management of correctional institutions and the criminal justice system?
3. What do you believe are the most promising areas of future technology that will evolve in prison and jail management?
4. Should citizens who are visiting confined family members or friends be subject to intrusive electronic security screening before receiving approval for visitation?
5. What are some of the challenges in protecting and securing information systems in the correctional environment?

ADDITIONAL RESOURCES

American Civil Liberties Union. (2001). *Q & A on Facial Recognition*, http://www.aclu.org/privacy/spying/14875res20030902.html

American Correctional Association, https://www.aca.org/

Electronic Surveillance Manual: Procedures and Case Law, http://www.justice.gov/criminal/foia/docs/elec-sur-manual.pdf

Justice Technology Information Network, http://www.nlectc.org

National Institute of Corrections, http://www.nicic.org

National Institute of Justice, *Topical Collection: Corrections Technology*, http://nij.ncjrs.gov/App/publications/Pub_search.aspx?searchtype=basic&category=99&location=top&PSID=42

NOTES

1. National Security Research, Inc. (2004). *Department of defense nonlethal weapons and equipment review: A research guide for civil law enforcement and corrections*. Retrieved from http://www.ncjrs.gov/pdffiles1/nij/205293.pdf
2. JustNet: Justice Technology Information Network, National Institute of Justice. Retrieved from http://www.justnet.org; see also Office of Law Enforcement Technology Commercialization (OLETC). Retrieved from http://www.oletc.org
3. The Federal Bureau of Investigation's Law Enforcement National Data Exchange (N-DEx) (combines data from federal and state law enforcement agencies, including booking, corrections, and incident data). Retrieved from http://www.fbi.gov/about-us/cjis/n-dex
4. National Information Exchange Model. Retrieved from https://www.niem.gov

5. Karuppannan, J. (2005). Mapping and corrections: Management of offenders with geographic information systems. *Corrections Compendium*, *30*(1). Retrieved from http://www.iaca.net/Resources/Articles/drjaishankarmaparticle.pdf

6. For example, Aegis Corrections Management solution. Retrieved from http://newworldsystems.com/Public_Safety/Aegis/Corrections_Management/article.asp; see also 3M Inmate Tracking System. Retrieved from http://solutions.3m.com/wps/portal/3M/en_US/ElectronicMonitoring/Home/ProductsServices/OurProducts/InmateTrackingSystem/

7. See American National Standards Institute (ANSI) Standard ANSI/HPS N43.17-2009. (2009). *Radiation safety for personnel security screening systems using x-ray or gamma radiation*; National Council on Radiation Protection and Measurements (NCRP) Commentary No.; 16. (2003). *Screening of humans for security purposes using ionizing radiation scanning systems*; and Interagency Steering Committee on Radiation Standards (ISCORS) Technical Report 2008-1. (2008, July). *Guidance for security screening of humans utilizing ionizing radiation*. Retrieved from http://www.iscors.org/doc/GSSHUIR%20July%202008.pdf

8. Saylor, W. G., & Gaes, G. G. (1997, Spring). PREP: Training inmates through industrial work participation, and vocational and apprenticeship instruction. *Corrections Management Quarterly*, *1*(2). Retrieved from http://www.bop.gov/news/research_projects/published_reports/recidivism/oreprprep_cmq.pdf; see also Gordon, H., & Weldon, B. (December 2003). Impact of career and technical education programs on adult offenders: Learning behind bars. *Journal of Correctional Education*, *54*(4), abstract retrieved from https://www.ncjrs.gov/App/Publications/abstract.aspx?ID=203952

9. Levine, S., Center for Technology and National Security Policy, & National Defense University. (2009, June). *The active denial system: A revolutionary, non-lethal weapon for today's battlefield*. Retrieved from http://www.ndu.edu/CTNSP/docUploaded/DTP%2065%20Active%20Defense-%20PO%2060032.pdf

10. See 18 U.S.C. Sec. 1791, amended by Public Law 111-225. See also California Penal Code Section 4576.

11. Department of Commerce, National Telecommunications and Information Administration. (2010, December). *Contraband cell phones in prisons: Possible wireless technology solutions*. Retrieved from http://www.ntia.doc.gov/files/ntia/publications/contrabandcellphonereport_december2010.pdf

12. Thomas, B. (2005). *Simple formula for strong passwords*. Bethesda, MD: SANS Institute.

Growth of the Private Sector

Douglas McDonald

CHAPTER OBJECTIVES

- Describe the factors that gave rise to the growth of the private prison industry in the 1980s.

- Explore research findings about the cost and quality of private prison operations.

- Discuss the complexities of the relationship around corrections between the government and the private sector.

Whether to turn the management and operation of entire prisons and jails over to private firms has become a hotly contested issue. Contracts for more narrowly focused services such as healthcare or food services have existed for some time and have raised few objections. However, in the mid-1980s, a vocal private correctional industry emerged and offered to take over entire correctional facilities and, indeed, entire state systems. Since then, the private correctional industry has grown rapidly, and although many still see the issue as government versus the private sector, a more apt description of current affairs in many jurisdictions is government *and* the private sector. Private facilities are now an established part of the correctional landscape.

■ Private Corrections—Repeating History

Private imprisonment is not a new invention; privately operated jails were commonplace in England until the 19th century.[1] In the United States, the government took sole responsibility for prisons and jails until wardens began leasing out convicts for work and housing assignments with private businesspeople in the early 19th century.[2] This practice was largely swept away by reform movements in the wake of scandals, but privately operated facilities continued to survive in low-security and community-based facilities and juvenile correctional systems.[3]

The modern private corrections industry got its start in the late 1970s when the U.S. Immigration and Naturalization Service (INS) began contracting with private firms to operate detention centers for illegal immigrants. In the mid-1980s, one of these new private firms offered to take over the entire state prison system in Tennessee and to run it more efficiently—an offer that was considered but ultimately declined. With slightly less notice, a number of small firms began to contract with local governments for private management of jails and with states for low-security and some medium-security prisons.[4] In many quarters, however, opposition to privatization remains powerful, as does the sense of battlement. For example, a national organization of public correctional employees, the Corrections and Criminal Justice Reform Task Force, declared at its third annual meeting in 1997 that privatization was the "number one threat to our profession in the nation."[5]

The emergence of the private imprisonment industry was the result of several factors.

- Demand for prison and jail beds had been growing, largely because of tougher sentencing laws and the war on drugs.
- State and local governments were slapped with expenditure caps.
- Public debt ceilings were being reached.
- Voters were declining to approve increases in public debt for prison and jail construction.[6]

Faced with conflicting demands caused by these phenomena, many public administrators welcomed the solution offered by private entrepreneurs. Private firms would build the needed facilities using their own capital and then charge the government a price that would recoup both the capital investment and ongoing operating costs. Governments could pay for these services using funds appropriated for operations, thereby avoiding the need to gain voters' approval of increased public debt.

In the mid-1980s, it looked as if the private sector was threatening to take over huge parts of the public correctional industry. This did not happen, but growth of the private correctional industry has still been strong, especially in some states. In 1987, there were about 3,000 state and federal prisoners in private facilities. By 1996, the number had soared to more than 85,000 and by 2010, to 128,200.[7] At last count, there were 415 private facilities operating under contract with state or federal correctional authorities during 2005, up from 264 only 5 years earlier.[8] In addition, there were others that contracted with county or city correctional agencies or with the Department of Homeland Security to house illegal immigrants.

By 2010, private facilities held 8% of all state and federal prisoners nationwide, but a number of states relied much more heavily on these facilities. Forty-four percent of New Mexico's state prisoners were held in private facilities that year. Proportions were also high in Montana (40%), Alaska (34%), Hawaii (33%), Idaho (30%), Vermont (27%), Mississippi (25%), Oklahoma (25%), and Colorado (20%).[9]

Growth in the private correctional industry's revenues was explosive: from about $650 million in 1996 to more than $1 billion in 1997.[10] By mid-1997, Wall Street and individual investors were impressed with these growth statistics and with the apparently bright prospects for future growth (private facilities had only about 3% of the market share of prisoners in the United States, compared with 8% in 2010). Stock prices of the four publicly traded firms had consequently been bid up very high, providing these companies with substantial amounts of cash to finance further expansion. By 2012, annual revenues received by the Corrections Corporation of America and the GEO Group, Inc. alone exceeded $3 billion.

The industry has long been dominated by a few big players. By the end of 1996, the Corrections Corporation of America, based in Nashville, held 49% of all prisoners in private adult facilities. The Wackenhut Corrections Corporation (now the GEO Group, Inc.) held 27%.[11] A few firms still capture most of the business.

The declining health of state government finances creates some uncertainty for the industry. State spending for institutional corrections stopped growing rapidly in 2001, when it leveled off and even declined in some years.[12] Growth in prisoner populations also leveled off in 2008 and declined in 2010 for the first time.[13] This new environment will pose some challenges to an industry that had been operating in a world where both numbers of prisoners and correctional budgets increased year after year.

Whereas the Corrections Corporation of America offered in 1986 to pay Tennessee $250 million for a 99-year lease on the state's prisons, most private facilities have either been newly constructed or are government owned and operated under a service contract. Unlike in the United Kingdom, government entities in the United States have not generally divested themselves of public properties. In 1997, however, exactly that happened. The District of Columbia sold its correctional treatment facility to the Corrections Corporation of America for $59 million, and the firm will operate it for the district under a 20-year leaseback arrangement. Proposals to do the same were being floated again in Tennessee in 1997 and in Florida as well. The National Performance Review has also stimulated greater attention to improving government performance. The review specifically supports privatization as one means of improving effectiveness and efficiency. Although the federal government cannot dictate programmatic preferences of state and local governments, this broad movement to improve government operations and support privatization of services is no doubt very influential. Indeed, surveys of state and local governments have found increased use of contracting for a broad range of social services.[14]

The effects of this increasing reliance on private imprisonment have not been studied extensively. Most research attention has focused on whether private facilities are less costly than public ones and, to a lesser extent, whether their services are better or worse. Little systematic research has addressed other questions such as whether privatization has furthered government objectives other than cost containment, or how the experience of relying on both government and privately operated facilities has changed or not changed correctional administrators' approaches to managing imprisonment services. Nor has there been a systematic study of what some call a new "correctional–industrial" complex, in which a well-financed private correctional industry lobbies for criminal sentencing legislation that expands the supply of prisoners and, by extension, the potential for greater profits. Concerns about such self-interested distortion of penal policymaking have been voiced for years,[15] but no studies have sought to determine the extent to which lawmakers are actually swayed by private industry lobbying. The political pressures to pass "get tough" legislation are already powerful in this country, even without any obviously self-interested lobbying by private correctional firms.

■ Cost Comparisons: Public Versus Private

Studies comparing the cost of private and public facilities have not reported consistent findings. Several reports find private facilities to be less costly. These include studies of Illinois work release centers and Logan and McGriff's study of a 350-bed minimum-security work camp in Tennessee.[16] (The latter study estimated that contracting was 3%–8% less costly than the public alternative.) In 1989, the Urban Institute conducted a study that compared a private minimum-security facility in Kentucky, a similar facility operated directly by the state, and two secure treatment facilities for serious juvenile offenders in Massachusetts—one public and the other private. It concluded that government-run facilities were 20%–28% more expensive than private ones.[17] Similarly, a study by the state of Texas estimated that the cost of contracting for four different privately operated prisons was about 15% lower than what direct government operation would have cost.[18] A study by Archambeault and Dies of two privately operated facilities in Louisiana and one government-operated one concluded that the privately operated facilities were cheaper by 12%–14% over a 5-year period.[19]

Still other studies found small or insignificant differences in costs. For example, an early study of the Eckerd Foundation's operation of the Florida School for Boys at Okeechobee found no cost savings attributable to private management compared with the cost of another publicly operated training school.[20] In his study of public and privately operated custodial facilities for juveniles in the United States, Donahue calculated the average cost per resident to be $22,600 in the public facilities and to be $22,845 in the private ones—an insignificant difference.[21] A statewide Tennessee study compared costs of a private multicustody facility and two state-run medium-security prisons and also found an insignificant difference.[22]

At least one study found private facilities to be more costly than their public counterparts. In a 1985 study, the Pennsylvania General Assembly's Legislative Budget and Finance Committee examined cost data provided by the INS for government-run centers and privately run centers for detaining illegal aliens. The study concluded that the average daily cost per inmate was 17% higher in the private facilities.[23] However, another study of INS detention centers estimated that private centers were 7%–19% less costly to the government.[24] This was confirmed in yet another study, which found the private facilities to be substantially less costly than INS-operated ones on average.[25]

Fewer studies have attempted to compare the quality of services delivered. In the Urban Institute's study, the authors reported that "by and large, both staff and inmates gave better ratings to the services and programs at the privately operated facilities; escape rates were lower, there were fewer disturbances by inmates; and in general, staff and offenders felt more comfortable at the privately operated ones."[26] Another study by Logan of public and privately operated facilities in New Mexico reported equivocal findings.[27] The Tennessee study found no difference in the level of performance among the privately operated and public facilities studied.[28] A comparison of a privately operated low-security federal facility in California with other low-security federal facilities found that the former rated higher on some measures of performance, no different on others, and worse on some. No single measure of "performance" was distilled from these findings, but the Federal Bureau of Prisons' (BOP's) evaluation of this closely monitored demonstration is probably the best indicator: the BOP awarded the contractor bonuses for its performance and renewed the 3-year contract.[29] One reason the findings regarding costs are inconsistent is that determining these costs is surprisingly difficult. Analysts have not always recognized the extent of this difficulty, which in part explains the variable findings in the research literature. Accounting practices followed in the public and private sectors differ in significant ways, which frustrates direct comparisons of costs.[30] In the private sector, accounting methods have been designed to value all inputs used to produce a good or a service, and most costs are thereby captured. In contrast, public sector accounting systems were designed not to identify costs but to monitor expenditures to ensure that funds are used for their intended purposes. The focus of accounting is therefore on the agency rather than the service being delivered. In many jurisdictions, a number of different agencies and government accounts provide funds or other resources used for correctional institutions; counting only those expenditures by correctional agencies produces an undercount of the true cost of publicly delivered imprisonment. For example, retirement fund contributions for employees in some places are paid not by the correctional agency's funds but from an overhead government account.[31] Other departments may provide medical or psychiatric care, utilities, transportation, or educational services. In nearly all governments, separate accounts are not kept for capital expenditures (as opposed to ongoing operating expenditures), and determining the cost of the capital assets "consumed" during a particular period of service is nearly impossible.

On the private side, other obstacles exist to identify the costs of contracting. The price charged to governments may not cover all costs, as firms may elect to experience shortfalls in hopes of winning more work in the longer run or may subsidize operations in one place with earnings obtained elsewhere. Still other costs of contracting, not always counted, include the government's expenditures to procure the contracts and to monitor their operations. A fair calculation would include all the government's costs of contracting, not just payments to contractors.

An additional methodological challenge faced by researchers is that comparable public and private facilities may not exist in the same jurisdiction for study. Consequently, researchers have had to estimate the costs of hypothetical public facilities or have compared costs from other facilities that are not precisely equivalent—which raises doubts about the validity of the inferences drawn.

McDonald and Carlson took advantage of a nearly unique opportunity to compare costs of private and public operation that was created when the BOP built three prisons using identical plans and then contracted with a private firm to operate one of them, located in Taft, California. Two others, operated directly by the BOP, were located in Mississippi and Arkansas. This offered a tightly controlled comparison of nearly identical prisons. The cost to the government of contracting was found to be slightly lower than what the government would have spent to operate the Taft facility directly. However, the cost would have been substantially lower if the government did not require that the contractor pay its employees a high wage that was ostensibly the local prevailing wage (which is mandated by the Service Contract Act). This "prevailing" wage was pegged at wages earned by California's state prison employees, the best paid in the nation. Had either of the facilities in Mississippi or Arkansas been given to the contractor, the differential between local prevailing wages and federal employee wages would have been very wide, resulting in much lower costs of contracting.[32]

With respect to costs and savings, students of the evaluation literature have not drawn consistent conclusions. For example, a study by the U.S. General Accounting Office examined five evaluations and reported that

> We could not conclude from these studies that privatization of correctional facilities will not save money. However, these studies do not offer substantial evidence that savings have occurred. . . . These studies offer little generalizable guidance for other jurisdictions about what to expect regarding comparative operational costs and quality of service if they were to move toward privatizing correctional facilities.[33]

Proponents of privatization, in contrast, read the research literature as showing "still more evidence that operating cost savings in the general range of 10 to 20 percent are typical" and that "these cost savings are often matched with performance improvements (e.g., few disturbances, few escapes, increased prisoner involvement in work programs, and more programs aimed at reducing recidivism)."[34]

There does not seem to be a universally prevalent cost advantage to public or private entities. Rather, because of various constraints (labor availability, restrictions on employee salary levels, regulatory requirements, government procurement procedures, etc.), private firms may be able to exploit opportunities in specific niches and find ways to deliver services at lower costs. In other places, such opportunities may not exist, and the publicly operated facilities may be less costly at a given level of service. Some governments are also more sophisticated than others in their contracting practices, which may result in lower relative costs and higher performance by the private firms.

■ Legal and Moral Issues

Critics have argued that privately operated correctional facilities are of questionable constitutionality or are improper, regardless of whether they are more cost-efficient. For example, in 1989, the American Bar Association (ABA) House of Delegates passed a resolution urging jurisdictions to proceed "with extreme caution in considering possible authorization of contracts with private corporations or other private entities for the operation of prisons or jails."[35] The accompanying report declared that

> *There can be no doubt that an attempt to delegate total operational responsibility for a prison or jail would raise grave questions of constitutionality under both the federal constitution and the constitutions of the fifty states. The more sweeping the delegation, the more doubtful would be its constitutionality.*[36]

For 50 years, the courts have allowed the federal government to delegate broad powers to private actors, and thus at the federal level, "private exercise of federally delegated power is no longer a federal constitutional issue."[37] Nor has delegation by state and local governments been seen as a federal constitutional issue since the 1920s. Not surprisingly, no federal court has found private imprisonment to be unconstitutional, despite the ABA's warning. Nor are there bans in most state constitutions against private delegation of correctional authorities. Nonetheless, judges in state courts have ruled inconsistently on issues regarding private delegation of state powers. To clarify this, legislatures in several states have passed laws authorizing delegation of correctional authority to private individuals or firms.[38] At least one state legislature (Washington) has passed laws explicitly banning privatization of formerly public functions.

Some critics argue that imprisonment is a core function of government, something that is intrinsically governmental in nature and should not be delegated to private actors.[39] However, the definition of what constitutes an intrinsically governmental function is being changed. Many policy makers find it entirely appropriate to delegate the administration of this function, while maintaining at the same time that the government has the responsibility for ensuring its provision. Accordingly, the courts have ruled that private imprisonment on behalf of government agencies constitutes "state action" and that governments retain the ultimate responsibility for what goes on in them.[40] Private facilities must comply with the same standards and laws that apply to public ones; they must conform to law and established standards.[41]

Still other objections to privatization have been voiced, arguing that the legitimacy of governmental authority is weakened in inmates' eyes by having private (and especially for-profit) corporations administer imprisonment.[42] Whether this actually occurs, however, is an empirical question that has not been studied. Moreover, it is reasonable to suspect that inmates' perceptions of legitimacy have more to do with whether the actions of the correctional workers conform to law and norms of fairness than whether they are public or private employees.

In most states, the question of whether to privatize turns not on matters of constitutionality or statutory law but on matters of policy. And whether one thinks it proper to delegate imprisonment authority to private actors ultimately depends on an individual's fundamental values and principles, as well as a consideration of the direct material interests of those engaged in delivering correctional services. Given that there is no clear national consensus for or against private delegation of imprisonment services, policy battles in legislative chambers are likely to continue.

■ A Sensitive Relationship

The performance of a contractor depends to some extent on the relationship between the contractor and the government and on the government's management of the contractor. In at least some jurisdictions, contracting out facility operations has been handled poorly; the government's specification of the services to be delivered has been poorly defined, silent on objectives, and long on procedures to be followed. Even when governments turn to contracting in hopes of reducing costs, they sometimes fail to establish an initial benchmark—the cost of direct government operation. Evaluation of bidders' proposals has sometimes emphasized cost over more general value, with the result that "lowballers" have been chosen against the better interests of the government. Monitoring has not always been adequate, despite the federal courts' clear insistence that governments cannot evade responsibility and liability for correctional services by delegating them to private actors. Contracting for both facilities and operations also gives the winning firm an edge on future competitions (because it will then own a facility while others will have to build one) and may reduce competition in the marketplace.

Therefore, rather than focusing on whether existing private facilities are less or more cost-effective than public ones, public managers should ask the following important question: How can government agencies obtain the results they seek to achieve? In contracting, governments have a tool for accomplishing any number of strategic objectives, which may include lower costs or improved correctional services. For example, a government seeking to lower correctional costs while maintaining service quality could establish a cost above which offers would not be entertained, explicit performance standards could be specified in the contract, monitoring systems could be designed to measure compliance with these standards, and actual costs could be monitored to ensure that targets have not been overrun. Governments can choose to terminate a contract if performance is not satisfactory.

Real life is more complicated and constrained than this simplified model suggests. For example, a commonplace observation is that government and businesses differ fundamentally in their purposes: Whereas private firms can be relatively single-minded in their pursuit of revenues or profit, government agencies and programs often strive to achieve multiple goals. This multiplicity of purposes stems, in part, from the genesis of programs in politics. That is, public programs are designed and enacted following a process by which different interests are accommodated. But this does not mean that government programs must operate with conflicting (or worse, unstated) missions. These missions can be clarified, and priorities can be established where multiple purposes exist.

■ Conclusion

How these developments in privatization will play out will probably depend as much on politics as on the merits or faults of private correctional facilities. Because prisons and jails claim such a large share of governments' budgets (especially at the state level), pressures for cost efficiency will probably continue. The threat of privatization may encourage public managers to find alternative ways of delivering correctional services, and organized public employees may succeed in staving off calls for their positions to be contracted out to private prison and jail operations. However, given the broad interest in relying on private firms to deliver public services, calls for privatization are likely to continue.

Chapter Resources

DISCUSSION QUESTIONS

1. What factors gave rise to the growth of the private prison industry in the 1980s?
2. What legal and moral issues surround the topic of prison privatization?
3. Why is the contractual relationship between the government and private prison operators sensitive?
4. What have research findings contributed to the discussion about the cost and quality of private prison operations?
5. Should privatization be encouraged or discouraged in the future?

ADDITIONAL RESOURCES

American Civil Liberties Union. (2011). *Banking on bondage: Private prisons and mass incarceration.* http://www.aclu.org/prisoners-rights/banking-bondage-private-prisons-and-mass-incarceration

Feeley, M. M. (2002). Entrepreneurs of punishment: The legacy of privatization. *Punishment & Society, 4*(3), 321–344.

Gaes, G. (2008). Cost, performance studies look at prison privatization. *NIJ Journal*, 259. https://www.ncjrs.gov/pdffiles1/nij/221507.pdf

McDonald, D. C. (1994). Public imprisonment by private means—The re-emergence of private prisons and jails in the United States, the United Kingdom, and Australia. *British Journal of Criminology, 34*, 28–48. http://heinonline.org/HOL/LandingPage?collection=journals&handle=hein.journals/bjcrim34&div=47&id=&page=

McDonald, D., & Carlson, K. (2005). *Contracting for imprisonment in the federal prison system: Cost and performance of the Taft Correctional Institution.* Cambridge, MA: Abt Associates. http://www.abtassociates.com/reports/TAFTPrisonEvalFINAL101805.pdf

McDonald, D., & Patten, C. (2003). *Governments' management of private prisons.* https://www.ncjrs.gov/pdffiles1/nij/grants/203968.pdf

Shichor, D. (1995). Punishment for profit: Private prisons/public concerns. London, UK: Sage Publications.

Stephan, J. (2008). *Census of state and federal correctional facilities.* Washington, DC: Bureau of Justice Statistics. http://www.bjs.gov/content/pub/pdf/csfcf05.pdf

NOTES

1. Crew, A. (1933). *London prisons of today and yesterday* (p. 50). London, UK: I. Nicholson & Watson; Feeley, M. (1991). The privatization of prisons in historical perspective. In W. Gormley (Ed.), *Privatization and its alternatives* (p. 397). Madison, WI: University of Wisconsin Press; Holdsworth, W. (1922–1924). *A history of English law* (vol. 4, 3rd ed.). London, UK: Cambridge University Press.

2. McKelvey, B. (1977). *American prisons: A history of good intentions*. Montclair, NJ: Patterson Smith; Blackmon, D. (2008). *Slavery by another name: The re-enslavement of black people in America from the civil war to world war II*. New York, NY: Doubleday.

3. McDonald, D. (1992). Private penal institutions. In M. Tonry (Ed.), *Crime and justice: A review of research*. Chicago, IL: University of Chicago Press.

4. Press, A. (1992). The good, the bad, and the ugly: Private prisons in the 1980s. In D. McDonald (Ed.), *Private prisons and the public interest*. New Brunswick, NJ: Rutgers University Press.

5. Corrections and Criminal Justice Reform Task Force, Report on the 3rd Round Table Conference, May 1997.

6. McDonald, D. (1990). Introduction. In D. McDonald (Ed.), *Private prisons and the public interest*. New Brunswick, NJ: Rutgers University Press.

7. Thomas, C., Bolinger, W., & Badalamenti, J. L. (1997). *Private adult correctional facility census* (10th ed.). Gainesville, FL: Center for Studies in Criminology and Law; Guerino, P., Harrison, P. M., & Sabol, W. J. (2011). *Prisoners in 2010*. Washington, DC: Bureau of Justice Statistics.

8. Stephan, J. J. (2008). *Census of state and federal correctional facilities, 2005*. Washington, DC: Bureau of Justice Statistics.

9. Guerino, P., Harrison, P. M., & Sabol, W. J. (2011). *Prisoners in 2010*. Washington, DC: Bureau of Justice Statistics.

10. Xiong, N. (1997, July 13). Private prisons: A question of savings. *New York Times*.

11. Thomas, C., Bolinger, W., & Badalamenti, J. L. (1997). *Private adult correctional facility census* (10th ed.). Gainesville, FL: Center for Studies in Criminology and Law.

12. Kyckelhahn, T. (2012). *State corrections expenditures, FY 1982–2010*. Washington, DC: Bureau of Justice Statistics.

13. Guerino, P., Harrison, P. M., & Sabol, W. J. (2011). *Prisoners in 2010*. Washington, DC: Bureau of Justice Statistics.

14. Council of State Governments. (1993). State trends and forecasts: Privatization, *2*(2). Lexington, KY: Author; Miranda, R., & Andersen, K. (1994). Alternative service delivery in local government, 1982–1992. *Municipal Year Book 1994*. Washington, DC: International City/County Management Association.

15. Schoen, K. (1985, March 28). Private prison operators. *New York Times*.

16. Chi, K. (1982). Private contractor work release centers: The Illinois experience. In *Innovations*. Lexington, KY: Council of State Governments; Logan, C., & McGriff, B. (1989). *Comparing costs of public and private prisons: A case study*. NIJ Reports no. 216.

17. Urban Institute. (1989). *Comparison of privately and publicly operated corrections facilities in Kentucky and Massachusetts*. Washington, DC: U.S. Department of Justice, National Institute of Justice.

18. State of Texas. (1991). *Recommendations to the Governor of Texas and members of the seventy-second legislature*. Austin, TX: Sunset Advisory Commission.

19. Archambeault, W., & Dies, D. Jr. (1996). *Cost effectiveness comparisons of private versus public prisons in Louisiana: A comprehensive analysis of Allen, Avoyelles, and Winn correctional centers*. Baton Rouge, LA: Louisiana State University, School of Social Work.

20. Brown, A., et al. (1985). *Private sector operation of a correctional institution: A study of the Jack and Ruth Eckerd youth development center, Okeechobee, Florida*. Washington, DC: U.S. Department of Justice, National Institute of Corrections.

21. Donahue, J. (1990). *The privatization decision*. New York, NY: Basic Books.

22. Tennessee Legislative Fiscal Review Committee. (1995). *Cost comparison of correctional centers*. Nashville, TN.

23. Joint State Government Commission. (1987). *Report of the private prison task force*. Harrisburg, PA: General Assembly of the Commonwealth of Pennsylvania.

24. McDonald, D. (1990). The costs of operating public and private correctional facilities. In D. McDonald (Ed.), *Private prisons and the public interest*. New Brunswick, NJ: Rutgers University Press.

25. McDonald, D. (1997). *Contracting for private detention services: The costs of private and government detention facilities*. Cambridge, MA: Abt Associates, Inc.

26. Urban Institute. (1989). *Comparison of privately and publicly operated corrections facilities in Kentucky and Massachusetts*. Washington, DC: U.S. Department of Justice, National Institute of Justice.

27. Logan, C. (1991). *Well-kept: Comparing the quality of confinement in a public and a private prison*. Washington, DC: U.S. Department of Justice, National Institute of Justice.

28. Tennessee Legislative Fiscal Review Committee. (1995). *Cost comparison of correctional centers*. Nashville, TN: Author.

29. McDonald, D., & Carlson, K. (2005). *Contracting for imprisonment in the federal prison system: Cost and performance of the privately operated Taft Correctional Institution*. Cambridge, MA: Abt Associates Inc., NCJ 211990; see also Federal Bureau of Prisons. (2005). *Evaluation of the Taft Demonstration Project: Performance of a private sector prison and the BOP*. Unpublished report 2005.

30. McDonald, D. (1992). Private penal institutions. In M. Tonry (Ed.), *Crime and justice: A review of research*. Chicago, IL: University of Chicago Press; McDonald, D. (1989). *The cost of corrections: In search of the bottom line*. Washington, DC: National Institute of Corrections.

31. McDonald, D. (1980). *The price of punishment: Public spending for corrections in New York*. Boulder, CO: Westview Press.

32. McDonald, D., & Carlson, K. (2005). *Contracting for imprisonment in the federal prison system: Cost and performance of the privately operated Taft Correctional Institution*. Cambridge, MA: Abt Associates Inc., NCJ 211990.

33. U.S. General Accounting Office. (1996). *Private and public prisons: Studies comparing operational costs and/or quality of service*. Washington, DC: Author.

34. Thomas, C., Bolinger, W., & Badalamenti, J. L. (1997). *Private adult correctional facility census* (10th ed.). Gainesville, FL: Center for Studies in Criminology and Law.

35. American Bar Association. (1989). *Report to the house of delegates*. Chicago, IL: Author.

36. American Bar Association. (1989). *Report to the house of delegates.* Chicago, IL: Author.

37. *Carter v. Carter Coal Company*, 298 U.S. 238 (1936); Lawrence, D. (1986). Private exercise of governmental power. *Indiana Law Journal*, *61*, 647–695.

38. National Criminal Justice Association. (1987). *Private sector involvement in financing and managing correctional facilities* (Exhibit 1). Washington, DC: Author.

39. Robbins, I. (1988). *The legal dimensions of private incarceration*. Washington, DC: American Bar Association.

40. *Medina v. O'Neill*, 569 F.Supp. 1028 (S.D. Texas, 1984); *Ancata v. Prison Health Services, Inc.*, 769 F.2d 700, 702 (11th Cir., 1985).

41. Logan, C. (1990). *Private prisons: Pro and con*. New York, NY: Oxford University Press; McDonald, When government fails: Going private as a last resort.

42. DiIulio, J. Jr. (1990). The duty to govern: A critical perspective on the private management of prisons and jails. In D. McDonald (Ed.), *Private prisons and the public interest*. New Brunswick, NJ: Rutgers University Press; Robbins, I. (1988). *The legal dimensions of private incarceration*. Washington, DC: American Bar Association.

Corrections in the 21st Century

Martin F. Horn

CHAPTER OBJECTIVES

- Describe the role and relevance of corrections to society as a whole.
- Identify the challenges faced by corrections systems today and in the future.
- Explain the importance of sound correctional leadership.

The field of corrections, and imprisonment in particular, is large. More than 2.5 million Americans (1 of every 136) are in prison or jail in the United States.[1] This includes 1 in 8 black men between the ages of 25 and 29 and 1 in 27 Hispanic males in that same age group.[2] Black men have a 32% chance of serving time in prison at some point in their lives—a greater chance than that of going to college. Local, state, and federal spending on corrections exceeds $60 billion annually, and corrections employs about 750,000 people nationally.[3] A 2007 estimate suggested that state and federal prison populations would grow by more than 192,000 by 2012, and that the cost of incarceration would balloon by an additional $27.5 billion.[4] In fact, by the end of 2011, the number of prisoners in state and federal custody declined by 0.9%, the second consecutive year the number of prisoners declined, and the incarceration rate in the United States stood at 492 per 100,000 U.S. residents, a decline of 1.7% from the 2010 rate.[*]

So many people enter and leave prisons and jails that their experiences of confinement and the administration of the facilities in which they are incarcerated are often ignored, placing the quality of civic life at grave risk. Increasingly, the public is demanding more transparency about how prisons and jails are managed. There is growing concern that the growth and operation of correctional systems are antithetical to democratic ideals. Following the atrocities at Abu Ghraib prison, the *New York Times* editorial board wrote, "The sickening pictures of American troops humiliating Iraqi prisoners have led inevitably to questions about the standards of treatment in the corrections system at home, which has grown tenfold over the last 30 years."[5]

It would be nice to live in a world where there were no prisons or jails, a world of perfect justice and harmony. But despite our best efforts, crime persists, and persons who would do harm to others have to be separated from the rest of society. It is important to remember that in its day, the prison was the great social reform of its time. Before that reform, penal institutions dealt with crime through corporal punishment, banishment, and social degradation. If the United States continued to respond to crime this way today, it would need fewer prisons. Because that is not the direction most Americans wish to go, correctional administrators and policy makers are faced with the challenge of making the prison and the jail places that serve shared democratic values and enhance public safety.

The first decade of the 21st century marked a remarkable change in America's attitudes and approach to punishment and imprisonment. In 2012, several states closed prisons or were in the process of doing so because of a decline in the number of prisoners in custody.[†] As the *Wall Street Journal* reported, these efforts cross party lines and reflect a new willingness to embrace diversion and treatment as alternatives to the use of imprisonment.[‡]

Additionally, new challenges emerged, making the administration of prisons and jails even more difficult. For example, advocates and families of prisoners drew attention to the high cost of inmate access to telephones provided in prisons.[||] At the same time, the first decade brought an onslaught of problems associated with new technology. Cell phones and smartphones found their way in to prisons and jails in alarming numbers, undermining the ability of correctional facilities to keep prisoners separate and apart from the community and incapacitated.[#]

The growth in the use of restrictive housing, administrative segregation, punitive segregation, and other forms of severe isolation came into question. This long-used tool of corrections administrators for keeping inmates safe may be in danger of attack because of its overuse, failure to administer it with an eye toward

---

[*] Carson, E. A., & Sabol, W. J. (2012, December). *Prisoners in 2011*. Washington, DC: U.S. Department of Justice, Bureau of Justice Statistics.

[†] Porter, N. (2012, December). *On the chopping block 2012: State prison closings*. Washington, DC: The Sentencing Project.

[‡] Fields, G., & Koppel, N. (2011, February 8). States seek prison breaks. *Wall Street Journal*.

[||] Shields, T. (2012, December 28). Prison phone rates charged by private equity may be cut. *Bloomberg Business Week*.

[#] Burke, T., & Owen, S. (2010, July). Cell phones as prison contraband. *FBI Law Enforcement Journal*. Washington, DC.

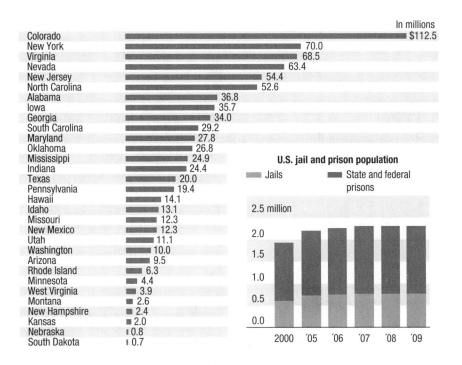

	In millions
Colorado	$112.5
New York	70.0
Virginia	68.5
Nevada	63.4
New Jersey	54.4
North Carolina	52.6
Alabama	36.8
Iowa	35.7
Georgia	34.0
South Carolina	29.2
Maryland	27.8
Oklahoma	26.8
Mississippi	24.9
Indiana	24.4
Texas	20.0
Pennsylvania	19.4
Hawaii	14.1
Idaho	13.1
Missouri	12.3
New Mexico	12.3
Utah	11.1
Washington	10.0
Arizona	9.5
Rhode Island	6.3
Minnesota	4.4
West Virginia	3.9
Montana	2.6
New Hampshire	2.4
Kansas	2.0
Nebraska	0.8
South Dakota	0.7

U.S. jail and prison population

Jails · State and federal prisons

2.5 million

2.0

1.5

1.0

0.5

0.0

2000 '05 '06 '07 '08 '09

FIGURE 53-1 Hard times: Thirty-one states made midyear cuts to corrections spending, totaling $805.9 million, in fiscal 2010.

Source: Courtesy of National Association of State Budget Officers.

human rights issues, and its use for purposes for which it was not intended. The United Nations' Special Rapporteur on torture likened the American use of segregation to torture,[**] and according to the Department of Justice, in 2005, more than 80,000 prisoners were held in what some call "solitary confinement."[††] Inmates in California, possibly coordinating their actions using cell phones and smartphones, went on a hunger strike to protest the practice of the Department of Corrections and Rehabilitation of placing inmates suspected of being gang members in segregation unless and until they renounced gang membership and revealed other gang members.[‡‡] And, as noted below, the continuing rise in the number of mentally ill persons in prison and jail, and for whom segregation is inappropriate, further complicates the situation.

On a more positive note, there is evidence that America's prisons and jails are safer than they have been in many years.[§§] And the reentry movement and use of evidence-based practice seem to have been institutionalized. Nonetheless, challenges remain.

[**] United Nations, Sixty-sixth session. (2011, August 5). *Promotion and protection of human rights: human rights questions, including alternative approaches for improving the effective enjoyment of human rights and fundamental freedoms.* Item 69 (b) of the provisional agenda. New York, NY.

[††] Stephan, J. J. (2008, October). *Census of state and federal adult correctional facilities, 2005.* Bureau of Justice Statistics, U.S. Department of Justice.

[‡‡] California starts emptying solitary confinement cells. (2013, January 4). *Los Angeles Times.*

[§§] Useem, B., & Piehl, A. (2008). *Prison state.* New York, NY: Cambridge University Press.

■ Leadership

The challenge of corrections administration is the challenge of leadership. According to John DiIulio, Jr., "prison management may be the single most important determinant of the quality of prison life."[6] Leadership determines what happens inside a prison. An institution as self-contained as a prison or jail, left to its own devices, can drift into a netherworld of danger and vice. Strong administrators and professional staff enable prisons and jails to be places where offenders are kept safely and are ultimately returned to their homes—no worse off, and hopefully better, than the day they arrived.

U.S. prisons and jails do an extraordinarily good job of performing their most basic missions. A study by the Bureau of Justice Statistics (BJS) found that the mortality rate among state prison inmates was almost 20% lower than for similar groups in the general population, with African Americans in prison experiencing a mortality rate 57% lower than their peers on the outside.[7] In a similar vein, an article in the *New England Journal of Medicine* found that persons are more likely to die when they leave prison than while they are in prison.[8] Such studies indicate that America's prisons are safe and getting safer.

■ Legitimacy

Prisons and jails are dependent on the legitimacy conferred on their leadership by the inmates. Legitimacy refers to the consensus among inmates that the administration is fair and has the best interests of the inmates in mind. Inmates, by and large, are adult and sentient; it is a mistake to infantilize them or treat them as incapable of understanding. They understand regimentation and rules, as long as those rules are evenly applied and reasonably related to their welfare. That is why effective managers speak about being firm, fair, and consistent. It is also why they recognize the importance of providing quality food and medical care to inmates. Correctional administrators do these things not only because they are the right thing to do and are constitutionally required; they do it to show inmates that they care about them as people.

Anne Owens, Her Majesty's Inspector of Prisons, has identified four key aspects of legitimacy:

1. Safety—All prisoners, even the most vulnerable, are held safely.
2. Respect—Prisoners are treated with respect for their human dignity.
3. Purposeful activity—Prisoners are able, and expected, to engage in activity that is likely to benefit them.
4. Resettlement—Prisoners are prepared for release into the community and are helped to reduce the likelihood of reoffending.[9]

■ Safety

Human beings are social by nature, interested in belonging to a group. People join groups for many reasons, safety not the least among them. Accordingly, one way correctional managers earn legitimacy is by keeping inmates safe. If administrators do not keep them safe, inmates will find alternative means, often in the form of arming themselves or joining a group, such as a gang, to gain protection.

Corrections administrators are keenly aware of the need to protect vulnerable inmates. In a diverse country such as the United States, members of any minority are potentially vulnerable in a prison setting. It is the responsibility of the conscientious prison administrator to be attentive to the risks associated with racial and ethnic biases. Changing definitions of gender and sexual orientation pose new challenges to accommodate the identity of individuals while still acknowledging and dealing with the prejudices and hostility they may face in a prison environment. In the future, protecting vulnerable inmates from harm without compromising their right to move freely in a prison population will continue to pose problems for administrators.

The prison must achieve a balance of the rights of the few and the needs of the many. Unfortunately, a single predatory inmate can make all the other inmates feel unsafe. When inmates feel unsafe, management loses its legitimacy, and inmates will do what they have to in order to feel safe again. Thus, the institution may have to isolate and contain predators for the majority of inmates have a safe environment.

The Mentally Ill

In the 1960s, the United States embarked on a remarkable social transformation with respect to its treatment of the mentally ill. The invention of psychotropic medications and the gradual loss of confidence in the traditional "talking therapies" combined with the high cost of running large state hospitals led to a national movement to deinstitutionalize mentally ill persons. Unfortunately, in the rush to deinstitutionalize, there was inadequate time to build the community safety net necessary to support these individuals. Pursuant to the law of unintended consequences, the burden of treating persons with mental illness today falls heavily on prisons and jails.

The prevalence of mental illness in correctional institutions is high, with a recent BJS study finding mental health problems in 56% of state prisoners and 64% of local jail inmates.[10] This is in part due to the trans-institutionalization that occurred in the last century. Trans-institutionalization is defined as

> *The movement of mentally ill from publicly funded mental health hospitals to nursing homes and correctional institutions. The increase in mental health illnesses in prisons not only burdens the prison health care system, but it further compromises the mental health status of prisoners with mental health diseases. Mental health care providers are also in short supply within correctional institutions, despite the fact that courts have mandated the treatment of mentally ill offenders. Additionally, correctional officers, who are in charge of security issues, often lack an understanding about appropriate management of mental health illnesses....*

> *Source:* Understanding Prison Health Care: Mental Health revised June 13, 2002, available at http://movementbuilding.org/prisonhealth/mental.html, accessed July 26, 2007.

Bernard E. Harcourt, professor of law and criminology at the University of Chicago, observed, "It should be clear why there is such a large proportion of mentally ill persons in our prisons: individuals who used to be tracked for mental health treatment are now getting a one-way ticket to jail."[12] When one looks at the combined institutionalization rates for prisons and jails as well as mental health and retardation facilities over the last half of the 20th century, it is obvious that the overall rate has not changed. What has changed is where these persons are held.

The experience of imprisonment for a mentally ill person can be an especially hard one. Many small jails in rural counties do not have access to psychiatric hospitals or physicians. Persons confined in those jails are condemned to a cruel and isolating existence made all the more difficult by the inability of the jailer to meet their needs. Untreated, the mentally ill inmate becomes a strain on the very fabric of the institution. Other inmates are disturbed by his or her symptoms, and staff are frustrated and exasperated by their inability to make the mentally ill individual and the other inmates comfortable. In this troubling mix, the seeds of bad outcomes are sown, and violence and suicide can ensue.

It is a sad commentary on 21st-century America if jails are the best healthcare option offered to the mentally ill. Prison and jail administrators need to be in the forefront of advocacy for diversion of the mentally ill from jail and prison to the kinds of caregiving settings where they can find appropriate treatment.

Sexual Violence and Harassment

The deprivation of contact with members of the opposite sex and the prohibition on all sexual activity in confinement create another dangerous dynamic where integrity is easily lost. Allowing sex among inmates is wrong for many reasons, not least that it creates destabilizing jealousies and competition among inmates. Because sex is a basic human need, it is highly sought and valued. Unfortunately, many members of today's corrections staff do not understand the simple concept that inmates are incapable of consent to sexual activity with a staff member. A prison or jail is, by its very nature, inherently coercive. It is naïve and uninformed to believe that inmates can consent to sexual contact as an act of free will. Staff need to understand this concept because it is another area where prison and jail administrators have been silent for too long.

More importantly, leadership must set an example for appropriate human relations in the institutional setting. Sexual harassment and sexual relationships among managers and subordinates send a mixed message to staff and are often at the root of sexual liaisons between staff and inmates. In today's work environment where cross-gender supervision is more common, the need to address this issue is acute.

The enactment of the Prison Rape Elimination Act reflects a growing concern around this issue.[13] In 2010, the Department of Justice began issuing significant new research about the frequency and prevalence of sexual assault inside America's prisons and jails.[||||] The Attorney General issued final regulations for implementation of the Prison Rape Elimination Act in 2012. According to the BJS "Nationwide, 2.1 percent of all prison inmates and 1.5 percent of all jail inmates reported at least one incident involving another inmate; 2.8 percent of prison inmates and 2.0 percent of jail inmates reported having had sex or sexual contact with facility staff."[##] And, "Among all prison inmates, the reported use or threat of physical force to engage in sexual activity was generally low. An estimated 1.3 percent of prison inmates reported the use or threat of force during inmate-on-inmate victimization and 1.0 percent during staff sexual misconduct. Among all jail inmates, 1.0 percent reported the use or threat of force during inmate-on-inmate victimization and staff sexual misconduct."

Correctional administrators have zero tolerance for sexual abuse of inmates. The anger and terror engendered by widespread sexual abuse can lead to more violence, suicide, homicide, and riots. The respect for inmates—respect for them as individuals and for their personal safety—is the most fundamental and critical correlate of legitimacy. Inmates would soon withdraw their grant of legitimacy from any correctional organization where such violations of their personal safety were widespread and condoned.

Nonetheless, because of society's homophobia and the shame and embarrassment that victims experience, there is no doubt that the incidence of inmate sexual encounters and sexual assault is underreported. Creating a prison or jail environment where these behaviors are not tolerated and where reporting is safe and easy for victims continues to be a challenge. As a first step, staff members must integrate the abhorrence of this behavior into their culture, combined with aggressive prosecution of violators.

Drugs and Alcohol

The overwhelming majority of prison and jail inmates are addicted to alcohol and other drugs.[14] Often, drug and alcohol use is related to mental illness. Sometimes, the addiction is an attempt at self-medication. The need to keep inmates sober while confined remains an ongoing challenge to corrections agencies.

Federal law mandated the creation of random drug testing protocols in prisons receiving federal residential substance abuse treatment funds.[15] Addiction is a primary problem for most prison and jail inmates, and if they continue to get high upon release, they will most certainly fail. If they are getting high in jail and

---

[||||] U.S Department of Justice. (2012, May 16). *National standards to prevent, detect, and respond to prison rape.* 28 CFR Part 115, Washington, DC.

[##] U.S. Department of Justice, Bureau of Justice Statistics. (2010, August 26). *4.4 percent of prison inmates and 3.1 percent of jail inmates reported one or more incidents of sexual victimization during 2008–2009.* Press release. Washington, DC; Beck, A., & Harrison, P. (2010, August). *Sexual victimization in prisons and jails reported by inmates, 2008–09.* Washington, DC: U.S. Department of Justice, Bureau of Justice Statistics.

prison, the likelihood that they will continue to get high upon release is nearly 100%. Moreover, if inmates are getting high while confined, it suggests larger problems within a correctional facility.

The presence of drugs in a correctional facility means that someone, usually an inmate or gang of inmates, is in control of their sale and distribution. It means that there will be fights and extortion and that the control of the facility will be in the hands of inmates, not staff. More disconcertingly, it may indicate that staff are aware of the presence of drugs and, at best, are turning a blind eye, or worse, are actually participating in the offense. Inmates know which staff members participate in or allow illegal activities to occur. The permission of or participation by corrections officials in the sale and use in illegal drugs within a facility eliminates any pretense of inmate rehabilitation.

Corrections officials must take the strongest possible steps to eradicate drugs from a prison or jail environment. This requires strategic thinking, creative approaches, and most importantly, the creation of a value system among staff at all levels that drug use will not be tolerated. Only by creating a top-to-bottom culture that does not permit drugs to be introduced and used in the correctional setting can one begin to talk about "corrections."

No amount of searching of inmates, visitors, staff, and packages can substitute for the dedication of staff that understand the reasons drug use must be eradicated in confinement. Staff need to understand that their safety and that of their fellow officers, as well as their mission and reputation, depend on the elimination of drugs from the facility. Too often drugs are an institution's "dirty little secret" and are not discussed. If organizations are to eliminate drugs, senior leadership must first acknowledge that a problem exists and openly discuss it with staff.

■ Rehabilitation

The debate continues about whether prisons and, to a lesser extent, jails have a contribution to make to rehabilitation. Latessa and others argue that properly constructed efforts specifically directed to the most high-risk offenders and designed to eradicate "criminogenic" behaviors can affect outcomes.[16] Latessa and his colleagues may be correct, but current research is limited in quantity and in scope. What does seem clear is that in order for inmates to succeed upon release, several issues need to be addressed, namely, sobriety, education, work, and housing.

An individual who does not stay sober upon release will fail. That is one reason drug-free prisons and jails must be the norm. It is also why institutions must help the individual stay sober in the days immediately following release. Accordingly, reentry work programs must focus on helping inmates to understand their addiction and connecting them with organizations that can help them stay sober upon release. Prisons and jails must be places where sobriety is taught and addictions are treated. Postrelease supervision agencies have to understand that addiction is a recurring disease of the brain and that recovery does not proceed in a straight line.[17] Postrelease supervision strategies should be designed with this understanding.

In the 21st century, if you cannot read, you cannot work. It is that simple. The vast majority of inmates admitted to prisons and jails continue to lack a high school diploma and many still read below the eighth-grade level. If there is one positive thing prisons can do, it is to teach people how to read. Before an inmate can participate in optional prison or jail activities, he or she should first be taught how to read. That said, it would be unwise to predicate an inmate's release upon attainment of an educational milestone. How much time an individual serves in confinement should be based on the crimes for which he or she was incarcerated. Nonetheless, prison and jail administrators have tools at their disposal that can provide inmates with an incentive to obtain an education, and these tools should be utilized. Investments in educational resources for prisons and jails are sound investments of public monies.

If prison and jail administrations are serious about reentry, they have to be serious about helping inmates find work upon release. More importantly, probation and parole agencies need to invest in finding work for the persons subject to their supervision. The seriousness with which a probation or parole agency approaches its work can be determined quickly by the time, effort, and money it invests in finding work for offenders. Simply training probation or parole agents how to connect their clients to work or agencies that help them find work can often pay big dividends in offender employment outcomes. Prisons can assist with this challenge by offering prison work assignments and vocational opportunities. To work effectively, whether one is a neurosurgeon or a short-order cook, requires pride in one's work, the ability to work with others, reliability, and acceptance of supervisory criticism. These basic skills can be taught in prison and jails; expensive vocational training is not the only way to help inmates enter the world of work.

Additionally, the prospect of finding adequate, affordable housing is especially relevant today in many large urban areas where this concern can pose a significant barrier to reentry. This, too, should be a concern of correctional staff and leadership.***

The Correctional Workforce

Recruitment and retention of correctional staff is a growing challenge.[18] In an increasingly diverse society, staff should be diverse as well. Forging a unified team from a diverse workforce can be a daunting challenge for managers. Much is written about workers' desire for benefits, autonomy, and creativity. Nonetheless, the needs of today's workforce are, at heart, no different from those of yesterday. To recruit and retain qualified and motivated corrections workers, institutions need to pay them well. There is no substitute for a good living wage, good benefits, and the opportunity for career advancement in a safe workplace. If any of those components is missing, no number of rewards will compensate.

Unions representing corrections workers can be an asset. In those jurisdictions where responsible collective bargaining has resulted in good salary arrangements, good medical benefits, and a good pension, recruitment and retention are likely to be easier and more successful than in jurisdictions where those things are absent. Unions can focus on corrections policy or on working conditions. Any undue attention to the former can undermine the latter. The smart corrections administrator will not view a union as a menace or an enemy. Rather, labor relations can help achieve shared values and goals like a safe workplace, good training, and advancement opportunities. An environment of trust between administration and labor relations can set an example for staff and inmates about how individuals can relate to each other and settle their differences in civil society.

Integrity is at the heart of effective leadership and a professional workforce. Drug trafficking and sexual contact are examples of the ways in which integrity can be compromised. The top administrator of any corrections agency must put integrity first and foremost on his or her list of priorities. Integrity is easily lost and takes many forms. The simple failure to pay attention to what is going on is its simplest form. As mentioned previously, left to their own devices, total confinement institutions can devolve into places where bad things happen. Thus, the first duty of the administrator is to be aware.

Finally, integrity is lost when managers allow inmates to run the facility. Often understaffing is blamed, but poor training and lack of supervision are often contributing factors. The investment in a trained workforce—too often the first thing sacrificed in tight budget times—is the best insurance against a loss of integrity. A well-trained, well-motivated workforce that understands its mission is less likely to be corrupted than an ill-trained, unmotivated one.

Conclusion

The management of corrections always has been and will be the responsibility of government. The public must be confident that the deprivation of liberty that corrections institutions exercise reflects the values of

---

*** Corporation for Supportive Housing. *Emerging evidence and lessons learned*. Retrieved from January 29, 2013, http://www.csh.org/wp-content/uploads/2011/12/RHIUpdateReport_Finalpdf.pdf

constitutional democracy. The emergence of the correctional standards movement certainly began the process. However, too few correctional agencies, particularly local jails, are accredited. Critics argue that self-regulation by the profession leads to standards and an accreditation process that cannot satisfy the demand for transparency. The administration of accreditation must itself be legitimate and transparent. There are models to learn from in this area, including the system in place for higher education.

Increasingly there are calls for oversight by public or private bodies possessing the "golden key," that is, the authority to enter a prison or jail unannounced at any time. There is a federal requirement that each state have such a body to oversee mental health facilities receiving federal funds.[19] Some jurisdictions already have public bodies that perform this function in prisons and jails.[20] It is critical that, however the function is performed, it be accountable to elected officials and to the public. Care of the inmate is an important concern, but it is not the only consideration in the administration of correctional facilities. The public also holds correctional administrators accountable for the protection of the public and staff and for running an efficient, cost-effective organization.

Confinement of those accused of crimes and those serving sentences will continue to present challenges in a free society. The manner in which we address these challenges will define our values, as it has throughout history. In the early years of the 19th century, scholars and philosophers from throughout the world visited the United States to witness the revolution in punishment that began at the Walnut Street Jail in Philadelphia. Today, America's correctional leadership is being questioned. The struggle to regain legitimacy lies ahead, but American traditions create a sound basis on which to proceed; values-based leadership and integrity will take us the rest of the way.

Chapter Resources

DISCUSSION QUESTIONS

1. What are some of the greatest difficulties facing corrections departments today? How are these challenges likely to change in the future?

2. What key objectives does society expect corrections systems to address? Can corrections systems meet these objectives? Why or why not?

3. Why is leadership important in corrections? What are some of the key decisions that leaders have to make?

4. Why is the presence of drugs in an institution particularly problematic? What steps can staff take to prevent this problem?

5. What major issues must inmate programming address in order to improve the likelihood that releasing offenders will not recidivate?

NOTES

1. Carson, E. A., & Sabol, W. J. (2012). *Prisoners in 2011.* Washington, DC: U.S. Department of Justice, Bureau of Justice Statistics. NCJ239808.

2. Carson, E. A., & Sabol, W. J. (2012). *Prisoners in 2011.* Washington, DC: U.S. Department of Justice, Bureau of Justice Statistics. NCJ239808.

3. U.S. Department of Justice, Office of Justice Programs. *Direct expenditures by criminal justice function, 1982–2005.* Retrieved September 23, 2007, from http://www.ojp.usdoj.gov/bjs/glance/tables/exptyptab.htm

4. Pew Charitable Trusts. (2007, February). *Public safety, public spending.* Washington, DC: Public Safety Performance: A Project of the Pew Charitable Trusts.

5. Jehl, D. (2004, May 5). The struggle for Iraq: Prisoners, some Iraqis held outside control of top general. *New York Times,* A1.

6. DiIulio, J. Jr. (1987). *Governing prisons* (p. 255). New York, NY: The Free Press.

7. Mumola, C. (2006). *Medical causes of death in state prisons, 2001–2004.* Washington, DC: U.S. Department of Justice, Bureau of Justice Statistics.

8. Binswanger, I., et al. (2007). Release from prison—A high risk of death for former inmates. *New England Journal of Medicine, 356*(2), 157–165.

9. HM Inspectorate of Prisons. (2004). *Expectations* (p. 5). London: Author.

10. James, D., & Glaze, L. (2006). *Mental health problems of prison and jail inmates.* Washington, DC: U.S. Department of Justice, Bureau of Justice Statistics.

11. *Understanding prison health care: Mental health.* Revised June 13, 2002. Retrieved July 26, 2007, from http://movementbuilding.org/prisonhealth/mental.html

12. Harcourt, B. (2007, January 15). The mentally ill, behind bars. *New York Times.*

13. Prison Rape Elimination Act, 42 U.S.C. §15601 et. seq.

14. Karberg, J., & James, D. (2005, July). *Substance dependence, abuse, and treatment of jail inmates, 2002.* Washington, DC: U.S. Department of Justice, Bureau of Justice Statistics; Mumola, C. J., & Karberg, J. (2006, October). *Drug use and dependence, federal and state prisoners 2004.* Washington, DC: U.S. Department of Justice, Bureau of Justice Statistics.

15. Residential Substance Abuse Treatment for State Prisoners, 42 U.S.C. §3796 ff.

16. Latessa, E. (1999). What works in correctional intervention. *Southern Illinois University Law Review, 23,* 414–426.

17. Volkow, N. (2007). *Drugs, brains, and behavior—The science of addiction.* Bethesda, MD: U.S. Department of Health and Human Services, National Institute on Drug Abuse. Retrieved October 2, 2007, from http://www.drugabuse.gov/scienceofaddiction/sciofaddiction.pdf

18. Workforce Associates, Inc. (2004). *A 21st century workforce for America's correction profession.* Lanham, MD: American Correctional Association.

19. New York State 42 U.S.C. §10805, MHL §45.03(a).

20. Constitution of the State of New York, Art. XII, §5; Teeters, N. K. (1937, September–October). The Pennsylvania prison society: A century and a half of penal reform. *Journal of Criminal Law and Criminology, 28*(3), 374–379.

Index

Note: "Page numbers followed by *b*, *f*, or *t* indicate material in boxes, figures, or tables, respectively."